# SCHOLASTIC SCOPE
# LITERATURE

## A READING AND LITERATURE
## • PROGRAM •

### LEVEL · Z

### LEVEL · 1

### LEVEL · 2

### LEVEL · 3

### LEVEL · 4

### LEVEL · 5
AMERICAN
LITERATURE

### LEVEL · 6
WORLD
LITERATURE

# SCHOLASTIC SCOPE
## LITERATURE

## A READING AND LITERATURE
## · PROGRAM ·

LEVEL
·5·

EDITED BY
KATHERINE ROBINSON
Editorial Director,
Scope Magazine

## LITERATURE CONSULTANTS

Jane Yolen
Author

Theodore Hipple, Ph.D.
Department Chair
Curriculum and Instruction
University of Tennessee
Knoxville, Tennessee

## READING CONSULTANT

Virginia B. Modla, Ph.D.
Reading Curriculum Associate
School District of Cheltenham Township
Elkins Park, Pennsylvania

## LEVEL FIVE READERS

Cynthia Imes
Teacher
Appleton High School West
Appleton, Wisconsin

Ann Miller
Coordinator, Learning Resource Center
Aptos High School
Aptos, California

John Russell
Teacher
Blue Springs High School
Blue Springs, Missouri

## CURRICULUM CONSULTANTS

Barbara Coulter
Director of Language Education
Detroit Public Schools
Detroit, Michigan

Nora Forester
Reading Coordinator
North Side School District
San Antonio, Texas

William Horst
Secondary Section Committee
National Council of Teachers of English

Barbara Krysiak, Ed.D.
Principal
North Hampton Elementary School
North Hampton, New Hampshire

Nancy McHugh
Teacher
Grant High School
Van Nuys, California

## CONTRIBUTING WRITERS/EDITORS

Ellen Ashdown
Richard Foerster

Acknowledgments begin on page 787.

ISBN 0-590-35730-1

12  11  10  9  8  7  6  5  4

4/9

Printed in the U.S.A.

# Contents

# Contents

# *C*onten*s*

. . . . . . . . . . . . . . . . . . . . . . . . . . . . . . . . . . . . . . . . . . . . . . . . . . . . . . . . . . . . . .

# Contents

# Contents

# Contents

# Contents

# $C$ontents

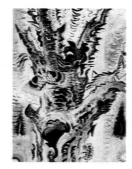

# *C*onten*t*s

# Scholastic Scope

## LITERATURE

### A Reading And Literature
### • Program •

# AN AMERICAN SAMPLER

*I hear America singing, the varied carols I hear.*
*Those of mechanics, each one singing his as it*
*should be blithe and strong.*
*The carpenter singing his as he measures his plank*
*or beam,...*
*The shoemaker singing as he sits on his bench,*
*the hatter singing as he stands...*
*The delicious singing of the mother, or of the young wife*
*at work, or of the girl sewing or washing,*
*Each singing what belongs to him or her*
*and to none else.*

— Walt Whitman

*The Jolly Flatboatmen in Port*
George Caleb Bingham (1811-1879)
Saint Louis Art Museum

# An American Sampler

This is a book about America and its people. It is not a history book, although it looks back at America's past. It is a book of literature, a sampling of works by America's most skillful writers.

The first section shows how American authors have approached different types of literature: short stories, personal narratives, poetry, and plays.

### Storytellers and Truth Tellers

As long as there have been people, there have been stories. The first stories were told aloud. Later, storytellers began to write down their tales. The term *short story* refers to any short work of fiction in which the author has made up a *plot*, a chain of events that leads to a satisfying ending; *characters*, people in the story; and *setting*, a time and place in which the events of the story occur.

O. Henry wrote nearly 100 years ago. His stories continue to be admired for their clever plots. Often his stories, such as the one you will read here, "After Twenty Years," have surprise endings or plot twists.

Toni Cade Bambara is a modern-day writer. Her story "Raymond's Run" has a plot and a setting, but what you will remember most is the people in the story — their personalities and feelings.

Fiction — short stories and novels — is not the only way authors can express their ideas. Through a form of nonfiction called the *personal narrative*, authors may directly describe their experiences and express their beliefs.

Helen Keller became blind and deaf in infancy. She learned about the world mostly through her sense of touch. The essay "Three Days to See" expresses Keller's ideas about the use of the sense of sight as she imagines it.

In 1858, Frederick Douglass wrote the story of his life, his *autobiography*, for a very important reason. He wanted all Americans to understand what it was like to grow up as a slave.

### Poets and Playwrights

Poetry is another way authors have chosen to express their feelings, describe their experiences, and tell their stories. In this section, you will sample the work of three of America's finest poets: Luis Palés Matos, Henry Wadsworth Longfellow, and Edna St. Vincent Millay. Poets choose words for their sounds as well as their meanings. Poetry should be read aloud.

Plays are another form of literature that is intended to be read aloud. The events

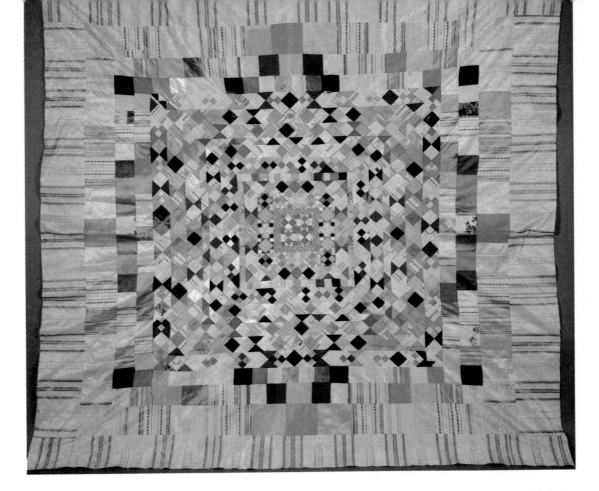

in a play are revealed through *stage directions*, descriptions of how the characters should move on the stage; and *dialogue*, what the characters say about their own feelings and actions, and the feelings and actions of the other people.

In "The Wind in the Rosebush," the dialogue and stage directions work together to reveal a shocking secret.

What is special about American literature is that it reflects the American spirit. What is the American spirit? You will find an idea of what it is in the poetry of Walt Whitman. His poem "I Hear America Singing" describes a complex and beautiful music, made up of as many different songs as there are different ways of life in our country.

The section includes a science-fiction selection, "Hail and Farewell," by a master of the genre, Ray Bradbury. Willie is an all-American boy—with a difference. Somehow Willie transforms the burden he bears into a generous advantage for the lonely people he meets.

Like the Americans in Whitman's poem, each author here "sings what belongs to him or her and to none else." Their songs are their stories, personal narratives, poems, and plays. Somehow all the pieces fit together like the many songs that blend to make a great musical work.

# After Twenty Years

*by O. Henry*

*O. Henry's real name was William Sydney Porter (1862–1910). He traveled throughout the United States and held many jobs. His varied experiences gave him a feeling for how different kinds of people spoke and thought. As you read "After Twenty Years," think about how the story will end. O. Henry is famous for stories with surprise endings.*

The policeman on the beat moved up the avenue. The streets were nearly empty. The time was barely 10:00 at night. Chilly gusts of wind with a taste of rain in them had chased people indoors.

Trying doors as he went, he twirled his club with many artful movements. He turned now and then to cast his watchful eye down the quiet street. The officer made a fine picture of a guardian of the peace. The vicinity was one that kept early hours. Now and then you might see the lights of an all-night lunch counter. But most of the doors belonged to stores that had long since been closed.

Midway on a certain block the policeman suddenly slowed his walk. In the doorway of a darkened hardware store a man leaned. As the policeman walked up to him, the man spoke up quickly.

"It's all right, Officer," he said. "I'm just waiting for a friend. It's an appointment made twenty years ago. Sounds a little funny to you, doesn't it? Well, I'll explain if you'd like to make certain it's

all straight. About that long ago there used to be a restaurant where this store stands — 'Big Joe' Brady's restaurant."

"Until five years ago," said the policeman. "It was torn down then."

The man in the doorway struck a match and checked his watch. The light showed a pale, square-jawed face with keen eyes, and a little white scar near his right eyebrow. His scarf-pin was a large diamond, oddly set.

"Twenty years ago tonight," said the man. "I dined here at 'Big Joe' Brady's with Jimmy Wells. He was my best chum, and the finest chap in the world. He and I were raised here in New York, just like two brothers, together. I was eighteen and Jimmy was twenty. The next morning, I was to start for the West to make my fortune. You couldn't have dragged Jimmy out of New York. He thought it was the only place on earth. Well, we agreed that night that we would meet here again exactly twenty years from that date and time, no matter what. We figured that in twenty years each of us ought to have our fortunes made, whatever they were going to be."

"It sounds pretty interesting," said the policeman. "Rather a long time between meets, though, it seems to me. Haven't you heard from your friend since you left?"

"Well, yes, for a time we wrote," said the other. "But after a year or two we lost track of each other. You see, the West is a pretty big place. I kept hustling around over it pretty lively. But I know Jimmy will meet me here if he's alive, for he always was the truest friend in the world. He'll never forget. I came a thousand miles to stand in this door tonight. It's worth it if my old partner turns up."

The waiting man again pulled out his handsome watch. The case was set with diamonds.

"Three minutes to ten," he announced. "It was exactly ten o'clock when we parted here at the restaurant door."

"Did pretty well out West, didn't you?" asked the policeman.

"You bet! I hope Jimmy has done half as well. He was a kind of plodder, though, as good a fellow as he was. I've had to compete with some of the sharpest wits going to get my pile. A man gets in a rut in New York. It takes the West to put a razor-edge on him."

The policeman twirled his club and took a step or two.

"I'll be on my way. Hope your friend comes around all right. Going to call time on him sharp?"

"I should say not!" said the other. "I'll give him half an hour at least. If Jimmy

is alive on earth he'll be here by that time. So long, Officer."

"Good night, sir," said the policeman. He passed on along his beat, trying doors as he went.

There was now a fine, cold drizzle falling. The wind had risen from its uncertain puffs into a steady blow. The few people astir on that street hurried along with coat collars turned high and pocketed hands. And in the door of the hardware store the man who had come a thousand miles to fill an appointment watched and waited.

About twenty minutes he waited. Then a tall man in a long overcoat, with collar turned up to his ears, hurried across from the opposite side of the street. He went directly to the waiting man.

"Is that you, Bob?" he asked, doubtfully.

"Is that you, Jimmy Wells?" cried the man in the door.

"Bless my heart!" exclaimed the new arrival, grasping both the other's hands with his own. "It's Bob, sure as fate. I was certain I'd find you here if you were still alive. Well, well, well! Twenty years is a long time. The old restaurant's gone, Bob; I wish it had lasted, so we could have had another dinner there. How has the West treated you, old man?"

"Bully; it has given me everything I asked it for. You've changed lots, Jimmy. I never thought you were so tall by two or three inches."

"Oh, I grew a bit after I was twenty."

"Doing well in New York, Jimmy?"

"Moderately. I have a position in one of the city departments. Come on, Bob;

we'll go around to a place I know of and have a good long talk about old times."

The two men started up the street, arm in arm. The man from the West was beginning to outline the history of his career. The other, submerged in his overcoat, listened with interest.

At the corner stood a drugstore, brilliant with electric lights. When they came into this glare each of them turned simultaneously to gaze upon the other's face.

The man from the West stopped suddenly and released his arm.

"You're not Jimmy Wells," he snapped. "Twenty years is a long time, but not long enough to change the shape of a man's nose."

"It sometimes changes a good man into a bad one," said the tall man. "You've been under arrest for ten minutes, 'Silky' Bob. Chicago thinks you may have dropped over our way and wires us she wants to have a chat with you. Going quietly, are you? That's sensible. Now, before we go to the station, here's a note I was asked to hand to you. You may read it here at the window. It's from Patrolman Wells."

The man from the West unfolded the little piece of paper handed to him. His hand was steady when he began to read, but it trembled a little by the time he had finished. The note was rather short.

Bob:
I was at the appointed place on time. When you struck the match to check the time, I saw your face. It was the face of the man wanted in Chicago. Somehow I couldn't do it myself. I went around and got a plain-clothes man to do the job.

Jimmy

## READING COMPREHENSION

**Summarizing.** Choose the best phrase to complete each sentence. Then write the complete statements on your paper.

1. The streets were nearly empty because _____ (people were afraid of crime late at night, most people had to go to work the next day, it was chilly and there was a chance of rain).

2. The waiting man and his friend had agreed to meet _____ (when both had made their fortunes, to share a meal and some drinks, exactly 20 years later).

3. After he arrested him, the plainclothesman handed "Silky" Bob _____ (a note from Jimmy Wells, a warrant for his arrest, a wire from Chicago).

**Interpreting.** Write the answer to each question on your paper.

1. How did "Silky" Bob know that his companion wasn't Jimmy Wells?

2. Why did the police officer walk up to the man in the doorway?

3. Why didn't "Silky" Bob recognize that the plainclothesman wasn't Jimmy Wells until they stood in the light?

### For Thinking and Discussing

1. It had been 20 years since Bob and Jimmy went their separate ways. How do you think Bob changed during that time?

2. Why do you think Jimmy Wells didn't want to arrest "Silky" Bob himself?

## UNDERSTANDING LITERATURE

**Plot in a Short Story.** "After Twenty Years" by O. Henry is an excellent example of a short story. In a few pages, it describes a particular *setting* (time and place), introduces *characters* (people), and tells the reader what happens to them through the *plot* (a series of events, usually involving a problem and its solution).

In a well-written short story, each incident in the plot has a purpose. That purpose may be one of the following:

**a.** to complicate the problem or conflict
**b.** to take the action a step further
**c.** to tell about the characters

On your paper, match each incident from "After Twenty Years" with the main purpose it serves in the plot.

1. The police officer began a conversation with the man in the doorway.

2. A tall man in a long overcoat went directly to the waiting man.

3. The man arrested "Silky" Bob and then gave him a note to read.

4. Bob read the note and learned that the police officer was the old friend for whom he had been waiting.

## WRITING

Think about how "Silky" Bob felt after he read the note from his old friend Jimmy Wells. Write an answer to Jimmy Wells, telling what "Silky" Bob might have said if he had had the chance.

# Raymond's Run

*by Toni Cade Bambara*

*Toni Cade Bambara (1939—) is well-known for her articles and stories about blacks in the United States. She has also written a full-length novel,* The Salt Eaters. *The story you are about to read is from her collection of short stories* Gorilla, My Love. *It is about the special love a teenage girl has for her mentally handicapped brother, Raymond.*

I don't have much work to do around the house like some girls. My mother does that. And I don't have to earn my pocket money by hustling; George runs errands for the big boys and sells Christmas cards. And anything else that's got to get done, my father does. All I have to do in life is mind my brother Raymond, which is enough.

Sometimes I slip and say my little brother Raymond. But as any fool can see he's much bigger and he's older, too. But a lot of people call him my little brother cause he needs looking after cause he's not quite right. And a lot of smart mouths got lots to say about that, too, especially when George was minding him. But now, if anybody has anything to say to Raymond, anything to say about his big head, they have to come by me. And I don't play the dozens* or believe in standing around with somebody in my face doing a lot of

talking. I much rather just knock you down and take my chances even if I am a little girl with skinny arms and a squeaky voice, which is how I got the name Squeaky. And if things get too rough, I run. And as anybody can tell you, I'm the fastest thing on two feet.

There is no track meet that I don't win the first-place medal. I used to win the 20-yard dash when I was a little kid in kindergarten. Nowadays, it's the 50-yard dash. And tomorrow I'm subject to run the quarter-meter relay all by myself and come in first, second, and third. The big kids call me Mercury cause I'm the swiftest thing in the neighborhood. Everybody knows that — except two people who know better, my father and me. He can beat me to Amsterdam Avenue with me having a two fire-hydrant headstart and him running with his hands in his pockets and whistling. But that's private information. Cause can you imagine some 35-year-old man stuffing himself into PAL shorts to race little kids? So as far as

---

* *The dozens* — a street-corner game that involves trading insults.

everyone's concerned, I'm the fastest and that goes for Gretchen, too, who has put out the tale that she is going to win the first-place medal this year. Ridiculous. In the second place, she's got short legs. In the third place, she's got freckles. In the first place, no one can beat me and that's all there is to it.

I'm standing on the corner admiring the weather and about to take a stroll down Broadway so I can practice my breathing exercises, and I've got Raymond walking on the inside close to the buildings, cause he's subject to fits of fantasy and starts thinking he's a circus performer and that the curb is a tightrope strung high in the air. And sometimes after a rain he likes to step down off his tightrope right into the gutter and slosh around getting his shoes and cuffs wet. Then I get hit when I get home. Or sometimes if you don't watch him he'll dash across traffic to the island in the middle of Broadway and give the pigeons a fit. Then I have to go behind him apologizing to all the old people sitting around trying to get some sun and getting all upset with the pigeons fluttering around them, scattering their newspapers and up- setting the wax-paper lunches in their laps. So I keep Raymond on the inside of me, and he plays like he's driving a stagecoach which is OK by me so long as he doesn't run me over or interrupt my breathing exercises, which I have to do on account of I'm serious about my running, and I don't care who knows it.

Now some people like to act like things come easy to them, won't let on that they practice. Not me. I'll high-prance down 34th Street like a rodeo pony to keep my knees strong even if it does get my mother uptight so that she walks ahead like she's not with me, don't know me, is all by herself on a shopping trip, and I am somebody else's crazy child. Now you take Cynthia Procter for instance. She's just the opposite. If there's a test tomor- row, she'll say something like, "Oh, I guess I'll play handball this afternoon and watch television tonight," just to let you know she ain't thinking about the test. Or like last week when she won the spelling bee for the millionth time, "A good thing you got 'receive,' Squeaky, cause I would have got it wrong. I completely forgot about the spelling bee." And she'll clutch the lace on her blouse like it was a narrow escape. Oh, brother. But of course when I pass her house on my early morning trots around the block, she is practicing the scales on the piano over and over and over and over. Then in music class she always lets herself get bumped around so she falls accidentally on purpose onto the piano stool and is so surprised to find herself sitting there that she decides just for fun to try out the ole keys. And what do you know — Chopin's waltzes just spring out of her fingertips and she's the most surprised thing in the world. A regular prodigy. I could kill people like that. I stay up all night studying the words for the spelling bee. And you can see me any time of day practicing running. I never walk if I can trot, and shame on Raymond if he can't keep up. But of course he does, cause if he hangs back someone's liable to walk up to him and get smart, or take his allowance from him, or ask him where he got that great big pumpkin head. People are so stupid sometimes.

So I'm strolling down Broadway breathing out and breathing in on counts of seven, which is my lucky number, and here come Gretchen and her sidekicks: Mary Louise, who used to be a friend of mine when she first moved to Harlem from Baltimore and got beat up by everybody till I took up for her on account of her mother and my mother used to sing in the same choir when they were young girls, but people ain't grateful, so now she hangs out with the new girl Gretchen and talks about me like a dog; and Rosie, who is fat as I am skinny and has a big mouth where Raymond is concerned and is too stupid to know that there is not a big deal of difference between herself and Raymond and that she can't afford to throw stones. So they are steady coming up

Broadway and I see right away that it's going to be one of those Dodge City scenes cause the street ain't that big and they're close to the buildings just as we are. First I think I'll step into the new candy store and look over the new comics and let them pass. But that's chicken and I've got a reputation to consider. So then I think I'll just walk straight on through them or even over them if necessary. But as they get to me, they slow down. I'm ready to fight, cause like I said I don't feature a whole lot of chit-chat, I much prefer to just knock you down right from the jump and save everybody a lotta precious time.

"You signing up for the May Day races?" smiles Mary Louise, only it's not a smile at all. A dumb question like that doesn't deserve an answer. Besides, there's just me and Gretchen standing there really, so no use wasting my breath talking to shadows.

"I don't think you're going to win this time," says Rosie, trying to signify with her hands on her hips all salty, completely forgetting that I have whupped her behind many times for less salt than that.

"I always win cause I'm the best," I say straight at Gretchen who is, as far as I'm concerned, the only one talking in this ventriloquist-dummy routine. Gretchen smiles, but it's not a smile, and I'm thinking that girls never really smile at each other because they don't know how and don't want to know how and there's probably no one to teach us how, cause grown-up girls don't know either. Then they all look at Raymond who has just brought his mule team to a standstill. And they're about to see what trouble they can get into through him.

"What grade you in now, Raymond?"

"You got anything to say to my brother, you say it to me, Mary Louise Williams of Raggedy Town, Baltimore."

"What are you, his mother?" sasses Rosie.

"That's right, Fatso. And the next word out of anybody and I'll be their mother too." So they just stand there and Gretchen shifts from one leg to the other and so do they. Then Gretchen puts her hands on her hips and is about to say something with her freckle-face self but doesn't. Then she walks around me looking me up and down but keeps walking up Broadway, and her sidekicks follow her. So me and Raymond smile at each other and he says, "Gidyap," to his team and I continue with my breathing exercises, strolling down Broadway toward the ice man on 145th with not a care in the world cause I am

Miss Quicksilver herself.

I take my time getting to the park on May Day because the track meet is the last thing on the program. The biggest thing on the program is the May Pole dancing, which I can do without, thank you, even if my mother thinks it's a shame I don't take part and act like a girl for a change. You'd think my mother'd be grateful not to have to make me a white organdy dress with a big satin sash and buy me new white baby-doll shoes that can't be taken out of the box till the big day. You'd think she'd be glad her daughter ain't out there prancing around a May Pole getting the new clothes all dirty and sweaty and trying to act like a fairy or a flower or whatever you're supposed to be when you should be trying to be yourself, whatever that is, which is as far as I'm concerned, a poor Black girl who really can't afford to buy shoes and a new dress you only wear once a lifetime cause it won't fit next year.

I was once a strawberry in a Hansel and Gretel pageant when I was in nursery school and didn't have no better sense than to dance on tiptoe with my arms in a circle over my head doing umbrella steps and being a perfect fool just so my mother and father could come dressed up and clap. You'd think they'd know better than to encourage that kind of nonsense. I am not a strawberry. I do not dance on my toes. I run. That is what I am all about. So I always come late to the May Day program, just in time to get my number pinned on and lay in the grass till they announce the 50-yard dash.

I put Raymond in the little swings,

which is a tight squeeze this year and will be impossible next year. Then I look around for Mr. Pearson, who pins the numbers on. I'm really looking for Gretchen if you want to know the truth, but she's not around. The park is jam-packed. Parents in hats and corsages and breast-pocket handkerchiefs peeking up. Kids in white dresses and light-blue suits. The parkees* unfolding chairs and chasing the rowdy kids from Lenox as if they had no right to be there. The big guys with their caps on backward, leaning against the fence swirling the basketballs on the tips of their fingers, waiting for all these crazy people to clear out the park so they can play. Most of the kids in my class are carrying bass drums and glockenspiels and flutes. You'd think they'd put in a few bongos or something for real like that.

Then here comes Mr. Pearson with his clipboard and his cards and pencils and whistles and safety pins and 50 million other things he's always dropping all over the place with his clumsy self. He sticks out in a crowd because he's on stilts. We used to call him Jack and the Beanstalk to get him mad. But I'm the only one that can outrun him and get away, and I'm too grown for that silliness now.

"Well, Squeaky," he says, checking my name off the list and handing me number seven and two pins. And I'm thinking he's got no right to call me Squeaky if I can't call him Beanstalk.

"Hazel Elizabeth Deborah Parker," I correct him and tell him to write it down on his board.

---

* *Parkees* — park attendants.

"Well, Hazel Elizabeth Deborah Parker, going to give someone else a break this year?" I squint at him real hard to see if he is seriously thinking I should lose the race on purpose just to give someone else a break. "Only six girls running this time," he continues, shaking his head sadly like it's my fault all of New York didn't turn out in sneakers. "That new girl should give you a run for your money." He looks around the park for Gretchen like a periscope in a submarine movie. "Wouldn't it be a nice gesture if you were . . . to ahh . . ."

I give him such a look he couldn't finish putting that idea into words. Grown-ups got a lot of nerve sometimes. I pin my number seven to myself and stomp away, I'm so burnt. And I go straight for the track and stretch out on the grass while the band winds up with "Oh, the Monkey Wrapped His Tail Around the Flagpole," which my teacher calls by some other name. The man on the loudspeaker is calling everyone over to the track and I'm on my back looking at the sky, trying to pretend I'm in the country, but I can't, because even grass in the city feels hard as sidewalk, and there's just no pretending you are anywhere but in a "concrete jungle" as my grandfather says.

The 20-yard dash takes all of two minutes cause most of the little kids don't know no better than to run off the track or run the wrong way or run smack into the fence and fall down and cry. One little kid, though, has got the good sense to run straight for the white ribbon up ahead so he wins. Then the second-graders line up for the 30-yard dash and I don't even

bother to turn my head to watch cause Raphael Perez always wins. He wins before he even begins by psyching the runners, telling them they're going to trip on their shoelaces and fall on their faces or lose their shorts or something, which he doesn't have to do since he is very fast, almost as fast as I am. After that is the 40-yard dash which I used to run when I was in the first grade. Raymond is hollering from the swings cause he knows I'm about to do my thing cause the man on the loudspeaker has just announced the 50-yard dash, although he might as well be giving a recipe for angel food cake cause you can hardly make out what he's sayin' for the static. I get up and slip off my sweat pants and then I see Gretchen standing at the starting line, kicking her legs out like a pro. Then as I get into place I see that ole Raymond is on line on the other side of the fence, bending down with his fingers on the ground just like he knew what he was doing. I was going to yell at him but then I didn't. It burns up your energy to holler.

Every time, just before I take off in a race, I always feel like I'm in a dream, the kind of dream you have when you're sick with fever and feel all hot and weightless. I dream I'm flying over a sandy beach in the early morning sun, kissing the leaves of the trees as I fly by. And there's always the smell of apples, just like in the country when I was little and used to think I was a choo-choo train, running through the fields of corn and chugging up the hill to the orchard. And all the time I'm dreaming this, I get lighter and lighter until I'm flying over the beach again, getting blown through the sky like a feather that weighs nothing at all. But once I spread my fingers in the dirt and crouch down over the Get on Your Mark, the dream goes and I am solid again and am telling myself: Squeaky, you must win, you must win, you are the fastest thing in the world, you can even beat your father up Amsterdam if you really try. And then I feel my weight coming back just behind my knees then down to my feet then into the earth and the pistol shot explodes in my blood and I am off and weightless again, flying past the other runners, my arms pumping up and down and the whole world is quiet except for the crunch as I zoom over the gravel in the track. I glance to my left and there is no one. To the right, a blurred Gretchen, who's got her chin jutting out as if it would win the race all by itself. And on the other side of the fence is Raymond with his arms down at his side and the palms tucked up behind him, running in his very own style, and it's the first time I ever saw that and I almost stop to watch my brother Raymond on his first run. But the white ribbon is bouncing toward me and I tear past it, racing into the distance till my feet with a mind of their own start digging up footfuls of dirt and brake me short. Then all the kids standing on the side pile on me, banging me on the back and slapping my head with their May Day programs, for I have won again and everybody on 151st Street can walk tall for another year.

"In first place . . ." the man on the loudspeaker is clear as a bell now. But then he pauses and the loudspeaker starts to whine. Then static. And I lean down to catch my breath and here comes Gretchen walking back, for she's overshot the finish line too, huffing and puffing with her hands on her hips, taking it slow, breathing in steady time like a real pro and I sort of like her a little for the first time. "In the first place . . ." and then three or four voices get mixed up on the loudspeaker and I dig my sneaker into the grass and stare at Gretchen who's staring back, we both wondering just who did win. I can hear old Beanstalk arguing with the man on the loudspeaker and then a few others running their mouths about what the stopwatches say. Then I hear Raymond yanking at the fence to call me and I wave to shush him, but he keeps rattling the fence like a gorilla in a cage, like in them gorilla movies, but then like a dancer or something he starts climbing up nice and easy but very fast. And it occurs to me, watching how smoothly he climbs hand over hand and remembering how he looked running with his arms down to his side and with the wind pulling his mouth back and his teeth showing and all, it occurred to me that Raymond would make a very fine runner. Doesn't he always keep up with me on my trots? And he surely knows how to breathe in counts of seven cause he's always doing it at the dinner table, which drives my brother George up the wall. And I'm smiling to beat the band cause if I've lost the race, or if me and Gretchen tied, or even if I've won, I can always retire as a runner and begin a whole new career as a coach with Raymond as my champion. After all, with a little more study I can beat Cynthia and her phony self at the spelling bee. And if I bugged my mother, I could get piano lessons and become a star. And I have a big rep as the baddest thing around. And I've got a roomful of ribbons and medals and awards. But what has Raymond got to call his own?

So I stand there with my new plans, laughing out loud by this time as Raymond jumps down from the fence and runs over with his teeth showing and his arms down to the side which no one before has quite mastered as a running style. And by the time he comes over I'm jumping up and down so glad to see him — my brother Raymond, a great runner in the family tradition. But of course everyone thinks I'm jumping up and down because the men on the loudspeaker have finally gotten themselves together and compared notes and are announcing, "In first place — Miss Hazel Elizabeth Deborah Parker." (Dig that.)

"In second place — Miss Gretchen P. Lewis." And I look over at Gretchen wondering what the "P" stands for. And I smile. Cause she's good, no doubt about it. Maybe she'd like to help me coach Raymond; she obviously is serious about running, as any fool can see. And she nods to congratulate me and then she smiles. And I smile. We stand there with this big smile of respect between us. It's about as real a smile as girls can do for each other, considering we don't practice real smiling every day, you know, cause maybe we're too busy being flowers or fairies or strawberries instead of something honest and worthy of respect . . . you know . . . like being people.

**Summarizing.** Choose the best phrase to complete each sentence. Then write the complete statements on your paper.

1. Hazel sometimes called Raymond her "little brother" because _____ (he liked to pretend he was small, she felt stronger than everyone, she had to look after him).

2. Hazel took her time getting to the park on May Day because _____ (the track meet was the last thing on the program, she liked to watch the May Pole dancing, she had to take Raymond with her).

3. As the announcement of the winner was being made, Hazel jumped up and down because she was _____ (not able to see over the crowd, excited at the thought of becoming Raymond's coach, very sure she had won).

**Interpreting.** Write the answer to each question on your paper.

1. Why did Hazel and Gretchen smile at each other after the race?

2. Why did it take so long to announce the winner?

3. What was Mr. Pearson about to suggest that Hazel do during the race?

**For Thinking and Discussing.** Why do you think Hazel got so excited about the idea of coaching her brother Raymond to become a runner?

**Characterization in a Short Story.** How do readers of a short story learn about its characters? A writer can portray a character directly by telling you what the character is like. Or the writer can portray a character indirectly by letting the character's own words and actions tell what he or she is like. Sometimes the way in which two or more characters react to one another helps you understand them.

Read each of the following statements. On your paper, identify the character each one tells you about. Then identify which technique of characterization is being used.

**Techniques of Characterization**
   a. character's actions
   b. character's own words
   c. how other characters react
   d. narrator's description of others

1. The big kids called her Mercury because she was the swiftest thing in the neighborhood.

2. "In the second place, she's got short legs. [Third,] she's got freckles."

3. She jumped up and down because she was so glad to see her brother.

4. "I always win cause I'm the best."

Pretend you are a sportscaster. Make up six questions that you would ask Hazel about herself. Then write the answers you think she would give.

# Three Days to See

*by Helen Keller*

*Helen Keller (1880-1968) became blind and deaf as the result of an illness when she was 19 months old. She learned to communicate through sign language and later through voice lessons. She also communicated quite effectively through her writing. In 1902 she published her autobiography,* The Story of My Life. *She also published several other books and many essays. As you will discover when you read this essay, Keller had an exceptional insight into people and the world around her.*

All of us have read thrilling stories in which the hero had only a limited time to live. Sometimes it was as long as a year; sometimes as short as 24 hours. I speak, of course, of free men who have a choice, not condemned criminals whose activities are strictly limited.

Such stories set us wondering what we should do under similar conditions. What should we crowd into these last hours? What happiness should we find in reviewing the past, what regrets?

Sometimes I have thought that we should live each day as if it were our last. Most of us, however, take life for granted.

The same casualness characterizes the use of all our senses. Only the deaf appreciate hearing. Only the blind realize the blessings that lie in sight. It's the same old story of not being grateful for what we have until we lose it.

I have often thought it would be a blessing if each human being were stricken blind and deaf for a few days. Darkness would make him appreciate sight. Silence would teach him the joys of sound.

Now and then I have tested my seeing friends to discover what they see. Recently I was visited by a good friend. She had just returned from a walk in the woods. "What did you see?" I asked. "Nothing in particular" was her reply.

How is it possible to walk for an hour and see nothing worthy of note? I cannot see, but I find hundreds of things that interest me. I feel the delicate patterns of a leaf. I pass my hand lovingly about the smooth skin of a birch or the rough bark of pine. In spring I touch the branches of trees in search of a bud. I feel the velvety texture of a flower. Occasionally, I place my hand on a small tree and feel the happy quiver of a bird in song.

At times I long to see all these things. If I can get so much pleasure from mere touch, how much more beauty must be revealed by sight. Yet those who have eyes see little. The panorama of color and action which fills the world is taken for granted.

If I were the president of a university I would set up a course called "How to Use Your Eyes." The teacher would show his pupils how they could add joy to their lives by really seeing what passes unnoticed before them.

Perhaps I can best illustrate by imagining what I should most like to see if I were given the use of my eyes, say, for just three days. And while I am imagining, suppose you, too, consider the problem.

How would you use your eyes if you had only three more days to see? How would you spend those three precious days?

I should want most to see the things which have become dear to me through my years of darkness. You, too, would want to let your eyes rest long on the things that are dear to you. Then you could take the memory of them with you into the long night that loomed ahead.

If by some miracle I were granted just three days to see, I should divide the period into three parts.

On the first day, I should like to see the people whose kindness and friendship have made my life worth living. First, I should

gaze long upon the face of my dear teacher, Mrs. Anne Sullivan Macy. She came to me when I was a child and opened the outer world to me. I should like to see in her eyes that strength of character and compassion for all which she has revealed to me so often.

I know my friends from the feel of their faces, through the thoughts they express to me, and through whatever their actions reveal to me. But I am denied that deeper understanding of them that I am sure would come through sight. I should like to call all my dear friends to me on that first day of sight. I should like to watch their eyes and faces react to expressed thoughts and events. I would look long into their faces, imprinting upon my mind the outward evidences of beauty within them. I should also let my eyes rest on a baby. I wish to see the eager, innocent beauty which precedes the awareness of the conflicts which develops later in life.

On that busy first day I should like to look into the loyal, trusting eyes of my dogs. I should also want to see the simple things in my home. I want to see the warm colors in the rugs under my feet. I want to see the pictures on the walls. My eyes would rest respectfully on the books in raised type which I have read and eagerly pore over the books that seeing people read. During the long night of my life books have built themselves into a great shining lighthouse. Books have revealed to me the deepest channels of human life and the human spirit.

In the afternoon of that first day I should take a long walk in the woods. I would

try desperately to absorb in a few hours the vast splendor which is constantly unfolding for those who can see. On the way home I would stop at a farm so that I might see the horses plowing in the field. (Perhaps I should see only a tractor!) And I should pray for the glory of a colorful sunset.

When dusk had fallen, I should experience the double delight of being able to see by artificial light. In the night of that first day I should not be able to sleep. My mind would be too full of the memories of the day.

The next day, the second day of sight, I should arise to watch the dawn.

This day I should devote to a hasty glimpse of the world, past and present. How can so much be compressed into one day? Through the museums, of course. Often I have visited the Museum of Natural History. I have touched with my hands many of the objects there exhibited. Now I would see the condensed history of earth displayed there — all the animals and the races of men pictured there.

My next stop would be the Metropolitan Museum of Art. Here in the vast chambers of the Metropolitan is unfolded the spirit people have expressed in their art. Oh, there is so much rich meaning and beauty in the art of the ages for you who have eyes to see!

Upon my short visit to this temple of art I should not be able to review a fraction of the great world of art. Artists tell me that for a true appreciation of art one must educate the eye. One must learn to consider line, form, color, and composi-

tion. If I had eyes, how happily would I take up this study. Yet I am told that, to many of you who have eyes to see, the world of art is unexplored.

Sadly, I would leave the Metropolitan Museum, which contains the key to beauty. Seeing persons do not need a Metropolitan to find this key to beauty. The same key lies waiting in smaller museums, and in books in even the smallest libraries. But naturally in my limited time of imaginary sight, I should choose the place where the key unlocks the greatest treasures in the shortest day.

The evening of my second day of sight I should spend at a theater or at the movies. Even now I often go to the theater, but the action of the play must be spelled into my hand by a companion. How I should like to see with my own eyes the actors moving gracefully or comically across the stage. I long to see the colorful costumes and scenery. I long to see how dancers move with rhythm and beauty.

How many of you, I wonder, when you gaze at a play or movie realize and give thanks for the miracle of sight that enables you to enjoy its color, grace, and movement?

So, through the evening of my second imaginary day of sight, the great figures of drama would crowd sleep from my eyes.

The following morning, I should again greet the dawn. I am sure that the dawn of each day must reveal a new beauty.

This is to be my third and last imagined day of sight. I shall have no time for regrets. There is too much to see. Today

I shall spend in the workaday world of the present. New York City is my destination.

I start from my home in the quiet little suburb of Forest Hills, Long Island. Here I see green lawns, trees, and neat little houses. I drive across the lacy structure of steel into the city. Below busy boats chug and scurry about the river. I look ahead and before me rise the fantastic towers of the city.

I hurry to the top of the Empire State Building. A short time ago, I "saw" the city below through the eyes of my secretary. I am eager to compare my fancy with reality. I am sure I should not be disappointed. It would be a vision of another world.

Now I begin my rounds of the city. First, I stand at a busy corner. I look at people and try to understand something of their lives. I see smiles, and I am happy. I see serious determination, and I am proud. I see suffering, and I am compassionate.

I stroll down Fifth Avenue. I see a seething mass of color. I am convinced that I should become a window shopper, too.

From Fifth Avenue I make a tour of the city. I see Park Avenue. I see the slums. I see factories, and parks where children play. My heart is full of the images of people and things. Some sights are pleasant. They fill my heart with happiness. Some sights are sad or ugly. To these I do not shut my eyes. They, too, are part of life. To close the eye on them is to close the heart and mind.

My third day of sight is drawing to an end. Perhaps there are many serious things I should study. Yet I should spend that last evening again at the theater. I should see a hilariously funny play.

At midnight I would again be blind. Naturally in those three short days, I should not have seen all I wanted to see. Only when darkness had again descended upon me should I realize how much I had left unseen. But my mind would be crowded with glorious memories. Thereafter the touch of every object would bring a glowing memory of how that object looked.

Perhaps this outline of how I should spend my three days of sight does not agree with the plan you would follow if you knew you were about to become blind. I am, however, sure that if you really faced that fate you would use your eyes as never before. Your eyes would touch and embrace every object that came within your range of vision. Then, at last, you would really see. A new world of beauty would open before you.

I who am blind can give one hint to those who see: Use your eyes as if tomorrow you would become blind. Use your other senses the same way. Hear the music of voices, the song of a bird as if you would be deaf tomorrow. Touch each object as if tomorrow this sense would fail. Smell the perfume of flowers, taste each morsel, as if tomorrow you could never taste or smell again. Make the most of every sense. Glory in the pleasure and beauty the world reveals to you through your senses. But of all the senses, I am sure that sight must be most delightful.

## READING COMPREHENSION

**Summarizing.** Choose the best phrase to complete each sentence. Then write the complete statements on your paper.

1. Helen Keller said she sometimes thought that _____ (it was a blessing to be blind, we should live each day as if it were our last, people talked too much about what they saw).

2. If she could see, on her second day of sight Helen Keller said she would arise to _____ (watch the dawn, go to the Museum of Natural History, see her friends standing around her).

3. After three days of being able to see, Helen Keller said she _____ (would now study more serious things, might wish she had never seen at all, would have glorious memories).

**Interpreting.** Write the answer to each question on your paper.

1. What were the first things that Helen Keller wanted to see?

2. What did Helen Keller mean when she said she saw the city through the eyes of her secretary?

3. Why does Helen Keller ask us to use our eyes as if tomorrow we would become blind?

**For Thinking and Discussing.** Why do you think Helen Keller asked her readers to pretend that they had only three more days to see?

## UNDERSTANDING LITERATURE

**Personal Narrative Essay.** An *essay* is a short work of literature in which the author makes a statement about an idea or subject and then gives reasons to support or prove that statement.

"Three Days to See" by Helen Keller is a *personal narrative essay*. Personal narrative essays are often informal in style. The author expresses his or her beliefs about a particular subject and gives examples to explain or support those beliefs.

Here are several beliefs expressed by Helen Keller in the essay you have just read. Go back to the text of the essay and find two examples or reasons that the author used to support each statement. Write them on your paper.

1. ". . . it would be a blessing if each human being were stricken blind and deaf for a few days."

2. "I cannot see, but I find hundreds of things that interest me."

3. ". . . those who have eyes see little."

4. "Make the most of every sense. Glory in the pleasure and beauty the world reveals to you through your senses."

## WRITING

Write a letter to a friend. Describe an experience you have had or something interesting you have seen. Try to paint a picture in your friend's mind of the experience or object you are describing.

# Learning to Read

*by Frederick Douglass*

*"I would rather be killed running than die a slave." So said Frederick Douglass (1817–1895). Frederick Douglass was born a slave. As a young man, he escaped from slavery in Maryland.*

*After winning his freedom, Douglass traveled all over the North, speaking out against slavery. In 1845, Douglass wrote about his life as a slave in* Narrative of the Life of Frederick Douglass. *This selection is part of his autobiography, telling about his experiences between the ages of eight and eighteen. During this time, he lived in Baltimore with relatives of his master. It was there that Douglass learned to read—and in doing so, gained the key to his freedom.*

My new mistress was a kind woman. She had never had a slave under her control before. She began, when I first went to live with her, to treat me the way she thought one human being ought to treat another. She did not seem to see that she must act like a slaveholder. For a slaveholder to treat me like a human being was wrong, and dangerous for her. Slavery proved as harmful to her as it was to me.

When I went to live there, she was religious, warm, and tenderhearted. But slavery took that away from her. Her soft heart turned to stone. Her gentleness turned into tiger-like fierceness.

At first, she had kindly taught me the ABC's, and to spell words of three or four letters. But her husband, Mr. Auld, found out. He told her she could not teach me any more. He said that it was not lawful, and not safe, to teach a slave to read.

"If you give him an inch, he'll take a yard," he said. "A slave should do nothing but obey his master. Learning to read will make him unfit to be a slave. And he will be discontented and unhappy."

From that moment I understood the pathway from slavery to freedom. My master had shown me the source of the white man's power. I knew it would be hard to learn without a teacher. But I set out with high hope and a fixed purpose, at whatever cost, to learn to read.

Mrs. Auld became even more against it than her husband himself. She was not satisfied in just doing what he had ordered.

Frederick Douglass, Elisha Hammond

She seemed anxious to do better. Nothing made her more angry than to see me with a newspaper. She would rush at me with a face of fury and snatch it from me. She was sure, now, that education and slavery could not mix.

I was narrowly watched. If I was in a separate room for any length of time, I was suspected of having a book. But it was too late. The first step had been taken. The alphabet had given me the inch. Nothing could keep me from taking the yard.

My plan worked very well. I made friends with all the little white boys I met in the street. As many of them as I could, I made into my teachers. When I was sent on an errand, I always took a book. I also took bread, for there was always plenty and I was welcome to it. In that way I was better off than many poor white children in the neighborhood. I would give bread to these hungry little boys. They, in turn, would teach me what they had learned in school.

I used to talk to them about slavery. I wished I could be as free as they would be when they were men.

"You will be free as soon as you are 21," I would say, "but I am a slave for life!"

These words used to trouble them. They would say, "Something may happen so you can be free."

I was now about 12 years old. The thought of being a slave for life weighed heavily upon my heart. I got hold of some books in which arguments for and against slavery were given. The more I read the more I was led to hate my masters. I saw them as robbers who had gone to Africa and stolen us from our homes and made us slaves in a strange land. Master Auld had been right. Discontentment had followed learning to read.

At times, I felt reading was a curse rather than a blessing. It had opened my eyes to the horrible pit I was in, with no ladder to climb out. Sometimes I even envied my fellow slaves who did not understand. I could think of nothing but my condition. Freedom had appeared, and would never disappear. I saw nothing without seeing it and felt nothing without feeling it. It looked from every star, breathed in every wind, and moved in every storm.

I would have killed myself if it were not for the hope of being free. Every little while, I would hear something about abolition. It was some time before I found out what it meant. If a slave ran away, or set fire to a barn, or did anything wrong in the mind of a slaveholder, it was said to be the fruit of abolition. I looked it up in the dictionary. I found it was "the act of abolishing." But what did that mean?

I did not dare ask anyone, for I was sure it was something they did not want me to know about. At last I got hold of a newspaper, which explained that Northerners were praying for the abolition of slavery. The light broke upon me.

I resolved to run away. But first, I had to learn how to write, so I could write my own pass.

I was often sent to a shipyard. I watched the ship carpenters get a piece of wood ready for use. They would write on it the name of the part of the ship it would be built into. When a piece of timber was meant for the larboard side they would write "L." For starboard, it was "S." For the larboard side forward, it would be "L.F." and so on. I soon learned the names of these letters, and began to copy them. Then, I would tell any boy I met who could write that I could write, too.

He would say, "I don't believe you. Let me see you try it." I would make the letters I had learned, and ask him to beat that. I got a good many lessons in writing. My copy books were board fences, walls, and pavements. My pen and ink was a lump of chalk.

By this time, little Master Thomas Auld was in school. When his mother went out, I would copy what he had written in his lesson books. Before long, I could write in a hand very like Master Thomas's.

In 1835, with six other slaves, I planned an escape from another master. Each of us had a "protection": "This is to certify that I, the undersigned, have given the bearer, my servant, full liberty to go to Baltimore and spend the Easter holidays. Written with mine own hand, &c, 1835. William Hamilton."

I wrote them.

## READING COMPREHENSION

**Summarizing.** Choose the best phrase to complete each sentence. Then write the complete statements on your paper.

1. When Mrs. Auld stopped teaching Frederick to read, he _____ (gave up learning to read and write, taught himself to read, made plans to escape).

2. Frederick made friends with white boys and often _____ (traded bread for lessons, invited them to his home, played games with them).

3. When Frederick Douglass escaped from his master in 1835, he _____ (went to work in a shipyard, wrote passes for himself and six other slaves, spent Easter with the Hamiltons).

**Interpreting.** Write the answer to each question on your paper.

1. Why did Mrs. Auld become angry when she saw Frederick with a newspaper?

2. What did Frederick believe was the path from slavery to freedom?

3. How did Frederick get the white boys to teach him how to write?

**For Thinking and Discussing**

1. Why do you think Frederick Douglass thought slavery was as harmful to Mrs. Auld as it was to him?

2. Why did knowing how to read make Frederick Douglass more unhappy and discontented?

## UNDERSTANDING LITERATURE

**Autobiography.** An *autobiography* is the story of a person's life written by himself or herself. An autobiography often tells how the author thinks or feels about significant events in his or her life.

Here are some ideas taken from "Learning to Read." Below them are Douglass's own words. On your paper, match the ideas to the quotes from his autobiography.

### Ideas

1. Education is the road to freedom.
2. Knowledge can make you sad as well as happy.
3. If you have something others want, you can get something from them in return.

### Quotes

a. "[Reading] had opened my eyes to the horrible pit I was in, with no ladder to climb out."

b. "I would give bread to these hungry little boys. They, in turn, would teach me what they had learned in school."

c. "My master had shown me the source of the white man's power. . . . I set out . . . at whatever cost, to learn to read."

## WRITING

Think about your own life, and choose one person or event that stands out in your mind. Write about that person or event as though it were going to be part of your own autobiography.

# Three American Poems

*Poetry expresses ideas and creates images, or pictures. It can stimulate your imagination by putting you in touch with events, places, and characters that are often beyond your everyday experience. Poetry can also reflect your own life and feelings. Here are three poems representing the work of three fine poets from different times and places in America.*

*Luis Palés Matos (1898–1959) is considered one of the greatest poets Puerto Rico has ever produced. His description in "Hurricane" gives you the feeling of being part of the event.*

*Edna St. Vincent Millay (1892–1950) wrote at about the same time as Matos. Her poetry conveys feelings so well that during her youth she was hailed as the voice of her generation. Perhaps her poem "Travel" captures a feeling that you have experienced when you have watched a train or an airplane speed by.*

*Henry Wadsworth Longfellow (1807–1882) is well known for his long poems that tell stories about famous people and events in American history. The poem included here, "The Tide Rises, The Tide Falls," tells a haunting story with few words but memorable insights.*

# The Hurricane   *by Luis Palés Matos*

When the hurricane unfolds
Its fierce accordion of winds,
On the tip of its toes,
Agile dancer, it sweeps whirling
Over the carpeted surface of the sea
With the scattered branches of the palm.

1. To what does the poet compare the winds of the hurricane?

2. Does this poem make a hurricane seem frightening? Why or why not?

**Palm Tree, Nassau,** Winslow Homer, 1898

# The Tide Rises, the Tide Falls

*by Henry Wadsworth Longfellow*

The tide rises, the tide falls,
The twilight darkens, the curlew calls;
Along the sea sands damp and
    brown
The traveler hastens toward the town,
  And the tide rises, the tide falls.

Darkness settles on roofs and walls,
But the sea, the sea in the darkness calls;
The little waves, with their soft, white
    hands,
Efface the footprints in the sands,
  And the tide rises, the tide falls.

The morning breaks; the steeds in their
    stalls
Stamp and neigh, as the hostler calls;
The day returns, but nevermore
Returns the traveler to the shore,
    And the tide rises, the tide falls.

**1.** The poem begins at what time of day? At what time of day does it end?

**2.** *Efface* means to destroy or take away. Explain how the waves can efface the footprints in the sand.

**Approaching Storm: Beach Near Newport,** Martin Johnson Heade, c. 1860

# Travel

*by Edna St. Vincent Millay*

The railroad track is miles away,
   And the day is loud with voices
     speaking,
Yet there isn't a train goes by all day,
   But I hear its whistle shrieking.

All night there isn't a train goes by,
   Though the night is still for sleep and
     dreaming,
But I see its cinders red on the sky,
   And hear its engine steaming.

My heart is warm with the friends I
   make,
   And better friends I'll not be knowing,
Yet there isn't a train I wouldn't take,
   No matter where it's going.

1. Why does the poet hear and see a train?
2. What words in the poem describe the sights and sounds of the train?

Rolling Power, Charles Sheeler, 1939

## READING COMPREHENSION

**Summarizing.** Choose the best phrase to complete each sentence. Then write the complete statements on your paper.

1. In "The Hurricane," the poet compares a hurricane to _____ (scattered palm trees, a dancer whirling about, thick carpeting).

2. In "The Tide Rises, the Tide Falls," the _____ (traveler heads for town, traveler lets out the horses, sea washes a town away).

3. Edna St. Vincent Millay's poem reveals that she _____ (enjoyed writing poems at home, took the train to work each day, loved the idea of traveling).

**Interpreting.** Write the answer to each question on your paper.

1. What does the last line of "The Hurricane" tell you about the storm's power?

2. What has probably happened to the traveler in "The Tide Rises, the Tide Falls"? Explain your answer.

3. In "Travel," the poet seems to find train travel a greater attraction than almost anything else. What details in the poem convey this idea?

**For Thinking and Discussing.** How does Longfellow's poem make you feel? What phrases help to create the poem's mood? How does the rhythm of the poem add to the effect?

## UNDERSTANDING LITERATURE

**Lyric and Narrative Poetry.** A *lyric poem* describes an object, an idea, or a feeling. The writer of lyric poetry uses words that create vivid pictures in the readers' minds. The descriptions in lyric poems, such as "The Hurricane" and "Travel," are often unusual.

Listed in Group A are some unusual descriptions from these poems. Write each item on your paper. Then, next to it, write the item from Group B that matches.

| Group A | Group B |
| --- | --- |
| "unfolds its fierce accordion" | spreading winds of a hurricane |
| "warm with the friends" | top of the sea during a storm |
| "carpeted surface" | the heart |

A *narrative poem* may also contain interesting or unusual descriptions. But, like a story, a narrative poem has a plot, characters, and a setting. On your paper, answer the following questions about "The Tide Rises, the Tide Falls."

1. Where and when does the action in the poem take place?

2. Who is the main character, and what happens to this character?

## WRITING

Choose "The Hurricane" or "Travel" and write a paragraph explaining how the poet felt about the subject of the poem. Give examples from the poem.

# The Wind in the Rosebush

*by Mary Wilkins Freeman*

*Mary Wilkins Freeman (1852–1930) was one of the busiest writers of the late 19th and early 20th centuries. She wrote over 230 short stories, 12 novels, and two volumes of poetry. Almost all of her work was about life in her native New England.*

*Like many American writers before her, she was fascinated by supernatural legends, especially those about ghosts. In one of her most famous stories, "The Wind in the Rosebush," she wrote about the strange happenings in an old New England house. Here is a dramatization of that story.*

## CHARACTERS

**Rebecca Flint,** a middle-aged woman
**Maria Orton,** a woman from Porter's Falls
**Thomas Orton,** husband of Maria Orton
**Emmeline Dent,** a middle-aged widow
**Postmaster**

**Time:** the 1890's.
**Place:** New England.

### Scene One

*A ferry boat is crossing a small New England river. Rebecca Flint sits stiff and straight on one bench. Near her sit Maria and Thomas Orton. Maria stares at Rebecca for a while. Then she speaks.*

**Maria:** It's a pleasant day, isn't it?
**Rebecca:** Yes. Very pleasant.
**Maria:** Have you come far?
**Rebecca:** From Michigan.
**Maria:** Oh, that's a long way from Porter's Falls. A long way to come and leave your family.
**Rebecca:** I don't have any family to leave.
**Maria:** Then — you're not married.
**Rebecca** *(proudly):* No, I am not married.
**Maria:** That's too bad.
**Rebecca:** I have never thought so.
**Maria:** Oh. Are you visiting somebody in Porter's Falls?
**Rebecca:** Yes, as a matter of fact. John Dent's widow. Her husband died about three years ago.

**Maria** (looking frightened): Oh. Yes — yes — I — I do know her. Thomas — we — we know her, don't we?

**Thomas** (hastily): Not very well. You're not related to Mrs. Dent, are you?

**Rebecca:** Not by blood. John Dent's first wife was my sister.

**Maria:** Was she? She was her sister, Thomas.

**Thomas:** I heard, Maria. (He shakes his head as if to warn his wife to be silent.)

**Rebecca:** I'm going to see the present Mrs. Dent, and take my niece Agnes home with me.

**Maria:** What? You're going to do what?

**Rebecca:** What's the matter? Is there some reason why I shouldn't?

**Maria:** Thomas —

**Thomas** (very softly): Let it rest, Maria.

**Maria:** But Thomas —

**Thomas:** Maria. I said, let it rest.

**Rebecca:** Is there something I should know about? Is my niece sick?

**Maria:** No, no, no — she's not sick. You can be sure of that. Everything's — all right with her.

**Rebecca** (relieved): Well, that's good to know. When did you last see her?

**Maria:** I — I haven't seen her for some time. (She is very flustered.)

**Rebecca:** She must have grown up real pretty, if she takes after my sister. Grace was such a pretty woman.

**Maria:** Yes. She did grow up pretty. Thomas —

**Thomas** (very softly): It's none of our business, Maria.

**Rebecca:** What kind of woman is the second wife?

**Maria:** I — guess she's a nice woman. I don't see much of her.

**Rebecca:** I felt kind of hurt that John married again so soon after my sister died. But I guess Agnes had to be taken care of. I couldn't take her then . . . . I was teaching school and I had my mother with me. But Mother's gone now, and I've given up teaching. I inherited a little money, and now I've come for Agnes. I think she'll be glad to come with me. Though as far as I know, her stepmother, Emmeline, is a good woman.

**Maria:** I — I guess so.

**Rebecca:** John wrote that his new wife was beautiful, too.

(The passengers react to a jolt as the ferry boat grates on the shore. Thomas grabs Maria by the arm, and hurries her off. Rebecca follows with her carpetbag.)

**Thomas:** Thank heaven we've landed. (To Rebecca) Over there, Miss. That's Mrs. Dent's horse and wagon. She's sent it for you.

**Rebecca:** Oh, thank you. (Calling) Young man, I'm the one you're waiting for. (She hurries off.)

**Maria** (looking after her): Thomas, I think I should have told her.

**Thomas:** Let her find it out herself. Don't go burning your fingers in other folks' pudding, Maria.

**Maria:** But suppose what folks say is true? And suppose she's a nervous woman? She might lose her mind.

**Thomas:** If she can lose her mind that easy, it's not too strong to begin with. You just keep out of it, Maria.

## Scene Two

*Rebecca starts up the walk to a fine-looking house. Mrs. Dent opens the door and comes partway down the walk to meet her.*

**Mrs. Dent:** You are Miss Rebecca Flint, I suppose.
**Rebecca:** Yes, I am. I wrote you —
**Mrs. Dent:** Your letter didn't get here until this morning. I wish you had given me more notice.
**Rebecca:** I'm sorry, but I just couldn't wait for you to answer. I felt I must come for Agnes, now that I could. She's my own flesh and blood, you know. And from her picture, she looks so much like my sister. *(Mrs. Dent begins to gasp.)*
**Mrs. Dent** *(clutching at her heart):* Oh!
**Rebecca:** Are you sick? Can I get you some water?
**Mrs. Dent:** No, no. I'm all right now. I have these spells. I'm over it already. Come in, Miss Flint. *(She stands back, and Rebecca starts toward the house before her. She stops at a rosebush growing beside the walk.)*
**Rebecca:** What a big rosebush. And look, it's late in the season, but that red rose is perfect. *(She reaches out to touch the rose.)*
**Mrs. Dent:** Don't you pick that rose!
**Rebecca:** I do not pick other people's roses without permission, Mrs. Dent.

*(Suddenly, the rosebush begins to move, as if blown by a strong wind. The hydrangea bush next to it does not move at all.)*

**Rebecca:** Mrs. Dent, look at that. There's not a bit of wind —
**Mrs. Dent:** Go into the house, Miss Flint! *(She pushes Rebecca ahead of her toward the house.)*
**Rebecca:** But why is the rosebush blowing when there's no wind?
**Mrs. Dent:** It's not blowing. *(The rosebush is still.)*
**Rebecca:** But the leaves were moving —
**Mrs. Dent:** And now they're not. I can't be responsible for every passing breeze, Miss Flint. Go on in.

## Scene Three

*A beautifully furnished room inside the Dent house.*

**Mrs. Dent:** Sit down. Take off your hat.
**Rebecca:** You have a fine home here. *(She sits and begins to unpin her hat.)* But where is Agnes?
**Mrs. Dent:** She went over to Addie Slocum's. No telling when she'll get back.
**Rebecca:** Oh, I did hope she'd be here. Is Addie her best friend?
**Mrs. Dent:** You might say that. When did you say you were going home?
**Rebecca** *(startled):* Why, I didn't say. As soon as Agnes is ready, I guess. I thought maybe a week.
**Mrs. Dent:** You don't have to wait for her, you know. You can go on home, and she can come later. She's 16. She can take care of herself.
**Rebecca:** No. I won't have her travel alone. She'll come when I do. *(She is annoyed.)* And if I can't wait here, in the

house that was my sister's home, I'll go somewhere else and stay.

**Mrs. Dent:** I didn't mean that. You can stay as long as you want to.

*(Suddenly, Rebecca jumps up and points to something in a mirror that is across from the window.)*

**Rebecca:** Look! In the mirror! It's Agnes. She's right outside. *(She runs to the door.)* I'll stand right here so I'll be the first thing she sees when she opens the door. *(She waits. But the door does not open. She opens it and looks out.)* Where is she? I saw her pass the window. *(She closes the door.)*

**Mrs. Dent:** You must have been mistaken.

**Rebecca:** No. I saw a shadow go over the ceiling, and I saw her in that mirror there. And then the shadow passed the window.

**Mrs. Dent:** How did she look in the mirror?

**Rebecca:** Little, light-haired — isn't that what Agnes looks like?

**Mrs. Dent:** Yes, it is. But you couldn't really have seen her. You've been thinking so much about her, you imagined it. It's too early for her to get home from Addie Slocum's. Let me show you to your room, Miss Flint. You can see Agnes tomorrow morning.

**Scene Four**

*The next morning. Mrs. Dent is in the kitchen, preparing breakfast. Rebecca comes downstairs into the room.*

**Rebecca:** Is Agnes here? I thought I heard a girl laughing in the night.

**Mrs. Dent:** No, she stayed with Addie. She often does that. She'll be along pretty soon. Have some breakfast, Miss Flint.

**Rebecca:** I'm not hungry, thank you. I'll just go out and look down the road. Maybe Agnes is on her way home. *(She goes out. Mrs. Dent stands and stares after her with a hard, strange look. She turns back to the wood stove. Rebecca runs in.)*

**Rebecca:** That rosebush! It's blowing again!

**Mrs. Dent:** What of it?

**Rebecca:** But there's no wind!

**Mrs. Dent:** Miss Flint, I told you I have no time for such nonsense. Now if you'll just sit down and eat this —

**Rebecca:** The window! There she is now! *(She runs to the door and throws it open. A breeze ruffles her hair and a paper is blown off the table.)* Agnes? Agnes? *(To Mrs. Dent)* There's nobody there again. And I saw somebody pass that window.

**Mrs. Dent:** You were mistaken again. Please shut that door. *(Rebecca shuts the door and sits down.)*

**Rebecca:** Are there roses somewhere in this kitchen? I smell roses.

**Mrs. Dent:** I don't smell a thing, Miss Flint. Why don't you settle down and eat your breakfast?

**Rebecca:** No. Mrs. Dent, I've come a long way, and I've waited long enough. I want you to send for Agnes.

**Mrs. Dent:** Why, of course. I'll do better. I'll go get her myself. *(She wipes her hands on her apron and takes it off. She reaches for a shawl hanging on the back of a door.)* I'll just — what's that paper there on the floor?

**Rebecca:** I don't know. *(She bends to pick it up. Mrs. Dent grabs it from her hand.)*

**Mrs. Dent:** Why, it's a note from Mrs. Slocum. She must have pushed it under the door and it blew in when you opened it. *(Looks at the paper.)* It says that Addie and Agnes have gone over to Lincoln on the train to visit Addie's uncle for a few days. They'll be gone till Thursday. *(She tears up the paper and puts it in the wood stove to burn.)*

**Rebecca:** Thursday. I won't see her till then. That's a long time.

**Mrs. Dent:** Now, if you're worried about getting home, I told you I could send Agnes on after you. If you'd like to help her get ready, there's a nightgown over in that basket she's been working on. You can sew the lace on it. Everything's right there.

**Rebecca** *(goes to a basket on the table and takes out a white nightgown and a length of lace):* If you'll just give me a needle and thread, I'd love to finish it for dear Agnes.


**Scene Five**

*Midnight. Rebecca lies in bed in her room. In the distance, piano music begins. Rebecca stirs and sits up. She gets up and throws a shawl over her old-fashioned nightgown. She tiptoes out into the hall and looks down over the bannister of the stairs. She screams.*

**Rebecca:** Mrs. Dent! Mrs. Dent! *(Mrs. Dent, in her long nightgown, her hair in curl papers, comes into the hall.)*

**Mrs. Dent:** What is the matter with you? It's after midnight.

**Rebecca** *(pointing over the railing):* The piano — the piano — down in the parlor —

**Mrs. Dent:** Well, what about it?

**Rebecca:** It was playing by itself! I heard music — I came out to look — I thought Agnes might have come home. I could see the keys moving — but nobody was playing!

**Mrs. Dent:** Miss Flint, your imagination is getting the best of you. I didn't hear any music, and neither did you. You dreamed it. Now go back to bed. *(Mrs. Dent goes back toward her room. Rebecca walks to her room and over to the bed. She begins to scream again.)*

**Rebecca:** Mrs. Dent! Mrs. Dent! *(Mrs. Dent appears. She goes to the doorway of Rebecca's room.)* Look! Look at my bed!

**Mrs. Dent** *(looking in):* Oh! *(She gasps, then quickly calms herself.)* It's the nightgown you finished for Agnes. What about it?

**Rebecca:** It's lying there, as if she was going to wear it. And the rose — the rose — the red rose from the rosebush! It's lying in the lace!

**Mrs. Dent:** Miss Flint, this is the last straw. You picked that rose, and you dropped the nightgown on your bed and forgot it. When you dreamed you heard that music, you knocked the rose onto your bed, and it happened to fall on the gown. Now that's the only sensible explanation.

**Rebecca:** No! No! I left the nightgown downstairs. I didn't pick the rose. And I didn't dream that music. It woke me up.
**Mrs. Dent** (*in a hard and commanding voice*): Miss Flint, go back to bed. We will talk about this in the morning.

## Scene Six

*The next morning. Mrs. Dent stands in the kitchen, working. Rebecca enters wearing her hat and shawl and carrying her carpetbag.*

**Rebecca:** Mrs. Dent. Early this morning I came downstairs and went out into the front yard. The red rose was still on the rosebush.

**Mrs. Dent:** Oh, dear. If I'd known you weren't well, Miss Flint, I wouldn't have let you stay in my house.

**Rebecca:** Well, I won't stay any longer. I'm leaving now. But on my way home, I will get off the train in Lincoln and find my niece and take her with me. I will thank you, Mrs. Dent, to give me the address of Addie Slocum's uncle.

**Mrs. Dent:** I don't have his address, Miss Flint.

**Rebecca:** Then tell me where the Slocums live. I'll go there and get the address.

**Mrs. Dent:** No. I will not have you going to the Slocums and raving about pianos that play by themselves and roses that leap on and off bushes. Go home, Miss Flint. When Agnes gets back, I'll tell her about you. If she wants to go and live with you, that will be her business. She's old enough to make up her own mind.

**Rebecca:** I will find her in Lincoln and take her home with me. Good-bye, Mrs. Dent. (*She stalks out the door. Mrs. Dent stands looking after her, a strange expression on her face.*)

**Scene Seven**

*The Porter's Falls post office. The post-master stands behind a barred window. Rebecca enters and goes to the window.*

**Rebecca:** Are you the postmaster here?

**Postmaster:** Yes, I've been postmaster for 30 years. What can I do for you?

**Rebecca:** I'm looking for some people I have business with. I wonder if you could tell me where they live. Their name is Slocum.

**Postmaster:** Slocum? No. No Slocums live in Porter's Falls.

**Rebecca:** You must be mistaken. They have a daughter named Addie, a girl about 16.

**Postmaster:** Addie Slocum. Oh, yes, I remember now. Ma'am, your business with these people must have waited a long time. Addie Slocum died 10 years ago, and her parents died a few years later. Nobody's lived in their house since then.

**Rebecca** (*very slowly*): And — Agnes Dent. Do you know a girl named Agnes Dent?

**Postmaster:** I'm sorry, ma'am, but that's a sad story, too. Poor little Agnes Dent got sick. It was real bad. The doctor prescribed some medicine that might have saved her. But it wasn't given to her. There was some talk of taking action against her stepmother, but there wasn't enough evidence. Ever since, people say there have been strange sights and sounds around the Dent house. Some say it's haunted.

**Rebecca:** But Agnes? What happened to Agnes?

**Postmaster:** Ma'am, Agnes Dent died a year ago. Just about this time. Pretty little thing. Sad. I remember she wore a white dress in her coffin. All trimmed with lace.

**Rebecca:** A white dress trimmed with lace. And — was there — a red rose?

**Postmaster:** Why, ma'am, it's funny you should ask that. Nobody knew how it got there. But just before they shut down the lid of the coffin, we all saw a red rose lying right over Agnes Dent's heart. (*Rebecca stands frozen in horror.*)

## READING COMPREHENSION

**Summarizing.** Choose the best phrase to complete each sentence. Then write the complete statements on your paper.

1. Rebecca Flint came to Porter's Falls to _____ (visit her sister, take her niece home with her, buy a house for Agnes and herself).

2. When Rebecca heard the music, Mrs. Dent told her _____ (that Agnes loved to play the piano, to turn down the volume, that she had imagined it).

3. When Agnes was buried, there was a red rose on her dress_____(that her stepmother had picked for her, like the rose Rebecca saw on Agnes's nightgown, that Rebecca had given her for her birthday).

**Interpreting.** Write the answer to each question on your paper.

1. What did Maria's husband mean when he said, "Don't go burning your fingers in other folks' pudding"?

2. What is suggested by the fact that the rosebush moved when Rebecca passed by it?

3. What are some of the unusual things that happened in this play? What or who might have been causing them?

**For Thinking and Discussing.** Do you think Mrs. Dent was responsible for Agnes's death? Why or why not? If so, what do you think Rebecca should do next?

## UNDERSTANDING LITERATURE

**Play.** The selection you have just read, "The Wind in the Rosebush," is a play, or drama. To understand what is going on in a play, you have to depend mainly on the conversations of the characters. These conversations are called *dialogue*.

In addition to the dialogue, the playwright includes *stage directions*, which give the actors and readers of the play more information about the plot and characters.

Stage directions are notes that describe the setting of a scene, tell how characters should say their lines, indicate what actions take place on the stage, and specify what props and scenery are needed.

Write the answers to the following questions on your paper.

1. In "The Wind in the Rosebush," find three examples of stage directions that reveal Rebecca's feelings.

2. Find three examples of stage directions that give insight into Mrs. Dent's character.

3. Find three references to the setting or props that tell about Agnes.

## WRITING

Think about what happened in "The Wind in the Rosebush." Suppose that Agnes were able to speak for herself and tell her story about what happened. Write the lines for her part. Include stage directions if you wish.

# Hail and Farewell

*by Ray Bradbury*

*Ray Bradbury, the famous science-fiction author, presents us with an unusual protagonist in this story. What is Willie's secret that forces him to leave his happy home again and again?*

**B**ut of course he was going away; there was nothing else to do; the time was up; the clock had run out, and he was going very far away indeed. His suitcase was packed; his shoes were shined; his hair was brushed; he had expressly washed behind his ears; and it remained only for him to go down the stairs, out the front door, and up the street to the small-town station where the train would make a stop for him alone. Then Fox Hill, Illinois, would be left far off in his past. And he would go on, perhaps to Iowa, perhaps to Kansas, perhaps even to California; a small boy, twelve years old, with a birth certificate in his valise to show he had been born forty-three years ago.

"Willie!" called a voice downstairs.

"Yes!" He hoisted his suitcase. In his bureau mirror he was a face made of June dandelions and July apples and warm summer-morning milk. There, as always, was his look of the angel and the innocent, which might never, in the years of his life, change.

"Almost time," called the woman's voice.

"All right!" And he went down the stairs, grunting and smiling. In the living room sat Anna and Steve, their clothes painfully neat.

"Here I am!" cried Willie in the parlor door.

Anna looked like she was going to cry. "Oh, good Lord, you can't really be leaving us, can you, Willie?"

"People are beginning to talk," said Willie quietly. "I've been here three years now. But when people begin to talk, I know it's time to put on my shoes and buy a railway ticket."

"It's all so strange. I don't understand. It's so sudden," Anna said. "Willie, we'll miss you."

"I'll write you every Christmas, so help me. Don't you write me."

"It's been a great pleasure and satisfaction," said Steve, sitting there, his words the wrong size in his mouth. "It's a shame it had to stop. It's a shame you had to tell us about yourself. It's an awful shame you can't stay on."

"You're the nicest folks I ever had," said Willie, four feet high, in no need of a shave, the sunlight on his face.

And then Anna *did* cry. "Willie, Willie." And she sat down and looked as if she wanted to hold him but was afraid to hold him now; she looked at him with shock and amazement and her hands empty, not knowing what to do with him now.

"It's not easy to go," said Willie. "You get used to things. You want to stay. But it doesn't work. I tried to stay on once after people began to suspect. 'How horrible!' people said. 'All these years, playing with our innocent children,' they said, 'and us not guessing! Awful!' they said. And finally I had to just leave town one night. It's not easy. You know darned well how much I love both of you. Thanks for three swell years."

They all went to the front door. "Willie, where're you going?"

"I don't know. I just start traveling. When I see a town that looks green and nice, I settle in."

"Will you ever come back?"

"Yes," he said earnestly with his high voice. "In about twenty years it should begin to show in my face. When it does, I'm going to make a grand tour of all the mothers and fathers I've ever had."

They stood on the cool summer porch, reluctant to say the last words. Steve was looking steadily at an elm tree. "How many other folks've you stayed with, Willie? How many adoptions?"

Willie figured it, pleasantly enough. "I guess it's about five towns and five couples and over twenty years gone by since I started my tour."

"Well, we can't holler," said Steve. "Better to've had a son thirty-six months than none whatever."

"Well," said Willie, and kissed Anna quickly, seized his luggage, and was gone up the street in the green noon light, under the trees, a very young boy indeed, not looking back, running steadily.

The boys were playing on the green park diamond when he came by. He stood a little while among the oak-tree shadows, watching them hurl the white, snowy baseball into the warm summer air, saw the baseball shadow fly like a dark bird over the grass, saw their hands open in mouths to catch this swift piece of summer that now seemed most especially important to hold on to. The boys' voices yelled. The ball lit on the grass near Willie.

Carrying the ball forward from under the shade trees, he thought of the last three years now spent to the penny, and the five years before that, and so on down the line to the year when he was really eleven and twelve and fourteen and the voice saying: "What's wrong with Willie, missus?" "Mrs. B., is Willie late agrowin'?" "Willie, you smokin' cigars lately?" The echoes died in summer light and color. His mother's voice: "Willie's twenty-one today!" And a thousand voices saying: "Come back, son, when you're fifteen; *then* maybe we'll give you a job."

He stared at the baseball in his trembling hand, as if it were his life, an interminable ball of years strung around and around and around, but always leading back to his twelfth birthday. He heard the kids walking toward him; he felt them blot out the sun, and they were older, standing around him.

"Willie! Where you goin'?" They kicked his suitcase.

How tall they stood in the sun. In the last few months it seemed the sun had passed a hand above their heads, beckoned, and they were warm metal drawn melting upward; they were golden taffy pulled by an immense gravity to the sky, thirteen, fourteen years old, looking down upon Willie, smiling, but already beginning to neglect him. It had started four months ago:

"Choose up sides! Who wants Willie?"

"Aw, Willie's too little; we don't play with 'kids.' "

And they raced ahead of him, drawn by the moon and the sun and the turning seasons of leaf and wind, and he was twelve years old and not of them anymore. And the other voices beginning again on the old, the dreadfully familiar, the cool refrain: "Better feed that boy vitamins, Steve." "Anna, does shortness *run* in your family?" And the cold fist knocking at your heart again and knowing that the roots would have to be pulled up again after so many good years with the "folks."

"Willie, where you goin'?"

He jerked his head. He was back among the towering, shadowing boys who milled around him like giants at a drinking fountain bending down.

"Goin' a few days visitin' a cousin of mine."

"Oh." There was a day, a year ago, when they would have cared very much indeed. But now there was only curiosity for his luggage, their enchantment with trains and trips and far places.

"How about a coupla fast ones?" said Willie.

They looked doubtful, but, considering the circumstances, nodded. He dropped his bag and ran out; the white baseball was up in the sun, away to their burning white figures in the far meadow, up in the sun again, rushing, life coming and going in a pattern. Here, *there*! Mr. and Mrs. Robert Hanlon, Creek Bend, Wisconsin, 1932, the first couple, the first year! Here, *there*! Henry and Alice Bolts, Limeville, Iowa, 1935! The baseball flying. The Smiths, the Eatons, the Robinsons! 1939! 1945! Husband and wife, husband and wife, husband and wife, no children, no children! A knock on this door, a knock on that.

"Pardon me. My name is William. I wonder if — "

"A sandwich? Come in, sit down. Where are you *from*, son?"

The sandwich, a tall glass of cold milk, the smiling, the nodding, the comfortable, leisurely talking.

"Son, you look like you been traveling. You run *off* from somewhere?"

"No."

"Boy, are you an orphan?"

Another glass of milk.

"We always wanted kids. It never worked out. Never knew why. One of those things. Well, well. It's getting late, son. Don't you think you better hit for home?"

"Got no home."

"A boy like you? Not dry behind the ears? Your mother'll be worried."

"Got no home and no folks anywhere in the world. I wonder if — I wonder — could I sleep here tonight?"

"Well, now, son. I don't just know. We never considered taking in — " said the husband.

"We got chicken for supper tonight," said the wife, "enough for extras, enough

for company. . . ."

And the years turning and flying away, the voices, and the faces, and the people, and always the same first conversations. The voice of Emily Robinson, in her rocking chair, in summer-night darkness, the last night he stayed with her, the night she discovered his secret, her voice saying:

"I look at all the little children's faces going by. And I sometimes think, What a shame, what a shame, that all these flowers have to be cut, all these bright fires have to be put out. What a shame these, all of these you see in schools or running by, have to get tall and unsightly and wrinkle and turn gray or get bald, and finally, all bone and wheeze, be dead and buried off away. When I hear them laugh I can't believe they'll ever go the road I'm going. Yet here they *come*! I still remember Wordsworth's poem: 'When all at once I saw a crowd, A host of golden daffodils;

Beside the lake, beneath the trees, Fluttering and dancing in the breeze.' That's how I think of children, cruel as they sometimes are, mean as I know they can be, but not yet showing the meanness around their eyes or *in* their eyes, not yet full of tiredness. They're so eager for everything! I guess that's what I miss most in older folks, the eagerness gone nine times out of ten, the freshness gone, so much of the drive and life down the drain. I like to watch school let out each day. It's like someone threw a bunch of flowers out the school front doors. How does it feel, Willie? How does it feel to be young forever? To look like a silver dime new from the mint? Are you happy? Are you as fine as you *seem*?"

The baseball whizzed from the blue sky, stung his hand like a great pale insect. Nursing it, he heard his memory say:

"I worked with what I had. After my folks died, after I found I couldn't get man's work anywhere, I tried carnivals, but they only laughed. 'Son,' they said, 'you're not a midget, and even if you are, you look like a *boy*! We want midgets with midgets' *faces*! Sorry, son, sorry.' So I left home, started out, thinking: What *was* I? A boy. I looked like a boy, sounded like a boy, so I might as well go on being a boy. No use fighting it. No use screaming. So what could I do? What job was handy? And then one day I saw this man in a restaurant looking at another man's pictures of his children. 'Sure wish I had kids,' he said. 'Sure wish I had kids.' He kept shaking his head. And me sitting a few seats away from him, a hamburger in my hands. I sat there, *frozen*! At that very instant I knew what my job would be for all the rest of my life. There *was* work for me, after all. Making lonely people happy. Keeping myself busy. Playing forever. I knew I had to play forever. Deliver a few papers, run a few errands, mow a few lawns, maybe. But *hard* work? No. All I had to do was be a mother's son and a father's pride. I turned to the man down the counter from me. 'I beg your pardon,' I said. I *smiled* at him. . . ."

"But, Willie," said Mrs. Emily long ago, "didn't you ever get lonely? Didn't you ever want — things — that grown-ups wanted?"

"I fought that out alone," said Willie. "I'm a boy, I told myself, I'll have to live in a boy's world, read boys' books, play boys' games, cut myself off from everything else. I can't be both. I got to be only one thing — young. And so I played that way. Oh, it wasn't easy. There were times — " He lapsed into silence.

"And the family you lived with, they never knew?"

"No. Telling them would have spoiled everything. I told them I was a runaway; I let them check through official channels, police. Then, when there was no record, let them put in to adopt me. That was best of all; as long as they never guessed. But then, after three years, or five years, they guessed, or a traveling man came through, or a carnival man saw me, and it was over. It always had to end."

"And you're very happy and it's nice being a child for over forty years?"

"It's a living, as they say. And when you make other people happy, then you're almost happy, too. I got my job to do and I do it. And anyway, in a few years now I'll be in my second childhood. All the fevers will be out of me and all the unfulfilled things and most of the dreams. Then I can relax, maybe, and play the role all the way."

He threw the baseball one last time and broke the reverie. Then he was running to seize his luggage. Tom, Bill, Jamie, Bob, Sam — their names moved on his lips. They were embarrassed at his shaking hands.

"After all, Willie, it ain't as if you're going to China or Timbuktu."

"That's right, isn't it?" Willie did not move.

"So long, Willie. See you next week!"

"So long, so long!"

And he was walking off with his suitcase again, looking at the trees, going away from the boys and the street where he had lived, and as he turned the corner a train whistle screamed, and he began to run.

The last thing he saw and heard was a white ball tossed at a high roof, back and forth, back and forth, and two voices crying out as the ball pitched now up, down, and back through the sky. "Annie, Annie, over! Annie, Annie, over!" like the crying of birds flying off to the far south.

In the early morning, with the smell of the mist and the cold metal, with the iron smell of the train around him and a full night of traveling shaking his bones and his body, and a smell of the sun beyond the horizon, he awoke and looked out upon a small town just arising from sleep. Lights were coming on, soft voices muttered, a red signal bobbed back and forth, back and forth in the cold air. There was that sleeping hush in which echoes are dignified by clarity, in which echoes stand nakedly alone and sharp. A porter moved by, a shadow in shadows.

"Sir," said Willie.

The porter stopped.

"What town's this?" whispered the boy in the dark.

"Valleyville."

"How many people?"

"Ten thousand. Why? This your stop?"

"It looks green." Willie gazed out at the cold morning town for a long time. "It looks nice and quiet," said Willie.

"Son" said the porter, "you know where you *going*?"

"Here," said Willie, and got up quietly in the still, cool, iron-smelling morning, in the train dark, with a rustling and stir.

"I hope you know what you're doing, boy," said the porter.

"Yes, sir," said Willie. "I know what I'm doing." And he was down the dark aisle, luggage lifted after him by the porter, and out in the smoking, steaming-cold, beginning-to-lighten morning. He stood looking up at the porter and the black metal train against the few remaining stars. The train gave a great wailing blast of whistle, the porters cried out all along the line, the cars jolted, and his special porter waved and smiled down at the boy there, the small boy there with the big luggage who shouted up to him, even as the whistle screamed again.

"What?" shouted the porter, hand cupped to ear.

"Wish me luck!" cried Willie.

"Best of luck, son," called the porter, waving, smiling. "Best of luck, boy!"

"Thanks," said Willie, in the great sound of the train, in the steam and roar.

He watched the black train until it was completely gone away and out of sight. He did not move all the time it was going. He stood quietly, a small boy twelve years old, on the worn wooden platform, and only after three entire minutes did he turn at last to face the empty streets below.

Then, as the sun was rising, he began to walk very fast, so as to keep warm, down into the new town.

**Summarizing.** Choose the best phrase to complete each sentence. Then write the complete statements on your paper.

1. Willie had been born 43 years ago, but he _____ (had the mind of a child, looked like a 12-year-old, acted too old for his age).

2. Willie had to leave Anna and Steve because _____ (people were beginning to talk, the couple no longer wanted him, he had a new job to go to).

3. Willie thought of his life as a boy as a _____ (curse, blessing, job).

4. Willie got off the train in Valleyville because _____ (it looked nice and green, he knew someone there, it was the last stop).

**Interpreting.** Write the answer to each question on your paper.

1. Why did people get suspicious after Willie was with Anna and Steve for three years?

2. How did Willie feel each time he had to leave his "parents"?

3. What did Willie mean when he said he would soon be in his second childhood and his job would be easier?

**For Thinking and Discussing.** What do you think would be the most difficult part of being a 12-year-old forever? What do you think would be the best part?

**Imagery.** Imagery in a literary work is the use of *figurative language,* or language that creates images or mental pictures. Imagery is used especially by poets but is often used by writers of stories as well.

Two special kinds of images are *similes* and *metaphors.* In a simile, the writer compares two different things using the word *like* or *as.* In a metaphor, two things are compared without using *like* or *as.* One thing is said to *be* another thing.

In *personification,* human qualities or actions are given to an object, animal, or idea. Often, similes and metaphors include the use of personification.

Below are images from "Hail and Farewell." On your paper, label each a simile or metaphor. If the comparison uses personification, write this word as well.

1. "In his bureau mirror he saw a face made of June dandelions and July apples and warm summer-morning milk."

2. "He stared at the baseball. . .as if it were his life, an interminable ball of years strung around and around. . . ."

3. "The baseball whizzed from the blue sky, stung his hand like a great pale insect."

Create your own images for the following subjects in the story: time, a young boy, a childless couple, a baseball, a train, a small town. Use at least one example of each type of figurative language.

# Section Review

## VOCABULARY

**Prefixes and Suffixes.** Some words are made up of a root, or base, and a prefix and/or a suffix. A *prefix* is added to the beginning of the root word, and it changes the word's meaning. A *suffix* is added to the end. For example, the prefix *re-* means "again." In the Section *Review,* you view, or look at, again what you have learned. The suffix *-er* means "one who." A *reviewer* looks again at something.

Here are some additional prefixes, suffixes, and their meanings. Read the following sentences from this section. On your paper, write each italicized word, circling its prefix and/or suffix. Then write the meaning of each word.

**Prefixes**  *non-, dis-* = not
*un-* = not; opposite of

**Suffixes**  *-ness* = state of being
*-ment* = resulting

1. "The same *casualness* characterizes the use of all our senses."

2. ". . . I should choose the place where the key *unlocks* the greatest treasures. . . ."

3. "*Discontentment* had followed learning to read."

4. "Miss Flint, I told you I have no time for such *nonsense.*"

## READING

**Fact and Opinion.** A *fact* is something that exists or that has happened. A fact is definitely true. It is a fact that O. Henry wrote "After Twenty Years." An *opinion* is a statement that tells what someone believes or feels about something. To say that "After Twenty Years" is O. Henry's best story is to state an opinion. Statements that have specific dates and figures are likely to be facts. Statements containing value words like *good, better, best, bad, worse, most,* and *lovely* are likely to be opinions.

Read each of the following statements about the selections in this section. Number your paper from 1 to 9. Identify each statement as *fact* or *opinion.*

1. It was 10:00 p.m. when Jimmy Wells and "Silky" Bob had parted at the restaurant door.

2. "Raymond's Run" is a great story.

3. Helen Keller was blind and deaf.

4. It would be a blessing if everyone were stricken blind for three days.

5. Frederick Douglass loved reading more than any other boy in Baltimore.

6. "The Hurricane" is a poem by Luis Palés Matos.

7. Riding on a train is better than making friends.

8. Emmeline Dent is a sinister character.

9. Willie is the name of the main character in "Hail and Farewell."

# WRITING

**The Writing Process.** Learning to write is easier if you view writing as a process, or series of steps. A good writing plan involves four steps: (1) Set your goal; (2) Make a plan; (3) Write the first draft; and (4) Revise. These are the steps that you will follow in completing the writing assignment in each Section Review.

## Step 1: Set Your Goal

Your first task in writing is to decide what to write. You can set a goal for yourself by (1) choosing a topic, (2) defining your purpose, and (3) identifying your audience.

Get started by considering which selection in Section 1 interests you most. Also consider which selection you know most about. Then choose one of the following topics for a composition:

1. the ending of "After Twenty Years"

2. the rivalry between Hazel and Gretchen in "Raymond's Run"

3. Helen Keller's plan in "Three Days to See"

4. the education of Frederick Douglass in "Learning to Read"

5. the rose in "The Wind in the Rosebush"

6. Willie's profession in "Hail and Farewell"

When you have made a choice, define your purpose for writing your composition. Decide how you want to focus your composition and what you want to communicate to your readers. Your purpose might be to inform, describe, explain, entertain, or persuade. Write a statement of purpose to keep you on track as you develop your ideas. Use the following examples as a model:

TOPIC:     Hazel's relationship to Raymond in "Raymond's Run"

PURPOSE:  To prove that the race changed the relationship between Hazel and Raymond

With your topic and purpose in mind, identify your audience, or your readers. You will want to adjust both the tone and content of your composition to the person or people who will read your work. In this case, assume that the audience will be your teacher and your classmates.

## Step 2: Make a Plan

Making a plan involves gathering and organizing ideas. Generally, you can gather ideas for a composition in two ways: (1) by reviewing your subject and taking notes, or (2) by brainstorming and taking notes. You can then organize your notes into a rough outline.

Since your composition is based on a selection that you have read, gather ideas by reviewing the story and taking notes. Look through the story for events and statements that relate to your topic, and jot down details that you might include in your paper. Then organize your notes in a rough outline, listing details under main ideas.

## Step 3: Write a First Draft

Think of the first draft of your paper as an experiment in which you develop your ideas by trying to express them in different ways. Let your rough outline guide you, but feel free to make changes as you write. Keep your ideas flowing. Refer to your statement of purpose to keep you on track.

Notice how the statement of purpose is reflected in the first paragraph of a paper about Hazel and Raymond:

> The race in "Raymond's Run" is a turning point in Raymond's relationship with his sister Hazel. Before the race, Hazel is Raymond's caretaker, and he is her responsibility. After the race, Hazel is Raymond's coach, and he is a runner in his own right. "Hazel's Run" has become "Raymond's Run," and their relationship is off to a new start.

**Step 4: Revise**

If you can, set aside your first draft for a day or two. Then return to it with a "fresh eye." Try to put yourself in the place of a first-time reader, and read your paper aloud. Change words and sentences that don't say exactly what you mean. Add new ideas that occur to you.

Ask yourself these questions as you revise your composition:

1. Have I used complete sentences?

2. Are my points clear and well stated?

3. Does each point relate to a main idea?

4. Have I fulfilled my statement of purpose?

When you are satisfied with your revision, proofread your paper. Correct errors in grammar, spelling, and punctuation. Then make a final copy of your work.

The following is a quiz for Section 1. Write the answers in complete sentences on your paper.

## Reading Comprehension

1. In "After Twenty Years," why was "Silky" Bob waiting in a doorway?

2. In "Raymond's Run," why did Hazel change her opinion of Gretchen?

3. List five of Helen Keller's plans in "Three Days to See."

4. In "The Wind and the Rosebush," did Rebecca achieve her aim in traveling to Porter's Falls?

5. In "Hail and Farewell," why was Willie forced to leave Fox Hill?

## Understanding Literature

6. What unexpected turn of events led to the surprise ending in "After Twenty Years"?

7. Identify two major characters in "Raymond's Run," and write one or two sentences describing each.

8. What is the most important message of Helen Keller's essay? Explain your answer.

9. Identify three important events from Frederick Douglass's autobiography.

10. Which poem is a narrative poem, "The Hurricane" or "The Tide Rises, the Tide Falls"? Explain your answer.

# ACTIVITIES

**Word Attack.** Raymond in "Raymond's Run" would sometimes slosh around in rainwater. *Slosh*, meaning "to splash about," is a *portmanteau word* — a word made by blending two other words and their meanings. *Slosh* is a blend of *slop* and *slush*.

Define each portmanteau word on the left by matching the word with its blended parts on the right. Then use each word in a sentence.

| | | | |
|---|---|---|---|
| 1. chortle | a. | gleam | + shimmer |
| 2. clump | b. | chuckle | + snort |
| 3. squiggle | c. | squirm | + wriggle |
| 4. glimmer | d. | chunk | + lump |

## Speaking and Listening

1. To appreciate fully the poetry in this section, read each poem more than once *and* read it aloud. As you read, pay careful attention to both what the poem says and how it sounds. Read slowly enough that each word is clear and distinct. Treat each line as a rhythmical unit. Be prepared to read your favorite poem to the class.

2. Perhaps you have had an experience with someone blind or deaf which helped you to understand that person's disability. Think about how you would tell others about what happened to you. Then describe your experience to the rest of the class.

## Researching

1. In "Three Days to See," Helen Keller planned to look at the books in raised type that she had read. The raised type that she mentioned is *braille* — a system of writing and printing for the blind. Do library research to learn about braille and its creator, Louis Braille. If your local library has braille books, practice touching the letters and trying to identify them. Share your findings with the class.

2. "Learning to Read" describes Frederick Douglass's life until the age of 18 when he escaped from slavery. Douglass fled to Massachusetts but continued to encounter racial discrimination. Read more about Douglass in your school or local library to learn how he protested racial and religious discrimination as a noted author and speaker.

## Creating

1. Author William Sydney Porter used the pseudonym O. Henry for his short stories. If you were a writer, what pseudonym might you assume? Jot down five fictitious names that appeal to you.

2. In "The Hurricane," Luis Palés Matos gave you the feeling that you were experiencing the storm. Longfellow described a haunting story in "The Tide Rises, the Tide Falls." And the yearning to travel was expressed in Millay's poem "Travel." Write a poem of your own about the weather, an experience, travel, or a subject of your own choice.

**69**

# THE NIGHT THE GHOST GOT IN

## JAMES THURBER

*We usually associate ghosts with creepy haunted houses and tales that make the skin crawl. The ghost that haunts the house in this story, however, starts a chain reaction of events that results in humor rather than horror.*

THE ghost that got into our house on the night of November 17, 1915, raised such a hullabaloo of misunderstandings that I am sorry I didn't just let it keep on walking, and go to bed. Its advent caused my mother to throw a shoe through a window of the house next door and ended up with my grandfather shooting a patrolman. I am sorry, therefore, that I ever paid any attention to the footsteps.

They began about a quarter past one o'clock in the morning, a rhythmic, quick-cadenced walking around the dining-room table. My mother was asleep in one room upstairs, my brother Herman in another; grandfather was in the attic, in the old walnut bed, which, as you will remember, once fell on my father. I had just stepped out of the bathtub and was busily rubbing myself with a towel when I heard the steps. They were the steps of a man walking rapidly around the dining-room table downstairs. The light from the bathroom shone down the back steps, which dropped directly into the dining-room; I could see the faint shine of plates on the plate-rail; I couldn't see the table. The steps kept going round and round the table; at regular intervals a board creaked, when it was trod upon. I supposed at first that it was my father or my brother Roy, who had gone to Indianapolis but were expected home at any time. I suspected next that it was a burglar. It did not enter my mind until later that it was a ghost.

After the walking had gone on for perhaps three minutes, I tiptoed to Herman's room. "Psst!" I hissed, in the dark, shaking him. "Awp," he said, in the low, hopeless tone of a despondent beagle—he always half suspected that something would "get him" in the night. I told him who I was. "There's something downstairs!" I said. He got up and followed me to the head of the back staircase. We listened together. There was no sound. The steps had ceased.

Herman looked at me in some alarm: I had only the bath towel around my waist. He wanted to go back to bed, but I gripped his arm. "There's something down there!" I said. Instantly the steps began again, circled the dining-room table like a man running, and started up the stairs toward us, heavily, two at a time. The light still shone palely down the stairs; we saw nothing coming; we only heard the steps. Herman rushed to his room and slammed the door. I slammed shut the door at the stairs top and held my knee against it. After a long

He Always Half Suspected That Something Would Get Him

minute, I slowly opened it again. There was nothing there. There was no sound. None of us ever heard the ghost again.

The slamming of the doors had aroused mother: she peered out of her room. "What on earth are you boys doing?" she demanded. Herman ventured out of his room. "Nothing," he said gruffly, but he was, in color, a light green. "What was all that running around downstairs?" said mother. So she had heard the steps, too! We just looked at her. "Burglars!" she shouted, intuitively. I tried to quiet her by starting lightly downstairs.

"Come on, Herman," I said.

"I'll stay with mother," he said. "She's all excited."

I stepped back onto the landing.

"Don't either of you go a step," said mother. "We'll call the police." Since the phone was downstairs, I didn't see how we were going to call the police—nor did I want the police—but mother made one of her quick, incomparable decisions. She flung up a window of her bedroom which faced the bedroom windows of the house of a neighbor, picked up a shoe, and whammed it through a pane of glass across the narrow space that separated the two houses. Glass tinkled into the bedroom occupied by a retired engraver named Bodwell and his wife. Bodwell had been for some years in rather a bad way and was subject to mild "attacks." Most everybody we knew or lived near had *some* kind of attacks.

It was now about two o'clock of a moonless night; clouds hung black and low. Bodwell was at the window in a minute, shouting, frothing a little, shaking his fist. "We'll sell the house and go back to Peoria," we could hear Mrs. Bodwell saying. It was some time before mother "got through" to Bodwell. "Burglars!" she shouted. "Burglars in the house!" Herman and I hadn't dared to tell her that it was not burglars but ghosts, for she was even more afraid of ghosts than of burglars. Bodwell at first thought that she meant there were burglars in his house, but finally he quieted down and called the police for us over an extension phone by his bed. After he had disappeared from the window, mother suddenly made as if to throw another shoe, not because there was further need of it but, as she later explained, because the thrill of heaving a shoe through a window glass had enormously taken her fancy. I prevented her.

The police were on hand in a commendably short time: a Ford sedan full of them, two on motorcycles, and a patrol wagon with about eight in it and a few reporters. They began banging at our front door. Flashlights shot streaks of gleam up and down the walls, across the yard, down the walk between our house and Bodwell's. "Open up!" cried a hoarse voice. "We're men from Headquarters!" I wanted to go down and let them in, since there they were, but mother wouldn't hear of it. "You haven't a stitch on," she pointed out. "You'd catch your death." I wound the towel around me again. Finally the cops put their shoulders to our big heavy front door with its thick beveled glass and broke it in: I could hear a rending of wood and a splash of glass on the floor of the hall. Their lights played all over the living-room and criss-crossed nervously in the dining-room, stabbed into hallways, shot up the front stairs and finally up the back. They caught me standing in my towel at the top. A heavy policeman bounded up the steps. "Who are you?" he demanded. "I live here," I said. "Well, whattsa matta, ya hot?" he asked. It was, as a matter of fact, cold; I went to my room and pulled on some trousers. On my way out, a cop stuck a gun into my ribs. "Whatta you doin' here?" he demanded. "I live here," I said.

The officer in charge reported to mother. "No sign of nobody, lady," he said. "Musta got away—what'd he look like?" "There were two or three of them," mother said, "whooping and carrying on and slamming doors." "Funny," said the cop. "All ya windows and doors was locked on the inside tight as a tick."

Downstairs, we could hear the tromping of the other police. Police were all over the place; doors were yanked open, drawers were yanked open, windows were shot up and pulled down, furniture fell with dull thumps. A half-dozen policemen emerged out of the darkness of the front hallway upstairs. They began to ransack the floor: pulled beds away from walls, tore clothes off hooks in the closets, pulled suitcases and boxes off shelves. One of them found an old zither[1] that Roy had won in a pool tournament. "Looky here, Joe," he said, strumming it with a big paw. The cop named Joe took it and turned it over. "What is it?" he asked me. "It's an old zither our guinea pig used to sleep on," I said. It was true that a pet guinea pig we once had would never sleep anywhere except on the zither, but I should never have said so. Joe and the other cop looked at me a long time. They put the zither back on a shelf.

"No sign o' nuthin'," said the cop who had first spoken to mother. "This guy," he explained to the others, jerking a thumb at me, "was nekked. The lady seems historical."[2] They all nodded, but said nothing; just looked at me. In the small silence we all heard a creaking in the attic. Grandfather was turning over in bed. "What's 'at?" snapped Joe. Five or six cops sprang for the attic door before I could intervene or explain. I realized that it would be bad if they burst in on grandfather unannounced, or even announced. He was going through a phase in which he believed that General Meade's[3] men, under steady hammering by Stonewall Jackson,[4] were beginning to retreat and even desert.

When I got to the attic, things were

---

1. **zither** (zith′ ər): a kind of stringed musical instrument.
2. **historical:** The policeman means *hysterical*.
3. **General Meade** (mēd): George Gordon Meade (1815–72) was a Union general during the American Civil War.
4. **Stonewall Jackson:** Thomas Jonathan "Stonewall" Jackson (1824–63) was a Confederate general during the American Civil War.

Police Were All Over the Place

pretty confused. Grandfather had evidently jumped to the conclusion that the police were deserters from Meade's army, trying to hide away in his attic. He bounded out of bed wearing a long flannel nightgown over long woolen underwear, a nightcap, and a leather jacket around his chest. The cops must have realized at once that the indignant white-haired old man belonged in the house, but they had no chance to say so. "Back, ye cowardly dogs!" roared grandfather. "Back t' the lines, ye lily-livered cattle!" With that, he fetched the officer who found the zither a flat-handed smack alongside his head that sent him sprawling. The others beat a retreat, but not fast enough; grandfather grabbed Zither's gun from its holster and let fly. The report[5] seemed to crack the rafters; smoke filled the attic. A cop cursed and shot his hand to his shoulder. Somehow, we all finally got downstairs again and locked the door against the old gentleman. He fired once or twice more in the darkness and then went back to bed. "That was grandfather," I explained to Joe, out of

5. **report:** gunshot.

74

breath. "He thinks you're deserters." "I'll say he does," said Joe.

The cops were reluctant to leave without getting their hands on somebody besides grandfather; the night had been distinctly a defeat for them. Furthermore, they obviously didn't like the "layout"; something looked—and I can see their viewpoint—phony. They began to poke into things again. A reporter, a thin-faced, wispy man, came up to me. I had put on one of mother's blouses, not being able to find anything else. The reporter looked at me with mingled suspicion and interest. "Just what the heck is the real low-down here, Bud?" he asked. I decided to be frank with him. "We had ghosts," I said. He gazed at me a long time as if I were a slot machine into which he had, without results, dropped a nickel. Then he walked away. The cops followed him, the one grandfather shot holding his now-bandaged arm, cursing and blaspheming. "I'm gonna get my gun back from that old bird," said the zither-cop. "Yeh," said Joe. "You—and who else?" I told them I would bring it to the station house the next day.

"What was the matter with that one policeman?" mother asked, after they had gone. "Grandfather shot him," I said. "What for?" she demanded. I told her he was a deserter. "Of all things!" said mother. "He was such a nice-looking young man."

Grandfather was fresh as a daisy and full of jokes at breakfast next morning. We thought at first he had forgotten all about what had happened, but he hadn't. Over his third cup of coffee, he glared at Herman and me. "What was the idee of all them cops tarryhootin' round the house last night?" he demanded. He had us there.

# THINKING ABOUT THE STORY

*Recalling*

1. What does the **narrator**—the person telling the story—say the ghost raised on the night of November 17, 1915?

2. How does the narrator become aware of the ghost's presence in the house? Who does the mother suspect is in the house instead?

3. Explain how the mother succeeds in summoning the police. What damage do they do to the house when they arrive?

4. Who does the grandfather think the police are? How does he add to the confusion in the house?

5. How does the reporter react when the narrator finally reveals "We had ghosts"?

*Interpreting*

6. What evidence does the narrator offer during the course of the story to prove that a ghost was really in the house?

7. A story has a **first-person point of view** when the person telling the story—the "I"—is one of the characters. Who is the narrator in this story? In general, what is his attitude toward the ghost and the incident involving the police? In your opinion, what does Thurber achieve by having this character tell the story?

8. A **satire** is any literary work in which human vices or follies are held up to ridicule. When the ridicule is gentle and good-natured, the satire is often called a **spoof.** What human follies do you think Thurber is spoofing in this story?

*Applying*

9. In this ghost story, a haunting begins a chain reaction of comic events that the narrator calls "a hullabaloo of misunderstandings." What other situations can you think of that might begin such a hullabaloo?

# ANALYZING LITERATURE

*Understanding the Elements of Humor*

The American writer Max Eastman defined **humor** as a "pleasant disappointment of expectation." In other words, we find something funny when our usual expectations, through some sudden or clever twist, result in a pleasant surprise. Humorists use many techniques to create comic twists. For example, they may *treat a serious subject lightheartedly*, or they may *raise a trivial subject to the level of high seriousness*. They may *exaggerate details*, stretching reality out of proportion. Or they may *relate absurd events in a deadpan fashion*, without emotional expression.

*Wordplay*, or the clever and unexpected use of words, is another important element of humor. Wordplay might take the form of an outrageous comparison or a pun (a play on words with double meanings) or a malapropism (an inappropriate use of a word in place of one with a similar sound).

If you found yourself smiling or laughing as you read "The Night the Ghost Got In," you were responding to the various elements of humor that Thurber used. Now go back and take a closer look at how he achieved the humorous effects.

1. What serious subject does Thurber treat in a particularly lighthearted way in the story?

2. Find at least two examples of exaggeration in the story.

3. Find passages in the story in which Thurber uses a deadpan technique to downplay the characters' expected emotional responses to the events.

4. Find one example each of an outrageous comparison, a pun, and a malapropism in the story.

5. How is the entire story itself a "pleasant disappointment of expectation"?

. . . . . . . . . . . . . . . . . . . . . . . . . . . . . . . . .

## CRITICAL THINKING AND READING

*Determining Character Motivation*
**Motivation** is the combination of character traits and circumstances that cause a character to act in a particular way. Sometimes an author may clearly state a character's motivation. At other times the author may allow readers to draw their own conclusions about a charac-

ter's motivation based on their understanding of the character and the plot. Often, however, the author will use a combination of these two methods.

For example, in "The Night the Ghost Got In," Thurber has the narrator clearly state one reason that the grandfather attacks the policemen: "Grandfather had evidently jumped to the conclusion that the police were deserters from Meade's army, trying to hide away in his attic." But is this all that motivates the grandfather? Thurber expects readers to conclude for themselves that the grandfather is somewhat out of touch with reality, eccentric, or even crazy.

As you read, look for details that explain motivation, and continually ask yourself why the characters are behaving as they do. By thinking not only about the circumstances to which a character must respond but also about that character's personality traits, you will better understand character motivation.

Locate the following passages in the story. Review the plot up to that point, and then draw on your knowledge of the characters to answer the questions.

1. " 'Come on, Herman,' I said.
'I'll stay with mother,' he said. 'She's all excited.'
I stepped back onto the landing."
What besides concern for his mother motivates Herman to stay behind?

2. "It was true that a pet guinea pig we once had would never sleep anywhere except on the zither, but I should never have said so."

What do you suppose motivates the narrator to wish he had kept silent?

3. "I had put on one of mother's blouses, not being able to find anything else. The reporter looked at me with mingled suspicion and interest."

What thoughts do you suspect motivate the reporter's suspicion? His interest?

························

## DEVELOPING LANGUAGE SKILLS

*Irregular Verbs*
Some of the oldest and most common verbs in English—words that express action or existence—indicate past time not in the regular way of adding *-ed* (play, played) but in irregular ways. The verb *go*, for example, changes not to *goed* but to *went* or *gone* to express action in the past.

The following irregular verbs appear in the first two paragraphs of "The Night the Ghost Got In." For each one, write the other present or past forms of the verb. Use a dictionary if you need help. Then list five other irregular verbs that Thurber uses in the story.

| | |
|---|---|
| 1. got | 6. heard |
| 2. am | 7. shone |
| 3. paid | 8. see |
| 4. began | 9. kept |
| 5. fell | 10. trod |

························

## THINKING AND WRITING

**1. Writing About an Author's Purpose.** What do you think was Thurber's purpose in writing "The Night the Ghost Got In"? Was it merely to amuse readers, or was it perhaps to reveal something about human nature, or was it perhaps a combination of both? Write a brief essay in which you discuss your understanding of Thurber's purpose in the story and show how he achieves it.

**Prewriting.** Begin by thinking about the effect the story as a whole had on you. Were you entertained? If so, by what in particular? Did you gain some insight into an aspect of human nature? Try to express that insight in a precisely worded sentence. Then list the various aspects of the story that you might want to discuss in relation to Thurber's purpose, such as the elements of humor, the way the plot develops, and the way the characters behave.

**Writing.** As you write, remember that the assignment asks you both to discuss Thurber's purpose and to show how he accomplishes it. Organize your paragraphs accordingly.

**Revising.** After you have finished a first draft, make sure your essay begins with a clear statement that expresses your understanding of Thurber's purpose. Then check to see if you have shown how Thurber conveyed that purpose. Are there sentences you can cut? Do you need to add additional details?

**Proofreading.** Reread your essay, and correct any mistakes in grammar, spelling, and punctuation. Be sure that you have used quotation marks correctly. If necessary, prepare a neat final copy.

**Publishing.** Read your paper to a group of your classmates. Do they agree with your analysis of the story?

### 2. Writing a Ghost Story.
Ghost stories are as old as literature itself. Try your hand at writing one.

**Prewriting.** Think about the overall effect you want to achieve: Do you want to frighten your audience, to amuse them as Thurber did, or to create a mood of mystery and wonder? Then think about the ghost itself: Will it interact with other characters or merely be perceived, as in Thurber's story? Will it be friendly or nasty or indifferent to the other characters? Finally, think about your plot in terms of a beginning, a middle, and an end.

**Writing.** As you write, do not hesitate to change your plan as you discover new possibilities for making your ghost story better. Give your imagination free rein.

**Revising.** As you revise, think about the story as a whole: Does the plot develop logically? Is it suspenseful in order to keep your audience's interest? Are your characters believable? Is their behavior logically motivated? Do all of the elements of your story work to convey an overall effect?

Next, concentrate on polishing your sentences. Read the story aloud to yourself. Are there rough spots that need your attention?

**Proofreading.** Reread your story, and correct any mistakes in grammar, spelling, and punctuation. If necessary, prepare a neat final copy.

**Publishing.** Read your story to the class. Consider assembling a class anthology of ghost stories or contributing your story to the school literary magazine.

# AMERICA'S EARLY VOICES

## *LITERATURE BEFORE 1840*

*Pleasant it looked,
this newly created world.
Along the entire length and breadth
of the earth, our grandmother,
extended the green reflection
of her covering.*

— Traditional Winnebago Song

*The Notch of the White Mountains*
Thomas Cole (1801-1848)
National Gallery of Art, Washington
Andrew W. Mellon Fund

# America's Early Voices: Literature Before 1840

**T**he earliest Americans lived in a land of great beauty and promise. Thousands of years ago, this land offered peace and plenty to the first people to settle in America, the Native Americans.

Each Native American group, or tribe, developed its own way of life, its own government, its own beliefs. Its members told stories and created poems that expressed their ideas about life.

About 400 years ago, colonists from England, Spain, and other nations began coming to America. They also came with hope for peace and opportunity. Here was a land where people could live according to their principles. Eventually they, too, would produce their own poets, thinkers, and storytellers. And, like the Native Americans, their literature would reflect their most deeply held beliefs.

### The Earliest American Literature

Many Native American groups stressed living in harmony with other people and with nature. An ancient Native American tale, the story "Godasiyo, the Woman Chief," is retold here. This story tells of people who cannot agree and the sad consequences of their disagreement.

The earliest colonists read books and newspapers that came from England and Europe. But in the early 1700's, Americans began printing their own.

Two of the most popular authors of this era were Jonathan Edwards and Benjamin Franklin. Edwards was a Puritan minister concerned with perfecting an ideal life. The Puritans came from England, eager to practice religion as they saw fit. They valued plainness. They did not like fancy churches, homes, clothing, or language. Edwards was an exciting speaker who would make his listeners groan and shriek with terror as he described the punishment that was awaiting all "sinners." Franklin was not concerned with the ideal or perfect life. He was practical. Whatever honest method worked best to achieve a goal was the method Franklin valued.

In this section, you will read Edwards's "Resolutions"—his rules for a perfect life, and two excerpts from Franklin's writing that reflect his cleverness, humor, and practical nature.

### The Revolutionary Era

The growth of American literature helped the colonists feel that they were more like one another than they were like the people of England. Many colonists began to feel that they wanted their own government,

**The Sentinel,** Albert Bierstadt, 1830–1902

and the writings of Americans began to reflect this desire. In this section, you will read selections by two of the authors of the revolutionary period who were famous for expressing their ideas and ideals very well: Abigail Adams and Thomas Paine.

### Writing After the Revolution

After America was firmly established as a nation, her people felt a great pride in themselves and their new country. The exploits of Davy Crockett, told in *Davy Crockett's Almanac*, and the writing of Jean de Crèvecoeur suggest in very different ways that Americans saw themselves as the strongest people in the world.

In the early 1800's, a young New York writer named Washington Irving began publishing stories. His stories drew on European, colonial, and Native American traditions. The stories were funny and exciting. He became the first American author to win worldwide fame. His story in this section, "The Legend of Sleepy Hollow," has remained popular since it was first published in 1819.

Nathaniel Hawthorne, born in 1804 in Salem, Massachusetts, wrote many short stories in addition to his classic novel *The Scarlet Letter*. One of them, "Dr. Heidegger's Experiment," is presented in play form. This story uses an element of fantasy to explore human nature.

The early Americans were searching for a better way of life — a way of life that was truly their own. Every generation makes this search in its own way.

# Godasiyo, the Woman Chief

### a Seneca legend retold by Dee Brown

*Dee Brown, a modern author and historian, retells this ancient story in language that reflects the way this story was first told aloud centuries ago by the Seneca people, one of the five Iroquois tribes of upstate New York.*

At the beginning of time when America was new, a woman chief named Godasiyo ruled over an Indian village beside a large river in the East. In those days all the tribes spoke one language and lived in harmony and peace. Because Godasiyo was a wise and progressive chief, many people came from faraway places to live in her village, and they had no difficulty understanding one another.

At last, the village grew so large that half the people lived on the north side of the river, and half on the south side. They spent much time canoeing back and forth to visit, attend dances, and exchange gifts of venison, hides, furs, and dried fruits and berries. The tribal council house was on the south side, which made it necessary for those who lived on the north bank to make frequent canoe trips to consult with their chief. Some complained about this, and to make it easier for everybody to cross the rapid stream, Godasiyo ordered a bridge to be built of saplings and tree limbs carefully fastened together. This bridge brought the tribe close together again, and the people praised Godasiyo for her wisdom.

Not long after this, a white dog appeared in the village, and Godasiyo claimed it for her own. Everywhere the chief went the dog followed her, and the people on the north side of the river became jealous of the animal. They spread stories that the dog was possessed by an evil spirit that would bring harm to the tribe. One day, a delegation from the north bank crossed the bridge to the council house and demanded that Godasiyo kill the white dog. When she refused to do so, the delegates returned to their side of the river, and that night they destroyed the bridge.

From that time on people on the north bank and those on the south bank began to distrust each other. The tribe divided into two factions, one renouncing Godasiyo as their chief, the other supporting her. Bad feelings between them grew so deep that Godasiyo foresaw that the next step would surely lead to fighting and war. Hoping to avoid bloodshed, she called all members of the tribe who supported her to a meeting in the council house.

"Our people," she said, "are divided by more than a river. No longer is there good will and contentment among us. Not

wishing to see brother fight against brother, I propose that those who recognize me as their chief follow me westward up the great river to build a new village."

Almost everyone who attended the council meeting agreed to follow Godasiyo westward. In preparation for the migration, they built many canoes of birch bark. Two young men who had been friendly rivals in canoe races volunteered to construct a special watercraft for their chief. With strong poles they fastened two large canoes together and then built a platform which extended over the canoes and the space between them. Upon this platform was a seat for Godasiyo and places to store her clothing, extra leggings, belts, robes, moccasins, mantles, caps, awls, needles, and adornments.

At last everything was ready. Godasiyo took her seat on the platform with the white dog beside her, and the two young men who had built the craft began paddling the double canoes beneath. Behind them the chief's followers and defenders launched their own canoes, which contained all their belongings. This flotilla of canoes covered the shining waters as far as anyone could see up and down the river.

After they had paddled a long distance, they came to a fork in the river. Godasiyo ordered the two young canoeists to stop in the middle of the river until the others caught up with them. In a few minutes the flotilla was divided, half of the canoes on her left, the others on her right.

The chief and the people on each side of her began to discuss the advantages of the two forks in the river. Some wanted to go one way; some preferred the other way. The arguments grew heated with anger. Godasiyo said that she would take whichever fork her people chose, but they could agree on neither. Finally those on the right turned the prows of their canoes up the right channel, while those on the left began paddling up the left channel. And so the tribe began to separate.

When this movement started, the two young men paddling the two canoes carrying Godasiyo's float disagreed as to which fork they should take, and they fell into a violent quarrel. The canoeist on the right thrust his paddle into the water and started toward the right, and at the same time the one on the left swung his canoe toward the left. Suddenly, Godasiyo's platform slipped off its supports and collapsed into the river, carrying her with it.

Hearing the loud splash, the people on both sides turned their canoes around and tried to rescue their beloved chief. But she and the white dog, the platform, and all her belongings had sunk to the bottom, and the people could see nothing but fish swimming in the clear waters.

Dismayed by this tragic happening, the people of the two divisions began to try to talk to each other. But even though they shouted words back and forth, those on the right could not understand the people on the left, and those on the left could not understand the people on the right. When Godasiyo drowned in the great river her people's language had become changed. This was how it was that the Indians were divided into many tribes spreading across America, each of them speaking a different language.

## READING COMPREHENSION

**Summarizing.** Choose the best phrase to complete each sentence. Then write the complete statements on your paper.

1. When Godasiyo first ruled the Indian village, _____ (her people wanted another chief, strangers caused much trouble, people understood each other and there was peace).

2. Godasiyo decided to build a new village _____ (because the old one was too shabby, to stop the fighting among her people, far from the old hunting grounds).

3. Godasiyo and her dog drowned because her people _____ (couldn't agree on which way to go, pushed her out of the boat, refused to try to rescue her).

**Interpreting.** Write the answer to each question on your paper.

1. Why did the people on the north side of the river spread stories that Godasiyo's white dog was possessed by an evil spirit?

2. Why did Godasiyo refuse to kill the white dog?

3. What does the behavior of Godasiyo tell you about her?

**For Thinking and Discussing.** Do you think that things would have been different if Godasiyo's village had stayed small? Explain your answer.

## UNDERSTANDING LITERATURE

**Point of View in a Legend.** Every story is told from a certain point of view. Legends, such as the Native American tale "Godasiyo, the Woman Chief," are usually told or written in the third person (*he, she, they, it*). The storyteller speaks in this "all-knowing" point of view in order to convince the reader or listener that the story might be true by relating what each character is thinking.

A legend often tries to explain why something happened. The third-person point of view allows the narrator to explain why different actions occur in the story.

Answer the following questions in complete sentences on your paper.

1. Why did Godasiyo's village increase in size?

2. What happened at the fork in the river?

3. After Godasiyo's death, why were the people unable to understand each other even when they tried?

## WRITING

Imagine that Godasiyo had not drowned, but had managed to swim to the river bank with her dog. Write a paragraph to give the legend a different ending. Be sure to use the third-person point of view. If you wish, you may begin your paragraph with "Godasiyo and her dog rose to the top of the water. They . . ."

# Resolutions

*by Jonathan Edwards*

*In the early 1700's, a great religious movement swept the American colonies. This period was called the "Great Awakening." People took a fresh interest in religion, founded hundreds of new churches, and became more concerned with religious liberty. One of the greatest figures of the Great Awakening was Jonathan Edwards (1703–1758). To Edwards, God was everything and people were nothing. Edwards preached and wrote that humans were basically sinners and needed to be constantly on guard against the devil. The selection below is adapted from Edwards's* Resolutions. *The* Resolutions *were meant to be a series of rules that people could follow to avoid becoming sinners.*

Being aware that I am unable to do anything without God's help, I do humbly beg him by his grace, to help me to keep these *Resolutions,* so far as they are agreeable to his will, for Christ's sake.

### REMEMBER TO READ OVER THESE RESOLUTIONS ONCE A WEEK.

**RESOLVED** Never *to do* anything, whether in soul or body, less or more, but what tends to the glory of God, nor *be,* nor *suffer* it, if I can possibly avoid it.

**RESOLVED** Never to lose one moment of time, but to improve it in the most profitable way I possibly can.

**RESOLVED** To live with all my might, while I do live.

**RESOLVED** Never to do any thing, which I should be afraid to do, if it were the last hour of my life.

**RESOLVED** To act, in all respects, both speaking and doing, as if nobody had been so vile as I. To act as if I had committed the same sins, or had the same infirmities or failings as others:

I will let the knowledge of their failings promote nothing but shame in myself, and prove only an occasion of my confessing my own sins and misery to God.

**RESOLVED** When I feel pain, to think of the pains of Martyrdom, and of Hell.

**RESOLVED** Never to do any thing out of revenge.

**RESOLVED** That I will live so, as I shall wish I had done when I come to die.

**RESOLVED** To maintain the strictest temperance, in eating and drinking.

**RESOLVED** Whenever I do any really evil action, to trace it back, till I come to the original cause: And then, both carefully try to do so no more, and to fight and pray with all my might against the original of it.

**RESOLVED** To study the Scriptures so steadily, constantly, and frequently, as that I may find, and plainly see myself grow in the knowledge of it.

**RESOLVED** Never to utter any thing that is sportive, or matter of laughter, on a Lord's day.

**RESOLVED** To ask myself, at the end of every day, week, month, and year, how I could possibly, in any respect, have done better.

**RESOLVED** That no other end but religion, shall have any influence at all on any of my actions.

## READING COMPREHENSION

**Summarizing.** Choose the best phrase to complete each sentence. Then write the complete statements on your paper.

1. In *Resolutions*, Jonathan Edwards gave his guidelines for _____ (making and keeping friends, becoming wealthy and wise, living a life free from sin).

2. Edwards believed people could improve themselves by _____ (examining their actions, relaxing more, thinking less).

3. Edwards felt that time _____ (should be used to rest, shouldn't be wasted, caused much suffering).

4. If Edwards did something wrong, he would try to _____ (trace its cause, forget about it, avoid getting caught).

**Interpreting.** Write the answer to each question on your paper.

1. Why did Jonathan Edwards write his *Resolutions*?

2. How do the writings of Jonathan Edwards indicate that he was a very religious man?

3. How did Jonathan Edwards think people could improve themselves?

**For Thinking and Discussing.** Edwards wrote, "RESOLVED    To live with all my might, while I do live." Give some examples of how a person might live as fully as possible. Do you recommend following this resolution? Why or why not?

## UNDERSTANDING LITERATURE

**Point of View.** Jonathan Edwards's *Resolutions* presented his personal views on religion and the rules by which he believed he and everyone else should live. Edwards expressed these resolutions in a personal way. He used the first-person point of view, referring to himself as "I."

Edwards chose not to write his beliefs in the form of orders to others (direct address, or second person, i.e., "*You* should . . .") or as comments on the world using the third person (i.e., "People should . . .").

Here are three of Edwards's resolutions expressed as orders to others. On your paper, first rewrite each as a personal expression using the first person and then as a comment on life using the third person.

1. You should never do anything out of revenge.

2. Ask yourself, at the end of every day, week, month, and year, how you could possibly, in any respect, have done better.

3. Live so, as you shall wish you had done when you come to die.

## WRITING

Choose five values that are important in your life. Write each as a resolution using the first-person point of view. For example, "I will try to respect the rights and values of my friends."

# The Writing of Benjamin Franklin

Benjamin Franklin (1706–1790) was one of the best loved and most influential Americans of his day. The literature he created suggests why he was so popular. His writing is full of both wisdom and humor.

# Sayings

*by Benjamin Franklin*

*Benjamin Franklin first published* Poor Richard's Almanack *at the age of 26. In it, a fictional character named Poor Richard gave advice to people on everyday living. Here is a sample.*

### 1
Three may keep a Secret,
if two of them are dead.

### 2
Early to bed and early to rise,
makes a man healthy, wealthy and wise.

### 3
He that scatters thorns,
let him not go barefoot.

### 4
Take this remark from *Richard*
poor and lame,
Whate'er's begun in anger ends in shame.

### 5
The worst wheel of the cart
makes the most noise.

### 6
He that falls in love with himself
will have no Rivals.

### 7
An open Foe may prove a curse;
But a pretended friend is worse.

### 8
Dost thou love Life?
then do not squander Time;
for that's the Stuff Life is made of.

# A Vegetable Diet

*by Benjamin Franklin*

*Franklin wrote the story of his own life in his* Autobiography of Benjamin Franklin. *The autobiography was written in bits and pieces throughout his lifetime. It was later collected and put into a single volume. "A Vegetable Diet" was adapted from Franklin's autobiography. In it, he explains his practical approach to living. As you read the selection, compare Franklin's approach to life with that of Jonathan Edwards.*

When about 16 years of age, I happened to meet with a book, written by one Tryon, recommending a vegetable diet. I determined to go into it. My brother, being yet unmarried, did not keep house, but boarded himself and his apprentices in another family. My refusing to eat flesh was an inconvenience, and I was frequently chided for it.

I made myself acquainted with Tryon's ways of preparing some of his dishes, such as boiling potatoes or rice, making hasty pudding, and a few others. Then I proposed to my brother, that if he would give me, weekly, half the money he paid for my board, I would board myself. He instantly agreed to it, and I presently found out that I could save half what he paid me.

This was an additional fund for buying books. But I had another advantage in it. Since my brother and the rest went from the printing house to their meals, I remained there alone.

After eating my light meal, which often was no more than a biscuit or a slice of bread, a handful of raisins or a tart from the pastry-cook's, and a glass of water, I had the rest of the time till their return for study. I made great progress in my study since my mind was clear from my moderation in eating and drinking.

In my first voyage from Boston, being becalmed off Block Island, our people set about catching cod, and hauled up a great many. Until then, I had stuck to my resolution of not eating animal food, and on this occasion I considered the taking of every fish as a kind of unprovoked murder, since none of them had, or ever could, do us any injury that might justify the slaughter. All of this seemed very reasonable.

But I had formerly been a great lover of fish, and, when this came hot out of the frying pan, it smelled admirably well. I balanced some time between principle

and inclination, till I remembered that, when the fish were opened, I saw smaller fish taken out of their stomachs. Then, thought I, "If you eat one another, I don't see why we may not eat you." So I dined upon cod very heartily, and continued to eat with other people, returning only now and then occasionally to a vegetable diet. So convenient a thing is it to be a *reasonable creature,* since it enables one to find or make a reason for everything one has a mind to do.

**Summarizing.**  Choose the best phrase to complete each sentence. Then write the complete statements on your paper.

1. Because Franklin did not eat meat, he often _____ (had to go hungry, got sick to his stomach, was scolded by his friends).

2. When Franklin smelled fish frying, he _____ (thought he would faint, became angry at the fishermen, remembered how much he liked to eat fish).

3. Franklin wrote that people are reasonable creatures because they _____ (eat meat when they can get it, find or make a reason for anything they want to do, usually have enough education).

**Interpreting.**  Write the answer to each question on your paper.

1. What event led Benjamin Franklin to eat the codfish?

2. What do the sayings from *Poor Richard's Almanack* suggest about what Benjamin Franklin might have been like as a person?

3. What did Ben Franklin think about a person's ability to keep a secret?

**For Thinking and Discussing.**  It's possible to be a vegetarian and to have a sound diet, but Franklin's approach to eating was not one that promoted good health. How might he have improved his diet while still saving money and time?

**Autobiographical Point of View.**  An *autobiography* is the story of a person's life, told in his or her own words. It is written in the first person (*I, me, my*).

Autobiographies are rarely *objective* — giving only the facts. Personal opinions make autobiographies *subjective* — giving personal impressions of things.

Write the answers to the following questions on your paper.

1. Franklin called his refusal to eat meat an "inconvenience." His choice of words tells you _____.
   a. why he didn't like to eat meat
   b. that those who fed him were angry
   c. he preferred his own way to conforming to the ways of others

2. ". . . my mind was clear from my moderation in eating and drinking." Franklin's words show that he _____.
   a. believed his way to be correct
   b. had studied the science of nutrition
   c. had great native intelligence

3. "I considered the taking of every fish as a kind of unprovoked murder." These words express _____.
   a. commonly accepted fact
   b. Franklin's personal views
   c. complete untruth

What special rules do you rely on to guide you in your life? Write three of them, using the first-person point of view.

# Two Voices of the Revolution

By 1775 Americans felt a great deal of pride in their ability to run their own affairs. The idea emerged that the colonies could band together to free themselves of English rule. They did not wish to be ruled by any king; they believed that people should rule themselves. American authors of the Revolution spread these ideas by creating literature that appealed to the emotions of their readers. On the following pages you will read examples of work by two of the most persuasive writers of this period: Abigail Adams and Thomas Paine.

The Surrender of General Burgoyne at Saratoga, John Trumbull, 1822

# Letter to Her Husband, John

*by Abigail Adams*

*Abigail Adams (1744–1818) was the wife of John Adams, who became the second President of the United States. While her husband was away during the American Revolution, she managed his business affairs. She was also an able writer who sent her husband many letters during his absence. Her letters have been collected and published because they deal with important issues of the times. This selection is taken from one of her letters to John Adams. In it, she discusses some of the issues that were important to her.*

If a new form of government is to be established here, which one will it be? Will it be left to our assemblies to choose one? Will there not be many differing opinions as to which government should be chosen? And shall we not run into arguments among ourselves?

I am more and more convinced that man is a dangerous creature; and that power, whether vested in many or a few, is ever grasping, and, like the grave, cries, "Give, give. . . ."

If we separate from Britain, what code of laws will be established? How shall we be governed so as to keep our liberties? Can any government be free which is not governed by general, stated laws? Who shall make these laws? . . . Give them force and energy? It is true your resolutions, as a body, have until now had the force of laws; but will they continue to have?

When I consider these things, and the prejudices of people in favor of ancient customs and laws, I feel anxious for the fate of our monarchy or democracy, or whatever is to take place. . . .

By the way, in the new code of laws which I suppose it will be necessary for you to make, I desire you would remember the ladies, and be more generous and favorable to them than your ancestors. Do not put such unlimited power into the hands of the husbands. Remember, all men would be tyrants if they could.

**Abigail Adams,** Benjamin Blythe, 1766

# The American Crisis
## Number 1

*by Thomas Paine*

*What kept the American soldiers fighting when they needed food, wore rags, and lost battles? One way they kept up their courage was by reading Thomas Paine's series of articles called* The American Crisis.

*Thomas Paine (1737–1809) was an Englishman who had come to the colonies only one year before the Declaration of Independence was written. Soon after arriving, he wrote a pamphlet called* Common Sense, *which urged Americans to rise up and throw out the British. In 1776, Paine joined the American army. Sitting by his tent, he wrote the following passage. Later, George Washington ordered that it be read to the American army. As you read it, ask yourself which words and phrases most inspired the American soldiers.*

These are the times that try men's souls. The summer soldier and the sunshine patriot will, in this crisis, shrink from the service of his country; but he that stands it now deserves the love and thanks of man and woman.

Tyranny, like hell, is not easily conquered; yet we have this consolation with us — that the harder the conflict, the more glorious the triumph. What we obtain too cheap, we esteem too lightly: It is dearness only that gives everything its value. Heaven knows how to put a proper price upon its goods; and it would be strange indeed if so celestial an article as freedom should not be highly rated.

Britain, with an army to enforce her tyranny, has declared that she has a right not only to tax but "to bind us in all cases whatsoever," and if being bound in that manner is not slavery, then is there not such a thing as slavery upon earth. . . .

## READING COMPREHENSION

**Summarizing.** Choose the best phrase to complete each sentence. Then write the complete statements on your paper.

1. Abigail Adams believed that power _____ (is necessary for happiness, should not be shared, is grasping and makes demands).

2. Abigail Adams asked her husband to _____ (make laws that share power with women, keep power from all tyrants, make as few laws as possible).

3. Part of Thomas Paine's message is that _____ (great sacrifices make victories more meaningful, war should be avoided, taxation is worse than slavery).

**Interpreting.** Write the answer to each question on your paper.

1. What did Abigail Adams think was dangerous about giving men unlimited power?

2. To whom was Thomas Paine referring when he said, ". . . summer soldier and the sunshine patriot"? What did he mean by this?

3. What did Thomas Paine mean when he said, "These are the times that try men's souls"?

**For Thinking and Discussing.** After reading the selection by Abigail Adams and the selection by Thomas Paine, what do you think was the major political concern of their time?

## UNDERSTANDING LITERATURE

**Point of View in Persuasive Writing.** Abigail Adams's letter to her husband and the excerpt from the pamphlet by Thomas Paine are examples of persuasive personal writing. Both use the first-person point of view and are designed to convince the reader to agree with the ideas stated.

In persuasive writing, the writer expresses an opinion that he or she hopes to make the reader believe and then provides details to support that opinion.

Write the answers to the following questions on your paper.

1. Abigail Adams wanted her husband to agree that _____.
   a. all men would be tyrants
   b. man is a dangerous creature
   c. laws should be fairer to women

2. Thomas Paine wrote, ". . . the harder the conflict, the more glorious the triumph." Identify which of the following support this statement.
   a. Things obtained too easily have less value.
   b. Summer soldiers will shrink from service.
   c. Britain declared the right to tax.

## WRITING

Choose a controversial issue of today, such as the driving age, unemployment, or saving the environment. Write a persuasive paragraph to convince others of your point of view. Use the first-person point of view.

# Two Voices of the New Nation

After the United States won the Revolutionary War, Americans felt full of pride and strength. In 1812 they again faced England in war — and again they won. Now Americans and Europeans began to believe that there was nothing that Americans could not do. During the early 1800's, many took on the challenge of exploring and settling new territory.

Jean de Crèvecoeur and Davy Crockett were two very different Americans, but both created literature that helped Americans feel proud of themselves and their nation.

He That Tilleth His Land Shall Be Satisfied, Unknown Artist, c. 1850

# What Is an American?

*by Jean de Crèvecoeur*

*Jean de Crèvecoeur (1735–1813) left his native France at the age of 19 to serve in the French army then fighting against the British in Canada. In 1759 he decided to remain in the New World. After exploring the Ohio and Great Lakes region, he settled down as a farmer in New York.*

*The selection here is taken from Crèvecoeur's* Letters From an American Farmer. *In it, he predicts that America will become a "melting pot" — a place where many nationalities will blend together into one new nationality: the American.*

What then is the American, this new man? He is either a European, or the descendant of a European. I could point out to you a family whose grandfather was English, whose wife was Dutch, whose son married a French woman, and whose present four sons now have four wives from different nations.

He is an American, who left behind him all his ancient prejudices and manners. Here individuals of all nations are melted into a new race of men, whose labors and heritage will one day cause great changes in the world. Americans are the western pilgrims, who are carrying along with them that great mass of arts, sciences, vigor, and industry.

The Americans were once scattered all over Europe. Here they are part of one of the finest systems which has ever appeared.

The American ought therefore to love this country much better than that where either he or his forefathers were born. Here his industry will be quickly rewarded. Children, who before demanded of him a morsel of bread, are now fat and frolicsome. They gladly help their father to clear those fields where crops will rise. No cruel prince, rich abbot, or mighty lord will claim part of their riches.

The American is a new man, who acts upon new principles. He must therefore entertain new ideas and form new opinions. From idleness, dependence, poverty, and useless labor, he has passed to toils for which he will be amply rewarded. This is an American.

# The Day the Sun Froze

*by David Crockett*

*David (Davy) Crockett (1786–1836) was an American fron-
tiersman who became a folk hero and political figure; he
served three terms in Congress. Certainly the tall tales that
were written about him in* Davy Crockett's Almanac *contributed greatly to his popularity. Many people believed that
Crockett himself wrote these stories. Some even believed the
stories were true. Yet the tales contain fantastic events, and
many new issues actually appeared after Crockett's death.
But the stories do tell of someone resourceful enough to meet
any challenge, however unusual. And Americans of that time
liked to think of themselves in that way.*

I'm that same David Crockett that is fresh from the backwoods. I'm half horse, half alligator — and part snapping turtle, too. I can wade the Mississippi River and leap over the Ohio River. I can ride upon a streak of lightning. Thorns wouldn't dare to scratch me. I can whip my weight in wild cats, and — if anyone pleases — I'll wrestle a panther, or hug a bear too close for comfort. Here is what I did on the day the sun froze.

One January morning, it was so cold the trees were too stiff to shake. The very daybreak froze solid just as it was trying to dawn. The tinder-box I used to light my fire wouldn't spark. It would no more catch fire than a raft sunk to the bottom of the sea.

Well, I decided the only way I was going to get some fire was to make it myself. I brought my knuckles together like two thunderclouds, but the sparks froze before I could collect them. So out I walked whistling "Fire in the Mountains!" as I went along in double quick time. Well, after I had walked about 20 miles I came to Daybreak Hill and discovered what was the matter.

The earth had actually frozen fast on her axis. She couldn't turn round. The sun

had gotten jammed between cakes of ice under the wheels. The sun had been shining and working to get loose until he froze in his cold sweat.

"C-r-e-a-t-i-o-n!" thought I. "This is the toughest form of suspension. It mustn't be endured. Something must be done or human creation is done for!"

It was so cold that my teeth and tongue were all collapsed together as tight as an oyster. But I took a fresh bear from my back. (I had picked it up along the road.) I beat the animal against the ice until the hot oil began to pour out of it on all sides. I then held the bear over the earth's axis.

I squeezed the hot bear oil out until I'd thawed the earth loose. Then, I poured about a ton of the hot bear oil over the sun's face.

I gave the earth's cogwheel one kick backward until I got the sun loose. I whistled, "Push along; keep moving!" In about 15 seconds the earth gave a grunt and began to move.

The sun walked back up into the sky. It saluted me with such gratitude that it made me sneeze. Then I shouldered my bear and saluted back. As I walked home, I introduced people to the fresh daylight with a piece of sunrise in my pocket.

## READING COMPREHENSION

**Summarizing.** Choose the best phrase to complete each sentence. Then write the complete statements on your paper.

1. According to Crèvecoeur, an American is a European who _____ (has brought culture but left prejudice behind, believes in Davy Crockett's spirit, intends to make a fortune and return to Europe).

2. Crèvecoeur suggested that hard work in America _____ (would lead to poverty, was easier than in Europe, would be rewarded).

3. According to Davy Crockett, one day it was extremely cold because _____ (the sun froze and the earth couldn't turn, it was an especially bad January, his tinder-box wouldn't spark and he couldn't build a fire).

**Interpreting.** Write the answer to each question on your paper.

1. What was Crèvecoeur's definition of an American?

2. How did Davy Crockett describe himself? Are these details believable?

3. Why did Davy Crockett sneeze at the end of the story "The Day the Sun Froze"?

**For Thinking and Discussing.** When early Americans read these two selections, what kinds of feelings do you think they experienced about themselves?

## UNDERSTANDING LITERATURE

**Point of View.** Davy Crockett used the first-person point of view in his account of frontier life. His story is subjective — a product of his imagination, not of outside reality — and uses exaggeration to make its point. The stories in *Davy Crockett's Almanac* were originally published as autobiographies, not as fiction. The people of Crockett's day wanted heroes to inspire them, and Crockett obliged.

Jean de Crèvecoeur's writing also uses the first person. "What Is an American?" was written as his answer to the question in the title. He did not use exaggeration in the way that Crockett did but commented seriously on what he believed. Nevertheless, Crèvecoeur's comments are subjective. They are his opinions.

Write the answers to the following questions on your paper.

1. List five exaggerations in the description of Davy Crockett that could not possibly be fact.

2. Find two sentences in "What Is an American?" that are the author's personal opinions and not necessarily facts that can be proved.

## WRITING

Using the first-person point of view, describe yourself in terms that would impress Davy Crockett. Exaggerate the qualities that you describe and make comparisons that are unusual and hard to believe.

# The Legend of Sleepy Hollow

*by Washington Irving*

*Stories about ghosts and magic spells have always been popular, but there was a time when few people wrote about them. Washington Irving (1783–1859) thought that since people liked telling ghost stories, they also might like reading them. He was right. His stories about the supernatural made him the first really popular American writer. The fact that many of Irving's stories were humorous added to their popularity.*

*Irving's home, which he called Sunnyside, is on the banks of the Hudson River. He made this area the setting for his most famous story, "The Legend of Sleepy Hollow."*

Sleepy Hollow was one of the quietest places in the world. The only sounds were the whisper of a brook or the whistle of a bird. It was in the high hills of upper New York State. A sleepy, dreamy power seemed to hang over the land.

The people of Sleepy Hollow were the great-grandchildren of the Dutch who had come to New York in the 1600's. Stories told how the Dutch took the land from an old Indian wizard. It might have been his spell that made the people walk as if always in a dream. They saw visions and strange sights. They heard music and voices in the air. And they told tales about haunted places and shadowy beings.

The strongest spirit that moved in the valley was the ghost of the Headless Horseman. It was said that he was a German soldier who had fought for the British in the Revolutionary War. His head had been shot off by a cannonball. Ever after, he rode through the night, hunting for his lost head. Sometimes he rode through the Hollow with speed like the wind, for he had to be back in his grave in the churchyard before the sun came up.

Ichabod Crane was the schoolmaster of Sleepy Hollow. He was not Dutch, like those he taught. He had come from New England. A crane is a tall bird with thin

legs, and Ichabod's name fitted him. He, too, was tall and very thin. He had long arms and legs. His hands hung a mile out of his sleeves.

His feet looked as big as shovels. His head was small, and flat on top. He had huge ears and large, green, glassy eyes. His nose was long and narrow. His clothes were baggy.

Ichabod earned extra money by teaching singing. He was thought to know more than most of the men around, and to be more of a gentleman. So the young women paid him a lot of attention.

He had read a lot about witches. He believed in their power. After school, he had to walk through the woods to reach the farmhouse where he boarded. It often seemed to him that the forest was full of evil spirits. To drive them away, he sang. He sang through his nose. Even so, the people of Sleepy Hollow liked to listen to his voice drifting on the wind.

On long winter evenings, old Dutch couples liked to sit by the open fire. The schoolmaster was often invited to spend the evening. They roasted apples and told ghost stories. Ichabod loved to listen to them, and to tell stories of his own. Best of all, he liked the talk about the Headless Horseman.

But then he had to walk home. Awful shapes and shadows filled his path in the pale light of a snowy night. A bush, covered with snow, could look like a ghost. He shook with fear at the sound of his own steps on the hard snow. And the howl of the wind in the trees was surely the Headless Horseman himself!

In the daytime, Ichabod forgot about ghosts and spirits. But he had another problem — a woman.

Among those he taught to sing was Katrina Van Tassel. She was the only child of a wealthy Dutch farmer. She was just 18, round and red-cheeked and pretty. She dressed to show off her beauty. Everyone admired her — and also the money that would one day be hers.

Ichabod Crane had a soft heart for pretty girls. And, too, he had visited her father's great house. Baltus Van Tassel was not proud of his wealth, but he liked to live well. His home looked over the river, and everything about it spoke of plenty.

Ichabod Crane looked at the rich fields and the well-filled barns. He watched the pigs and the ducks and the turkeys. He thought of how they could all be turned into cash. With that money, he could buy huge tracts of land in the wilderness. He could build a palace. He saw himself riding a fine horse with Katrina beside him.

From the moment Ichabod saw the Van Tassel farm, his peace of mind was over. He wanted only one thing. He wanted to win Katrina. It was not an easy task. Katrina was spoiled. She wanted this today, that tomorrow. She had many admirers, too. They all kept an eye on each other. They would not welcome Ichabod to their number.

One of them was a big, loud-mouthed country fellow named Brom Van Brunt. He was the hero of Sleepy Hollow. He was handsome, tough, and the strongest man around. Because of his size and strength, he was called Brom Bones. He rode a horse with great grace and skill. He won races, and was often called on to settle arguments. Brom himself was always ready for either a fight or some fun. He had a merry sense of humor.

Brom and his friends liked to dash through the valley on horses at midnight. They would shout and yell, waking the sleeping farmers. Still, everyone liked him. In cold weather he wore a fur cap with a long foxtail. When people saw it coming, they got ready for some excitement.

Brom had, for some time, been interested in the lovely Katrina. Though he seemed as big and rough as a bear, people said that Katrina held out some hope to him. When his horse was seen tied outside the Van Tassel house, other young men rode away.

But Ichabod Crane did not go away. He was the kind of person who bends, but does not break. Ichabod knew he could not openly fight Brom Bones. But, as singing teacher, he could go to the Van Tassels' often. Baltus Van Tassel and his wife let Katrina have her way in everything. So Ichabod sat with Katrina under the elm tree beside the spring. Or he took her walking in the soft evening light.

From the day Ichabod began to visit Katrina, Brom Bones fell from favor. His horse was no longer seen tied outside her house. He became Ichabod's deadly enemy.

Brom would have liked to fight the schoolmaster. But he knew Ichabod was too smart for that. So Brom had to find other ways to get back at him.

Brom and his friends began to play jokes on Ichabod. They stopped up the chimney of the school, so it filled with smoke. They broke in at night and turned everything upside down. Worst of all, Brom trained a dog and took it to singing classes. When Katrina sang, the dog howled. "It thinks it can teach her better than Ichabod," Brom said.

In school, Ichabod sat on a high stool. He held a ruler in his hand, to scare the children. One day, as he sat there, a man brought him a message. There would be a party at the Van Tassels' that night. Ichabod was invited.

He rushed the children through their lessons, and let them out early. Then he spent an hour brushing his best black suit and getting himself ready. He borrowed a horse from the old farmer he boarded with, Hans Van Ripper.

Ichabod and the horse were well matched. The horse was thin and rough-coated. His mane and tail were matted. One eye was blind, but it glowed with a wild light. The other had a gleam of evil in it.

The horse was old, but once he had been full of fire. His name was Gunpowder. He looked worn out but he still had more of the devil in him than any young horse in the Hollow.

Ichabod rode so that his knees were nearly up to the saddle. His sharp elbows stuck out like a grasshopper's. He carried his whip straight up in his hand, like his ruler. As the horse bumped along, his arms flapped like a pair of wings. A small wool hat rested on the top of his nose. The skirts of his black coat fluttered out almost to the horse's tail. Few people had ever seen such a sight in broad daylight.

It was a fine autumn day. The trees were turning orange, red, and purple. Apples hung on the trees, and pumpkins lay in the fields. Golden ears of corn were ready to pick. It made Ichabod think of pudding and pies, handed to him by Katrina Van Tassel.

Toward evening, Ichabod reached the castle of Baltus Van Tassel. Almost everyone from the Hollow and the country around it was there. The hero of the scene was Brom Bones. He had come to the party on his horse, Dare-devil. No one but Brom could ride the high-spirited animal. Brom thought that a gentle horse was not worthy of him.

In the Van Tassels' parlor, Ichabod found much to charm him. There were many lovely girls. But he saw only the heaped-up plates of cakes and pies, ham and smoked beef. There were dozens of dishes, and Ichabod tried them all.

One day, he thought as he ate, he might own all this. He would turn his back on the school. He would snap his fingers in the face of Hans Van Ripper and all the other farmers. He would kick out any teacher who dared to call him "friend"!

Music began in the hall. Ichabod was thought to be a great dancer. So he led the dancing, with Katrina. Brom Bones sat in a corner, angry and in love.

After the dancing, Ichabod sat down with the older people. The round of ghost stories began. There were tales of screams heard at the spot where a spy had been hanged. There were stories of a woman in white who wept where she had died in the snow. But the favorite was still the Headless Horseman. He had, the old wives said, been heard several times lately. Every night, he tied up his horse among the graves in the churchyard.

Brom Bones broke in. He said that the Headless Horseman had caught up with him one night. Brom offered to race with the ghost.

Dare-devil was beating the ghost horse easily, until they came up to a little bridge. It crossed a brook in front of the church. The Headless Horseman disappeared in a flash of fire.

The party began to break up. The old farmers loaded their families into wagons. Some of the young girls rode horseback behind the young men. Laughter rang through the woods, dying away with the sound of the horses' hoofs.

Ichabod stayed behind for a talk with Katrina. He thought that he was well on the way to winning her. Something, though, had gone wrong. Ichabod walked out of the house, looking sad and hurt. He went to the stable and woke up Gunpowder. With a heavy heart, he started to ride home.

It was almost midnight. From far off, he could hear sounds. But there was no sign of life near him. All the stories about ghosts crowded into his mind. The night grew darker and darker. The stars seemed to sink into the sky. Ichabod had never felt so lonely. And just ahead was the big tree on which the spy had been hanged.

Ichabod began to whistle. As he got nearer, he thought he saw something hanging. But it was only a scar, where lightning had hit the tree. Then he heard a groan. His teeth chattered. His knees hit the saddle. It was only one tree branch rubbing against another.

Ichabod rode on. He came to a rough log bridge. It crossed a stream that was thought to be haunted. His heart began to pound. He kicked his horse in the ribs, and tried to dash across the bridge. Instead, the old horse ran across the road, into the bushes.

The schoolmaster used his whip and his heels. Old Gunpowder dashed forward. Then he came to a sudden stop. His rider nearly went over his head.

Ichabod heard a noise. In the dark shadows, he saw something. It was huge, crooked, dark, and tall. It did not move.

Ichabod's hair stood up. What was to be done? It was too late to turn and run. And what chance was there to escape a ghost?

With a show of courage, he croaked, "Who are you?" There was no answer. He said it again. Still there was no answer. He kicked Gunpowder in the sides, and began to sing. The shadow moved. Now it stood in the middle of the road.

He seemed to be a horseman of great size. He was mounted on a powerful black horse. He began to trot on the blind side of old Gunpowder.

Ichabod wanted to get away from this strange companion. He thought about Brom Bones's adventure with the Headless Horseman.

He rode faster. The stranger rode faster, too. Ichabod pulled up, and fell into a walk. The stranger did the same. Ichabod

tried to sing. His tongue stuck to the roof of his mouth.

They reached a rise in the ground. The figure of the stranger stood out against the sky. He was wrapped in a cloak. He was very tall. And he had no head. The head, which should have been on his shoulders, was resting on the front of his saddle.

Ichabod kicked Gunpowder. Away they dashed. Stones flew and sparks flashed from the horse's hoofs. Ichabod's clothes fluttered in the air. He leaned his long body over his horse's head. And the stranger rode beside him.

On they rode. Ichabod felt his saddle loosen and slip to the ground. He hung on to old Gunpowder's neck, slipping from side to side. Up ahead, he saw the walls of the church. Just before him was the brook and the bridge. This was where Brom said the Horseman had gone up in a flash of fire.

"If I can reach it," Ichabod thought, "I'm safe."

He heard the black horse close behind him. Gunpowder leaped onto the bridge. They were across! Ichabod looked back. He wanted to see the flash.

The ghost rose in the saddle. He reached down, and picked up his head. He threw it at Ichabod. Ichabod tried to jump out of the way. He was too late. The round thing hit his head. He was knocked into

the dust. Gunpowder, the ghost rider, and the black horse passed by him like the wind.

Next morning, the old horse was found eating grass at his master's gate. They traced his path back to the bridge. The little brook was searched. Near it, they found Ichabod's hat, and a broken pumpkin. But the body of the schoolmaster was never found.

The mystery caused much talk. People went to look at the bridge and the place where the hat and pumpkin had been found. They decided that Ichabod must have been carried off by the Headless Horseman.

Several years later, an old farmer went to New York City. He came back saying that he had heard that Ichabod Crane was still alive. Afraid of the ghost, and unhappy over losing Katrina, he had gone away. In another part of the country, he had studied law. Now he was a judge.

Brom Bones always had a knowing look when anyone spoke of Ichabod. He would burst into a laugh when people wondered about the pumpkin. He married Katrina very soon after Ichabod had gone.

Old country people, however, believe to this day that Ichabod was taken away by a ghost. They still say that his voice can sometimes be heard singing in the silence of Sleepy Hollow.

## READING COMPREHENSION

**Summarizing.** Choose the best phrase to complete each sentence. Then write the complete statements on your paper.

1. Ichabod often got to spend time with Katrina because _____ (he helped her with her spelling, she took singing lessons from him, he was very good-looking).

2. When Ichabod left the Van Tassels' party, he was very sad because _____ (he thought parties shouldn't end, something had gone wrong between him and Katrina, Brom Bones had threatened him).

3. After the party, Ichabod met what he thought was the Headless Horseman, and Ichabod _____ (disappeared, died of fright, threw a pumpkin at the rider).

**Interpreting.** Write the answer to each question on your paper.

1. What was one possible explanation for why the people of Sleepy Hollow acted as if they were in a dream?

2. What does the behavior of Katrina Van Tassel tell you about her?

3. What probably *really* happened to Ichabod on his way home from the Van Tassels' party?

**For Thinking and Discussing.** What were some of the humorous details that Washington Irving included in his supernatural story, "The Legend of Sleepy Hollow"?

## UNDERSTANDING LITERATURE

**Point of View.** "The Legend of Sleepy Hollow," like many other legends, is told from the third-person point of view. This "all-knowing" point of view allows the storyteller to include everything he or she wants the reader or listener to know, and to be as objective as possible.

Here are some statements from "The Legend of Sleepy Hollow." On your paper, identify those that would not have been included if Ichabod himself had been telling the story.

1. "His feet looked as big as shovels. His head was small, and flat on top."

2. "He was thought to know more than most of the men around, and to be more of a gentleman."

3. "She was just 18, round and red-cheeked and pretty. She dressed to show off her beauty."

4. "From the moment Ichabod saw the Van Tassel farm, his peace of mind was over."

5. "Brom . . . liked to dash through the valley on horses at midnight."

6. "Next morning, the old horse was found eating grass at his master's gate."

## WRITING

Imagine that you are Ichabod Crane. Write a paragraph using the first-person point of view to explain your disappearance.

# Dr. Heidegger's Experiment

*a stage play by Ev Miller*
*based on the story by Nathaniel Hawthorne*

*Dr. Heidegger's experiment is of a social nature. But there is also an element of magic at work. At first it seems as if the magic might change four lives. Even magic, however, has its limits.*

## CHARACTERS

**Dr. Heidegger,** a scientist
**Mr. Medbourne,** a merchant who has lost all his money
**Colonel Killigrew,** a man who eats and drinks too much
**Mr. Gascoigne,** a ruined politician
**Widow Wycherly,** a former beauty

NOTE: During this play, four of the elderly characters grow young, then old again. Since they are always on stage, they cannot change their makeup or put on wigs. But old age can be represented by cracked voices and bent-over postures.

*Scene: Dr. Heidegger's study. It is an old-fashioned room that is filled with bookcases and books. At the center is a table. On it are four wine glasses and a silver pitcher. As the curtain rises, Dr. Heidegger answers the door, and two old men enter.*

**Heidegger:** Mr. Medbourne! Colonel Killigrew! It's good to see both of you again. Did you come over here together?

**Medbourne:** I should say not! We met out in front. If I had known that Killigrew had been invited, I would not be here.

**Killigrew:** I feel the same way about Medbourne.

**Heidegger:** Gentlemen, it's been at least 20 years since we've seen each other. Can't we be civilized?

**Medbourne:** Well . . .

**Killigrew:** I can if he can.

**Heidegger:** Good. Make yourselves at home. How are you, Colonel?

**Killigrew:** Awful. My gout is killing me.

**Medbourne:** Perhaps you shouldn't have drunk so much when you were young.

**Killigrew:** I thought you said you were going to try to get along.

**Heidegger:** That's right, no more fighting. How have you been, Medbourne?

**Medbourne:** Not so good. I invested all

115

my money — and lost it. Now, in my old age, I must beg from relatives.

**Killigrew:** You were always too greedy for money.

**Medbourne:** That's a lie!

**Heidegger:** Gentlemen, please! *(There is a knock on the door.)* Ah, my other guests have arrived.

**Killigrew:** I hope they are better company than this oaf.

**Medbourne:** Are you calling me an oaf?

**Killigrew:** I'm certainly not calling the doctor an oaf.

**Heidegger:** These guests are old friends of yours.

*(He opens the door. Mr. Gascoigne and Widow Wycherly enter.)*

**Heidegger:** Mr. Gascoigne, thank you for bringing Madame Wycherly over.

**Gascoigne:** It was my pleasure. It's not every day that I have the company of such a lovely woman.

**Wycherly** *(pleased):* You were always one for words, Wilbert.

**Killigrew:** Clara! What a wonderful surprise!

**Wycherly:** John! Is it really you? It's been so long.

**Killigrew:** It's been much too long. You are as lovely as ever.

**Wycherly:** I am a wrinkled old woman, and you know it!

**Killigrew:** I still regret the fact that you did not marry me 50 years ago.

**Heidegger:** Madame, you remember Mr. Medbourne, don't you?

**Wycherly:** Why, of course. How are you, Charles?

**Medbourne:** I feel much better now that I've seen you, Clara.

**Wycherly:** What a lovely thing to say.

**Medbourne:** Gascoigne, how are you?

**Gascoigne:** I am in perfect health for a man my age. I plan to run for office again.

**Medbourne:** Really? I didn't know that a man could run for public office after being convicted of corruption.

**Gascoigne** *(angry):* I was innocent of those charges! And I resent your bringing this up in front of Clara.

**Medbourne:** I'm sure Clara knows all about it.

**Gascoigne:** Well, what about you? Your shady dealings were investigated by the law more than once.

**Medbourne:** I was never charged!

**Killigrew:** That's because you paid off the officials.

**Medbourne:** Stay out of this, you fat old fool!

**Gascoigne:** He may be fat. But at least he didn't steal money from every widow in the country.

**Killigrew:** I am not fat!

**Heidegger:** Gentlemen, please stop quarreling.

**Killigrew** *(still angry):* Dr. Heidegger, I don't understand this little party of yours. Medbourne, Gascoigne, and I are not exactly good friends. Don't you remember that all three of us wanted to marry Madame Wycherly when we were young?

**Heidegger:** I am aware of that. But I do have a reason for inviting all of you here. I hope you will help me perform an experiment. Please sit down and make yourselves comfortable.

*(He picks up a large black book. He opens it and takes a faded rose from between the pages.)*

**Medbourne:** What is that?

**Heidegger:** It is a rose that bloomed 55 years ago.

**Wycherly:** Why have you saved it all these years?

**Heidegger:** It was given to me by Sylvia Ward. As you know, she died before our wedding. I kept the rose in her memory. Now, do you believe that it could ever bloom again?

**Wycherly:** Nonsense!

**Killigrew:** Of course not!

**Gascoigne:** Do you take us for fools?

**Heidegger:** Watch.

*(He drops the rose into the pitcher on the table. After a long moment, he reaches in and takes out a fresh, red rose.)*

**Wycherly:** It is a miracle!

**Gascoigne:** It's a trick!

*(Killigrew looks into the pitcher.)*

**Killigrew:** How did you do that?

**Heidegger:** Have you ever heard of the Fountain of Youth?

**Medbourne:** What?

**Heidegger:** Ponce de Leon, the Spanish explorer, searched for it several centuries ago.

**Medbourne:** I've heard that tale, but I believe it is a fantasy.

**Heidegger:** No, it is not.

**Wycherly:** Did Ponce de Leon actually find the Fountain of Youth?

**Heidegger:** No, because he didn't search in the right place. The Fountain of Youth is in the southern part of Florida.

**Killigrew:** You are joking.

**Heidegger:** No, I am not. The fountain is surrounded by several huge magnolia trees. They have been kept alive for thousands of years by the wonderful water.

**Gascoigne:** How did you get it, Doctor?

**Heidegger:** A friend of mine knew of my interest in such matters. He sent me what's in this pitcher.

**Medbourne:** I don't believe it.

**Heidegger:** It is true.

**Killigrew:** What would be the effect of this water on the human body?

**Heidegger:** You can judge that for yourself. All of you are welcome to drink as much as you need to restore your youth.

**Gascoigne** *(suspicious):* Why haven't you used it yourself?

**Heidegger** *(laughs):* I've had enough trouble growing old. I am in no hurry to grow young again. I'd rather just watch this experiment.

**Killigrew:** That's fine with me. Just give me some of that water.

**Gascoigne:** Do you really believe this story, Killigrew?

**Killigrew:** Can it hurt to try the water? I don't think Dr. Heidegger would try to poison us.

**Heidegger:** I assure you that the water is not poisonous.

**Gascoigne:** Well . . .

**Wycherly:** If it will convince you, Wilbert, I will drink first.

**Killigrew:** I will join her.

*(They move toward the table.)*

**Heidegger:** Wait. Before you drink, maybe you should decide upon some rules for passing through the perils of youth again. After all, you each have a lifetime of experience to direct you.

**Medbourne:** What kind of rules?

**Heidegger:** Rules of behavior.

**Medbourne:** Are you suggesting that we might make the same mistakes twice?

**Heidegger:** Perhaps.

**Wycherly:** We have learned lessons from our past mistakes. I know *I* have. I've often thought that if only I could live those times over again, I would change them completely.

**Heidegger:** Would you really?

**Wycherly:** I *know* I would.

**Killigrew:** I would, too.

**Heidegger:** Very well. Drink, then.

*(He pours the water into the four glasses. Each guest picks up a glass.)*

**Killigrew:** To our youth!

**Medbourne:** To a new life!

**Gascoigne:** To vigor!

**Wycherly:** To beauty!

*(They drink the water. As the following conversation takes place, their voices become more youthful. They stand straighter.)*

**Wycherly:** I can feel it! I'm beginning to feel younger!

**Killigrew:** My gout has gone! I no longer feel the pain!

**Gascoigne:** I must admit that I do feel a bit strange.

**Medbourne:** Strange? You are simply feeling younger.

119

**Wycherly:** But I want to feel younger than this. I want to be a girl again.

**Killigrew:** And I want to be the handsome young man I was 50 years ago.

**Wycherly:** Give us more, Doctor. We are still too old!

**Medbourne:** Yes! Quick! Give us more!

**Heidegger:** Be patient. You took a long time growing old. Surely you can be content to grow young in half an hour.

*(He fills their glasses, and they drink the water quickly. Now they begin to act like people in their 20's.)*

**Medbourne:** It's been years since I've felt so positive about life.

**Gascoigne:** I feel like climbing a mountain.

**Wycherly:** I have begun to feel pretty again.

**Killigrew:** My dear, you are charming!

**Wycherly** *(blushing):* Why, thank you. Does anyone have a mirror?

**Heidegger** *(pointing):* There is one on the wall over there.

**Wycherly** *(looking in the mirror):* It's true!

**Killigrew:** I feel like singing the songs I knew as a youth.

**Medbourne:** I suppose that means tavern songs. Didn't you spend most of your youth drinking in taverns?

**Killigrew:** Of course not!

**Medbourne:** Then sing another kind of song.

**Killigrew:** Well, I . . . I can't think of any others.

**Medbourne:** Ha! I knew it!

**Gascoigne:** Forget it. There are more important things than singing.

**Killigrew:** Like what?

**Gascoigne:** Like politics. There is nothing greater than a man who serves his country.

**Medbourne:** Spoken like a true thief.

**Gascoigne:** I resent that. I served my country well. Poverty has made you a rude man, Medbourne.

**Medbourne:** I won't be poor for long. I am young again, and I already have a deal in mind.

**Gascoigne:** A deal! Have you ever done an honest day's work?

**Medbourne:** Look who's talking!

**Killigrew:** You are both too serious about life. Life is filled with good wine and good times. Why waste it on boring matters?

**Medbourne:** Killigrew, you are a fool!

**Killigrew:** And you are a miser!

**Wycherly** *(turning away from the mirror):* Gentlemen, please don't quarrel. We are lucky to be young again. But, Dr. Heidegger, please give me another glass of that water. I am not yet young enough.

**Heidegger:** There is plenty of water left.

*(He fills their glasses. Then he returns to his chair, holding the rose. After his guests drink again, they begin to act like teenagers.)*

**Wycherly** *(posing before the mirror):* Look how young I am!

**Killigrew:** But we look foolish in these old clothes.

**Medbourne:** Only old codgers wear clothes like these. And there is only one old codger in this room.

*(The others laugh as he points at Dr. Heidegger.)*

**Wycherly:** Thank goodness we're not old like that!

**Gascoigne** *(pretending to walk with a cane)*: Thank goodness we don't have to walk like this!

**Medbourne:** The old look so foolish.

**Wycherly:** I must get a new dress.

**Killigrew:** We'll all get new clothes. Then we'll have a party.

**Wycherly:** Yes! I love to dance. *(She dances over to Dr. Heidegger and holds out her hands to him.)* Doctor, you dear, *old* soul, get up and dance with me. *(The others laugh.)*

**Heidegger:** No, thank you. My dancing days are over.

**Wycherly** *(like a spoiled child)*: Dance with me!

**Heidegger:** I'm sure that one of these young men would be glad to have such a pretty partner.

**Killigrew:** Dance with me, Clara!

**Gascoigne:** No! She is my partner!

**Medbourne:** Wait! She promised to marry me many years ago.

**Killigrew:** She promised me!

*(Gascoigne grabs one of her hands. Medbourne grabs her other hand. Killigrew grabs her by the waist. They pull her in different directions.)*

**Wycherly** *(pleased by all the attention):* Gentlemen! Please don't fight over me!

**Medbourne** *(pushing Killigrew):* Stay away from her, you fool!

**Killigrew** *(shoving Medbourne into Gascoigne):* Don't push me around!

**Gascoigne** *(getting into the fight):* She doesn't belong to either of you!

*(They fall against the table as they fight. The table turns over, and the water spills from the pitcher.)*

**Heidegger:** Gentlemen! Madame Wycherly! Please stop fighting!

*(They all stand still. Then they look confused as old age begins to return.)*

**Heidegger:** Look. *(He holds up a faded rose.)* My poor Sylvia's rose has faded again.

**Wycherly** *(aging as she speaks):* It has grown old.

**Killigrew:** Does the water's magic wear off?

**Heidegger:** Yes. *(He touches the rose to his lips.)* Still, I love this rose whether fresh or faded.

**Medbourne:** Are we old again so soon?

**Killigrew:** Ow! My gout!

**Heidegger:** Yes, you are old again.

**Gascoigne:** Give us more water.

**Heidegger:** I cannot. It's all over the floor.

**Wycherly:** You mean you have no more?

**Heidegger:** That's right. But I am not sorry. If the Fountain of Youth were at my doorstep, I would not drink from it. That is the lesson you have taught me.

**Killigrew:** But we must have more of it!

**Heidegger:** There is no more.

**Gascoigne:** But you said the Fountain of Youth was . . . where?

**Medbourne:** He said the southern part of Florida.

**Wycherly:** We can find it.

**Killigrew:** We'll travel there together. Dr. Heidegger, will you come with us?

**Heidegger:** Haven't you learned a lesson from all this?

**Medbourne:** There is only one lesson to be learned. Being young is far, far better than being old.

**Wycherly:** I must be beautiful again. I cannot stand being old and ugly.

**Heidegger:** Madame Wycherly, being old does not necessarily mean being ugly.

**Gascoigne** *(leading the others toward the door):* There is no time to lose. We will find the Fountain of Youth, and we will stay near it. We will drink from it morning, noon, and night. We will be young forever!

**Heidegger** *(holding up the faded rose):* Good luck to you, my dear, *old* friends.

*(The curtain falls.)*

THE END

## READING COMPREHENSION

**Summarizing.** Choose the best phrase to complete each sentence. Then write the complete statements on your paper.

1. The three men that Dr. Heidegger invited over _____ (were good friends, had never met one another, were not on good terms).

2. When the four guests began to grow young, they felt _____ (wonderful, awful, frightened).

3. At the end of the play, Heidegger's guests _____ (were satisfied with being old, parted as enemies, went off together to find the Fountain of Youth).

**Interpreting.** Write the answer to each question on your paper.

1. Why did Dr. Heidegger invite the four people to his home?

2. What did the four guests have in common?

3. When the guests became young again, did they show that they had learned from their past mistakes? Explain.

**For Thinking and Discussing**

1. What was the lesson Dr. Heidegger learned from his experiment?

2. Suppose that instead of a Fountain of Youth, there was a Fountain of Age. You could grow older little by little, and the effect would be only temporary. Would you drink from it? Why or why not?

## UNDERSTANDING LITERATURE

**Point of View.** In a play, every character speaks about himself or herself in the first person. This means there can be several different points of view. We learn how each character thinks through what he or she says and does and through what other characters say about him or her.

Based upon your reading of "Dr. Heidegger's Experiment," who do you think might have made each statement below? Write your answers on your paper.

1. "If you would just give me a small loan, I could double your money."

2. "Let's have a party and celebrate our new-found youth! I'll make a toast!"

3. "There is no such thing as aging gracefully. Oh, to be young and beautiful again!"

4. "You can learn a great deal about people just by observing them. But what you learn can be discouraging."

5. "It's high time people started respecting the good men in public office again."

## WRITING

Imagine that you are Dr. Heidegger. After your old friends leave, you sit down to write about the experiment. Write a diary entry in the first person, describing your thoughts and feelings about the events that took place. Include your impressions of the success or failure of the experiment.

# Section Review

## VOCABULARY

**Context Clues.** Sometimes you can tell the meaning of a word you're not sure of by the meaning of the rest of the sentence or paragraph. This is called using *context clues.* For example, suppose you read:

> It's best to use temperance when you eat or drink because too much food or wine could harm you.

If you don't know what *temperance* means, you can probably figure it out. It means "self-control," or "moderation."

Read the passages below from this section. Select the best meaning for each italicized word. On your paper, rewrite the sentences using the meaning you have chosen.

1. "In those days all the tribes spoke one language and lived in *harmony* and peace."
   agreement    danger    villages

2. "Dost thou love Life? Then do not *squander* Time; for that's the Stuff Life is made of."
   discuss    waste    enjoy

3. ". . . To act as if I had . . . the same *infirmities* or failings as others."
   happiness    pleasures    weaknesses

4. "It might have been his *spell* that made the people walk as if always in a dream."
   jokes    magic    story

**Author's Purpose.** When you read, it's often useful to try to figure out the *author's purpose.* It may help you to understand a selection better if you think about why the author wrote it.

As you read, you have to think about what the author is trying to tell you. Does it make sense? Should you believe it? Do you agree with what it says? Evaluating what you read in this way is called *critical reading.*

Select the best choice to complete each statement. Write your answers on your paper.

1. The legend of Godasiyo and "The Legend of Sleepy Hollow" both contain _____ .
   a. a dog as a minor character
   b. proof for the important facts
   c. explanations that may not be true

2. Ben Franklin and Jonathan Edwards both thought _____ .
   a. their beliefs were valuable
   b. people should enjoy their food
   c. sinners should be hanged

3. The writings of Abigail Adams, Thomas Paine, and Jean de Crèvecoeur are similar because they _____.
   a. deal with women in politics
   b. attempt to persuade the reader
   c. criticize the British

4. Davy Crockett's autobiography is _____ .
   a. his true life story
   b. accurate about life in the woods
   c. really a work of fiction

**A Persuasive Letter.** Persuasion is the gentle art of convincing others that your point of view is correct. When you are trying to persuade someone, it is important that you consider the other person's point of view. In this way, you demonstrate that you understand and respect what is important to him or her. Present your point of view fairly and honestly. Nothing will damage a persuasive argument more than a lie or half-truth. Demonstrate your knowledge of the subject or issue by giving your audience convincing reasons for accepting your point of view. Finally, always be polite and adopt a calm and reasonable attitude.

### Step 1: Set Your Goal

The best topics for persuasive writing are ones you have definite opinions about. It is unlikely that you will persuade others of your point of view if you do not feel strongly about it yourself. You should also be familiar enough with the topic so you have facts to support your arguments.

In order to make an effective persuasive argument, you need to know something about your audience. Ask yourself what they know about the topic and how they feel about it. Try to put yourself in their places and think as they think.

Choose one of the following topics for a persuasive letter:

1. Pretend that Abigail Adams, Thomas Paine, and Benjamin Franklin are all living today and are running for mayor of your town or city. Choose the one you would vote for. Then write a persuasive letter to your classmates, telling them why you think they should vote the same way.

2. Dr. Heidegger said that if the Fountain of Youth were at his doorstep, he would not drink from it. On the other hand, Gascoigne and the others were ready to move to Florida so they could be near the Fountain of Youth.

   Decide which side of the issue you would take. Then write a letter to a friend persuading him or her of your point of view.

### Step 2: Make a Plan

A good way to begin gathering ideas for persuasive writing is to jot down the arguments against your point of view. Then jot down convincing counterarguments of your own. Whenever possible, use specific facts to support your arguments.

Sometimes, in addition to facts, you may want to make an emotional appeal. A decision to use emotion depends in part on your audience. For example, if you are writing to someone you don't know, you should probably stick to the facts. If you are writing to a friend, you might want to include an emotional appeal.

An emotional appeal may also depend on the situation. An emotional situation might require an emotional response. For example, read the passage from Thomas Paine's "The American Crisis" again. Notice how he appeals to the emotions when he talks about tyranny and freedom.

Once you know what your arguments are going to be, organize them in the order of their importance. You may begin with your most important point. Or if you want to leave your reader with a strong impression, present your strongest argument last.

### Step 3: Write a First Draft

Now that you have gathered your ideas and organized your arguments, it is time to write the first draft of your persuasive letter. Begin with a clear statement of your point of view. Then present your arguments in their order of importance. Don't forget to consider the point of view of your audience as you write. Make sure the proportions of facts and emotional appeals are appropriate for the reader. Keep the tone of your letter positive.

### Step 4: Revise

By revising your persuasive letter, you will have a chance to make your arguments even more convincing. As you revise, ask yourself the following questions:

☐ Is my point of view clear?

☐ Do my ideas flow logically?

☐ Have I countered each possible objection with a response?

☐ Is the tone of my letter sincere?

When you feel that your letter is as persuasive as possible, proofread it carefully for errors. Then make a neat, final copy.

## QUIZ

The following is a quiz for Section 2. Write the answers in complete sentences on your paper.

## Reading Comprehension

1. Why did Godasiyo build the bridge over the river in "Godasiyo, the Woman Chief"?

2. What was Edwards's advice in "Resolutions" about eating and drinking?

3. What was the main point Abigail Adams was making in her "Letter to Her Husband, John"?

4. In "The Legend of Sleepy Hollow," what traces of Ichabod's presence were found the morning after the Van Tassels' party?

5. In "Dr. Heidegger's Experiment," what did Dr. Heidegger take out of a big black book? What did he use it for?

## Understanding Literature

6. What is a legend? From what point of view is a legend written?

7. From what point of view are Edwards's "Resolutions" written?

8. In what ways are Abigail Adams's letter and Thomas Paine's pamphlet "The American Crisis" alike?

9. From whose point of view is an autobiography written? Is an autobiography objective? Give an example from Benjamin Franklin's work to support your answer.

10. What kind of literary work do you think Davy Crockett's "The Day the Sun Froze" really is? Give an example from the story to support your answer.

## ACTIVITIES

### Word Attack

1. In "Godasiyo, the Woman Chief," Godasiyo was described as "a wise and progressive chief. . . ." The word *progressive* is made up of the base word *progress* and the suffix *-ive*. In this case, the suffix *-ive* means "having a tendency or inclination to act in a certain way." A *progressive* chief is one who acts in a way that promotes progress. The suffix *-ive* changes a base word to an adjective or a noun.

   Below are some words formed with the suffix *-ive*. Write a simple definition for each. Then use each word in a sentence.

   | | |
   |---|---|
   | objective | selective |
   | expensive | defensive |
   | exclusive | offensive |

2. In "What Is an American?" children are described as being "frolicsome." *Frolicsome* is made up of the base word *frolic* and the suffix *-some*. The suffix *-some* usually changes a base word to an adjective and means "showing or displaying a certain characteristic." *Frolicsome* means "behaving in a frolicking manner."

   Add the suffix *-some* to each of the following base words. Check a dictionary if you are uncertain about the spelling. Then use each of the words you wrote in a sentence.

   | | |
   |---|---|
   | trouble | awe |
   | lone | loath |
   | tire | burden |

### Speaking and Listening

1. George Washington ordered that Thomas Paine's "The American Crisis" be read to the American soldiers fighting the British. Practice reading it aloud, and prepare to present it to your class. Keep in mind that the piece is an emotional appeal meant to increase the morale of the troops.

2. "Dr. Heidegger's Experiment" is a play for four actors and one actress. Get together with four classmates and rehearse the play. Be prepared to perform it for the class.

**Researching.** Many of the people you read about in this section played an important role in the formation of our country. Select one of the people from the list below. Do some research about him or her and write a short biography.

Jonathan Edwards
Benjamin Franklin
Thomas Paine
Abigail Adams

### Creating

1. "The Day the Sun Froze" is a tall tale written by Davy Crockett. Tall tales were popular on the American frontier. They described exaggerated and impossible events as if they were actual happenings. Write a tall tale of your own. Make it as humorous as you can.

2. Think about what is necessary in order to do well in the world you now live in. Write your own set of resolutions. Use the first-person point of view.

# SPEECH TO THE VIRGINIA CONVENTION

## PATRICK HENRY

*On March 23, 1775, a few weeks before the American Revolution began, Virginia politicians were discussing the growing political crisis. Patrick Henry had proposed arming the militia against the British. Henry's words were not recorded at the time. His speech was reconstructed after his death. What has been passed down is one of the most stirring speeches ever delivered by an American.*

MR. President:[1] No man thinks more highly than I do of the patriotism, as well as abilities, of the very worthy gentlemen who have just addressed the House. But different men often see the same subject in different lights; and, therefore, I hope that it will not be thought disrespectful to those gentlemen, if, entertaining as I do, opinions of a character very opposite to theirs, I shall speak forth my sentiments freely and without reserve. This is no time for ceremony. The question before the House is one of awful moment to this country. For my own part I consider it as nothing less than a question of freedom or slavery; and in proportion to the magnitude of the subject ought to be the freedom of the debate. It is only in this way that we can hope to arrive at truth, and fulfill the great responsibility which we hold to God and our country. Should I keep back my opinions at such a time, through fear of giving offense, I should consider myself as guilty of treason toward my country, and of an act of disloyalty toward the majesty of heaven, which I revere above all earthly kings.

Mr. President, it is natural to man to indulge in the illusions of hope. We are apt to shut our eyes against a painful truth, and listen to the song of that

---

1. **Mr. President:** the president of the Virginia Convention.

siren, till she transforms us into beasts.[2] Is this the part of wise men, engaged in a great and arduous struggle for liberty? Are we disposed to be of the number of those who, having eyes, see not, and having ears, hear not,[3] the things which so nearly concern their temporal salvation? For my part, whatever anguish of spirit it may cost, I am willing to know the whole truth; to know the worst and to provide for it.

I have but one lamp by which my feet are guided; and that is the lamp of experience. I know of no way of judging of the future but by the past. And judging by the past, I wish to know what there has been in the conduct of the British ministry for the last ten years, to justify those hopes with which gentlemen have been pleased to solace themselves and the House? Is it that insidious smile with which our petition[4] has been lately received? Trust it not, sir; it will prove a snare to your feet. Suffer not yourselves to be betrayed with a kiss.[5] Ask yourselves how this gracious reception of our petition comports with these warlike preparations which cover our waters and darken our land. Are fleets and armies necessary to a work of love and reconciliation? Have we shown ourselves so unwilling to be reconciled, that force must be called in to win back our love? Let us not deceive ourselves, sir. These are the implements of war and subjugation; the last arguments to which kings resort.

I ask gentlemen, sir, what means this martial array, if its purpose be not to force us to submission? Can gentlemen assign any other possible motives for it? Has Great Britain any enemy, in this quarter of the world, to call for all this accumulation of navies and armies? No, sir, she has none. They are meant for us; they can be meant for no other. They are sent over to bind and rivet upon us those chains which the British ministry have been so long forging. And what have we to oppose to them? Shall we try argument? Sir, we have been trying that for the last ten years. Have we anything new to offer on the subject? Nothing. We have held the subject up in every light of which it is capable; but it has been all in vain. Shall we resort to entreaty and humble supplication?[6] What terms shall we find which have not been already exhausted? Let us not, I beseech you, sir, deceive ourselves longer. Sir, we

---

2. **listen . . . beasts:** an allusion to Homer's *Odyssey* in which the sirens lured sailors to their death with their sweet songs and in which the enchantress Circe transformed men into beasts.
3. **having eyes . . . hear not:** an allusion to the Bible, Jeremiah 5:21.
4. **our petition:** the First Continental Congress had petitioned King George III to revoke new tax laws. The King repealed the laws conditionally.
5. **betrayed with a kiss:** an allusion to the Bible, Luke 22:47-48, and Judas's betrayal of Jesus.

6. **supplication:** petitioning or begging.

*Patrick Henry Before the Virginia House of Burgesses, 1851.* Peter F. Rothermel.
Red Hill-The Patrick Henry National Memorial, Brookneal, Virginia.

have done everything that could be done, to avert the storm which is now coming on. We have petitioned; we have remonstrated;[7] we have supplicated; we have prostrated ourselves before the throne, and have implored its interposition[8] to arrest the tyrannical hands of the ministry and Parliament. Our petitions have been slighted; our remonstrances have produced additional violence and insult; our supplications have been disregarded; and we have

---

7. **remonstrated:** complained.

8. **interposition:** intervention.

been spurned, with contempt, from the foot of the throne. In vain, after these things, may we indulge the fond[9] hope of peace and reconciliation. There is no longer any room for hope. If we wish to be free—if we mean to preserve inviolate[10] those inestimable privileges for which we have been so long contending—if we mean not basely to abandon the noble struggle in which we have been so long engaged, and which we have pledged ourselves never to abandon until the glorious object of our contest shall be obtained, we must fight! I repeat it, sir, we must fight! An appeal to arms and to the God of Hosts is all that is left us!

They tell us, sir, that we are weak; unable to cope with so formidable an adversary. But when shall we be stronger? Will it be the next week, or the next year? Will it be when we are totally disarmed, and when a British guard shall be stationed in every house? Shall we gather strength by irresolution and inaction? Shall we acquire the means of effectual resistance, by lying supinely on our backs, and hugging the delusive phantom of hope, until our enemies shall have bound us hand and foot? Sir, we are not weak, if we make proper use of the means which the God of nature hath placed in our power. Three millions of people, armed in the holy cause of liberty, and in such a country as that which we possess, are invincible by any force which our enemy can send against us. Besides, sir, we shall not fight our battles alone. There is a just God who presides over the destinies of nations; and who will raise up friends to fight our battles for us. The battle, sir, is not to the strong[11] alone; it is to the vigilant, the active, the brave. Besides, sir, we have no election.[12] If we were base enough to desire it, it is now too late to retire from the contest. There is no retreat, but in submission and slavery! Our chains are forged! Their clanking may be heard on the plains of Boston! The war is inevitable—and let it come! I repeat it, sir, let it come!

It is in vain, sir, to extenuate the matter. Gentlemen may cry peace, peace—but there is no peace. The war is actually begun![13] The next gale that sweeps from the north will bring to our ears the clash of resounding arms! Our brethren are already in the field! Why stand we here idle? What is it that gentlemen wish? What would they have? Is life so dear, or peace so sweet, as to be purchased at the price of chains and slavery? Forbid it, Almighty God! I know not what course others may take; but as for me, give me liberty, or give me death!

---

9. **fond:** foolish.
10. **inviolate:** intact; whole.

11. **battle . . . to the strong:** an allusion to the Bible, Ecclesiastes 9:11.
12. **election:** choice.
13. **war . . . begun:** Boston had recently been occupied by British troops under the leadership of General Howe.

# THINKING ABOUT THE SPEECH

*Recalling*

**1.** According to the first paragraph, how does Henry characterize the "question before the House"? What does he say he would be guilty of if he should keep back his opinions?

**2.** According to the third paragraph, by what does Henry say he judges the future? Of what "last argument" does he accuse the British and their king?

**3.** What reason does Henry give in the fourth paragraph against further compromises with the British? What does he say must be done instead?

**4.** What evidence does Henry offer in the next-to-last paragraph to prove that America is invincible?

**5.** At the end of his speech, what does Henry ask God to forbid? What course does he say he himself will take?

*Interpreting*

**6.** Henry's speech consists of an opening, four paragraphs of development, and a conclusion. In the four middle paragraphs, Henry touches on the main points of "the very worthy gentlemen" who spoke before he did. What four arguments do you think they offered for favoring compromise with the British? Briefly summarize how Henry counters each of these arguments.

**7.** Henry makes several *allusions*, or references, to the Bible in his speech. What effect do you suppose Henry wanted these allusions to have on his audience?

**8.** An effective persuasive speech uses not only logical arguments but also emotional appeals to sway listeners. The speaker's delivery—his or her voice and body movements—have much to do with a speech's emotional impact, but so do the words and sentences themselves. Find various passages in Henry's speech which convey the following emotions: bewilderment, concern, frustration, outrage, confidence, determination.

*Applying*

**9.** What situations in present world affairs would you argue to fight about rather than compromise? To compromise rather than fight?

# ANALYZING LITERATURE

*Understanding the Elements of a Speech*

When Thomas Jefferson was a college student, he had the opportunity to hear Patrick Henry speak. "He appeared to me," Jefferson later wrote, "to speak as Homer wrote." Jefferson's comparison of Henry to the greatest epic poet of ancient Greece was high praise indeed. Greek poetry began as a spoken art. Moreover, the Greeks, and the Romans after them, considered public speaking, or **oratory**, an art. It was a requirement in every school and the basic means of debating public issues in a society in which only a small minority could read and write. Handbooks were written to explain not only how best to organize a speech's ideas but also how to make the language artful and eloquent. In Patrick Henry's day, these ancient handbooks were still widely studied, especially by preachers and politicians. Accordingly, Henry's speech contains several of the devices that would have been found in the speech of an ancient Greek.

**Repetition** is an important device in oratory, both for emphasizing ideas and for creating an effective rhythm. Henry, for example, often repeats words or phrases at the beginning of sentences or clauses to join related ideas. The ancients called this kind of repetition *anaphora* (ə **nǎf'** ə rə): But *when* shall we be stronger? *Will it be* the next week, or the next year? *Will it be when* we are totally disarmed, and *when* a British guard shall be stationed in every house?

The passage above illustrates another device of oratory, the rhetorical question. A **rhetorical question** is one that does not require a reply since the answer is obvious and usually the only one possible. The question is meant to make listeners instantly respond in their minds and agree with the speaker's viewpoint. By asking "when shall we be stronger," Henry in effect was stating "we shall not be stronger than we are right now." Henry also uses a device called a **periodic sentence**—a sentence which builds suspense by delaying the main idea until the very end, usually after a series of opening phrases or clauses meant to arouse the listeners' curiosity. A periodic sentence adds particular emphasis and dignity to an important idea. Good orators are careful not to overuse this device. Accordingly, Henry's speech contains only one periodic sentence, which he used to convey his single most important idea.

1. Find the periodic sentence in Patrick Henry's speech. What central point does it convey?
2. Find at least one other example each of repetition and rhetorical questions in Henry's speech.

......................................

# CRITICAL THINKING AND READING

*Author's Purpose: Persuasion*
**Persuasion** is the type of composition in which the author's main purpose is to convince an audience to support a particular line of action. How effective the author is in convincing the audience depends on how well he or she handles certain elements.

**Identifying the Controversy.** A controversy exists when groups of people hold two or more opposing views on an issue. An author of persuasion must be aware of the opposing views before he or she can muster effective arguments against them and in support of his or her own point of view.

**Targeting the Audience.** The author must address a particular audience: those who do not share the author's point of view. He or she must be careful not to offend this target audience. Instead, the author must take into consideration their feelings and beliefs.

**Appealing to the Intellect and the Emotions.** Persuasion relies on a blend of reasoned argument and emotional appeal. The audience must be convinced that the author has carefully thought about the controversy and assumed a reasonable point of view. At the same time, the audience must be convinced that the way the author feels about the issue is the way that they feel too.

Whenever you read or listen to a work of persuasion, think about these three elements. By thinking critically, you will be able to judge the effectiveness of an author's argument and decide whether you want to agree or disagree with the views presented.

**1.** What controversial issue is the subject of Patrick Henry's speech? Where does he identify the controversy in broad, general terms? Where does Henry discuss the controversy in specific terms?

**2.** Who make up Henry's target audience? Explain how Henry carefully avoids offending this audience.

**3.** Find two details in the speech that would have appealed to the audience's intelligence. Then find two details that appeal to the audience's emotions.

**4.** On a scale of 1 to 10, how effective in your opinion is Henry's speech? Cite specific passages in the speech to support your evaluation.

*Dictionaries and the Changing Meanings of Words*

A living language is always changing. New words are always entering the language; old ones fall into disuse. Some words even change meaning. For these reasons, a dictionary will often label certain words as "Obsolete" or "Archaic," meaning "no longer in current use," and list more than one definition or meaning for a given word. A dictionary, therefore, is a record of both a language's present and its past. When you are reading the literature of earlier centuries, a good college dictionary can help you unlock the meanings of obsolete words as well as familiar words with uncommon meanings.

The following passages from Patrick Henry's speech contain familiar words with meanings that are no longer the most commonly used. Use a college dictionary to determine the exact meaning of each italicized word.

1. "The question before the house is one of awful *moment* to this country."

2. "Are we *disposed* to be of the number of those who, having eyes, see not. . . ."

3. "In vain, after these things, may we indulge the *fond* hope of peace and reconciliation."

4. "If we were base enough to desire it, it is now too late to *retire* from the *contest*."

# THINKING AND WRITING

**Writing a Persuasive Speech.**
Select a controversial issue of current concern to you and your classmates. Compose a five- to ten-minute speech in which you try to persuade your classmates to agree with your view of the issue.

**Prewriting.** After you select a topic, make sure the issue is controversial—one in which people, as Henry says, can "often see the same subject in different lights." Next, decide which side of the controversy you will support. List the beliefs and feelings that you suspect those who disagree with you will have. Finally, list arguments that you think will counter those beliefs and feelings.

**Writing.** Use Henry's speech as a model. Begin with an introduction followed by a series of reasoned arguments and ending with a rousing summary of your main point.

**Revising.** After you have completed a first draft, consider the following questions as you polish your speech: Have you clearly identified the controversy and the course of action you favor? Have you supported your position with reasoned arguments? Have you dealt with your opponents' point of view by presenting counterarguments? Is your conclusion memorable?

Next, focus on the emotional aspects of your speech: Have you avoided offending your audience? Have you appealed to their feelings as well as their intelligence?

Finally, consider your language. Have you used repetition and rhetorical questions effectively? Would a periodic sentence at a crucial point in your speech add emphasis and dignity?

**Proofreading.** Reread your speech and correct any mistakes in grammar, spelling, and punctuation. If necessary, prepare a neat, final copy.

**Publishing.** Deliver your speech to the class.

# EARLY AMERICA IMAGINED

## HISTORICAL FICTION

*Isn't it strange some people make
you feel so tired inside,
Your thoughts begin to shrivel up
Like leaves all brown and dried!*

*But when you're with some other ones,
It's stranger still to find
Your thoughts are thick as fireflies
All shiny in your mind!*

—Rachel Field

*Winter Scene in Brooklyn*
Francis Guy (1760-1820)
The Brooklyn Museum
Gift of the Brooklyn Institute of Arts and Sciences

# Early America Imagined: Historical Fiction

When some people read history, their imaginations come alive. They feel the joys and sorrows of the past. When other people read history, they find it difficult to go beyond a list of facts: dates, places, and famous names.

Authors of *historical fiction* use their imaginations to create stories that make history come alive for everyone. Famous places, events, and dates take on new meaning when you consider the people who really lived during those times. They were people with feelings, fears, dreams, and personalities.

### Fact and Fiction in Plot

Historical fiction combines facts about history with made-up details. Authors use their imaginations and their understanding of how people live today to explain how and why certain events in history may have happened. Thus the plot — the chain of events in the story — usually blends fiction and facts from history.

It is a fact that people in the 17th century believed in witches. The first story in this section, "Salem Village, Massachusetts," tells us something about how and why the famous Salem witch trials happened. Twentieth-century writer Stephen Vincent Benét probably read reports of the trials by people who were there, as well as many history books about that time and place, before he wrote his story. But he used his own judgment and ideas to explain the details of the story — why the characters did what they did. You will also read Benét's poem about Cotton Mather, which shows how he felt about Mather's part in the trials.

### Fictional Characters and Real Feelings

The second story in this section, "April Morning," was written in the 1960's, but it describes April 19, 1775, in Lexington, Massachusetts. The modern author, Howard Fast, made up a fictional person, Adam Cooper. In this exciting, realistic story, you will feel, through Adam, the terror and excitement of the day as the people of Lexington probably experienced it over 200 years ago.

Midnight Ride of Paul Revere, Grant Wood, 1931

## Real Characters and Fictional Details

The third story in this section also takes place during the Revolutionary War. The people and events in this story are real. The author, Jane Yolen, used historical sources to gather the facts which she used in the story. These facts told her about the setting—where and when the story took place. The facts also gave her the names of her main characters and some idea of the events in the plot. Yolen then used her imagination to make up details and dialogue to bring to life the story of Fanny Campbell, a young woman who staged a daring rescue and became a heroine in the Revolutionary War.

Historical fiction is fun to read because it provides a sense of visiting another time and place. Often historical fiction includes memorable events and characters. However, authors of historical fiction write about the concerns of their own time and place as well as about the past. The authors of historical fiction try to give us guidelines for our own lives. They seem to say, "Look at the mistakes that fear, pride, foolishness, or greed have led to in the past. Let's not make these mistakes again. Look at the people in our past who valued freedom and loyalty, acted with courage, and learned new skills. They accomplished much. Let's use these abilities to improve the quality of life in our own era."

# Salem Village, Massachusetts

*by Stephen Vincent Benét*

*Stephen Vincent Benét (1898–1945) is famous for his stories and poems about our nation's past. In the story that follows, he vividly describes what took place in Salem Village, Massachusetts, in 1692.*

*In the 17th century, people had no doubt that witches were real. Thousands of people in Europe were accused of witchcraft and were burned at the stake, hanged, or tortured. Thirty people were found guilty of witchcraft in Salem Village in 1692. Nineteen were hanged. The panic ended almost as soon as it had begun. All Salem admitted to making a tragic error. It was the end of witchcraft trials in America.*

**S**alem Village had a new minister — the Reverend Samuel Parris. He brought with him to Salem Village two West Indian servants — a man known as John Indian and a woman named Tituba. And when he had bought those two or their services in the West Indies, he was buying a rope that was to hang 19 people of New England.

Perhaps the nine-year-old Elizabeth Parris, the minister's daughter, boasted to her new friends of the odd stories Tituba told and the strange things she could do. Perhaps Tituba herself let the report of her magic powers be spread about the village.

During the winter of 1691–92 a group of girls and women began to meet nightly at the parsonage, with Tituba and her fortune-telling as the chief attraction. The winters were long and white — and any diversion was welcome. Elizabeth Parris, at nine, was the youngest. Then came Abigail Williams, 11, and Ann Putnam, 12. The rest were older — Mercy Lewis, Mary Wolcott, and Elizabeth Hubbard were 17; Elizabeth Booth and Susan Sheldon, 18; and Mary Warren and Sarah Churchill, 20. Three were servants — Mercy Lewis, Mary Warren, and Sarah Churchill.

The elder women included a pair of gossipy, superstitious busybodies — Mrs. Pope and Mrs. Bibber; and young Ann Putnam's mother, Ann Putnam, Sr.

The circle met no doubt with the usual giggling, whispering, and gossip. From mere fortune-telling it proceeded to other and more serious matters — table rapping,

perhaps, and a little West Indian voodoo. Weird stories were told by Tituba and weird things were shown, while the wind blew outside and the big shadows flickered on the wall.

Soon the members of the circle began to show hysterical symptoms. They crawled under tables and chairs. They made strange sounds. They shook and trembled with nightmare fears. Something strange and out of nature was happening — who had ever seen normal young girls behave like these young girls?

Serious ministers were called in to look at the afflicted children. A Dr. Gregg gave his opinion. It was almost too terrible to believe, and yet what else could be believed? *Witchcraft!*

Meanwhile, one may suppose, the "afflicted children," like most hysterical subjects, enjoyed the stares, the horrified looks, the respectful questions that greeted them. They had been unimportant girls of a little town; now they were the center of attention. There was only one catch about it. If they were really bewitched, somebody must be doing the bewitching.

On the 29th of February, 1692, in the midst of a storm of thunder and lightning, three women — Sarah Good, Sarah Osburn, and Tituba — were arrested on the deadly charge of bewitching the children.

The next day, March 1, two judges, Justice Hawthorne and Justice Corwin, arrived. The first hearing was held in the crowded meetinghouse of the village, and all Salem swarmed to it.

The children had picked their first victims well. Sarah Good and Sarah Osburn were old women of no particular standing in the community.

The Justices must have arrived with their minds made up. For the first question addressed to Sarah Good was, bluntly: "What evil spirit have you familiarity with?"

"None," said the piping old voice.

"Have you made no contracts with the devil?" proceeded the Justice.

"No."

The Justice went to the root of the matter at once.

"Why do you hurt these children?"

"I do not hurt them. I scorn it," said Sarah Good defiantly. But the Justice had her now. He was not to be brushed aside.

"Who, then, do you employ to do it?"

"I employ nobody."

The Justice returned to the main charge, like any prosecuting attorney.

"Have you made no contract with the devil?"

"No."

It was time for Exhibit A. The Justice turned to the children. Was Sarah Good one of the persons who tormented them? And then, before the amazed eyes of all, they began to be tormented. They twisted; they grew stiff; they were stricken moaning or speechless.

"Sarah Good, do you see now what you have done? Why do you not tell us the truth? Why do you torment these poor children?"

And with these words Sarah Good was already hanged. For all that she could say was, "I do not torment them." And yet everyone had seen her, with their own eyes.

Sarah Osburn's examination followed the same course — the same questions, the same useless denial, the same fits of the afflicted children, the same end.

Then Tituba was examined and gave them their fill of strange stories and horrors.

The West Indian woman, a slave in a strange land, was fighting for her life. She admitted, repentantly, that she had tormented the children. But she had been forced to do so. By whom? By Goody Good and Goody Osburn.* Everyone could see that she spoke the truth. For, when she was first brought in, the children were tormented at her presence. But as soon as she had confessed and turned king's evidence, she was tormented herself. To jail with her — but she had saved her neck.

The hearing was over. The men and women of Salem went back to their homes to discuss the fearful workings of God's will. Here and there a common-sense voice murmured a doubt or two — to convict two old women of a terrible crime on the word of young girls and a West Indian slave!

But, on the whole, the villagers of Salem felt relieved. The cause of the problem had been found. It would be stamped out and the afflicted children would recover. The children slept after a tiring day — they were not used to such performances.

As for the accused women, they went to Boston Jail — to be chained there while awaiting the gallows.

Meanwhile, on an outlying farm, Giles Corey, 81 years of age, began to argue

the case with his wife, Martha. He believed in the afflicted children. She did not, and said so — even going so far as to say that the judges were blinded. It was one of those marital arguments that occur between strong-willed people. And it was to bring Martha Corey to the gallows and Giles Corey to an even stranger doom.

As for what went on in the minds of the afflicted children, we cannot say. But this much is sure. They had seen and felt their power. The hearing had been the greatest and most exciting event of their

---

* "Goody" was a polite title used to refer to a married woman.

narrow lives. And it was so easy to do. You twisted your body and groaned — and grown people were afraid.

On March 19, Martha Corey and Rebecca Nurse were arrested on the charge of witchcraft. On March 21, they were examined and committed. And with that the real reign of terror began.

Salem Village, as a community, was no longer sane.

Let us get it over quickly. The Salem witches stopped being Salem's business. They became a matter affecting the whole colony. Sir William Phips, the new governor, appointed a special court to try the cases. And the hangings began.

Through the summer the accusations, the arrests, the trials, came thick and fast till the jails were crowded. Nor were those now accused friendless old women like Sarah Good. They included Captain John Alden, who saved himself by breaking jail, and the wealthy and prominent Englishes, who saved themselves by running away.

The most disgraceful scenes occurred at the trial of the saintly Rebecca Nurse.

Thirty-nine citizens of Salem were brave enough to sign a petition for her, and the jury brought in a verdict of "not guilty." The mob in the sweating courtroom immediately began to cry out, and the judge told the jury to reverse their verdict. They did so, to the mob's delight. Rebecca Nurse was hanged on Gallows Hill on July 19 with Sarah Good, Sarah Wilds, Elizabeth How, and Susanna Martin.

Susanna Martin's only witchcraft seems to have been that she was an unusually tidy woman and had once walked a muddy road without getting her dress dirty. As for Elizabeth How, the children cried, "I am stuck with a pin. I am pinched," when they saw her — and she was hanged.

One hanging on June 19, five on July 19, five on August 18, eight on September 22, including Mary Easty and Martha Corey. But for stubborn Giles Corey a different fate was waiting.

The old man had begun by believing in the whole hocus-pocus. He had quarreled with his wife about it. He had seen her arrested as a witch, insulted by the judges, and condemned to die. Now he himself was in danger.

Well, he could die as his wife would. But there was the property — his goods, his prosperous farm. By law, the goods and property of those convicted of witchcraft were taken by the state. Giles Corey drew up a will leaving that property to the two sons-in-law who had not joined in the madness. And then at the trial, he said, "I will not plead. I am condemned already in courts where ghosts appear as witnesses and swear men's lives away."

Those who refused to plead either guilty or not guilty were given an old English punishment. It was heaping weights or stones upon the unhappy victim till he pleaded guilty or not guilty — or until his chest was crushed. And exactly that happened to old Giles Corey. They heaped the stones upon him until they killed him — and two days before his wife hanged, he died. But his property went to the loyal sons-in-law. So died Giles Corey.

And then, suddenly and strangely as the madness had come, it was gone.

The afflicted children, at long last, had gone too far. They had accused the governor's lady, and they had accused Mrs. Hall, a minister's wife who was known in the colony for her goodness. There comes a point when men and women revolt against blood and horror. If it went on, no one but the afflicted children and their friends would be left alive.

In 1706 Ann Putnam made a public confession that she had been tricked by the devil in testifying as she had. She had testified in every case but one.

We have no reason to hold Salem up to judgment. It was a town, like any other — and a strange madness took hold of it. But it is no stranger a thing to hang people for witchcraft than to hang them for the shape of their nose or the color of their skin. Persecution follows superstition and intolerance, as fire follows the fuse. And once we light that fire, we cannot foresee where it will end any more than they could in Salem Village almost 300 years ago.

## READING COMPREHENSION

**Summarizing.** Choose the best phrase to complete each sentence. Then write the complete statements on your paper.

1. At first, Tituba's stories and fortune-telling were viewed as _____ (matters of life and death, harmless entertainment, cures for sick children).

2. Tituba was sent to prison instead of being hanged because she _____ (continued to claim her innocence, confessed and implicated others, told everyone she loved children).

3. The "afflicted" children went too far when they _____ (accused two respected women, refused to speak to the doctor, would not attend school).

**Interpreting.** Write the answer to each question on your paper.

1. What was Doctor Gregg's diagnosis of the "afflicted" children?

2. Why did the "afflicted" children behave as if they were victims of witchcraft?

3. What role did Ann Putnam play in the Salem witchcraft trials?

### For Thinking and Discussing

1. What did the author mean when he wrote, "Persecution follows superstition and intolerance, as fire follows the fuse"?

2. Do you think the reign of terror could have been stopped earlier? How?

## UNDERSTANDING LITERATURE

**Historical Fiction.** "Salem Village, Massachusetts" is historical fiction. The author has woven together material from his imagination with real characters, settings, and events from history.

Sometimes the characters and incidents in a work of historical fiction are real. Sometimes they are invented to suit the purposes of the author. Because a work of historical fiction is set before the lifetime of the person who is writing it, its dialogue is usually created by the author. Often the author makes inferences about what the characters are thinking or feeling. These inferences are usually based on historical fact, but they can't always be proved.

On your paper, label each of the following statements that can be found in history books as *fact*. Label the items created by the author to help tell the story as *fiction*.

1. "Salem Village had a new minister. . . ."

2. "The circle met . . . with the usual giggling, whispering, and gossip."

3. "In 1706 Ann Putnam made a public confession. . . ."

4. "As for Elizabeth How, the children cried, 'I am stuck with a pin. I am pinched. . . .'"

## WRITING

Use historical facts that you know about the witchcraft trials and your imagination to write Ann Putnam's confession.

# Cotton Mather
## 1663—1728

*by Stephen Vincent Benét*

Grim Cotton Mather
Was always seeing witches,
Daylight, moonlight,
They buzzed about his head,
Pinching him and plaguing him
With aches and pains and stitches,
Witches in his pulpit,
Witches by his bed.

Nowadays, nowadays,
We'd say that he was crazy,
But everyone believed him
In old Salem town
And nineteen people
Were hanged for Salem witches
Because of Cotton Mather
And his long, black gown.

Old Cotton Mather
Didn't die happy.
He could preach and thunder,
He could fast and pray,
But men began to wonder
If there had been witches —
When he walked in the streets
Men looked the other way.

---

What sort of a person was Cotton Mather?
What details in the poem give you clues about
his occupation and his character?

# April Morning

*by Howard Fast*

*Howard Fast (1914— ) is best known for his historical
novels, although he has also written numerous plays, poems,
film scripts, and short stories. In the retelling of April Morning that follows, Fast describes the experiences of 15-year-old
Adam Cooper during the battles of Lexington and Concord.
After the bloody fighting has ended, Adam knows that his
life will never be the same again.*

We could hear the sound of British
drums in the distance. It was very soft at
first, but it kept getting louder.

Morning mist covered the road. When
it cleared, we saw them for the first time.
They were marching up the road as if they
were on parade. Their coats were as red
as fire, and their rifles gleamed in the sun.
There were row after row of them as far
as we could see.

In front were three officers on horses.
Then came soldiers carrying flags. Behind
them were the drummers. Then came the
regular soldiers, maybe 1,000 in all. My
hands began to sweat, and my heart was
beating fast.

Suddenly, a British officer saw us. He
held up his arm. The drums stopped. So
did the soldiers. Then the officer rode up
to us. We were standing in a small park
in the center of our village — Lexington,
Massachusetts.

It was April, 1775. About 70 of us were
lined up in two rows. We had our rifles,
but we didn't expect a fight.

Before the British arrived, the Reverend
had told us, "Our duty is to be firm and
calm, but not to die. Ours is a way of life,
not of death."

My father, Moses Cooper, had agreed.
"We are not here to start a war, but to
prevent one," he said.

Our plan was to let the Reverend speak
to the British when they came. He didn't
carry a gun, so they would know we
wanted peace. We had our rights, and we
wanted the British to know it. But none
of us wanted war.

Now the British officer began to shout
orders to his men. They marched into the
park facing us. Their first line was only
30 steps away. For the first time, I felt
something awful was going to happen.

Then the officer yelled at us, "Put down
your guns, you filthy rebels! Break up and
go to your homes!"

The Reverend tried to speak, but he did not get a chance. The officer rode right at him and almost knocked him down. It was my father who kept him from falling. I heard a shot fired. Then I saw my father grab his chest and fall to the ground.

I started to scream, but I couldn't hear myself. All I could hear was the roar of British guns. The whole world seemed to be crashing down on me. I turned and ran. Everyone else ran, too.

I didn't see the ditch ahead of me, and fell into it. When I looked up, I saw Sam Hodley standing above me. He had a hole in his neck, and blood was pouring out. We looked at each other for a second. Then he fell dead into the ditch right beside me.

"No!" I screamed. Then I vomited.

I was sick, but I could see redcoats running toward the ditch. So I jumped out and began running again. I came to an empty hut and crawled into a corner. Then I cried. I hadn't cried that much since I was small.

When you are 15, like me, you can still pretend a little. For a while, I pretended my father wasn't dead. That was the only way I could stop crying. But I knew my father would never come home again.

I thought about yesterday. Things that seemed so important then didn't seem that way now. I remembered my father calling me when I started back to the house.

"Adam Cooper," he said. "Have you finished your work?"

"Yes," I said, and kept on walking.

"Adam," he said. "Don't walk away and talk with your back to me."

"Yes, sir," I said, and turned around.

"Get some water from the well and take it to your mother. Wasting steps is as foolish as wasting time."

"Yes, Father," I said.

I wanted to say, "Why do you always cut me down to half my size? Maybe I would try harder to please you if you were kinder to me." But I didn't say that, of course.

Slowly I pulled a pail of water from the well. As I did, I said some magic words. That was in case the devil had put a curse on our water. My father and mother didn't believe in magic. They said that people who do are ignorant. Maybe so, but I wasn't taking any chances.

Just then my younger brother, Levi,

came by. "Give me some water," he said. "Or else I'll tell Father about the magic. I heard you."

"You little brat," I said. But I gave him a drink anyway.

I knew I was in trouble when we sat down to eat that night. My father looked angry. And Levi was quiet, which was unusual for him. I guessed he had told my father about the magic.

Soon my father asked, "How tall are you, Adam? As tall as a man?"

"Yes, sir," I said.

"And as strong as a man, too," he said. "Then you should also have the mind of a man. Don't you think so, Adam?"

"Yes, sir," I said. "That makes sense."

When my father started asking questions like that, it was a danger sign. Both my mother and grandmother knew it. But only Granny wasn't afraid of him.

"Oh, eat your pudding, Moses," she told him. "All these questions will just spoil your digestion."

"I'm talking to Adam," my father said firmly. Then he gave me a speech. We were plain people, he said, but intelligent just the same. And intelligent people didn't believe in magic. It went against our religion. It also went against the truth.

Granny got angry. "All this fuss about some foolishness by a fifteen-year-old boy," she said. "I never saw a man who liked to argue so much. You don't have enough sense to enjoy your wife's cooking."

It was lucky my father had to go to a meeting that night. That finally ended the quarrel. The meeting was to talk about our rights, and how to defend them against the British. My father believed in fighting with ideas, not guns. If you could win an argument, he said, you could win a war.

I asked my father if I could go with him to the meeting. He said, "When you start acting like a man, I'll take you. Not before." Then he walked out.

"Why does he hate me so?" I asked my mother.

"Hate you?" she said. "Adam, he *loves* you. You're his son."

"Then I guess I've got love and hate mixed up," I said. "No matter what I do, he finds fault."

"That's just his way," Granny said. "He expects too much from everyone."

"Well, it's not my way to like it," I said. Then I walked out and slammed the door. Levi was standing outside.

"Are you going to lick me?" he asked.

"Just stay out of my sight, you little skunk," I said. "Next time I *will* lick you."

I needed some sympathy, and I knew where to get it. Ruth Simmons would always say something kind to me. We had known each other since we were little children. Once, when we were 13, she asked me whom I wanted to marry. I told her I hadn't thought about it. She said she had already picked me because she loved me. That made me pretty nervous for a while. But then Granny told me I was too young to worry about getting married. And Ruth stopped talking about it.

I took Ruth for a walk in the village park. I told her how my father had made me feel so bad. Then I talked about going to sea on my uncle's ship.

"You can't be serious," Ruth said.

"Why not?" I asked. "Would it make any difference to you?"

"It would make me the loneliest girl in Massachusetts if you went away."

When she said that, I felt good for the first time in days. I took her hand in mine and kissed her. I kept her hand in mine all the way back to her house.

Late that night, Levi woke me up. "Adam," he said. "I hear a horse coming up the road."

"So what?" I said. "Travelers ride at night, don't they?"

"Travelers don't race their horses in the dark," Levi said.

He was right. This horse was racing fast. The sound of its hoofs got louder. I saw the rider stop outside the village inn. He was shouting, but I could not make out his words. I saw lights going on in all the houses.

My father got dressed and went outside. I got dressed, too. But my mother stopped me at the front door.

"Where do you think you're going?" she asked. "Go back upstairs."

"Mother," I said, "all the men are going outside. Don't make me stay here."

My mother was going to say I was just a boy. But Granny stopped her.

"I think Adam is right," Granny said. "He ought to be there."

Outside, there was a crowd around the rider. He said that British troops were marching this way from Boston. They wanted to grab all the guns and gunpowder stored in Concord. That was just a few miles from our village.

"How many redcoats are there?" someone asked.

"At least a thousand," the rider said. Then he rode off to Concord to warn the people there.

Now everyone began to argue about what we should do. Our village was on the road to Concord. Jonas Parker said we should get ready to fight. Then the Reverend spoke. He asked what chance 70 of *us* would have against 1,000 of

*them*? He said we should learn all the facts before we did anything foolish.

After him, my father spoke. He said that no one wanted to see men get killed. We didn't want to, and he was sure the British didn't, either. But, he said, we believed in our rights and liberties. We had to stand up to the British, or they would not respect us. That was the way to avoid a war, he said. Everyone cheered my father, and I felt very proud of him.

Then Jonas Parker told the men to sign up as soldiers. You had to be at least 16 to sign up. But I knew how to use a gun, and I wanted to join the men. Jonas Parker and my father were in charge of the signing. They could stop me because of my age.

"Your name?" Parker asked.

"Adam Cooper," I said.

My father looked at me real hard. Then he nodded his head at Parker.

"Sign your name here and get your gun," Parker said. That was all.

When I got home, Ruth Simmons was waiting for me. She said she was afraid I would be killed. I told her she was being silly. There wasn't going to be a war, I said. We were just going to stand up for our rights.

"Just the same," she said, "wars happen. Suppose one starts tomorrow."

"If it does," I said, "I do not intend to be killed."

"You don't have to pretend to be so brave and manly," she said. "It's natural to be scared at a time like this."

"Ruth Simmons, let me tell you something," I said. But she didn't let me finish. She threw her arms around me and kissed me. Then she ran home. I chased her part of the way, just for fun.

When I got home, Mother and Father were arguing. She said the men had all gone crazy. How could they stop a large British army? Most of all, she was angry because my father had let me sign up.

"He's just a boy," she said.

"Yesterday he was a boy," my father said. "Tonight he's not. You can't shelter him anymore. If you try, you will lose a son."

When my father went out, I kissed my mother on the cheek. She started to cry. That made me cry, too.

Granny wiped away my tears, and I kissed her, too. Then she pushed me out the door.

My father and I walked to the village park together. When we got there, he said, "Adam . . . ," but the rest of the words stuck in his throat.

Then he put his arm around my shoulder and held me close. It was the first time he had ever tried to say that he loved me. I knew then that he really did.

Well, you know what happened when the British came. My father and others killed. Everybody running. Me hiding in a hut. I knew I had to get out of there. The British were still around, and it wasn't safe.

I looked out the door. I saw a field with some trees and ran toward it. I ran so fast, I didn't see the two redcoats standing nearby. One of them shouted, "Halt!" The other raised his rifle and pulled the trigger. Lucky for me, the rifle didn't fire. I jumped over a stone fence as if I had wings. The way I kept running, you'd think the devil was behind me.

Suddenly, I felt two strong arms grab me. I struggled, but I couldn't break away. Then I heard the man say, "Easy, lad. I'm not going to harm you. My name is Solomon Chandler. I live near here. I saw you running from those redcoats like a deer. But they're not chasing you. How could they? Those packs on their backs weigh more than forty pounds. Besides, it's two of us now against two of them. The odds are even."

I stared at him. He was a tall, skinny man. Half of his teeth were missing.

"You don't know them," I said. "They shot us down like dogs, and killed my father. And we ran away like cowards."

"They killed your father, did they?" he said. "That's a terrible thing. But I don't agree that you were cowards. You don't have to be brave to pull a trigger. It's harder for decent people to do it than for others.

Half the regular British soldiers are convicts. They are serving time in the army instead of in jail. The rest are poor, ignorant lads who just do what they're told. Few of them can read or write."

Chandler asked me my name. Then he gave me something to eat. He had cold chicken, ham, and bread in his bag. They tasted better than anything I had ever eaten before. I guess I was pretty hungry and tired.

Solomon Chandler had fought against the French years before. He seemed to know a lot about what was happening right now. He said that the British were marching on to Concord. So far, it had been easy for them. But it would be different when they tried to march back.

"Come with me," he said. "I'll show you what I mean."

We walked through the fields toward Concord. Along the way, other men with

guns joined us. They came from farms and towns all over. When I saw some men from Lexington, I almost cried for joy. Until then, I was afraid the whole village was dead.

Soon there were more than 100 of us. We made a camp. Chandler told us that there were other camps like this between Lexington and Concord.

"The redcoats will march back down that road," he said. "When they do, we'll make it hot for them. There are stone walls and trees all along the road. We'll stay behind them and fire as the British pass by."

Our plan was to fight in small groups. We would shoot, run ahead, then shoot again. It would be "hit and run." We couldn't fight them any other way. Their army was too strong.

A man on a horse rode into our camp. He came from Concord. He said the British were already there. They hadn't found the guns and powder they were looking for. The guns and powder were hidden in another place. There had been some fighting at the river. But now the British were "having a picnic."

"When do they march back to Boston?" Chandler asked.

The rider guessed it would be soon. So we got behind the stone wall near the road and waited. It seemed like a long time. Then we heard the sound of shooting up the road. The shooting got nearer and nearer.

"Here they come," Chandler cried out to warn us.

A minute later, we could see the redcoats. They had changed since I saw them in Lexington. They weren't beating any drums now. They looked scared and angry. Some of them were hurt and bleeding. Dust from the road had made them dirty.

Now they were passing in front of us. Solomon Chandler fired at a British officer. The officer fell from his horse, dead. Then we all started to fire. Smoke covered the road, but I could hear the redcoats screaming.

Then some of them ran toward us with their bayonets. I was so dazed, I just stood there. It was a good thing that Joseph Simmons — Ruth's father — saw me. He grabbed my arm and dragged me away.

"Don't you know when it's time to get out of a place?" he asked.

We started running. And I ran a lot faster than he.

Later, we rested and loaded our guns again. We could hear firing all up and down the road. I took a look around. Under a tree, I saw the body of a dead redcoat. He was a young boy. His face was very thin, as if he had never had enough to eat. His eyes were wide open, and his lips had turned purple. Then I got sick again.

"I've had a bellyful of war and killing," I told Simmons. "I'm sick of this whole bloody business."

"I know," Simmons said. "But we can't stop now, Adam. There's been too much shooting for either side to turn back. It's too late for arguments. There won't be any peace for a long time."

"When will that be?" I asked.

"When the British stop trying to control us. When they sail away in their ships and leave us for good. When we can call this land our own. Not before then."

The fighting that day kept up a long time. I saw other men get killed. Maybe I killed a redcoat myself. I don't know.

We won the battle. But all of us were sad going home. There is less joy in winning a battle than history books tell you.

Levi was the first to see me enter the house. "Adam!" he cried. "We thought you were dead!"

"Do I look dead?" I asked. "I'm awful tired, but I'm alive."

Then my mother took me in her arms. She held me so tightly, I thought my ribs would break. When she let go, she started to cry. Granny didn't say a word. I could see she was trying to hold back her own tears.

Later, I went upstairs to look at my father for the last time. His body was laid out on a bed. I didn't cry. I had seen so many bodies that day that I just felt numb. I would always remember my father alive, but not that body on a bed.

I didn't know what would happen the next day. Would the British come back? Would there be more fighting? No one knew. But I was sure of one thing.

Since that morning, everything had changed. The warm, sunny world of my childhood had gone away. It would never come back again.

## READING COMPREHENSION

**Summarizing.** Choose the best phrase to complete each sentence. Then write the complete statements on your paper.

1. At first, the American patriots wanted to _____ (kill as many British soldiers as possible, prevent a war by talking, prepare the army to fight well).

2. When the men signed up as soldiers, Adam _____ (signed up even though he was too young, was permitted to remain at home, learned how to use a gun).

3. When Adam told Joseph Simmons that he was sick of war and killing, Simmons said that _____ (things had gone too far to be stopped, the war would be over soon, Adam was too young to fight).

**Interpreting.** Write the answer to each question on your paper.

1. What battle of the Revolutionary War did Adam Cooper fight in during April 1775?

2. Why was Adam confused about how his father felt about him?

3. How did Adam feel about the war when the battle was over?

**For Thinking and Discussing.** Solomon Chandler told Adam, "You don't have to be brave to pull a trigger. It's harder for decent people to do it than for others." Do you agree with him? Explain why or why not.

## UNDERSTANDING LITERATURE

**Characters in Historical Fiction.** In historical fiction, the characters — even though they may be invented by the writer — must be true to the period in which the story is set. For example, Adam Cooper *could* have been a real person. He fits into the time and place in which the events occur.

On your paper, select the best choice to complete each statement about the characters in the selection you have just read.

1. The British soldiers had _____.
   a. many wealthy people among them
   b. jackets that were hard to see
   c. many convicts among them

2. Ruth Simmons told Adam she was _____.
   a. eager to see the fighting start
   b. afraid he would be killed
   c. too young to get married

3. Solomon Chandler _____.
   a. understood the enemy and the land
   b. learned fighting in France
   c. was thrown out of the British army

4. Adam showed no emotion when he saw his father's body because _____.
   a. he hadn't really liked his father
   b. boys weren't supposed to cry
   c. the fighting had dulled his senses

## WRITING

Imagine you are a British soldier in the battle this story describes. Write two or three paragraphs about the day's events.

# She Sailed for Love

*by Jane Yolen*

*Pirates were a real threat to 18th-century sailors. Yet in this story by Jane Yolen (1939— ), a rather unusual pirate reunites a young man with the woman he loves, and also manages to aid the American war effort.*

**R**evolutionary America saw the birth of many heroes. War often breeds greatness. One of these brave souls was a pirate. Once you have heard her story, you are not likely to forget her. Her name was Fanny Campbell and she sailed for love. The story of her adventures is an old New England tale still told in Massachusetts.

It all started in Lynn, a little town outside of Boston, where two fishermen, Henry Campbell and Richard Lovell, were neighbors. Their houses stood side by side in a section of Lynn called High Rock. Side by side their children grew up — Fanny Campbell and William Lovell.

Fanny was a bright-eyed girl. She was slender with the kind of face that is both honest and strong. William was a wiry New Englander, forthright and outspoken. As they grew up, Fanny and William fell in love. Their parents and neighbors were all in favor of their marriage. Things seemed so simple — then.

William wanted to become a deep-sea sailor. He received permission from his father to go to Boston and ship aboard a New England merchant ship. For six months he sailed. In the seventh, he returned home to Fanny.

"Fanny," he said, "you must come sailing with me. The sea is an open road to the world."

She went, of course. Fanny was an active girl. She knew how to ride a horse. She knew how to shoot. She had even killed a wildcat in the Lynn woods. Sailing, too, came easily to her.

The two young people spent their days on the sea. William taught Fanny all there was to know about sailing. He taught her to handle a ship in any weather. But then the time to part came again.

"Fanny," said William one day, taking her hands in his, "now you know as much about the sea as I do. Promise you will never be afraid when I am on a voyage."

"Promise," said Fanny. "You're going off again, aren't you?"

"Yes," he answered. "I've been offered a berth on the *Royal Kent*. She's bound for South America and the Indies. It's —

it's a fine chance. I really want to take it."

"Then you must," Fanny said, smiling.

William hesitated a moment. "When this trip is over, I'm coming back to marry you."

"Of course, William," Fanny said. "But don't look so grim and serious. You must learn to laugh more. Don't worry. I'll be waiting for you."

William sailed the next day. He was gone for more than two years. While he was away, Fanny had another caller, Captain Robert Burnet, an officer in the British Navy. Burnet fell in love with Fanny and courted her for those two years. Although she did not hear from William, Fanny was faithful. Captain Burnet's suit was refused again and again.

Late one night, two years after William Lovell had gone to sea, a stranger knocked on the Campbell door. He was gaunt and tired-looking, with a face that seemed chiseled from granite.

The door opened and Fanny stood framed in the moonlight.

"Beggin' your pardon, ma'am, but my name is Jack Herbert," said the stranger. "Are you Fanny Campbell?"

"I am," she said.

"At last," he murmured. "I come from William Lovell."

"Oh," said Fanny. For a moment that was all she could say. Then she invited the stranger in. He followed her into the warmth of the kitchen.

"Where is William? Is he well?" Fanny asked.

"It's a long story, Miss Campbell. William is well but he's not well off. I was on the *Royal Kent* with him."

"Was?" said Fanny, interrupting him.

"Was, ma'am. The *Royal Kent* is no more. We were coming out of Port au Plate when a pirate schooner came in sight. We turned to run but it was no use. She caught and boarded us. We weren't meant for fighting, you know. Anyhow, there were four pirates to every one of us. We tried, though. Killed a good number. We even got their leader. But they killed our captain — a fine man, may he rest in peace. They scuttled our ship."

"But what happened to William?"

"I'm getting to that, ma'am," Herbert said. "Bill was wounded. Pretty badly, too. The pirates took him aboard. We were all taken aboard, to make up for the men they lost."

"We headed toward Cuba, but the wind died before we reached the bay. We were laying becalmed. That's when Bill and Henry Breed and I (Henry's a fine lad, too) were chosen for watch. It was the late watch, ma'am. Called the 'graveyard watch.' We were the only people up. It was then that Bill thought of a plan. He said we could make a break and find the governor of Cuba. If we told him what happened, he'd get us home safely. So, we decided to try."

"Then what happened?" asked Fanny.

"Well, we headed the schooner into the light wind. We tied the wheel so the ship would stay on course. Then the three of us put a small boat over the side. We lowered some provisions, enough to get us through to shore, and climbed down a rope ladder to the dinghy. We rowed for about half a mile, till we were out of range of the pirates. Then we hoisted sail for Cuba."

"William is safe in Cuba, then," said Fanny, looking hopefully at Herbert.

"Well, ma'am, not exactly. That is, he is in Cuba. But when we got to Havana, we were arrested as suspicious characters. If you had been in an open boat for a few days and were dirty and ragged, you might have looked suspicious, too. Not meaning any offense, ma'am. And we had served aboard a pirate ship.

"They threw us in jail for six months. Jail! It was more like a black hole. We fought with the rats for possession of the straw beds. Then the Cubans took us out for trial. But there wasn't any evidence so they put us back in jail. They figured to get some in a little while, I guess."

"Why, that's ridiculous," said Fanny indignantly.

"Yes, ma'am. Only that's the way it was," Herbert said. "We were in jail over a year. Bill kept count of the days by scratching a mark on the wall with his spoon. Then I managed to escape by myself. I hid aboard an American ship and got to Boston. I came to you because Bill asked me to give you this note if I made it."

He dug into his pocket and pulled out a small, dirty slip of paper. Fanny reached for the crumpled note. She did not dare open it in front of Herbert. She was afraid she might cry. Instead, she faced him

squarely and asked, "Where are you staying, Mr. Herbert?"

"I'm in Boston, ma'am. At Copp's Hill."

A plan had begun to form in Fanny's mind. "Mr. Herbert, stay at Copp's Hill until you hear from me. I won't be longer than a week in sending word. We are going to get William and Mr. Breed out of jail; that is, if you are with me."

"Miss Campbell, Bill and Breed are fine lads. They helped me out more than once. I won't let them rot in a Cuban jail. No, ma'am, I'll be ready!"

"Fine, Mr. Herbert. You won't be sorry!" Fanny led the sailor to the door.

"And Mr. Herbert — "

"Yes, ma'am?"

"God bless you!" said Fanny. Herbert walked off into the darkness. Fanny shut the door after him. Then she leaned against it and opened the note. William had written that he was well, that he would return, and that he loved her.

Two days later, in Copp's Hill, Jack Herbert received a midnight visitor. The visitor was a slender deep-eyed sailor who reminded him of his promise to Fanny Campbell. The sailor brought Herbert to the brig *Constance,* anchored in Boston Harbor. She was ready to sail for England by way of Cuba and she was well-armed. The captain of the *Constance* was a tyrannical and cruel man named Brownless. Banning, the first mate, was an ignorant sailor who cared little for the ship and less for the men. But the second mate, a bright-eyed youth named Channing, was well-skilled in the ways of the sea. Channing was new to the *Constance.* He had joined the crew the day before, but the men already admired him for his ease on board ship. His beardless, tanned face was always covered with a big smile, and he always had a joke or a story ready. An officer, he still mixed well with the men, and they would have liked him for that alone.

Jack Herbert went aboard the ship as a common sailor. He heard nothing more of Fanny's plan but he had faith in her. After all, she had gotten him aboard a ship bound for Cuba. That was a start. The next move, too, he decided to leave to her.

The *Constance* set sail for Cuba. She was not out a week when the crew became restless. Captain Brownless, a hardhearted man, delighted in punishing the men. In the waters of the West Indies, a day's sail from Cuba, the likeable young second mate took his pistol and went to the captain's quarters.

"Captain Brownless," said Channing in a gentle voice, "because I am an officer you have confided in me. But I think it's time we shared this confidence with the men — don't you?"

The captain muttered, "Mutiny!" under his breath, but in the face of the pistol he had little choice. Channing mustered the crew and stood the captain in front of him, facing the men.

"Men," Channing shouted over the roar of the sea, "the captain has not told you the truth about this trip. I learned it because I am an officer, but I am not too pleased. We are headed for England, as you know. But there, as you do not know, Brownless intended to have you pressed into service in the British Navy. That's a three-year hitch, men, and nothing you could have done about it. No questions. No volunteers. No way out. Just the word from Brownless here and you'd be British sailors. What do you say to that?"

"Pressed into service?"

"Aye."

"No getting out of it?"

"No."

The sailors buzzed the idea around. Slowly a roar arose that challenged the noise of the sea.

"Hang him! Hang the captain! Drown him! Cast him overboard!"

The captain turned pale as the men moved toward him menacingly.

Channing put up his hand to stop the noise. He smiled broadly. "All right. I see what your mood is. But I have a better — and a more just — solution. We will take over the ship and sail on to Cuba. There we can turn Brownless over to the proper authorities. If you want me, I'll be your captain till then."

The men cheered their agreement. Then Channing pointed to Herbert, who was standing in the midst of the crew. "Herbert there will be mate. Brownless goes into his cabin to stay. You realize, though, this means we're a mutiny ship and a mutiny crew. The law calls us pirates. So, if we are pirates, we will pirate our way to Cuba. Hoist up the black flag!"

Brownless was locked in his cabin. That night, the cook, who had remained loyal, sneaked to Channing's cabin to try to murder the new captain. Brownless, meanwhile, had gotten out past the guard and was intent on the same bloody errand. In

the darkness outside of Channing's door, the two men came upon each other. Mistaking each other for Channing, they exchanged blows with their knives. The next morning, on his way to wake the new captain, a sailor stumbled on their bodies. They were buried at sea.

The *Constance* was a renegade ship. She sailed pirate's colors. With Channing as captain, the crew overpowered the British bark *George of Bristol* and put the sailors in irons below decks. Jack Herbert was put in charge of the new ship.

Late one night, the *George* and the *Constance* sailed into Havana Bay. The two ships anchored a half-mile from the fort where William Lovell and Henry Breed were imprisoned. In the dark, Herbert and eight loyal crewmen rowed to the fort.

Leaving one man on guard at the rowboat, they crept along the beach toward the fort. A mute form was seen ahead. The first sentry! Herbert signaled silently with one hand and a sailor sneaked to the rear of the guard. Quickly his hand went over the guard's mouth. It was over in seconds. No one had heard.

Three more guards were gagged and tied up quickly and quietly, and locked in the guardhouse. Herbert searched their pockets and found the keys.

The sailors opened the jail door. The large iron door let out a harsh, protesting squeak.

The men raced to the cell where two men lay sleeping and opened the door.

"Breed? Billy? Are you alive, lads? Are you alive?"

The men stirred in their hay beds. They winked open their eyes and stared. "Herbert . . . is it. . . ?"

Herbert ran into the cell and clapped the men heartily on the back. They laughed and cried with disbelief, relief.

"No time, sir. No time," called one of the sailors in a harsh whisper.

"He's right," said Herbert. "Get your things together, boys. We're leaving this place for good!"

The men raced out of the jail, down to the beach, and into the boat. They grabbed the oars and within minutes they were at the *Constance*. Just as the two ships started out of the harbor, there was a loud cry from the fort. The escape had been discovered! But it was too late. The American ships sailed free with their booty — two very tired and happy ex-prisoners.

The cabin boy found Herbert, William, and Breed top side. They were watching as the fort vanished below the horizon.

"Sir, if you please, sir," said the boy. "The captain says to tell Mr. Lovell that he is to be first mate of the *Constance* and to come to his cabin at once."

Herbert shrugged his shoulders. "Guess the captain knows what he is doing. He is the one who plotted the escape. I'm sure he's under orders from your Fanny Campbell."

William shrugged, too. "You know him better than I," he said. "I'd be his cabin boy and scrub the deck from stem to stern for what he's done. And I hope to tell him so. If he wants me to be his mate, he's got the most loyal mate about."

William made his way to the captain's cabin and knocked on the door. When there was no answer, he walked in, somewhat timidly. The captain had his back to the door, his hands clasped behind him.

"Lovell here, sir," William began.

"Oh, yes, Lovell," replied the captain. "You seem to know your way around ships. Been a sailor most of your life?"

"Thank you, sir. No, sir, but since I've been at sea I've loved it."

"That's fine, Lovell," said Channing, his back still to the door. "Speaking of love, do you have a girl at home? It's been some time since you've been there."

"Yes, sir, I do."

"And you're sure she is still waiting for you after all this time?"

"I hope so, sir. More than anything else, I hope so."

"What is your girl like?"

"Begging your pardon, sir, but I don't think this discussion should go on. . . ."

"You're not ashamed of her, are you, Lovell?"

"Sir, I won't take that, not even from you," roared William. His hands tensed into fists.

"Oh, William," laughed the captain. "You've really got to learn to laugh. Don't you know me?"

The captain turned around. He took off his hat. "I'm Fanny!"

It was true — Channing was Fanny. Her hair had been cropped short, her skin dyed a dark brown.

"Oh, William! Herbert told me about Cuba and the prison. I couldn't trust anyone else to find you. I had to do it myself." Fanny began to cry.

"It's all right, Fanny. I'm here. I'm here. We're together again," said William.

And they were. Together, William and Fanny captained the *Constance* and the *George*. They captured a British merchantman and learned from the crew that the Revolutionary War was in full swing. A vote from the men convinced them that they should give up their pirating ways — and turn privateer. That meant that instead of stopping any ship that came along and robbing it for their own profit, the crew would work for the American government, capturing only enemy ships. Then they would turn over a share of the booty to the new government. As loyal Americans, they could rob any British ships they could capture.

The *Constance* and the *George* soon came upon an armed British sloop. After a short battle they captured it. The captain of the sloop was none other than Fanny's former suitor, Robert Burnet. He recognized Fanny, but because he still loved her, he never told. He was clapped in chains below deck with the rest of the British prisoners. And the crew of the *Constance* did not learn that their captain was a woman.

The two ships sailed toward Boston, but changed course when they discovered that the British had taken the harbor. Instead, Fanny headed the *Constance* and the *George* toward Marblehead Harbor, not far from Boston, where the crew became legal privateers.

Boston still rings with the true tales of many Revolutionary War heroes, but few people know of Fanny Campbell. Yet she was America's first female pirate — a pirate who sailed for freedom, justice, and love aboard the good ship *Constance*.

## READING COMPREHENSION

**Summarizing.** Choose the best phrase to complete each sentence. Then write the complete statements on your paper.

1. William did not return from his trip on the *Royal Kent* because he _____ (had mutinied and switched sides, no longer loved Fanny, was in prison in Cuba).

2. Fanny disguised herself as a man because she _____ (yearned to go to sea, didn't trust anyone else to rescue William, wanted to be a captain).

3. Fanny and William helped the American cause by _____ (refusing to sell goods to the British, capturing and robbing British ships, enlisting in the army).

**Interpreting.** Write the answer to each question on your paper.

1. What was the message in the note delivered to Fanny by Jack Herbert?

2. Why did the *Constance* become a pirate ship after Channing became captain?

3. What was the secret plan that Captain Brownless had shared with Channing?

**For Thinking and Discussing.**

1. Do you think it would have made a difference to the crew if they had known their captain was a woman? Why or why not?

2. Do you think Fanny was right or wrong to encourage mutiny? Explain.

## UNDERSTANDING LITERATURE

**Details in Historical Fiction.** Sometimes historical fiction portrays a real person in a fictionalized way. The author creates a character based on a person who really lived and invents dialogue and details to make the character come alive.

"She Sailed for Love" is historical fiction in which the main characters are thought to have really existed. The major events may have happened much as the author depicted them. Many of the specific details, however, are created by the author.

In developing a real character in a fictionalized way, a writer often gives the character feelings that anyone in a similar situation would have. This adds a note of authenticity to the character portrayal.

Answer the questions on your paper.

1. Go back to the story "She Sailed for Love." Find five examples of statements that the author used to describe the feelings of a character.

2. In the story, locate three examples of dialogue that the author probably created.

## WRITING

Imagine that you are Fanny or William and that you have been reunited on the *Constance*. Write a letter to your family telling them what has happened. In the last paragraph, mention your plans for the immediate future. Include details to make your letter sound authentic.

# Section Review

**Synonyms and Antonyms.** Two words that have the same or almost the same meaning are called *synonyms*. For example, *trembling* and *shaking* are synonyms.

*Antonyms* are two words that have opposite meanings. For example, *dirty* and *clean* are antonyms.

Here are some sentences from the selections you have just read. Write each italicized word on your paper. Then write its synonym from the list below.

agreements    selfish    slim    amusement

1. "The winters were long and white — and any *diversion* was welcome."

2. " 'Have you made no *contracts* with the devil?' "

3. "She was *slender* with the kind of face that is both honest and strong."

Write each italicized word on your paper. Then write its antonym from the list given below.

shouted    smooth    devoted    disloyal

1. "Although she did not hear from William, Fanny was *faithful*."

2. "Fanny reached for the *crumpled* note."

3. "The captain *muttered*, 'Mutiny!' under his breath, . . ."

**Cause and Effect.** Everything happens for a reason. This reason is called the *cause*. Every cause produces a result, or *effect*. Understanding cause-and-effect relationships helps you to understand how and why things happen in a story.

Words and phrases like *because, since, so, as a result of, therefore,* or *then* may signal cause-and-effect relationships:

People ran from the streets *because* the redcoats were coming.

**Cause:**   The redcoats were coming.
**Effect:**   People ran from the streets.

Each statement below expresses a cause-and-effect relationship. Make two columns on your paper. Label one Cause and the other Effect. Then write the appropriate phrase in each column.

1. I heard a shot fired. Then I saw my father grab his chest and fall.

2. I didn't see the ditch ahead of me; as a result, I fell into it.

3. Then I cried because I knew my father would never come home again.

4. My father had to go to a meeting, so our quarrel ended.

5. Ruth Simmons said she wanted to marry me since she loved me.

6. My mother was angry because my father let me sign up.

7. I was underage and therefore trusted in my father to keep silent when I enlisted.

170

**A Firsthand Report.** A firsthand report is an eyewitness account of an experience or an event. As an "on-the-scene" reporter, you describe what you have personally experienced or carefully observed.

Your report is *objective* when you include only the facts in describing what has taken place. It is *subjective* when you express your feelings and opinions as well.

## Step 1: Set Your Goal

Choose one of the following topics for both an objective and a subjective first-hand report:

a. You lived in Salem, Massachusetts, in the winter of 1692 at the time of the witch trials. You attended the first hearing in the village meetinghouse on March 1. Report on the examination of at least one of the three women accused of witchcraft. Describe the defendant's testimony. Draw from the details in the story "Salem, Massachusetts."

b. Like Levi in "April Morning," you were awakened by the sound of hoof-beats on April 18, 1775. You joined the men of Lexington outside the village inn and heard the rider's warning. You watched the mustering of troops. Report on the historical event that you witnessed. Be sure to record the high points of the speeches made by the villagers.

## Step 2: Make a Plan

Generally, you gather information for a report by carefully observing an event and by interviewing the participants. In this case, you can gather information by taking notes on what has taken place.

First, prepare a list of questions that you want answered about the event. Include the questions that journalists ask: *Who? What? When? Where? Why? How?* Then, use your imagination and the information in the appropriate story to answer the questions that you have listed.

## Step 3: Write a First Draft

Review your notes and use the information you gathered to write the first draft of an objective firsthand report. Organize your report as a news article. In the first paragraph, include the answers to the most important *Who? What? When? Where? Why?* and *How?* questions. After the first paragraph, add others in which you provide less important supporting information. Be neutral and report only the facts.

Notice the objective tone of this first paragraph of a report on a childhood adventure of Fanny Campbell, the heroine of "She Sailed for Love":

With a single blast of her father's musket, 14-year-old Fanny Campbell killed a wildcat in the Lynn woods this morning. Fanny, daughter of fisherman Henry Campbell, shot the crazed animal as it ran toward her growling. "I had no choice," the slender hunter earnestly explained.

Now use your notes to write a subjective firsthand report. This time, concentrate on setting the scene, rather than on listing the facts. Feel free to express your opinion of the event or character that you are describing. Let the reader know right away that your report is subjective by writing in the first person. Use the following first paragraph as a model:

Call her young. Call her lovely. Call her lucky. Above all, call her brave. To whom do I refer? That young, lovely, lucky, and, above all, brave Lynn girl who shot a crazed wildcat in the woods this morning.

## Step 4: Revise

When you revise your objective report, ask yourself these questions:

1. Have I answered the important questions in the first paragraph and presented supporting information in the paragraphs that follow?

2. Have I included only facts, leaving out my opinions and feelings?

When you revise your subjective report, ask yourself these questions:

1. Have I written my report in the first person?

2. Have I captured the feeling of the event or person and included my own feelings as well?

After you revise your objective and subjective firsthand reports, check for grammatical errors, as well as for errors in punctuation and spelling.

## QUIZ

The following is a quiz for Section 3. Write the answers in complete sentences on your paper.

## Reading Comprehension

1. In "Salem Village, Massachusetts," what did the Rev. Samuel Parris do that led to the deaths of 19 people?

2. Why did the madness in Salem finally stop?

3. In "April Morning," what changed Adam Cooper's life on that fateful morning?

4. In "She Sailed for Love," why did William Lovell teach Fanny Campbell to sail?

5. How did Fanny's sailing lessons save William's life?

## Understanding Literature

6. In what ways is the story "Salem Village, Massachusetts" an example of historical fiction?

7. What did Benét say about the thoughts of the afflicted children in his story? What interpretation did he give to their actions?

8. List one example of fact and one example of fiction in Benét's epitaph to Cotton Mather.

9. The characters in "April Morning" are fictional. What about the story is factual?

10. In "She Sailed for Love," how did William discover that Captain Channing was really Fanny? Are the exact details of this scene fact or fiction? Explain your answer.

## ACTIVITIES

**Word Attack.** The sentences below are taken from "She Sailed for Love." The words in parentheses are written as phonetic respellings. Use the pronunciation key in the glossary to help you decode the words. On your paper, list the words as they are actually spelled, and underline any silent consonants.

a. It all started in Lynn . . . (hwâr) two fisherman . . . (wûr) (nā′bərz).

b. He (tôt) her to (hăn′dl) a ship in any weather.

c. "We rowed for about (hăf) a mile. . . ."

d. William had (rĭt′n) that . . . he (wŏŏd) return. . . .

e. "You seem to (nō) your way (ə round′) ships."

f. As (loi′əl) Americans, they (kŏŏd) rob any British ships they (kŏŏd) capture.

## Speaking and Listening

1. A firsthand report may be oral as well as written. Prepare to deliver your subjective firsthand report as a newscast to a television audience. First, revise your report so that it sounds like an on-the-scene news broadcast. Introduce yourself, and tell your audience where you are and what you are reporting on. If you can, recruit a classmate and include an interview with a bystander.

2. Courtroom trials are real-life dramas, and the Salem witch trials were particularly dramatic. Get together with several classmates and dramatize one of the trials mentioned in "Salem Village, Massachusetts." Call both the defendant and at least one child to the witness stand. Model the testimony on the dialogue included in the story. Be prepared to perform the scene for the class.

## Researching

**Researching.** Twentieth-century playwright Arthur Miller explored the Salem tragedy in his play *The Crucible.* Locate a copy of the play in your library. Read about the Salem witch trials from Miller's point of view. How does Miller's interpretation of people and events compare with that of Benét? What does Miller's play add to your understanding of historical Salem? Share your findings with the class.

## Creating

1. In "April Morning," Adam Cooper willingly enlisted in the army. The pirates in "She Sailed for Love" voted to become privateers. Recruit more colonists for the American cause. Design a colorful recruitment poster that will encourage people to join one of the newly created armed forces.

2. In "She Sailed for Love," Jane Yolen described Fanny Campbell as an unsung Revolutionary War hero. Sing Fanny's praises in an inscription for her tombstone. Describe her character, her accomplishments, and the love of her life. You might model your statement after Benét's epitaph for Cotton Mather.

# THE DEVIL AND DANIEL WEBSTER

## STEPHEN VINCENT BENÉT

*As a U.S. Congressman and Senator, Daniel Webster was a strong defender of the Constitution. So great were his skills as an orator that whenever he rose to speak his audience instantly fell silent. By the time of his death, Webster had become a legendary figure.*

*This story combines historical fact, humor, and supernatural elements to create a larger-than-life portrait of Webster.*

IT'S a story they tell in the border country, where Massachusetts joins Vermont and New Hampshire.

Yes, Dan'l Webster's dead—or, at least, they buried him. But every time there's a thunderstorm around Marshfield, they say you can hear his rolling voice in the hollows of the sky. And they say that if you go to his grave and speak loud and clear, "Dan'l Webster—Dan'l Webster!" the ground'll begin to shiver and the trees begin to shake. And after a while you'll hear a deep voice saying, "Neighbor, how stands the Union?" Then you better answer the Union stands as she stood, rock-bottomed and copper-sheathed, one and indivisible, or he's liable to rear right out of the ground. At least, that's what I was told when I was a youngster.

You see, for a while, he was the biggest man in the country. He never got to be President, but he was the biggest man. There were thousands that trusted in him right next to God Almighty and they told stories about him that were like the stories of patriarchs and such. They said when he stood up to speak, stars and stripes came right out in the sky, and once he spoke against a river and made it sink into the ground. They said when he walked the woods with his fishing rod, Killall, the trout would jump out of the streams right into his pockets, for they knew it was no use putting up a fight against him; and, when he argued a case, he could turn on the harps of the blessed and the shaking of the earth underground. That was the kind of man he was, and his big farm up at Marshfield was suitable to him. The chickens he raised were all white meat down through the drumsticks, the cows were tended like children, and the big ram he called Goliath[1] had horns with a curl like a morning-glory vine and could butt through an iron door. But Dan'l wasn't one of your gentlemen farmers; he knew all the way of the land, and he'd be up by candlelight to see that the chores got done. A man with a mouth like a mastiff,[2] a brow like a mountain and eyes like burning anthracite[3]—that was Dan'l Webster in his prime. And the biggest case he argued never got written down in the books, for he argued it against the devil, nip and tuck and no holds barred. And this is the way I used to hear it told.

There was a man named Jabez Stone, lived at Cross Corners, New Hampshire. He wasn't a bad man to start with, but he was an unlucky man. If he planted corn, he got borers;[4] if he planted potatoes, he got blight.[5] He had good enough land, but it didn't prosper him; he had a decent wife and children, but the more children he had, the less there was to feed them. If stones cropped up in his neighbor's field, boulders boiled up in his; if he had a horse with spavins,[6] he'd trade it for one with the staggers[7] and give something extra. There's some folks bound to be like that, apparently. But one day Jabez Stone got sick of the whole business.

He'd been plowing that morning and he'd just broke the plowshare on a rock that he could have sworn hadn't been there yesterday. And, as he stood looking at the plowshare, the off horse[8] began to cough—that ropy kind of cough that means sickness and horse doctors. There were two children down with the measles, his wife was ailing, and he had a whitlow[9] on his thumb. It was about the last straw for Jabez Stone. "I vow," he said, and he looked around him kind of desperate—"I vow it's enough to make a man want to sell his soul to the devil! And I would, too, for two cents!"

Then he felt a kind of queerness come over him at having said what he'd said; though, naturally, being a New Hampshireman, he wouldn't take it back. But, all the same, when it got to be evening and, as far as he could see, no notice had been taken, he felt relieved in his mind, for he was a religious man. But notice is always taken, sooner or later, just like the Good Book says. And,

---

1. **Goliath:** in the Bible (I Samuel 17), a giant slain by the young David.
2. **mastiff:** a large, powerful dog with short, square jaws.
3. **anthracite:** hard coal.
4. **borer:** an insect that is harmful to corn.
5. **blight:** a disease that destroys plants.
6. **spavins** (spăv' ĭnz): a disease that can make a horse lame.
7. **staggers:** a disease of a horse's nervous system that makes it lose coordination, stagger, or fall down.
8. **off horse:** the horse on the right in a double harness.
9. **whitlow** (hwĭt' lō): painful, infected swelling.

sure enough, next day, about supper-time, a soft-spoken, dark-dressed stranger drove up in a handsome buggy and asked for Jabez Stone.

Well, Jabez told his family it was a lawyer, come to see him about a legacy. But he knew who it was. He didn't like the looks of the stranger, nor the way he smiled with his teeth. They were white teeth, and plentiful—some say they were filed to a point, but I wouldn't vouch for that. And he didn't like it when the dog took one look at the stranger and ran away howling, with his tail between his legs. But having passed his word, more or less, he stuck to it, and they went out behind the barn and made their bargain. Jabez Stone had to prick his finger to sign, and the stranger lent him a silver pin. The wound healed clean, but it left a little white scar.

After that, all of a sudden, things began to pick up and prosper for Jabez Stone. His cows got fat and his horses sleek, his crops were the envy of the neighborhood, and lightning might strike all over the valley, but it wouldn't strike his barn. Pretty soon, he was one of the prosperous people of the county; they asked him to stand for selectman,[10] and he stood for it; there began to be talk of running him for state senate. All in all, you might say the Stone family was as happy and contented as cats in a dairy. And so they were, except for Jabez Stone.

---

10. **stand for selectman:** run for the office of selectman. A selectman is one of a board of officers elected in many New England towns to manage municipal affairs.

The stranger came up through the lower field, switching his boots with a cane—they were handsome black boots, but Jabez Stone never liked the look of them, particularly the toes. And after he'd passed the time of day, he said, "Well, Mr. Stone, you're a hummer! It's a very pretty property you've got here, Mr. Stone."

"Well, some might favor it and others might not," said Jabez Stone, for he was a New Hampshireman.

"Oh, no need to decry your industry!" said the stranger, very easy, showing his teeth in a smile. "After all, we know what's been done, and it's been according to contract and specifications. So when—ahem—the mortgage falls due next year, you shouldn't have any regrets."

"Speaking of that mortgage, mister," said Jabez Stone, and he looked around for help to the earth and sky, "I'm beginning to have one or two doubts about it."

"Doubts?" said the stranger, not quite so pleasantly.

"Why, yes," said Jabez Stone. "This being the USA and me always having been a religious man." He cleared his throat and got bolder. "Yes, sir," he said, "I'm beginning to have considerable doubts as to that mortgage holding in court."

"There's courts and courts," said the stranger, clicking his teeth. "Still, we might as well have a look at the original document." And he hauled out a big black pocketbook, full of papers. "Sherwin, Slater, Stevens, Stone," he muttered. "I, Jabez Stone, for a term of seven years—Oh, it's quite in order, I think."

But Jabez Stone wasn't listening, for he saw something else flutter out of the black pocketbook. It was something that looked like a moth, but it wasn't a moth. And as Jabez Stone stared at it, it seemed to speak to him in a small sort of piping voice, terrible small and thin, but terrible human. "Neighbor Stone!" it squeaked. "Neighbor Stone! Help me! For heaven's sake, help me!"

But before Jabez Stone could stir hand or foot, the stranger whipped out a big bandanna handkerchief, caught the creature in it, just like a butterfly,[11] and started tying up the ends of the bandanna.

"Sorry for the interruption," he said. "As I was saying—"

But Jabez Stone was shaking all over like a scared horse.

"That's Miser Stevens' voice!" he said, in a croak. "And you've got him in your handkerchief!"

The stranger looked a little embarrassed.

"Yes, I really should have transferred him to the collecting box," he said with a simper, "but there were some rather unusual specimens there and I didn't want them crowded. Well, well, these little contretemps[12] will occur."

"I don't know what you mean by contertan," said Jabez Stone, "but that was Miser Stevens' voice! And he ain't dead! You can't tell me he is! He was just as spry and mean as a woodchuck, Tuesday!"

"In the midst of life—"[13] said the stranger, kind of pious. "Listen!" Then a bell began to toll in the valley and Jabez Stone listened, with the sweat running down his face. For he knew it was tolled for Miser Stevens and that he was dead.

"These long-standing accounts," said the stranger with a sigh; "one really hates to close them. But business is business."

He still had the bandanna in his hand, and Jabez Stone felt sick as he saw the cloth struggle and flutter.

"Are they all as small as that?" he asked hoarsely.

"Small?" said the stranger. "Oh, I see what you mean. Why, they vary." He measured Jabez Stone with his eyes, and his teeth showed. "Don't worry, Mr. Stone," he said. "You'll go with a very good grade. I wouldn't trust you outside the collecting box. Now, a man like Dan'l Webster, of course—well, we'd have to build a special box for him, and even at that, I imagine the wingspread would astonish you. But, in your case, as I was saying—"

"Put that handkerchief away!" said Jabez Stone, and he began to beg and to

---

11. **butterfly**: in classical mythology, the butterfly was a symbol for the soul.
12. **contretemps** (kôn′ trə tän′): embarrassing occurrences.

13. **"In the midst of life"**: "we are in death" finishes the quotation, from the burial service in *The Book of Common Prayer.*

pray. But the best he could get at the end was a three years' extension, with conditions.

But till you make a bargain like that, you've got no idea of how fast four years can run. By the last months of those years, Jabez Stone's known all over the state and there's talk of running him for governor—and it's dust and ashes in his mouth. For every day, when he gets up, he thinks, "There's one more night gone," and every night when he lies down, he thinks of the black pocketbook and the soul of Miser Stevens, and it makes him sick at heart. Till, finally, he can't bear it any longer, and, in the last days of the last year, he hitches up his horse and drives off to seek Dan'l Webster. For Dan'l was born in New Hampshire, only a few miles from Cross Corners, and it's well known that he has a particular soft spot for old neighbors.

It was early in the morning when he got to Marshfield, but Dan'l was up already, talking Latin to the farmhands and wrestling with the ram, Goliath, and trying out a new trotter and working up speeches to make against John C. Calhoun.[14] But when he heard a New Hampshireman had come to see him, he dropped everything else he was doing, for that was Dan'l's way. He gave Jabez Stone a breakfast that five men couldn't eat, went into the living history of every man and woman in Cross Corners, and finally asked him how he could serve him.

Jabez Stone allowed that it was a kind of mortgage case.

"Well, I haven't pleaded a mortgage case in a long time, and I don't generally plead now, except before the Supreme Court," said Dan'l, "but if I can, I'll help you."

"Then I've got hope for the first time in ten years," said Jabez Stone, and told him the details.

Dan'l walked up and down as he listened, hands behind his back, now and then asking a question, now and then plunging his eyes at the floor, as if they'd bore through it like gimlets.[15] When Jabez Stone had finished, Dan'l puffed out his cheeks and blew. Then he turned to Jabez Stone and a smile broke over his face like the sunrise over Monadnock.[16]

"You've certainly given yourself the devil's own row to hoe, Neighbor Stone," he said, "but I'll take your case."

"You'll take it?" said Jabez Stone, hardly daring to believe.

"Yes," said Dan'l Webster. "I've got about seventy-five other things to do and the Missouri Compromise[17] to straighten out, but I'll take your case. For if two New Hampshiremen aren't a match for the devil, we might as well

---

14. **John C. Calhoun:** (1782–1850), U.S. vice president, senator from South Carolina, and great orator who often clashed with Webster, particularly on the issue of slavery.

15. **gimlet** (gĭm′ lĭt): a small tool used for boring holes.
16. **Monadnock** (mō năd′ nŏk): southern New Hampshire's highest mountain.
17. **Missouri Compromise:** a Congressional act of 1820 that tried to ensure a balance between slave states and free states entering the Union.

give the country back to the Indians."

Then he shook Jabez Stone by the hand and said, "Did you come down here in a hurry?"

"Well, I admit I made time," said Jabez Stone.

"You'll go back faster," said Dan'l Webster, and he told 'em to hitch up

Constitution and Constellation to the carriage. They were matched grays with one white forefoot, and they stepped like greased lightning.

Well, I won't describe how excited and pleased the whole Stone family was to have the great Dan'l Webster for a guest, when they finally got there. Jabez Stone had lost his hat on the way, blown off when they overtook a wind, but he didn't take much account of that. But after supper he sent the family off to bed, for he had most particular business with Mr. Webster. Mrs. Stone wanted them to sit in the front parlor, but Dan'l Webster knew front parlors and said he preferred the kitchen. So it was there they sat, waiting for the stranger, with a jug on the table between them and a bright fire on the hearth—the stranger being scheduled to show up on the stroke of midnight, according to specifications.

Well, most men wouldn't have asked for better company than Dan'l Webster and a jug. But with every tick of the clock Jabez Stone got sadder and sadder. His eyes roved round, and though he sampled the jug you could see he couldn't taste it. Finally, on the stroke of 11:30 he reached over and grabbed Dan'l Webster by the arm.

"Mr. Webster, Mr. Webster!" he said, and his voice was shaking with fear and a desperate courage. "For heaven's sake, Mr. Webster, harness your horses and get away from this place while you can!"

"You've brought me a long way,

neighbor, to tell me you don't like my company," said Dan'l Webster, quite peaceable, pulling at the jug.

"Miserable wretch that I am!" groaned Jabez Stone. "I've brought you a devilish way, and now I see my folly. Let him take me if he wills. I don't hanker after it, I must say, but I can stand it. But you're the Union's stay and New Hampshire's pride! He mustn't get you, Mr. Webster! He mustn't get you!"

Dan'l Webster looked at the distracted man, all gray and shaking in the firelight, and laid a hand on his shoulder.

"I'm obliged to you, Neighbor Stone," he said gently. "It's kindly thought of. But there's a jug on the table and a case in hand. And I never left a jug or a case half finished in my life."

And just at that moment there was a sharp rap on the door.

"Ah," said Dan'l Webster, very coolly, "I thought your clock was a trifle slow, Neighbor Stone." He stepped to the door and opened it. "Come in!" he said.

The stranger came in—very dark and tall he looked in the firelight. He was carrying a box under his arm—a black, japanned[18] box with little air holes in the lid. At the sight of the box, Jabez Stone gave a low cry and shrank into a corner of the room.

"Mr. Webster, I presume," said the stranger, very polite, but with his eyes glowing like a fox's deep in the woods.

"Attorney of record for Jabez Stone,"

said Dan'l Webster, but his eyes were glowing too. "Might I ask your name?"

"I've gone by a good many," said the stranger carelessly. "Perhaps Scratch will do for the evening. I'm often called that in these regions."

Then he sat down at the table and poured himself a drink from the jug. The liquor was cold in the jug, but it came steaming into the glass.

"And now," said the stranger, smiling and showing his teeth, "I shall call upon you, as a law-abiding citizen, to assist me in taking possession of my property."

Well, with that the argument began— and it went hot and heavy. At first, Jabez Stone had a flicker of hope, but when he saw Dan'l Webster being forced back at point after point, he just scrunched in his corner, with his eyes on that japanned box. For there wasn't any doubt as to the deed or the signature— that was the worst of it. Dan'l Webster twisted and turned and thumped his fist on the table, but he couldn't get away from that. He offered to compromise the case; the stranger wouldn't hear of it. He pointed out the property had increased in value, and state senators ought to be worth more; the stranger stuck to the letter of the law. He was a great lawyer, Dan'l Webster, but we know who's the King of Lawyers, as the Good Book tells us, and it seemed as if, for the first time, Dan'l Webster had met his match.

Finally, the stranger yawned a little. "Your spirited efforts on behalf of your

_____

18. **japanned:** enameled or lacquered.

client do you credit, Mr. Webster," he said, "but if you have no more arguments to adduce,[19] I'm rather pressed for time"—and Jabez Stone shuddered.

Dan'l Webster's brow looked dark as a thundercloud.

"Pressed or not, you shall not have this man!" he thundered. "Mr. Stone is an American citizen, and no American citizen may be forced into the service of a foreign prince. We fought England for that in '12[20] and we'll fight all hell for it again!"

"Foreign?" said the stranger. "And who calls me a foreigner?"

"Well, I never yet heard of the dev— of your claiming American citizenship," said Dan'l Webster with surprise.

"And who with better right?" said the stranger, with one of his terrible smiles. "When the first wrong was done to the first Indian, I was there. When the first slaver put out for the Congo, I stood on her deck. Am I not in your books and stories and beliefs, from the first settlements on? Am I not spoken of, still, in every church in New England? 'Tis true the North claims me for a Southerner and the South for a Northerner, but I am neither. I am merely an honest American like yourself—and of the best descent—for, to tell the truth, Mr. Webster, though I don't like to boast of it, my name is older in this country than yours."

"Aha!" said Dan'l Webster, with the veins standing out in his forehead. "Then I stand on the Constitution! I demand a trial for my client!"

"The case is hardly one for an ordinary court," said the stranger, his eyes flickering. "And, indeed, the lateness of the hour—"

"Let it be any court you choose, so it is an American judge and an American jury!" said Dan'l Webster in his pride. "Let it be the quick[21] or the dead; I'll abide the issue!"

"You have said it," said the stranger, and pointed his finger at the door. And with that, and all of a sudden, there was a rushing of wind outside and a noise of footsteps. They came, clear and distinct, through the night. And yet, they were not like the footsteps of living men.

"In God's name, who comes by so late?" cried Jabez Stone, in an ague[22] of fear.

"The jury Mr. Webster demands," said the stranger, sipping at his boiling glass. "You must pardon the rough appearance of one or two; they will have come a long way."

And with that the fire burned blue and the door blew open and twelve men entered, one by one.

If Jabez Stone had been sick with terror before, he was blind with terror now. For there was Walter Butler, the Loyalist, who spread fire and horror through the Mohawk Valley in the times of the Revolution; and there was Simon

---

19. **adduce:** offer; present.
20. **'12:** the War of 1812.

21. **quick:** living.
22. **ague** (ā' gyoo): a feverish chill.

Girty, the renegade, who saw white men burned at the stake and whooped with the Indians to see them burn. His eyes were green, like a catamount's,[23] and the stains on his hunting shirt did not come from the blood of the deer. King Philip[24] was there, wild and proud as he had been in life, with the great gash in his head that gave him his death wound, and cruel Governor Dale,[25] who broke men on the wheel. There was Morton of Merry Mount, who so vexed the Plymouth Colony, with his flushed, loose, handsome face and his hate of the godly. There was Teach, the bloody pirate, with his black beard curling on his breast. The Reverend John Smeet, with his strangler's hands and his Geneva gown,[26] walked as daintily as he had to the gallows. The red print of the rope was still around his neck, but he carried a perfumed handkerchief in one hand. One and all, they came into the room with the fires of hell still upon them, and the stranger named their names and their deeds as they came, till the tale of twelve was told. Yet the stranger had told the truth—they had all played a part in America.

"Are you satisfied with the jury, Mr. Webster?" said the stranger mockingly, when they had taken their places.

The sweat stood upon Dan'l Webster's brow, but his voice was clear.

"Quite satisfied," he said. "Though I miss General Arnold from the company."

"Benedict Arnold is engaged upon other business," said the stranger, with a glower. "Ah, you asked for a justice, I believe."

He pointed his finger once more, and a tall man, soberly clad in Puritan garb, with the burning gaze of the fanatic, stalked into the room and took his judge's place.

"Justice Hathorne is a jurist of experience," said the stranger. "He presided at

---

23. **catamount:** a wild cat.
24. **King Philip:** (1639?–1676), name given to Metacomet, chief of the Wampanoag. After trying to live in peace with the English settlers, he led an uprising against the colonists in 1675. He was killed in a surprise attack by the English, and his head was mounted on a pole in Plymouth, Massachusetts, where it remained on public display for more than 20 years.
25. **Governor Dale:** Sir Thomas Dale, English Deputy Governor of Virginia, 1611–1616, who was known for his severe laws.
26. **Geneva gown:** minister's robe.

certain witch trials once held in Salem. There were others who repented of the business later, but not he."

"Repent of such notable wonders and undertakings?" said the stern old justice. "Nay, hang them—hang them all!" And he muttered to himself in a way that struck ice into the soul of Jabez Stone.

Then the trial began, and, as you might expect, it didn't look anyways good for the defense. And Jabez Stone didn't make much of a witness in his own behalf. He took one look at Simon Girty and screeched, and they had to put him back in his corner in a kind of swoon.

It didn't halt the trial, though; the trial went on, as trials do. Dan'l Webster had faced some hard juries and hanging judges in his time, but this was the hardest he'd ever faced, and he knew it. They sat there with a kind of glitter in their eyes, and the stranger's smooth voice went on and on. Every time he'd raise an objection, it'd be "Objection sustained," but whenever Dan'l objected, it'd be "Objection denied." Well, you couldn't expect fair play from a fellow like this Mr. Scratch.

It got to Dan'l in the end, and he began to heat, like iron in the forge. When he got up to speak he was going to flay that stranger with every trick known to the law, and the judge and jury too. He didn't care if it was contempt of court or what would happen to him for it. He didn't care any more what happened to Jabez Stone. He just got madder and

madder, thinking of what he'd say. And yet, curiously enough, the more he thought about it, the less he was able to arrange his speech in his mind.

Till, finally, it was time for him to get up on his feet, and he did so, all ready to bust out with lightnings and denunciations. But before he started he looked over the judge and jury for a moment, such being his custom. And he noticed the glitter in their eyes was twice as strong as before, and they all leaned forward. Like hounds just before they get the fox, they looked, and the blue mist of evil in the room thickened as he watched them. Then he saw what he'd been about to do, and he wiped his forehead, as a man might who's just escaped falling into a pit in the dark.

For it was him they'd come for, not only Jabez Stone. He read it in the glitter of their eyes and in the way the stranger hid his mouth with one hand. And if he fought them with their own weapons, he'd fall into their power; he knew that, though he couldn't have told you how. It was his own anger and horror that burned in their eyes; and he'd have to wipe that out or the case was lost. He stood there for a moment, his black eyes burning like anthracite. And then he began to speak.

He started off in a low voice, though you could hear every word. They say he could call on the harps of the blessed when he chose. And this was just as simple and easy as a man could talk. But he didn't start out by condemning or reviling. He was talking about the things that make a country a country, and a man a man.

And he began with the simple things that everybody's known and felt—the freshness of a fine morning when you're young, and the taste of food when you're hungry, and the new day that's every day when you're a child. He took them up and he turned them in his hands. They were good things for any man. But without freedom, they sickened. And when he talked of those enslaved, and the sorrows of slavery, his voice got like a big bell. He talked of the early days of America and the men who had made those days. It wasn't a spread-eagle[27] speech, but he made you see it. He admitted all the wrong that had ever been done. But he showed how, out of the wrong and the right, the suffering and the starvations, something new had come. And everybody had played a part in it, even the traitors.

Then he turned to Jabez Stone and showed him as he was—an ordinary man who'd had hard luck and wanted to change it. And, because he'd wanted to change it, now he was going to be punished for all eternity. And yet there was good in Jabez Stone, and he showed that good. He was hard and mean, in some ways, but he was a man. There was sadness in being a man, but it was a proud thing too. And he showed what the pride of it was till you couldn't help feeling it. Yes, even in hell, if a man was a man, you'd know it. And he wasn't

---

27. **spread-eagle:** blindly patriotic.

pleading for any one person any more, though his voice rang like an organ. He was telling the story and the failures and the endless journey of mankind. They got tricked and trapped and bamboozled, but it was a great journey. And no demon that was ever foaled could know the inwardness of it—it took a man to do that.

The fire began to die on the hearth and the wind before morning to blow. The light was getting gray in the room when Dan'l Webster finished. And his words came back at the end to New Hampshire ground, and the one spot of land that each man loves and clings to. He painted a picture of that, and to each one of that jury he spoke of things long forgotten. For his voice could search the heart, and that was his gift and his strength. And to one, his voice was like the forest and its secrecy, and to another like the sea and the storms of the sea; and one heard the cry of his lost nation in it, and another saw a little harmless scene he hadn't remembered for years. But each saw something. And when Dan'l Webster finished he didn't know whether or not he'd saved Jabez Stone. But he knew he'd done a miracle. For the glitter was gone from the eyes of the judge and jury, and, for the moment, they were men again, and knew they were men.

"The defense rests," said Dan'l Webster, and stood there like a mountain. His ears were still ringing with his speech, and he didn't hear anything else till he heard Judge Hathorne say, "The jury will retire to consider its verdict."

Walter Butler rose in his place and his face had a dark, gay pride on it.

"The jury has considered its verdict," he said, and looked the stranger full in the eye. "We find for the defendant, Jabez Stone."

With that, the smile left the stranger's face, but Walter Butler did not flinch.

"Perhaps 'tis not strictly in accordance with the evidence," he said, "but even the damned may salute the eloquence of Mr. Webster."

With that, the long crow of a rooster split the gray morning sky, and judge and jury were gone from the room like a puff of smoke and as if they had never been there. The stranger turned to Dan'l Webster, smiling wryly.

"Major Butler was always a bold man," he said. "I had not thought him quite so bold. Nevertheless, my congratulations, as between two gentlemen."

"I'll have that paper first, if you please," said Dan'l Webster, and he took it and tore it into four pieces. It was queerly warm to the touch. "And now," he said, "I'll have you!" and his hand came down like a bear trap on the stranger's arm. For he knew that once you bested anybody like Mr. Scratch in fair fight, his power on you was gone. And he could see that Mr. Scratch knew it too.

The stranger twisted and wriggled, but he couldn't get out of that grip. "Come, come, Mr. Webster," he said, smiling palely. "This sort of thing is ridic—ouch!—is ridiculous. If you're worried about the costs of the case, naturally, I'd be glad to pay—"

"And so you shall!" said Dan'l Webster, shaking him till his teeth rattled. "For you'll sit right down at that table and draw up a document, promising never to bother Jabez Stone nor his heirs or assigns[28] nor any other New Hampshireman till doomsday! For any hades[29] we want to raise in this state, we can raise ourselves, without assistance from strangers."

"Ouch!" said the stranger. "Ouch! Well, they never did run very big to the barrel, but—ouch!—I agree!"

So he sat down and drew up the document. But Dan'l Webster kept his hand on his coat collar all the time.

"And, now, may I go?" said the stranger, quite humble, when Dan'l'd seen the document was in proper and legal form.

"Go?" said Dan'l giving him another shake. "I'm still trying to figure out what I'll do with you. For you've settled the costs of the case, but you haven't settled with me. I think I'll take you back to Marshfield," he said, kind of reflective. "I've got a ram there named Goliath that can butt through an iron door. I'd kind of like to turn you loose in his field and see what he'd do."

Well, with that the stranger began to beg and to plead. And he begged and he pled so humble that finally Dan'l, who was naturally kindhearted, agreed to let him go. The stranger seemed terrible grateful for that and said, just to show they were friends, he'd tell Dan'l's fortune before leaving. So Dan'l agreed to that, though he didn't take much stock in fortunetellers ordinarily. But, natu-

rally, the stranger was a little different.

Well, he pried and he peered at the lines in Dan'l's hands. And he told him one thing and another that was quite remarkable. But they were all in the past.

"Yes, all that's true, and it happened," said Dan'l Webster. "But what's to come in the future?"

The stranger grinned, kind of happily, and shook his head.

"The future's not as you think it," he said. "It's dark. You have a great ambition, Mr. Webster."

"I have," said Dan'l firmly, for everybody knew he wanted to be President.

"It seems almost within your grasp," said the stranger, "but you will not attain it. Lesser men will be made President and you will be passed over."

"And, if I am, I'll still be Daniel Webster," said Dan'l. "Say on."

"You have two strong sons," said the stranger, shaking his head. "You look to found a line. But each will die in war and neither reach greatness."

"Live or die, they are still my sons," said Dan'l Webster. "Say on."

"You have made great speeches," said the stranger. "You will make more."

"Ah," said Dan'l Webster.

"But the last great speech you make will turn many of your own against you," said the stranger. "They will call you Ichabod;[30] they will call you by

---

28. **assigns:** inheritors of money or property.
29. **hades** (hā′ dēz): hell. In Greek mythology, Hades was the underworld kingdom of the Greek god Hades.

30. **Ichabod** (ĭk′ ə bŏd): a Hebrew name meaning "inglorious," and the title of a poem by John Greenleaf Whittier critical of Webster's speech of March 7, 1850, in which Webster denounced the abolitionists.

other names. Even in New England, some will say you have turned your coat and sold your country, and their voices will be loud against you till you die."

"So it is an honest speech, it does not matter what men say," said Dan'l Webster. Then he looked at the stranger and their glances locked.

"One question," he said. "I have fought for the Union all my life. Will I see that fight won against those who would tear it apart?"

"Not while you live," said the stranger, grimly, "but it will be won. And after you are dead, there are thousands who will fight for your cause, because of words that you spoke."

"Why, then, you long-barreled, slab-sided, lantern-jawed, fortunetelling note shaver!" said Dan'l Webster, with a great roar of laughter, "be off with you to your own place before I put my mark on you! For, by the thirteen original colonies, I'd go to the Pit[31] itself to save the Union!"

And with that he drew back his foot for a kick that would have stunned a horse. It was only the tip of his shoe that caught the stranger, but he went flying out of the door with his collecting box under his arm.

"And now," said Dan'l Webster, seeing Jabez Stone beginning to rouse from his swoon, "let's see what's left in the jug, for it's dry work talking all night. I hope there's pie for breakfast, Neighbor Stone."

But they say that whenever the devil comes near Marshfield, even now, he gives it a wide berth. And he hasn't been seen in the state of New Hampshire from that day to this. I'm not talking about Massachusetts or Vermont.

---

31. **the Pit:** Hell.

# THINKING ABOUT
# THE STORY

*Recalling*

**1.** According to the narrator, where do "they" tell the story of Daniel Webster's encounter with the Devil? When did the narrator first hear the story told?

**2.** What are some of the misfortunes that lead Jabez Stone to sell his soul to the Devil?

**3.** Explain the bargain that Jabez Stone makes with "the stranger." In what ways does Stone's life change between the time he signs the agreement and the time it expires?

**4.** Explain what Jabez Stone sees flutter out of the Devil's black pocketbook. What does Stone realize will happen to him after his agreement with the Devil expires?

**5.** What proof does the Devil offer that he is an American citizen?

**6.** What tactics does Daniel Webster consider using to win his case before the Devil's jury? What does he realize will happen if he fights using the Devil's own weapons?

**7.** What are some of the "simple things" that Daniel Webster mentions in his argument before the jury? What "miracle" does he realize he has accomplished when he finishes his speech?

**8.** What is the jury's decision? After the verdict, how does Daniel Webster treat the Devil, and what does he get from him?

*Interpreting*

**9.** According to the second and third paragraphs, what details depict Daniel Webster as a larger-than-life personality? Which details seem factual and historically accurate?

**10.** Find two or more details in the story that reveal Jabez Stone as basically a good man. Why is this characterization of Stone important to the story?

**11.** A **foil** is a character whose traits are in direct contrast to those of another character. What traits do the men on the Devil's jury all share? Explain how the jury is a foil for Daniel Webster.

**12.** What practices in real life is the author criticizing by characterizing the Devil as the kind of businessman that he is?

**13.** By depicting Daniel Webster as victorious over the forces of evil, what American values is the author affirming as good?

*Applying*

**14.** Imagine that you were asked to update the characters and circumstances in this story for a television play. What modern American hero would you use to replace Daniel Webster? What twentieth-century Americans would you choose to form the Devil's jury? How would you characterize the Devil and Jabez Stone?

# ANALYZING LITERATURE

*Understanding a Tall Tale*

A **tall tale** is a humorous story that describes outrageously unbelievable happenings in a literal manner. It is told using colloquial or everyday language and makes much use of exaggeration. The main character in a tall tale is sometimes a historical figure whose abilities have been so exaggerated as to seem superhuman. The stories about Davy Crockett wrestling bears and about George Washington throwing a silver dollar across the Delaware River fall into this category.

Tall tales were a popular form of entertainment among the settlers on the American frontier. Many writers, such as Mark Twain, often recorded the tall tales that they heard and added embellishments of their own. In "The Devil and Daniel Webster," Stephen Vincent Benét drew upon the tradition of the American tall tale as well as older folk beliefs about contracts with the Devil. By using the elements commonly found in tall tales, Benét was able to create an entertaining short story while making an important point about basic American values.

**1.** Find three details in the story that strike you as particularly humorous. Why is the story's lighthearted mood better suited to Benét's purpose than an eerie and terrifying mood?

**2.** Benét uses many **similes**—comparisons between basically dissimilar things using *like* or *as*—to describe Daniel Webster. For example, Benét says that Webster's "hand came down like a bear trap on the stranger's arm." Find four or five other similes that describe Webster's appearance or actions. Explain why these similes are especially suited for a tall tale.

**3.** Explain how Benét makes use of a first-person narrator to create the impression that his short story is actually a traditional tall tale.

**4.** What events in "The Devil and Daniel Webster" would seem entirely unbelievable if Benét had not chosen to use the elements associated with traditional tall tales?

**5.** Describe the overall impression you have of Daniel Webster by the end of the story. Do you think of him more as a complex human being or more as someone exaggerated into superhuman proportions?

# CRITICAL THINKING AND READING

*Making Inferences*

An **inference** is an informed guess. When you read, you will often have to make guesses about what an author means based on the details the author provides. By thinking carefully about particular details, you will be able to make the logical leap and correctly guess the meaning.

Consider again the following details from "The Devil and Daniel Webster." Then answer the questions that ask you to make an inference based on the details.

**1.** When Jabez Stone and the Devil are discussing the sizes of the various specimens in his collecting box, the Devil says, "Now, a man like Daniel Webster, of course—well, we'd have to build a special box for him, and even at that, I imagine the wingspread would astonish you." Based on the Devil's statement, what inferences can you make regarding Daniel Webster's soul?

**2.** After the jury enters, the Devil asks Daniel Webster if he is satisfied. "Quite satisfied," Webster says. "Though I miss General Arnold from the company." Why should Webster expect Benedict Arnold in particular to be among the Devil's jurors?

**3.** When Mrs. Stone wants to entertain Daniel Webster in the front parlor, the narrator adds that "Dan'l Webster knew front parlors and said he preferred the kitchen." What can you infer about Webster's personality from this detail?

· · · · · · · · · · · · · · · · · · · · · · · · · · · · · ·

## DEVELOPING VOCABULARY SKILLS

*Legal Terms*
Benét portrays the Devil as a businessman who does everything "according to contract and specifications" and refers to him as "the King of Lawyers." Accordingly, the story contains several words often found in legal contexts. Test your understanding of these words by matching the legal term on the left with its definition on the right.

**1.** legacy    **a.** to present a case in a court of law

**2.** mortgage    **b.** a document that transfers property

**3.** plead    **c.** a person to whom property is transferred

**4.** deed    **d.** money or property left to someone through a will

**5.** assign    **e.** a pledge of property to a creditor as security for a debt

· · · · · · · · · · · · · · · · · · · · · · · · · · · · · ·

## THINKING AND WRITING

**1. Writing About a Character.**
What impression of Daniel Webster do you think Stephen Vincent Benét wanted people to have after reading his story? Write an essay in which you respond to this question, and cite evidence from the story to support your opinion.

**Prewriting.** Begin by thinking about and listing the various traits that Benét gives Daniel Webster. Which seem the traits of an ordinary man? Which seem those of someone truly extraordinary? What shortcomings, if any, does Benét's Daniel Webster have? Find passages in the story that illustrate each of the traits you have listed.

**Writing.** Begin by writing a clear statement that answers the question posed in the assignment. You might, for example, begin by completing this sentence: "In 'The Devil and Daniel Webster,' the impression Stephen Vincent Benét wants readers to have of Daniel Webster is of a man who _____." Use your list of character traits to support your statement, and be sure to support your claims by quoting appropriate passages from the story.

**Revising.** Check to make sure you have organized your ideas convincingly. Have you backed up each of your opinions with evidence from the story?

**Proofreading.** Reread your essay and correct any mistakes in grammar, spelling, and punctuation. Be sure that you have used quotation marks correctly. If necessary, prepare a neat final copy.

**Publishing.** Read your essay to the class. How many of your classmates agree with your analysis of Webster's character in the story?

## 2. Writing an Adaptation.

Stephen Vincent Benét adapted "The Devil and Daniel Webster" as a folk opera, then as a stage play, and finally as a film under the title *All That Money Can Buy* (1941). Try your hand at writing an adaptation of Benét's story. Prepare a script for a radio performance of "The Devil and Daniel Webster." You might work with one or two classmates, each adapting different scenes.

**Prewriting.** Think about how you can best divide the story into dramatic scenes. Consider scenes for Jabez Stone's initial meetings with the Devil, Stone's visit to enlist Daniel Webster's help, the jury trial, and the outcome after the jury's verdict. Remember that as a radio play, your script must rely on dialogue and sound effects and possibly a narrator to link the scenes.

**Writing.** After you have planned your scenes, write the dialogue for the various characters. Draw on Benét's story as much as possible, but feel free to add whatever you think is necessary to make your radio play an effective but faithful adaptation. Be sure to indicate sound effects that will enliven the drama.

**Revising.** When you have completed a first draft, make changes to improve your script. Does the dialogue generate suspense? Does each character's own personality emerge through what he or she says? Do the sound effects add to the drama? Is the script faithful to the spirit of Benét's original story?

**Proofreading.** Reread your radio play, and correct any mistakes in spelling and punctuation. If possible, type a neat final copy.

**Publishing.** Participate in organizing a performance of your adaptation for the class.

# VOICES OF EXPERIENCE

### *1840-1898*

*Trust thyself: Every heart*
*vibrates to that iron string.*

— Ralph Waldo Emerson

*Chenago Valley, New York*
William Louis Sonntag (1822-1900)
The Hunter Museum of Art, Chattanooga
Anonymous Gift

# Voices of Experience: 1840–1898

**A**merica was growing and changing rapidly in the years 1840–1898. There were more and more Americans — Americans born here and new Americans who came from other nations. More and more territory was being explored and settled as people moved westward. Great advances in science and technology helped farms, factories, and cities grow. The steamboat and the railroad made travel faster and safer than ever before.

Yet despite all this growth, the years 1840–1898 were not a happy time. Americans found that they were growing apart. What was good for one section of the country was somehow bad for another. The Civil War years, from 1861 to 1865, were the most dramatic expression of these differences. The choices and conflicts of American life were reflected in the literature created during these years.

### Life Before the Civil War

Mark Twain lived in the South, the West, and finally settled in the East. In his writing, he captured the flavor of life in different places in America. Two of the selections in this section are based on his early experiences in Hannibal, Missouri.

Walt Whitman's poetry celebrates America and the ideals of democracy. In "There Was a Child Went Forth," he describes the many different kinds of experiences that shape a person as he or she grows up.

Democratic ideals were part of two very important movements in the 19th century: the abolitionist movement and the movement to give women the vote. Abolitionists believed that all people should have freedom and equal rights.

As they campaigned for an end to slavery, many abolitionists began to realize that women, too, were being treated unfairly in America. Women could not own land, inherit money, or vote in elections. Many abolitionists also began speaking out for women's suffrage (the right to vote). In the 1850's, Sojourner Truth, a former slave, was a tireless crusader for both abolition and women's suffrage. Her witty speech "Ain't I a Woman?" is included in this section.

### The Civil War and Its Aftermath

Louisa May Alcott was a nurse in an army hospital during the Civil War. The selection "Civil War Nurse" describes her experiences and her search for a way to make sense of war. Ambrose Bierce was also affected by the Civil War. He himself

Guerrilla Warfare, Civil War, Albert Bierstadt, 1862

fought in the Union Army and was seriously wounded. In his story "A Horseman in the Sky," Bierce recreates one of the most painful dilemmas the war created for many Americans.

Chief Joseph of the Nez Percé tribe may not have taken part in the Civil War, but he certainly understood the pain and loss caused by war. The United States government had again and again broken agreements and taken tribal lands away from Native Americans, often by force. In the 1870's, Chief Joseph spoke out against these conditions in his speech "I Will Fight No More Forever."

"A Christmas Love Story" is a true story retold by Julius Lester. Slaves Ellen and William Craft formulate a daring plan to escape to freedom, but at every turn, obstacles arise to frighten and delay them. Will their love and courage triumph over an evil system?

The two main characters in the story "A White Heron" both love birds, but in very different ways. To the tall young man, each bird is a potential trophy, to be shot or snared, stuffed and preserved, and added to his collection. To the young girl, each bird is a friend, to be watched, listened to, and, if it will trustingly come close enough, fed from the hand. Both of these bird-lovers have seen the beautiful white heron, but only one has the power to decide its fate.

# A Dose of Pain-Killer

*by Mark Twain*

*One of America's best and best-loved writers is Mark Twain (1835–1910), who grew up in the small Mississippi River town of Hannibal, Missouri. The river and the towns along it became the setting for much of Twain's later work, including* The Adventures of Huckleberry Finn *and* The Adventures of Tom Sawyer. *Here is an excerpt from* The Adventures of Tom Sawyer, *a book based on Twain's memories of his own boyhood in Hannibal. As the story begins, Tom has just lost his girl friend, Becky, and witnessed a murder — both in the same day! Understandably, he is troubled and confused. His guardian, Aunt Polly, thinks he is sick, and therefore deserving of one of her cures.*

Tom Sawyer's Aunt Polly was one of those people who are infatuated with patent medicines and all new-fangled methods of producing health or mending it. She was always experimenting in these things. When something fresh in this line came out she wanted to try it right away; not on herself, for she was never sick, but on anybody else that came handy.

The water treatment was new now, and Tom's low condition was a windfall to her. She had him out at daylight every morning, stood him up in the woodshed, and drowned him with cold water; then she scrubbed him down with a scratchy towel; then she rolled him up in a wet sheet and put him away under blankets till she sweated his soul clean.

In spite of all this, the boy grew more and more melancholy and pale and dejected. Now she heard of Pain-Killer for the first time. She ordered a lot at once. She tasted it and was filled with gratitude. It was simply fire in a liquid form.

She dropped the water treatment and pinned her faith to Pain-Killer. She gave Tom a teaspoonful, and watched with deepest anxiety for the result. Her troubles were instantly at rest, her soul at peace again; for the "indifference" was broken up. The boy could not have shown a wilder, heartier interest if she had built a fire under him.

Tom thought over various plans for relief, and finally hit upon that of pretending to be fond of Pain-Killer. He asked for it so often that he became a nuisance, and his aunt ended by telling him to help himself and quit bothering her.

She watched the bottle secretly. She found that the medicine did really diminish, but it did not occur to her that the boy was mending the health of a crack in the sitting-room floor with it.

One day Tom was in the act of dosing the crack, when his aunt's yellow cat came along, purring, eyeing the teaspoon greedily, and begging for a taste. Tom said, "Don't ask for it unless you want it, Peter."

But Peter signified that he did want it.

"You better make sure."

Peter was sure.

"Now you've asked for it, and I'll give it to you, because there ain't anything mean about *me*. But if you find you don't like it, you mustn't blame anybody but your own self."

Peter was agreeable. So Tom pried his mouth open and poured down the Pain-Killer. Peter sprang a couple of yards in the air. He delivered a war-whoop and set off round and round the room, banging against furniture, upsetting flowerpots, and making general havoc.

Next he rose on his hind feet and pranced around, in a frenzy of enjoyment, with his head over his shoulder and his voice proclaiming his happiness. Then he went tearing around the house again, spreading chaos and destruction in his path.

Aunt Polly entered just in time to see him throw a few double somersaults, deliver a final mighty hurrah, and sail through the open window, carrying the rest of the flowerpots with him. The old lady stood peering over her glasses in astonishment. Tom lay on the floor, expiring with laughter.

"Tom, what on earth ails that cat?"

"*I* don't know, Aunt," gasped the boy.

"Why, I've never seen anything like it. What *did* make him act so?"

" 'Deed I don't know, Aunt Polly. Cats always act so when they're having a good time."

"They do, do they?" There was something in the tone that made Tom uneasy.

"Yes'm. That is, I believe they do."

"You *do*?"

The old lady was bending down, Tom watching anxiously. Too late he realized her "drift." The handle of the tell-tale teaspoon was visible under the bedspread. Aunt Polly took it, held it up. Tom winced, and dropped his eyes. Aunt Polly raised him by the usual handle — his ear — and cracked his head soundly with her thimble.

"Now, sir, why do you want to treat that poor dumb beast so?"

"I done it out of pity for him — because he hadn't any aunt."

"Hadn't any aunt — you numbskull! What has that got to do with it?"

"Heaps. Because if he'd a had one she'd a burst him out herself! She'd a roasted his bowels out of him 'thout any more feeling than if he was a human!"

Aunt Polly felt a sudden pang of remorse. This was putting the thing in a new light. What was cruelty to a cat *might* be cruelty to a boy, too. She began to soften; she felt sorry. Her eyes watered a little, and she put her hand on Tom's head and said gently, "I was meaning for the best, Tom. And, Tom, it *did* do you good."

"I know you was meaning for the best, Aunty, and so was I with Peter. It done *him* good, too. I never see him get around so since — "

"Oh, go 'long with you, Tom, before you aggravate me again. And you try and see if you can't be a good boy, for once, and you needn't take any more medicine."

## READING COMPREHENSION

**Summarizing.** Choose the best phrase to complete each sentence. Then write the complete statements on your paper.

1. Aunt Polly was one of those people who was always trying out new methods for _____ (making money, staying healthy, training cats).

2. Peter reacted to Pain-Killer by _____ (falling asleep, asking for more, racing all over the house knocking things over).

3. When Aunt Polly realized what happened to Peter, she understood how _____ (dangerous the medicine was, Tom felt about taking the medicine, sick Peter was).

**Interpreting.** Write the answer to each question on your paper.

1. Why did Aunt Polly give Tom Pain-Killer?

2. Was Tom helped in any way by Pain-Killer?

3. What did Tom do with Pain-Killer when Aunt Polly let him help himself to the medicine?

4. How did Aunt Polly know that Tom had given a dose of Pain-Killer to Peter?

**For Thinking and Discussing.** What other means could Tom have used to convince Aunt Polly that Pain-Killer medicine was awful? How might you deal with a similar situation?

## UNDERSTANDING LITERATURE

**Plot.** The events in a story are called the *plot*. Each event is responsible for resulting in another. The first event is known as the *cause*. The cause produces the next event, or the result, known as the *effect*. Cause and effect make a story logical. Events happen for a reason. In "A Dose of Pain-Killer," Aunt Polly was "infatuated with patent medicines." The effect was that she gave the new medicines to "anybody . . . that came handy."

On your paper, match each of the following causes to the effect it produced.

### Causes

1. Aunt Polly gave Tom his first dose of Pain-Killer.
2. Tom pretended to like Pain-Killer.
3. Tom gave Peter some of the medicine.
4. Aunt Polly found the teaspoon under the bed.

### Effects

a. Peter raced around the house, knocking over furniture and flowerpots.
b. Aunt Polly cracked Tom's head with a thimble.
c. Aunt Polly let Tom give himself the medicine.
d. Tom felt as if he'd been drinking fire.

## WRITING

What would have happened if Aunt Polly had taken Pain-Killer herself? Describe the events that might have occurred as a result of her action.

# Life on the Mississippi

*by Mark Twain*

*Here is a play based on Mark Twain's book* Life on the Mississippi. *Like the main character in the play, Twain was a riverboat pilot as a young man. (In fact, the name Mark Twain comes from a term that was used on riverboats. "Mark twain" means that the water is deep enough for the pilot to steer in safely.) Mark Twain's real name was Samuel Clemens; Sam is also the name of the pilot in the play. In many of Twain's books, the main character is an innocent person learning about life. In this play, Sam learns to be a pilot, but he also learns about friendship, responsibility, danger, and death.*

## CHARACTERS

**Sam,** a steamboat steersman
**Bixby,** the pilot who trains Sam
**Ritchie,** another steersman
**Brown,** another pilot
**Tom,** another steersman
**Emmeline,** a passenger
**Klinefelter,** a steamboat captain

*It is 1857. Sam Clemens is at the riverboat landing in Hannibal, Missouri. He walks onto the* Paul Jones, *a steamboat that is headed down the Mississippi River. As the boat pulls away from shore, Sam goes to the wheelhouse, where the steering wheel is. Bixby, the pilot, is behind the wheel. The second pilot, George Ealer, and his steersman, Ritchie, are also there.*

**Sam:** Mr. Bixby?

*(Bixby ignores Sam and rings a bell. Then he speaks into a tube that goes down to the engine room.)*

**Bixby** *(into the tube):* Hold her where she is, Ben.

**Sam:** Mr. Bixby, could I speak to you? The captain said I could. He says you don't have a steersman.

**Bixby:** He did?

**Sam:** How would you like to teach me about the river?

**Bixby:** I wouldn't.

**Sam:** I could be your apprentice.

**Bixby:** You boys think that being a pilot just means standing at the wheel and ringing bells. Well, there's more to it than that.

**Sam:** I expect there is.

**Bixby:** Being a pilot is no job for a coward. It can be awfully terrifying at times. Have you got the nerve for that, boy?

**Sam** *(gulping):* I hope so.

**Bixby:** "Hope so" and "think so" have got no place on the river. "Know so" is the only thing we care about.

**Sam:** I'm willing to pay for the learning. I've got $100.

**Bixby:** You kids are more trouble than you're worth. Have you ever done any steering?

**Sam:** I was raised on the river. I've steered everything that floats — except a steamboat. And I reckon I could do that, once I've learned how.

**Bixby:** What's your name, son?

**Sam:** Sam, sir.

**Bixby:** Do you drink?

**Sam:** No.

**Bixby:** Do you gamble?

**Sam:** No, but I could learn how to.

**Bixby:** Do you tell the truth?

**Sam:** Do I lie? No, sir. Now and then I tell whoppers, but only when there's no harm in it.

**Bixby:** Well, I reckon Horace Bixby is your man. You can have the bunk next to Ritchie. *(Sam and Ritchie grin at each other.)* Now stand over here next to me.

*(He points.)* That's 12-Mile Point behind us. We stay by the bank until we get to Sheep-Nose Point. Here's where we start to cross the river. The water gets shallow around here. See where those ripples flatten out? That's a reef. There's a break in the reef where we can go through. Otherwise, we'd run aground. *(Bixby steers the boat through the reef, as Sam watches.)*

*(The next morning before dawn, Sam is asleep. Ritchie steps into their cabin and shakes Sam awake.)*

**Sam** *(sleepy):* What are you doing?

**Ritchie:** Get up to the wheelhouse.

**Sam:** But it's the middle of the night.

**Ritchie:** It's past four o'clock, and it's your watch again.

**Sam:** But I've only had four hours of sleep. I thought steamboats tied up for the night.

**Ritchie:** Some of them do. It's up to the pilots. Bixby and Ealer can steer at midnight as well as by daylight. It makes no difference to them.

*(Still yawning, Sam goes to the wheelhouse.)*

**Bixby:** All right, Sam. What's the name of the first point above Harrison's landing?

**Sam:** I don't know.

**Bixby:** What's the name of the next point?

**Sam:** I don't know that, either.

**Bixby:** Well, what do you know?

**Sam:** I guess I don't know anything.

**Bixby:** I believe that. You are the stupidest dunderhead I've ever seen. What makes you think you could be a pilot? You couldn't steer a cow down a lane. Now why do you think I told you the names of those points?

**Sam** *(puzzled):* I thought you did it to be entertaining.

**Bixby:** Do you think you're in this wheelhouse to learn funny songs and dances? No, by dogs! You're here to learn the river. There it is, boy — the Mississippi. *(Sam looks at the river.)* It's 1,200 miles long from New Orleans to St. Louis. It's filled with the ghosts of dead steamboats and bad pilots. You'd better know where you are out there, boy.

**Sam:** Yes, sir.

**Bixby:** You must get a notebook. When I tell you something, put it down right away. There's only one way to be a pilot. You must learn this river by heart.

*(A few days later, Sam is sitting on the deck with a notebook. Ritchie walks up and reads it over his shoulder.)*

**Ritchie:** You've got the whole river written down here!

**Sam:** It's in the book, all right. I just wish it were in my head. I can't remember any of it. At this rate, I'll never learn it.

**Ritchie:** Don't worry. Look at the river now. Isn't it beautiful?

**Sam:** Once, I would have said it was romantic. But now, the river appears different. Mr. Bixby has changed it all. Take that sunset. I used to feel holy just looking at a sight like that. Now, I look at it and wonder if the color means rain tomorrow. Do you see that silver streak on the water? It's like something a painter would put in, just to look pretty. But I know it's really a new reef that's there to catch steamboats. Beauty is fine, Ritchie, but it doesn't count for much on the river.

*(Later, Bixby asks Sam more questions.)*

**Bixby:** What's the shape of Walnut Bend?

**Sam** *(startled):* I didn't know it had a special shape.

**Bixby:** You're too much, boy! The shape of the river is the most important thing. Of course, it never looks the same.

**Sam:** Then how in creation am I ever going to learn it?

**Bixby:** How do you follow a hallway at home in the dark? You learn the shape of it. You steer through the dark hall by the shape you remember.

**Sam:** My hallway is the same shape going

in or coming out. The river is different going upstream or downstream.

**Bixby:** It's also different at day and at night. Do you hear that dog barking?

**Sam:** Yes, sir.

**Bixby:** Remember the sound. You'll know where you are if you hear it on a dark night.

**Sam:** Do you expect me to remember things like that?

**Bixby:** Yes, if you want to be a pilot.

**Sam:** I might as well quit right now. I haven't got brains enough to be a pilot.

**Bixby** (angry): Stop that! When I say I'll teach a man the river, I mean it. I'll teach him or kill him!

(One day, the boat stops to pick up a group of men. Ritchie explains to Sam who they are.)

**Ritchie:** They call themselves "river inspectors." They're really pilots out of work, going to Memphis for new jobs. They get to ride free. They pretend they're inspecting the river. Mostly they just lie around and eat and bother the pilot. (He points at a thin, mean-looking man.) His name is Brown. He's a pretty good pilot, but he's meaner than a snake!

(At the next landing, Bixby goes ashore. He has told Sam to meet him at a restaurant later. When Sam heads toward the restaurant, Brown stops him.)

**Brown:** You're Bixby's cub, aren't you?

**Sam:** Yes, sir.

**Brown:** I just got a job on the *Anna Louise*. I need someone who knows the river below Goose Island. How would you like to steer for me?

**Sam:** I can't leave Mr. Bixby. He's teaching me the river.

**Brown:** I'll pay you 50 cents a week, with the teaching thrown in.

**Sam:** I've got a responsibility to Mr. Bixby. He's always fair to me. I can't let him down. Besides, I wouldn't work for someone who would try to steal me away from another pilot.

**Brown:** Don't get smart with me! (Sam begins to walk away.) I won't forget you. It's a big river, but we'll meet on it someday. Then you'll be sorry!

(Sam meets Bixby at the restaurant.)

**Bixby:** I'm leaving the *Paul Jones*. I've just signed onto the *Aleck Scott*.

**Sam** (disappointed): That's nice.

**Bixby:** I thought you'd be happy for me. The *Aleck Scott* is the finest boat on the lower Mississippi.

**Sam** (politely): Is that so? Will you be needing someone to steer for you?

**Bixby:** Yes, but it can't be just anybody. The *Aleck Scott* needs someone who knows his stuff.

**Sam:** It won't be hard for you to find someone good.

**Bixby:** On the other hand, he doesn't have to be too smart. Any fool will do. (He grins.) Were you thinking of applying?

**Sam:** If you thought I'd leave you behind, you're more of a fool than I thought.

(Sam and Bixby join the Aleck Scott. The other steersman, Tom, is Sam's age. Right away, the two of them start bragging.)

**Tom:** My pilot, Thornburg, is the best pilot on the river. I guess Bixby's all right, though.

**Sam:** Bixby's the best pilot since Noah steered the Ark. Bixby holds the record for the run from Natchez to New Orleans.

**Tom:** Skill is more important than speed. Some people call Thornburg "Low-Water Thornburg." Once he took the *Sally Henry* right across a swamp. There were only three inches of water. He is famous for that, all right. (*Sam hasn't swallowed this tale. He decides to make up a taller tale.*)

**Sam:** There are lots of swamps you can go through. What really takes skill is going where there's no water at all.

**Tom** (*sarcastically*): I'd like to hear about that.

**Sam:** I'm surprised you haven't heard about it already. A boat got stranded two miles up a dry creek after a flash flood. The captain hired Bixby to get it back into the river. So Bixby put an ad in the papers for the saddest woman in the country. She soon turned up, crying away.

**Tom:** What was she crying about?

**Sam:** She married a man with seven children and a hundred debts. Then he ran off with a pretty girl from the circus, leaving his wife with all the problems. Well, Bixby put this woman at the back of the boat, right by the paddle wheel. He told her to cry for all she was worth. He put his mate beside her to sing sad songs. Well, Bixby brought the boat back two miles on the tears of a weeping woman.

**Tom:** I didn't know you could tell a whopper like that. You've got a real talent.

(*At the next stop, a girl named Emmeline and her parents get on. Tom and Sam compete for her attention. Tom shows her around the boat, and tells her tall tales about himself. One day, she goes to the wheelhouse to draw a picture. Sam can't help showing off.*)

**Sam** (*into the speaking tube*): Ben, how are we fixed for wood?

**Bixby:** You know we just picked up a full load. (*Then he sees how embarrassed Sam is in front of Emmeline.*) I'm going outside. Do you know the river along here?

**Sam:** I could run this stretch with my eyes closed.

**Bixby:** It will be okay if you keep them open. (*He leaves.*)

**Emmeline:** I'm beginning to think that Tom makes up those stories about his heroic deeds. I'd hate to think he was lying to me.

**Sam:** I know what you mean.

**Emmeline:** What's that in the water over there?

**Sam:** That's what's left of a boat that ran aground on an alligator reef.

**Emmeline:** An alligator reef?

**Sam:** Sure. Alligators ripped the bottom out of that boat.

**Emmeline:** That's too much to believe.

**Sam:** I'm not a liar like Tom. I just know about it because my first job was on an alligator boat.

**Emmeline:** What is that?

**Sam:** It's a boat that clears out alligators from a river. There aren't nearly as many now as there used to be.

**Emmeline** (*impressed*): You must be very strong to turn that wheel.

**Sam:** I can do it one-handed. (*He tries to*

*steer with one hand. The boat goes out of control, and he has to fight to get it straight again.)*

**Emmeline:** Why is this boat going so slowly? Can't you go faster?

**Sam:** If we use too much steam, the boat could blow up.

**Emmeline:** Are you scared? *(Sam can't resist a dare.)*

**Sam** *(into the speaking tube):* Ben, open up to full speed.

*(The boat speeds up. On the deck, Captain Klinefelter turns to Bixby.)*

**Klinefelter:** What's that young fool up to?

**Bixby** *(starting to walk toward the wheelhouse):* He's showing off for some little missy.

**Klinefelter:** Wait, he's slowing down again now.

**Bixby:** I still think we should teach him a lesson. Do you know the stretch of river around Island 66?

**Klinefelter:** Of course. It's so deep there, you couldn't touch the bottom with a church steeple.

**Bixby:** Right. It's perfect.

*(Later on, Sam is alone in the wheelhouse. Klinefelter shouts up to him.)*

**Klinefelter:** Steersman, isn't that shallow water up ahead?

**Sam:** No, sir. It can't be. *(He looks ahead.)* I can't see it.

**Klinefelter:** We'd better have it measured. *(He pretends to have the river's depth measured as they go ahead.)* It's only a quarter twain deep!

**Sam** *(shocked):* What did you say? *(He yells into the speaking tube.)* Stop all the engines! Back her up! Oh, Ben, if you love me, back her up!

*(He hears Ben laughing down in the engine room. He turns around and sees Bixby, Klinefelter, Tom, and Emmeline laughing at him.)*

**Sam** *(hurt):* That was a dirty trick to play.

**Bixby:** Didn't you know there was no bottom at this crossing?

**Sam:** Yes, sir, I did.

**Bixby:** Then you shouldn't have let anyone talk you out of it. When you set your course, follow it. And when you think you're in danger, don't turn coward.

*(For days, everyone teases Sam. A week later, they stop at a landing. Ritchie comes on board and walks up behind Sam.)*

**Ritchie:** Oh, Ben, if you love me, back her up!

**Sam** *(turning around):* Ritchie! How are you? Where is the *Paul Jones*?

**Ritchie:** We just landed. It took us three days longer than you. But at least we didn't get held up at Island 66.

**Sam** *(embarrassed):* Everyone along this river must have heard that story by now. Well, what are you doing here?

**Ritchie:** Didn't you hear? Thornburg is leaving the *Aleck Scott*. He's going down to Natchez to help the pilots form a union. Mr. Ealer has been hired to take his place, and he brought me with him.

**Sam** *(grinning):* That's great! Wait till I tell old Bixby. *(Just then, Bixby appears.)*

**Bixby:** "Old Bixby" already knows about it. As it happens, I'm going with Thornburg. For the rest of this trip, another pilot is taking my place.

**Sam:** Do you mean I'll have to steer for someone else? Who will it be?

*(Bixby points at the wheelhouse. Sam goes inside — and finds Brown.)*

**Sam** *(shocked):* Mr. Brown!

**Brown:** So, you were Bixby's cub. Well, you're Brown's cub now. *(Pause.)* Are you going to stand there all day?

**Sam:** I've had no orders, sir.

**Brown:** I didn't order any smart-talk, that's for sure. Don't put on airs with me, you derned puppy. Go to the kitchen, and get me a cool drink. And you'd better learn to jump lively!

*(A few days later, Sam and Ritchie sit on the deck together. Sam is writing in his notebook.)*

**Ritchie:** Are you still writing down the river in your notebook?

**Sam:** No. Now I'm writing down ways to murder Brown. I've got 16 ways listed so far. *(He shows the list to Ritchie.)*

**Ritchie:** Shouldn't you use a secret code? If somebody found this, it could be used for evidence.

**Sam:** I haven't done anything against the law — yet. Hey, how about "pounding him into the deck with a hammer"? That makes 17.

*(Sam and Brown are in the wheelhouse. The clerk, Henry, looks in the door. He has a message from the captain, but he is terrified of Brown. He tries to tell Brown to cross the river to a landing, but Brown ignores him. Sam gives a sign to Henry that he will tell Brown. Henry slips away.)*

**Sam:** Mr. Brown?

**Brown:** What do you want?

**Sam:** The captain's clerk was here, sir.

**Brown:** Do you think I'm blind? I saw him. I don't like you chattering while you're on duty. Don't speak until you're spoken to.

**Sam:** But —

**Brown:** Keep your mouth shut!

*(On the deck, Captain Klinefelter is watching the shore. He turns and goes into the wheelhouse.)*

**Klinefelter** *(angry):* Mr. Brown, didn't Henry give you my message? You were supposed to stop at Jones's landing across the river.

**Brown:** That's the first I've heard of it.

**Klinefelter:** I sent him to tell you.

**Brown:** I saw him, but the fool never said a thing.

**Klinefelter** *(to Sam):* Didn't you hear him?

**Sam:** Yes, sir.

**Brown:** Shut your mouth, boy! You never heard anything of the kind!

*(Klinefelter leaves.)*

**Sam** *(to Brown):* You lied. Henry did tell you. *(Brown tries to hit Sam, and Sam knocks him down. As they fight, Sam notices that no one is steering the boat. He runs to the wheel and begins steering.)*

**Brown:** You tried to kill me, you devil. I'll charge you with an attempt to murder. You'll be in prison for life, you butter-faced pup. Give me that wheel. *(He tries to push Sam away from the wheel.)* I'll give you a taste of my temper.

**Sam:** I've had all of your temper I want. You're a miserable old tyrant. You can have your old steamboat back. *(He stops when he sees Klinefelter watching them from the deck and frowning.)*

*(Later, Sam is called into Klinefelter's cabin.)*

**Klinefelter:** Have you been fighting with Mr. Brown?

**Sam:** Yes, sir.

**Klinefelter:** Do you know that that is a very serious matter?

**Sam:** Yes, sir.

**Klinefelter:** This boat was going down the river with no one steering at one point.

**Sam:** Yes, sir.

**Klinefelter:** Did you hit him first?

**Sam:** Yes, sir.

**Klinefelter:** Did you hit him hard?

**Sam:** You might say so, sir.

**Klinefelter:** I'm glad you did. *(He grins.)* Don't tell anyone I said that. I don't ever want you to fight on this boat again. But wait for Brown on shore sometime. Then give him a good beating. *(He winks at Sam. Sam is surprised and relieved. Klinefelter opens the cabin door and speaks loudly in case anyone outside the cabin is listening.)* Now get out of here, you puppy! *(Sam leaves, and Brown enters Klinefelter's cabin.)*

**Brown:** I hope you ordered him to get off the boat. I won't turn the wheel while that cub stays.

**Klinefelter:** He doesn't have to be in the wheelhouse while you're there.

**Brown:** I won't stay on the same boat with him! One of us must go ashore.

**Klinefelter:** Very well.

*(In a short while, Sam and Klinefelter stand on the deck. They watch Brown being taken to shore in a rowboat.)*

**Klinefelter:** Thanks to you, this boat has only one pilot now.

**Sam** *(trying to look sorry)*: Yes, sir, I know.

**Klinefelter:** I think you should take over until Mr. Bixby gets back.

**Sam:** Yes, sir. *(Now he looks excited.)* Thanks!

*(Meanwhile, Ritchie has been made pilot of the* Paul Jones. *One night in a terrible river accident, the boat explodes. Seeing the explosion, Sam races the* Aleck Scott *to the scene — only to find that Ritchie is dead. He is shocked and very saddened.)*

*(A few weeks later, Bixby returns to the* Aleck Scott. *He has heard about Ritchie's death, and he is concerned about Sam. He hurries to the wheelhouse, where Sam is steering.)*

**Bixby:** Hello, Sam.

**Sam** *(cool and calm)*: Hello, Mr. Bixby.

**Bixby:** I heard about Ritchie, and I'm sorry. *(There's an awkward pause. Then Bixby changes the subject.)* I see you're steering on your own now. When I heard about Brown, I wasn't sure I'd still find you on the river. But I hoped so.

**Sam:** Someone once told me that "hope so" has no place on the river.

**Bixby** *(looking out at the river)*: Hey, where are you going?

**Sam:** I'm starting to cross.

**Bixby:** It's too soon. Wait until you reach that point up there.

**Sam:** That was three weeks ago. The river has been rising since then. The easy water is down here now.

**Bixby:** Oh, you think so? *(They smile at each other, and Bixby shakes Sam's hand. Sam is a real pilot now.)*

**Summarizing.** Choose the best phrase to complete each sentence. Then write the complete statements on your paper.

1. When Sam told Bixby that sometimes he told "whoppers," he meant that he told _____ (lies, fishing stories, amusing tall tales).

2. After Bixby played a trick on Sam about the depth of the river, he said that in the future Sam should _____ (never pilot again, trust his own judgment, follow Klinefelter's directions).

3. At the end of the story, Sam was capable of being a riverboat pilot because of his _____ (experience and confidence, appreciation of the river, interest in riverboats).

**Interpreting.** Write the answer to each question on your paper.

1. What did Sam ask Bixby to teach him?

2. Why did Bixby tell Sam that he should get a notebook?

3. Why did Brown leave the *Aleck Scott* soon after he and Sam fought in the wheelhouse?

**For Thinking and Discussing**

1. What did Sam learn from his experiences on the *Paul Jones* and the *Aleck Scott*?

2. What was Sam's attitude toward the Mississippi before he began learning to pilot? How did it change?

**Sequence.** The order of the events in a story or play is called *sequence*. Placing events in the correct sequence ensures an understanding of *what* happened and *when* it happened in a story.

Group A and Group B below are lists of events from "Life on the Mississippi." On your paper, place the events in the proper sequence for each group. Then combine the two groups and see if the entire list is in the correct sequence.

### Group A

Ritchie woke Sam for his first night shift.
Sam began using a notebook.
Bixby took Sam along to the *Aleck Scott*.
Sam asked Bixby for a chance to learn how to be a pilot.
Sam told Brown he'd stay with Bixby.

### Group B

Bixby and Klinefelter tricked Sam.
Sam became Brown's "cub."
Sam told the whopper about how a woman's tears helped Bixby free a boat.
Sam and Brown fought in the wheelhouse.
Sam became the pilot.
The captain commanded the boat.

Imagine that you are Sam. Write a letter to a friend about your experiences on the river. Explain how you feel about Bixby, Klinefelter, Ritchie, and Brown. Be sure to put the events in the proper sequence.

# There Was a Child Went Forth

*by Walt Whitman*

There was a child went forth every day,
And the first object he look'd upon, that object he became,
And that object became part of him for the day or a certain
    part of the day,
Or for many years or stretching cycles of years.


The early lilacs became part of this child,
And grass and white and red morning-glories, and white and
    red clover, and the song of the phoebe-bird,
And the third-month lambs and the sow's pink-faint litter, and
    the mare's foal and the cow's calf,
And the noisy brood of the barnyard or by the mire of the
    pond-side,
And the fish suspending themselves so curiously below there,
    and the beautiful curious liquid,
And the water-plants with their graceful flat heads, all became
    part of him. . . .


And the schoolmistress that pass'd on her way to the school,
And the friendly boys that pass'd, and the quarrelsome boys,
And the tidy and fresh-cheek'd girls, and the barefoot Negro
    boy and girl,
And all the changes of city and country wherever he went.


The mother at home quietly placing the dishes on the supper-
    table,
The mother with mild words, clean her cap and gown, a
    wholesome odor falling off her person and clothes as she
    walks by,

The father, strong, self-sufficient, manly, mean, anger'd, unjust,
The blow, the quick loud word, the tight bargain, the crafty
    lure,
The family usages, the language, the company, the furniture, the
    yearning and swelling heart . . .
The doubts of day-time and the doubts of night-time, the
    curious whether and how,
Whether that which appears so is so, or is it all flashes and
    specks?
Men and women crowding fast in the streets, if they are not
    flashes and specks what are they?

**Weaning the Calf,** Winslow Homer, 1875

The streets themselves and the facade of houses, and goods in
    the windows,
Vehicles, teams, the heavy-plank'd wharves, the huge crossing at
    the ferries,
The village on the highland seen from afar at sunset, the river
    between . . .
The hurrying tumbling waves, quick-broken crests, slapping . . .
The horizon's edge, the flying sea-crow, the fragrance of salt
    marsh and shore mud,
These became part of that child who went forth every day, and
    who now goes, and will always go forth every day.

1. This poem describes the many influences upon a child's life, from things in nature like the early lilacs to the people in his family. How do they all become a "part of him"?

2. This poem is filled with descriptions of the world around the child. What was this world like? Is it like a child's world today?

3. The poem points out many contrasts, or opposites, in the boy's life. For example, the father is both strong and mean, and the boys are both friendly and quarrelsome. What contrasts have you observed in your daily life?

# Ain't I a Woman?

*by Sojourner Truth*

*Sojourner Truth (1795–1883) was born a slave. She changed her name from Belle to Sojourner Truth when she won her freedom in 1827. A sojourner is a traveler, and she traveled throughout the country raising support for the abolitionist movement and for women's rights. She delivered the following speech at a women's-rights convention in 1851.*

Well, Children, where there is so much racket there must be something out of kilter. I think that between the Negroes of the South and the women at the North, all talking about rights, the white men will be in a fix pretty soon. But what's all this here talking about?

That man over there says that women need to be helped into carriages, and lifted over ditches, and to have the best place everywhere. Nobody ever helps me into carriages, or over mud puddles, or gives me any best place! And ain't I a woman? Look at me! Look at my arm! I have ploughed and planted. I have gathered into barns, and no man could head me! And ain't I a woman? I could work as much as a man — when I could get it — and bear the lash as well! And ain't I a woman? I have borne 13 children, and seen them most all sold off to slavery. When I cried out with my mother's grief, none but Jesus heard me! And ain't I a woman?

Then they talk about this thing in the head; what's this they call it? [Intellect, someone whispers.] That's it, honey. What's that got to do with women's rights or Negro's rights? If my cup won't hold but a pint, and yours holds a quart, wouldn't you be mean not to let me have my little half-measure full?

Then that little man in black there, he says women can't have as much rights as men, 'cause Christ wasn't a woman! Where did your Christ come from? Where did your Christ come from? From God and a woman! Man had nothing to do with Him.

If the first woman God ever made was strong enough to turn the world upside down all alone, these women together ought to be able to turn it back, and get it right side up again! And now they is asking to do it, the men better let them.

Obliged to you for hearing me, and now old Sojourner ain't got nothing more to say.

**Sojourner Truth,** Unknown Artist

1. How did Sojourner Truth describe her life? How did this compare with how a male speaker had said women should be treated?

2. Do you think Sojourner agreed that women should be "helped into carriages . . . and have the best place everywhere"? Why or why not?

# Civil War Nurse

*by Louisa May Alcott*

*Louisa May Alcott (1832–1888) is best known as the author of the famous novels* Little Women *and* Little Men. *Raised in Massachusetts, she spent about a year working in Union Army hospitals during the Civil War. In 1863 she wrote a book about her experiences called* Hospital Sketches. *The following selection comes from that book. It describes her work as a nurse and her feelings about her patients.*

The hours I like best are at night, and so I was soon promoted to night nurse. I usually found the men in the most cheerful state of mind their condition allowed.

The evenings were spent in reading aloud and writing letters. I waited on and amused the men, and went with Dr. P. as he made his second daily rounds. I cared for my dozens of wounds, giving last doses of medicine and making the men cozy for the long hours to come.

I had managed to sort out the patients in the ward into three rooms. One I visited with a tray full of bandages and pins. Another I visited with books, flowers, games, and happy talk. To the third room I brought lullabies, kind words, and sometimes a helping hand in time of death.

The night I am writing about opened with a little comedy and closed with a little tragedy. I was watching beside the bed of a 12-year-old drummer boy who had come to us after a dreadful battle. A slight wound in the knee brought him there, but his mind had suffered more than his body. For days he had been reliving in his thoughts the scenes he could not forget. Then he would break out in terrible sobs which were pitiful to hear.

As I sat by him, I tried to soothe his poor brain by the constant touch of my hands over his hot forehead. In his mind he was cheering his comrades on, then counting them as they fell around him. He often grabbed my arm to drag me from the neighborhood of a bursting shell. His face burned with fever, his eyes were restless, and his head was never still. A constant stream of shouts, warnings, and broken cries poured from his lips.

It was past 11:00 and my patient was slowly wearing himself into periods of quiet. In one of these pauses, I heard a curious sound. I looked over my shoulder and saw a one-legged man hopping around the room. I recognized a soldier whose fever had taken a turn for the worse and left his mind in a state of confusion. At this point he informed me he was heading for home. When his mind was clear, the least movement produced a roar of pain. But the loss of reason seemed to have caused a change in the man and in his manner. He balanced himself on one leg like a stork and refused any suggestion of mine to return to bed.

I couldn't think what to do with this creature. I was about to run for help when another wounded soldier came to the rescue. He put an end to the crisis by carrying the lively one-legged man to his bed. The one-legged soldier was worn out from his efforts and soon fell asleep.

My rescuer and I enjoyed a great laugh together, then returned to our places. Then the sound of a sob came from a bed in the corner. It was the little drummer boy. He was trying to control the sad sounds that kept breaking out.

"What is it, Teddy?" I asked, as he rubbed the tears away.

"I've got a pain, ma'am, but I'm not crying for that, because I'm used to it. I dreamed Kit was here, and when I woke up he wasn't, and I couldn't help it then."

Kit was a good friend, badly hurt himself, who would not leave the drummer behind. He had wrapped him in his own blanket and carried him in his arms to the ambulance. Kit died at the door of the hospital which promised care and comfort for the drummer boy.

For 10 days Teddy refused to be comforted because he had not been able to thank Kit for his protection, which may have cost him his life. This thought had been troubling him in secret. I told him that his friend probably would have died in any case, but I couldn't end his sorrow.

As I was comforting him, a message I had been fearing came for me.

"John is going, ma'am, and wants to see you, if you can come."

"I'll be there the moment this boy is asleep. Tell John so, and let me know if I am in danger of being too late."

The messenger left and while I quieted the drummer, I thought of John. He had come in a day or two after the others and was put in my "pitiful" room. He was a large man with a fine face and the most peaceful eyes I have ever seen.

When he came, I watched him for a night or two before I made friends with him. He seldom spoke and never complained. He was thoughtful and concerned while watching the sufferings of others, as if he forgot his own.

One night, as I went on my rounds with Dr. P., I asked which man in the room probably suffered most. To my great surprise, the doctor glanced at John.

"Every breath he draws is like a stab, for the bullet went into his left lung and broke a rib. The poor man can find no rest because he must lie on his wounded back or else he can't breathe. It will be a long, hard struggle because of his great strength, but even this can't save him."

"You don't mean he must die, Doctor?"

"There's not the slightest hope for him, and you'd better tell him so before long.

**The Letter Home,** Eastman Johnson, 1863

You have a way of doing such things comfortably, so I leave it to you. He won't last more than a day or two at the most."

I could have sat down on the spot and cried if I had not learned to save my tears for spare moments. Such an end seemed very hard for such a fine man. The army needed men like John who fight for freedom with both heart and hand. I could not give him up so soon. It was an easy thing for Dr. P. to say, "Tell him he must die," but a hard thing to do. I didn't have the heart to do it then, and I hoped that some change for the better might take place in spite of what Dr. P. had said.

A few minutes later I came in and saw John sitting up with no one to support him. The doctor was changing the bandage on his back.

The doctor's words made me feel sad that I had not given John those little cares and kindnesses that make the heavy hours pass easier. He looked very lonely just then, as he sat with bent head and hands folded on his knee. I saw no sign of suffering till I looked nearer. Then I saw great tears roll down and drop upon the floor. It was a new sight there. Though I had seen many men suffer in silence or with groans of pain, none of them cried. It did not seem weak, only very moving. My heart opened wide and took him in. I gathered the bent head in my arms as freely as if he had been a little child and said, "Let me help you bear it, John."

Never on any human face have I seen so beautiful a look of thanks, surprise, and comfort, as that which he gave me.

"Thank you, ma'am," he whispered. "This is just what I wanted!"

"Then why not ask for it before?"

"I didn't like to be a trouble. You seemed so busy, and I could manage to get on alone."

"You shall not want it anymore, John."

Now I understood the sad look he sometimes gave me as I went out after a brief pause beside his bed. I had been used to stopping with those who seemed to need me more than he did. But now I knew that I brought as much comfort to him as to the others. I took the place of his mother, wife, or sister. Now while I cared for his wounds, he leaned against me, holding my hand tightly. If pain brought forth tears from him, no one saw them fall but me. I found him the manliest man of all of them, shy and brave and natural. I saw his goodness and his dreams, which had helped to make him what he was.

After that night I gave an hour of each evening that remained of his life to his comfort and pleasure. He could only speak in whispers, but what he told me added to the warmth and respect I felt for him.

Once I asked him, "Do you ever regret that you came, when you lie here suffering so much?"

"Never, ma'am," he answered. "I have not helped a great deal, but I've shown I was willing to give my life, and maybe I have to. But I don't blame anybody, and if it was to do over again, I'd do it."

Then he suddenly asked: "This is my first battle. Do they think it's going to be my last?"

"I'm afraid they do, John."

It was the hardest question I ever had been called upon to answer. His clear eyes were fixed on mine, forcing a truthful answer by their own truth. He seemed a little surprised at first, as he considered the terrible fact. Then he shook his head and spoke.

"I'm not afraid, but it's difficult to believe all at once. It doesn't seem possible for such a little wound to kill me."

But John had never seen the great holes between his shoulders. He saw only the awful sights about him, and he could not believe his own wound was worse than these.

"Shall I write your mother now?" I asked, thinking that the news I had just given him might change all his plans. But I think I should have guessed his answer, knowing him as I did.

"No, ma'am, to my brother just the same. He'll break the news to her best, and I'll add a line to her myself when you get done. I hope the answer will come in time for me to see it."

These things had happened two days earlier. Now John was dying, and the letter had not come. I had been called to many deathbeds in my life, but to none that made my heart ache as it did then. As I went in, John stretched out both hands.

"I knew you would come! I guess I'm moving on, ma'am."

He was dying so quickly that even as he spoke I saw his face grow paler. I sat down by him and wiped the drops from his forehead. I stirred the air about him with a slow wave of the fan, and waited to help him die. He stood in need of help, and I could do so little. As the doctor had said, the strong body fought against death every inch of the way. He was forced to draw each breath with pain. For hours he suffered, yet through it all, his eyes never lost their perfect calm, and his strong spirit showed in them.

Suddenly he rose up in his bed and cried out with a bitter cry that broke the silence with its terrible suffering: "For God's sake, give me air!"

It was the only cry that pain or death had squeezed from him, the only favor he had asked. None of us could grant it, for all the airs that blew were useless now. We threw up the window. The first red light of dawn was warming the sky, and we could see the rising sun. John saw it, and laid himself gently down and sighed deeply. We knew then that for him suffering was forever past. He died then, and though the heavy breaths still continued, he never spoke again. To the end he held my hand close, so close that when he was asleep at last, I could not draw it away. I felt glad that perhaps my touch had eased his hardest hour.

When they had gotten him ready for the grave, John looked to me like a hero. I felt a tender pride in my lost patient. The lovely expression on his face soon replaced the marks of pain. I longed for those who loved him best to see him as he had accepted Death.

As we stood looking at him, a letter was handed to me which had been forgotten the night before. It was John's letter, come just an hour too late for him to see it. Yet he did have it, for after I had cut some of his hair for his mother, I took off his ring to send to her. Then I kissed him for her sake, and laid the letter in his hand. I felt that its place was with him. I made myself happy with the thought that even now he would have some token of the love which makes life beautiful and lives on past death.

Then I left him, glad to have known so fine a man, and carrying with me a lasting memory of him. I remembered John as he lay calmly waiting for the dawn of that long day which knows no night.

**Summarizing.** Choose the best phrase to complete each sentence. Then write the complete statements on your paper.

1. The "little comedy" Alcott described was created by a _____ (drummer boy, one-legged soldier, group of nurses).

2. The drummer boy suffered most from his _____ (wounds, memories, loneliness).

3. Alcott was surprised at how much John suffered because he had _____ (slept so much, been so cheerful, not complained).

4. John accepted the news that his death was near without _____ (surprise, fear, feeling).

**Interpreting.** Write the answer to each question on your paper.

1. What experience from the war caused Teddy's sadness?

2. Why did Alcott prefer working at night?

3. Why did John ask Alcott to send a letter to his brother rather than to his mother?

**For Thinking and Discussing.**
1. What were some of the qualities required for a good Civil War nurse? Do you think many people could have done Alcott's job? Why or why not?

2. What do you think was in the letter that had come for John?

**Ironic Turn of Events.** A series of events makes up a story. Each event helps us anticipate, or expect, what will happen next. Sometimes what happens is different from what was expected. This is called an *ironic turn of events*. For example, in "Civil War Nurse," John complained the least of all the soldiers, but he was in the greatest pain.

An ironic turn of events often occurs when something is not expected because it seems so unfair. For example, Kit carried Teddy off the battlefield only to die on the hospital steps.

Read the following sentences. On your paper, tell why each is ironic.

1. Teddy screamed out in anguish at the memory of his friend's wounds.

2. John's tears demonstrated his manliness.

3. John said that he had no regrets about coming to war.

4. John's letter arrived too late, but he still received it.

Imagine you are Alcott. Write a letter to John's family to inform them of his death. What would you say about John and the way he died? Be sure to describe both John's personality and the nature of his injuries. Also explain what you felt was ironic about John's stay in the hospital.

# A Horseman in the Sky

*by Ambrose Bierce*

*Born and raised in the Midwest, Ambrose Bierce (1842–1914) enlisted in the Union Army at the age of 19. He fought bravely in many battles and was seriously wounded in 1865. By the end of the war, the death and suffering he had seen on the battlefield made Bierce a bitter man, and he had begun to doubt whether the Northern cause was right. In the story you are about to read, Bierce describes the tragedy that results when two members of the same family fight on opposite sides in the war.*

**A** soldier lay by the side of a road in western Virginia. It was a sunny autumn afternoon in 1861. The soldier's right hand loosely held his rifle. People might have thought him dead. But he had fallen asleep while on guard duty. If discovered by his men, he would be shot.

The road where the soldier lay ran west along the top of a cliff. Then it turned south, zigzagging down through a green forest. But before the road turned south, there was a large flat rock. Looking down from the rock, one could see a deep, wooded valley. A stone dropped from this point would have fallen 1,000 feet. The valley was surrounded by other high cliffs. It looked as if there were no way in and no way out.

But five regiments of Union soldiers were hidden in the valley. They had marched all day and night. Now they were resting. When it was dark, they would climb to where their guard now slept. Then they would walk quietly down the southern side of the mountain. This road would lead them to the rear of the enemy camp. Their surprise attack was planned for midnight.

The sleeping soldier was a young Virginian named Carter Druse. He was the only child of rich parents. And he had always lived in the mountain country of western Virginia. His home was only a few miles from where he now lay.

Carter usually ate a peaceful breakfast

with his father. But one morning had been different. Carter got up from the table. He watched his father eating. Then he said: "Father, there are Union soldiers at Grafton. I am going to join them."

Carter's father stopped eating. His face was pale and sad. It was a long time before he spoke. "You must do what you think is right. But . . . you are a traitor to Virginia."

Carter Druse said nothing.

"Virginia," his father said, "will get along without you. But your mother is very ill. She won't live longer than a few weeks. Please don't upset her with your news."

Carter Druse bowed to his broken-hearted father. He left his childhood home to go to war. Carter was courageous and did well in the Union Army. Up until now. . . .

Now he was asleep at his guard duty. But something somewhere woke him up. Carter quietly raised his head from his arm and looked around him. His first feeling was of great delight. For at the edge of the rock was a horse and rider of great dignity.

The rider looked like a Greek god carved in marble. His gray costume blended with the sky. The face of this horseman was turned slightly away. He was looking down to the bottom of the valley. The rider and the horse appeared much larger than they actually were.

Carter had a strange feeling. He felt as if he'd slept till the end of the war. And now he was looking at a great work of art that honored the deeds of the past.

This feeling left him as the horse moved slightly backward. The man remained motionless. Carter was now wide awake. He carefully brought the butt of the rifle against his cheek. He cocked the gun. A touch upon the trigger and the other man would be dead.

But the horseman turned his head and looked in Carter's direction. He seemed to look into Carter's face, into his eyes. It was as if the horseman could see into Carter's brave, sympathetic heart.

Is it so terrible to kill an enemy in war? Carter asked himself that question. After all, this horseman was a threat to Carter and his fellow soldiers. Carter Druse grew pale. He was trembling and felt faint. His hand fell away from his gun. His head slowly dropped until his face rested on a pile of leaves.

But these frightened feelings did not last long. In another moment, Carter raised his face from the leaves. He put his hands around the rifle. His finger found the trigger. His mind, heart, and eyes were clear. His conscience was sound. He could not hope to capture that enemy. If Carter alarmed the horseman, he would go dashing to the enemy camp. Carter's duty was plain. The man must be shot dead without warning. But . . .

Perhaps the man had discovered nothing. Perhaps he was only admiring the scenery. If allowed, the horseman might turn and ride away. Carter looked down the bottom of the valley. Creeping along the green meadow were a line of men and horses. Some foolish commander was letting the soldiers water their horses in the open. They were in plain view of the horseman.

Carter looked away from the valley. He steadied his rifle, staring again at the man and horse. His father's words came back to him: "You must do what you think is right." Carter was calm now. His nerves were like a sleeping baby's. His breathing was regular and slow. Duty had won. He fired.

A Union officer, looking for adventure, left his hidden camp in the valley. He made his way to an open space near the foot of the cliff. The officer looked up dizzily to the top of the gigantic cliff. It was then that he saw an amazing sight. A man on horseback was riding down into the valley through the air!

The rider sat straight in his saddle. He held the reins firmly. His long hair streamed upward. His hands were hidden in the horse's lifted mane. The animal's body was level. Its movements were those of a wild gallop. The horse threw its legs forward as if it were leaping. But this was flight!

The officer was filled with amazement and terror by the horseman in the sky. His legs failed him, and he fell. Almost at the same time, he heard a crashing sound

in the trees. Then all was still. There was no echo.

Trembling, the officer rose to his feet. He ran away from the cliff to a point where he expected to find the horseman. But there was no sign of him. The officer had forgotten that the horse and its rider would fall directly downward. He could have found them at the very foot of the cliff. A half-hour later he returned to camp.

The officer was a smart man. He knew better than to tell what might seem an impossible lie. He said nothing of what he had seen.

After firing his shot, Private Carter Druse reloaded his rifle. He continued his watch over the valley. Ten minutes later a Union sergeant crept carefully to him on hands and knees. Carter didn't turn his head or look at him.

"Did you fire?" the sergeant whispered.

"Yes."

"At what?"

"A horse. It was standing on that rock, pretty far out. It's no longer there. It went over the cliff."

Carter's face was white. He showed no other sign of emotion. Having answered, he turned away and said no more. The sergeant did not understand.

"See here, Druse," he said. "It's no use making a mystery. I order you to report. Was there anybody on the horse?"

"Yes."

"Well?"

"My father. . . . My father was on the horse."

The sergeant rose to his feet and walked away. "Good God!" he said.

## READING COMPREHENSION

**Summarizing.** Choose the best phrase to complete each sentence. Then write the complete statements on your paper.

1. If Carter Druse's men found him asleep while he was on guard duty, he would be _____ (dismissed from duty, disgraced, shot).

2. Carter's father told him that if he joined the Union Army, he would be _____ (treated badly, a traitor to Virginia, sent away).

3. Carter's first feeling when he saw the horse and rider was _____ (fear, anger, great delight).

4. Carter was finally convinced to shoot by his sense of _____ (honor, power, duty).

**Interpreting.** Write the answer to each question on your paper.

1. Why was Carter's father saddened when his son told him he was joining the Union soldiers?

2. Why did Carter have difficulty deciding whether or not to shoot the horseman?

3. What did Carter fear would happen if he did not shoot the horseman?

4. Why didn't the officer who saw the horseman falling through the air tell anyone about what he had seen?

**For Thinking and Discussing.** What other choices could Carter have made if he had not shot the horse?

## UNDERSTANDING LITERATURE

**Surprise Ending.** The conclusion of a story that causes some form of shock is called a *surprise ending*. A surprise ending is achieved when an author creates anticipation for an expected ending. In "A Horseman in the Sky," Carter questioned whether he should kill the man on the horse. Carter resolved his conflicts, deciding to do what was "right." We know Carter was very unhappy about taking another man's life. We are shocked to find that Carter's sorrow was not just for another soldier but for his own *father*.

There are usually small clues that warn a reader about a surprise ending. On your paper, choose the events from the following list that are hints of the surprise ending in "A Horseman in the Sky."

1. Carter had been asleep on guard duty.

2. Carter felt a "great delight" when he first saw the man on the horse.

3. Carter was a private.

4. Carter's father's words came to him, and he was able to fire his gun.

5. "Carter Druse grew pale. He was trembling and felt faint. His hand fell away from his gun."

## WRITING

Write a paragraph describing a different surprise ending for the story. You might write the ending as you would have liked it to be.

# I Will Fight No More Forever

*by Chief Joseph*

*The Nez Percé Indians lived in the beautiful Wallowa Valley in Oregon. Although they had an agreement with the U.S. government that the valley belonged to them, the government, under pressure from settlers moving west, broke the treaty. The Nez Percé were told they had to move to a reservation many miles away. War broke out between the Nez Percé and U.S. troops. Anxious to avoid more bloodshed, Chief Joseph (1841–1904) led his people to Canada. Thousands of soldiers gave chase and caught up with them only a few miles from the Canadian border. Chief Joseph surrendered on October 5, 1877, and made the following speech to his captors.*

Tell General Howard I know his heart. What he told me before, I have in my heart. I am tired of fighting. Our chiefs are killed. Looking Glass is dead. Toohoolhoolzote is dead. The old men are all dead. It is the young men who say yes and no. He who led on the young men is dead. It is cold and we have no blankets. The little children are freezing to death. My people, some of them, have run away to the hills and have no blankets, no food; no one knows where they are — perhaps freezing to death. I want to have time to look for my children and see how many I can find. Maybe I shall find them among the dead. Hear me, my chiefs. I am tired; my heart is sick and sad. From where the sun now stands I will fight no more forever.

1. What were the reasons given by Chief Joseph for his surrender? Which reason do you feel is the strongest? Explain your opinion.

2. From the evidence you are given in the speech, how would you describe Chief Joseph? What kind of leader do you think he was?

3. Instead of saying, "I will never fight again," Chief Joseph said: "From where the sun now stands I will fight no more forever." How does the wording of the phrase affect its meaning?

# A Christmas Love Story

*a true story retold by Julius Lester*

*It is pre-Civil War America. Ellen and William Craft, a married couple, are black slaves. William has been apprenticed to John Knight, a cabinetmaker; Ellen has been given to Rebecca as a maid. Ellen does not look like a slave — her skin is creamy white, her eyes are gray-green, and her hair is straight. These features are the legacy of the white man who is her father — but to him, Ellen is as much a slave as any of the others he "owns."*

*Ellen and William decide to take advantage of Ellen's looks in a clever plan to escape from slavery in Macon, Georgia. During one Christmas, they make a bold and courageous attempt to spend all their future holidays as free people. William cuts Ellen's hair short, and she dresses as a young white southern gentleman. Then they wrap white cloth around her right hand and wrist and tie it over her shoulder into a sling. Ellen is to travel as a cultivated young man on his way to Philadelphia for medical treatment with William as his faithful manservant along to assist him. It is a frightening prospect, but Ellen and William are strengthened and encouraged by their love for each other.*

*The two have asked for and received four-day passes from their "masters," so they will not be missed. They have some money saved, and Ellen has bought them two tickets for the train to Savannah — the first leg of their journey. On their trip, they both just manage to evade people who might guess their true identities, including John Knight, the cabinetmaker.*

It was evening when the train arrived in Savannah. As William put on his white hat and walked off the car, he could smell a heavy saltiness to the air. That could only be the ocean, he concluded, though he had never smelled it before.

He walked slowly forward to the car where his "master" was. When "he" descended the steps, William did not look up into that face he loved so completely, but with one hand reached for "his" hand, while taking the suitcase from "him" with the other. As Ellen stepped onto the station platform, she squeezed William's hand before releasing it.

"Were you able to rest, Master?"

"I'm afraid not, William."

"Perhaps you'll be able to sleep tonight on the steamer."

"I hope so."

The station platform was crowded with disembarking passengers and friends and family who'd come to meet them. It was Christmastime, Ellen remembered, a time for reunions and cheeriness. Or so she had observed.

She wondered why William was standing there holding the valises. Then she remembered. She was the "master" and had to find the carriage to take them to the dock to the steamer for Charleston, South Carolina.

She started slowly across the platform and through the station, William a discreet two paces behind. Once on the street, a man standing beside a carriage stepped forward quickly.

"Going to the Charleston steamer, sir?"

Ellen nodded. "Yes."

"Right this way. That your nigger?"

"Yes, he is. And a more faithful servant cannot be found in all of Georgia."

The man opened the door of the carriage. "Well, consider yourself blessed by God."

"I do," Ellen responded, smiling to herself as William took her hand and squeezed it tightly as he helped her inside.

"You can ride up top with me, boy," the carriage driver told William.

As the carriage moved slowly through the streets of Savannah, William wished it had been daylight so he might see something of this city by the ocean. It was a place favored by many wealthy whites, especially at this time of year, when the weather might turn chilly in central Georgia. He'd overheard whites in the cabinet

shop talk of plants and trees growing in this city that must be wondrous to see — palm trees, oak trees with hanging moss. It was odd to be in a place and not know exactly where he was.

If whites had not talked so casually around him at the shop and around Ellen at Rebecca's, as if slaves did not have ears or brains, they would not have known what to do. But by putting together the conversations they had overheard so many times, they learned how to travel from the South to the North and freedom. At least he hoped they had.

When they arrived at the wharf, William leaped down and opened the door to assist his "master." While he took the valises, Ellen paid the driver. They walked up the gangplank in silence, and William waited nervously while his "master" bought the tickets. The ship's captain directed the ill-looking "white man" toward "his" cabin.

Once inside, Ellen threw her free arm around William and they clung to each other for a moment.

"How are you?" William wanted to know.

"Good, I suppose," she said, weariness in her voice.

Ellen sank down onto the bed. "Could you take the sling off?"

William shook his head. "I don't think that's a good idea. What if something happens and someone comes in the middle of the night and you don't have it on?"

She sighed. "You're right. But my arm is so stiff, I wonder if I will ever have feeling in it again."

"Once we're in Philadelphia, I'll kiss it back to life," he said, smiling broadly.

"William Craft!" she exclaimed, laughing and blushing.

"I love you, wife," he said, kissing her softly. "Now, it's about time for you to go down to supper, isn't it?"

She shook her head. "Not tonight, William. I just don't think I could carry off being the young slave owner tonight."

"But you haven't eaten all day," he protested.

"I'll be fine," she reassured him. "Sleep is what I need."

"Very well. I'll see you at breakfast."

"Must you go so soon?"

"It's best not to arouse suspicion."

She nodded. "Be careful, husband."

"I will."

When William returned to the deck, he was surprised that he could not see the wharf. It took him a moment to realize that the ship was moving. How could that be? To move and not feel the motion. Was this what it felt like to be a white, fluffy cloud on an endless blue sky?

He stood at the rail for a moment, looking out into a black nothingness that he knew was the ocean. What did it look like? He couldn't imagine water so wide that there was nothing else to be seen. So dark was it, he would've thought that he had become a star against the night if he had not been able to see the stars above him.

The breeze carrying the smells of the unseen ocean was chilly now, and just as he was wondering where the colored passengers slept, the captain came up to him.

"Your master didn't look too well, boy," he said roughly.

"No, sir. He sick." William deliberately responded with the poor grammar expected of him.

The captain laughed harshly. "You'd have to be blind not to see that. What's wrong with him?"

"He sick, sir," William said, grinning. "I don't know he sickness."

"Well, I just hope he doesn't die on my boat."

"Massa die?" William exclaimed, laughing. "Aw, sir. Massa not gon' die. No, sir! He just don't look so good right now, because of all the traveling. That's all, sir."

The captain nodded. "Hope you're right," he said, and turned to walk away.

"Begging your pardon, sir?" William called after him.

The captain stopped and turned around. "What is it?"

"Where is the place the niggers sleep at?"

The captain laughed. "Boy, you know how to sleep on your feet, don't you? That's all niggers good for anyway. Sleeping and eating. Ain't no cabins on my boat for niggers." Laughing loudly, he walked away.

William walked the deck until he saw a pile of cotton sacks lying near the steamer's funnel. It was warm there and he lay down, placing his hat beside him. As tired as he was, he did not sleep, but gazed into the night sky. He remembered when he was a child, before his parents were sold. He remembered the summer nights he stared up into the night as he was doing now. It had made him feel that he wasn't a slave anymore, but just a little boy wondering why the stars did not fall out of the sky. He remembered wondering why he had been born a slave and not a star.

He wasn't a child any longer, but he wondered still, not only about that, but if the stars could see him as clearly as he saw them. Did he twinkle in the night to their eyes as they did to his?

When the sun rose, he got up and went to the rail to look at the ocean. He was disappointed that it looked scarcely different from a large, wrinkled piece of cloth. Unlike the night sky, which made him wonder about himself and the world, the ocean was simply there. It did not twinkle or brood. It just lay there.

He did not know how much time passed before he heard voices. He walked into the dining hall. Five men were sitting down to breakfast. William moved forward quickly to help his "master," who was just taking a place next to the captain.

"You seem to be feeling better this morning," the captain said to Ellen.

"Yes, thank you."

"I hope your ailment is not serious."

"I don't think so. My doctor believes it to be an attack of inflammatory rheumatism," she added, using a term she'd overheard once from one of Rebecca's dinner guests. "He recommended that I see a physician in Philadelphia."

Breakfast was served and William leaned over to cut his "master's" food into small pieces.

"Will there be anything else for now?" William asked.

"No, William."

As soon as he returned to the deck, the captain said, "You have a very attentive boy, sir. But you had better watch him like a hawk when you reach Philadelphia. I know several gentlemen who have lost valuable niggers in the North."

Before Ellen could muster a reply, a man opposite, with a long mustache that curled downward to the corners of his mouth, both elbows on the table, a large chicken breast in his hands, and a fair portion in his mouth, sputtered, "Good advice, Captain. Very good advice." He dropped the chicken breast into the plate and leaned across the table, staring intently at Ellen. "I would not take a nigger to the North under any circumstances. I have dealt with many niggers in my time. I never saw one who put his heel upon free soil that either didn't run away or amounted to a hill of beans when he came back to these parts." He picked up the piece of chicken. "Now, sir, if you wanted to sell that nigger of yours, I'm the man to talk to. Name your price, and if it's reasonable, I'll put the silver dollars on the table right this minute."

The man took a large bite out of the chicken breast, but his eyes did not waver from Ellen's face. She forced herself to meet his gaze, though she felt she was staring into Death's very own face.

"I do not wish to sell, sir," she said calmly. "I cannot get on well without him."

The man snorted. "You'll do without him pretty quick if you take him to the North. I have seen lots of niggers in my time, and I guarantee you that that is a keen nigger. I can see from the cut of his eye that he is certain to run away. You'd better sell him to me and let me put him on the market down in New Orleans."

"I think not, sir," Ellen responded firmly. "I have great confidence in his fidelity."

"Fi*devil*!" the slave trader exploded, banging his fist on the table and accidentally catching the edge of his saucer, sending the cup of hot coffee spilling into the lap of the man seated next to him. The scalded man jumped up with a sudden shriek.

The slave trader patted him on the arm. "Sit down, neighbor," he said brusquely. "Accidents will happen in the best of families." Then, pointing his finger directly at Ellen, he continued, "It makes me mad to hear a man talking about fidelity in niggers. There isn't a one who wouldn't run away, given a chance. If I was President of these United States, I wouldn't let any man take a nigger into the North and bring him back to the South. These are my flat-footed, everyday, right-up-and-down sentiments. I am a southern man, every inch of me to my backbone."

Suddenly the men at the table stood, shouting, "Three cheers for the sunny South! Hooray! Hooray! Hooray!"

Alone in the midst of the raucous yells stood a portly, balding man, the front of his trousers wet and stained with coffee. Ellen thought he looked as if he wanted to cry, and when he noticed the "young gentleman's" look of sympathy, he smiled gratefully.

Just then someone opened the dining-room door and announced that the steamer was approaching Charleston harbor. The men dispersed and Ellen returned to the cabin, grateful to find William waiting for her there.

"That was an ordeal!" she exclaimed after they embraced.

"The noise had me a little nervous."

Ellen chuckled. "Oh, they were worried about your fidelity, William. You aren't going to get up North and fall in love with some fancy northern girl, are you?"

"What are you talking about?" he asked, bewildered.

Suddenly her body slumped and William held her to him. "I was just trying to make a joke before I became hysterical," she said weakly.

"Three more days," William whispered.

"Three hundred years would not seem so long."

Knowing there would be a crowd at the dock, William and Ellen were afraid to disembark immediately, fearing they might be recognized, or that Knight had acted on his suspicion and telegraphed a message for the authorities to be on the lookout for them.

The wharf was practically deserted when they finally left the boat, William holding Ellen by the arm. A carriage took them to the hotel, one which Ellen had heard Rebecca mention as the best in Charleston.

Ellen rested through the day. That evening she and William returned to the wharf for the next part of their journey.

"A ticket for myself and my slave to Philadelphia, sir," Ellen told the ticket agent.

The agent's face was the color and texture of cheese, and he scowled through the grill. "Boy!" he yelled suddenly at William, who stood to the side.

"Sir?" William responded quickly.

"Do you belong to this gentleman?"

"Yes, sir!"

The agent turned back to Ellen. "You have to register your name here, sir, the name of your nigger, and pay a dollar duty on him."

Ellen paid the dollar and, pointing to her bandaged hand, said, "As you see, I am not able to write." This was literally true. She was glad now that she had thought of having her arm and hand bandaged. Nothing would have given them away as escaping slaves more quickly than the inability to write. "I would be grateful if you would sign for me, sir."

The agent shook his head vigorously. "I won't do it! No, sir! I won't do it!"

Ellen wondered if he suspected something. Or was he one of those people who enjoyed being contrary? Whatever his motive, it didn't matter. What would she do if he continued to refuse? Would it be something ridiculous like this that would lead to their undoing?

Just then a man with a round, pudgy face wearing a top hat walked up to Ellen, smiling. "Having a problem?" he asked warmly, patting Ellen on the back.

For an instant Ellen was confused. Then she recognized the man on whom the coffee had been spilled that morning. She smiled warmly.

"The ticket agent says I must register my slave, but as you can see, my infirmity prevents me from writing and the agent will not do the writing for me."

"Nonsense!" the man exclaimed. "See here, sir!" he continued, pointing his finger at the ticket agent. "I know this young

man's people. Good family. One of the best in the South. Now, kindly enter his and his slave's name in the register so he may be on his way."

Ellen couldn't believe what she was hearing. Why was he telling such a lie? Was he that grateful for the look of sympathy she had given him as he stood at the table looking very foolish and alone?

The ticket agent appeared confused now, and looked over his shoulder at someone Ellen could not see.

"That's good enough for me, Eli." Ellen heard a voice, then saw the captain of the steamer come into view. "I will register the gentleman's name and take the responsibility myself."

Ellen thanked the captain and her companion from the boat warmly, and William moved forward quickly to assist his "master" from the terminal and onto the steamer.

Once the steamer was under way, the captain came to Ellen and explained. "I hope that you will not take what happened as a sign of disrespect, Mr. Johnson. They make it a rule to be very strict at Charleston. I have known families to be detained there with their slaves until reliable information could be received respecting them. You know, it would be mighty easy for an abolitionist to come down here, pose as a slave owner, and take off with a lot of valuable slaves."

"Yes, you're quite right," Ellen agreed. "Quite right. I appreciate your assistance more than I can say."

William slept fitfully that night, curled in a corner of the deck near the funnel. He awoke often, however, not only concerned that they had come closer to being caught, but worried even more about Ellen. If his own nerves were frayed, Ellen's must be near to unraveling.

"Only two more days," he whispered through the night to her. "Two more days, my love."

The steamer reached Wilmington, North Carolina, after breakfast the next morning. William and Ellen transferred without incident to the train for Richmond, Virginia.

Ellen settled wearily onto the lumpy train seat. She had thought by now she would be accustomed to her role. But the closer they came to freedom, the more nervous and frightened she was. How much worse to be caught now than at the beginning. And the closer they came, the more she doubted that they would succeed. How could they? How could everyone not see there was a woman behind the bandages and green spectacles?

But maybe there was something about her that looked like a man. She wanted to take her mirror from the valise and look at herself closely to reassure herself that there was something womanly about her. She needed William to tell her how beautiful she was. When these four days were ended, she would want to hear him tell her that for the next 40,000 days, and then make him begin again.

A young woman and a man with a full and neatly trimmed black beard sat down in the seat across from her. The woman looked to be only a year or two younger than Ellen, and with her sparkling blue eyes and cheeks flushed red from the morning chill, she was quite lovely.

Though Ellen didn't want to talk, she found herself in yet another conversation about the bandages and her "health." The young woman chattered a little too eagerly, Ellen noticed, her cheeks flushing red long after the chill should've left them. When the young woman shyly and gravely offered "Mr. Johnson" an apple, her eyes cast downward, Ellen couldn't help blushing. The girl was attracted to William Johnson!

Ellen thanked the girl warmly, and didn't know what else to say, embarrassed for herself and the girl who was being deceived. Ellen pleaded fatigue, closed her eyes, and pretended to sleep.

After some moments Ellen heard a deep sigh.

"Papa, Mr. Johnson seems to be a very nice young gentleman." She sighed again. "I have never felt so much for a gentleman in my life!"

Ellen was greatly relieved when the train came to the next stop and she opened her eyes to see the man and his daughter preparing to get off.

The girl's father handed Ellen his card. "The next time you are traveling this way, Mr. Johnson, I would be honored if you would do us the kindness of calling on us. I would be pleased to see you." Smiling, he added, "I believe my daughter would be too."

The girl's face turned a deep red. "Oh, Papa!" she exclaimed. Then, trying to muster her dignity, she looked at "Mr. Johnson" and said solemnly, "It has been

a pleasure meeting you, and I will pray for your health."

"Thank you," Ellen said, holding the card in her hand, afraid to cast a glance at it for fear that she might be holding it upside down and would not know. Only when the man and his daughter had left the train did Ellen put the card in her pocket.

The ride from Richmond to Fredericksburg, Virginia, was quiet, and Ellen slept. A little beyond Fredericksburg she and William transferred without incident to the steamer for Washington, D.C.

Only two more changes, Ellen thought, as she settled into a chair on the deck. Maybe they were going to make it.

Perhaps she was more optimistic because, for the first time in three days, she was able to share part of her trip with William. He was leaning against the rail at the other end of the deck. He looked so handsome in his black suit, black cravat, and white beaver hat. When she'd seen it in the store window in Macon, she had insisted he buy it. He had been afraid it would attract too much attention on the trip. She wanted him to dress as handsome as he was, and he was the most wonderful sight she had ever seen.

"Sir!"

The harsh voice was at Ellen's shoulder, and though it startled and frightened her, she willed her body not to tremble.

"I am speaking to you, sir!"

She turned slowly to look into the angry face of a thin man peering at her through wire-rimmed spectacles. "Sir?" she responded with a coolness she couldn't feel.

"Is that your nigger?" he asked, pointing at William.

She inclined her head in a curt nod.

"What are you trying to do?" the man

sputtered, spittle flecking his lips. "Spoil him by letting him wear such a fine hat? Just look at the quality of it. The President couldn't wear a better hat. If I had my way, I'd go and kick it overboard."

A man sitting a few chairs away came over and said mildly, "Come, come, my good fellow. Don't speak in such a way to a gentleman."

"And why not?" the thin man shouted, his tiny eyes bulging. "It makes me itch all over, from head to toe, to get hold of every nigger I see dressed like a white man. That nigger ought to be sold to New Orleans and have the Devil whipped out of him."

Ellen rose quickly but calmly. "Please excuse me, gentlemen." She walked to her cabin, where she fell across the bed, her body trembling, as she bit her lip to hold back the sobs that wanted to escape from her body.

There was a knock on the cabin door. She sat up, but was afraid to know who was on the other side.

The knock came again. "Master?"

"Oh, thank God!" she sobbed, hurrying to unlock the door and admit William. "Thank God!" she repeated, clinging to him.

"It's almost over," William said softly. "It's almost over."

When the boat docked at Washington, they transferred quickly to the train for Baltimore, the last major slave port before they would enter the North.

It was night when the train arrived in Baltimore. The station was crowded with people arriving and leaving, carrying bas-kets with brightly wrapped presents.

It's Christmas Eve, William remembered, but he did not pause to look at the large Christmas tree in the station, its boughs holding tiny lighted candles. He knew that Ellen would not endure much longer, and he could feel her body trembling as he guided her through the station and onto the train for Philadelphia. There were too many people around to risk whispering to her, but he squeezed her upper arm tightly as he helped her to a seat.

As he came off the train and made his way to the Negro car, a white-haired man in a gold-braided uniform stopped him. "Where are you going, boy?" he asked sternly.

"Philadelphia with my master, sir," William replied, the quiet calm in his voice hiding the rising fear that something was wrong.

"Where is your master?"

"In the carriage I just left, sir." William smiled.

"You'd better get him out," the stationmaster said firmly. "And be quick about it! No man can take a slave past Baltimore unless he can prove that he has the right to take him along. Get him off now and bring him to my office."

William watched the stationmaster walk into the terminal. He didn't know what to do. He had never overheard any slave owner in Macon speak of needing proof of slave ownership to go from the South to the North. Maybe he should quietly disappear now. Ellen would be free, at least, and he would take his chances of finding his own way.

238

But if he just disappeared, Ellen would never know what had happened to him. He couldn't do that to her. Slowly he stepped back onto the train and saw Ellen sitting alone at the far end of the coach. She looked up and smiled when she saw him. He managed a weak smile, wondering how he was going to tell her.

"How are you feeling?" he whispered, leaning over the seat.

"Much better." Her smile was radiant. "We did it, William."

"Not quite," he said solemnly. Quickly he told her what had happened.

"No!" Ellen exclaimed loudly, then lowered her voice. "No, no, no!"

William feared she was going to dissolve into uncontrollable sobbing as she kept repeating, "No, no, no! No, William; No!"

They were less than twelve hours from Philadelphia and freedom. They couldn't have come so close to be stopped now. Could they?

William grasped her hand. "Let's go," he said gently.

"Go where?" Ellen demanded to know. "What are we going to do?"

"I don't know. Let's go to the office."

She gripped his hand fiercely. "You aren't going to trick me, are you, and run off or do something foolish? I don't want freedom without you, William Craft."

"No. Let's go to the office. We've come this far. I just can't believe that we are not meant to go all the way."

The stationmaster's office was crowded with travelers exchanging holiday greetings with the white-haired man seated behind the large desk at the end of the room. Ellen noticed the bottle of liquor on the edge of the desk, and the glasses of amber-colored liquid in the hands of the dozen or so men jammed into the tiny room. She noticed, too, that the sounds of joviality diminished as she and William made their way through the crowd. There was only silence when she and William stopped before the stationmaster.

"Did you wish to see me, sir?" she asked, her voice tiny and barely audible in her ears.

"Yes, I did," the stationmaster said. "It is against the rules of this railroad, sir, to allow any person to take a slave out of Baltimore and into Philadelphia unless he can satisfy us that he has a right to take him along."

Ellen looked at the stationmaster, at the white hair and pale blue eyes that looked at her kindly. He was just an old man doing his job, anxious for the train to leave so he could get home to spend Christmas Eve with his family. There wouldn't be any problem, she was sure.

"And why is that, sir?" she asked, her voice strong now. "Isn't the word of a white gentleman worth anything in Baltimore?" she asked indignantly.

The pale soft eyes of the stationmaster hardened so quickly that Ellen was startled, and when he spoke, his voice was so cold, Ellen could feel the warmth leaving her body. She had made a mistake, a fatal one.

"Sir, a gentleman would not question the rules of this railroad or the laws of this great city. But if you are so dense that you don't understand, let me explain. If we allowed any gentleman to take a slave past here into Philadelphia, and should the gentleman not be that slave's rightful owner, and should the lawful owner come prove that his slave escaped on our railroad, the railroad would have to pay that man what he said his slave was worth. And that money would come out of my pocket! Now do you understand?" he asked with sarcastic finality.

Ellen felt the eyes of everyone in the room on her. Suddenly there was the sound of a chuckle.

"Now, now, Arnold," someone said to the stationmaster. "That's not the proper Christmas spirit, is it?"

"Hear, hear," came another voice. "Arnold, you can plainly see the state of the gentleman's health. A gentleman in his condition needs his faithful servant."

"Furthermore," came a third voice, "you don't really think a nigger would try to run away by riding the train, do you?"

Everyone laughed at such a ridiculous idea.

"All I know," countered the stationmaster, "is that if a nigger escapes on one of my trains, the railroad will hold me responsible. A nigger like that one there probably goes for a thousand dollars. And that's a thousand dollars I don't have."

It was an argument none of the men could refute.

"Sir," one of the men said, addressing Ellen, "isn't there someone in Baltimore who can vouch for you and your slave?"

"No. I am a stranger passing through to seek medical treatment in Philadelphia." Ellen looked at the stationmaster, who was pouring himself another drink. "Sir, I bought tickets in Charleston to pass

us through to Philadelphia. Therefore you have no right to detain me here. None whatsoever!"

The words were not out of her mouth before she knew she had made another mistake. But she hadn't gotten this close to be stopped! The man had to be made to change his mind.

The stationmaster leaped up from behind the desk. "Right or no right!" he shouted. "I will not let you pass!" His face flushed red, and his arm trembled as he pointed at her and shouted even louder, "I will not let you pass!"

Everyone in the room seemed frozen. No one moved or spoke or even dared breathe, it seemed. Ellen knew that she was supposed to turn and walk out. She would have had she been able to. But she couldn't move. To turn and walk out was the end.

So she stood and stared at the stationmaster. He stared back. Leave, she told herself. Leave. There might be another way to Philadelphia. Maybe William was right. She could go ahead and, once in Philadelphia, find some means to locate him and help him escape.

If she didn't walk out soon, the stationmaster would summon the police to eject her and maybe arrest her even. And that would be the worst thing that could happen. Leave!

But she could not move. The only sound in the room was the tick-tick of the pendulum of the tall clock behind the stationmaster's desk.

The door of the office opened. Certain that the police had been summoned somehow, Ellen turned. But she had scarcely

moved before she noticed that it was only the conductor who'd been on the train from Washington to Baltimore.

He sauntered in, laughing when he saw the bottle sitting on the stationmaster's desk. "Just the thing I was looking for, Arnold," he said brightly.

"Did these two ride in with you from Washington?" the stationmaster asked abruptly, pointing to Ellen and William.

Someone handed the conductor an empty glass and he poured himself a drink. He turned and looked at Ellen and William.

"These two?" he asked, swallowing the drink quickly. He chuckled and wiped his mouth with the back of his hand. "Now, that'll keep me warm for a while." He set the glass on the desk and, nodding at Ellen and William, said, "Come in from Wash-

ington same as I did. Come all the way from Macon, Georgia, believe he said. Going to Philadelphia to see some doctor up there."

Just then the bell rang, announcing that it was time for the train to leave. "Well, time for me to go to work," the conductor said. "Merry Christmas, everyone."

"Merry Christmas," various ones called out, their minds not on Christmas at that moment but the scene in the office.

As the conductor left, the stationmaster threw up his arms and let them fall to his sides.

"I don't know what to do," he said, his voice soft now. He looked at Ellen and shrugged. "I suppose it is all right. Since you are not well, it would be a pity to stop you here."

241

A great cheer went up in the room. "That's the spirit, Arnold!" "I knew you were a good man!"

Quickly the office emptied as the men hurried to board the train, many patting Ellen on the shoulder and back as they left.

"You better hurry," the stationmaster said to Ellen. "That train isn't going to wait for you."

"Thank you, sir," Ellen said warmly. "You'll never know how deeply grateful I am."

Ellen was the center of much attention on the train. She didn't know how she managed to smile, laugh, and make conversation. She was empty now, so drained by the terror of the four days minus twelve hours, that she feared she might laugh at some harmless remark and, unable to stop, her laughter would tumble over and down into hysterical sobbing.

"You look a little pale," someone observed.

"I am somewhat weary."

"Well, we'll let you rest now."

"You're very thoughtful."

Ellen went almost immediately into a sound sleep and was startled when she heard a voice saying, "Wake up. Wake up."

"What is it?" she asked too loudly, afraid that the stationmaster had changed his mind and she was being ordered off the train.

"You have to get off, sir."

She looked into the conductor's face, panic threatening her sanity. "Is something wrong?"

"No, no," the conductor said. "We're at Havre de Grace. We have to ferry across the Susquehanna River. For the safety of the passengers, we ask them to ride on the ferry itself rather than remain in the coaches."

It was dark and cold when she stepped outside. A fine mist was falling, which chilled her quickly. She looked around for William, who always came to her whenever the train stopped. Ellen had never needed him as she did now, as the ferry moved into the cold, misty blackness of the river.

This wasn't like him. Where was he? She could make out the passengers in the light from the lanterns hanging along the ferry railing. He wasn't there! William was not there! He had been caught! She knew it!

She hurried around the ferry until she found the conductor. "Have you seen my servant, sir?"

The conductor chuckled. "Oh, he's probably run off and is in Philadelphia by now."

Ellen ignored his remark. "Could you find him for me?" she commanded.

The conductor was indignant. "I'm no slave hunter! If I had my way, every slave in the South would go free tomorrow. You'll get no help or sympathy from me!"

When the ferry stopped on the other side of the river, Ellen had not found William. She wondered if she should board the train or stay and see if she could learn what had happened to him.

She knew, however, that if he had been captured, his only solace would be knowing she was free. Reluctantly she got on the train. She was grateful for the darkness that hid the tears flowing down her face.

She didn't know that she had fallen asleep or how long she had been asleep when a voice awakened her. "Master?"

Her eyes opened quickly to see William bending over her. "Oh, William!" she exclaimed in a hushed whisper. "Where were you? I thought you—"

He put a finger to her lips to silence her, then smiled sheepishly. "I fell asleep. The conductor didn't bother to wake me when we came to the ferry. I woke up a few minutes ago and he told me that he'd told you I'd run away."

Tears flowed down her face again, but these were of relief. In the darkness she found his hand and squeezed it so tightly that he winced.

"It won't be long now," he told her.

When he returned to the Negro car, the conductor came in, chuckling. "Your master feel better now?"

"Yes, sir."

"Well, let me give you some advice, boy. When you get to Philadelphia, run away and leave that cripple and have your freedom."

"No, sir," William said indifferently. "I can't do that, sir."

"Why not?" the conductor asked, surprised. "Don't you want to be free?"

"Massa good to nigger, sir. Massa good massa, him."

The conductor was outraged. "Well, of all the dumb things I've heard in my life," he said before storming out of the car.

William was sorry he could not tell the conductor the truth. He seemed like a good man, but one could never tell.

"That was good advice he gave you," William heard a voice say.

He looked around to see a black man seated across the aisle.

"Oh?" William said noncommittally, hiding his eagerness to talk to this well-dressed black, who by the erect way he sat showed that he had never lived a day in slavery. "I be better off with massa than free nigger any day," William said, hoping the man would take the bait.

The free black needed to hear no more to begin telling William about the black churches, fraternal organizations, businesses, and social life among the blacks of Philadelphia. "Why, there are blacks and whites eager to help someone like yourself escape from slavery." He told William the name and address of a white man who had helped many runaway slaves.

William listened intently, remembering everything he heard. When the man finished, his face eagerly awaiting William's response, William said, "Massa, he good massa to nigger. Me and massa grow up like brothers, me and massa did."

The free black got up in disgust. "You've got as much sense as a brick." He moved to the other end of the coach to be as far away from William as possible.

William regretted that the man would never know the truth, nor how helpful he had been. But they were too close to take any unnecessary risks.

William drifted off to sleep, repeating the name and address of the white man over and over.

When the shrill whistle of the train awakened him, William opened his eyes and there, through the window, at the beginning of a day as gray as pewter, he saw the buildings of a large city. Philadelphia!

The train had scarcely slowed to a stop before he was out of the coach and hurrying to Ellen. Quickly they found a carriage and were being taken through the streets of the still city.

William put his arm around Ellen, and she began to cry. It was over, and she could cry now. Her body heaved with the force of the tears, as if the demons of fear and doubt were being torn from her body. She cried and William held her as if she were a child.

When the carriage stopped at the address, Ellen was so weak that William lifted her from the carriage. Through her tears she smiled, the green spectacles on her nose looking ridiculous now.

"Merry Christmas, husband," she said, feeling light in his arms, her arms around his neck.

Then she took the spectacles from her nose and tossed them high into the air. "Merry Christmas!" she shouted. "Merry Christmas, everybody!"

And she did not know her laughter from her crying, and the tears on her face shone like a smile.

## READING COMPREHENSION

**Summarizing.** Choose the best phrase to complete each sentence. Then write the complete statements on your paper.

1. The story Ellen gave for traveling North was that "he" was going to _____ (visit "his" family, seek medical treatment in Philadelphia, sell "his" slave).

2. Ellen and William almost got caught in Charleston because Ellen _____ (didn't know how to write, took off the bandages, was seen holding William's hand).

3. Ellen was embarrassed when _____ (people remarked on "his" ill health, William told her he loved her, a young woman admired "him").

**Interpreting.** Write the answer to each question on your paper.

1. How did the man on whom the coffee had been spilled help Ellen and William?

2. How did Ellen and William learn to travel from the South to the North?

3. Why were the rules about white people traveling North with slaves so strict?

4. Why did the conductor who'd been on the train from Washington to Baltimore help Ellen and William?

**For Thinking and Discussing.** If you had been Ellen or William, would you have told the last conductor and the free black man the truth? Why or why not?

## UNDERSTANDING LITERATURE

**Plot.** The plot of a story is usually centered on a problem that the character or characters face. This part of a story is called the *conflict*. When we read a story, we become interested in how the conflict will be resolved.

Many events in a story serve to develop or complicate the conflict. This adds interest and suspense. In "A Christmas Love Story," the main conflict is Ellen and William's struggle to reach the North and freedom. However, they face many problems that stand in their way.

Below are some events from the story. Write the events that serve to complicate the conflict. Then, for each event that you write, tell how the problem was resolved.

1. A slave trader wanted to buy William.

2. William deliberately spoke with the poor grammar expected of a slave.

3. In Charleston, Ellen had to register their names.

4. In Baltimore, Ellen had to show proof of slave ownership to travel on.

5. A free black man gave William the name of someone who had helped many runaways.

## WRITING

What might have happened in Georgia when Ellen and William were discovered missing? Write a paragraph describing the reactions of their masters and what they might have done to track the runaways.

# Section Review

**Idioms and Ironic Speech.** A phrase with a special meaning is called an *idiom. Kick the bucket* literally means "to knock over a bucket." But this phrase is also an idiom that means "to die." A phrase that either exaggerates or understates is called *ironic speech.* The phrase *simply fire in a liquid form* is an example of ironic speech. It exaggerates the awful taste of the medicine in "A Dose of Pain-Killer."

On your paper, write the meaning of each italicized idiom or example of ironic speech.

1. "Her troubles were instantly at rest, *her soul at peace again.*"

2. "The boy could not have shown a wilder, heartier interest if she had *built a fire under him.*"

3. "Tom lay on the floor, *expiring with laughter.*"

4. "You couldn't *steer a cow down a lane.*"

5. "You must learn this river *by heart.*"

6. ". . . he's *meaner than a snake!*"

7. "Bixby's the best pilot *since Noah steered the Ark.*"

8. "You'll be in prison for life, you *butter-faced pup.*"

**Sequence and Predicting Outcomes.** The plot of a story usually has many events, or incidents. Knowing the order in which these events happen is important in understanding the story. The order in which things happen is called *sequence.*

When you read, keep in mind the sequence of the events in the story. As you are reading, think about what might come next in the sequence. This is called *predicting outcomes.* See if you can guess what is going to happen before it does.

Here are some events from "Civil War Nurse." On your paper, write the numbers from 1 to 7, and then write the statements in the order in which they happened in the story. One statement is a prediction of something that probably happened after the story ended. One statement is unlikely to have happened and you should leave it out.

☐ Teddy's friend Kit carried the boy to safety.

☐ Alcott remembered John and her nursing experiences for the rest of her life.

☐ Alcott became the night nurse.

☐ Alcott told John he was going to die.

☐ Alcott soothed Teddy after a bad dream.

☐ Alcott and John decided to marry after he got out of the hospital.

☐ Alcott gave John his mother's letter.

☐ John asked Alcott to write a letter to his brother.

**Answers on an Essay Test.** You write a short composition whenever you answer an item on an essay test. You can prepare for a test by going through a practice run. You can focus and organize the answers you write by using the four steps of the writing process.

## Step 1: Set Your Goal

Before you begin to write an essay answer, you should read the instructions and the questions carefully. Check the instructions for guidelines about the number of items you should answer, the length of your essays, and the amount of time you have for writing. Look for key words such as *compare* or *summarize* to cue you to the kinds of answers required. You can then decide which questions to answer and how much time to devote to each one.

Read the following essay-test questions and choose one as a topic for an essay. Notice that the key word in each question has been italicized.

a. *Describe* the effect of the pain-killer in "A Dose of Pain-Killer."

b. *Compare* the characters of Bixby and Brown in "Life on the Mississippi."

c. *Summarize* the plot in "A Christmas Love Story."

d. *Discuss* the theme of bravery in "Civil War Nurse."

e. *Explain* why Carter hesitated before shooting the horseman in "A Horseman in the Sky."

## Step 2: Make a Plan

When you have chosen a question, read it at least twice, paying special attention to the key word. Then, on a piece of scrap paper or on the margins of your test paper, jot down the points that you want to include in your answer. Organize your ideas by numbering the points in the order in which you plan to present them. The key word should provide a clue to an appropriate organization.

You might follow these suggestions for focusing and organizing answers to each of the five questions.

a. *Describe* by using sensory details. Mention details in the order a viewer would notice them.

b. *Compare* by stating both similarities and differences. Choose one of these plans: (1) First state similarities and then differences. (2) First discuss one character and then the other. (3) Discuss each point of comparison, one at a time.

c. *Summarize* by listing all the main events in sequence.

d. *Discuss* by writing down your ideas as well as examples from the story that support your ideas. List each example beneath the appropriate main idea. List the main ideas in a logical order.

e. *Explain* by stating reasons. Provide examples that support your reasons. List your reasons and the supporting examples in a logical order.

## Step 3: Write a First Draft

Start your essay with an opening sentence that repeats or rephrases the test question and includes the first point you want to make. Use the following example to guide you:

Q: Describe the child's world in "There Was a Child Went Forth."

A: The child's world in "There Was a Child Went Forth" is a combination of nature at its best and people as they are.

Continue writing, using your numbered list of points. Try to stick to your plan. While you might expand on or skip over a point as you write, you probably will not have time to rethink or reorganize your answer completely.

### Step 4: Revise
Even if you don't have time for a second draft, you may have time to review your test answers for clarity and organization. Ask yourself these questions:

1. Does the opening sentence rephrase the question and introduce my first point?
2. Have I paid attention to the key word and responded to the question correctly?
3. Have I touched on all the points I want to make?

Always proofread your answers and correct mistakes in spelling, grammar, and punctuation.

## QUIZ

The following is a quiz for Section 4. Write the answers in complete sentences on your paper.

## Reading Comprehension

1. What caused the fight in the wheelhouse between Sam and Brown in "Life on the Mississippi"?

2. In "Civil War Nurse," why was Teddy haunted by his memories of Kit?

3. In "A Horseman in the Sky," why did the Union captain who saw the rider and horse fall through the air decide not to say anything?

4. What right was Sojourner Truth arguing for in "Ain't I a Woman?"

5. In "A Christmas Love Story," why did William hide his true intentions from both the sympathetic conductor and the free black man?

## Understanding Literature

6. List the sequence of events in "A Dose of Pain-Killer."

7. What emotions were presented in "There Was a Child Went Forth" and "Ain't I a Woman?" Which emotions are the most important to the poem? To the speech?

8. What effect did John's look of gratitude have on Alcott in "Civil War Nurse"? What did it cause her to do?

9. Give an example of an ironic turn of events in "A Horseman in the Sky."

10. How does the phrase "there are only losers in war" apply to "I Will Fight No More Forever"?

248

# ACTIVITIES

**Word Attack.** In "Life on the Mississippi," Sam called Brown a tyrant. The word *tyrant* is derived from the Greek word *tyrannos*. A tyrant is a harsh, cruel person.

The following words are also forms of the word *tyrannos*. Use each one in a sentence.

tyrannical

tyranny

tyrannize

What dinosaur's name is derived from *tyrannos*?

## Speaking and Listening

1. Both Sojourner Truth and Chief Joseph were great leaders; they evidently were great speakers as well. Practice reading aloud the speech given either by Sojourner Truth or Chief Joseph. As you read, try to relay the deep convictions felt by the speaker. Be prepared to deliver the speech in front of the class.

2. In 1863, President Abraham Lincoln gave one of the greatest speeches ever written when he attended the dedication of a national cemetery at Gettysburg, the site of a great but costly Union victory. Locate a copy of "The Gettysburg Address" and prepare for an oral presentation.

## Researching

1. Harriet Tubman and Frederick Douglass were both born into slavery. They escaped and became leaders of the anti-slavery movement. Do research on one of these figures and write your findings in a report.

2. Like Carter Druse in "A Horseman in the Sky," Robert E. Lee was forced to choose between his country and his family at the time of the Civil War. Unlike Druse, however, Lee decided to join the Confederacy. Use your history text and other sources to find out why Lee made this decision and how it affected his family, the South, and the entire nation.

## Creating

1. One of Mark Twain's talents was telling the kinds of "whoppers" so often invented by the characters in his stories. Make up a whopper of your own in which you explain an unusual occurrence, boast about an extraordinary feat, or exaggerate a rather ordinary feat. Trade whoppers with your classmates.

2. Suppose Sojourner Truth were alive today. How do you think she would feel about modern society? Pretend you are a talk-show host interviewing her. What questions would you ask her about her reactions to modern-day life, and what do you think her responses might be? Write down your imaginary interview.

3. If Chief Joseph had kept a diary, it would be filled with pain, hurt, and disillusionment. Suppose the Nez Percé were given back their homeland. Write this entry in the diary the way Chief Joseph would have written it.

# A WHITE HERON

## SARAH ORNE JEWETT

*Poet and essayist Ralph Waldo Emerson once wrote:*

*Most persons do not see the sun. . . . The sun illuminates only the eye of the man, but shines into the eye and the heart of the child. The lover of nature is he . . . who has retained the spirit of infancy even into the era of manhood.*

*Read about two characters who seem to be lovers of nature.*

THE woods were already filled with shadows one June evening, just before eight o'clock, though a bright sunset still glimmered faintly among the trunks of the trees. A little girl was driving home her cow, a plodding, dilatory,[1] provoking creature in her behavior, but a valued companion for all that. They were going away from the western light, and striking deep into the dark woods, but their feet were familiar with the path, and it was no matter whether their eyes could see it or not.

There was hardly a night the summer through when the old cow could be found waiting at the pasture bars; on the contrary, it was her greatest pleasure to hide herself away among the high huckleberry bushes, and though she wore a loud bell she had made the discovery that if one stood perfectly still it would not ring. So Sylvia had to hunt for her until she found her, and call "Co'! Co'!" with never an answering "Moo," until her childish patience was quite spent. If the creature had not given good milk and plenty of it, the case would have seemed very different to her owners. Besides, Sylvia had all the time there was, and very little use to make of it. Sometimes in pleasant weather it was a consolation to look upon the cow's pranks as an intelligent attempt to play hide and seek, and as the child had no playmates she lent herself to this amusement with a good deal of zest. Though this chase had been so long that the wary animal herself had given an un-

---

1. **dilatory** (dĭl′ ə tôr′ē): inclined to delay; slow.

*The Red Lane, 1918.* John Sloan.
Private Collection, courtesy of Kennedy Galleries, New York.

usual signal of her whereabouts, Sylvia had only laughed when she came upon Mistress Moolly at the swampside, and urged her affectionately homeward with a twig of birch leaves. The old cow was not inclined to wander farther; she even turned in the right direction for once as they left the pasture, and stepped along the road at a good pace. She was quite ready to be milked now, and seldom stopped to browse. Sylvia wondered what her grandmother would say because they were so late. It was a great while since she had left home at half past five o'clock, but everybody knew the difficulty of making this errand a short one. Mrs. Tilley had chased the horned torment too many summer evenings herself to blame anyone else for lingering, and was only thankful as she waited that she had Sylvia, nowadays, to give such valuable assistance. The good woman suspected that Sylvia loitered occasionally on her own account; there never was such a child for straying about out-of-doors since the world was made! Everybody said that it was a good change for a little maid who had tried to grow for eight years in a crowded manufacturing town, but, as for Sylvia herself, it seemed as if she never had been alive at all before she came to live at the farm. She thought often with wistful compassion of a wretched dry geranium that belonged to a town neighbor.

"'Afraid of folks,'" old Mrs. Tilley said to herself, with a smile, after she had made the unlikely choice of Sylvia from her daughter's houseful of children, and was returning to the farm. "'Afraid of folks,' they said! I guess she won't be troubled no great with 'em up to the old place!" When they reached the door of the lonely house and stopped to unlock it, and the cat came to purr loudly, and rub against them, a deserted pussy, indeed, but fat with young robins, Sylvia whispered that this was a beautiful place to live in, and she never should wish to go home.

The companions followed the shady woodroad, the cow taking slow steps, and the child very fast ones. The cow stopped long at the brook to drink, as if the pasture were not half a swamp, and Sylvia stood still and waited, letting her bare feet cool themselves in the shoal water, while the great twilight moths struck softly against her. She waded on through the brook as the cow moved away, and listened to the thrushes with a heart that beat fast with pleasure. There was a stirring in the great boughs overhead. They were full of little birds and beasts that seemed to be wide awake, and going about their world, or else saying good night to each other in sleepy twitters. Sylvia herself felt sleepy as she walked along. However, it was not much farther to the house, and the air was soft and sweet. She was not often in the woods so late as this, and it made her feel as if she were a part of the gray shadows and the moving leaves. She was just thinking how long it seemed since she first came to the farm a year ago, and wondering if everything went on in the noisy town just the same as when she was there; the thought of the great red-faced boy who used to chase and frighten her made her hurry along the path to escape from the shadow of the trees.

Suddenly this little woods girl was horror stricken to hear a clear whistle not very far away. Not a bird's whistle, which would have a sort of friendliness, but a boy's whistle, determined, and somewhat aggressive. Sylvia left the cow to whatever sad fate might await her, and stepped discreetly aside into the bushes, but she was just too late. The enemy had discovered her, and called out in a very cheerful and persuasive tone, "Halloa, little girl, how far is it to the road?" and trembling Sylvia answered almost inaudibly, "A good ways."

She did not dare to look boldly at the tall young man, who carried a gun over his shoulder, but she came out of her bush and again followed the cow, while he walked alongside.

"I have been hunting for some birds," the stranger said kindly, "and I have lost my way, and need a friend very much. Don't be afraid," he added gallantly. "Speak up and tell me what your name is, and whether you think I can spend the night at your house, and go out gunning early in the morning."

Sylvia was more alarmed than before. Would not her grandmother consider her much to blame? But who could have foreseen such an accident as this? It did not appear to be her fault, and she hung her head as if the stem of it were broken, but managed to answer "Sylvy," with much effort when her companion again asked her name.

Mrs. Tilley was standing in the doorway when the trio came into view. The cow gave a loud moo by way of explanation.

"Yes, you'd better speak up for yourself, you old trial! Where'd she tuck herself away this time, Sylvy?" Sylvia kept an awed silence; she knew by instinct that her grandmother did not comprehend the gravity of the situation. She must be mistaking the stranger for one of the farmer lads of the region.

The young man stood his gun beside the door, and dropped a heavy game bag beside it; then he bade Mrs. Tilley good evening, and repeated his wayfarer's story, and asked if he could have a night's lodging.

"Put me anywhere you like," he said. "I must be off early in the morning, before day; but I am very hungry, indeed. You can give me some milk at any rate, that's plain."

"Dear sakes, yes," responded the hostess, whose long slumbering hospitality seemed to be easily awakened. "You might fare better if you went out on the main road a mile or so, but you're welcome to what we've got. I'll milk right off, and you make yourself at home. You can sleep on husks or feathers," she proffered graciously. "I raised them all myself. There's good pasturing for geese just below here towards the

253

*Cobb House, 1942.* Edward Hopper.
Worcester Art Museum, Massachusetts. Gift of Stephen C. Clarke.

ma'sh.[2] Now step round and set a plate for the gentleman, Sylvy!" And Sylvia promptly stepped. She was glad to have something to do, and she was hungry herself.

It was a surprise to find so clean and comfortable a little dwelling in this New England wilderness. The young man had known the horrors of its most primitive housekeeping, and the dreary squalor of that level of society which does not rebel at the companionship of hens. This was the best thrift of an old-fashioned farmstead, though on such a small scale that it seemed like a hermitage.[3] He listened eagerly to the old woman's quaint talk, he watched Sylvia's pale face and shining gray eyes with ever growing enthusiasm, and insisted that this was the best supper he had eaten for

---

2. **ma'sh:** marsh. The grandmother's New England speech omits certain sounds, such as the *r* sound, in many words.

3. **hermitage** (hûr′ mĭ tĭj): a place where a person lives alone in an isolated area; a monastery.

a month; then, afterward, the new-made friends sat down in the doorway together while the moon came up.

Soon it would be berry time, and Sylvia was a great help at picking. The cow was a good milker, though a plaguy[4] thing to keep track of, the hostess gossiped frankly, adding presently that she had buried four children, so that Sylvia's mother, and a son (who might be dead) in California were all the children she had left. "Dan, my boy, was a great hand to go gunning," she explained sadly. "I never wanted for pa'tridges or gray squer'ls while he was to home. He's been a great wand'rer, I expect, and he's no hand to write letters. There, I don't blame him, I'd ha' seen the world myself if it had been so I could.

"Sylvia takes after him," the grandmother continued affectionately, after a minute's pause. "There ain't a foot o' ground she don't know her way over, and the wild creatures counts her one o' themselves. Squer'ls she'll tame to come an' feed right out o' her hands, and all sorts o' birds. Last winter she got the jaybirds to bangeing[5] here, and I believe she'd 'a' scanted herself of her own meals to have plenty to throw out amongst 'em, if I hadn't kep' watch. Anything but crows, I tell her, I'm willin' to help support—though Dan he went an' tamed one o' them that did seem to have reason same as folks. It was round here a good spell after he

went away. Dan an' his father they didn't hitch[6]—but he never held up his head ag'in after Dan had dared him an' gone off."

The guest did not notice this hint of family sorrows in his eager interest in something else.

"So Sylvy knows all about birds, does she?" he exclaimed, as he looked round at the little girl who sat, very demure but increasingly sleepy, in the moonlight. "I am making a collection of birds myself. I have been at it ever since I was a boy." (Mrs. Tilley smiled.) "There are two or three very rare ones I have been hunting for these five years. I mean to get them on my own ground if they can be found."

"Do you cage 'em up?" asked Mrs. Tilley doubtfully, in response to this enthusiastic announcement.

"Oh, no, they're stuffed and preserved, dozens and dozens of them," said the ornithologist,[7] "and I have shot or snared every one myself. I caught a glimpse of a white heron three miles from here on Saturday, and I have followed it in this direction. They have never been found in this district at all. The little white heron, it is," and he turned again to look at Sylvia with the hope of discovering that the rare bird was one of her acquaintances.

But Sylvia was watching a hoptoad in the narrow footpath.

"You would know the heron if you

---

4. plaguy (plā′ gē): annoying.
5. bangeing (bănj′ ĭng) *(Maine dialect)*: taking advantage of another's hospitality.

6. **hitch:** get along well together.
7. **ornithologist** (ôr′ nə **thŏl′** ə jĭst): a person who studies birds.

saw it," the stranger continued eagerly. "A queer tall white bird with soft feathers and long thin legs. And it would have a nest perhaps in the top of a high tree, made of sticks, something like a hawk's nest."

Sylvia's heart gave a wild beat; she knew that strange white bird, and had once stolen softly near where it stood in some bright green swamp grass, away over at the other side of the woods. There was an open place where the sunshine always seemed strangely yellow and hot, where tall, nodding rushes grew, and her grandmother had warned her that she might sink in the soft black mud underneath and never be heard of more. Not far beyond were the salt marshes and beyond those was the sea, the sea which Sylvia wondered and dreamed about, but never had looked upon, though its great voice could often be heard above the noise of the woods on stormy nights.

"I can't think of anything I should like so much as to find that heron's nest," the handsome stranger was saying. "I would give ten dollars to anybody who could show it to me," he added desperately, "and I mean to spend my whole vacation hunting for it if need be. Perhaps it was only migrating, or had been chased out of its own region by some bird of prey."

Mrs. Tilley gave amazed attention to all this, but Sylvia still watched the toad, not divining, as she might have done at some calmer time, that the creature wished to get to its hole under the doorstep, and was much hindered by the unusual spectators at that hour of the evening. No amount of thought, that night, could decide how many wished-for treasures the ten dollars, so lightly spoken of, would buy.

The next day the young sportsman hovered about the woods, and Sylvia kept him company, having lost her first fear of the friendly lad, who proved to be most kind and sympathetic. He told her many things about the birds and what they knew and where they lived and what they did with themselves. And he gave her a jackknife, which she thought as great a treasure as if she were a desert islander. All day long he did not once make her troubled or afraid except when he brought down some unsuspecting singing creature from its bough. Sylvia would have liked him vastly better without his gun; she could not understand why he killed the very birds he seemed to like so much. But as the day waned, Sylvia still watched the young man with loving admiration. She had never seen anybody so charming and delightful; the woman's heart, asleep in the child, was vaguely thrilled by a dream of love. Some premonition of that great power stirred and swayed these young foresters who traversed the solemn woodlands with soft-footed silent care. They stopped to listen to a bird's song; they pressed forward again eagerly, parting the branches, speaking to each other rarely and in whispers; the young man going first and Sylvia following, fascinated, a few steps behind, with her gray eyes dark with excitement.

She grieved because the longed-for white heron was elusive, but she did not lead the guest, she only followed, and there was no such thing as speaking first. The sound of her own unquestioned voice would have terrified her—it was hard enough to answer yes or no when there was need of that. At last evening began to fall, and they drove the cow home together, and Sylvia smiled with pleasure when they came to the place where she heard the whistle and was afraid only the night before.

Half a mile from home, at the farther edge of the woods, where the land was highest, a great pine tree stood, the last of its generation. Whether it was left for a boundary mark, or for what reason, no one could say; the woodchoppers who had felled its mates were dead and gone long ago, and a whole forest of sturdy trees, pines and oaks and maples, had grown again. But the stately head of this old pine towered above them all and made a landmark for sea and shore miles and miles away. Sylvia knew it well. She had always believed that whoever climbed to the top of it could see the ocean; and the little girl had often laid her hand on the great rough trunk and looked up wistfully at those dark boughs that the wind always stirred, no matter how hot and still the air might be below. Now she thought of the tree with a new excitement, for why, if one climbed it at break of day, could not one see all the world, and easily discover whence the white heron flew, and mark the place, and find the hidden nest?

What a spirit of adventure, what wild ambition! What fancied triumph and delight and glory for the later morning when she could make known the secret! It was almost too real and too great for the childish heart to bear.

All night the door of the little house stood open, and the whippoorwills[8] came and sang upon the very step. The young sportsman and his old hostess were sound asleep, but Sylvia's great design kept her broad awake and watching. She forgot to think of sleep. The short summer night seemed as long as the winter darkness, and at last when the whippoorwills ceased, and she was afraid the morning would after all come too soon, she stole out of the house and followed the pasture path through the woods, hastening toward the open ground beyond, listening with a sense of comfort and companionship to the drowsy twitter of a half-awakened bird, whose perch she had jarred in passing. Alas, if the great wave of human interest which flooded for the first time this dull little life should sweep away the satisfactions of an existence heart to heart with nature and the dumb[9] life of the forest!

There was the huge tree asleep yet in the paling moonlight, and small and hopeful Sylvia began with utmost bravery to mount to the top of it, with tin-

_____

8. **whippoorwills:** birds that are active at night; their call sounds like their name.
9. **dumb:** silent.

gling, eager blood coursing the channels of her whole frame, with her bare feet and fingers, that pinched and held like bird's claws to the monstrous ladder reaching up, up, almost to the sky itself. First she must mount the white oak tree that grew alongside, where she was almost lost among the dark branches and the green leaves heavy and wet with dew; a bird fluttered off its nest, and a red squirrel ran to and fro and scolded pettishly at the harmless housebreaker. Sylvia felt her way easily. She had often climbed there, and knew that higher still one of the oak's upper branches chafed against the pine trunk, just where its lower boughs were set close together. There, when she made the dangerous pass from one tree to the other, the great enterprise would really begin.

She crept out along the swaying oak limb at last, and took the daring step across into the old pine tree. The way was harder than she thought; she must reach far and hold fast, the sharp dry twigs caught and held her and scratched her like angry talons, the pitch made her thin little fingers clumsy and stiff as she went round and round the tree's great stem, higher and higher upward. The sparrows and robins in the woods below were beginning to wake and twitter to the dawn, yet it seemed much lighter there aloft in the pine tree, and the child knew that she must hurry if her project were to be of any use.

The tree seemed to lengthen itself out as she went up, and to reach farther and farther upward. It was like a great mainmast[10] to the voyaging earth; it must truly have been amazed that morning through all its ponderous frame as it felt this determined spark of human spirit creeping and climbing from higher branch to branch. Who knows how steadily the least twigs held themselves to advantage this light, weak creature on her way! The old pine must have loved his new dependent. More than all the hawks, and bats, and moths, and even the sweet-voiced thrushes, was the brave, beating heart of the solitary gray-eyed child. And the tree stood still and held away the winds that June morning while the dawn grew bright in the east.

Sylvia's face was like a pale star, if one had seen it from the ground, when the last thorny bough was past, and she stood trembling and tired but wholly triumphant, high in the treetop. Yes, there was the sea with the dawning sun making a golden dazzle over it, and toward that glorious east flew two hawks with slow-moving pinions.[11] How low they looked in the air from that height when before one had only seen them far up, and dark against the blue sky. Their gray feathers were as soft as moths; they seemed only a little way from the tree, and Sylvia felt as if she too could go flying away among the clouds. Westward, the woodlands and farms reached miles and miles into the distance; here and there were church steeples, and

---

10. **mainmast:** the principal pole that supports the sails on a sailing ship.
11. **pinion** (pĭn′ yən): a bird's wing.

white villages; truly it was a vast and awesome world.

The birds sang louder and louder. At last the sun came up bewilderingly bright. Sylvia could see the white sails of ships out at sea, and the clouds that were purple and rose-colored and yellow at first began to fade away. Where was the white heron's nest in the sea of green branches, and was this wonderful sight and pageant of the world the only reward for having climbed to such a giddy height? Now look down again, Sylvia, where the green marsh is set among the shining birches and dark hemlocks; there where you saw the white heron once you will see him again; look, look! a white spot of him like a single floating feather comes up from the dead hemlock and grows larger, and rises, and comes close at last, and goes by the landmark pine with steady sweep of wing and out-stretched slender neck and crested head. And wait! wait! do not move a foot or finger, little girl, do not send an arrow of light and consciousness from your two eager eyes, for the heron has perched on a pine bough not far beyond yours, and cries back to his mate on the nest, and plumes his feathers for the new day!

The child gives a long sigh a minute later when a company of shouting cat-birds comes also to the tree, and vexed by their fluttering and lawlessness the solemn heron goes away. She knows his secret now, the wild, light, slender bird that floats and wavers, and goes back like an arrow presently to his home in the green world beneath. Then Sylvia, well satisfied, makes her perilous way down again, not daring to look far below the branch she stands on, ready to cry sometimes because her fingers ache and her lamed feet slip. Wondering over and over again what the stranger would say to her, and what he would think when she told him how to find his way straight to the heron's nest.

"Sylvy, Sylvy!" called the busy old grandmother again and again, but nobody answered, and the small husk bed was empty, and Sylvia had disappeared.

The guest waked from a dream, and remembering his day's pleasure hurried to dress himself that it might sooner begin. He was sure from the way the shy little girl looked once or twice yesterday that she had at least seen the white heron, and now she must really be persuaded to tell. Here she comes now, paler than ever, and her worn old frock is torn and tattered, and smeared with pine pitch. The grandmother and the sportsman stand in the door together and question her, and the splendid moment has come to speak of the dead hemlock tree by the green marsh.

But Sylvia does not speak after all, though the old grandmother fretfully rebukes her, and the young man's kind appealing eyes are looking straight in her own. He can make them rich with money; he has promised it, and they are poor now. He is so well worth making happy, and he waits to hear the story she can tell.

No, she must keep silence! What is it that suddenly forbids her and makes her dumb? Has she been nine years growing, and now, when the great world for the first time puts out a hand to her, must she thrust it aside for a bird's sake? The murmur of the pine's green branches is in her ears, she remembers how the white heron came flying through the golden air and how they watched the sea and the morning together, and Sylvia cannot speak; she cannot tell the heron's secret and give its life away.

Dear loyalty, that suffered a sharp pang as the guest went away disappointed later in the day, that could have served and followed him and loved him as a dog loves! Many a night Sylvia heard the echo of his whistle haunting the pasture path as she came home with the loitering cow. She forgot even her sorrow at the sharp report[12] of his gun and the piteous sight of thrushes and sparrows dropping silent to the ground, their songs hushed and their pretty feathers stained and wet with blood. Were the birds better friends than their hunter might have been—who can tell? Whatever treasures were lost to her, woodlands and summertime, remember! Bring your gifts and graces and tell your secrets to this lonely country child.

---

12. **report:** gunshot.

## THINKING ABOUT THE STORY

*Recalling*
1. How old is Sylvia, and where had she lived before coming to her grandmother's farm? How does Sylvia feel about living there?
2. Describe how Sylvia reacts when she first encounters the young man. How does the grandmother respond to his request to spend the night?
3. What does the young man do with the birds he shoots? How does he want Sylvia to help him?
4. Why does Sylvia decide to climb the great pine tree? What does she see when she reaches the treetop?
5. What does Sylvia do when she is urged to reveal the location of the white heron's nest?

*Interpreting*
6. Compare Sylvia's and the young man's attitudes toward nature. How are they similar? How are they different?
7. Identify Sylvia's **internal conflict**. Between what opposing loyalties must she decide?
8. Reread the story's last three sentences. What "treasures" do you suppose Sylvia lost by resolving her internal conflict as she did? What "gifts and graces" do you suppose she gained?
9. What do you suppose the great pine tree and the white heron **symbolize** in this story?

*Applying*
10. What situations can you imagine in which loyalty to one's self and principles is more important than loyalty to friends or family?

## ANALYZING LITERATURE

*Understanding Realism*
Today, so many works of fiction have a true-to-life quality about them that it is difficult to believe that realism became an important movement in American literature little more than a hundred years ago. As a style of literature, **realism** attempts to depict characters and events as they would be in real life. Settings are described in objective detail and resemble places that may seem familiar to readers or even ordinary. Realist writers avoid idealizing and glamorizing their subjects and do not shy away from depicting real human suffering.

In your opinion, how realistic is "A White Heron"? Consider the following questions in your analysis of the story.
1. Which details of setting might a reader have expected to find on a real New England farm in the late 1800's? Which details, if any, seem glamorized?
2. Do the characters seem like people you might meet in real life? Explain.
3. Do the events of the story seem truly possible? Which events, if any, seem far-fetched or fanciful?

261

## CRITICAL THINKING AND READING

*Drawing Conclusions*

Though Sarah Orne Jewett grew up in rural Maine and lived in South Berwick, she often visited Boston and was familiar with the nearby manufacturing centers, such as Lowell, Massachusetts, where the Industrial Revolution began in the United States. What evidence can you find in "A White Heron" to support the following proposition?

Sarah Orne Jewett believed that the spread of urban society in America threatened not only traditional rural values but also the human spirit itself.

In answering, consider these points:
• where Sylvia was born
• where and how the young man probably lives when he is not on vacation
• the young man's attitudes toward "primitive housekeeping" and nature
• how Jewett describes the pine tree that Sylvia climbs

## DEVELOPING LANGUAGE SKILLS

*Dialect and Regionalisms*

A **dialect** is a variation within a language. It includes pronunciations, grammatical constructions, and words peculiar to a particular group within the general population. A dialect also includes regionalisms. According to the *Dictionary of American Regional English*, a **regionalism** is "any word or phrase whose form or meaning is not used generally throughout the United States but only in part (or parts) of it."

In "A White Heron," the speech of Mrs. Tilley, Sylvia's grandmother, is characteristic of the dialect of English spoken in Maine. For example, she drops her *r*'s after an open *a* sound, as in "pa'tridges." She uses unusual grammatical expressions, such as "while he was to home" instead of the more usual "while he was home." And she uses regionalisms that might puzzle someone not from Maine, such as "bangeing." Jewett's ability to re-create Maine dialect in her writing is one way she gives her stories local color and realism.

1. Find at least one other example each of a pronunciation, grammatical expression, and regionalism that characterizes Mrs. Tilley's speech as dialect.

2. Make a list of several pronunciations, grammatical constructions, and regionalisms that are characteristic of your particular area of the country.

## THINKING AND WRITING

**1. Writing About an Author's Purpose.**

What purpose do you think the author had in telling the story of Sylvia's decision to keep the white heron's secret?

Write a short essay in which you identify Jewett's purpose and support your opinion with evidence from the story.

**Prewriting.** In determining Jewett's purpose, think about Jewett's depiction of nature in the story and the different ways that Sylvia and the young man respond to nature. Think also about the attitudes that Jewett reveals in the story regarding rural life versus urban life.

**Writing.** Make sure your essay begins with a clear statement that identifies Jewett's purpose. Support your opinion by citing at least three items of evidence from the story.

**Revising.** Check that you have organized your ideas logically. Can you strengthen your argument by adding additional evidence from the story?

**Proofreading.** Reread your essay, and correct any mistakes in grammar, spelling, and punctuation. Be sure that you have used quotation marks correctly. If necessary, prepare a neat final copy.

**Publishing.** Read your essay to the class.

## 2. Writing a Personal Essay.
In "A White Heron," the author uses the elements of fiction to convey a belief regarding human attachment to nature. She could have written of her own beliefs directly, using personal observations to support her opinions. Write a personal essay in which you express your feelings and beliefs about nature.

**Prewriting.** Begin by making notes for yourself. What central point about nature do you wish to convey to your audience? What personal observations can you use not only to prove your central point but also to make your essay lively and interesting for your readers?

**Writing.** Begin your essay with an appropriate **anecdote**, a short, entertaining account of an incident that bears some relation to the central point of your essay. Follow this anecdote with a statement of your central point, or main idea. Then support your statement with observations drawn from your personal experience and from your reading.

**Revising.** Make your essay a pleasure for your audience to read. Are your examples interesting as well as informative? Do they all relate to the main idea you wish to get across?

**Proofreading.** Reread your personal essay and correct any mistakes in grammar, spelling, and punctuation. If necessary, prepare a neat final copy.

**Publishing.** Submit your essay to the school or local newspaper for publication on its opinion page.

# VOICES OF IMAGINATION

## *1840-1898*

*A Light exists in Spring*
*Not present in the year*
*At any other period*
*When March is scarcely here.*

*A Color stands abroad*
*On Solitary Fields*
*That Science cannot overtake*
*But Human Nature Feels.*

— Emily Dickinson

*Landscape with Rainbow*
Robert Scott Duncanson (1821/1822-1872)
National Museum of American Art/Smithsonian Institution
Gift of Leonard Granoff

# Voices of Imagination: 1840–1898

**S**cience and reason can't fully explain everything that people think and feel. Storytellers and poets have always understood this. During the years 1840–1898, many of America's finest authors explored the unreasonable side of the human mind.

### Creating an Effect

Edgar Allan Poe is famous for his suspenseful tales. His ideas for stories came not from the events of everyday life, but from his desire to create a certain effect. Often the effect he aimed for was terror. As you will see when you read "The Pit and the Pendulum," he was very successful.

Unlike Edgar Allan Poe, mountain man Jim Bridger did use his life experiences as the basis for his fantastic tales. In 1844, Bridger told St. Louis newspaper reporters of the hot springs, geysers, and other natural wonders that he had found when exploring the Yellowstone region. When people didn't believe him, Bridger began telling tall tales about highly exaggerated events and fantastic places. These tales were amazing and funny. They were retold again and again in newspapers of his era. In this section, you will read a tall tale based on one of Bridger's original tales.

Emily Dickinson never explored the West, never saw a spouting geyser or a giant redwood tree. She seldom left her home in Amherst, Massachusetts. Her poetry presents a unique vision of everyday events and things. She shares her emotions in her poems and reminds us that we, too, have powerful feelings that are not always easy to understand.

### The Supernatural

Supernatural tales — stories that involve ghosts, witches, or magic — all deal with the clash of the forces of good and evil. Sometimes these tales remind us of the good and evil in real life.

Charles W. Chestnutt's parents were born in slavery. He grew up hearing true stories about the lives of slaves and fantastic stories based on the ancient African tales of magic, or conjuring. His supernatural tales do more than create a mood of terror or a vivid image of an unusual event. His conjure stories are set on Southern plantations before the Civil War. Like "Poor Sandy," the story included here, these tales reflect the evils of slavery.

Another author whose work often re-

**The Grand Canyon of the Yellowstone,** Thomas Moran, 1872

flects the struggle between good and evil is Henry James. "The Turn of the Screw" vividly describes the thoughts and feelings of a young woman who believes she is surrounded by evil forces.

Certainly James did not model this tale on his own experience, but it did stem from his own emotions. In the 1870's and 1880's, he had suffered many personal tragedies, including the deaths of his sister and several of his closest friends. He was living in an old English country house and felt surrounded by doom. In "The Turn of the Screw," his feelings and imagination join forces to create one of the most suspenseful ghost stories ever written.

Frank Stockton's stories are typically offbeat, and "The Griffin and the Minor Canon" is no exception. His unlikely hero, a modest clergyman, wins the respect of a fearsome monster, but this admiration could prove dangerous to his health!

Realistic literature may describe people's feelings. But the realistic literature of the 19th century almost always reflected the way people *should* feel and the way they *should* behave. Writers of imaginative literature freed themselves from the boundaries of reality. They proved that real feelings and emotions can come alive in impossible places and through supernatural events.

# The Pit and the Pendulum

*by Edgar Allan Poe*

*Edgar Allan Poe (1809–1849) is one of the most popular American authors of all time. His tales of horror and suspense are widely read today. They have also been made into popular movies and teleplays. The story you are about to read is a retelling of Poe's famous tale of terror and torture "The Pit and the Pendulum." We begin this story after a prisoner who has been condemned to death faints and awakens in a strange cell. Poe describes the torment of this man as he awaits his execution by methods almost too horrible to imagine. . . .*

**I** awakened, but did not open my eyes. I reached out my hand and it fell upon something damp and hard. I struggled to imagine where I could be. I longed to, yet dared not, open my eyes. It was not that I feared to look upon things horrible, but that I was terrified that there might be *nothing* to see.

At length, with a wild desperation, I quickly opened my eyes. My worst thoughts, then, were confirmed. The blackness of eternal night enclosed me. I struggled for breath. The intensity of the darkness seemed to overwhelm me.

I rose to my feet and stepped cautiously about my prison. As I walked, there came rushing into my memory a thousand tales told of the horrors of the dungeons of Toledo. Was I left to perish of starvation in this underground world of darkness? Perhaps a fate even more fearful awaited me. That the result would be death, I had no doubt. The method and the hour were all that now occupied my mind.

My outstretched hands at length touched something solid. It was a wall — very smooth, slimy, and cold. I felt along it, but I could get no idea of the size of my dungeon.

At first, I walked with extreme caution, for the floor was treacherous with slime. At length, however, I took courage, and stepped firmly — trying to walk as direct a line as possible. I had advanced some

10 or 12 paces in this manner when I slipped and fell violently on my face.

In the confusion, I did not at first realize a somewhat startling fact. In a few seconds it came to me: my chin rested upon the floor of the prison, but my lips, and the upper portion of my head, touched nothing. At the same time, the smell of decayed fungus rose to my nostrils. I put forward my arm, and shuddered to find that I had fallen at the edge of a circular pit.

Groping about the floor I was able to dislodge a small fragment, and let it fall into the pit. For many seconds, I listened to its sounds as it dashed against the sides of the wall in its descent. At length, there was a gloomy plunge into water, followed by loud echoes. At the same moment, there came the sound of the quick opening, and rapid closing, of a door overhead, while a faint gleam of light flashed suddenly through the blackness, and as suddenly faded away.

I saw clearly the doom which had been prepared for me, and congratulated myself upon the timely accident by which I had escaped. Another step before my fall, and the world would have been no more!

Shaking in every limb, I felt my way back to the wall — deciding there to die rather than risk the terrors of the wells. My imagination now pictured them to be in many places about the dungeon.

Terror kept me awake for many long hours, but at length I again slumbered. Upon arousing, I found by my side, as before, a loaf and a pitcher of water. A burning thirst consumed me, and I emptied the vessel at a swallow. It must have been drugged — for scarcely had I drunk, before a deep sleep fell upon me — a sleep like that of death. How long it lasted, I know not; but when, once again, I opened my eyes, the objects around me were visible. A hellish light now lit the interior of the prison.

It was not more than 25 yards around. The walls were made of iron, or some other metal, in huge plates. I now noticed the floor, too, which was of stone. In the center yawned the circular pit from whose jaws I had escaped.

All this I saw unclearly and by much effort — for my personal condition had been greatly changed during slumber. I now lay upon my back, and at full length, on a low, wood frame. To this I was securely tied by a long strap resembling a belt. It wound many times around my body, leaving only my head and my left arm free, so that I could, with much effort, supply myself with food from an earthen dish which lay by my side on the floor.

Looking upward, I surveyed the ceiling of my prison. It was some 30 or 40 feet overhead, and from a heavy steel rod was hung a huge pendulum, such as we see on old clocks. There was something about the thing which caused me to look at it more closely. While I gazed directly upward at it (for its position was directly over my own) I thought that I saw it move. In an instant, I realized that I was right. Its sweep was brief and slow. I watched it for some minutes somewhat in fear, but more in wonder.

A slight noise attracted my notice, and looking to the floor, I saw several enormous rats crossing it. They had entered from the well which lay just within view to my right. Even while I gazed, they came up in troops, hurriedly, with ravenous eyes, attracted by the scent of the meat. It required much effort to scare them away.

It might have been half an hour, perhaps even an hour, before I again looked upward. What I then saw confused and amazed me. The sweep of the pendulum had increased by nearly a yard, and its speed was, as a result, much greater. But what mainly disturbed me was that it had noticeably *descended*. I now observed — with what horror I need not say — that its lower edge was a crescent-shaped blade of glittering steel, about a foot long; the lower edge as sharp as that of a razor. The whole thing *hissed* as it swung through the air. I could no longer doubt the doom prepared for me.

What matters it to tell of the long, long hours of horror during which I counted the rushing movements of the steel! Inch by inch, down and still down it came! Many days passed — before it swept so closely over me as to fan me with its breath. The odor of the sharp steel forced itself into my nostrils. I prayed for it to descend faster. I grew frantically mad, and struggled to force myself upward against the sweep of its fearful blade. And then I fell suddenly calm, and lay smiling at the glittering death.

I saw that the blade was designed to cross my body at the heart. It would cut the threads of my clothing — it would return and repeat its operations — again — again. In spite of its wide sweep (some

30 feet or more) and the hissing speed of its descent, still the cutting of my clothing would be all that, for several minutes, it would accomplish.

Down — steadily down it swept. To

the right — to the left — far and wide —
with the shriek of a spirit of the damned,
I laughed and howled.

Down — certainly, relentlessly down!
It swung within three inches of my chest.

I saw that some 10 or 12 sweeps would
bring the steel in actual contact with my
clothing — and now there suddenly came
over my spirit the calmness of despair.
For the first time in many hours — or
perhaps days — I *thought*. There flashed
upon my mind the idea of release. I began
at once to free myself.

For many hours the immediate area
where I lay had been swarming with rats.
They were wild, bold, ravenous — their
red eyes glaring upon me. "To what food,"
I thought, "have they been accustomed in
the well?"

They had devoured, in spite of all my
efforts to prevent them, all but a small
portion of the contents of the dish. With
the bits of the oily and spicy food which
now remained, I rubbed the belt wherever
I could reach it; then, raising my hand
from the floor, I lay breathlessly still.

At first, the ravenous animals were
startled and terrified at the change — in
the stoppage of movement. But this was
only for a moment. Observing that I did
not move, one or two of the boldest leaped
upon the framework, and sniffed at the
belt. This seemed the signal for the general
rush.

Up from the well they hurried in fresh
troops. They leaped in hundreds upon my
body. The movements of the pendulum
did not disturb them at all. Avoiding its
strokes, they busied themselves with the
belt. They swarmed upon me in ever
greater heaps. They gathered upon my
throat; their cold lips sought my own.
Disgust swelled my chest and chilled my

heart. Yet one minute more, and I felt that the struggle would be over. Plainly I felt the loosening of the belt. With a more than human effort, I lay *still*.

At length, I felt that I was *free*. The belt hung in shreds from my body. But the stroke of the pendulum already pressed upon my chest. It had cut through the threads of my clothing. Twice again it swung, and pain shot through every nerve. But the moment of escape had arrived. At a wave of my hand the rats quickly scurried away. With a slow steady movement, I slid from the hold of the belt and beyond the reach of the blade. For the moment, at least, *I was free*.

I had scarcely moved from my wooden bed of horror when the pendulum stopped. I saw it drawn up, by some invisible force, through the ceiling. This was a chilling lesson. My every motion was being watched. I had escaped death in one form of agony, only to be delivered to worse than death in some other.

With that thought, I looked nervously around at the wall of iron that hemmed me in. Something unusual — some change had taken place in the dungeon. I became aware, for the first time, of the origin of the strange rays which lit up the cell. They came from a crack, about half an inch wide, extending entirely around the prison at the base of the walls. The walls were completely separated from the floor.

Even while I breathed there came to my nostrils the steam of heated iron! A suffocating odor filled the prison! I panted! I gasped for breath! I shrank from the glowing metal to the center of the cell.

Amid the thought of fiery destruction that approached, the idea of the coolness of the well came over my soul. I rushed to its deadly edge and peered over. For a wild moment, my spirit refused to understand the meaning of what I saw. At length it forced its way into my soul. Oh — any horror but this! With a shriek, I rushed from the edge and buried my face in my hands — weeping bitterly.

The heat rapidly increased, and once again I looked up. There had been a second change in the cell — and now the change was in the shape. With a low rumbling or moaning sound, the dungeon had shifted its shape as the walls began to steadily press in upon themselves. I could have clasped the red walls to my chest as a garment of eternal peace. "Death," I said, "any death but that of the pit!"

Flatter and flatter grew the walls, with a speed that left me no time for thought. I shrank back from the pit — but the closing walls pressed me steadily onward.

Soon there was no longer an inch of footing on the firm floor of the prison. I struggled no more, but the agony of my soul was voiced in one loud, long, and final scream of despair. I felt that I swayed upon the edge — I looked away.

There was a loud hum of human voices! There was a loud blast as of many trumpets! There was a harsh grating as of a thousand thunders! The fiery walls rushed back! An outstretched arm caught my own as I fell, fainting, into the well. It was that of General LaSalle. The French army had entered Toledo. The city was in the hands of its enemies.

## READING COMPREHENSION

**Summarizing.** Choose the best phrase to complete each sentence. Then write the complete statements on your paper.

1. At first the prisoner walked cautiously because he _____ (knew he was being watched, was very weak from his ordeal, found the floor very slippery).

2. The purpose of the pendulum was to _____ (frighten the rats, torture and kill, keep the prison clock going).

3. The prisoner rubbed his belt with food so that _____ (he could save some for later, the oils would rot the material, the rats would chew the belt loose).

4. The prisoner was finally saved by _____ (a French general, a kind guard, falling into the well).

**Interpreting.** Write the answer to each question on your paper.

1. How did the prisoner know that, in the cell, there was a deep pit with water at the bottom of it?

2. Which torture was the prisoner saved from by luck? Which by cleverness?

3. How did darkness contribute to the prisoner's terror?

**For Thinking and Discussing.** What do you think was the most terrifying part of the prisoner's experience? Was his torture mental or physical? Why do you think Poe set up the story in this way?

## UNDERSTANDING LITERATURE

**Mood and Imagery.** In a literary selection, *mood* is the feeling the author creates with the words that he or she uses. The mood influences the way the reader feels when reading. For example, the mood could be lighthearted and make the reader happy. Or the mood could be terrifying and make the reader uneasy or fearful.

In "The Pit and the Pendulum," Poe created a mood of horror by using *imagery*, words that appeal to the senses.

Read each sentence below. On your paper, write which one of your senses is affected: sight, smell, hearing, touch, or taste.

1. "The blackness of eternal night enclosed me."

2. "It was a wall — very smooth, slimy, and cold."

3. "At the same time, the smell of decayed fungus rose to my nostrils."

4. "At length, there was a gloomy plunge into water, followed by loud echoes."

5. "A burning thirst consumed me, and I emptied the vessel at a swallow."

6. "Flatter and flatter grew the walls, with a speed that left me no time for thought."

## WRITING

Write a few paragraphs about either a very good or very bad experience you've had. Create a mood by including descriptive sentences that appeal to the five senses.

# Jim Bridger and the Fiddler Who Wouldn't Fiddle

*a Jim Bridger tale retold by Sid Fleischman*

*Jim Bridger (1804–1881) was a fur trapper and mountain man, a skilled pathfinder who became the first white man to see the Yellowstone region and other areas of the West. He was also a famous storyteller. A newspaper reporter named Ned Buntline wrote his stories down and made them famous. Here, Sid Fleischman, a modern writer with a great fondness for the Old West, retells one of Jim's tales.*

Jim Bridger was a long-haired mountain man. In fringed buckskins and Indian moccasins, he wandered through the wilderness of the Old West before almost anyone else. It was Jim who brushed the hair out of his eyes and first discovered the Great Salt Lake. They might have named it after him, but no one believed he'd found water you couldn't sink in. Jim shrugged his big, bony shoulders and headed back to the mountains.

One day his horse broke three front teeth grazing on a patch of green grass. That's how Jim discovered a petrified forest. The grass and trees had turned to stone for miles around. "Petrified, all petrified," he reported when he got back to civilization. "The bees and the wild flowers, and yes, sir, in some of those trees sat petrified birds singing petrified songs."

But he's not famous for all those things.

Jim Bridger was a ramshackle, sharp-eyed army scout. In time they named a fort and a forest after him, and a pass and a creek and a mountain or two.

He once pointed to a mountain in the distance, flat-topped and red as a Navajo blanket. "Stranger," he said. (Jim liked to talk to strangers; they were so few and far between in the wilderness.) "Stranger, look how that mountain has grown! When I first came out here, it was nothing but a red anthill."

And that's what Jim Bridger's famous for. That mountain. He made an alarm clock out of it.

The way it happened, Jim was out in the wilderness as usual, when a blizzard whipped down out of Canada. He traveled through the snow for days and nights. He didn't dare to stop and rest. He knew a man could sleep himself to death in the blizzard and bitter cold.

Jim was all tuckered out, and he knew he couldn't go much farther. Then, through the chill daylight, he caught sight of that red, flat-topped mountain in the distance. It was slab-sided, too, and he had bounced echoes off it many a time. He reckoned from where he now stood, it would take about eight hours for an echo to return.

Jim Bridger gave a yip of joy and made camp. He laid out his bedroll on the snow. Then he gave an ear-quivering yell.

"WAKE UP! WAKE UP, JIM BRIDGER, YOU FROSTBIT, NO-ACCOUNT RASCAL!"

Then he climbed into his bedroll, clamped his eyes shut, and fell away to snoring. Oh, he snored thunderbolts, and dreamed of hot biscuits and gravy.

Exactly seven hours and 56 minutes later, Jim Bridger's alarm clock went off.

"WAKE UP!" roared the echo. "WAKE UP, JIM BRIDGER, YOU FROSTBIT, NO-ACCOUNT RASCAL!"

Jim roused from his bedroll, refreshed and feeling strong as a new rope. It was a week before he reached Fort Bridger, where the sun was shining and no one believed his story.

But a trapper came straggling in and said, "It's true, every word. I found the coals of Jim's campfire and bundled up in furs to catch some shut-eye. Next thing, I knew, that mountain commenced booming. I didn't get a wink of sleep. Doggonit, Jim, you snore loud enough to drive pigs to market!"

Some time later Jim Bridger was coming back from exploring Yellowstone when he bumped into a brand-new town. It stood smack-dab on the spot where he'd camped the day of the big blizzard. But folks didn't know he'd been there first, so they didn't name the place after him. They called it Blue Horizon.

Blue Horizon didn't amount to much, but it did have a general store, a stable, a blacksmith, and a funeral parlor.

Jim said his howdys, but everyone he met had the grumbles. Sitting around the stove in the general store, he tried to cheer them up by reporting the wonders seen in the Yellowstone.

"Durn my gizzard if steaming water didn't shoot up out of the earth. And boiling water flows out of the rocks into the prettiest lake full of trout you ever saw."

"Can't no trout live in boiling water," grumbled the mayor, chewing a cigar as if it were beef jerky.

"You're exactly right," Jim answered. "Down below, the water's cold as a frog. The hot spring floats on top. Oh, I ate a mess of trout and never once had to build a cook fire and get out my skillet."

The mayor kept chomping his cigar. Jim could see nobody gave a hoot about his hot-and-cold lake. They didn't even accuse him of lying.

"Something bothering you gents?" he asked.

The mayor nodded. "We got to call off the barn dance tonight. The fiddler won't fiddle."

Now Jim Bridger loved a frolic, and it had been a long time since he'd kicked his heels to a jolly tune.

"Who's the fiddler?" he asked.

"Buryin' John Potter, the undertaker. He's hornet-mad because folks didn't elect him mayor instead of me."

The more Jim Bridger thought about it, the more his feet hankered for fiddle music. So he sauntered across the street to the undertaker's parlor.

"You can't fool me, Buryin' John Potter," said Jim. "I see your fiddle on the wall, but that don't mean you can play a note. On purpose, I mean."

"Can, but won't," grumbled Potter. He was hollow-cheeked, sharp-chinned, and long in the arms. Wearing his black claw-hammer coat, he looked like a crow, except that he chewed tobacco.

"No, sir," Jim said. "If you was to saw your fiddling bow across those catgut

music. Once heard Jingle-Bob Earl play a frolic back in Missouri, and I guess you'll agree he's the best fiddler who ever was."

"Faw," snorted Buryin' John Potter. "He couldn't play high C if he was standing on a stepladder. I'm the mightiest fiddler who ever was — but I ain't fiddlin' tonight."

And Jim said, "I brought a gourd plugged full of hot steam from the Yellowstone, and it's still perishin' hot. That Yellowstone steam takes years to cool off. I figured to use that gourd as a foot warmer. The nights are turning chilly already, wouldn't you say? Buryin' John, that Yellowstone foot warmer is yours if you can play the screen box half as clever as Jingle-Bob Earl. Come outside and prove it."

The undertaker took down his fiddle, and the two men rode out to a distant spot west of town not far from Jim's echo mountain. Buryin' John tuned his strings, clamped his sharp jaw on the edge of the fiddle box and began beating time with one foot as if he were pounding a stake into the ground. He spit tobacco juice and ripped out "Turkey in the Straw."

Jim thought he'd never heard it played so sweet, but he said, "Won't do. Jingle-Bob Earl played louder 'n that. His fiddling rattled windows for miles around. Do you know 'Scooping Up Pawpaws'? Or 'Have You Seen My New Shoes?'"

"Both," Buryin' John muttered, and commenced sawing away twice as loud as before. The music raised the sap in Jim's feet. It was all he could do to keep from leaping to his heels and raising dust.

Then the undertaker lifted his chin

strings, I'll wager you couldn't hit two notes out of five."

"Haw," said the undertaker, smirking.

"Reckon you don't even know 'Chicken in the Bread Tray Pickin' Up Dough.' "

"By heart," said the undertaker sourly. "But I ain't fiddlin' tonight. Don't think you can sweet-word me into changing my mind."

"Wouldn't think of it," Jim replied. "But I'm a powerful fine judge of fiddle from the fiddle and shot tobacco juice to one side. "Reckon that gourd foot warmer is mine," he declared.

"Not so hasty," said Jim. "You call that a contest? Why, Jingle-Bob Earl could fiddle all night without playing the same tune twice."

The undertaker rosined his horsetail bow, tucked the fiddle back under his jaw, and scraped away. Hour after hour the bow cut wild figures in the air. Now and then Buryin' John squirted tobacco juice without missing a note. Jim had never heard such limber-armed fiddling. It was an ear-quivering wonder.

Finally the sun began to dive for home. Jim jumped up, stomped his feet to the music and sang out.

*You could fiddle down a possum*
*from a mile-high tree.*
*You could fiddle up a whale*
*from the bottom of the sea!*

And he said, "Buryin' John, you win! You're the mightiest fiddler that ever was! The Yellowstone foot warmer is yours."

When Jim got back to the general store, it was falling dark. "Head for the barn!" he exclaimed. "The frolic's about to commence."

The barn filled up in no time. Folks stood around waiting for Buryin' John. They'd heard him practicing his fiddle all day long. A mule began to bray, but they couldn't dance to that. Dogs began to bark, but they couldn't dance to that.

Finally, the mayor, who was there to do the fiddle calling, said, "Can't be a frolic without a fiddler. We might as well go home."

"Keep your hair on, Mayor, and the barn doors open. All the windows, too," said Jim, cupping an ear. "Coming this way is the grandest, mightiest fiddling you ever heard. Caller, clear your throat!"

Suddenly, bounding back from Jim's slab-sided echo mountain, came the first notes of "Turkey in the Straw." So taken by surprise were the folks in the barn that they stood frozen like bird dogs on point.

Then Jim leaped to the center of the floor with hours of stored-up frolic in his feet. He kicked his heels and the dance was on. The fiddle caller aired his lungs.

*Grab your partners, make a square,*
*Music's comin' from I don't know where!*

The rafters shook with a romping and a stomping, and the barn was aswirl with calico skirts. The mayor shucked his coat and kept calling.

*Dive for the oyster; dig for the clam.*
*Dive for the sardine; take a full can.*

Suddenly the undertaker, in his black claw-hammer coat, loomed up in the doorway. When he saw all the jollification, the wad of tobacco jumped out of his mouth.

"Durn my gizzard, if it ain't Buryin' John!" Jim called out.

"That's my fiddlin'!"

"Oh, you're a sly one." Jim laughed, thinking fast. "That was eternally clever of you to echo your fiddling so you could kick your heels to your own music. Had everybody fooled, you did! They thought you was hornet-mad. Don't stand there stiff as a crowbar. Grab a partner, Buryin' John, and lift your hooves to the mightiest fiddler that ever was."

**Summarizing.** Choose the best phrase to complete each sentence. Then write the complete statements on your paper.

1. Jim was able to use the mountain as an alarm clock because _____ (the mountain used to be an anthill, no one else knew it was there, noises echoed from its flat sides).

2. The undertaker agreed to play his fiddle for Jim because _____ (he needed the money, no one else could do it, Jim bet that the undertaker wasn't the best fiddler).

3. The music for the square dance came from _____ (the mayor and his helpers, the echoes of the undertaker's playing, Jim Bridger himself).

**Interpreting.** Write the answer to each question on your paper.

1. Why did everyone in Blue Horizon have "the grumbles" when Jim Bridger walked into town?

2. Why didn't Jim Bridger tell Buryin' John that he'd never heard "Turkey in the Straw" played so well?

3. Why did Jim Bridger give Buryin' John credit for thinking up the idea of echoing his fiddle music off the mountain?

**For Thinking and Discussing.** Do you think this story would be as funny without the exaggerations? Could the story be told without exaggeration?

**Mood.** An author creates a mood by the way he or she tells a story. The mood of the tall tale about Jim Bridger is lighthearted and humorous.

Read the following pairs of sentences. On your paper, tell which one in each pair creates a humorous mood.

1. a. One day his horse broke three front teeth grazing on a patch of green grass.
   b. One day his starving horse was trying to chew a mouthful of grass when his three front teeth shattered.

2. a. Jim felt like dancing after having been in the wilderness for so long.
   b. The music raised the sap in Jim's feet.

3. a. Then Jim leaped to the center of the floor with hours of stored-up frolic in his feet.
   b. Jim stomped angrily to the middle of the floor and kicked for hours.

Write an exaggerated description of a person, place, or thing. Create a mood that makes the reader laugh. Here is an example to get you started. You may build on this or you may create a totally original paragraph.

The car was very fast. When I drove it somewhere, I always arrived two minutes before I left home.

# Three poems by Emily Dickinson

*Emily Dickinson (1830–1886) had a happy childhood and went to college. As an adult, she stayed in her house in Amherst most of the time, seeing only family members. She wrote many letters, however, and hundreds of short poems. Her poems are about the timeless themes of love, nature, and the human soul.*

## "Hope" Is the Thing With Feathers

*by Emily Dickinson*

"Hope" is the thing with feathers —
That perches in the soul —
And sings the tune without the words —
And never stops — at all —


And sweetest — in the Gale — is heard —
And sore must be the storm —
That could abash the little Bird
That kept so many warm —

I've heard it in the chillest land —
And on the strangest Sea —
Yet, never, in Extremity,
It asked a crumb — of Me.

---

1. The poet says, "Hope is the thing with feathers." To what is she comparing hope?
2. What words and phrases does she use in the poem to further this comparison?

# A Word Is Dead

*by Emily Dickinson*

A word is dead
When it is said,
Some say,
I say it just
Begins to live
That day.

1. We use words to express our ideas and feelings. What does the image of a dead word suggest?

2. What does the image of a living word suggest? Do all words live on after they are spoken, or just some? Explain.

**The Conversation**, Eastman Johnson, 1875–1880

# The Wind Tapped Like a Tired Man

*by Emily Dickinson*

The wind tapped like a tired man,
And like a host, "Come in,"
I boldly answered; entered then
My residence within.

A rapid, footless guest,
To offer whom a chair
Were as impossible as hand
A sofa to the air.

No bone had he to bind him,
His speech was like the push
Of numerous humming-birds at once
From a superior bush.

His countenance a billow,
His fingers, if he pass
Let go a music, as of tunes
Blown tremulous in glass.

He visited, still flitting;
Then, like a timid man,
Again he tapped — 'twas flurriedly —
And I became alone.

---

**1.** What words and phrases does Dickinson use to describe the wind?

**2.** Was the movement of the wind strong or gentle? Which words in the poem show this?

---

**Summarizing.** Choose the best phrase to complete each sentence. Then write the complete statements on your paper.

1. Hope, according to Emily Dickinson, _____ (is a very costly and rare thing, needs to find shelter in a storm, gives much and asks for nothing).

2. Emily Dickinson believed that words _____ (should always be written, are often quickly forgotten, come alive when spoken).

3. Dickinson compared the wind to _____ (a warm summer's day, bits of broken glass, a tired man with a bird-like voice).

4. The poet didn't offer her guest a chair because he _____ (would rather have had a sofa, couldn't sit down, told her he didn't want one).

**Interpreting.** Write the answer to each question on your paper.

1. How long does hope's tune go on for, once hope "perches in the soul"?

2. What imagery does Dickinson use in " 'Hope' Is the Thing With Feathers" to describe the difficult times we all go through?

3. What is timid about the wind?

**For Thinking and Discussing.** Why do you think the poet compared the wind to a tired man?

**Personification.** Imagery in literature is the use of words or details to create pictures in the reader's mind. One type of imagery is *personification*.

Personification means treating ideas, animals, or other objects as though they were human.

For example, Emily Dickinson talked about words as though they could live or die, and she described the wind by comparing it to a tired man.

Reread the poem "The Wind Tapped Like a Tired Man." On your paper, make a list of the phrases Emily Dickinson used to describe the wind as though it were a man. Then tell which of your senses each comparison appeals to. One example is:

"His speech was like the push/Of numerous humming-birds at once/From a superior bush." This image helps you feel and hear the wind. It appeals to your senses of touch and hearing.

Write a short poem or paragraph in which you use personification to describe one of the following subjects:

a rainstorm
a motorcycle
a guitar

Through your use of imagery, make sure you treat your subject as though it were human.

# Poor Sandy

*by Charles W. Chestnutt*

*Charles Chestnutt (1858–1932) began publishing his stories in*
The Atlantic Monthly *magazine in 1887. The story that
follows is set in North Carolina just before the Civil War.
Chestnutt called "Poor Sandy" a conjure tale because the
story draws on ancient African legends of conjure doctors
who had supernatural powers. A conjure woman mixed roots
and herbs into a "goopher" mixture to make powerful
magic. As you will see in this story, however, the results of
conjuring were not always predictable.*

**S**andy used to belong to old Master
Marlboro. You know the old Marlboro
place on the other side of the swamp.
Well, Sandy was a mighty good hand, he
could do many things around the plantation. In fact, he did his work so well
that when Master Marlboro's children
grew up and married, they all wanted their
daddy to give them Sandy for a wedding
present. But Master Marlboro knew the
rest wouldn't be satisfied if he gave Sandy
to just one of them. So when they were
all married, Master Marlboro gave Sandy
to each of his children for a month or so.
When they all had had him the same
length of time, he was passed around again
and again. Once in a while, Master Marlboro would lend Sandy to some of his
other kinfolks when they were short-
handed. Well, this went on until it got so
Sandy didn't hardly know where he was
going to stay from one day to the other.

One time when Sandy was lent out as
usual, a speculator came along with a lot
of slaves, and Master Marlboro swapped
Sandy's wife off for a new woman. When
Sandy came back Master Marlboro gave
him a dollar and allowed he was mighty
sorry to break up the family, but the
speculator had given him a good offer,
and times were hard and money scarce,
so he was best to make the trade. Sandy
took on something about losing his wife,
but he soon saw it wasn't no use crying
over spilt molasses. And being as he liked
the looks of the new woman, he took up
with her after she had been on the plantation a month or so.

Sandy and his new wife got on mighty
well together, and the rest of the slaves
all commenced to talk about how loving
they were. When Tenie took sick once,
Sandy set up all night with her, and then
went to work in the morning just like he

had his regular sleep, and Tenie would have done anything in the world for her Sandy.

Sandy and Tenie hadn't been living together for more than two months before Master Marlboro's old uncle, who lived down in Robinson County, sent word up if Master Marlboro couldn't let him hire him a good hand for a month or so. Sandy's master was one of these here easygoing folks who wanted to please everybody, so he says yes, he could lend him Sandy. So Master Marlboro told Sandy to get ready to go down to Robinson County the next day to stay for a month.

It was mighty hard on Sandy to be taken away from Tenie. It was so far down to Robinson County that he didn't have no chance of coming back to see her until the time was up. He wouldn't mind coming 10 or 15 miles at night to see Tenie, but Master Marlboro's uncle's plantation was more than 40 miles off. Sandy was mighty sad and cast down after what Master Marlboro had told him.

He told Tenie, "I'm getting tired of this here going around so much. Here I am lent to Master James this month, and I got to do so and so. Then to Master Archie the next month, and I got to do so and so. Then I got to go over to Miss Jenny's, and it's Sandy this and Sandy that, and Sandy here and Sandy there, until it appears to me that I ain't got no home, no master, no mistress, no nothing. I can't even keep a wife. My other woman was sold away without my getting a chance to tell her good-bye. And now I got to go off and leave you, Tenie, and I don't know whether I'm ever going to see you again

or not. I wish I was a tree, or a stump, or a rock, or something that could stay on the plantation for a while."

After Sandy got through talking, Tenie didn't say a word, but just sat there by the fire, thinking and thinking. Finally she upped and said:

"Sandy, I ain't never told you I was a conjure woman?"

Of course Sandy had never dreamed of nothing like that, and he made a great admiration when he heard what Tenie had said.

By and by, Tenie went on. "I ain't goophered nobody, nor done no conjure work, for fifteen years or more. When I got religion I made up my mind I wouldn't work no more goopher. But there are some things I don't believe it's no sin to do, and if you don't want to be sent around from pillar to post, and if you don't want to go down to Robinson County, I can fix things so you won't have to. If you'll say the word, I can turn you into whatever you want to be, and you can stay right where you want to as long as you got a mind to."

Sandy didn't care, he was willing to do anything to stay close to Tenie. So Tenie asked him if he didn't want to be turned into a rabbit.

Sandy said, "No, the dogs might get after me."

"Shall I turn you into a wolf?"

"No, everybody is scared of a wolf, and I don't want nobody to be scared of me."

"Shall I turn you into a mockingbird?"

"No, a hawk might catch me. I want to be turned into something that will stay in one place."

"I can turn you into a tree," said Tenie. "You wouldn't have no mouth nor ears, but I can turn you back once in a while so you could get something to eat, and hear what was going on."

"Well," said Sandy, "that'll do."

And so Tenie took him down by the swamps, not far from the slave quarters, and turned him into a big pine tree, and set him out among some other trees. The next morning, as some of the field hands were going along there, they saw a tree that they didn't remember, or else one of the saplings had been growing mighty fast.

When Master Marlboro discovered that Sandy was gone, he thought he had run away. He got the dogs out, but the last place they could track Sandy to was the foot of that pine tree. And there the dogs stood and barked and bayed and pawed at the tree, and tried to climb up on it. When they were taken around through the swamp to look for the scent, they broke loose and made for the tree again. It was the darnedest thing the white folks had ever heard of, and Master Marlboro figured that Sandy must have climbed up on the tree and jumped off on a mule or something, and rode far enough to spoil the scent. Master Marlboro wanted to accuse some of the other slaves of helping Sandy run off, but they all denied it to the last, and everybody knew Tenie set too much in store by Sandy to help him run away where she couldn't never see him no more.

When Sandy had been gone long enough for folks to think he done got clean away, Tenie used to go down to the woods at night and turn him back. Then they would slip up to the cabin and sit by the fire and talk. But they had to be careful, or else somebody would see them, and that would spoil the whole thing. So Tenie always turned Sandy back in the morning early, before anybody was stirring.

But Sandy didn't get along without his trials and tribulations. One day a woodpecker came along and started to peck at the tree. The next time Sandy was turned back he had a little round hole in his arm, just like a sharp stick had been stuck in it. After that, Tenie set a sparrow hawk to watch the tree, and when the woodpecker came along the next morning to finish his nest, he got gobbled up before he stuck his bill in the bark.

Another time, Master Marlboro sent a slave out in the woods to chop turpentine boxes. The man chopped a box in this here tree and hacked the bark up two or three feet, in order to let the turpentine run. The next time Sandy was turned back he had a big scar on his left leg, and it took Tenie about all night to make a mixture to fix him up. After that Tenie set a hornet to watch the tree, and when the slave came back again to cut another box on the other side of the tree, the hornet stung him so hard that the axe slipped and cut his foot about off.

When Tenie saw so many things happening to the tree, she concluded she would have to turn Sandy into something else. And after studying the matter over, and talking with Sandy one evening, she made up her mind to fix up a goopher mixture that would turn herself and Sandy into foxes, or something, so that they could run away and go someplace where

they would be free and live like white folks.

Tenie had got the night set for her and Sandy to run away, when that very day young Master Dunkin, one of Master Marlboro's sons, rode up to the big house in his buggy and said his wife was mighty sick and he wanted his mama to lend him a woman to nurse his wife. The mistress said to send Tenie, since she was a good nurse. Of course the young master was in a terrible hurry to get back home. Tenie said she would go right along with her young master, but she tried to make some excuse to get away and hide until night, when she would have everything fixed up for her and Sandy. She said she wanted to go to her cabin to get her bonnet. Her missus said it didn't matter about the bonnet, her head-handkerchief was good enough. Then Tenie said she wanted to get her best frock; her missus said no, she didn't need no more frocks, when that one got dirty she could get a clean one where she was going. So Tenie had to get in the buggy and go along with young Master Dunkin to his plantation, which was more than 20 miles away. There wasn't no chance for her seeing Sandy no more until she came back home. The poor woman felt mighty bad about the way things was going on and she knew Sandy

must be wondering why she didn't come and turn him back no more.

While Tenie was away nursing young Master Dunkin's wife, Master Marlboro took a notion to build him a new kitchen and being as he had lots of timber on his place, he began to look around for a tree to have the lumber sawed out. I don't know how it came to be so, but he happened to hit on the very tree Sandy was turned into. Tenie was gone, and there wasn't nobody near to watch the tree.

The two men that cut the tree down said they never had such a time with a tree before. Their axes would glance off

and didn't appear to make no progress through the wood. And the creaking, shaking, and wobbling you ever did see, that tree did when he commenced to fall. It was the darnedest thing!

When they got the tree all trimmed up, they chained it up to a timber wagon and started for the sawmill. But they had a hard time getting the log there. First they got stuck in the mud when they were going across the swamp and it was two or three hours before they could get out. When they started on again the chain kept coming loose, and they had to keep stopping to hitch the log up again. When they commenced to climb the hill to the sawmill, the log broke loose and rolled down the hill and in among the trees, and it took about half a day more to get it hauled up to the sawmill.

The next morning after the day the tree was hauled to the sawmill, Tenie came home. When she got back to her cabin, the first thing she did was to run down to the woods and see how Sandy was getting on. When she saw the stump standing there with sap running out of it, and the limbs laying there scattered around, she almost went out of her mind. She ran to her cabin and got her goopher mixture, then followed the tracks of the timber wagon to the sawmill. She knew Sandy couldn't live no more than a minute or so if she turned him back, for he was all chopped up so he had to be dying. But she wanted to turn him back long enough for her to explain that she hadn't gone off on purpose and left him to be chopped down and sawed up. She didn't want him to die with hard feelings toward her.

The men at the sawmill had just got the big log on the carriage, and was starting up the saw, when they saw a woman running up the hill all out of breath, crying and going on just like she was plumb distracted. It was Tenie. She came right into the mill and threw herself on the log, right in front of the saw. She was hollering and crying to her Sandy to forgive her, and not think hard of her for it wasn't no fault of hers. Then Tenie remembered the tree didn't have no ears, and she was getting ready to work her goopher mixture so as to turn Sandy back, when the mill hands caught ahold of her and tied her arms with a rope, fastened her to one of the posts in the sawmill, and then they started the saw up again and cut the log up into boards right before her eyes. But it was mighty hard work, for all the squeaking and moaning and groaning that log did while the saw was going through it.

The saw was one of these there old-timers, up and down saws, and it took them days longer to saw a log then it does now. They greased the saw, but that didn't stop the fuss. It kept right on, until finally they got the log all sawed up.

When the overseer who ran the sawmill came from breakfast, the hands told him about the crazy woman that had come running into the sawmill, a-hollering and going on, and tried to throw herself before the saw. The overseer sent two or three of the hands to take Tenie back to her master's plantation.

Tenie appeared to be out of her mind for a long time, and her master had to lock her up in the smokehouse until she got over her spells. Master Marlboro was mighty mad. It would have made your flesh crawl to hear him cuss, because he said the speculator had fooled him by working a crazy woman off on him. While Tenie was locked up in the smokehouse, Master Marlboro took and hauled the lumber from the sawmill and put up his new kitchen.

When Tenie got quieted down, so she could be allowed to go around the plantation, she up and told her master all about Sandy and the pine tree. When Master Marlboro heard it, he allowed she was the most distracted slave he had ever heard of. He didn't know what to do with Tenie. First he thought he would put her in the poorhouse, but finally, seeing as she didn't do no harm to nobody nor nothing, but just went around moaning and groaning and shaking her head, he decided to let her stay on the plantation and nurse the little black children while their mothers were working in the cotton fields.

The new kitchen Master Marlboro built wasn't much used. It hadn't been put up long before the slaves started to notice queer things about it. They could hear something moaning and groaning about the kitchen in the nighttime, and when the wind would blow they could hear something hollering and squeaking like it was in great pain and suffering. It got so after a while that it was all Master Marlboro's wife could do to get a woman to stay in the kitchen in the daytime long enough to do the cooking. There wasn't a slave on the plantation that wouldn't rather take 40 lashes than to go about that kitchen after dark, that is, except Tenie. She didn't

appear to mind the spirits. She used to slip around at night and sit on the kitchen steps leaning up against the door, talking to herself with a kind of foolishness that nobody could make out. Master Marlboro had threatened to send her off the plantation if she said anything to any of the other slaves about the pine tree. But somehow or another the slaves found out all about it and they all knew the kitchen was haunted by Sandy's spirit. It even got so that Master Marlboro's wife herself was scared to go out in the yard after dark.

When it came to that, Master Marlboro tore the kitchen down and used the lumber to build a schoolhouse. The schoolhouse wasn't supposed to be used except in the daytime, but on dark nights folks going along the road would hear queer sounds and see queer things. Poor old Tenie used to go down there at night and wander around the schoolhouse. The slaves all knew that she went to talk with Sandy's spirit.

One winter morning when one of the boys went to school early to start the fire, what should he find but poor old Tenie, lying on the floor, stiff and cold and dead. There didn't appear to be nothing particular the matter with her. She had just grieved herself to death for her Sandy.

## READING COMPREHENSION

**Summarizing.** Choose the best phrase to complete each sentence. Then write the complete statements on your paper.

1. Tenie turned Sandy into a tree _____ (because she hated him, so he wouldn't have to leave her, so he could talk about his roots).

2. Tenie did not come to Sandy one night because she _____ (was tired of him, had to take care of a sick woman, ran away).

3. When Tenie ran into the sawmill to save Sandy, the men _____ (tried to help her, stopped the saw, tied her up).

4. Tenie died from _____ (sadness over the loss of Sandy, old age, Master Marlboro's anger).

**Interpreting.** Write the answer to each question on your paper.

1. Why did Master Marlboro want Sandy's tree chopped down?

2. How did Master Marlboro treat Sandy?

3. Why was everyone afraid of the kitchen and the schoolhouse made from the pine tree?

**For Thinking and Discussing.**

1. What did Sandy learn from his first marriage that influenced the way he behaved in his second marriage?

2. What did you learn about the life of a slave from "Poor Sandy"?

## UNDERSTANDING LITERATURE

**Imagery.** Imagery is the use of words that appeal to the senses and stir the reader's imagination. An author's use of imagery often helps create a mood, or atmosphere. Imagery can influence the reader's feelings about what he or she is reading. In parts of the story "Poor Sandy," the author painted such vivid word pictures that you may have found yourself horrified.

Read the following passages. On your paper, identify the sense each one appeals to. Then tell how each makes you feel.

1. "When she saw the stump standing there with sap running out of it, and the limbs laying there scattered around, she almost went out of her mind."

2. "One winter morning when one of the boys went to school early to start the fire, what should he find but poor old Tenie, lying on the floor, stiff and cold and dead."

## WRITING

Imagine that you are Tenie. Think of something other than a tree to turn Sandy into. Write one paragraph telling about the advantages of what you have chosen. Write another paragraph telling of the disadvantages. In your description, use imagery to help your readers know what Sandy is like. In his new form, what will he look like? What sounds will he make? How will he feel to the touch? Will he have an odor? A taste?

# The Turn of the Screw

*by Henry James*

*One of the best-known stories by Henry James (1843–1916) is "The Turn of the Screw." As you will discover in reading this retelling of the story, "The Turn of the Screw" is more than a ghost story. It shows a struggle between the forces of good and evil.*

*After a brief introduction, the story is told from the point of view of a young woman. She tells you what she thinks is going on. But it is up to you, the reader, to decide how much is real and how much is her imagination. As you read this story, ask yourself these questions: Are the ghosts real or imaginary? Who is good and who is evil in the story?*

A group of friends was sitting around a fireplace one night, telling ghost stories. A man named Douglas said he knew a ghost story that no one there had ever heard before. "For horror," he said, "there is nothing like it. Perhaps because it involves children, the strangeness and terror of the tale are given another twist, another turn of the screw."

His friends begged him to tell them the story. He said it had been written by a governess he had known many years ago. She had sent it to him before she died. He kept it locked in a drawer in his house in London. He would send a messenger with a key to get it. Then he would read it to them.

Meanwhile, he would tell his friends what he knew about her. This is what he said that night.

When her story began, she was 20 years old and the daughter of a poor minister. She needed a job, so she went to London to answer a newspaper ad in person. The gentleman she met was a handsome bachelor who lived in a fine house.

He told her that he had a young niece and nephew who were orphans. The little girl, Flora, was living at his home in the country. The housekeeper, Mrs. Grose,

was taking care of her. The boy, Miles, was at boarding school. He would join them when the summer vacation began.

The uncle said the children needed a governess to look after them and be their teacher. Their first governess, Miss Jessel, had died.

At first, the young woman did not want to take the job. It would be lonely caring for two children in the country. Also, the uncle said he did not want to be bothered about them. She would have to take care of everything herself.

She wasn't sure she could handle the job. But the uncle was so charming and such a gentleman that she could not refuse.

The next night, the story written by the governess arrived. Douglas began to read it to his friends. From now on, the story is told in her own words.

Did I make a mistake in taking the job? I thought so during the long ride to the uncle's house in the country. I was sure the house would be small and gloomy. But when I arrived, I had a pleasant surprise. The house was large and sunny.

I was welcomed by a stout, wholesome woman — Mrs. Grose. She introduced me to Flora, the younger of my two pupils. Flora was the most beautiful and charming child I had ever seen. She looked like an angel in a painting. It would be a joy, I thought, to teach such a girl.

My room was one of the best in the house. It had a large bed for me and a small one for Flora.

That night, I had trouble sleeping. Near dawn, I thought I heard the cry of a child from far away. A little later, I heard a light footstep outside my door. But I did not think much of those sounds then. I was too happy thinking of the wonderful child whose life I would share.

In the morning, I asked Mrs. Grose about Flora's brother, Miles. "Is he as remarkable as Flora?"

Mrs. Grose smiled and said, "Oh, yes. He'll be home from school in a couple of days. Then you'll see for yourself."

Later, Flora showed me around the house. I began to feel that the house was like a castle. I kept wondering, "Is this all a dream?"

A letter arrived from the children's uncle that evening. Inside the envelope was a second letter addressed to him. It was unopened.

The uncle wrote, "I know this letter is from Miles's school principal. That man is an awful bother. Please read this letter and answer it yourself. Don't tell me anything about it — not one word."

I read the principal's letter before going to bed. It upset me so much that again I had trouble sleeping.

In the morning, I told Mrs. Grose, "Miles has been dismissed from school. They will not take him back again — ever."

Mrs. Grose's eyes filled with tears. "What has he done?"

"The letter doesn't say," I said. "It just says they are sorry they cannot keep him there anymore. That must mean he is doing some harm to the other boys."

Mrs. Grose became angry. "Miles wouldn't harm anyone. Why, he's only ten years old."

"Yes, it's hard to believe," I said. "Have you ever known him to be bad?"

"Yes, thank goodness. A boy who has never been bad is no boy for me!"

I still had some doubts. Later, I asked Mrs. Grose some more questions. "Did the first governess, Miss Jessel, ever have trouble with the boy?"

"If she did, she never told me," Mrs. Grose said.

"What was she like?"

"She was almost as young and as pretty as you."

"Did she die here?"

Mrs. Grose shook her head. She said that one day Miss Jessel left for a short vacation. She never came back. Later, Mrs. Grose heard from the children's uncle that Miss Jessel was dead.

"What did she die of?" I asked.

Mrs. Grose seemed upset. "He never told me. Now, I must get back to my work."

The next day, Miles came home from school. The moment I saw him, all my doubts about him disappeared. I had never seen such sweetness and innocence in a boy. It was impossible not to love him.

I told Mrs. Grose that I would ignore the letter from school. I would not tell the boy's uncle about it, which made Mrs. Grose very relieved.

The next few weeks were the happiest of my life. The children were charming, giving me no trouble at all. The weather was perfect, the days sunny and long.

Then one evening, everything changed. The children had gone to bed, and I was taking a walk near the house. It was still light enough for me to enjoy the scenery. As I walked, I dreamed I might meet a handsome man who would smile at me. He would be just like the children's uncle.

At that moment, I looked up at the house. What I saw gave me a great shock. A man was looking out of one of the two towers on the roof. It was not the children's uncle. It was someone I had never seen before.

He stared at me for a full minute. As he did, everything became as quiet as death. Then he turned away, and I could see him no more.

Who was this man? Was some insane person kept in the tower? Or had some stranger sneaked into the house, looked around, and then sneaked out again?

I decided it must have been a nosy stranger. I was glad I would never see him again.

For a few days, I thought no more about him. Then it was Sunday, and time to go to church. I remembered that I had left my gloves in the dining room. When I entered the room, I saw someone standing outside the window. It was the man I had seen in the tower!

He stared at me again, but then began to look around the room. I realized he was not looking for me, but for someone else.

I was very frightened, but I had a duty to protect the children. I ran outside to challenge the stranger. But when I got to the window, he was gone.

Something made me look inside the window, as he had done. Just then, Mrs.

Grose walked into the room. When she saw me, her face turned white.

She ran outside to meet me. "What is the matter?" she asked. "You look awful!"

I could not keep the secret to myself anymore. I told Mrs. Grose the whole story.

"What did the stranger look like?" she asked.

I said, "He is tall and has red, curly hair and a long face. His mouth is wide, and his lips are thin. He has little whiskers on his chin. He is handsome in a slick sort of way, but he is no gentleman."

Mrs. Grose looked amazed. She said, "It's Peter Quint! He was the uncle's personal servant. When the uncle left, Quint stayed on with us. Then he went, too."

"Went where?" I asked.

Mrs. Grose looked very odd. Finally she said, "He died."

I nearly screamed. "Died?"

"Yes, Mr. Quint is dead."

That night, Mrs. Grose and I talked some more. She had seen nothing herself. But she fully believed that I had seen something.

I told her I felt that Quint was looking for Miles. I wondered, though, why the children had never mentioned Quint to me.

Mrs. Grose said that Flora was too young to remember him. But he and Miles had been "great friends." She herself had never liked Quint. He was an evil fellow.

His life came to an end one winter night. He had been drinking heavily in the village. On his way home, he slipped on an icy hill, and the fall killed him.

Several days later, I found more proof that the children were in danger. I had left Miles inside the house to read. Flora and I had walked to a small lake. While Flora played, I sat on a bench and did some sewing. Suddenly I knew, without looking up, that someone was on the other side of the lake. It was someone, I was sure, who had no right to be there.

I looked at Flora to see if she noticed anything. She showed no sign of it. But she had become very quiet and had turned her back to the lake. Finally, I looked up to face the figure on the other shore. . . .

I could hardly wait to tell Mrs. Grose what I had seen. When I found her, I cried, "It's awful! The children know what we know — and maybe a lot more. Just two hours ago, Flora saw! Yet she kept it to herself."

"Then how do you know she saw anything?" Mrs. Grose asked.

"I could tell she was aware."

"You mean aware of Quint?"

"No, it was a woman this time. She was dressed all in black, and her face was very evil. She kept looking at Flora. It was as if she wanted to get hold of her."

"Was she someone you've ever seen before?" Mrs. Grose asked.

"No, but it was someone the child has seen. I'm sure it was the governess who died — Miss Jessel."

"How do you know that?"

I described her to Mrs. Grose. "She was beautiful, but very pale and dreadful. Her eyes were evil. Everything about her was evil."

Mrs. Grose now seemed to believe me. "Miss Jessel was evil," she said. "She and Quint were both evil, and they were attracted to each other."

"It's much worse than I thought," I said. "The children are lost. I can't save them."

That night, I tried to get more information from Mrs. Grose. I wanted to know especially about Miles and Peter Quint. She said that for several months, they had always been together. She thought this was wrong, and once said so to Miss Jessel. Miss Jessel had told her to mind her own business.

Sometimes Mrs. Grose scolded Miles for spending so much time with Quint. Then Miles would deny it.

"You mean he lied?" I asked.

"Yes, but he's such an angel now. You don't think he's hiding anything from you, do you?"

"I'm not sure," I said.

For several days, I saw no more of either Quint or Miss Jessel. I began to feel more at ease. The children were wonderful. They tried hard to please me, and they learned their lessons perfectly.

I tried hard not to show that I had any fears about them. But sometimes I thought they knew.

Late one night, I heard a footstep outside my door. It was the same sound I had heard the first night I was in the house. I picked up a candle and went out into the hall. At the top of the stairs, the candle

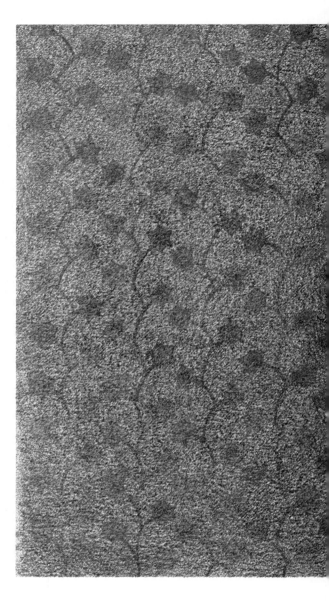

blew out. But dawn was beginning, and a little light came through the window.

I looked down the stairs and saw — the ghost of Quint! In the pale light, he seemed very dangerous. We stared at each other, but this time I was not afraid, and

298

he knew it. Suddenly, he turned his back on me and disappeared.

For the next few nights, I hardly slept. I kept going out into the hall, wondering if I would find Quint again. But there was no sign of him.

At last, I became so tired that one night I fell fast asleep. Later, I woke up suddenly. I had left a candle burning, but now it was out. Had Flora blown it out?

I went to her bed, but she was not in it. I looked around and saw her standing at the window, staring outside. She was so interested in someone on the lawn that she did not notice me.

Was Miss Jessel out there? I had to find out, so I slipped out of the room. I went to an empty room that also faced the lawn, and I looked out the window.

In the moonlight, I could see a figure watching the tower. I was sure that Quint was up there again. With horror, I now saw that the figure on the lawn was Miles!

I ran outside, took Miles by the hand, and led him to his room. I wondered what to say to him. Could I accuse him of keeping company with an evil ghost? If I did, people would say I was crazy.

Finally, I said, "Tell me the truth. What were you doing out there?"

He smiled and looked at me with his beautiful eyes. "If I tell you, will you understand?"

I nodded.

"It's very simple," he said. "For a change, I wanted you to think I was *bad*."

He explained that it was a joke that he and Flora had planned to scare me. For the moment, I believed him.

Then I asked, "But weren't you afraid of catching a cold out there?"

"When I'm bad," he said, "I am *very* bad." Then he kissed me good night.

The next morning, my fears about the children came back. There was only one person I could tell them to — Mrs. Grose. I told her that the children's sweetness and goodness were all an act. The truth was, I said, that the children constantly met Quint and Miss Jessel.

"But whatever for?" asked Mrs. Grose.

"For the love of all the evil those two put into them. Quint and Miss Jessel come back to keep up their evil work. They are like demons, tempting the children to join them in their world. If the children join them, they will be destroyed."

Mrs. Grose said I should write to the children's uncle for help. But how could I tell him that his house was haunted? Could I say that his niece and nephew kept company with ghosts? No, I would have to save the children myself.

I was sure that Miles and Flora were aware that I knew their secret. Yet they never spoke of Quint or Miss Jessel, and I did not dare to.

For a few weeks, I did not see Quint or Miss Jessel at all. But I was certain that the children saw them, even when we were together. At times, everything would become very quiet. It was then, I believe, that the children had visitors.

Sometimes I wanted to say, "They're here. You can't deny it." But I always stopped myself. The strain almost made me hate the children. Yet they were as charming as ever.

During this time, I kept a close watch over Miles and Flora. I was like a prison guard, and I wondered when Miles would demand more freedom.

It happened on an autumn Sunday as we were walking to church. Suddenly, he asked, "When am I going back to school?"

It was natural for him to ask this. But I feared writing to his uncle about it. The uncle did not know that Miles had been dismissed from school. He would ask *why* this had happened. Then *everything* would come out — Quint, Miss Jessel, all the horrors.

I did not say this to Miles. Instead, I said that his uncle was very busy. I could not bother him.

"Well," Miles said, "if *you* won't write him, I will." Then he marched into the church without me.

Instantly I was in a panic. I could not face Miles's uncle. Miles knew I was afraid. He would make use of my fear to get his own way.

I had to escape and never see the children again. Now that everyone was in church, I could pack up and leave unseen.

I hurried to the house. I went to the study for my books. What I found sent a chill through me.

Miss Jessel was sitting at my table. She looked very sad and tired. She stared at me as if to say, "This is *my* room. You have no right to be here."

I screamed at her, "You terrible woman!"

A moment later, she was gone. I knew then that I had to stay to protect the children.

That night, I told Mrs. Grose, "I'm going to send for the children's uncle. I will show him the letter from Miles's principal. It's not my fault that Miles was dismissed because he was wicked."

"But we really don't know that he was wicked," Mrs. Grose said.

"What other reason is there?" I asked. "Is he stupid? Is he sick? Is he a trouble-maker? No. He's clever and perfect. So he must have been wicked."

Tears came into Mrs. Grose's eyes. But she agreed that I should write to the uncle.

I began the letter that night, but I became restless. I picked up a candle and walked into the hall.

For a moment, I paused outside Miles's door. From inside, he called, "Come in."

I went in and found him in bed. "How did you know I was out there?" I asked.

"I heard you. Do you think you make no noise?"

I told him that I had begun a letter to his uncle. He laughed and said, "Well, then, finish it."

His laughter sounded so innocent. Perhaps I could still save him.

"Miles, what happened at school? Why haven't you ever talked about it?"

He looked at me, but said nothing.

"Miles, I want to help you. I'd rather die than hurt you. Help me to save you."

Just then, I felt an icy gust of air. Miles screamed, and the candle went out. It was very strange, because the window was shut.

"How did the candle go out?" I cried.

"I blew it out," Miles said.


The next day, Miles was very charming. He offered to play the piano for me, and I agreed. He played so well that I lost track of time. Suddenly, I wondered where Flora was. It was the first time she had been out of my sight.

I looked all over the house for her, but could not find her. I told Mrs. Grose, "She's gone out. She's with her."

"With Miss Jessel?"

"Yes. Miles and Flora planned it. He played the piano for me so Flora could sneak out alone. We must find her."

I knew that Flora would be at the lake where I first saw Miss Jessel. But when we got there, we could not find Flora.

"She must have rowed over to the other side. The rowboat is missing."

"How could she? She's just a child."

"She's not alone, and at such times, she's not a child. She's an old, old woman."

We walked around the lake to the other side. Soon we found the rowboat. A little farther on, we saw Flora. When she saw us, she started picking flowers.

Mrs. Grose ran to her and hugged her.

Flora looked at me as if she thought I might no longer trust her. Then she smiled sweetly and asked, "Where is Miles?"

That was too much for me. I asked, "Where is Miss Jessel?"

I had never mentioned this name before to Flora, and she was shocked. Mrs. Grose screamed.

Then I saw the figure of Miss Jessel across the lake. I pointed to her and shouted, "She's there!"

Flora looked at me in horror. I told her, "You see her as well as you see me."

Flora didn't bother to look across the lake. But Mrs. Grose looked and looked where I had pointed. Finally she said, "She isn't there. Nobody's there. You've never seen her. Poor Miss Jessel is dead and buried."

Then she tried to calm Flora. "It's all a mistake, love. We'll go home right away."

Flora was holding tightly to Mrs. Grose. All her beauty seemed to have disappeared. The look in her eyes made her old and ugly.

She said to me, "I see nobody. I never have. You're cruel, and I don't like you!" She hugged Mrs. Grose and cried, "Take me away. Take me away from *her*!"

Flora's words hurt me, even though I knew they came from that figure across the lake. I said, "I've done my best, but I've lost you. Good-bye."

I cried after they left. It was almost dark when I got back to the house. Flora's things were gone from my room. She would now stay with Mrs. Grose.

Later in the evening, Miles came into my room and sat down. I felt he wanted to tell me something, but he said little.

The next morning, Mrs. Grose told me that Flora had a fever.

"She was awake most of the night," Mrs. Grose said. "She was afraid you would come in."

"Flora will never speak to me again," I said. "You must take her away from here, away from me. Take her to her uncle."

"But why?"

"I need some time with Miles — alone. I believe he wants to tell me everything. He tried last night, but couldn't. A day or two more will bring it all out."

"You are right," Mrs. Grose said. "Flora must leave this place. Since yesterday, I've heard such awful things from her — about you. I have no idea where she learned such shocking words."

"From them," I said.

"She must get away from this house — and *them*," she said.

I almost hugged her with joy. The day before she had seen nothing at the lake. Yet she still believed in me.

Mrs. Grose had more to say. The letter I had written to the children's uncle had disappeared. She was sure that Miles had taken it.

"Now I know what he must have done at school," she said. "He stole letters."

I was sure it was worse than that. But I simply said, "I think he is already ashamed of himself and wants to confess. If he confesses, he's saved. And if he's saved, I am, too."

Mrs. Grose said good-bye and then left.

All that day, I left Miles alone. I wanted him to feel free.

That evening, we ate together in the dining room. Miles asked, "Is Flora really very sick?"

"She'll be better soon," I said. "She just needs to get away from this place."

Miles got up and walked to the window where I had seen Quint. By this time, the servants had left the room.

Miles said, "So now we are alone. I hope it won't be too lonely for you."

I told him that I always enjoyed his company. Then I asked, "Don't you remember what I told you the other night? I said I would do anything to help you."

"I remember. You wanted me to tell you something."

"That's it. Tell me what's on your mind."

"Do you mean now — here?"

"There couldn't be a better time or place."

Suddenly, he seemed afraid of me. "I will tell you everything you want to know," he said. "But not right now."

"Why not?"

"I have to see one of the servants about something."

I knew he was lying, and I felt ashamed for making him lie. "I'll wait for you to come back," I said. "But first, will you tell me one little thing? Did you take the letter I wrote to your uncle?"

Just then, Peter Quint appeared outside the window. I jumped up and grabbed Miles. I held him with his back to the window, so he could not see Quint's awful face. I felt I was fighting a demon for a human soul.

Poor Miles began to sweat, and he became very pale, but he answered my question. "Yes, I took the letter. I wanted to see what you said about me."

I looked out the window again, but Quint was gone. I was winning the battle! I was saving Miles!

I asked him more questions. "Is that what you did at school — take letters or other things?"

"No," Miles said.

"Then what did you do?"

"I said things. Some of the boys must have repeated them, and the teachers found out."

"What things did you say?"

Before Miles could answer, I saw Quint's face outside the window again. I screamed at it, "No more! No more!"

I could feel Miles's heart pounding as I held him. "Is she here?" he asked. "Is it Miss Jessel?"

"It's not Miss Jessel. But it's *there* — for the last time."

Miles turned his head and looked around the room. "Is it *he*?" he asked.

My victory was now almost complete. "Whom do you mean by *he*?" I asked.

"Peter Quint, you devil!" Miles cried. Then he looked puzzled and asked, "Where is he?"

"What does he matter now, my own? What will he *ever* matter?" I asked. "I have you, but he has lost you forever." Then, to prove that I was right, I pointed outside. "There, *there*!" I said to Miles.

Miles turned round to the window, stared, and glared again, and saw nothing but the quiet day. Then he let out a cry like a creature hurled over a cliff. I grasped him as if to catch him in his fall, and I held him in my arms.

But at the end of a minute I began to feel what it truly was that I held. We were alone with the quiet day, and his little heart — dispossessed — had stopped.

**Summarizing.** Choose the best phrase to complete each sentence. Then write the complete statements on your paper.

1. The young woman took the job as governess because she _____ (wanted to be in the country, knew the job would be easy, was completely charmed by the uncle).

2. The strange sounds didn't bother the governess the first night in her new home because she was _____ (too tired to hear them, too afraid, so happy about her new job).

3. Miles came home early from school _____ (to meet the new governess, because he was dismissed, for his uncle's birthday).

4. The man the governess saw in the tower _____ (was a relative of the uncle, fit the description of a dead man, was a friend of Mrs. Grose).

5. The woman ghost was _____ (a governess who had died, the kitchen maid, the uncle's wife).

6. The governess felt the ghosts had come to _____ (scare her, kill her, harm the children).

7. Miles played the piano for the governess so that Flora could _____ (go to her room and read by herself, talk to Mrs. Grose alone, meet with Miss Jessel).

8. The governess did not tell the uncle about the ghosts because she was afraid he would _____ (take the children away, think she was crazy, blame Mrs. Grose).

9. When the governess saw Peter Quint appear outside the window, she _____ (chased after him, ran away, held Miles so that he could not see Quint's awful face).

10. At the end of the story, _____ (Flora ran away, Miles died, Mrs. Grose sent for the police).

**Interpreting.** Write the answer to each question on your paper.

1. What did the governess decide to do with the letter from Miles's principal?

2. When did the governess become sure that the children were in some kind of danger?

3. Why did Mrs. Grose believe the governess, even though she had never seen the ghosts herself?

4. Why did Miles seem to become afraid of the governess when she asked him to tell her what was on his mind?

**For Thinking and Discussing.**

1. There is a fight between good and evil in "The Turn of the Screw." Which side wins the struggle?

2. Why do you think the author changes the point of view from which the story is told? What difference does this make to the story?

**Imagery.** "The Turn of the Screw" is a story about the conflict between good and evil. The mood of the story shifts back and forth from the sense that all is well to feelings that evil is going to win.

The images the author used to describe the setting and the characters help the mood change from peace to horror. Some images seem lovely and beautiful, while others are unpleasant and frightening.

Read the passages below. On your paper, label the mood of each as *good* or *evil*.

1. "Flora was the most beautiful and charming child I had ever seen."

2. " 'He is handsome in a slick sort of way, but he is no gentleman.' "

3. "He stared at me. . . . As he did, everything became as quiet as death."

4. "I had never seen such sweetness and innocence in a boy. It was impossible not to love him."

5. "[Miss Jessel] kept looking at Flora. It was as if she wanted to get hold of her."

## WRITING

Pretend you are the governess. Write two letters to your family. Write one on the first day of the job. Tell how wonderful everything is. Write the second one after you've seen the ghosts. Use pleasant images in the first letter. Use frightening ones in the second.

# The Griffin and the Minor Canon

*by Frank Stockton*

*If you know Frank Stockton's stories, you expect the unexpected. If this is your first encounter with the master storyteller, prepare to be entertained! Enjoy this tale of an unusual encounter between monster and man.*

Over the great door of an old, old church which stood in a quiet town of a faraway land there was carved in stone the figure of a large griffin. The old-time sculptor had done his work with great care, but the image he had made was not a pleasant one to look at. It had a large head, with enormous open mouth and savage teeth. From its back arose great wings, armed with sharp hooks and prongs. It had stout legs in front, with projecting claws. But there were no legs behind — the body running out into a long and powerful tail, finished off at the end with a barbed point. This tail was coiled up under him, the end sticking up just back of his wings.

The sculptor, or the people who had ordered this stone figure, had evidently been very much pleased with it, for little copies of it, also in stone, had been placed here and there along the sides of the church, not very far from the ground, so that people could easily look at them and ponder on their curious forms. There were a great many other sculptures on the outside of this church — saints, martyrs, grotesque heads of men, beasts, and birds, as well as those of other creatures which cannot be named, because nobody knows exactly what they were. But none were so curious and interesting as the great griffin over the door and the little griffins on the sides of the church.

A long, long distance from the town, in the midst of dreadful wilds scarcely known to man, there dwelt the Griffin whose image had been put up over the church door. In some way or other, the old-time sculptor had seen him and afterward, to the best of his memory, had copied his figure in stone.

The Griffin had never known this, until, hundreds of years afterward, he heard from a bird, from a wild animal, or in some manner which it is not now easy to find out, that there was a likeness of him on the old church in the distant town.

Now, this Griffin had no idea how he looked. He had never seen a mirror, and the streams where he lived were so turbulent and violent that a quiet piece of water, which would reflect the image of anything looking into it, could not be found. Being, as far as could be ascertained, the very last of his race, he had never seen another griffin. Therefore it was that, when he heard of this stone image of himself, he became very anxious to know what he looked like, and at last he determined to go to the old church and see for himself what manner of being he was.

So he started off from the dreadful wilds and flew on and on until he came to the countries inhabited by men, where his appearance in the air created great consternation; but he alighted nowhere, keeping up a steady flight until he reached the suburbs of the town which had his image on its church. Here, late in the afternoon, he lighted in a green meadow by the side of a brook and stretched himself on the grass to rest. His great wings were tired, for he had not made such a long flight in a century, or more.

The news of his coming spread quickly over the town, and the people, frightened nearly out of their wits by the arrival of so strange a visitor, fled into their houses and shut themselves up. The Griffin called loudly for someone to come to him, but the more he called, the more afraid the people were to show themselves. At length he saw two laborers hurrying to their homes through the fields, and in a terrible voice he commanded them to stop. Not daring to disobey, the men stood, trembling.

"What is the matter with you all?" cried the Griffin. "Is there not a man in your town who is brave enough to speak to me?"

"I think," said one of the laborers, his voice shaking so that his words could hardly be understood, "that — perhaps — the Minor Canon — would come."

"Go, call him, then!" said the Griffin; "I want to see him."

The Minor Canon, who was an assistant in the old church, had just finished the afternoon services and was coming out of a side door with three aged women who had formed the weekday congregation. He was a young man of a kind disposition, and very anxious to do good to the people of the town. Apart from his duties in the church, where he conducted services every weekday, he visited the sick and the poor, counseled and assisted persons who were in trouble, and taught a school composed entirely of the bad children in the town with whom nobody else would have anything to do. Whenever the people wanted something difficult done for them, they always went to the Minor Canon. Thus it was that the laborer thought of the young priest when he found that someone must come and speak to the Griffin.

The Minor Canon had not heard of the strange event, which was known to the whole town except himself and the three old women. When he was informed of it and was told that the Griffin had asked to see him, he was greatly amazed and frightened.

"Me!" he exclaimed. "He has never heard of me! What should he want with me?"

"Oh, you must go instantly!" cried the two men. "He is very angry now because he has been kept waiting so long. Nobody knows what may happen if you don't hurry to him."

The poor Minor Canon would rather have had his hand cut off than go out to meet an angry Griffin; but he felt that it was his duty to go, for it would be a woeful thing if injury should come to the people of the town because he was not brave enough to obey the summons of the Griffin. So, pale and frightened, he started off.

"Well," said the Griffin, as soon as the young man came near, "I am glad to see that there is someone who has the courage to come to me."

The Minor Canon did not feel very brave, but he bowed his head.

"Is this the town," said the Griffin, "where there is a church with a likeness of myself over one of the doors?"

The Minor Canon looked at the frightful creature before him and saw that it was, without doubt, exactly like the stone image on the church. "Yes," he said, "you are right."

"Well, then," said the Griffin, "will you take me to it? I wish very much to see it."

The Minor Canon instantly thought that if the Griffin entered the town without the people's knowing what he came for, some of them would probably be frightened to death, and so he sought to gain time to prepare their minds.

"It is growing dark now," he said, very much afraid, as he spoke, that his words might enrage the Griffin, "and objects on the front of the church cannot be seen clearly. It will be better to wait until morning, if you wish to get a good view of the stone image of yourself."

"That will suit me very well," said the Griffin. "I see you are a man of good sense. I am tired, and I will take a nap here on this soft grass, while I cool my tail in the little stream that runs near me. The end of my tail gets red-hot when I am angry or excited, and it is quite warm now. So you may go; but be sure and come early tomorrow morning and show me the way to the church."

The Minor Canon was glad enough to take his leave and hurried into the town. In front of the church he found a great many people assembled to hear his report of his interview with the Griffin. When they found that he had not come to spread ruin, but simply to see his stony likeness on the church, they showed neither relief nor gratification but began to upbraid the Minor Canon for consenting to conduct the creature into the town.

"What could I do?" cried the young man. "If I should not bring him he would come himself and, perhaps, end by setting fire to the town with his red-hot tail."

Still the people were not satisfied, and a great many plans were proposed to prevent the Griffin from coming into the town. Some elderly persons urged that the young men should go out and kill him, but the young men scoffed at such a ridiculous idea.

Then someone said that it would be a good thing to destroy the stone image, so that the Griffin would have no excuse for entering the town. This plan was received with such favor that many of the people

ran for hammers, chisels, and crowbars, with which to tear down and break up the stone griffin. But the Minor Canon resisted this plan with all the strength of his mind and body. He assured the people that this action would enrage the Griffin beyond measure, for it would be impossible to conceal from him that his image had been destroyed during the night. But the people were so determined to break up the stone griffin that the Minor Canon saw that there was nothing for him to do but to stay there and protect it. All night he walked up and down in front of the church door, keeping away the men who brought ladders, by which they might mount to the great stone griffin and knock it to pieces with their hammers and crowbars. After many hours the people were obliged to give up their attempts, and went home to sleep. But the Minor Canon remained at his post till early morning, and then he hurried away to the field where he had left the Griffin.

The monster had just awakened, and, rising to his forelegs and shaking himself, he said that he was ready to go into the town. The Minor Canon, therefore, walked back, the Griffin flying slowly through the air at a short distance above the head of his guide. Not a person was to be seen in the streets, and they went directly to the front of the church, where the Minor Canon pointed out the stone griffin.

The real Griffin settled down in the little square before the church and gazed earnestly at his sculptured likeness. For a long time he looked at it. First he put his head on one side, and then he put it on the other. Then he shut his right eye and gazed with his left, after which he shut his left eye and gazed with his right. Then he moved a little to one side and looked at the image, then he moved the other way. After a while he said to the Minor Canon, who had been standing by all this time:

"It is, it must be, an excellent likeness! That breadth between the eyes, that expansive forehead, those massive jaws! I feel that it must resemble me. If there is any fault to find with it, it is that the neck seems a little stiff. But that is nothing. It is an admirable likeness — admirable!"

The Griffin sat looking at his image all the morning and all the afternoon. The Minor Canon had been afraid to go away and leave him and had hoped all through the day that he would soon be satisfied with his inspection and fly away home. But by evening the poor young man was very tired and felt that he must eat and sleep. He frankly said this to the Griffin and asked him if he would not like something to eat. He said this because he felt obliged in politeness to do so; but as soon as he had spoken the words, he was seized with dread lest the monster should demand half a dozen babies, or some tempting repast of that kind.

"Oh, no," said the Griffin, "I never eat between the equinoxes. At the vernal and at the autumnal equinox I take a good meal, and that lasts me for half a year. I am extremely regular in my habits and do not think it healthful to eat at odd times. But if you need food, go and get it, and I will return to the soft grass where I slept last night and take another nap."

The next day the Griffin came again to the little square before the church, and remained there until evening, steadfastly regarding the stone griffin over the door. The Minor Canon came out once or twice to look at him, and the Griffin seemed very glad to see him; but the young clergyman could not stay as he had done before, for he had many duties to perform. Nobody went to the church, but the people came to the Minor Canon's house and anxiously asked him how long the Griffin was going to stay.

"I do not know," he answered, "but I think he will soon be satisfied with regarding his stone likeness, and then he will go away."

But the Griffin did not go away. Morning after morning he came to the church; but after a time he did not stay there all day. He seemed to have taken a great fancy to the Minor Canon and followed him about as he worked. He would wait for him at the side door of the church, for the Minor Canon held services every day, morning and evening, though nobody came now. "If anyone should come," he said to himself, "I must be found at my post." When the young man came out, the Griffin would accompany him in his visits to the sick and the poor, and would often look into the windows of the schoolhouse where the Minor Canon was teaching his unruly scholars. All the other schools were closed, but the parents of the Minor Canon's scholars forced them to go to school because they were so bad they could not endure them all day at home — Griffin or no Griffin. But it must be said they generally behaved very well when that great monster sat up on his tail and looked in at the schoolroom window.

When it was found that the Griffin showed no sign of going away, all the people who were able to do so left the town. The canons and the higher officers of the church had fled away during the first day of the Griffin's visit, leaving behind only the Minor Canon and some of the men who opened the doors and swept the church. All the citizens who could afford it shut up their houses and traveled to distant parts, and only the working people and the poor were left behind. After some days these ventured to go about and attend to their business, for if they did not work they would starve.

They were getting a little used to seeing the Griffin; and having been told that he did not eat between equinoxes, they did not feel so much afraid of him as before.

Day by day the Griffin became more and more attached to the Minor Canon. He kept near him a great part of the time and often spent the night in front of the little house where the young clergyman lived alone. This strange companionship was often burdensome to the Minor Canon; but, on the other hand, he could not deny that he derived a great deal of benefit

and instruction from it. The Griffin had lived for hundreds of years, and had seen much, and he told the Minor Canon many wonderful things.

"It is like reading an old book," said the young clergyman to himself. "How many books I would have had to read before I would have found out what the Griffin has told me about the earth, the air, the water, about minerals, and metals, and growing things, and all the wonders of the world!"

Thus the summer went on and drew toward its close. And now the people of the town began to be very much troubled again.

"It will not be long," they said, "before the autumnal equinox is here, and then that monster will want to eat. He will be dreadfully hungry, for he has taken so much exercise since his last meal. He will devour our children. Without doubt, he will eat them all. What is to be done?"

To this question no one could give an answer, but all agreed that the Griffin must not be allowed to remain until the approaching equinox. After talking over the matter a great deal, a crowd of the people went to the Minor Canon at a time when the Griffin was not with him.

"It is all your fault," they said, "that the monster is among us. You brought him here, and you ought to see that he goes away. It is only on your account that he stays here at all; for, although he visits his image every day, he is with you the greater part of the time. If you were not here, he would not stay. It is your duty to go away, and then he will follow you, and we shall be free from the dreadful danger which hangs over us."

"Go away!" cried the Minor Canon, greatly grieved at being spoken to in such a way. "Where shall I go? If I go to some other town, shall I not take this trouble there? Have I a right to do that?"

"No," said the people, "you must not go to any other town. There is no town far enough away. You must go to the dreadful wilds where the Griffin lives; and then he will follow you and stay there."

They did not say whether or not they expected the Minor Canon to stay there also, and he did not ask them anything about it. He bowed his head and went into his house to think. The more he thought, the more clear it became to his mind that it was his duty to go away and thus free the town from the presence of the Griffin.

That evening he packed a leathern bag full of bread and meat, and early the next morning he set out on his journey to the dreadful wilds. It was a long, weary, and doleful journey, especially after he had gone beyond the habitations of men; but the Minor Canon kept on bravely and never faltered.

The way was longer than he had expected. His provisions soon grew so scanty that he was obliged to eat but a little every day; but he kept up his courage and pressed on. After many days of toilsome travel, he reached the dreadful wilds.

When the Griffin found that the Minor Canon had left the town, he seemed sorry but showed no desire to go and look for him. After a few days had passed he became much annoyed and asked some of the people where the Minor Canon had gone. But, although the citizens had been so anxious that the young clergyman should go to the dreadful wilds, thinking that the Griffin would immediately follow him, they were now afraid to mention the Minor Canon's destination, for the monster seemed angry already, and if he should suspect their trick he would, doubtless, become very much enraged. So everyone said he did not know, and the Griffin wandered about disconsolate. One morning he looked into the Minor Canon's schoolhouse, which was always empty now, and thought that it was a shame that everything should suffer on account of the young man's absence.

"It does not matter so much about the church," he said, "for nobody went there; but it is a pity about the school. I think I will teach it myself until he returns."

It was the hour for opening the school, and the Griffin went inside and pulled the rope which rang the school bell. Some of the children who heard the bell ran in to see what was the matter, supposing it to be a joke of one of their companions. When they saw the Griffin they stood astonished and scared.

"Go tell the other scholars," said the monster, "that school is about to open, and that if they are not all here in ten minutes I shall come after them."

In seven minutes every scholar was in place.

Never was seen such an orderly school. Not a boy or girl moved or uttered a whisper. The Griffin climbed into the master's seat, his wide wings spread on each side of him, because he could not lean back in his chair while they stuck out behind. His great tail coiled around in front of the desk, the barbed end sticking up, ready to tap any boy or girl who might misbehave.

The Griffin now addressed the scholars, telling them that he intended to teach them while their master was away. In speaking he tried to imitate, as far as possible, the mild and gentle tones of the Minor Canon. But it must be admitted that in this he was not very successful. He had paid a good deal of attention to the studies of the school, and he determined not to try to teach them anything new, but to review them in what they had been studying. So he called up the various classes, and questioned them upon their previous lessons. The children racked their brains to remember what they had learned. They were so afraid of the Griffin's displeasure that they recited as they had never recited before. One of the boys, far down

in his class, answered so well that the Griffin was astonished.

"I should think you would be at the head," said he. "I am sure you have never been in the habit of reciting so well. Why is this?"

"Because I did not choose to take the trouble," said the boy, trembling in his boots. He felt obliged to speak the truth, for all the children thought that the great eyes of the Griffin could see right through them, and that he would know when they told a falsehood.

"You ought to be ashamed of yourself," said the Griffin. "Go down to the very tail of the class; and if you are not at the head in two days, I shall know the reason why."

The next afternoon this boy was Number One.

It was astonishing how much these children now learned of what they had been studying. It was as if they had been educated over again. The Griffin used no severity toward them, but there was a look about him which made them unwilling to go to bed until they were sure they knew their lessons for the next day.

The Griffin now thought that he ought to visit the sick and the poor, and he began to go about the town for this purpose. The effect upon the sick was miraculous. All, except those who were very ill indeed, jumped from their beds when they heard he was coming and declared themselves quite well. To those who could not get up he gave herbs and roots, which none of them had ever before thought of as medicines, but which the Griffin had seen used in various parts of

316

the world; and most of them recovered. But, for all that, they afterward said that, no matter what happened to them, they hoped that they should never again have such a doctor coming to their bedsides, feeling their pulses and looking at their tongues.

As for the poor, they seemed to have utterly disappeared. All those who had depended upon charity for their daily bread were now at work in some way or other. Many of them offered to do odd jobs for their neighbors just for the sake of their meals — a thing which before had been seldom heard of in the town. The Griffin could find no one who needed his assistance.

The summer had now passed, and the autumnal equinox was rapidly approaching. The citizens were in a state of great alarm and anxiety. The Griffin showed no signs of going away, but seemed to have settled himself permanently among them. In a short time the day for his semiannual meal would arrive, and then what would happen? The monster would certainly be very hungry and would devour all their children.

Now they greatly regretted and lamented that they had sent away the Minor Canon. He was the only one on whom they could have depended in this trouble, for he could talk freely with the Griffin, and so find out what could be done. But it would not do to be inactive. Some step must be taken immediately. A meeting of the citizens was called, and two old men were appointed to go and talk to the Griffin. They were instructed to offer to prepare a splendid dinner for him on equinox day — one which would entirely satisfy his hunger. They would offer him the fattest mutton, the most tender beef, fish, and game of various sorts, and anything of the kind that he might fancy. If none of these suited, they were to mention that there was an orphan asylum in the next town.

"Anything would be better," said the citizens, "than to have our dear children devoured."

The old men went to the Griffin, but their propositions were not received with favor.

"From what I have seen of the people of this town," said the monster, "I do not think I could relish anything which was prepared by them. They appear to be all cowards and, therefore, mean and selfish. As for eating one of them, old or young, I could not think of it for a moment. In fact, there was only one creature in the whole place for whom I could have had any appetite, and that is the Minor Canon, who has gone away. He was brave, and good, and honest, and I think I should have relished him."

"Ah!" said one of the old men very politely, "in that case I wish we had not sent him to the dreadful wilds!"

"What!" cried the Griffin. "What do you mean? Explain instantly what you are talking about!"

The old man, terribly frightened at what he had said, was obliged to tell how the Minor Canon had been sent away by the people, in the hope that the Griffin might be induced to follow him.

When the monster heard this, he became furiously angry. He dashed away from the old men, and, spreading his wings, flew backward and forward over the town. He was so much excited that his tail became red-hot and glowed like a meteor against the evening sky. When at last he settled down in the little field where he usually rested, and thrust his tail into the brook, the steam arose like a cloud, and the water of the stream ran hot through the town. The citizens were greatly frightened and bitterly blamed the old man for telling about the Minor Canon.

"It is plain," they said, "that the Griffin intended at last to go and look for him, and we should have been saved. Now who can tell what misery you have brought upon us."

The Griffin did not remain long in the little field. As soon as his tail was cool, he flew to the town hall and rang the bell. The citizens knew that they were expected to come there. And although they were afraid to go, they were still more afraid to stay away. They crowded into the hall. The Griffin was on the platform at one end, flapping his wings and walking up and down, and the end of his tail was still so warm that it slightly scorched the boards as he dragged it after him.

When everybody who was able to come was there, the Griffin stood still and addressed the meeting.

"I have had a very low opinion of you," he said, "ever since I discovered what cowards you are, but I had no idea that you were so ungrateful, selfish, and cruel as I now find you to be. Here was your Minor Canon, who labored day and night for your good and thought of nothing else but how he might benefit you and make you happy. As soon as you imagine yourselves threatened with a danger — for well I know you are dreadfully afraid of me — you send him off, caring not whether he returns or perishes, hoping thereby to save yourselves. Now, I had conceived a great liking for that young man and had intended, in a day or two, to go and look him up. But I have changed my mind about him. I shall go and find him, but I shall send him back here to live among you, and I intend that he shall enjoy the reward of his labor and his sacrifices.

"Go, some of you, to the officers of the church, who so cowardly ran away when I first came here, and tell them never to return to this town under penalty of death. And if, when your Minor Canon comes back to you, you do not bow yourselves before him, put him in the highest place among you, and serve and honor him all his life, beware of my terrible vengeance! There were only two good things in this town: the Minor Canon and the stone image of myself over your church door. One of these you have sent away, and the other I shall carry away myself."

With these words he dismissed the meeting, and it was time, for the end of his tail had become so hot that there was danger of it setting fire to the building.

The next morning the Griffin came to the church, and tearing the stone image of himself from its fastenings over the great door he grasped it with his powerful forelegs and flew up into the air. Then, after hovering over the town for a moment, he gave his tail an angry shake and took up his flight to the dreadful wilds. When he reached this desolate region, he set the stone griffin upon a ledge of a rock which rose in front of the dismal cave he called his home. There the image occupied a position somewhat similar to that it had had over the church door. The Griffin, panting with the exertion of carrying such an enormous load to so great a distance, lay down upon the ground and regarded it with much satisfaction. When he felt somewhat rested, he went to look for the Minor Canon. He found the young man, weak and half starved, lying under the shadow of a rock. After picking him up and carrying him to his cave, the Griffin flew away to a distant marsh, where he procured some roots and herbs which he well knew were strengthening and beneficial to man, though he had never tasted them himself. After eating these the Minor Canon was greatly revived and sat up and listened while the Griffin told him what had happened in the town.

"Do you know," said the monster, when he had finished, "that I have had, and still have, a great liking for you?"

"I am very glad to hear it," said the Minor Canon, with his usual politeness.

"I am not at all sure that you would be," said the Griffin, "if you thoroughly understood the state of the case; but we will not consider that now. If some things were different, other things would be otherwise. I have been so enraged by discovering the manner in which you have been treated that I have determined that you shall at last enjoy the rewards and honors to which you are entitled. Lie down and have a good sleep, and then I will take you back to the town."

As he heard these words, a look of trouble came over the young man's face.

"You need not give yourself any anxiety," said the Griffin, "about my return to the town. I shall not remain there. Now that I have that admirable likeness of myself in front of my cave, where I can sit at my leisure and gaze upon its noble features and magnificent proportions, I have no wish to see that abode of cowardly and selfish people."

The Minor Canon, relieved from his fears, lay back and dropped into a doze. When he was sound asleep, the Griffin took him up and carried him back to the town. He arrived just before daybreak, and putting the young man gently on the grass in the little field where he himself used to rest, the monster, without having been seen by any of the people, flew back to his home.

When the Minor Canon made his appearance in the morning among the citizens, the enthusiasm and cordiality with which he was received were truly wonderful. He was taken to a house which had been occupied by one of the banished high officers of the place, and everyone was anxious to do all that could be done for his health and comfort. The people crowded into the church when he held services, so that the three old women who used to be his weekday congregation could not get to the best seats, which they had always been in the habit of taking; and the parents of the bad children determined to reform them at home, in order that he might be spared the trouble of keeping up his former school. The Minor Canon was appointed to the highest office of the old

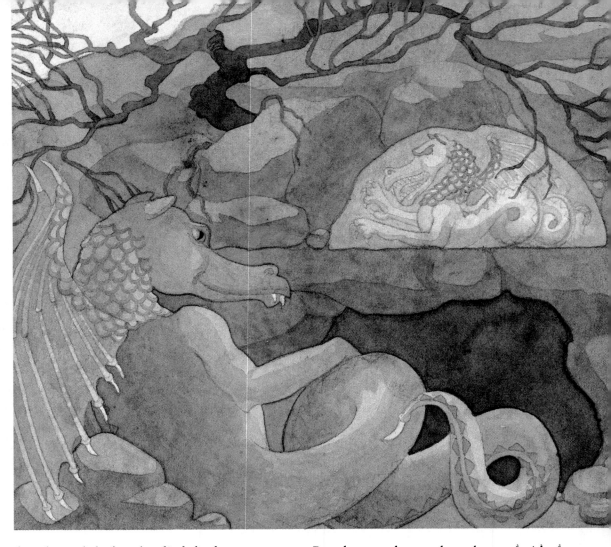

church, and, before he died, he became a bishop.

During the first years after his return from the dreadful wilds, the people of the town looked up to him as a man to whom they were bound to do honor and reverence; but they often, also, looked up to the sky to see if there were any signs of the Griffin coming back. However, in the course of time, they learned to honor and reverence their former Minor Canon without the fear of being punished if they did not do so.

But they need never have been afraid of the Griffin. The autumnal equinox day came round, and the monster ate nothing. If he could not have the Minor Canon, he did not care for anything. So, lying down, with his eyes fixed upon the great stone griffin, he gradually declined and died. It was a good thing for some of the people of the town that they did not know this.

If you should ever visit the old town, you would still see the little griffins on the sides of the church; but the great stone griffin that was over the door is gone.

**Summarizing.** Choose the best phrase to complete each sentence. Then write the complete statements on your paper.

1. The Griffin came to the town because he wanted to _____ (meet the Minor Canon, find a good meal, see his carved likeness over the church door).

2. The Griffin did not leave the town because _____ (he couldn't take his eyes off the stone figure, the townspeople wanted him to stay, he had become fond of the Minor Canon).

3. The people became upset again when _____ (it was time for the Griffin's meal, the Griffin began to teach the children, the Minor Canon left town).

4. The Griffin had no appetite for anyone but the Minor Canon because the townspeople were all _____ (poor, brave, and good, cowardly and selfish).

**Interpreting.** Write the answer to each question on your paper.

1. Why did the Minor Canon guard the church door when the Griffin arrived?

2. Why did the Minor Canon go to the wilds where the Griffin lived?

3. Why did the Griffin change his mind about eating the Minor Canon?

**For Thinking and Discussing.** How do you think the Minor Canon would have felt if he learned what had happened to the Griffin?

**Imagery and Mood.** Imagery is the use of language that appeals to the reader's senses and emotions. Images help to create a picture in the reader's mind. They also help to create a mood, or atmosphere. A writer can make you feel peaceful, for example, by describing peaceful sights and sounds. The mood of a story may be cheerful, sad, humorous, solemn, or frightening.

In "The Griffin and the Minor Canon," there are several moods which change as different parts of the story are told.

Read the following passages from the story. Write the mood that best describes each passage on your paper.

1. "A long, long distance from the town, in the midst of dreadful wilds scarcely known to man, there dwelt the Griffin whose image had been put up over the church door."

   joyful    excited    mysterious

2. "The news of his coming spread quickly over the town, and the people, frightened out of their wits . . . fled into their houses and shut themselves up."

   fearful    peaceful    cheerful

## WRITING

Choose one of the following subjects: an empty beach, a stranger in town, an airplane ride, or a ghost. Write two paragraphs about the subject. In one, create a gloomy mood. In the other, create a cheerful mood. Be sure to use images that appeal to the senses in your descriptions.

# Section Review

**Similes, Metaphors, and Personification.** A *simile* is a direct comparison using the word *like* or *as*. In the line "The wind tapped like a tired man," the poet implies that the wind is like a person.

A *metaphor* is a suggested comparison.

"Hope" is the thing with feathers —
That perches in the soul —

The poet does not use *like* or *as*. She suggests that hope and a bird are alike.

*Personification* is the description of an object, animal, or idea as though it were human. Personification may be in the form of either a simile or a metaphor. Emily Dickinson compared the wind to a man.

Read these lines. On your paper, label each a *metaphor* or *simile*. If the comparison is also *personification*, write that word as well. Then explain each comparison.

1. "In the center yawned the circular pit from whose jaws I had escaped."

2. "Jim roused from his bedroll, refreshed and feeling strong as a new rope."

3. ". . . when the wind would blow they could hear something hollering and squeaking like it was in great pain and suffering."

4. "She looked like an angel in a painting."

**Making Inferences.** Sometimes an author does not say something directly. Rather, the author suggests something.

When you try to figure out what the author is suggesting, you are *making inferences*. Inferences are guesses based on the information the author gives you in a selection.

Read the following sentences about the selections in this section. On your paper, write what each author was inferring.

1. In the "Pit and the Pendulum," the narrator was freed when the French took over the town. You can guess, or infer, that the man was _____ .
   a. guilty of a terrible crime
   b. a prisoner of war
   c. a madman

2. In "Poor Sandy," Sandy's first wife was sold. Sandy's second wife was sent away to work for someone else. You can infer that slaves were _____ .
   a. free to work anywhere
   b. difficult to control
   c. treated like property, not people

3. In "The Turn of the Screw," the governess saw ghosts that others did not see. She believed that it was her duty to protect the children from these demons. One inference you could make is that she _____ .
   a. disliked the children in her care and wanted to hurt them
   b. took her job too seriously and it affected her mind
   c. liked communication with spirits

## WRITING

**A Description.** The main purpose of a description is to recreate a scene or event so vividly that your readers can experience it in their imaginations. A good description revolves around a single main idea, with vivid words and phrases providing the details that make the description come alive. Using words that appeal to the five senses — sight, sound, taste, touch, and smell — helps you to paint a word picture that seems real to those who read it.

### Step 1: Set Your Goal

The first step in writing a description is to choose a topic. The best topics for descriptive writing are concrete topics. A concrete topic is a specific person, place, thing, or event that can be described by using words that appeal to the five senses. In addition, you should choose a topic that you are interested in and know well.

Choose one of the following topics for a description:

☐ The narrator in Edgar Allan Poe's "The Pit and the Pendulum"
☐ The dance or the barn where the dance was held in "Jim Bridger and the Fiddler Who Wouldn't Fiddle"
☐ The plantation setting for "Poor Sandy"
☐ The uncle in "The Turn of the Screw"
☐ The dreadful wilds in "The Griffin and the Minor Canon"

Once you have chosen a topic, think about the overall impression or feeling you want your description to make. You may want your reader to feel as if he or she is seeing the object or event exactly as you did. Or, you might want to evoke a certain emotion, such as amusement or sadness. The purpose of your description will, to some extent, determine the words and phrases you use.

### Step 2: Make a Plan

Once you have decided on the impression you want your description to make, you need to list details that communicate that impression. Begin by writing a main-idea sentence that states the overall impression of your topic. Then list details that support the main-idea sentence. For example, in "The Griffin and the Minor Canon," the following main-idea sentence introduces a description of the Minor Canon: "He was a young man of kind disposition, and very anxious to do good to the people of the town."

Details that support the main idea include the following:

☐ performs church services every day
☐ visits sick and poor
☐ counsels persons who are in trouble
☐ teaches a school of unruly children
☐ always handles the difficult tasks

Note how each detail supports the overall impression of the main-idea sentence.

Next, you need to organize the details in your list. If you are describing an event, you may want to put the details in time order — the order in which things happen. If you are describing a person, place, or thing, you may want to use spatial order to guide the reader's attention from one place to another. For example, in describing a house, you might begin with the yard and end with the roof.

Look over your list of details. Cross out any that do not seem to fit your overall impression. Add others, if you wish. Then organize your details in the way you want to present them.

### Step 3: Write a First Draft

Remember that the purpose of a first draft is to get your thoughts down on paper. Don't worry about choosing the best words or writing perfect sentences. Use the following checklist as a guide:

- ☐ State your main idea in the beginning.
- ☐ Use your organized list of details as a guide, but feel free to make changes.
- ☐ Try to use as many sensory and descriptive words as possible.
- ☐ Be sure each detail supports the impression made in the main-idea sentence.

### Step 4: Revise

As you revise your first draft, think about how you can make your description more vivid. Use specific nouns and verbs in place of general ones, such as *oak* instead of *tree* or *muttered* instead of *said*. Make your nouns and verbs even more specific by adding adjectives and adverbs.

When you have finished your revision, reread it. Will it leave the reader with the right impression, or are there other changes to be made? When you have made all the changes that you feel are necessary, proofread your description for mistakes in grammar, spelling, and punctuation. Correct any errors and make a clean copy.

### QUIZ

The following is a quiz for Section 5. Write the answers in complete sentences on your paper.

## Reading Comprehension

1. What role did the rats play in "The Pit and the Pendulum"?

2. In "Jim Bridger and the Fiddler Who Wouldn't Fiddle," what was Bridger's alarm clock? To what use did he put it besides waking himself up?

3. In "Poor Sandy," why did Tenie turn Sandy into a tree?

4. What happened to Miles at the end of "The Turn of the Screw"?

5. In "The Griffin and the Minor Canon," why did the townspeople send the Minor Canon away? How did their action backfire?

## Understanding Literature

6. What mood did Poe create in "The Pit and the Pendulum"? Where did the story take place? Identify three details that added to the mood.

7. To what did Emily Dickinson compare hope in " 'Hope' Is the Thing With Feathers"?

8. What effect does the story "Poor Sandy" have on its readers? Mention three details of the plot that add to this effect.

9. Between what two forces is the struggle, or conflict, in "The Turn of the Screw"? Identify two details that help describe each of the forces.

10. What was ironic about the fear the townspeople had of the Griffin in "The Griffin and the Minor Canon"?

# ACTIVITIES

**Word Attack.** Every word is made up of syllables. Each syllable contains a single vowel sound. Look at these words:

limb          wa•ter          cir•cu•lar

The word *limb* has one vowel sound (*i*) and, therefore, one syllable. *Water* has two vowel sounds and two syllables. The word *circular* has three vowel sounds and, therefore, three syllables. The following words are from "The Pit and The Pendulum." Write each word and draw a line between each syllable. Then check a dictionary to see if you were correct.

| | |
|---|---|
| horrible | ravenous |
| dungeon | suffocate |
| hellish | immediate |
| terror | relentless |
| pendulum | descended |

## Speaking and Listening

1. Tall tales, legends, and ghost stories were often told, not read. Reread one of the following stories, take notes, and practice giving your version of the story orally.

☐ "Jim Bridger and the Fiddler Who Wouldn't Fiddle"

☐ "Poor Sandy"

☐ "The Turn of the Screw"

Be prepared to present your version of the story to the class.

2. When you read poetry aloud, you often appreciate elements of the poem that you might not notice through silent reading. Repetition of the lines helps you to hear the sounds of the words and the rhythm they create when they are arranged together. Choose one of the following poems by Emily Dickinson to read aloud. Practice reading the poem until you feel familiar enough with it to share it with others. Then present the poem aloud to the class.

☐ " 'Hope' Is the Thing With Feathers"

☐ "A Word Is Dead"

☐ "The Wind Tapped Like a Tired Man"

**Researching.** A griffin is a creature from Greek mythology. Choose one of the following mythological creatures to research, and write a short report on it. From what culture did it originate? What did it represent? What did it look like?

| | |
|---|---|
| dragon | gorgon |
| hippogriff | centaur |
| chimera | unicorn |

## Creating

1. Emily Dickinson wrote a poem about hope. Hope is an abstract noun difficult to define. Select one of the following abstract nouns, and write a poem to express its meaning.

| | |
|---|---|
| love | courage |
| happiness | freedom |
| anger | beauty |

2. In the first paragraph of "The Griffin and the Minor Canon," the Griffin is described in detail. Using the description as a guide, draw what you think the Griffin looked like.

# THE RAVEN
## EDGAR ALLAN POE

*In addition to his tales of horror and suspense, like "The Pit and the Pendulum" (page 268), Edgar Allan Poe is famous for his hauntingly musical poems. By far his most celebrated poem is "The Raven," which was first published in 1845 in a New York newspaper. Like many of Poe's tales, "The Raven" depicts a drama that rages within a character's mind.*

*Suddenly There Came a Tapping.* Edouard Manet.
Courtesy, Museum of Fine Arts, Boston. Gift of W. G. Russell Allen.

Once upon a midnight dreary, while I pondered, weak and weary,
Over many a quaint and curious volume of forgotten lore—
While I nodded, nearly napping, suddenly there came a tapping,
As of some one gently rapping, rapping at my chamber door.
"'Tis some visitor," I muttered, "tapping at my chamber door—
      Only this and nothing more."

Ah, distinctly I remember it was in the bleak December;
And each separate dying ember wrought[1] its ghost upon the floor.
Eagerly I wished the morrow;—vainly I had sought to borrow
From my books surcease[2] of sorrow—sorrow for the lost Lenore—
For the rare and radiant maiden whom the angels name Lenore—
      Nameless *here* for evermore.

And the silken, sad, uncertain rustling of each purple curtain
Thrilled me—filled me with fantastic terrors never felt before;
So that now, to still the beating of my heart, I stood repeating,
"'Tis some visitor entreating entrance at my chamber door—
Some late visitor entreating entrance at my chamber door;—
      This it is and nothing more."

Presently my soul grew stronger; hesitating then no longer,
"Sir," said I, "or Madam, truly your forgiveness I implore;
But the fact is I was napping, and so gently you came rapping,
And so faintly you came tapping, tapping at my chamber door,
That I scarce was sure I heard you"—here I opened wide the door;—
      Darkness there and nothing more.

Deep into that darkness peering, long I stood there wondering, fearing,
Doubting, dreaming dreams no mortal ever dared to dream before;
But the silence was unbroken, and the stillness gave no token,
And the only word there spoken was the whispered word, "Lenore?"
This I whispered, and an echo murmured back the word, "Lenore!"
      Merely this and nothing more.

---

1. **wrought:** past tense of *work*.
2. **surcease:** an end; discontinuation.

*Perched Upon a Pallid Bust of Pallas.* Edouard Manet.
Courtesy, Museum of Fine Arts,
Boston. Gift of W. G. Russell Allen.

Back into the chamber turning, all my soul within me burning,
Soon again I heard a tapping somewhat louder than before.
"Surely," said I, "surely that is something at my window lattice;
Let me see, then, what thereat is, and this mystery explore—
35 Let my heart be still a moment and this mystery explore—
      'Tis the wind and nothing more!"

Open here I flung the shutter, when, with many a flirt[3] and flutter,
In there stepped a stately Raven of the saintly days of yore;[4]
Not the least obeisance[5] made he; not a minute stopped or stayed he;
40 But, with mien[6] of lord or lady, perched above my chamber door—
Perched upon a bust of Pallas[7] just above my chamber door—
      Perched, and sat, and nothing more.

---

3. **flirt:** abrupt, jerking movement.
4. **yore:** time long past.
5. **obeisance** (ō bā′ səns): a bow, curtsy, or other sign of respect.
6. **mien** (mēn): manner.
7. **Pallas** (păl′ əs): Pallas Athena, the goddess of wisdom in Greek mythology.

Then this ebony bird beguiling my sad fancy into smiling,
By the grave and stern decorum of the countenance[8] it wore,
45 "Though thy crest be shorn and shaven, thou," I said, "art sure no craven,[9]
Ghastly grim and ancient Raven wandering from the Nightly shore—
Tell me what thy lordly name is on the Night's Plutonian[10] shore!"
      Quoth the Raven, "Nevermore."

Much I marveled this ungainly fowl to hear discourse so plainly,
50 Though its answer little meaning—little relevancy bore;
For we cannot help agreeing that no living human being
Ever yet was blessed with seeing bird above his chamber door—
Bird or beast upon the sculptured bust above his chamber door,
      With such name as "Nevermore."

55 But the Raven, sitting lonely on the placid bust, spoke only
That one word, as if his soul in that one word he did outpour.
Nothing farther then he uttered—not a feather then he fluttered—
Till I scarcely more than muttered, "Other friends have flown before—
On the morrow *he* will leave me, as my Hopes have flown before."
60       Then the bird said, "Nevermore."

Startled at the stillness broken by reply so aptly spoken,
"Doubtless," said I, "what it utters is its only stock and store
Caught from some unhappy master whom unmerciful Disaster
Followed fast and followed faster till his songs one burden[11] bore—
65 Till the dirges of his Hope that melancholy burden bore
      Of 'Never—nevermore.' "

But the Raven still beguiling my sad fancy into smiling,
Straight I wheeled a cushioned seat in front of bird and bust and door;
Then, upon the velvet sinking, I betook myself to linking
70 Fancy unto fancy, thinking what this ominous bird of yore—
What this grim, ungainly, ghastly, gaunt, and ominous bird of yore
      Meant in croaking "Nevermore."

---

8. **countenance:** appearance, especially facial features.
9. **craven:** coward.
10. **Plutonian** (plo͞o tō′ nē ən): referring to Pluto, the god of the dead and ruler of the underworld (the land of darkness) in Roman mythology.
11. **burden:** a refrain of a song.

This I sat engaged in guessing, but no syllable expressing
To the fowl whose fiery eyes now burned into my bosom's core;
75 This and more I sat divining, with my head at ease reclining
On the cushion's velvet lining that the lamplight gloated o'er,
But whose velvet-violet lining with the lamplight gloating o'er,
    *She* shall press, ah, nevermore!

Then, methought,[12] the air grew denser, perfumed from an unseen censer[13]
80 Swung by seraphim[14] whose footfalls tinkled on the tufted floor.
"Wretch," I cried, "thy God hath lent thee—by these angels he hath sent thee
Respite[15]—respite and nepenthe[16] from thy memories of Lenore;
Quaff,[17] oh, quaff this kind nepenthe and forget this lost Lenore!"
    Quoth the Raven, "Nevermore."

85 "Prophet!" said I, "thing of evil!—prophet still, if bird or devil!—
Whether Tempter[18] sent, or whether tempest tossed thee here ashore,
Desolate yet all undaunted, on this desert land enchanted—
On this home by Horror haunted—tell me truly, I implore—
Is there—*is* there balm in Gilead?[19]—tell me—tell me, I implore!"
90     Quoth the Raven, "Nevermore."

"Prophet!" said I, "thing of evil!—prophet still, if bird or devil!
By that Heaven that bends above us—by that God we both adore—
Tell this soul with sorrow laden if, within the distant Aidenn,[20]
It shall clasp a sainted maiden whom the angels name Lenore—
95 Clasp a rare and radiant maiden whom the angels name Lenore."
    Quoth the Raven, "Nevermore."

---

12. **methought:** an old-fashioned expression meaning "I thought to myself."
13. **censer:** a container in which incense is burned.
14. **seraphim** (sĕr′ ə fĭm): angels of the highest rank.
15. **respite:** a period of temporary relief from pain.
16. **nepenthe** (nĕ pĕn′ thĕ): a drug which the ancient Greeks believed gave relief from pain and sorrow.
17. **quaff** (kwŏf): to drink heartily.
18. **Tempter:** that is, the Devil.
19. **balm in Gilead** (gĭl′ ē əd): a line from the Bible (Jeremiah 8:22), referring to
a healing ointment (a balm) made in a region in ancient Palestine called Gilead.
The question means, "Is there relief from my sorrow?"
20. **Aidenn** (ā′ dĕn): Arabic for *Eden; heaven; paradise.*

"Be that word our sign of parting, bird or fiend!" I shrieked, upstarting—
"Get thee back into the tempest and the Night's Plutonian shore!
Leave no black plume as a token of that lie thy soul hath spoken!
100 Leave my loneliness unbroken!—quit the bust above my door!
Take thy beak from out my heart, and take thy form from off my door!"
       Quoth the Raven, "Nevermore."

And the Raven, never flitting, still is sitting, *still* is sitting
On the pallid bust of Pallas just above my chamber door;
105 And his eyes have all the seeming of a demon's that is dreaming,
And the lamplight o'er him streaming throws his shadow on the floor;
And my soul from out that shadow that lies floating on the floor
       Shall be lifted—nevermore!

# THINKING ABOUT
# THE POEM

*Recalling*

1. This poem tells a story and has a **setting**. At what time of day and year do the events happen? Where does the action take place?

2. What is the speaker doing when he first hears the tapping? According to stanza 2, why is he engaged in this activity?

3. In stanzas 4 and 5, the speaker opens his door and looks out. What does he find there? Who does he think might be outside?

4. When the Raven enters, where does he perch? What one word does he speak? What explanation does the speaker give in stanza 11 for what the Raven says?

5. According to lines 81–83, what does the speaker imagine has been sent to him? What questions does he ask the Raven in lines 88–89 and 93–95? How does the bird reply?

6. What does the Raven do after the speaker orders him to leave? According to the last stanza, where will the speaker's soul stay forever?

*Interpreting*

7. From what the speaker thinks and says, who do you imagine Lenore was? What do you suppose happened to her?

8. The details that Poe uses to describe the **setting** in this poem create a general **mood** or feeling. Considering these details of setting, describe the mood that they convey.

9. Like a story, this poem describes a **conflict**, or struggle between opposing forces. Although the speaker seems to be involved in an external struggle with the Raven, the real conflict is internal, within the speaker's own mind. What two opposing ideas are struggling for control of the speaker's mind? Which side wins?

10. Pallas Athena was the Greek goddess of wisdom. What is the significance of having the Raven perch atop a bust of her rather than some other god? What does the Raven come to **symbolize**, or represent, within the poem?

*Applying*

11. What advice would you give to someone like the speaker, whose grief over the loss of a loved one had led to hopelessness?

# ANALYZING
# LITERATURE

*Music in Poetry*

In his essay "The Poetic Principle," Poe stressed the importance of "the union of Poetry With Music." He believed that poets who sang their poems or used musical instruments were able to give their listeners "a shivering delight." Poe also knew, however, that the words themselves in a poem could have a musical effect. As you listened to "The Raven," you probably felt the effect of Poe's *word music* even before you began to understand what the poem was about. The very sounds of Poe's words helped to create the poem's eerie mood, to convey particular ideas, and to reveal the speaker's highly nervous and obsessive nature.

Like regular music, the music in poetry is usually based on **repetition**. A poet, for example, may repeat a word or phrase to emphasize a particular idea:

From my books surcease of *sorrow*—
*sorrow* for the lost Lenore—

Consonant sounds may be repeated at the beginnings of nearby words or within words. This kind of repetition is called **alliteration**. In this line the *s*-sounds let you hear the movement of the curtain:

the *s*ilken, *s*ad, un*c*ertain ru*s*tling of each purple *c*urtain

The repetition of nearby vowel sounds is called **assonance**. The long *a*-sounds in the following line suggest the deep admiration the speaker had for his lost Lenore:

the r*a*re and r*a*diant m*a*iden whom the *a*ngels n*a*me Lenore

When the words in a poem form a repeating pattern of stressed and unstressed syllables, the poem is said to have **meter**. Throughout "The Raven," Poe uses a pattern of eight stressed sylla-

bles per line (except in each stanza's last line, which has four). Each stressed syllable (′) is usually followed by one unstressed syllable (˘):

Ŏnce ŭpón ă mídnĭght dréarў, whĭle Ĭ pónderĕd, wéak ănd wéarў,

**Rhyme** is yet another kind of repetition in poetry. Words rhyme when they end with the same or nearly the same sound, such as *remember* and *December* or *enchanted* and *haunted*. Notice how Poe rhymes the *or*-sound throughout "The Raven": *lore, door, more, floor, Lenore, evermore,* and so on to the final *nevermore*! Poe chose this rhyming sound because it conveys a mournful mood. It also suggests the speaker's obsession with his grief. Poe also uses rhymes within lines. The first line and the third and fourth lines of each stanza contain **internal rhymes**:

This I sat engaged in *guessing*, but no syllable *expressing*
This and more I sat *divining*, with my head at ease *reclining*
On the cushion's velvet *lining* that the lamplight gloated o'er,

Together all these different kinds of repetition create the distinctive music that Poe thought would be appropriate for the story he tells in "The Raven."

Identify at least one more example of each of the following kinds of repetition in "The Raven": repeated words or phrases, alliteration, assonance, internal rhyme. Explain the particular effect that Poe creates with each example.

## CRITICAL THINKING AND READING

*Drawing Conclusions*

Authors often present details and incidents in their stories and poems and leave it up to readers to draw their own conclusions. For example, Poe describes the Raven in such a way that readers must decide for themselves whether the bird is indeed a "thing of evil" and a "devil" or just someone's escaped pet.

On a piece of paper, make two columns with the headings "Natural Bird" and "Supernatural Demon." Next, find details in the poem that serve as evidence regarding the Raven's true nature. List the details under the appropriate heading. When you complete your list, consider your evidence and draw a conclusion regarding the Raven: Do you agree with the poem's speaker that the bird is a demon? Why or why not?

## DEVELOPING VOCABULARY SKILLS

*Antonyms*

The somber mood that Poe creates in "The Raven" depends not only on the poem's sound, but also on descriptive words like *bleak* and *dying*. To understand how important Poe's word choices are in creating the poem's overall effect, try listing one or more **antonyms**, or words with opposite meanings, for each adjective below. Use a dictionary if you need help.

1. dreary (line 1)
2. melancholy (line 65)
3. gaunt (line 71)
4. ominous (line 71)
5. desolate (line 87)

## THINKING AND WRITING

**1. Writing a Poem.**

Imagine that the speaker in "The Raven" is himself a poet. What kind of poem do you think he might write about his "lost Lenore." Try writing a short poem about Lenore using the speaker's point of view.

**Prewriting.** Poe believed that a poem should convey a single overall emotional effect. Think about the one emotion that you want to convey in your poem, such as love, despair, or joy. Then jot down words and phrases that might help you convey that emotion.

**Writing.** Draw on your list of words and phrases to write your poem, but feel free to add or change words as you go along. Concentrate on expressing a single strong emotion about Lenore.

**Revising.** Reread your poem aloud. Listen closely to the sounds of your words. Does your word music suit the emotion you are expressing? Decide whether or not you want to revise your lines using rhyme and meter. Can any phrases be made more musical by using alliteration and assonance? Do you want to repeat certain words or phrases for emphasis? Experiment with different wordings until you feel you have created the right effect.

**Proofreading.** Correct any mistakes in grammar, spelling, and punctuation in your poem. Prepare a neat, final copy.

**Publishing.** You might contribute your poem to a class anthology of Lenore poems. As an alternative, you might participate in a group poetry reading in which you read your poem or someone else's for the class's enjoyment. The class might then vote for the best poem.

## 2. Analyzing a Character.

In "The Raven" Poe never actually describes the main character who speaks the poem. Nevertheless, readers can tell much about his personality from the way he addresses and responds to the Raven, from the description he gives of his chamber, and from the feelings he expresses for Lenore. Write a short essay in which you first identify the speaker's main character traits and then support your analysis with evidence from the poem.

**Prewriting.** Reread "The Raven" and make notes regarding the way the speaker reacts to the Raven, describes his room, and talks of Lenore. Then ask yourself questions: What kind of man reacts this way, lives in such surroundings, and has these emotions? Use your responses as the basis for your essay's main idea.

**Writing.** Organize your prewriting notes into paragraphs—one for each topic: reactions to the Raven, descriptions of the room, and feelings for Lenore. Begin each paragraph with a straightforward topic sentence. For example, you might begin one paragraph like this: "The way the speaker reacts to the Raven reveals a personality that is increasingly _____." Then support your topic sentence by quoting evidence from the poem.

**Revising.** Make sure that your essay begins with a general statement that introduces all of the points that you raise later on. Check to be sure that you have included enough evidence from the poem to make your arguments convincing. Consider sharing your draft with a classmate to get his or her input.

**Proofreading.** Reread your composition, and correct any mistakes in grammar, spelling, and punctuation. Make sure you have quoted passages from the poem accurately. If necessary, prepare a neat, final copy.

**Publishing.** Read your paper to the class, and compare your character analysis to those of your classmates. What overall picture of the speaker's personality emerges?

# A VOICE OF COURAGE

## STEPHEN CRANE (1871-1900)

*A man said to the universe:*
*Sir, I exist!*

— Stephen Crane

*John Biglen in a Single Scull*
Thomas Eakins (1844-1916)
Metropolitan Museum of Art
Fletcher Fund

# Biography

# Stephen Crane

Stephen Crane believed that each person sees the world in his or her own way. His goal as a writer was to present his personal view as honestly as he could.

Anyone who reads Crane's works gets the feeling of sharing his vision. His power as a writer comes from the way he uses simple language to describe his characters' feelings and experiences.

## Crane's Early Life

Born on November 1, 1871, in Newark, New Jersey, Crane became a strong swimmer and an excellent baseball player.

Crane's two oldest brothers worked as newspaper reporters, and as a young teenager, he began to help them gather facts for stories. Like all good reporters, Crane trained himself to find the facts and report them objectively, to describe events as accurately and unemotionally as possible.

After one year of college, Crane became a reporter in New York City. For a while, he lived in the streets with the homeless people of the Bowery. He wanted to make sure his stories about life in the slums were correct in every detail.

When he was 21, he wrote a *novel*—a long work of fiction—that would tell people more about what it was like to live in the slums. The book was called *Maggie:*
*A Girl of the Streets,* and its realistic descriptions shocked many people.

Just one year later, Crane completed another novel. *The Red Badge of Courage* is about a teenage soldier who faces his first battle during the Civil War.

Crane himself had no personal experience with war. But he remembered his older brothers' tales of their experiences as Civil War soldiers, and he had studied Mathew Brady's photographs of the Civil War again and again. At last Crane could imagine every detail of what it would be like to be in the midst of a battle. *The Red Badge of Courage* captures his vision of the experience of war.

By 1895, *The Red Badge of Courage* had become one of the most popular books in America. At the age of 23, Stephen Crane was respected as one of America's greatest writers.

## Fame and Adventure

Fame brought Crane many new assignments as a reporter. He traveled to Texas and Mexico to write about life in the West. There he narrowly escaped being killed by bandits. Crane wrote several stories based on his experiences in Texas.

Crane also traveled to Greece to cover the Turkish War and to Cuba to report

on the Spanish-American War. This last assignment again brought him close to death when the ship he was on sank. Crane wrote a newspaper article as well as a story called "The Open Boat" based on the tragedy and the ordeal he experienced. Both the article and the story are included in this section.

All this travel and hardship took its toll on Crane's health. He became ill with tuberculosis. Yet he continued to travel and to write articles, stories, and poems.

Crane's poetry, like his stories and articles, uses simple words and vivid images. He wrote poetry because he felt that it presented his ideas more directly than other forms of writing. Two of his poems, "A Man Said to the Universe" and "The Wayfarer," are included in this section.

Crane spent the last two years of his life in Europe. He hoped the change in climate would cure him. It did not. He continued to write until his death in 1900, a few months before his 29th birthday.

In his brief lifetime, he had come face to face with poverty, failure, great danger, and illness. He had also known great adventure and literary success. He did not expect life to be fair or easy. He lived out his 29 years with honesty and courage. Like his most admirable characters, Crane faced life head on.

# The Red Badge of Courage

*by Stephen Crane*

*As you read this dramatization of the novel* The Red Badge of Courage, *think about the fears of the soldiers, their loyalties, and their sense of duty. Ask yourself why this story about young Henry Fleming has moved so many people since its publication in 1893.*

## CHARACTERS

Jim Conklin
Soldier 1
The Youth (Pvt. Henry Fleming)
Wilson
The Youth's Mother
Colonel
Soldier 2, on firing line
Lieutenant
Sergeant
Soldier 3, on firing line
General
Tattered Man
Corporal
Soldier 4
Soldier 5
Soldier 6
Narrator

*It is a cold spring morning in 1863. The smoke of several campfires drifts among the soldiers of the 304th New York regiment, Union Army. Some of the men are bent over their plates, eating their breakfast. Others are shaving and getting washed. The Youth, Pvt. Henry Fleming, is startled by the shouts of a soldier running up, waving a bright red shirt.*

**Jim:** We're movin' out! We're movin' out!

**Others:** Who told yeh? Who says so? Don't believe it. Me neither.

**Jim:** I tell yeh we're movin' out t'morrah! Got it from a friend, see, who got it from a cavalryman who got it from his brother who jest happens to be one of the orderlies at division headquarters.

**Soldier 1:** This here army ain't never gonna move again. I've got m'self ready t' go eight times in the last four weeks and we ain't moved yet.

**Jim:** Look here, I don't much care whether you believe it or not. Don't give a hang. You jest suit yerselves. (*He walks off.*)

(*Later that morning, the Youth is inside his hut as Jim Conklin and a soldier named Wilson enter. A third soldier follows them.*)

**Youth:** Jim?

**Jim:** Huh? What's that? You say somethin', Henry?

**Youth:** I . . . I was jest . . . yeh think there's goin' to be a real battle?

**Wilson** (*unbelieving*): Huh!

**Jim:** Oh, you'll see fightin' this time, m' boy. I mean what'll be out-and-out fightin'.

**Youth:** Jim?

**Jim:** What's th' matter?

**Youth** (*pauses*): How do yeh think th' reg'ment'll do?

**Jim:** Oh, they'll fight all right, I guess. After they oncet get into it.

**Youth:** Do yeh think . . . I mean . . . yeh think any of the boys'll run?

**Jim:** Oh, there may be a few of 'em run. 'Specially when they first goes under fire. Of course, it might happen the hull kit-and-boodle starts to run. . . . I mean if some big fightin' comes first off. And then again they might jest stay and fight like fun.

**Youth:** Nobody knows.

**Jim:** Huh? What's that?

**Youth:** What's it like?

**Jim:** Well now, lookee here, I don't figger we're goin' t' lick th' hull Rebel Army all-to-oncet th' first time out. No, sir. But we'll fight though, I reckon. Better than some and worse than others. Oh, sure. They call us "fresh fish" and everything.

But th' boys come of good stock and most of 'em'll fight like sin after they oncet get shootin'.

**Youth:** Have yeh . . . have yeh ever thought yeh might run yourself?

**Jim:** Well . . . I've thought it might get too hot for ol' Jim Conklin in some of them scrimmages, and if a whole lot of boys started to run, why I s'pose I'd start and run. And if I oncet started to run, I'd run like th' devil and no mistake. But if everybody else was a standin' and fightin', why, I'd stand and fight. B' jiminey, I sure would. Wouldn't *you*, Henry?

(*The next morning, the regiment moves out. At noon, the troops stop for lunch. The Youth, seated off by himself, pulls off a boot and looks down at a hole in his sock. He hears a voice.*)

**Voice of Mother:** Yeh send 'em back. (*The Youth looks up to see who's speaking.*) Yeh git a hole in 'em, you send 'em right back to me, hear?

(*The mother appears. But she is standing at the doorway to the Youth's home. The Youth imagines himself at home.*)

**Mother:** I've knit yeh eight pairs of socks, Henry, and I've put in all yer best shirts, b'cause I want my boy to be jest as warm and comfortable as anybody in th' army. Whenever they get holes in 'em, I want yeh to send 'em right-away back to me, so's I kin dern 'em.

**Youth:** Yes, ma'am.

**Mother:** An' be careful now t' choose yer company. There's lots of bad men in th' army, Henry. Th' army makes 'em wild and they like nothin' better than th' job

of leadin' off a young feller like yeh, who ain't never been away from home much, and a-learning 'em to drink and swear. Keep clear of them folks, Henry.

**Youth:** Yes, ma'am.

**Mother:** And take good care of yerself in this here fightin' business. Don't yeh go shirkin', child, on my account. If th' time comes when yeh have to be kilt or do a mean thing, why, don't yeh think of anything 'cept what's right.

**Youth:** Yes, ma'am.

**Mother:** Here. Here's yer Bible. I don't presume yeh'll be a-settin' readin' it all day, but comes a time yeh'll want advice, there's wisdom in it, child. There's wisdom with little or no searchin'.

**Youth:** I'll read it, Ma.

**Mother:** Well, then. Be a good boy. An' don't forget about yer socks. All right?

*(There are tears in the mother's eyes. The Youth is about to embrace her, but as he reaches forward, she disappears.)*

**Wilson:** What's that yer saying?

*(The Youth, looking bewildered, shakes his head.)*

**Wilson:** Boy, I don't know, Henry, yer sure actin' peculiar. Come on, now. We're movin' again.

*(The troops are on the move when the sound of artillery is heard. The Colonel comes riding down the line on horseback.*

**Colonel:** The grove! Make for the grove!

*(The men run for the grove and form a firing line.)*

**Soldier 2** *(on the Youth's right)*: Hey, yeh know what I heard? I heard th' Colonel say he's goin' t' shoot th' first man who turns and runs.

**Wilson:** Henry? *(The Youth turns to Wilson, puzzled.)* You do me a favor? *(The Youth stares at Wilson.)* It's my first and last . . . battle.

**Youth:** What?

**Wilson:** I can feel it. My first and last battle, Henry. Something tells me. I'm a goner this first time and I . . . Henry, I want yeh to take these here things . . . to my folks. *(He holds up a small packet of letters.)*

**Youth:** Why . . . what th' devil . . . ?

**Lieutenant:** Here they come!

**Soldier 2:** Oh, Lordy, Lordy. We're in for it now.

**Lieutenant:** Fire!

**Sergeant:** Fire!

*(The troops open fire. Men drop here and there like bundles. A soldier on the line screams a wild, barbaric scream and starts to run.)*

**Lieutenant:** Get back! Get back!

*(Soldiers continue to fire. But there is little fire from the enemy.)*

**Youth:** What's happenin'?

**Soldier 3** *(on the Youth's left)*: They've stopped.

**Youth:** Huh?

**Soldier 3:** Oh, dear Gawd, they've stopped.

**Sergeant:** Hold your fire! Hold your fire!

*(The Youth looks down the line of soldiers. He sees fallen soldiers, then turns to the soldier on his left, feeling sudden tenderness and goodwill toward him.)*

**Youth:** Gee . . . ain't it hot, huh?

**Soldier 3:** You bet. I never seen sech dumb hotness. *(He laughs.)*

**Lieutenant:** They're coming back!

*(Soldiers, their faces smudged, reload and fire. Suddenly the soldier on the Youth's left cries out.)*

**Soldier 3:** Oh, Gawd . . . they've kilt me. Oh, Gawd. . . .

*(The Youth stares in horror as the soldier slumps over. The soldier on the Youth's right lets out a howl of anguish and runs off. The gunfire is now a pounding roar. The Youth panics, stands up, bewildered and terrified. Then, taking a deep breath, he starts to run. Like a blind man, he trips, falls, rises again, crosses an open field, plunges into a grove of trees, then hears the sound of approaching horses. In the clearing beyond, the Youth sees the Colonel and the Division General.)*

**Colonel:** We're holdin' 'em, sir. Right down the line.

**General:** By heaven we are! We'll wallop 'em now! We've got 'em sure!

*(The Youth is stunned by the news. Tears come to his eyes. He stumbles on through the brush. He comes to a dusty road where a procession of wounded soldiers is approaching. Bloodstained and tattered, the men are cursing and groaning and wailing to themselves. The Youth watches the wounded pass by, then steps into line beside a soldier fouled with dust and in a tattered uniform.)*

**Tattered Man:** Pretty good fight.

**Youth:** What? . . . What?

**Tattered Man:** It was a pretty good fight, wasn't it?

**Youth:** Yes.

**Tattered Man:** I was talkin' cross pickets with a boy from Georgia one night, an' that boy he sez, "Yer fellers'll run like th' devil when they oncet hear a gun," he sez. An I sez back to 'um, "Maybe yer fellers'll all run like th' devil, too!" Well . . . he larfed. No, sir. They didn't run today. They stood and fit, b' Gawd.

*(The Youth tries to move ahead, but the Tattered Man keeps right up with him.)*

**Tattered Man:** Where yeh hit? *(The Youth, in panic, looks the other way.)* Hey, I sed, where yeh hit, ol' boy?

**Youth:** I . . . I . . .

*(The Youth turns away and moves back down the line. Because of the Tattered Man's question, he is now sure everyone knows his guilt. He wishes that he, too, had a wound, a red badge of courage. He falls into line next to a gravely wounded soldier.)*

**Youth:** Jim! Jim Conklin!

**Jim:** Well . . . hello, Henry.

**Youth:** I'm so glad to see yeh, Jim.

**Jim:** What a circus it was, huh? An' yeh know, b' jiminey, I got shot.

**Youth:** Let me help you, Jim.

**Jim** *(clutches the Youth's arm)*: I'll tell yeh what I'm 'fraid of, Henry. I'm 'fraid I'll fall down an' . . . an' then them artillery wagons . . . they'll like as not run me over.

*(The Tattered Man appears at the Youth's side.)*

**Tattered Man:** Yeh better take 'im outta th' road. He'll git run over sure.

**Youth:** Jim, yeh come with me. Please!

*(Jim tries to wrench himself free.)*

**Jim:** Wha'sa matter?

**Youth:** Please!

**Jim:** Oh? Into th' field. Th' field, huh?

*(Jim breaks away and runs off blindly into the field, the Youth and Tattered Man following. Suddenly Jim's body stiffens and straightens. Shaking all over, he meets death.)*

**Youth** *(filled with grief, faces toward the sound of battle)*: Damn you! Damn you!

*(The Youth, weary and forlorn, walks away. He comes upon a company of infantry, charging across the field. He tries to question them, but they will not stop. When he grabs one by the arm, the soldier yells at the Youth to let him go, and finally hits the Youth over the head with his rifle. When the Youth regains consciousness, a friendly soldier is standing over him, who helps him find his way back to his regiment.)*

**Wilson:** Halt! Halt there!

**Youth:** Hello, Wilson.

**Wilson:** Henry. That yeh, Henry?

**Youth:** It's me.

**Wilson:** Well now, I give yeh up for a goner, that's sure. I thought yeh was dead, Henry.

**Youth:** Well . . . I've had an awful time. I got separated from th' reg'ment. I got shot. In th' head. I never seen sech fightin' an' awful time.

**Wilson:** Here, let me have a good look at it first, Henry. You set yerself down there an' I'll see how bad it is. *(The Youth sits down.)* Henry, it's as I thought. Yeh've been grazed by a ball. It's raised a queer lump jest as if some feller had lammed yeh on th' head with a club. But it stopped bleedin' a long time ago. *(He bandages the wound.)* Good. That's good. And yeh never hollered 'er nothin'. Yer a good 'un, Henry. Most men would a been in th' hospital long ago. A shot in th' head ain't foolin' business. Come on, now, I'm goin' t' see yeh git a good night's sleep.

*(The next morning, the soldiers line up to move out. Wilson steps up with an extra gun for the Youth.)*

**Wilson:** Here you go, Henry.
**Youth:** Did yeh ever think . . .
**Wilson:** Huh? What's that?
**Youth:** . . . that some people are chosen maybe?
**Wilson:** Chosen? Fer what?
**Youth:** I mean like chosen of th' gods. People jest meant to be picked out from all th' rest and no matter what happens they get through jest fine. You can't kill 'em b'cause they're chosen of the gods. Do you believe in that?
**Wilson:** Henry, I don't know what th' devil yer even talkin' about.
**Corporal:** Keep it movin'. Move along there!

*(The sound of gunfire grows louder. The soldiers take cover. Wilson is suddenly at the Youth's side.)*

**Wilson:** Henry, I uh . . . if it's all th' same to yeh . . . well, I guess yeh might as well give me back them letters.
**Youth:** All right. *(He hands the packet to Wilson, whose face is turned away from him in shame. Seeing his friend's embarrassment, the Youth says nothing.)*

*(A loud volley of gunfire is heard in the woods. The order is given to fire, and the Youth, with wild hatred in his eyes, fires directly at the oncoming line of enemy soldiers. The gray line falters, and falls back in retreat. The order is given to charge. The soldiers run into a tremendous volley of enemy gunfire. Several soldiers are struck. One by one, the soldiers come to a halt.)*

**Lieutenant:** Come on, yeh fools! Yeh can't stay here! Move! *(No one moves.)* Skulkin' cowards! Yeh want t' die right here? We've got t' move! Got to!
**Wilson:** Well, Henry . . . I guess we're finished.
**Youth:** Oh, shut up! Come on, let's go! Let's go!

*(The Youth charges forward like a madman. Wilson and others follow. A color sergeant carrying the flag is struck down. The Youth wrenches the flag away, and charges directly into the line of fire. The soldiers in blue hurl themselves recklessly on toward the gray line. The gray line breaks and runs. A hoarse and frantic cheer goes up from the blue line. The Youth surveys the battlefield where gray corpses are scattered about. The cheers die out. The guns grow silent.)*

*(The next day, the battle-weary soldiers make their way back to permanent camp. The Youth and Wilson trudge alongside each other when three soldiers come up alongside, faces shining with excitement.)*

**Soldier 4:** You fellers jest oughta heard!
**Soldier 5:** Right next to us. Th' Colonel and th' Lieutenant was talkin'.

**Soldier 6:** Th' Colonel, he sez, "Who was th' lad who carried th' flag?"

**Soldier 5:** That's jest what he said. An' th' Lieutenant speaks right up an' sez, "That was Fleming, sir. Private Fleming carried th' flag."

**Soldier 6:** An' th' Colonel sez, "If I had 10,000 wildcats like him, I could tear th' stomach outta this war in less'n a week."

**Soldier 4:** You and Wilson, sez th' Lieutenant. You two was headin' th' charge an' howlin' like Injuns all th' time.

**Soldier 6:** An' yeh know what th' Colonel sez then? He sez, "They both deserve to be major generals." That's exactly what he sez. Major generals.

**Wilson:** Yer lyin'.

**Soldier 5:** Swear to God.

**Youth:** He never said it.

**Soldier 4:** He did, by Gawd. We heard 'em!

*(The Youth and Wilson glance at each other. Despite their embarrassment, their eyes are glistening and their faces are flushed with pleasure.)*

**Narrator:** The Battle of Chancellorsville lasted four days and ended on May 4, 1863. Twenty-five thousand men were killed or wounded including a Southern general known to his troops as Stonewall Jackson. All the wounded on these fields of battle had received their red badge of courage. But the Youth, however, emerged from his struggles with something else. He knew that he would never again quail before his guides wherever they should point him. He had been to touch the great death, and found out that after all, it was but the great death. He was a man.

**Summarizing.** Choose the best phrase to complete each sentence. Then write the complete statements on your paper.

1. In the Youth's dream, his mother urged him to _____ (return home immediately, answer her last letter, stand up and fight when the time came).

2. After the soldier next to him was killed, the Youth _____ (started to shoot, panicked and ran, was wounded).

3. The Youth was wounded in the head because _____ (a friendly soldier hit him over the head with a rifle, a friendly soldier shot him by mistake, an enemy soldier shot him).

4. When the soldiers stopped their charge against the enemy, the Youth _____ (ran away, carried the flag into battle, also stopped fighting).

**Interpreting.** Write the answer to each question on your paper.

1. Why did the Tattered Man tell the Youth to try to pull Jim Conklin off the road?

2. Why did the Youth want to have his own "red badge of courage"?

3. In the beginning, how did Jim Conklin's feelings about the coming battle contrast with the Youth's feelings?

**For Thinking and Discussing.** How do you think the Youth would behave in future battles? Explain your answer.

349

# UNDERSTANDING LITERATURE

**Theme.** The *theme* of a play or story is the main idea or message the author is writing about. It is the point, usually about life or nature, that the author feels strong about. The author uses the characters, the setting, and the plot to make the point.

Some stories and plays contain more than one theme. *The Red Badge of Courage* contains several intertwined themes about courage, war, and growing up. Each theme is supported by the character Henry Fleming and the setting—the battle. Stephen Crane used Henry's actions and feelings to express several themes.

Here are three themes from *The Red Badge of Courage*:

**a.** Confusion, fear, and luck are as much a part of war as bravery and planning.

**b.** A child becomes an adult when he or she acts from a sense of what is right rather than out of fear or ignorance.

**c.** You must conquer the fear of death before you can think clearly enough to face battle bravely.

Below are passages that contain stage directions and dialogue from the play. On your paper, match each passage with the theme or themes listed above that the passage suggests.

1. "**Mother:** . . . Don't yeh go shirkin', child, on my account. If th' time comes when yeh have to be kilt or do a mean thing, why, don't yeh think of anything 'cept what's right."

2. "(. . . *Bloodstained and tattered, the men are cursing and groaning and wailing to themselves. The Youth watches the wounded pass by, then steps into line beside a soldier fouled with dust and in a tattered uniform.*)"

3. "**Tattered Man:** . . . They didn't run today. They stood and fit, b'Gawd."

4. "**Youth:** Did yeh ever think . . . that some people are chosen maybe? . . . People jest meant to be picked out from all th' rest and no matter what happens they get through fine. . . ."

5. "**Wilson:** Well, Henry . . . I guess we're finished.
"**Youth:** Oh, shut up! Come on, let's go! Let's go!
"(*The Youth charges forward like a madman. Wilson and others follow. A color sergeant carrying the flag is struck down. The Youth wrenches the flag away, and charges directly into the line of fire. . . .*)"

6. "**Narrator:** . . . He knew that he would never again quail before his guides wherever they should point him. He had been to touch the great death, and found out that after all, it was but the great death. He was a man."

# WRITING

Pretend that you are Henry. Describe the following situations in your diary: the time before battle, the time you panicked and ran away, and your feelings after fighting in a battle. Write a paragraph for each situation.

# The Wayfarer

*by Stephen Crane*

The wayfarer
Perceiving the pathway to truth
Was struck with astonishment.
It was thickly grown with weeds.
"Ha," he said,
"I see that none has passed here
In a long time."
Later he saw that each weed
Was a singular knife.
"Well," he mumbled at last,
"Doubtless there are other roads."

---

1. What does the fact that "the pathway to truth was thickly grown with weeds" suggest?

2. In this poem, the way to truth is described as a pathway. How do people search for truth in real life? Do you think the search is as difficult as Crane suggests? Why or why not?

# The Wreck of the Commodore
## Stephen Crane's Own Story

*The following story first appeared in a newspaper called The New York Press on January 7, 1897. Stephen Crane had sailed on the Commodore to write a story about gunrunners during the Spanish-American War. As you will see, the news story he wrote is very different from the one he had expected to write.*

JACKSONVILLE, FLA., JAN. 6 — It was the afternoon of New Year's Eve. The *Commodore* was docked in Jacksonville. As stevedores steadily loaded box after box onto the ship, her hatch, like the mouth of a monster, engulfed them.

Everything was perfectly open. The *Commodore* was cleared with a cargo of arms and munitions for Cuba. The boat loaded up as calmly as if she were carrying oranges to New York.

### Exchanging Farewells

There was some difficulty at the customs house. The ship was detained until twilight had settled upon the bay. The lights of Jacksonville blinked dimly through a heavy fog. At last the *Commodore* swung clear of the dock amid a chorus of good-byes. As she turned toward the distant sea, the Cubans ashore cheered. In response, the *Commodore* gave three long blasts of her whistle. Somehow they sounded sad.

There was danger in carrying guns to Cuba. Yet we were all enveloped in a gentle cheerfulness. Twice the *Commodore* was beached* before we reached open sea, on the night of January 1.

### Sleep Impossible

Now huge waves came lashing at the ship and a certain lightheartedness departed from the men aboard. That night I could not sleep. I was far too excited. When I did try to get some rest in my bunk, I found I had to hold on to the bed to keep from being pitched around the room.

I went into the galley and found the cook sleeping on a bench. He had used a

---

* *Beached*—stuck in the mud.

**Eight Bells,** Winslow Homer, 1886

checkerboard to wedge himself in so that the motion of the ship would not dislodge him. He awoke when I entered. "I don't feel right about this ship," he said. "It strikes me that something is going to happen to us. This old ship is going to get it in the neck."

"Well, how about the men on board?" said I. "Are any of us going to get out, prophet?"

"Yes," said the cook. "Sometimes I have these feelings come over me. They are always right. It seems to me that somehow you and I will both get out and meet again somewhere."

Next I went to the pilot house. An old seaman, Tom Smith, was then at the wheel. In the darkness I could not see Tom's face. "Well, Tom," I said, "how do you like the sea?"

He said, "I've been on a number of these trips. The pay is pretty good, but I

353

think if I ever get back safe this time, I will cut it."

I sat down in a corner of the pilot house and I almost went to sleep. The captain came on duty and he was standing near me. Suddenly the chief engineer rushed in and cried that there was something wrong in the engine room. He and the captain left at once.

I was drowsing in my corner when the captain returned. He went to the room just beyond the pilot house and called to the Cuban leader, "Come get those fellows to work. I can't talk their language and I can't get them going."

## No Panic on Board

The Cuban leader turned to me and said, "Go help in the fireroom. They are going to bail with buckets."

The engine room looked like the middle kitchen of hell. It was very hot. The lights burned faintly, casting strange shadows. Soapish seawater swirled and swished among machinery that roared and clattered and steamed.

Here I first came to know a young oiler named Billy Higgins. He was sloshing around, filling buckets with water and passing them to a chain of men that extended up the ship's side.

During this time there was much talk of pumps and machines. I did not understand all of it, but I did understand that there was a general and sudden ruin in the engine room.

There was no panic at this time, and even later there was never any panic on board the *Commodore*.

## Lowering Boats

The heat and hard work in the fireroom affected me and I had to come on deck again. I saw the first boat about to be lowered. A certain man sat alone in the boat with a valise about as large as a hotel. I had not entirely recovered from the astonishment of witnessing this "noble deed" when I saw another valise go to him.

Now I heard the order to getaway the lifeboat which was stowed on top of the deckhouse. The deckhouse was very slippery. With each roll of the ship the men there thought themselves likely to fall into the deadly sea.

Higgins was on top of the deckhouse and with the first mate and two other men we wrestled with the lifeboat. We could have pushed a little brick schoolhouse down a road as easily as we could have moved the lifeboat. But the first mate rigged up a block and tackle. On the deck below the captain corralled enough men to move the boat. We were ordered to stop hauling.

In this lull the cook of the ship asked me, "What are you going to do?"

I told him of my plans, and he said, "Well, that's what I am going to do, too."

Now the whistle of the *Commodore* began to blow. If ever there was a voice of death and despair it was the voice of this whistle.

It was now that the first mate showed a sign of losing his grip: He raged at us who were trying to launch the lifeboat. But the boat moved at last and swung down into the water.

Afterward, I saw the captain standing with his arm in a sling, holding onto a stay with his one good hand. He directed the launching of the boat. Then he gave me a gallon jug of water to hold, and asked me what I was going to do.

I told him what I planned and he told me the cook had the same idea. Then he ordered me to go forward and be ready to launch the 10-foot dinghy.

### In the 10-Foot Dinghy

I went forward with my jug of water. When the captain came we launched the dinghy, and they put me over the side to fend her off from the ship with an oar.

They handed me down the water jug, and then the cook came into the boat. We sat there in the darkness, wondering why the captain had not yet come and ordered us away from the doomed ship.

The captain was waiting for the other boats to go. Finally he hailed in the darkness, "Are you all right, Mr. Graines?"

The first mate answered, "We are all right, sir."

"Shove off, then," cried the captain.

The captain was just about to swing over the rail when a dark form came forward and a voice said, "Captain, may I go with you?"

The captain answered, "Yes, Billy, you may get in."

It was Billy Higgins, the oiler. Billy dropped into the boat and a moment later the captain followed. He brought with him an end of about 40 yards of lead line. The other end was attached to the rail of the ship.

As we swung back the captain said, "Boys, we will stay right near the ship till she goes down." Of course, this cheerful information filled us all with glee. The line kept us headed properly into the wind. As we rode over the monstrous waves, we saw upon each rise the swaying lights of the dying *Commodore*.

When the gray dawn came, the form of the *Commodore* grew slowly clear to us. We had gone a bit farther away from the ship and now she was floating with such an air of comfort. We laughed when we had time, and said, "What a gag it would be on those other fellows if she did not sink at all."

But later we saw men aboard her, and later still they began to hail us. The men on board were a mystery to us. We had seen all the boats leave the ship. We rowed back to the ship, but we did not go too near. We were four men in a 10-foot boat, and we knew that the touch of a hand on our gunwale would surely swamp us.

### Helping Their Mates

The first mate cried out from the ship that the third boat had broken alongside the ship. He cried that these men had rafts, and they wished us to tow them.

The captain said, "All right."

Their rafts were floating astern. "Jump in!" cried the captain. But there was a strange hesitation. In the gray light of morning the seven men on board looked like ghosts. They were silent save for the words of the mate to the captain. Here

Early Morning After a Storm at Sea, Winslow Homer, 1902

was death, but here also was an indefinable kind of strength.

Four men clambered over the rails. They stood there watching the cold, steely sheen of the sweeping waves.

"Jump," cried the captain again.

The old chief engineer first obeyed the order. He landed on the outside raft and the captain told him how to grip the raft. He obeyed as promptly as a child in school.

A stoker followed him, and then the first mate threw his hands over his head and plunged into the sea. He had no life belt. I somehow felt that I could see in the expression of his hands, and in the very toss of his head, rage, rage, rage. He was full of rage as he leaped to death.

And then I saw Tom Smith, the man who was going to quit filibustering* after this trip. He jumped to a raft and turned his face toward us. On board the *Commodore* three men remained. Silently, they gazed at us. One man had his arms folded and was leaning against the deckhouse. The stoker on the first raft threw us a line and we began to tow. Of course, we all

_____

* *Filibustering*—gun running.

on the raft ready to spring. His face was the face of a lost man reaching upward. And we knew that the weight of his hand on our gunwale would doom us.

## The *Commodore* Sinks

The cook let go of the line. We rowed around to see if we could not get a line from the chief engineer. All this time there were no shrieks, no groans. And then the *Commodore* sank.

She lurched and swung, righted and dove into the sea. The rafts and the men on them were suddenly swallowed by the ocean. And then the men in the dinghy uttered words that were something far beyond words.

The lighthouse of Mosquito Inlet stuck above the horizon like the point of a pin. We turned our dinghy toward the shore.

The story of life in an open boat for 30 hours would be instructive for the young. But none of it is to be told here and now. For my part I would prefer to tell the story at once. From it would shine the splendid courage of Captain Edward Murphy and of William Higgins, the oiler. At this time, however, let us say that when we were swamped in the surf, the captain gave orders amid the wildness of the waves as clearly as if he had been on the deck of a battleship.

John Kitchell of Daytona came running down the beach. He dashed into the water and dragged the cook. Then he went after the captain, but the captain sent him to me. Then we saw Billy Higgins lying with his forehead on the sand. His head was clear of water, but he was dead.

knew that it was impossible for the dinghy to pull the rafts to safety. Our dinghy was within six inches of the water's edge. Enormous waves were breaking all around us. I knew that a tugboat would have a hard time moving the rafts.

But we tried it and would have continued but something happened. Suddenly the boat began to go backward. A man on the first raft was pulling the line hand over hand. He was drawing us toward him.

He had turned into a demon. He was wild — wild as a tiger. He was crouched

357

**Summarizing.** Choose the best phrase to complete each sentence. Then write the complete statements on your paper.

1. The *Commodore* was going to Cuba with a cargo of _____ (food, arms and munitions, medicine).

2. The captain wanted to stay near the ship until _____ (help arrived, the men launched the last lifeboat, it sank).

3. The dinghy began to go backward because _____ (the waves pulled it, the *Commodore* was sinking, a man on the raft was pulling the line).

4. After the *Commodore* sank, the _____ (men on the rafts drowned, dinghy pulled the rafts to shore, author saved the captain's life).

**Interpreting.** Write the answer to each question on your paper.

1. Why were men still trapped on the *Commodore*?

2. What might have been in the valises carried by the man in the lifeboat?

3. How did the first mate, who jumped into the ocean, feel?

4. What did the actions of the men in the dinghy show about their characters?

**For Thinking and Discussing.** The captain of the *Commodore* was compared to the captain of a battleship. What was the captain of the *Commodore* battling against?

**Theme and Foreshadowing.** The theme of a story is the author's main idea or message. Symbols are often used to *foreshadow* an event that will happen later in the story. Foreshadowing is a device that suggests what will happen later. It is the author's way of creating suspense and emphasizing the theme of the story.

In "The Wreck of the *Commodore*," the ship's whistle is used to foreshadow the fate of the *Commodore*. The theme of this story is that the sinking of the ship was a terrible tragedy. At the beginning of the story, "the *Commodore* gave three long blasts of her whistle. Somehow they sounded sad." Later, Crane writes, "If ever there was a voice of death and despair it was the voice of this whistle."

Read these passages. On your paper, tell what event each passage foreshadows.

1. "Now huge waves came lashing at the ship and a certain lightheartedness departed from the men aboard."

2. "He [Tom] said, 'I've been on a number of these trips. The pay is pretty good, but I think if I ever get back safe this time, I will cut it.' "

3. "In the gray light of morning the seven men on board looked like ghosts."

## WRITING

Write at least two paragraphs about a real event you have seen on TV. Use foreshadowing to suggest the end of your story.

# The Open Boat

*by Stephen Crane*

*"The Open Boat" was written a few months after Crane's report of the sinking of the* Commodore. *He wrote this story because he wanted to go beyond the facts of a news story to describe how it really felt to be adrift in an open boat.*

None of them knew the color of the sky. Their eyes were on the waves that swept before them. The waves were a dull gray, except for the tops, which were foaming white. The boat wasn't much bigger than a bathtub.

The cook sat at one end, bailing out water. On one side, the oiler handled one of the oars. The reporter, sitting next to him, pulled at the other oar. They both watched the waves and wondered why they were there. They had been rowing for hours.

At the other end was the injured captain. He could not forget seeing his ship sink lower and lower, and finally go down. His voice was deep and sad.

"Steer a little more south," the captain said.

"A little more south, sir," said the oiler.

One thing wrong with the sea is that when you get over one wave, another is right behind it. Each wave is just as eager to swamp your boat as the one before it.

The men were not aware of the dawn. They knew it was morning only because the sea had changed from gray to green.

"It's a good thing the wind is blowing toward shore," the cook said. "Otherwise, we wouldn't have a chance."

The reporter and the oiler agreed. The captain chuckled, but he didn't sound amused.

Gulls flew around them. Sometimes they sat on the sea. The anger of the sea meant nothing to them, and the men envied them.

One gull tried to land on the captain's head. The captain wanted to knock it away, but a sudden movement would turn the boat over. So he gently waved his arm over his head. When the bird flew away, the four men breathed more easily.

All the while, the oiler and the reporter rowed — and rowed and rowed. Sometimes they had one oar each. Sometimes the oiler handled both oars. Sometimes the reporter did.

The hardest part was changing places. It's easier to steal eggs from under a hen than it was to change seats in that boat.

After a while, the captain said he saw a lighthouse. Soon the cook said he could see it, too. At the oars, the reporter turned and looked, but he couldn't see it.

At the top of a wave, he turned and looked again. This time, he saw something very small on the horizon.

"Do you think we'll make it, Captain?" the cook asked.

"Yes," said the captain, "if the wind holds and the boat doesn't swamp with water."

The cook bailed faster.

"I wish we had a sail," the captain said. "We could tie my coat on the end of an oar. That would give you boys a chance to rest."

So the cook and the reporter made a sail. The oiler steered with the other oar, and the boat made good speed.

Slowly, the lighthouse grew larger. At last, from the top of each wave, the men could see land.

Then the wind died down. So the reporter and the oiler started rowing again.

The reporter wondered how anyone could think of rowing as an amusement. It was not an amusement. It was a horror to the muscles and a crime against the back.

"Easy now, boys," said the captain. "When we reach the surf, we'll have to swim for it. Save your strength."

"They'll see us soon," the cook said. "They'll be out after us."

A quiet cheerfulness surrounded the men. They would probably be ashore in an hour.

After a while, the cook said, "It's funny they don't see us yet."

The cheerfulness faded. Land was within

sight, but no one was there to help them.

The men now felt very angry. Each, in his own way, wondered, "If I am going to drown, why was I allowed to come this far? Why didn't it happen at the beginning, before all this suffering?"

When they got near the surf, the oiler said, "We won't last another three minutes. We're about to swamp with water, and we're too far out to swim to shore."

"Take us back out to sea," the captain said sadly.

The reporter and the oiler took turns rowing. Their backs ached so much that they no longer feared the ocean. By now, it looked a lot more comfortable than the boat. It seemed like a great, soft mattress.

"Look!" cried the cook. "There's a man on shore! He's waving at us!"

"Now we're all right," the oiler said. "There will be a boat for us in a half hour."

"Now there are some more people," the cook said. "One of them is waving his coat."

"Why don't they send a boat out after us?" the reporter asked.

"Maybe they think we're out fishing," the captain said. "Maybe they're just waving to be friendly."

The people stood on the shore waving. Soon, it began getting dark. The people on shore blended into the gloom. The oiler and the reporter kept taking turns rowing.

Late at night, it was the reporter's turn. The other three men were asleep. The reporter imagined that he was the only man afloat on all the oceans.

There was a swishing sound near the boat. Then the reporter saw a large fin cut through the water. He stared at it without feeling. He only wished one of the others was awake. He didn't want to be alone with the shark.

Long after the shark swam away, the oiler woke up. The reporter asked him, "Will you take over?"

The oiler took over. The reporter fell asleep as soon as he touched the bottom of the boat.

It seemed only a moment later when the oiler asked, "Will you take over?"

"Sure," the reporter said.

Later, the reporter got some more sleep. When he opened his eyes again, it was dawn. Land was once again in sight. They could see little cottages and a tall windmill on a beach. But no one, not even a dog, appeared on the beach.

"I guess no help is coming," the captain said. "We'd better try to go through the surf anyway. If we stay out much longer, we'll be too weak to swim at all."

The others agreed. The oiler, who was now rowing, turned the boat toward the beach.

The reporter looked at the tall windmill. It was a giant, standing with its back to their struggles, as if they were ants. It seemed neither cruel nor kind. It simply did not care about them.

The captain spoke again. "All we can do is row as far as possible. When she swamps, we'll swim for the beach. We won't get in very close before we turn over."

As they headed toward the shore, the waves tossed the boat higher and higher.

The reporter knew he should be afraid. But his mind was ruled by his muscles, and his muscles did not care. His only thought was that if he should drown, it would be a shame.

"When you jump," the captain warned, "get clear of the boat."

The tumbling white water caught the boat and whirled it almost straight up and down. Water poured in from all sides. The reporter went overboard.

The January water was icy. To the reporter, this seemed to be an important fact. It was colder than he had expected to find it off the coast of Florida.

When he came to the surface, he saw the others. The oiler, swimming rapidly, was ahead in the race. The cook paddled nearby him. Behind the reporter, the captain hung on to the overturned boat with his good hand.

The reporter paddled slowly. Suddenly, he felt himself caught in a current. He looked at the shore as if it were a piece of stage scenery. Although he swam, he was not moving forward.

The captain, holding onto the boat, passed the reporter. The reporter stayed in the grip of this new enemy, the strange current.

"Am I going to drown?" he wondered. "Can it be possible?"

Then a wave whirled him out of the current. Now he could make progress toward the shore again.

The captain yelled to him, "Swim for the boat!"

The reporter struggled to reach the boat. He noticed a man running along the shore.

The man threw off his coat, shoes, and pants — and ran into the water.

The reporter kept paddling toward the boat. Suddenly, a large wave caught him up and flung him over the boat and far past it.

To the reporter, this seemed to be a miracle. He came down in water that was only up to his waist. But he was too weak to stand. Each time he got up, he was knocked down by a wave.

Then he saw the man who had been running along the shore. The man dragged the cook ashore. Then he waded toward the captain. The captain waved him away and sent him to the reporter.

The man grabbed the reporter's hand and pulled. The reporter thought he saw a halo behind the man's head.

"Thanks, old man," the reporter said.

Then they saw the oiler. He was lying face down in the shallow water.

The reporter wasn't sure of all that happened afterward. When he reached safe ground, he fell. He could feel every part of his body hit the sand.

Now the beach was filled with people, blankets, clothes, and coffee. The land gave a warm and generous welcome to the men from the sea.

One dripping shape, though, was carried slowly up the beach. For the oiler, the only welcome from the land would be a grave.

That night, the white waves moved back and forth in the moonlight. The wind brought the sound of the sea's voice to the three men on shore. Now they felt they could be interpreters of that voice.

## READING COMPREHENSION

**Summarizing.** Choose the best phrase to complete each sentence. Then write the complete statements on your paper.

1. The captain warned his men to save their strength so they could _____ (swim to shore, signal for help, row through the surf).

2. Although land was in sight, the men realized _____ (they would drown, there was no one to help them, their supplies were gone).

3. When the reporter was rowing, he saw _____ (another boat, the large fin of a shark, a sea gull).

4. When the men reached the beach, _____ (it was deserted, people helped them, the captain was found dead).

**Interpreting.** Write the answer to each question on your paper.

1. What did the captain do when the oiler told him their boat wouldn't make it to shore?

2. How did the reporter feel just before he jumped out of the boat to swim to shore?

3. What did the captain's reaction to his would-be rescuer show about his character?

**For Thinking and Discussing.** Do you think Crane succeeded in describing how it really felt to be adrift in a boat? Explain your answer.

## UNDERSTANDING LITERATURE

**Allegory.** An *allegory* is a kind of story that has at least two meanings or interpretations.

"The Open Boat" is an allegory. On one level, the story is about four men at sea. But another interpretation of the story is that these men represent all people, or humanity. The sea and land can be interpreted as symbols of nature or life. Crane is telling two stories at the same time.

Read these passages from the story. On your paper, tell what the author is saying about these men in each situation. Then tell what the author might be saying about people and about nature or life in general.

1. ". . . when you get over one wave, another is right behind it."

2. "So the cook and the reporter made a sail. The oiler steered with the other oar, and the boat made good speed."

3. "The reporter looked at the tall windmill. It was a giant, standing with its back to their struggles, as if they were ants. It seemed neither cruel nor kind. It simply did not care about them."

## WRITING

Imagine that you were the man on the shore who first spotted the boat. Describe what you thought you saw. Try to write your description in the form of an allegory that reflects this theme: When people fail to understand one another, tragedy can occur.

# A Man Said to the Universe

*by Stephen Crane*

A man said to the universe:
"Sir, I exist!"
"However," replied the universe,
"The fact has not created in me
A sense of obligation."

1. Why would a man announce his existence to the universe?

2. A sense of obligation means that someone feels he or she must or should do something. What did Crane mean in the last three lines of this poem?

**In Nature's Wonderland,** Thomas Doughty, 1835

# Section Review

## VOCABULARY

**Shades of Meaning.** Authors use words the same way artists use paint. Both must pick the exact color or shade they want to create the picture they have in mind. The word *run,* for example, has a meaning slightly different from the word *jog.* A police officer does not jog after a thief. He or she runs after the thief. The difference between the two words is what is called *shades of meaning.*

Read each pair of sentences. Then, on your paper, write the letter of the sentence that has the more precise meaning.

1.  **a.** The lights of Jacksonville *blinked dimly* through the night.
    **b.** The lights of Jacksonville *were visible* through the night.

2.  **a.** He *looked angry.*
    **b.** He *had turned into a demon.*

3.  **a.** He was *crouched* on the raft ready to *spring.*
    **b.** He *sat* on the raft ready to *jump.*

4.  **a.** All this time there were *no shrieks, no groans.*
    **b.** All this time there was *no noise.*

5.  **a.** The engineer *came in* and *said* that there was something wrong.
    **b.** The engineer *rushed in* and *cried* that there was something wrong.

## READING

**Main Ideas and Supporting Details.** The main idea is what a paragraph is about. The supporting details are pieces of information that are used to back up or explain the main idea.

Read the paragraph below.

Although it was the first day of spring, it snowed. The streets were slick with ice. I wished that I had worn warm boots. It seemed that summer would never come. I watched some kids build a snowman and use an old garbage-can top as a sled. The birds sat glumly on icy tree branches.

The main idea in the paragraph is: It snowed on the first day of spring. The supporting details are: streets were icy; kids built a snowman; they made a sled.

Read the paragraphs below. On your paper, write the main idea of each. Then list at least two supporting details.

1.  "The old chief engineer first obeyed the order. He landed on the outside raft and the captain told him how to grip the raft. He obeyed as promptly as a child in school."

2.  "The reporter wondered how anyone could think of rowing as an amusement. It was not an amusement. It was a horror to the muscles and a crime against the back."

3.  "The tumbling white water caught the boat and whirled it almost straight up and down. Water poured in from all sides. The reporter went overboard."

# WRITING

**An Autobiographical Narrative.** An autobiographical narrative is a story based on your personal experiences. When you write an autobiographical narrative, you should tell who was involved, what happened, and where and when the story took place. Like any story, an autobiographical narrative should have a beginning, middle, and end. The beginning should establish the scene, the middle should describe the action, and the end should tell how the story turned out. Your narrative will have more meaning for the reader if you tell how you felt about the experience.

## Step 1: Set Your Goal

In many ways, writing an autobiographical narrative is easy since all the information you need is stored in your memory. However, it is very important that you choose a topic that will capture your reader's interest. Choose an event that was important and had meaning for you.

Think of a personal experience about which you would like to write. Answering the following questions might help you decide on a topic.

- ☐ Is there one experience that you will never forget?
- ☐ Have you ever witnessed an important news event?
- ☐ Did you ever do something that you thought was impossible?
- ☐ Has something very funny or frightening ever happened to you?

Once you have decided on a topic, determine what the purpose of your narrative will be. Usually your purpose will be to make a point or give your readers some new insight. You also want to share the special meaning the experience had for you. For example, Stephen Crane wrote "The Open Boat" to show how it really felt to be adrift at sea.

## Step 2: Make a Plan

Once you have decided on your topic and your purpose for writing, you need to begin gathering details for your story. A story, however, is more than a list of events. It must have a plot.

A plot has four basic elements: action, conflict, climax, and resolution. The action of a story is made up of what the characters do and what happens to them. The conflict is the struggle between two opposing forces. For example, in "The Open Boat," the conflict was between the forces of nature and the men in the boat struggling to stay alive. The climax, or turning point, is the highest point of action and the point at which the outcome of the conflict is decided. In "The Open Boat," the climax occurred when the boat capsized and its occupants swam for shore. The resolution shows the result of what happened at the climax. It brings the story to a satisfying close now that the action is over. In "The Open Boat," the resolution occurred when the occupants of the boat were dragged ashore.

Write a plot outline for your personal narrative by listing all the events that might be part of your story. Be sure there are events for each element of the plot. Then go over your list and group the events according to those that belong in the beginning, middle, and end of the story.

Finally, number the events in chronological order.

### Step 3: Write a First Draft

Remember, a story is more than a list of events. The details should make it come alive for the reader. As you write your first draft, be sure to use descriptive language — specific nouns, verbs, adjectives, and adverbs — to make the story seem real. Include dialogue to give your readers the feeling that they're hearing live action rather than just reading about it.

### Step 4: Revise

When you revise your first draft, put yourself in your readers' place. Check to see if you included all the information they need to follow the plot easily. Here is a checklist to help you revise your story:

- ☐ Does your story have a plot that is easy to follow?
- ☐ Does your story have a beginning, middle, and end?
- ☐ Does the dialogue sound natural?
- ☐ Does your story make a point? Is the point clear?

When you have finished revising your story, proofread it for errors in spelling, grammar, and punctuation. Make sure you punctuated the dialogue correctly. Then make a final copy.

## QUIZ

The following is a quiz for Section 6. Write the answers in complete sentences on your paper.

## Reading Comprehension

1. Why did Wilson take back his letters from Henry in "The Red Badge of Courage"?

2. What did Henry's mother expect of him in "The Red Badge of Courage"?

3. Why did the wayfarer say ". . . there are other roads" in the poem "The Wayfarer"?

4. Why were some men left on the ship in "The Wreck of the *Commodore:* Stephen Crane's Own Story"?

5. Why didn't the people on shore rush to save the men in the lifeboat in the story "The Open Boat"?

## Understanding Literature

6. After Henry ran away, he met a group of wounded soldiers. How did this meeting affect the theme of the play?

7. In what ways are the man in "A Man Said to the Universe" and the wayfarer in "The Wayfarer" alike?

8. Why didn't the sailors panic when the *Commodore* began to sink? How did their calmness add to the theme of the story?

9. Describe the windmill as a symbol in "The Open Boat." Discuss how this symbol adds to the theme.

10. Compare "The Wreck of the *Commodore:* Stephen Crane's Own Story" and "The Open Boat." Which story is more suspenseful? Which story states its theme more powerfully? Explain your answers.

## ACTIVITIES

### Word Attack

1. Words created by combining two or more words are called *compound words*. Compound words that are written as one word are called *closed compounds*. For example, in "The Red Badge of Courage," you read, *"The smoke of several campfires drifts among the soldiers. . . ."* The word *campfires* is a closed compound because the two words *camp* and *fires* are written as one word.

   Copy each of the following closed compound words on your paper. Then draw a line between the two words that make up each compound.

   | | |
   |---|---|
   | cavalryman | headquarters |
   | horseback | goodwill |
   | battlefield | wildcats |
   | checkerboard | gunfire |

2. Two or more words that have a special meaning when used together but are written separately are called *open compound words*. Use the following open compound words in sentences of your own.

   | | |
   |---|---|
   | firing line | pilot house |
   | first mate | block and tackle |
   | lead line | engine room |

**Speaking and Listening.** Act out one of these scenes from "The Red Badge of Courage."

1. The opening scene — the morning that the soldiers are told they will be moving out. You will need people to play the parts of Jim, Soldier 1, Wilson, and the Youth. Pay particular attention to the dialect used in the dialogue.

2. The scene that recalls the conversation between the Youth and his mother as she prepares to send him off to fight.

   Be prepared to perform the scene for the class.

### Researching

1. "The Red Badge of Courage" takes place during the Civil War. Choose one of the following Civil War topics to research, and prepare a short report to give to your class.

   The Battle of Bull Run
   The Battle of Antietam
   The Emancipation Proclamation
   The Battle of Gettysburg

2. Several nautical terms were used in "The Wreck of the *Commodore*." The words below name some of the parts of a sailboat. Find the meaning of each word, and then draw a diagram of a sailboat in which you label each part listed. Find a picture of a sailboat to use as a guide.

   | | | |
   |---|---|---|
   | bow | foresail | keel |
   | stern | mast | tiller |
   | hull | yard | rigging |

**Creating.** Pretend you are Henry Fleming. Write a letter to your mother after the Battle of Chancellorsville. Describe your experience, and tell about your feelings and how you have changed.

# VOICES OF EXPERIENCE

## *1898-1939*

*We have tomorrow
Bright before us
Like a flame.*

— Langston Hughes

*The Green Car*
William James Glackens (1870-1938)
Metropolitan Museum of Art
Arthur H. Hearn Fund

# Voices of Experience: 1898–1939

The American people faced the beginning of the 20th century with bright hopes. By 1898, there were nearly 75 million people in the United States. Millions of immigrants came to our shores each year, and America's territory now stretched from the gold fields of Alaska to the sugar plantations of Puerto Rico.

During this era, there was an outpouring of fine literature that represented the experiences and ideas of Americans from many different backgrounds. Here were authors who made the world take notice.

## The Changing American Scene

A gold rush in the frozen Klondike territory led some Americans to explore the last frontier on this continent. Jack London didn't find a wealth of gold in Alaska, but he did find a wealth of experience. These experiences became the basis of a number of powerful adventure stories, including the first story in this section, "Love of Life."

Sherwood Anderson created vivid, sympathetic portraits of people he knew well. His essay in this section, "Discovery of a Father," shows Anderson at his best.

Although Anderson was sympathetic to people's weaknesses, he felt very bitter about the changes that new machines and big business brought to small towns. Carl Sandburg, another Midwestern writer, interpreted the changes in American life differently. Sandburg loved Chicago and city life. His poetry became popular because it showed the American people as strong and flexible. During these years, Americans not only learned how to handle technology; they also had to deal with the losses resulting from the battles of World War I (1917–1919). Sandburg's poem "Under a Telephone Pole" shows how he used different elements of early 20th-century life to celebrate the American spirit, as Whitman had done before him.

## Changing American Goals

The 1920's brought many changes. Few American writers captured the spirit of the Roaring Twenties better than F. Scott Fitzgerald. As you will see when you read the play adapted from his story "Bernice Bobs Her Hair," Fitzgerald wrote about the young people of his day — their rebellion against accepted values and their love of pleasure.

During the 1920's, many black writers,

View up Broadway From Maiden Lane, Fogerty, circa 1890's

artists, and musicians settled in Harlem, a community in New York City. From their works emerged the movement, the Harlem Renaissance. This section contains poetry by two of its greatest poets: Langston Hughes and Countee Cullen. Their poems show the world something of the experience of being black in America.

During the 1930's, the American people suffered from an economy that could not provide enough jobs or food. Perhaps these hard times helped make Ernest Hemingway popular. His strong, independent characters showed a toughness that Americans claimed as their own. His story "A Day's Wait" is typical of his direct way of writing.

During the 1930's, Dorothy Parker created humor that helped Americans forget their troubles. Parker's story "The Standard of Living" reminds us that throughout this difficult period, Americans lost neither their sense of humor nor their dreams for a better future.

Sam Levenson's memoir "Everything But Money" closes this section. His heartwarming recollections of family life provide a true glimpse of the love and humor that held the Levensons together in spite of their very modest means.

# Love of Life

*by Jack London*

*In his short lifetime, Jack London (1876–1916) wrote hundreds of short stories and dozens of novels. Much of his writing is based on things that happened in his own life. Born in San Francisco, London received almost no formal education as a boy. He loved to read, though, and educated himself by constantly reading books. As a young man, he went to the Klondike region of Alaska during the Alaskan Gold Rush. He turned his experiences in the Klondike into tales of adventure.*

*A central theme in London's writing is survival — surviving the harsh conditions of nature and the cruelty that humans sometimes inflict upon one another. The following story takes place during the Gold Rush and describes one man's powerful will to live — and the desperate things he does in order to survive.*

They limped painfully down the bank. They were tired and weak, and their faces had the expression of hardship long endured. They were heavily burdened with blanket packs that were strapped to their shoulders. Each man carried a rifle. They walked in a stooped posture, their eyes bent upon the ground.

The first man stepped into the milky stream that foamed over the rocks. The other man followed at his heels. In places the water dashed against their knees, and both men staggered for footing.

The man who followed slipped on a smooth boulder, nearly fell, but recovered himself. At the same time, he uttered a sharp cry of pain. When he had steadied himself, he stepped forward, but nearly fell again.

He called out, "I say, Bill, I've sprained my ankle."

Bill staggered on through the milky water. He limped up the farther bank and continued straight without looking back. The man in the stream watched him.

"Bill!" he cried out.

Bill's head did not turn. The man watched him go till he passed over the crest and disappeared.

He turned his gaze slowly and looked at the world that remained to him now that Bill was gone. There were no trees, no shrubs, no grasses — nothing but a tremendous desolation that sent fear swiftly dawning into his eyes.

He hitched his pack farther over his left shoulder to take a portion of its weight from the injured ankle. Then he proceeded to the bank, slowly and carefully, wincing with pain.

With a desperation that was madness, unmindful of the pain, he hurried up the slope to the crest of the hill over which his comrade had disappeared. But at the crest he saw a shallow valley, empty of life. He fought with his fear again, overcame it, hitched the pack still farther over his left shoulder, and lurched on down the slope.

Farther on he knew he would come to a small stream. He would follow it until it emptied into the river Dease, and here he would find a cache under an upturned canoe. And in this cache would be ammunition for his empty gun, fishhooks and lines and a small net. Also, he would find flour — not much — a piece of bacon, and some beans.

He stubbed his toe on a rocky ledge, and from weariness and weakness staggered and fell. He slipped out of the packstraps. Then he built a fire and put a tin pot of water on to boil.

His feet were raw and bleeding. His ankle was throbbing, and he gave it an examination. It had swollen to the size of his knee. He tore a long strip from one of two blankets and bound the ankle tightly. He tore other strips and bound them about his feet to serve for both moccasins and socks. Then he drank the pot of water, steaming hot, and crawled between his blankets. He slept like a dead man.

At 6:00 he awoke. He knew that he was hungry. He had not eaten for two days; for a far longer time he had not had all he wanted to eat.

He put his pack into shape for traveling. He looked at his moose-hide sack. It was not large, but it weighed 15 pounds — as much as all the rest of the pack. He set it to one side and rolled the pack. When he rose to his feet to stagger on into the day, the sack was included in the pack on his back.

His ankle had stiffened, his limp was more noticeable, but the pain of it was nothing compared with the pain of his stomach.

Late in the afternoon he followed a stream which ran through patches of rush grass. Grasping these rushes firmly near the root, he pulled up what looked like a young onion sprout no larger than a nail. But its fibers were tough. It was composed of stringy filaments without nourishment.

He made camp again on a rocky ledge. He built a fire and warmed himself by drinking quarts of hot water. His ankle pulsed with pain, but he knew only that he was hungry. Through his restless sleep he dreamed of feasts and banquets.

He awoke, chilled and sick. A raw wind was blowing, and the first flurries of snow were whitening the hilltops.

This was a signal for him to strap on his pack and stumble onward, he knew not where.

He had no fire that night. He crawled under his blanket to sleep the broken-hunger sleep.

Day came. The edge of his hunger had gone. There was a dull, heavy ache in his stomach, but it did not bother him so much.

He ripped one of his blankets into strips and bound his bleeding feet to prepare himself for a day of travel. When he came to his pack, he paused over the moose-hide sack, but in the end it went with him.

Though the hunger pangs were no longer so strong, he realized that he was weak. He had to pause for frequent rests.

In the middle of the day, he found two minnows in a large pool. He managed to catch them in his tin bucket. He was not particularly hungry. The dull ache in his stomach had been growing duller and fainter. He ate the fish raw, chewing carefully. He had no desire to eat, but he knew he must eat to live.

Another night. In the morning, he untied the leather string that fastened the moose-hide sack. From its open mouth poured a yellow stream of coarse gold

dust and nuggets. He divided the gold in halves, hiding one half on a ledge, wrapped in a piece of blanket, and returning the other half to the sack.

His hunger awoke in him again. He was very weak and often stumbled and fell. Stumbling once, he fell into a bird's nest. There were four newly hatched chicks, a day old. He ate them ravenously.

His hunger was driving him on. He wondered if Bill, too, was lost. By midday his pack became too heavy. Again he divided the gold, this time throwing half of it on the ground. In the afternoon he threw the rest of it away. Now he had only the half-blanket and the tin bucket and the rifle.

In the late afternoon he came upon some scattered bones where wolves had made a kill. He put a bone in his mouth and sucked at the shreds of life that still dyed it faintly pink. He closed his jaws on the bones and crunched. Sometimes the bone broke, sometimes his teeth.

He looked at the bones. Could it be that he might be like that before the day was done? There was no hurt in death. To die was to sleep. It meant rest. Then why was he not content to die?

It was the life in him unwilling to die that drove him on.

He awoke on a rocky ledge. The sun was shining bright and warm. A fine day, he thought. Perhaps he could manage to locate himself. By a painful effort he rolled over on his side. Below him was a wide river that flowed into a bright, shining sea. Most unusual, he thought, a trick of his disordered mind. He saw a ship lying at anchor in the midst of the shining sea! He knew that there were no seas or ships in the heart of the barren lands.

He heard a snuffle behind him — a half-choking gasp or cough. Very slowly, he rolled over on his other side. Again came the snuffle and cough. Outlined between two jagged rocks several feet away, he saw the gray head of a wolf. The head seemed to droop limply and forlornly. The animal blinked continually in the sunshine. It seemed sick. As he looked, it snuffled and coughed again.

This, at least, was real, he thought. He closed his eyes for a long while and thought, and then it came to him. He had been walking north by east. That shining sea was the Arctic Ocean and that ship was a whaler, lying at anchor.

He sat up and turned his attention to immediate affairs. He had worn through the blanket-wrappings, and his feet were shapeless lumps of raw meat. His last blanket was gone. Rifle and knife were both missing.

Though extremely weak, he had no feeling of pain. He was not hungry. The thought of food was not even pleasant to him, and whatever he did was done by his reason alone. He ripped off his pant legs to the knees and bound them around his feet before he began what he knew would be a terrible journey to the ship.

Every minute or so he had to rest. His steps were feeble and uncertain, just as the wolf's that trailed him were feeble and uncertain.

Throughout the night he heard the cough of the sick wolf. He knew the sick wolf clung to the sick man's trail in the hope that the man would die first. In the morning, he saw it looking at him with a hungry stare. It stood crouched, tail between its legs, like a miserable dog. It shivered in the chill morning wind, and grinned weakly when the man spoke to it in a voice no more than a hoarse whisper.

In the afternoon the man came upon a trail. It was of another man, who did not walk, but who dragged himself on all fours. The man thought it might be Bill. He had no curiosity. In fact, feeling and emotion had left him. Stomach and nerves had gone to sleep. Yet the life that was in him drove him on. It refused to die.

He followed the trail of the other man who dragged himself along, and soon came to the end of it — a few fresh-picked bones. The ground was marked by the footpads of many wolves. He saw a moose-hide sack, which had been torn by sharp teeth. Bill had carried it to the last. Ha! Ha! He would have the last laugh on Bill. He could survive and carry it on the ship in the shining sea.

He turned away. Well, Bill had deserted him — but he would not take the gold, nor would he suck Bill's bones. Bill would have sucked my bones though, had it been the other way around, the man thought as he staggered on.

That day he decreased the distance between him and the ship by three miles; the next day by two — for he was crawling now as Bill had crawled; and the end of the fifth day found the ship still seven miles away, and him unable to make even a mile a day. His knees had become raw meat like his feet.

Still the sick wolf coughed and wheezed at his heels. It was a grim tragedy of existence — a sick man that crawled, a sick wolf who limped — two dying creatures hunting each other's lives.

He was awakened by the wheezing sound of the sick wolf's breath. Without movement, he lay on his back listening. It drew closer, ever closer, and he did not move.

The patience of the wolf was terrible. The man's patience was no less terrible. For half a day he lay motionless, fighting off unconsciousness and waiting for the

thing that was to feed upon him and upon which he wished to feed.

He did not hear the breath. He slipped slowly from some dream to the feel of the tongue along his hand. He waited. The fangs pressed softly. The wolf was using its last strength to sink teeth in the food for which it had waited so long. But the man had waited long, and the hand closed on the jaw. Slowly, while the wolf strug-gled feebly and the hand clutched feebly, the other hand crept across to a grip.

Five minutes later the whole weight of the man's body was on top of the wolf. The hands had not enough strength to choke the wolf, but the face of the man pressed close to the throat of the wolf and the mouth of the man was full of hair. At the end of half an hour the man was aware of a warm trickle in his throat. It was not pleasant. It was like molten lead being forced into his stomach, and it was forced by his will alone. Later the man rolled over on his back and slept.

There were some members of a scientific expedition on the whaling ship *Bedford*. From the deck they saw a strange object on the shore. It was moving down the beach toward the water. It was blind, unconscious. It squirmed along the ground like some monstrous worm. It writhed and twisted and went ahead a few feet an hour.

A few weeks later, the man sat at the table with the scientific men and ship's officers. He was haunted by a fear that the food would not last. He asked the cook, the cabin boy, the captain, about the food stores. They reassured him countless times. But he did not believe them.

It was noticed that the man was getting fat. He grew stouter with each day. The scientific men shook their heads and wondered. They limited the man at his meals, but still his weight increased.

The scientific men set a watch on the man. They saw him stop a sailor. The sailor grinned and gave him part of a sea biscuit. The man clutched it greedily and put it into his shirt. Similar were the donations from other grinning sailors.

The scientific men secretly examined his bunk. It was lined with hardtack; the mattress was stuffed with hardtack; every nook and cranny was filled with hardtack. The man was taking precautions against another famine — that was all. He would recover from it, the scientific men said. And he did, before the *Bedford's* anchor rumbled down in San Francisco Bay.

**Summarizing.** Choose the best phrase to complete each sentence. Then write the complete statements on your paper.

1. After the injured man realized his ankle was sprained, his companion, Bill, _____ (went to get medical help, went on without him, stayed and took care of him).

2. Although the man was starving and in terrible pain, he was driven on by _____ (his fear of the wolves, the overwhelming desire for revenge, his will to survive).

3. The man's moose-hide sack contained _____ (gold, food, money).

4. After his rescue, the man hid food in his bunk because _____ (he feared starvation, he was still very hungry, the ship's food supply was running low).

**Interpreting.** Write the answer to each question on your paper.

1. Why did the sick wolf follow the injured man's trail?

2. What had the man and his companion been doing in the wilderness?

3. What did the man's refusal to take Bill's gold demonstrate about his character?

4. In what ways were the man and the wolf alike and different?

## For Thinking and Discussing.

1. What message did this story present about man's desire to survive despite the apparent hopelessness of his situation?

2. What was the effect of referring to the main character in the story as "the man," rather than by his name?

3. If helping someone else would mean endangering one's own survival, do you think it would be right not to help? Why or why not?

## UNDERSTANDING LITERATURE

**Style.** *Style* is a combination of what the author has to say and the particular way in which it is said.

In analyzing Jack London's style, it's difficult — if not impossible — to separate what he says from the way he says it. London wrote hundreds of short stories and a central focus of many of them is survival.

The way London presents conflict — person *vs.* nature and person *vs.* person (usually in a harsh natural setting) — is an essential element of his style. The details he presents are bold and brutal. His words are direct and blunt. As you read London's stories of survival, you can almost feel his characters' pain.

Some of the following sentences from "Love of Life" tell of the man's actions as he fought for survival. Others are descriptive details about nature. Divide your paper into two columns. Label one column *Efforts to Survive* and the other column *Forces of Nature*. Write each sentence below in the correct column. Then go back to the story and find two more entries for each column.

1. "He tore a long strip from one of two blankets and bound the ankle tightly."

2. "He ate the fish raw, chewing carefully."

3. "There were no trees, no shrubs, no grasses — "

4. "Outlined between two jagged rocks several feet away, he saw the gray head of a wolf."

5. "The man clutched it greedily and put it into his shirt."

6. "A raw wind was blowing, and the first flurries of snow were whitening the hilltops."

7. "Slowly, while the wolf struggled feebly and the hand clutched feebly, the other hand crept across to a grip."

## WRITING

Imagine that you were stranded for a week somewhere — on your own, under extremely harsh conditions. Pick whatever setting you wish — a desert, a forest, outer space, a jungle, the Arctic, or a mountain. Write two or three paragraphs about where you were and the steps you took to survive. Try to use bold words and details as Jack London would.

# Discovery of a Father

*by Sherwood Anderson*

*Sherwood Anderson (1876–1941) wrote many novels, stories, and essays that reflect life in small Midwestern towns like the one in which he grew up. Anderson's father had been a harness maker and a blacksmith, but as automobiles and trains did more of the work that horses had once done, he had less and less to do. In this autobiographical essay, Anderson skillfully describes the characteristics that made his father — and his relationship with his father — so special.*

You hear it said that fathers want their sons to be what they feel they cannot themselves be, but I tell you it also works the other way. A boy wants something very special from his father. I know that as a small boy I wanted my father to be a certain thing he was not. I wanted him to be a proud, silent, dignified father. When I was with other boys and he passed along the street, I wanted to feel a flow of pride. "There he is. That is my father."

But he wasn't such a one. He couldn't be. It seemed to me then that he was always showing off. Let's say someone in our town had got up a show. My father would manage to get the chief comedy part. It was, let's say, a Civil War play and he was a comic soldier. He had to do the most absurd things. They thought he was funny, but I didn't.

I thought he was terrible. I didn't see how mother could stand it. She even laughed with the others. Maybe I would have laughed if it hadn't been my father.

Or there was a parade, the Fourth of July or Decoration Day. He'd be in that, too, right at the front of it, on a white horse hired from a stable.

He couldn't ride. He fell off the horse. Everyone hooted with laughter, but he didn't care. He even seemed to like it. I remember once when he had done something ridiculous, and right out on Main Street, too. I was with some other boys, they were laughing and shouting at him, and he was shouting back. He was having as good a time as they were. I ran down an alley in back of some stores and had a good long cry.

Or I would be in bed at night and Father would come home and bring some men with him. He was a man who was never alone. Before he went broke, running a harness shop, there were always a lot of men loafing in the shop. He went broke, of course, because he gave too much credit. I thought he was a fool. I had got to hating him.

There'd be men I didn't think would want to be fooling around with him. There might even be the superintendent of our schools and a quiet man who ran the hardware store. Once, I remember, there was a white-haired man who was a cashier of the bank. It was a wonder to me that they'd want to be seen with such a wind-bag. That's what I thought he was. I know now what it was that attracted them. It was because life in our town, as in all small towns, was at times pretty dull and he livened it up. He made them laugh. He could tell stories. He'd even get them to singing.

If they didn't come to our house, they'd go off, say at night, to where there was a grassy place by a creek. They'd cook food there and sit about listening to his stories.

He was always telling stories about himself. He'd say this or that wonderful thing had happened to him. It might be something that made him look like a fool. He didn't care.

If an Irishman came to our house, right away father would say he was Irish. He'd tell what county in Ireland he was born in. He'd tell things that happened there when he was a boy. He'd make it seem so real that, if I hadn't known he was born in southern Ohio, I'd have believed him myself.

If it was a Scotchman, the same thing happened. He'd get a burr into his speech. Or he was a German or a Swede. He'd be anything the other man was. I think they all knew he was lying, but they seemed to like him just the same. As a boy that was what I couldn't understand.

And there was Mother. How could she stand it? I wanted to ask but never did. She was not the kind you'd ask such questions.

I'd be upstairs in my bed, in my room above the porch, and Father would be telling some of his tales. A lot of Father's stories were about the Civil War. To hear him tell it, he'd been in about every battle. He'd been great friends with General Grant. When Grant went to the East to take charge of all the armies, he took Father along.

"I was an orderly at headquarters and Sim Grant said to me, 'Irve,' he said, 'I'm going to take you along with me.'"

He'd tell about the day Lee surrendered and how, when the great moment came, they couldn't find Grant.

"Huh," said Father. "He was in the woods with me."

My father said that he was the one who told Grant about Lee. An orderly riding by had told him, because the orderly knew how thick he was with Grant. Grant was embarrassed.

"But, Irve, look at me. I'm all covered with mud," he said to Father.

That's just one of the kind of things he'd tell. The men knew he was lying, but they seemed to like it just the same.

When we got broke, down and out, do you think he ever brought anything home? Not he. If there wasn't anything to eat in the house, he'd go off visiting around at farmhouses. They all wanted him. Sometimes he'd stay away for weeks, Mother working to keep us fed, and then home he'd come bringing, let's say, a ham. He'd got it from some farmer friend. He'd slap it on the table in the kitchen. "You bet I'm going to see that my kids have something to eat," he'd say, and Mother would just stand smiling at him. She'd never say a word about all the weeks and months he'd been away, not leaving us a cent for

food. Once I heard her speaking to a woman on our street. Maybe the woman had dared to sympathize with her. "Oh," she said, "it's all right. He isn't ever dull like most of the men on this street. Life is never dull when my man is about."

But often, I was filled with bitterness, and sometimes I wished he wasn't my father. I'd even invent another man as my father. To protect my mother I'd make up stories of a secret marriage that for some strange reason never got known. As though some man, say the president of a railroad company or maybe a congressman, had married my mother, thinking his wife was dead and then it turned out she wasn't.

So they had to hush it up but I got born just the same. I wasn't really the son of my father. Somewhere in the world there was a wonderful man who was really my father. I even made myself half believe these fancies.

And then there came a certain night. He'd been off somewhere for two or three weeks. He found me alone in the house, reading by the kitchen table.

It had been raining and he was very wet. He sat and looked at me for a long time, not saying a word. I was startled, for there was the saddest look on his face

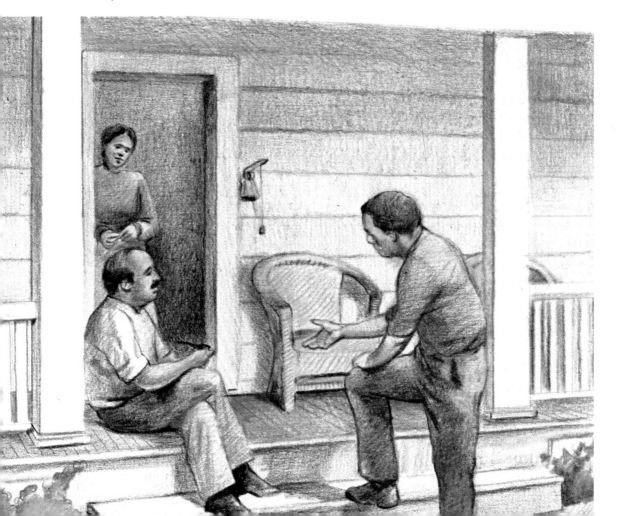

I had ever seen. He sat for a time, his clothes dripping. Then he got up.

"Come on with me," he said.

I got up and went with him out of the house. I was filled with wonder but I wasn't afraid. We went along a dirt road that led down to a pond. We walked in silence. The man who was always talking had stopped his talking.

I didn't know what was up. I had the queer feeling I was with a stranger. I didn't know whether my father intended it so. I don't think he did.

The pond was quite large. It was still raining hard. There were flashes of lightning followed by thunder. We were on a grassy bank at the pond's edge. Then my father spoke. In the darkness and rain his voice sounded strange.

"Let's go for a swim," he said. Still filled with wonder, I kicked off my shoes.

We went into the pond. Taking my hand he pulled me in. It may be that I was too frightened, too full of a feeling of strangeness, to speak. Before that night my father had never seemed to pay any attention to me.

"And what is he up to now?" I kept asking myself. I did not swim very well, but he put my hand on his shoulder and struck out into the darkness.

He was a man with big shoulders, a powerful swimmer. In the darkness I could feel the movement of his muscles. We swam to the far edge of the pond and then back. The rain continued and the wind blew. Sometimes my father swam on his back and when he did he took my hand in his large powerful one and moved it over so that it rested always on his shoulder. Sometimes there would be a flash of lightning and I could see his face quite clearly.

It was as it was earlier, in the kitchen, a face filled with sadness. There would be the momentary glimpse of his face and then again the darkness, the wind, and the rain. In me there was a feeling I had never known before.

It was a feeling of closeness. It was something strange. It was as though there were only we two in the world. It was as though I had been jerked suddenly out of myself, out of a world in which I was ashamed of my father.

He had become blood of my blood. He the strong swimmer and I the boy clinging to him in the darkness. We swam in silence and in silence we went home.

There was a lamp lighted in the kitchen and when we came in, the water dripping from us, there was my mother. She smiled at us. I remember that she called us "boys."

"What have you boys been up to?" she asked, but my father did not answer. As he had begun the evening's experience with me in silence, so he ended it. He turned and looked at me. Then he went, I thought, with a new and strange dignity out of the room.

I climbed the stairs to my own room, undressed in the darkness, and got into bed. I couldn't sleep and did not want to sleep. For the first time I knew that I was the son of my father.

He was a storyteller as I was to be. It may be that I even laughed a little softly there in the darkness. If I did, I laughed knowing that I would never again be wanting another father.

**Summarizing.** Choose the best phrase to complete each sentence. Then write the complete statements on your paper.

1. As a young boy, the writer wanted his father to be _____ (very funny, less argumentative, proud and dignified).

2. The boy's father always _____ (made up stories about his past, confided in his son, enjoyed his son's stories).

3. After they went swimming together, the boy _____ (was disappointed in his father, felt close to his father, enjoyed his father's jokes).

4. Like his father, the boy grew up to be a _____ (strong swimmer, good husband, storyteller).

**Interpreting.** Write the answer to each question on your paper.

1. How did the young boy first feel about his father?

2. Why did the boy make up stories, pretending he was someone else's son?

3. How did the boy's mother feel about her husband?

4. Why did the boy finally realize he "would never again be wanting another father"?

**For Thinking and Discussing.** How do you think you would have felt about your father if you were in the boy's place? Explain your answer.

**Style.** *Style* is the individual way an author puts words together to hold the reader's attention and to express intended ideas.

"Discovery of a Father" is a personal narrative essay. It is the author's personal comment on a part of his life and is written in the first person, as if the author were speaking directly to the reader.

Some of the statements below were written by Anderson. Others were not. On your paper, identify the ones that are from his work by the style in which they're written.

1. The absence of dignity can lead irreversibly to an absence of pride.

2. When the cast of characters of a local drama was announced, Irve Anderson was usually ready to step into a comic role.

3. My father would manage to get the chief comedy part. It was, let's say, a Civil War play and he was a comic soldier.

4. The boy's father was given to doing the unexpected.

5. "What have you boys been up to?" she asked, but my father didn't answer.

Describe someone in a simple, conversational style such as Anderson's. Tell your reader at least two things you like and two things you don't like about the person.

# Under a Telephone Pole

*by Carl Sandburg*

I am a copper wire slung in the air,
Slim against the sun I make not even a clear line of
    shadow.
Night and day I keep singing — humming and
    thrumming:
It is love and war and money; it is the fighting and the
    tears, the work and want,
Death and laughter of men and women passing through
    me, carrier of your speech,
In the rain and the wet dripping, in the dawn and the
    shine drying,
        A copper wire.

1. Who or what is the "I" in Carl Sandburg's poem? What does it look like and what does it do?

2. What sorts of things does the poem say men and women talk about? What sorts of things would you have mentioned if you were the poet?

# Bernice Bobs Her Hair

*a teleplay by Joan Micklin Silver*
*based on the story by F. Scott Fitzgerald*

*F. Scott Fitzgerald (1896–1940) has long been considered the leading American writer of the 1920's. He is the writer who best captured the feeling of those prosperous times, when for some people life was one big party.*

*The teleplay you are about to read is based on one of Fitzgerald's short stories, "Bernice Bobs Her Hair." In the 1920's, a young woman bobbed (cut) her hair in order to show how daring and modern she could be.*

## CHARACTERS

**Marjorie Harvey**
**Roberta**
**Genvieve Ormande**
**Otis Ormande**
**Charley Paulson**
**Carpenter Thompson**
**Bernice,** Marjorie's cousin
**Mrs. Deyo**
**Warren McIntyre**
**Mrs. Harvey**
**Annie,** the Harveys' maid
**G. Reece Stoddard**
**Draycott Deyo**

*Fade in on the women's powder room of a country club in a Midwestern town. Dance music can be heard in the background. It is the summer of 1919. Marjorie, 18, and Roberta, 18, enter. They wear their hair piled on top of their heads. They are not yet "flappers" — young women who wear short hair, short dresses, and makeup. But they consider themselves very modern. Marjorie takes a red jelly bean out of her purse and hands it to Roberta.*

**Roberta:** Marjorie, you saved my life. *(She licks the jelly bean and uses it as a lipstick. Then she sees Marjorie holding a flower up to her hair.)* Who gave you the flower?

**Marjorie:** Warren.

**Roberta:** I thought he'd get over you when he went away to school.

**Marjorie:** No. I got over him.

**Roberta:** I know about three girls in the East who are wild about him.

**Marjorie:** When you've grown up across the street from someone, he loses his mystery.

*(Genvieve enters.)*

**Genvieve** *(to Marjorie):* My brother Otis has been stuck with your cousin for an hour.

**Marjorie** *(dropping the flower into a wastebasket):* All right. *(As she leaves, Bernice enters. Marjorie barely nods at her and keeps going. Outside, she finds several boys waiting for the girls inside.)*

**Otis:** Marjorie!

**Marjorie:** I know, Otis. I'm going to take care of it. *(She looks at Charley.)*

**Charley:** Not me, Marjorie.

*(She looks at Carpenter.)*

**Carpenter:** Sorry, Marjorie. I'm waiting for Sara Hughes.

*(Marjorie moves off.)*

**Otis** *(to Charley and to Carpenter):* It wouldn't kill you.

**Charley:** Don't say that. It *might!*

*(Cut to Bernice, Roberta, and Genvieve in the powder room.)*

**Roberta** *(fixing her hair):* Are you having a nice time, Bernice?

**Bernice:** Yes. But it's so much warmer here than it is back home. Back home we have a breeze even in the hottest part of summer.

**Roberta:** I'll bet you do. Coming, Genvieve? *(She and Genvieve leave. Mrs. Deyo enters.)*

**Mrs. Deyo:** Bernice, dear, what a charming dress.

**Bernice:** Thank you, Mrs. Deyo.

**Mrs. Deyo:** I'm pleased to hear that you and Marjorie are such close cousins. I hope she turns to you for guidance.

**Bernice** *(embarrassed):* Well, not too often.

**Mrs. Deyo:** You could be a good influence on Marjorie.

*(Cut to Marjorie going up to Warren.)*

**Warren** *(eagerly):* I was looking for you, Marjorie.

**Marjorie:** Warren, will you do something for me?

**Warren:** Sure.

**Marjorie:** Dance with Bernice. *(He looks disappointed.)* Please? *(He nods.)* I'll see that you don't get stuck.

**Warren:** It's all right.

**Marjorie:** You're an angel! She's in the powder room. *(Warren moves toward a group of boys outside the powder room. Otis is among them, waving a piece of wood.)*

**Carpenter:** Be patient, Otis.

**Charley:** That's right, Otis. As soon as she fixes her hair, you'll get your chance.

**Warren:** What chance? What's the piece of wood for?

**Otis:** It's a club. When Bernice comes out, I'll hit her on the head — and back into the powder room. *(They all laugh.)*

**Warren:** Good news, Otis. I'm your relief hitter.

**Otis:** I'll never forget this, old man. *(He hands Warren "the club.")* In case you need it.

*(He hurries off. As the music starts again,*

*the others leave, too. Bernice comes out of the powder room.)*

**Warren** *(going over to her):* Bernice?
**Bernice:** Oh! I . . . I'm looking for Otis.
**Warren:** I told him this was my dance.
**Bernice** *(nervous because Warren is very handsome):* It's so hot in there. The floor is crowded.
**Warren:** Let's sit on the porch. There might be a breeze.
**Bernice:** I don't think so. Back home we have a breeze even in the hottest summer.
**Warren:** Well, you don't want to dance. And you don't want to sit out. Have a better idea?
**Bernice:** I didn't mean that. I meant . . . well, let's try the porch.

*(Cut to Bernice and Warren sitting at a table on the porch. She is silent. He can see Marjorie inside, talking to G. Reece Stoddard. Marjorie looks interested. Reece is older than Marjorie and her friends. He is also handsome. Warren is annoyed. Suddenly he pretends to be interested in Bernice.)*

**Warren:** Bernice, you've got an awfully kissable mouth.
**Bernice** *(looking shocked):* Fresh! *(Warren looks pained. He likes to joke with girls. And girls usually like to joke with him.)*

*(Cut to the Harvey house late that night. Bernice is going to her room. As she passes Marjorie's room, she hears voices. When she hears her name, she stops to listen.)*

*(Cut to Marjorie and her mother inside the room. Marjorie is brushing out her long hair.)*

**Marjorie:** She's ruining my summer.
**Mrs. Harvey:** I wish you wouldn't talk like that.
**Marjorie:** Otis Ormande is a fool. But he got stuck with her so long, I actually felt sorry for him. I had to beg Warren to take her off Otis's hands.
**Mrs. Harvey:** I'm sure Warren didn't mind too much. Mrs. Ormande was saying —
**Marjorie:** Don't tell me! All your friends think Bernice is "so sweet" and "so pretty." What difference does that make? Men don't like her.
**Mrs. Harvey:** Some things are more important than cheap popularity.
**Marjorie:** I can't think of any.
**Mrs. Harvey** *(smiles):* You're very young, Marjorie.
**Marjorie:** Thank heavens!
**Mrs. Harvey:** In my day, a girl from a good family —
**Marjorie:** But that was *then*, Mother. This is *now*. These days, it's every girl for herself. *(She begins fixing her hair in two heavy braids for the night.)*
**Mrs. Harvey:** I know Bernice isn't very outgoing.
**Marjorie:** Outgoing? I've never heard her say a word to boys except that it's hot. Or the dance floor is crowded.

*(Cut to Bernice outside. She has heard enough. She goes to her room and begins to braid her hair for the night.)*

*(Cut to the front door of the Harvey house the next morning. Warren rings the bell. Annie opens the door.)*

**Annie:** I'm sorry, Mr. Warren. Miss Marjorie isn't up yet.
**Warren:** Thanks. *(He starts to leave, then*

*turns back.)* Do you know if she's free this afternoon?

**Annie:** I believe she's going to the show.

*(Cut to the Harvey dining room. Marjorie is at the table, pouring milk on her cornflakes. Annie enters.)*

**Annie:** I told him you weren't up yet.

**Marjorie:** Aren't there any berries? *(Annie gets a bowl of blueberries from the sideboard. Bernice enters.)*

**Bernice** *(coldly):* Good morning.

**Marjorie:** Morning.

**Bernice:** I don't care for any breakfast, Annie.

**Annie** *(surprised):* No?

**Bernice:** No, thank you. *(When Annie leaves, Bernice turns to Marjorie.)* I heard what you said about me to your mother last night.

**Marjorie** *(calmly):* Where were you?

**Bernice:** In the hall. I didn't mean to listen . . . at first. *(Pause.)* I guess I'd better go home. *(She expects some sympathy. But she's come to the wrong person for it.)*

**Marjorie:** Well, if you aren't having a good time, I suppose you'd better go. *(Bernice bursts into tears and leaves.)*

*(Cut to the Harvey sitting room, later. Bernice enters.)*

**Bernice:** Do you think you've treated me well?

**Marjorie:** I've done my best. There's some excuse for an ugly girl whining. But you're not ugly. So don't expect me to weep for you.

**Bernice** *(angry):* You're hard and selfish. You haven't a feminine quality in you.

**Marjorie:** Bernice, girls our age divide into two groups. The ones like me have a good time. The ones like you sit around and criticize us for it. Go or stay, just as you like. *(She leaves.)*

*(Cut to Marjorie going downstairs. Carpenter and Reece are waiting for her in the front hall.)*

**Marjorie:** Who let these two parlor snakes in my house? *(They smile.)* My cousin can't go to the show with us. She's sick or something.

**Reece** *(politely):* Sorry to hear that.

**Carpenter:** That's too bad.

**Marjorie** *(whispers):* Hurry up. She might get better. *(They laugh as they leave.)*

*(Cut to Bernice writing to her mother. There is a knock on her bedroom door.)*

**Mrs. Harvey's voice:** Bernice, are you feeling better?

**Bernice** *(opens the door):* I'm all right, Aunt Josephine.

**Mrs. Harvey:** Will you come down? Mrs. Deyo and Draycott are here.

*(Cut to Mrs. Harvey and Mrs. Deyo on one side of the sitting room. Bernice and Draycott are on the other side.)*

**Bernice:** You weren't at the dance last night, were you?

**Draycott:** No. Mother said it was even noisier than usual.

**Bernice:** The dance floor was crowded.

**Draycott:** I hate a crowded dance floor.

**Mrs. Deyo** *(to Mrs. Harvey):* Bernice is a lovely child. I'm sure she's a good influence on Marjorie.

**Bernice** *(to Draycott):* How are your studies coming along?

**Draycott:** Very well, thank you.

**Mrs. Deyo** *(to Mrs. Harvey):* Have you noticed how thin some of the young girls are? They're dancing themselves to death. Next thing you know, one of them will bob her hair.

**Mrs. Harvey:** Oh, I don't think things will go that far.

**Mrs. Deyo:** Well, Draycott? (*She rises.*)

**Draycott** (*rising*): Good-bye, Bernice.

**Bernice:** Good-bye, Mrs. Deyo.

**Mrs. Deyo:** Just stay as sweet as you are, Bernice. Your mother must be proud of you.

**Bernice:** Thank you.

(*Cut to Marjorie's room. Marjorie enters. She is surprised to see Bernice waiting for her.*)

**Bernice:** I've decided that maybe you're right about things. If you'll tell me why your friends don't like me, I'll see what I can do.

**Marjorie** (*after a pause*): Will you do exactly as I say?

**Bernice:** If they are sensible things.

**Marjorie:** Forget sensible things. If I tell you to take boxing lessons, you'll have to. Well? (*Bernice nods.*) Now, the first thing is your appearance.

**Bernice:** Don't I look all right?

**Marjorie:** No. You're also boring. You lean on men when you dance. You haven't any idea of how to make a man fall in love with you. Are you willing to admit all that?

**Bernice:** Maybe.

**Marjorie:** No maybes.

**Bernice:** All right. But how are you going to fix all that in two weeks?

**Marjorie:** If you'll pay attention, I can fix it in two days. (*She looks closely at Bernice. Bernice grins, embarrassed. Marjorie*

*frowns.*) When you go home, have your teeth straightened. Meanwhile, smile with your mouth closed.

(*Cut to the Harvey dining room that evening. Annie is passing dessert.*)

**Mrs. Harvey:** Marjorie, Mrs. Deyo and Draycott were here this afternoon while you were out.

**Marjorie:** Lucky for me.

**Mrs. Harvey:** Mrs. Deyo wants to give a party in honor of Bernice. I think Draycott has a case on Bernice.

**Marjorie:** Let's not talk about it at the table. (*Bernice and Annie smile. Marjorie frowns at Bernice, who closes her mouth.*)

**Marjorie:** Mother, can we be excused?

**Mrs. Harvey:** I don't think Bernice is through.

**Marjorie:** Yes, she is. Aren't you?

**Bernice** (*puts down her fork*): Yes, thank you, Aunt Josephine. (*The two girls rise.*)

**Marjorie:** If any men call, tell them I'm busy. Bernice and I want to spend a quiet evening.

**Mrs. Harvey:** That's a good idea, dear. (*The girls leave. Mrs. Harvey turns to Annie.*) You see, Annie? I knew they would get to like each other in time.

**Annie:** Awful sudden-like, isn't it?

**Mrs. Harvey:** That's the way youngsters are.

(*Cut to Bernice's room. Marjorie is going through Bernice's clothes and tossing them aside. She comes to the dress Bernice wore to the dance last night.*)

**Marjorie:** Don't ever put this old-fashioned thing on again.

**Bernice:** But my mother —

**Marjorie:** Your mother's advice was fine

when you were a little girl. You're 17!
(She comes to a bright red dress.) What
is this?

Bernice: I know, it's awful.

Marjorie: It's divine! It's the only dress I
like in the whole bunch.

Bernice: I can't wear it every night.

Marjorie: You can wear some of mine.
(Cut to Marjorie's room. Marjorie gives
Bernice a red jelly bean.)

Marjorie: Lick it, and rub it on. (Bernice
licks it, and rubs it on her lips. Marjorie
frowns.) No. You don't want it all over
the place. Just follow the outline of your
mouth.

Bernice: Is it true you turned three cart-
wheels at the Pump and Slippers Dance?

Marjorie: Five. But that's old hat. We'll
think up something better for you to do.
(Pause.) I wonder whether we should bob

your hair. (*Bernice looks shocked.*) All right, it was just a thought. But it will make a terrific line!

(*Cut to the sitting room, the next day. Marjorie cranks up the record player. When the music starts, she dances with Bernice.*)

**Marjorie:** Don't lean. (*Bernice straightens up stiffly.*) Bend in a little. (*They keep dancing.*) Why aren't you saying anything?

**Bernice:** Well, you aren't, either.

**Marjorie:** I'm the man. The girl has to keep the talk going.

**Bernice:** It's hard to think of something.

**Marjorie:** When you're with a man, there are only three topics of conversation — you, me, and us.

**Bernice:** All right. (*Silence.*) Maybe it would be better if I knew who you were.

**Marjorie:** Pick someone.

**Bernice:** You pick.

**Marjorie:** Anybody. Warren McIntyre. (*Bernice is tongue-tied, as she is with the real Warren.*) Go on!

**Bernice:** Are you going back to school soon?

**Marjorie:** Oh, thrilling! (*She goes to the record player and lifts the needle from the record.*)

**Bernice:** You said you, me, and us.

**Marjorie:** But what can he say except "Yes, I am" or "No, I'm not"? And who cares anyway? Look, you be Warren. (*Bernice nods.*) Is it true what I hear about you, Warren McIntyre?

**Bernice:** What do you hear?

**Marjorie** (*with charm*): That you're fickle. (*She nudges Bernice.*) Ask who told me that.

**Bernice:** Who told you that?

**Marjorie:** Never mind. I just hope it's true. Fickle men are the only kind that interest me.

**Bernice** (*trying to be casual*): Marjorie, what would you say if someone said, "You've got an awfully kissable mouth"?

**Marjorie** (*again with charm*): Do you mean a mouth that looks as if it's been kissed a lot? Or one you'd like to kiss? (*Bernice is shocked, but she tries not to show it.*)

**Bernice:** Have you ever . . . ?

**Marjorie:** Lots of times.

**Bernice:** Did you ever kiss Warren?

**Marjorie:** Warren flunked my test. I think if you really love someone, you love him even when he isn't around. Well, Warren went away to school. Before he came home for Christmas, I fell in love with four men. I'm afraid he'll never get over me. Poor thing.

(*Cut to the dining room, the next evening. The table is set for eight. Bernice enters in her red dress. Marjorie, not dressed up yet, is fussing over the place cards.*)

**Bernice:** Where have you put me? (*She finds her card. Then she checks those on either side. At first she is pleased.*) G. Reece Stoddard. (*Then she frowns.*) Charley Paulson.

**Marjorie:** Sad birds like Charley are part of any crowd. And you can't afford to neglect them. Suppose you can get three sad birds to keep dancing with you. The attractive men will see there's no danger of getting stuck with you. Then *they'll* dance with you.

**Bernice:** I never thought of that. (*Pause.*)

You'd better get dressed. It's almost time.

**Marjorie:** I think I'll put Roberta on the other side of Charley. (*The doorbell rings.*) Good. Now I can get dressed.

(*Bernice realizes that Marjorie planned this. Now Bernice will have to greet the guests by herself. She opens the front door. Roberta, Genvieve, Charley, Carpenter, Warren, and Reece enter.*)

**Reece:** Hello, Bernice.

**Warren:** Where's Marjorie?

**Bernice:** She'll be right down. (*Everyone, except Bernice, starts talking about someone named Babs. Bernice shyly stands to one side. Marjorie finally comes downstairs and frowns at Bernice.*)

**Marjorie:** Bernice, could I see you for a minute? (*Bernice follows her into the kitchen. Marjorie turns on her.*) You aren't even trying! If you've been wasting my time, I'll never forgive you! You might as well go home!

**Bernice:** No!

(*Cut to the eight young people at the table. Marjorie glares at Bernice. Bernice takes a deep breath and turns to Charley.*)

**Bernice:** Mr. Charley Paulson, do you think I ought to bob my hair?

**Charley** (*surprised*): Why?

**Bernice:** I want to be a society vampire. And I don't know how I can unless I bob my hair. Do you? (*Charley looks at her with interest.*) I want your advice because I hear you're so critical of girls.

**Marjorie:** What are you all talking about over there?

**Bernice:** I was just saying that I'm going downtown to a barbershop. I'm going to have my hair bobbed. (*She looks around at everyone.*) Of course I'm charging admission. But if you'll all come and encourage me, I'll give out passes for the best seats. (*Everyone is amused. Bernice smiles her new smile.*)

**Carpenter:** I thought bobbed hair was just for movie vamps. Would you really do it, Bernice?

**Bernice:** I know it's not something good girls do. But I believe you have to amuse people, feed them, or shock them. (*The boys laugh. Bernice speaks to Charley in a low tone.*) Charley, I've been wanting to ask your opinion of several people. I hear you're a wonderful judge of character.

(*Cut to Charley dancing with Bernice.*)

**Charley:** What did you mean when you said I'm critical of girls?

**Bernice:** That's what I hear.

**Charley:** Who said it?

**Bernice:** Several people.

**Charley:** Who?

**Bernice:** Guess. (*Carpenter cuts in.*)

**Charley:** Hey, wait a minute.

**Carpenter:** Too bad, Charley. (*He begins dancing with Bernice.*) Are you really going to bob your hair?

**Bernice:** First thing next week. Can you come?

**Carpenter:** I wouldn't miss it.

**Bernice:** Carpenter, is it true what I hear about you?

**Carpenter:** What's that?

**Bernice** (*realizing they're dancing very close to Reece and Roberta*): Just promise me you won't tell Mr. G. Reece Stoddard.

**Reece:** Tell me what?

**Bernice** (*as though surprised*): Oh! (*Car-*

*penter dances her off. Reece looks after her with interest.)*

**Carpenter:** He can't hear. Go ahead.
**Bernice:** I'd better whisper it. *(She whispers something in his ear.)*
**Carpenter:** Who said that?
**Bernice:** Never mind. I hope it's true. Fickle men are the only kind that interest me.

*(We see Marjorie picking out some records to play. Warren is beside her.)*

**Warren:** But *you* said you wanted to drive out to the lake.
**Marjorie:** I did?
**Warren:** Yes, weeks ago.
**Marjorie:** I changed my mind. Stop being such a pest.

*(Suddenly Warren has had enough of*

398

*Marjorie. He looks at the dancing couples. He sees Charley cutting in on Bernice. Just then the record ends. Reece excuses himself from Roberta and comes over to Warren.)*

**Reece:** Cut in on Roberta and me, will you?

**Warren:** Sure. Why?

**Reece:** I want to dance with Bernice.

*(We see Marjorie and Genvieve. Genvieve's sash has come loose.)*

**Marjorie:** Do you want to sew it or pin it?

**Genvieve:** Pin it.

**Marjorie:** Come upstairs. *(As the two girls go upstairs, Warren moves toward Reece and Roberta. Reece looks relieved. But Warren passes by and cuts in on Bernice. They begin to dance.)*

**Bernice:** How do you think I'll look with my hair bobbed?

**Warren:** You weren't serious, were you?

**Bernice:** Of course! Did you think it was just a line? *(Warren shrugs.)* The person in this room with a line is Warren McIntyre.

**Warren:** Why do you say that?

**Bernice:** "Bernice, you've got an awfully kissable mouth." *(Warren grins.)* I meant to ask your opinion of a kissable mouth. Is it one that looks as if it's been kissed a lot? Or is it one you'd like to kiss?

**Warren:** Why . . . one I'd like to kiss.

**Bernice:** Thank you, Warren. That's very handy to know. *(They both laugh.)*

*(Cut to Bernice and Marjorie going upstairs after the party. Bernice looks very happy.)*

**Marjorie:** So it worked?

**Bernice:** Oh, yes! The only trouble was I ran out of things to say. I had to repeat myself with different men.

**Marjorie:** They'll never know. Anyway, I'll fix up some new things tomorrow.

**Bernice** *(feeling put down)*: Maybe I could. I thought up some of the things I said tonight.

**Marjorie** *(not interested)*: Good night. *(She goes into her room.)*

*(Cut to the Harvey front door the next day. Otis rings the bell. Annie answers.)*

**Annie:** Miss Marjorie has gone downtown with her mother.

**Otis:** That's funny. Charley Paulson's sister said Charley was over here.

**Annie:** He is.

**Otis:** What's he doing here if Marjorie is downtown? *(Annie holds the door open. Otis enters and sees Bernice and Charley in the sitting room. Bernice is wearing one of Marjorie's dresses. She is laughing at the story Charley is telling.)*

**Otis:** Hey, Paulson! What about our tennis game?

**Charley** *(surprised)*: I forgot all about it.

**Otis:** If you hurry, we can still play a set or two.

**Charley:** I'm busy right now. See you later. *(As Otis goes out the front door, he meets Carpenter.)*

**Otis:** Marjorie is downtown.

**Carpenter:** Where's Bernice?

**Otis:** Bernice? *(Carpenter goes into the house. Otis pauses, then goes back into the house.)*

*(Cut to Marjorie's room. The two cousins are braiding their hair for the night.)*

**Marjorie:** You've learned how to smile. But you've got to learn how to look very sad, too.

**Bernice:** Why?

**Marjorie:** You need it sometimes.

**Bernice:** How do you do it?

**Marjorie:** Open your eyes wide. Now droop your mouth a little. Then look into the man's eyes. Then say, "I hardly have any boy friends at all."

**Bernice:** But I thought the idea was to seem popular.

**Marjorie:** This *only* works if you're popular. Suppose an unpopular girl said she didn't have any boy friends. What could a man say? But if a popular girl says it. . . .

**Bernice:** I see. Do you think I'll ever know all these things the way you do?

**Marjorie:** I don't know. You got a late start.

*(Cut to the Harvey front door the next day. Annie is holding the door open. Warren is outside.)*

**Annie** *(surprised)*: You want to see Miss Bernice? *(Before Warren can answer, Bernice appears.)*

**Bernice** *(to Warren)*: Hello, shell shock.

**Warren:** Ready?

**Bernice:** Annie, please tell Aunt Josephine I'm going for a ride. *(She and Warren run toward his car.)*

*(Cut to Mrs. Harvey upstairs, leaning over the railing.)*

**Mrs. Harvey:** Annie? Who was that at the door?

**Annie:** Mr. Warren. He and Miss Bernice went for a ride. *(Mrs. Harvey goes into Marjorie's room. Marjorie is being fitted*

*for a skirt. A dressmaker is pinning up the hem.)*

**Marjorie:** Who was it?

**Mrs. Harvey:** Warren.

**Marjorie:** Well, I can't see him now.

**Mrs. Harvey:** He came for Bernice. Did you know he telephoned her twice yesterday?

**Marjorie:** I'm glad he's finally found someone who appreciates him. *(She looks down at her skirt.)* This still isn't right.

**Mrs. Harvey:** I agree. It's too short.

**Marjorie:** No, it's too long. *(She looks down at the dressmaker.)* Take it up another quarter of an inch.

*(Cut to a picnic. Bernice, Warren, Marjorie, Otis, and Roberta are sitting around.)*

**Otis:** Bernice, do you think you'll come back for Christmas vacation?

**Bernice:** I haven't been invited yet.

**Marjorie** *(trapped)*: You're welcome to come here.

**Otis:** Swell!

**Marjorie** *(to Bernice)*: But knowing you, you'll have to ask your mother first.

**Bernice:** No. I've explained to her that a modern girl needs a great deal of freedom.

*(Cut to Bernice and Warren walking away from the group.)*

**Bernice:** I don't think you're sincere.

**Warren:** I am sincere. Why wouldn't I be?

**Bernice** *(stops and gives him her newly learned sad look)*: You're very popular. I'm just the new girl in town. I hardly have any boy friends at all.

**Warren:** Are you kidding? Half the men in town are crazy about you.

**Bernice:** Who, for instance?

**Warren:** Me, for instance.

*(Cut to Marjorie and Roberta. They are watching Bernice and Warren from a distance.)*

**Marjorie:** I could get him back like that! *(She snaps her fingers.)*

**Roberta:** Could you? *(She doesn't sound so sure. Marjorie gets a hard look in her eyes.)*

*(Cut to Bernice in the Harvey bathroom, brushing her eyebrows. Marjorie enters without knocking.)*

**Marjorie** *(coldly)*: You may as well get Warren out of your head.

**Bernice** *(surprised)*: What?

**Marjorie:** Stop making a fool of yourself over him. He doesn't care a bit for you. *(She leaves. After a pause, Bernice goes to Marjorie's room and knocks on the door. Marjorie opens it.)*

**Bernice:** You seem to think I've stolen your private property.

**Marjorie:** I'm not interested in discussing it.

**Bernice:** But you told me Warren flunked your test. You fell in love with four men before he came home for Christmas — *(Before she can finish the sentence, Marjorie has closed the door.)*

*(Cut to the group at a picnic the next day. Otis is showing off in a childish way. The others — Bernice, Marjorie, Roberta, Genvieve, Warren, Charley, and Reece — groan.)*

**Reece:** Otis, when are you going back to kindergarten?

**Otis:** Me? The day Bernice gets her hair bobbed.

**Marjorie:** Then your education is over.

**Otis:** Huh?

**Marjorie:** She didn't mean it. I thought you realized.

**Roberta** *(to Bernice)*: You mean that was just a line?

**Bernice** *(embarrassed)*: I don't know.

**Marjorie:** You never meant it. Admit it. *(Bernice looks around. Everyone is watching her. Warren seems especially curious.)*

**Otis:** Tell her where to get off, Bernice.

*(Bernice looks around again. Now Warren looks doubtful.)*

**Warren:** That's funny. I thought Bernice was sincere.

**Bernice** *(suddenly)*: I am. I like bobbed hair, and I'm going to bob mine.

**Marjorie:** When?

**Bernice:** Any time.

**Roberta:** No time like the present.

**Charley** *(jumps up)*: Let's have a bobbing party.

*(Everyone stands up, except Bernice.)*

**Marjorie:** Don't worry. She'll back out.

**Otis:** Come on, Bernice.

**Bernice:** Sure. *(She leads the way.)*

*(Cut to the group of young people watching a barber chop off Bernice's beautiful long hair. They are speechless. They hadn't realized how shocking this would be. The barber has never before cut a woman's hair, and he's doing a poor job of it.*

*(Cut to Bernice getting down from the barber chair. She is trying to smile. Her short hair seems lifeless. It no longer seems to go with her face. The other young people just stare at her.)*

**Bernice:** Well, I did it. *(There is a silence. Then Marjorie turns to Warren.)*

**Marjorie:** Would you mind driving me to the cleaners? I've got to get a dress there before supper. Roberta can drive the others home.

**Warren** *(confused):* What? Oh, sure. I'd be glad to.

*(Cut to the Harvey dining room that evening.)*

**Mrs. Harvey** *(to Bernice):* I don't know why you had to do such a thing. But couldn't you have at least waited until after tomorrow night?

**Marjorie:** What's tomorrow night? *(She remembers.)* Mrs. Deyo's party for Bernice!

**Mrs. Harvey:** Bernice, she'll be so insulted.

**Bernice:** Why?

**Mrs. Harvey:** She feels bobbed hair is sinful. She gave a talk on the subject at the Ladies' Club.

**Bernice:** I didn't know that.

**Mrs. Harvey:** Oh, Bernice. What will your mother say? She'll think I let you do it.

**Bernice:** I'm sorry, Aunt Josephine.

*(Cut to Bernice's room that night. She is looking at her short hair in a mirror. There is a knock on the door. Then Marjorie enters. Her long hair is down.)*

**Marjorie:** Bernice, I'm sorry about Mrs. Deyo's party. I had forgotten all about it.

**Bernice:** It's all right.

**Marjorie** *(beginning to braid her long hair)*: I didn't think you'd really go through with it. I'm really sorry.

**Bernice:** It doesn't matter.

**Marjorie:** You'll get used to it, maybe.

**Bernice:** I'm used to it now, and I like it.

**Marjorie:** Good. Don't let it worry you.

**Bernice:** I won't.

**Marjorie:** Life is too short.

**Bernice:** Yes.

**Marjorie:** Good night. *(She leaves.)*

*(Later, we see Bernice dressed for traveling. She leaves an envelope on her pillow addressed to Aunt Josephine.*

*(Cut to Marjorie's room. Marjorie is asleep. Bernice enters silently with a pair of scissors. She goes over to Marjorie and cuts off her two braids.*

*(Cut to the sidewalk outside the Harvey house. Bernice appears. A suitcase is in one hand. Marjorie's braids are in the other hand. She crosses the street. Smiling, she throws the braids into Warren's car. Then she hurries down the street toward the train station.)*

**Summarizing.** Choose the best phrase to complete each sentence. Then write the complete statements on your paper.

1. Bernice wasn't popular with Marjorie's friends because she _____ (refused to dance with them, had a boyfriend back home, was boring and ill at ease).

2. Marjorie tried to teach Bernice _____ (how to drive, how to make a party dress, how to be attractive to men).

3. At the dinner party, Bernice announced her plans to _____ (leave town, return for Christmas, bob her hair).

4. When Marjorie was told Warren had stopped by, she _____ (assumed he wanted to see her, assumed he wanted to see Bernice, ran down to meet him).

5. Mrs. Deyo would have been insulted by Bernice because the older woman _____ (had planned a party in Bernice's honor, thought bobbed hair was sinful, didn't like Bernice's parents).

6. For revenge, Bernice _____ (took Warren's car, cut off Marjorie's hair, tore Marjorie's party dress).

**Interpreting.** Write the answer to each question on your paper.

1. Why did Mrs. Deyo like Bernice?

2. How did Marjorie finally react when Warren became interested in Bernice?

3. How did Bernice's relationship with Marjorie's friends change?

4. Why did Bernice finally agree to have her hair cut off?

5. How did Bernice really feel after her haircut?

**For Thinking and Discussing.** If Bernice had come to you for advice about ways to become more popular, what would you have told her to do?

## UNDERSTANDING LITERATURE

**Style.** The elements of F. Scott Fitzgerald's writing style can't be separated from the period in which he lived and set much of his work.

Fitzgerald was fascinated with the very wealthy, and many of his tales are about rich people in the 1920's.

An important element of Fitzgerald's style is his use of dialogue. He often revealed character by what people said to and about each other. Much of the action in his works is revealed through dialogue.

One of the devices of style Fitzgerald used well to convey the flavor of his times was his use of expressions that were popular in the 1920's. These added much realism to his dialogue.

Here are some lines from "Bernice Bobs Her Hair." On your paper, match each with the person who is speaking and the character(s) being revealed. Some choices may be used more than once. Then identify two or more expressions from the 1920's.

a. Marjorie about self

b. Marjorie/self and others

c. Bernice/self

d. Marjorie's mother/Marjorie

e. Warren/Bernice

f. Marjorie/Bernice

1. "Warren flunked my test. . . . Before he came home for Christmas, I fell in love with four men."

2. "Well, you don't want to dance. And you don't want to sit out. Have a better idea?"

3. "Some things are more important than cheap popularity."

4. "Who let these two parlor snakes in my house?"

5. "You're also boring. You lean on men when you dance. You haven't any idea of how to make a man fall in love with you."

6. "Sad birds like Charley are part of any crowd. And you can't afford to neglect them."

7. "I want to be a society vampire. And I don't know how I can unless I bob my hair."

## WRITING

Write a short scene about a party that takes place during your own lifetime. Use dialogue and include as many popular expressions as you can to convey the flavor of the occasion.

# Three Poems of the Harlem Renaissance

*Renaissance* is a French word that means "rebirth." It is usually used to refer to the time in history when Europe had a great rebirth of writing and art. During the 1920's, in Harlem, there was a great explosion of creativity in many art forms. Black painters, musicians, and writers from all over the country came to Harlem. Here you will sample the works of two of the greatest poets of the Harlem Renaissance: Langston Hughes (1902–1967) and Countee Cullen (1903–1946).

# Dream Variations

*by Langston Hughes*

To fling my arms wide
In some place of the sun,
To whirl and to dance
Till the white day is done.
Then rest at cool evening
Beneath a tall tree
While night comes on gently,
   Dark like me —
That is my dream!

To fling my arms wide
In the face of the sun,
Dance! Whirl! Whirl!
Till the quick day is done.
Rest at pale evening . . .
A tall, slim tree . . .
Night coming tenderly
   Black like me.

1. What kind of mood do the speaker's day-time activities suggest?

2. What kind of mood do the speaker's evening activities suggest?

# The Negro Speaks of Rivers

*by Langston Hughes*

I've known rivers:
I've known rivers ancient as the world and older than the
      flow of human blood in human veins.

My soul has grown     deep like rivers.

I bathed in the Euphrates when dawns were young.
I built my hut near the Congo and it lulled me to sleep.
I looked upon the Nile and raised the pyramids above it.
I heard the singing of the Mississippi when Abe Lincoln went
      down to New Orleans, and I've seen its muddy bosom
      turn all golden in the sunset.

I've known rivers:
Ancient, dusky rivers.

My soul has grown     deep like rivers.

---

1. When the poet uses *I*, does he mean just himself? For whom is he speaking? What does the poem have to say about the black heritage?
2. The Congo and the Nile rivers are in Africa. How is their location important to the poem?
3. In what ways can a soul be "deep like rivers"?

# Any Human to Another

*by Countee Cullen*

The ills I sorrow at
Not me alone
Like an arrow,
Pierce to the marrow,
Through the fat
And past the bone.

Your grief and mine
Must intertwine
Like sea and river,
Be fused and mingle,
Diverse yet single,
Forever and forever.

Let no man be so proud
And confident,
To think he is allowed
A little tent
Pitched in a meadow
Of sun and shadow
All his little own.

Joy may be shy, unique,
Friendly to a few,
Sorrow never scorned to speak
To any who
Were false or true.

Your very grief
Like a blade
Shining and unsheathed
Must strike me down.
Of bitter aloes wreathed,
My sorrow must be laid
On your head like a crown.

---

**1.** *Diverse* means different or varied. In what ways are people's troubles "diverse yet single"?

**2.** Does the poet think that there is more joy in the world or more sorrow? Explain your answer. Do you agree? Why or why not?

## READING COMPREHENSION

**Summarizing.** Choose the best phrase to complete each sentence. Then write the complete statements on your paper.

1. In "Dream Variations," the poet wants to _____ (dance during the day, sing all the time, work all the time).

2. In "Dream Variations," the poet rests _____ (during the day, all the time, at night).

3. In the poem "The Negro Speaks of Rivers," Langston Hughes compares _____ (rivers and his soul, rivers and his mind, rivers and world history).

4. The poem "Any Human to Another" says that people should _____ (compete with each other, care for each other, stand on their own).

**Interpreting.** Write the answer to each question on your paper.

1. To which rivers does the poet refer in "The Negro Speaks of Rivers"?

2. In what way are the rivers in "The Negro Speaks of Rivers" used to represent the passage of time?

3. In "Any Human to Another," what does the poet mean by "your very grief like a blade . . . must strike me down" and "my sorrow must be laid on your head like a crown"?

**For Thinking and Discussing.** Do you agree that people should not stand alone in sorrow? Explain.

## UNDERSTANDING LITERATURE

**Style and Rhythm in Poetry.** The rhythm of a poem reflects the poet's purpose. Poems about unhappiness often have heavy rhythms. Poems about joyful subjects often have musical rhythms.

In Langston Hughes's poem "The Negro Speaks of Rivers," the line "My soul has grown deep like rivers" is repeated, and each time it makes a powerful statement. The rhythm of the lines matches the pride and power this poem suggests.

Read the lines below, and on your paper, describe each rhythm you feel. Is it fast or slow? What mood does it suggest?

1. "To fling my arms wide
   In the face of the sun,
   Dance! Whirl! Whirl!
   Till the quick day is done."

2. "The ills I sorrow at
   Not me alone
   Like an arrow,
   Pierce to the marrow,
   Through the fat
   And past the bone."

3. "I've known rivers:/I've known rivers ancient as the world and older than the/flow of human blood in human veins."

## WRITING

Write two to four lines of poetry about love, using a light, joyous rhythm. Write two to four lines about loneliness, using a heavy rhythm.

# A Day's Wait

*by Ernest Hemingway*

*Ernest Hemingway (1898–1961) is one of America's great adventurer-writers who based much of his work on his own experiences. At different times in his life, he drove an ambulance and was wounded in World War I, hunted big game in Africa, covered the Spanish Civil War as a reporter, and went deep-sea fishing while living in Cuba. For a time, Hemingway also lived in France and got to know other Americans who were living abroad. The experiences he had and the people he met all found their way into his writing. The following story, told mostly in dialogue and short, clear sentences, is typical of Hemingway's style. In the story you meet a boy called Schatz. Hemingway used this nickname for his own sons.*

He came into the room to shut the windows while we were still in bed and I saw he looked ill. He was shivering, his face was white, and he walked slowly as though it ached to move.

"What's the matter, Schatz?"

"I've got a headache."

"You'd better go back to bed."

"No. I'm all right."

"You go to bed. I'll see you when I'm dressed."

But when I came downstairs he was dressed, sitting by the fire, looking a very sick and miserable boy of nine years. When I put my hand on his forehead I knew he had a fever.

"You go up to bed," I said, "you're sick."

"I'm all right," he said.

When the doctor came he took the boy's temperature.

"What is it?" I asked him.

"One hundred and two."

Downstairs, the doctor left three different medicines in different-colored capsules with instructions for giving them. One was to bring down the fever, another a purgative, the third to overcome an acid condition. The germs of influenza can only exist in an acid condition, he explained. He seemed to know all about influenza and said there was nothing to worry about if the fever did not go above one hundred and four degrees. This was a light epidemic of flu and there was no danger if you avoided pneumonia.

Back in the room I wrote the boy's temperature down and made a note of the time to give the various capsules.

"Do you want me to read to you?"

"All right. If you want to," said the boy. His face was very white and there were dark areas under his eyes. He lay still in the bed and seemed very detached from what was going on.

I read aloud from Howard Pyle's *Book of Pirates*; but I could see he was not following what I was reading.

"How do you feel, Schatz?" I asked him.

"Just the same, so far," he said.

I sat at the foot of the bed and read to myself while I waited for it to be time to give another capsule. It would have been natural for him to go to sleep, but when I looked up he was looking at the foot of the bed, looking very strangely.

"Why don't you try to go to sleep? I'll wake you up for the medicine."

"I'd rather stay awake."

After a while he said to me, "You don't have to stay in here with me, Papa."

"It doesn't bother me."

"No, I mean you don't have to stay if it's going to bother you."

I thought perhaps he was a little light-headed and after giving him the prescribed capsules at 11:00 I went out for a while.

It was a bright, cold day, the ground covered with a sleet that had frozen so that it seemed as if all the bare trees, the bushes, the cut brush, and all the grass and the bare ground had been varnished with ice. I took the young Irish setter for a little walk up the road and along a frozen creek, but it was difficult to stand or walk on the glassy surface and the red dog slipped and slithered and I fell twice, hard, once dropping my gun and having it slide away over the ice.

We flushed a covey of quail under a high clay bank with overhanging brush and I killed two as they went out of sight over the top of the bank. Some of the covey lit in trees, but most of them scattered into brush piles and it was necessary to jump on the ice-coated mounds of brush several times before they would flush. Coming out while you were poised unsteadily on the icy, springy brush they made difficult shooting, and I killed two,

missed five, and started back pleased to have found a covey close to the house and happy there were so many left to find on another day.

At the house they said the boy had refused to let anyone come into the room.

"You can't come in," he said. "You mustn't get what I have."

I went up to him and found him in exactly the position I had left him, white-faced, but with the tops of his cheeks flushed by the fever, staring still, as he had stared, at the foot of the bed.

I took his temperature.

"What is it?"

"Something like a hundred," I said. It was one hundred and two and four tenths.

"It was a hundred and two," he said.

"Who said so?"

"The doctor."

"Your temperature is all right," I said. "It's nothing to worry about."

"I don't worry," he said, "but I can't keep from thinking."

"Don't think," I said. "Just take it easy."

"I'm taking it easy," he said and looked straight ahead. He was evidently holding tight onto himself about something.

"Take this with water."

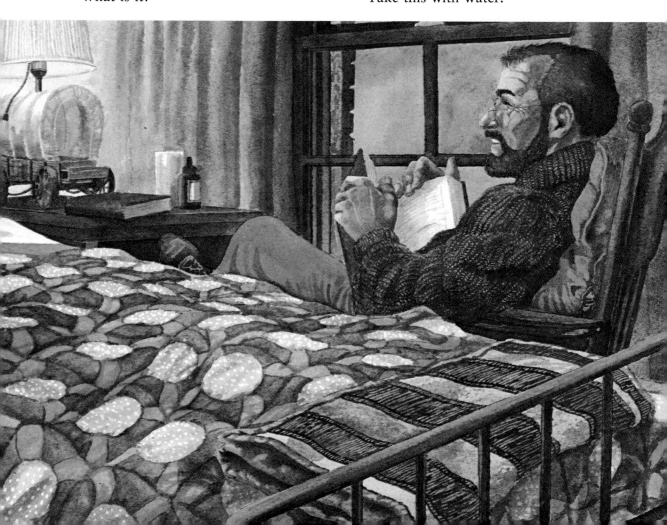

"Do you think it will do any good?"

"Of course it will."

I sat down and opened the *Pirate* book and commenced to read, but I could see he was not following, so I stopped.

"About what time do you think I'm going to die?" he asked.

"What?"

"About how long will it be before I die?"

"You aren't going to die. What's the matter with you?"

"Oh, yes, I am. I heard him say a hundred and two."

"People don't die with a fever of one hundred and two. That's a silly way to talk."

"I know they do. At school in France the boys told me you can't live with forty-four degrees. I've got a hundred and two."

He had been waiting to die all day, ever since 9:00 in the morning.

"You poor Schatz," I said. "Poor old Schatz. It's like miles and kilometers. You aren't going to die. That's a different thermometer. On that thermometer thirty-seven is normal. On this kind it's ninety-eight."

"Are you sure?"

"Absolutely," I said. "It's like miles and kilometers. You know, like how many kilometers we make when we do seventy miles in the car."

"Oh," he said.

But his gaze at the foot of the bed relaxed slowly. The hold over himself relaxed, too, finally, and the next day it was very slack and he cried very easily at little things that were of no importance.

416

**Summarizing.** Choose the best phrase to complete each sentence. Then write the complete statements on your paper.

1. The boy's father called the doctor because he _____ (thought his son was going to die, knew the child had the mumps, thought the child had a fever).

2. The doctor said there was nothing to worry about _____ (as long as the boy took the pills, if the fever didn't go above 104 degrees, because children recover quickly).

3. The father sat and read to him, but the boy _____ (dozed off, wanted a different book, couldn't pay attention).

4. After giving his son his medicine, the father _____ (took a nap, visited a friend, went hunting).

5. The boy was sure he was going to die because _____ (the doctor said flu is deadly, he felt worse than he ever had, he confused two different measures of temperature).

**Interpreting.** Write the answer to each question on your paper.

1. How did the father know the boy was sick?

2. Why wouldn't the boy let anyone into his room when his father went out?

3. When the boy told his father that he didn't have to stay "if it's going to bother you," what did he mean?

4. Why did the boy's father compare the two kinds of temperature reading to miles and kilometers?

5. After his father compared the temperature readings to miles and kilometers, why did the boy finally relax?

**For Thinking and Discussing**

1. Why do you think the boy "cried very easily at little things that were of no importance" the day after he found out about the different measures of temperature?

2. Why do you think the boy worried for an entire day before asking his father when he would die? Explain your answer.

## UNDERSTANDING LITERATURE

**Style.** Ernest Hemingway's work is well known for its spare, recognizable style. His style expresses his individuality and his own personal code. Hemingway believed that it was the job of a writer to face reality and to tell the truth.

Hemingway spoke of the need "to strip language clean, to lay it bare down to the bone." He revised his own writing again and again before publication and tried to eliminate any unneeded words or phrases. He tried to keep his sentences simple.

Hemingway's dialogue sounds natural and realistic. He communicates complicated human feelings with very few words.

Here are five characteristic elements of Hemingway's style, followed by some passages from the story you have just read. On your paper, match each passage to one or more of the elements of style that it demonstrates.

a. facing reality and telling the truth

b. simple sentence structure

c. no unnecessary words

d. natural dialogue

e. communication of feelings

1. "He was shivering, his face was white, and he walked slowly as though it ached to move."

2. " 'What's the matter, Schatz?'
'I've got a headache.'
'You'd better go back to bed.'
'No. I'm all right.' "

3. "I thought perhaps he was a little light-headed and after giving him the prescribed capsules at 11:00 I went out for a while."

4. "He had been waiting to die all day, ever since 9:00 in the morning."

5. " 'Poor old Schatz. It's like miles and kilometers. You aren't going to die. That's a different thermometer.' "

## WRITING

Imagine that you are the boy in this story and that you believe you are going to die of fever. Write one or two paragraphs describing the way you feel and your fears. Make sure your writing style is well suited to your subject.

# The Standard of Living

*by Dorothy Parker*

*Dorothy Parker (1893–1967) was known for the clever
way she poked fun at the people and social rules of her day.
Her writing also shows a real understanding of different kinds
of people. Here you will meet two young women of the 1930's
who wonder what it would be like to have a million dollars.*

**A**nnabel and Midge came out of the tea room with the arrogant slow walk of the leisured, for their Saturday afternoon stretched ahead of them. They had lunched, as usual, on sandwiches of spongy white bread with butter and mayonnaise; thick wedges of cake lying wet beneath ice cream; and melted chocolate gritty with nuts. Or they might have eaten meat patties sweating beads of oil, covered with pale, thick sauce. They chose no other sort of food, nor did they think of it. And their skin was like the petals of flowers, and their stomachs were as flat and their bodies as lean as those of young Indian braves.

Annabel and Midge had been best friends almost from the day that Midge had found a job as a secretary with the firm that employed Annabel. By now, Annabel, two years longer at the firm, had worked up to the wages of $18.50 a week; Midge was still at $16. Each girl lived at home with her family and paid half her salary to its support.

The girls sat side by side at their desks; they ate together every noon; together they set out for home after work. Many of their evenings and most of their weekends were passed in each other's company. Constant use had not worn ragged the fabric of their friendship.

Always the girls went to walk on Fifth Avenue on their free afternoons, for it was the ideal ground for their game. The game could be played anywhere, but the great shop windows inspired the two players to their best form.

Annabel invented the game. Basically, it was no more than the ancient sport of what-would-you-do-if-you-had-a-million-dollars? But Annabel had drawn a new set of rules for it, and made it stricter.

Annabel's version went like this: You must suppose that somebody dies and leaves you a million dollars, cool. But there is a condition to the gift. It is stated in the will that you must spend every nickel of the money on yourself.

There lay the difficulty of the game. If, when playing it, you forgot and said you would rent a new apartment for your family, for example, you lost your turn to the other player.

It was necessary, of course, that the game be played in complete seriousness. Each purchase must be carefully considered, and if necessary, supported by argument.

Annabel and Midge were surely born to be friends, for Midge played the game like a master from the moment she learned it. Midge played with a seriousness that was not only proper but extreme. The single strain on the girls' friendship was when Annabel once said that the first thing she would buy with her million dollars would be a silver fox coat. It was as if she had struck Midge across the mouth. When Midge recovered her breath, she said that she couldn't imagine how Annabel could do such a thing — silver fox coats were so common! She added that everybody had a silver fox coat. She said, with a slight toss of her head, that she herself wouldn't be caught dead in silver fox.

For the next few days, though the girls saw each other as constantly, they did not once play their game. Then one morning, as soon as Annabel entered the office, she came to Midge and said she had changed her mind. She would not buy a silver fox coat with any part of her million dollars. Instead, she would select a coat of mink. Midge smiled, and her eyes shone. "You're doing the right thing," she said.

Now, as they walked along Fifth Avenue, they played the game again. It was one of those hot, glaring September days, with slivers of dust in the wind. People drooped in the heat, but the girls carried themselves tall and walked a straight line, as was proper for rich young women on their afternoon stroll. There was no longer need for them to start the game at the beginning. Annabel went direct to the heart of it.

"All right," she said. "So you've got this million dollars. So what would be the first thing you do?"

"Well, the first thing I'd do," Midge said, "I'd get a mink coat." But she said it mechanically, as if she was giving the old answer to an expected question.

"Yes," Annabel said. "I think you ought to. The terribly dark kind of mink." But she, too, spoke without enthusiasm. It was too hot; fur, no matter how dark and sleek, was horrid to the thoughts.

They stepped along in silence for a while. Then Midge's eye was caught by a shop window. Cool, lovely gleamings were there set off by elegant darkness.

"No," Midge said, "I take it back. I wouldn't get a mink coat the first thing. Know what I'd do? I'd get a string of pearls. Real pearls."

Annabel's eyes turned to follow Midge's.

"Yes," she said slowly. "I think that's a kind of good idea. And it would make good sense, too. Because you can wear pearls with anything."

Together they went over to the shop window and stood pressed against it. It contained but one object — a double row of great, even pearls clasped by a deep emerald around a little pink velvet throat.

"What do you suppose they cost?" Annabel said.

"Gee, I don't know," Midge said. "Plenty, I guess."

"Like a thousand dollars?" Annabel said.

"Oh, I guess like more," Midge said. "On account of the emerald."

"Well, like ten thousand dollars?" Annabel said.

"Gee, I wouldn't even know," Midge said.

The devil nudged Annabel in the ribs.

"Dare you go in and price them," she said.

"Like fun!" Midge said.

"Dare you," Annabel said.

"Why a store like this wouldn't even be open this afternoon," Midge said.

"Yes, it is so, too," Annabel said. "People just came out. And there's a doorman on. Dare you."

"Well," Midge said. "But you've got to come, too."

They said their thanks, icily, to the doorman as he opened the door to the shop. It was cool and quiet, a lovely room with paneled walls and soft carpet.

A neatly dressed clerk came to them and bowed. "Good afternoon," he said in a soft-spoken greeting.

"Good afternoon," Annabel and Midge said together, coldly.

"Is there something — ?" the clerk said.

"Oh, we're just looking," Annabel said. It was as if she threw the words down from a throne.

The clerk bowed.

"My friend and I just happened to be passing," Midge said. "My friend here and myself just happened to be wondering how much those pearls are that you've got in your window."

"Ah, yes," the clerk said. "The double rope. That is two hundred and fifty thousand dollars, Madam."

"I see," Midge said.

The clerk bowed. "An unusually beautiful necklace," he said. "Would you care to look at it?"

"No, thank you," Annabel said.

"My friend and myself just happened to be passing," Midge said.

They turned to go. The clerk hurried ahead to open the door. He bowed as they swept by him.

"Honestly!" Annabel said as they walked along the avenue. "Can you imagine a thing like that?"

"Two hundred and fifty thousand dollars!" Midge said. "That's a quarter of a million dollars right there!"

"He's got his nerve!" Annabel said.

They walked on. Slowly the self-confidence went, completely drained from them, and with it went the proud walk. Their shoulders drooped and they dragged their feet; they bumped against each other without notice or apology. They were silent and their eyes were cloudy.

Suddenly Midge straightened her back, lifted her head high, and spoke, clear and strong.

"Listen, Annabel," she said. "Look. Suppose there was this terribly rich person, see? You don't know this person, but this person has seen you somewhere and wants to do something for you. Well, it's a terribly old person, see? And so this person dies just like going to sleep, and leaves you ten million dollars. Now, what would be the first thing you'd do?"

**Summarizing.** Choose the best phrase to complete each sentence. Then write the complete statements on your paper.

1. Annabel and Midge first met _____ (at work, in a tea room, in a jewelry store).

2. In Annabel's game, the million dollars could not be spent on _____ (anything for anyone else, silver fox coats, jewelry that was not pure gold).

3. The young women went into the jewelry store because they _____ (had a million dollars to spend, expected to buy some expensive jewelry, dared each other to price the necklace).

4. When they learned the price of the pearls, the girls _____ (never played their game again, asked to see them, pretended they had more money).

**Interpreting.** Write the answer to each question on your paper.

1. Why did Annabel and Midge once stop playing their game for several days?

2. Why did Annabel and Midge play their game?

3. Why did the girls feel so dejected when they learned the price of the pearls?

**For Thinking and Discussing.** What did the girls' new approach to their game at the end of the story show about their character?

**Ironic Tone.** Style is the particular way an author arranges words. In "The Standard of Living," the important elements of style are the way the author revealed character and her consistently *ironic tone*.

Parker wrote in the third person, "all knowing," point of view. She revealed her characters by describing them and their actions and using dialogue that let them speak for themselves. The dialogue includes an occasional adverb that describes the way the words are said.

On your paper, identify each sentence below that is in Parker's ironic style.

1. She said, with a slight toss of her head, that she herself wouldn't be caught dead in a silver fox coat.

2. Midge told Annabel that a silver fox coat wouldn't be her choice even though it was a magnificent fur.

3. They said their thanks, icily, to the doorman as he opened the door. . . .

4. "Those pearls are fantastic! May we look at them even though we'll never be able to dig up the cash?"

Imagine that someone has left *you* a million dollars. Write a paragraph telling what you would buy and why. Follow Annabel's rules: You're not allowed to buy anything for anyone else. Write in the first person and use a style that reflects your attitude toward the inheritance.

# Everything But Money

*by Sam Levenson*

*Sam Levenson makes you laugh out loud at the smallest event. And even though most of these episodes from his childhood occurred against a backdrop of poverty, we never feel sad about Sam and his family. Rather we admire their love, spirit, and wisdom.*

My parents came to America by invitation. Those who had landed here before them sent back picture postcards of a lady called Miss Liberty. Printed on them were these words:

> *Give me your tired, your poor,*
> *Your huddled masses yearning to breathe free,*
> *The wretched refuse of your teeming shore.*
> *Send these, the homeless, tempest-tost to me,*
> *I lift my lamp beside the golden door!*

It was signed Emma Lazarus, a name that sounded familiar to my parents — perhaps some second cousin on my mother's side. So Mama and Papa packed all their belongings and left for America. After all, who was more tired, poor, huddled, yearning to be free, wretched, homeless, and tempest-tost than they?

I was raised as a virtually free American in a section of New York that was called a slum by sight-seeing guides and a depressed area by sociologists. Both were right. Our neighborhood fulfilled all the sordid requirements with honors. We were unquestionably above average in squalid tenements, cold flats, hot roofs, dirty streets, and flying garbage. Yet, paradoxically, I never felt depressed or deprived. My environment was miserable; I was not.

I was a most fortunate child. Ours was a home rich enough in family harmony and love to immunize eight kids against the potentially toxic effects of the environment beyond our door.

Our home was a battleground in the relentless struggle not only for survival (which even beasts can manage) but for survival with dignity. This was the American Revolution fourth floor back.

Mama and Papa were the leaders of this band of freedom fighters consisting of seven sons and one daughter, whose homemade weapons were hard work, family pride and, above all, faith in education as the major weapon of our liberation movement.

Those were not the "good old days," but there were more victories than defeats, and each small victory was cause for a

large celebration around the dinner table at the end of the day. Each member of the clan would recount his conquests at the shop or in school to the great delight of the others, who responded with much back-slapping, hysterical laughter, and chants of victory.

According to studies made by social-service agencies, a good home is defined as one in which there are love, acceptance, belonging, high moral standards, good parental example, decent food, clothing, shelter, spiritual guidance, discipline, joint enterprises, a place to bring friends, and respect for authority. Today any child, rich or poor, who lives in such a home is considered a "lucky kid." By these standards, then, I was a "lucky kid," not in spite of my home but because of it.

It is also possible — and this is not unusual among poor children — that I went on my merry way being merry simply because I did not know any better. I had no idea, for instance, that I was entitled to a bed of my own. It was obvious even to an ordinary kid like me that the more kids you slept with the more fun you had in bed. I figured that was what they meant by "bedlam." I didn't know that beds were supposed to be soft. To me "bed and board" meant one and the same thing.

I didn't know there were good cuts of meat and bad. Our menu at mealtime offered two choices — take it or leave it — an approach that seemed to stimulate our appetites. I didn't know that meatballs were supposed to contain meat. To this day I don't like the taste of meatballs made of meat. They just don't taste like Mama's.

Our block had about twenty tenements; each building about thirty families; each family about 5.6 children (not counting stowaways) by government census — if the census taker could halt the increase long enough to write down the number. There are towns in the United States with smaller populations which have a post office of their own. Yet I never felt crowded in or crowded out. My neighbors never appeared as a crowd to me. To me they were individuals — not all good and kind and noble, but individuals. We knew all about them and they all about us.

I didn't know I needed some quiet place where I could do my homework. My brothers used to sit around the dining-room table in the evening doing homework en masse, noisily, bothering each other, correcting, helping. I didn't know I was supposed to be obsessed by sibling rivalries, so I admired my brothers and learned a great deal from them.

I learned from experience that if there was something lacking it might turn up if I went after it, saved up for it, worked for it, but never if I just waited for it. Of course, you had to be lucky, too, but I discovered that the more I hustled the luckier I seemed to get.

Lest all this appear as a defense of the notion that ignorance is bliss, I'd like to tell you what I *did* know. I knew that there were things I wanted badly, things I would ask for. Mama's answer to such requests usually came in two words: "Not now." (Later we came to refer to this approach as Mama's theory of postponement of pleasure.) First things first. First came the absolute *necessities* like books. Skates, sleds, and bicycles would have to wait. I know Mama didn't enjoy denying us the joys of childhood. She had to, in the interest of our adulthood. "You'll have to do *without* today if you want a tomorrow *with*."

Our parents set the moral tone of the family. They expected more of some of us and less of others, but never less than they thought we were capable of. The Levensons were different from each other, yet very much alike, as children and as adults. As brothers we were expected to collaborate rather than compete. Each was responsible not only to himself but to his brother, and all were responsible to our parents, who were prepared to answer to the world for all of us.

Mama and Papa hoped to derive joy from their children. "May you have joy from your children" was the greatest blessing conceivable. They were the parting words on happy and sad occasions. Honor brought to parents by their children was the accepted standard for measuring success. It also became an incentive for us. Our personal success was to a great extent predicated upon the happiness we could bring to our parents.

As the children of immigrants my brothers were aware of the fact that they represented the "undesirables," the "foreigners," as others had been "undesirables" in previous decades. They realized, too, that the only way to rise above undesirability was not merely to become desirable, but to become indispensable. This would require equal amounts of education and sacrifice.

Joe, the eldest, became a doctor. Jack, next in line, became a dentist. They were the first to break through the barbed-wire fence of poverty. Because of them it was easier for the rest of us.

Through all the bleak years that Joe spent in medical school Papa could contribute nothing but a regular allowance of moral support. Joe will tell you to this day that he sews up a wound just like his father, the tailor, did. The stitches never show. He has still retained one nasty habit, though—he bites off the thread, a trick he learned from Mama who, in turn, learned a lot from Joe. He used to show her medical pictures of man's insides. "Just like a chicken," Mama observed. Joe will also tell you about the skull he brought home. The brothers placed it in the bookcase. At night they would put a lighted candle into it to scare off burglars. It worked. The one burglar who got in was so terrified he forgot his tools. We gave them to Joe, who used them on us, his first patients.

Jack, immediately after graduation from dental school, was besieged by all the moneyless tenants of our building, who provided him with the kind of professional experience money couldn't buy. After a while he learned how to cope with the situation. He either told them that nothing was wrong, or that they needed a specialist—my cousin Alvin.

Our only sister's name is Dora. To this day none of us can remember where she got dressed. She is the clearing house for all news, gossip, birth announcements, and recipes. Dora has been the family historian, the curator of pictures, medals, legal

documents, and old silver. She knows everybody's age but her own.

David was the Horatio Alger kid of our family. He had only one job in all his life. At the age of sixteen he went to work as a bookkeeper for a clothing jobber. He is now a partner in the business. He has not gone out to lunch in forty years. He can't make it because during lunch hour all the poor relatives come for suits.

Michael, next in line, threw Mama completely. At about the age of fourteen he won a medal for art. An artist in the family? "From this you expect to make a living? Learn a trade!" But there was no stopping him. He studied art all day and worked in the post office all night. Mama used to leave his portion of chopped liver on a plate so that he could have "a little something" before he went to bed. This unprotected delicacy standing on the table for hours brought out the wolf in the rest of us. Each one would wait till no one else was around, scoop out a little section of the liver, gulp it down, and flatten out the remainder with the palm of his hand so it would cover the same area. By the time Mike sat down to eat he could see the design on the plate through the liver.

At the age of twenty-three Michael won a prize which sent him to study in Europe for five years. The relatives sent him off with about thirty-two hand-knit sweaters and sixty-seven jars of homemade jelly. From Paris he sent me some of his prize money to buy a violin. In subsequent years he has exhibited his work in group shows.

Bill, next in line, became a successful dental technician. At first he decided not to work for somebody else for ten hours a day — not him, boy — so he went into business and worked twelve hours a day — for himself, boy.

Albert, just ahead of me, has been at my side all my life. He had a genius for getting into trouble. He did not go looking for it. He didn't have to. It came looking for him. Somehow he was always available.

I was there when:

1. The revolving door at the Automat jammed on Albert when he was half-way through. In the presence of hundreds of people studying Albert under glass, a crew of mechanics had to release him.

2. Albert took two steps on the sidewalk to let an elderly man pass, and found himself in a cellar with a freshly delivered ton of coal for company.

3. Albert walked into the house carrying a jar of sour cream. He slipped on the freshly washed wooden planks and the jar hit the floor. Normally the cream would splash on the floor, but not for Albert. The jar hit the floor and the cream hit the ceiling. This may not work for you even if you try it, but for Albert this was a "natural."

I am the kid brother of the family. To this day when the boys get together they send me for ice cream, and I have to go. (Joe still calls me the "go-getter.") As the last of so many I presented a special problem to Mama, who in moments of anger often couldn't remember my name. She would stare at me and call off every name but mine: "Joe, no, Jack, no . . ." Out of sheer frustration, she would say: "You, what's your name?"

I became a schoolteacher and married Esther, who had waited eight years for me to get a job. It was customary at the time to get a job first, then a wife. I never claimed my college diploma. It cost $1.87. My cap-and-gown graduation picture is a further commentary on those days. Across the face are stamped the words "Proof Only."

## READING COMPREHENSION

**Summarizing.** Choose the best phrase to complete each sentence. Then write the complete statements on your paper.

1. The neighborhood Sam Levenson's family lived in was _____ (very dangerous, above average, poor and crowded).

2. The family's "weapons" were hard work, family pride, and _____ (religion, faith in education, good manners).

3. Sam Levenson never got his college diploma because _____ (he didn't finish college, he couldn't pay for the diploma, he didn't care about it).

**Interpreting.** Write the answer to each question on your paper.

1. What reasons did Levenson give to explain why his childhood was happy?

2. What did Mama mean when she said, "You'll have to do *without* today if you want a tomorrow *with*"?

3. Why was Sam Levenson's graduation picture stamped with the words "Proof Only"?

**For Thinking and Discussing.** In some ways the author's writing reflects the notion that "ignorance is bliss." In what cases would you agree with this notion? In what cases would you disagree? Give some examples from your own childhood to support your answers.

## UNDERSTANDING LITERATURE

**Style.** Style is the particular way in which an author uses language to express what he or she has to say. An author's style is what makes him or her unique or different from other writers. Style often reveals the author's personality and the theme or purpose of the writing.

In "Everything But Money," there is no mistaking Sam Levenson's humorous style. His style reveals the way he looks upon his childhood — with fond amusement. It also tells us that his purpose in writing was to entertain and amuse the reader.

Levenson uses various techniques to create humor. Sometimes he exaggerates, or overstates an idea beyond the limits of truth. Sometimes he writes in a tongue-in-cheek way and treats serious subjects lightly. And sometimes he uses puns or other plays on words.

Read the following passages. Write a sentence describing what makes each funny.

1. "I didn't know there were good cuts of meat and bad. Our menu at mealtime offered two choices — take it or leave it. . . ."

2. "It was customary at the time to get a job first, then a wife."

## WRITING

Give examples of the techniques the author used to create humor in his story. Then use your own brand of humor to write about an event from your childhood.

# Section Review

VOCABULARY

**Multiple Meanings.** Sometimes a word can have more than one meaning, and what the word means depends on the way it is used in the sentence. For example, *lean* can mean "without much flesh or fat." *Lean* can also mean "bend, or rest against." Dorothy Parker used the word *lean* to describe the slim characters in her story.

Read each sentence below. On your paper, select the correct meaning of each italicized word.

1. "He went *broke*, of course, because he gave too much *credit*."
   *broke*  **a.** smashed to bits
          **b.** without money
   *credit*  **a.** buying on time
         **b.** recognition

2. "The *single strain* on the girls' friendship was when Annabel once said . . . she would buy . . . a silver fox coat."
   *single*  **a.** not married
         **b.** only
   *strain*  **a.** melody or tune
         **b.** pressure or tension

3. "It contained but one *object*—a double *row* of . . . pearls . . ."
   *object*  **a.** disagree
         **b.** thing
   *row*  **a.** line or string
        **b.** to use an oar

READING

**Drawing Conclusions.** Sometimes when you read, the author tells you directly what he or she wants you to know. In other cases, you have to put together the details and draw your own conclusions.

Write the answers to the following questions on your paper.

1. In "Discovery of a Father," Anderson's mother laughed when her husband clowned. She worked and managed during his absences, and she smiled when he returned. You can conclude that she _____ .
   **a.** would have preferred a wealthy man
   **b.** loved her husband the way he was
   **c.** secretly desired a divorce

2. In "Love of Life," both men were carrying packs. Bill went on when his companion got hurt. The injured man kept going but lightened his load by leaving gold along the trail. You can conclude that Bill _____ .
   **a.** wanted to go for help quickly
   **b.** couldn't afford to wait for his friend
   **c.** valued gold more than his friend

3. In "A Day's Wait," the boy had the flu and a fever. He couldn't keep his mind on the story his father read to him, and he refused to go to sleep. Although the doctor and the boy's father were not concerned, you can conclude that the boy was _____ .
   **a.** in serious danger of death
   **b.** very worried about himself
   **c.** eager to return to school

# WRITING

**A Journal.** A journal or diary is a place where you record your personal experiences, thoughts, feelings, and dreams. Since no one is meant to read a journal but the person who wrote it, there are no strict rules about what to write or how to write it. What you write in your journal on a particular day is called a journal entry. Over the years, your journal entries can add up to a kind of personal history.

In addition to providing you with a place to write your personal thoughts, a journal can also help you with other kinds of writing. For example, writing freely in your journal can help you come up with topics for writing assignments. Your journal entries can also be the material for autobiographical narratives.

Think about the stories you have read in this section. It is not hard to imagine that some of the authors may have kept journals. Jack London, Sherwood Anderson, and Sam Levenson all drew upon personal experiences and how they felt about them.

## Step 1: Set Your Goal

Keep a journal of your own for a week. Be sure to date each entry so you will know when you wrote it.

The following is a list of possible topics you may want to record:

- ☐ your feelings about a particular person or thing that's on your mind
- ☐ conversations you have been involved in
- ☐ your opinions of movies or television programs you have seen or of things you have read about in the newspaper
- ☐ what you can recall about your dreams
- ☐ descriptions of activities that you participate in, such as sports, hobbies, or school activities
- ☐ events or other things that you've seen, such as an unusual happening on the street or a beautiful sunset

## Step 2: Make a Plan

Before you can begin your journal, you need to have something to write in. You might purchase a small notebook or diary or simply staple several sheets of paper together. Whatever you choose to use as your journal, it should be used for that purpose and nothing else.

Most people who have kept a journal for a while write in it whenever the mood strikes them. However, if you've never kept a journal before, you should probably start with a plan.

Think about a place that would provide a good environment for writing in your journal. A quiet place, such as your bedroom or a library, can offer a sense of peace and solitude. Some people feel that they write more freely if they are in a natural setting that they find inspiring, such as a favorite park, lake shore, or hilltop. Others feel that they need people around them for inspiration. You might choose to write in a cafeteria, coffee shop, or on a porch overlooking a busy street. The important thing is to think about how you feel and where you would be most comfortable writing.

At first, it's a good idea to get in the habit of writing in your journal at a particular time every day. That way, you can count on some personal time to relax and think about your feelings and experiences. Of course, you can write in your journal at other times, too, but be sure to try to save that special time.

## Step 3: Write a First Draft

Now you are ready to begin writing your first journal entry. If you have trouble getting started, you might like to try a method called "free writing." To begin, think of any word or topic and write it down. Then let the word trigger other words and thoughts, and let those trigger still others, and so on. Write everything down as it comes to mind. When you reread what you have written, you will probably be surprised at how much you had to say.

## Step 4: Revise

By this time, you should have written at least one entry a day in your journal for a week. Now look over your entries and choose the one you like best. Then revise it by making it into a story, a short composition, or some other more finished piece of writing. Remember that unlike your journal entries, which are private, this piece of writing may be read by others. Be sure to proofread your composition for spelling, grammar, and punctuation errors. Then prepare a final copy.

## QUIZ

The following is a quiz for Section 7. Write the answers in complete sentences on your paper.

## Reading Comprehension

1. Why did Bill leave his companion at the beginning of "Love of Life"?

2. In "Discovery of a Father," what comparison did the author make between his father and himself at the story's end?

3. Why did Bernice bob her hair in the teleplay "Bernice Bobs Her Hair"? How did she feel about it later?

4. In "A Day's Wait," what was the problem that the main character had? What did *he* think his problem was?

5. What was the game Annabel and Midge played in "The Standard of Living"?

## Understanding Literature

6. In Jack London's stories, what usually happened to the strong? What happened to the weak? Give an example of each from "Love of Life."

7. In whose words is "Discovery of a Father" told? Why do you think the author chose this style?

8. Give three details from "Bernice Bobs Her Hair" that show Fitzgerald's understanding of young people in the 1920's.

9. What are two important elements of Ernest Hemingway's style? Give an example of each from "A Day's Wait."

10. Give three examples of Sam Levenson's use of humor in "Everything But Money."

**Word Attack.** A base word is a word to which prefixes, suffixes, or inflectional endings such as *-ed* and *-ing* can be added. For example, in the word *unpleasantness*, the prefix *un-* and the suffix *-ness* have been added to the base word *pleasant*. Prefixes and suffixes change the meaning of a base word—*unpleasantness* means "the quality or state of being unpleasant," or "not pleasant."

The words below appear in the stories in this section. Find the base word in each and use it in a sentence of your own. Remember that the spelling of a base word may change when a suffix or inflectional ending is added.

> desolation
> momentary
> precautions
> indispensable
> disordered
> unconsciously
> unquestionably
> undesirability
> popularity

**Speaking and Listening**

1. Sam Levenson was famous as a radio and television humorist who told funny anecdotes about his family and early life. Think of a funny story you could tell about your early childhood or about a family experience. Make notes on the story, but don't write the story out. Practice telling your story aloud. Use your notes to refresh your memory as you speak. Be prepared to tell the story to your classmates.

2. The poems of Langston Hughes and Countee Cullen express their deep feelings about life. Practice reading one of their poems aloud. Try to capture the mood and feeling of the poem you have chosen. Be prepared to present the poem in class.

**Researching**

1. The story "Bernice Bobs Her Hair" is set in the 1920's at the beginning of the flapper era, also called "the Roaring 20's." Research that period of American history and prepare a brief report for your class. Answer these questions in your report: What was a flapper? What were the clothing styles of the period? Why was the period called the Roaring 20's? What date and event marked the end of the period? For what other things was the period known?

2. In "Everything But Money," Sam Levenson refers to the Statue of Liberty. Do some research on the statue to find out where it came from, why it was built, how big it is, how long it took to construct, and other facts about its history. Also find out who Emma Lazarus was and how she became associated with the statue.

**Creating.** In "Under a Telephone Pole," Carl Sandburg is able to give special meaning to something as commonplace as a telephone wire. Think of something ordinary that people take for granted, such as a pencil, a newspaper, or a sidewalk, and write a poem that conveys a special meaning about it.

# GEORGE GRAY

### EDGAR LEE MASTERS

*Have you ever wondered what the dead would say if they
could speak to us from their graves? In Edgar Lee Masters's
most famous collection of poems,* Spoon River Anthology
(1915), *the former inhabitants of a fictional Midwestern town
speak their own epitaphs—short verse compositions that sum
up their lives. Here are three voices from Masters's celebrated
book.*

I have studied many times
The marble which was chiseled for me—
A boat with a furled[1] sail at rest in a harbor.
In truth it pictures not my destination
5  But my life.
For love was offered me and I shrank from its disillusionment;
Sorrow knocked at my door, but I was afraid;
Ambition called to me, but I dreaded the chances.
Yet all the while I hungered for meaning in my life.
10  And now I know that we must lift the sail
And catch the winds of destiny
Wherever they drive the boat.
To put meaning in one's life may end in madness,
But life without meaning is the torture
15  Of restlessness and vague desire—
It is a boat longing for the sea and yet afraid.

---

1. **furled:** tightly rolled up.

*Evening, 1932.* Charles Burchfield.
Collection of The Newark Museum, New Jersey. Purchase 1944.

# LUCINDA MATLOCK

## EDGAR LEE MASTERS

I went to the dances at Chandlerville,
And played snap-out[1] at Winchester.
One time we changed partners,
Driving home in the moonlight of middle June,
5   And then I found Davis.
We were married and lived together for seventy years,
Enjoying, working, raising the twelve children,
Eight of whom we lost
Ere  I had reached the age of sixty.
10  I spun, I wove, I kept the house, I nursed the sick,
I made the garden, and for holiday
Rambled over the fields where sang the larks,
And by Spoon River gathering many a shell,
And many a flower and medicinal weed—
15  Shouting to the wooded hills, singing to the green valleys.
At ninety-six I had lived enough, that is all,
And passed to a sweet repose.
What is this I hear of sorrow and weariness,
Anger, discontent and drooping hopes?
20  Degenerate sons and daughters,
Life is too strong for you—
It takes life to love Life.

---

1. **snap-out:** a game, also known as "crack-the-whip," in which players
in a line, each holding the next, run or skate until the leader turns in
a new direction, causing the rest of the line to swing around rapidly
and those at the end to lose their hold.

# FIDDLER JONES

## EDGAR LEE MASTERS

The earth keeps some vibration going
There in your heart, and that is you.
And if the people find you can fiddle,
Why, fiddle you must, for all your life.
5   What do you see, a harvest of clover?
Or a meadow to walk through to the river?
The wind's in the corn; you rub your hands
For beeves[1] hereafter ready for market;
Or else you hear the rustle of skirts
10  Like little girls when dancing at Little Grove.
To Cooney Potter a pillar of dust
Or whirling leaves meant ruinous drouth;[2]
They looked to me like Red-Head Sammy
Stepping it off, to "Toor-a-Loor."
15  How could I till my forty acres
Not to speak of getting more,
With a medley of horns, bassoons and piccolos
Stirred in my brain by crows and robins
And the creak of a windmill—only these?
20  And I never started to plow in my life
That someone did not stop in the road
And take me away to a dance or picnic.
I ended up with forty acres;
I ended up with a broken fiddle—
25  And a broken laugh, and a thousand memories,
And not a single regret.

---

1. **beeves:** plural of *beef*; cattle.
2. **drouth:** drought.

# THINKING ABOUT THE POEMS

## GEORGE GRAY

### Recalling

**1.** Into what shape was George Gray's gravestone chiseled? What does he say it pictures "in truth"?

**2.** During his lifetime, what things were offered to George Gray, knocked at his door, or called to him? How did he react to each of these opportunities?

**3.** What does George Gray say he now knows?

**4.** How does George Gray define "life without meaning"?

### Interpreting

**5.** What do you think George Gray means in line 13: Specifically, what kinds of things "in one's life may end in madness"?

**6.** What do you think George Gray would say gives life meaning?

**7.** Explain why a "boat with a furled sail" is an appropriate **symbol** for George Gray himself.

### Applying

**8.** Do you agree with George Gray that catching the "winds of destiny / Wherever they drive the boat" is better than remaining safely "at rest in a harbor"? Why or why not?

## LUCINDA MATLOCK

### Recalling

**1.** How long were Lucinda Matlock and her husband Davis married? What happened to eight of their twelve children?

**2.** List five of the many things that Lucinda Matlock did during her lifetime.

**3.** What does Lucinda Matlock say she had done by the age of ninety-six?

**4.** What things does Lucinda Matlock say she hears from "degenerate sons and daughters"? What criticism does she level against them?

### Interpreting

**5.** In general, what kind of life did Lucinda Matlock have? How would you characterize her attitude toward that life?

**6.** Whom do you suppose Lucinda Matlock is referring to in line 20? Do you think she is right in saying "life is too strong" for them? Why or why not?

**7.** What does Lucinda Matlock mean by "life" in the poem's last line? By "Life"?

### Applying

**8.** The poem's last line seems an appropriate epitaph for Lucinda Matlock's gravestone. What do you think would be an appropriate epitaph for George Gray?

## FIDDLER JONES

### Recalling

**1.** According to the opening lines, what did Fiddler Jones feel in his heart?

**2.** What stirred in Fiddler Jones's brain whenever he heard crows, robins, and the creak of a windmill?

**3.** What invariably happened when Fiddler Jones began to plow?

**4.** What things does Fiddler Jones say he "ended up with"?

*Interpreting*

**5.** How successful was Fiddler Jones at farming? Why wasn't he more successful at farming than he was?

**6.** Why do you suppose Fiddler Jones ends up with "not a single regret"?

*Applying*

**7.** Do you admire people like Fiddler Jones—those who ignore practical matters to follow the vibrations in their hearts? What are the advantages and disadvantages of leading such a life?

## ANALYZING LITERATURE

*Free Verse*

**Free verse** is poetry that avoids the regular rhythms and predictable rhyming patterns usually found in traditional poetry like Edgar Allan Poe's "The Raven" on pages 326–331. Instead, free verse imitates the shifting rhythms of natural speech and relies on occasional rhymes and other sound devices—such as repetition and alliteration—to create musical effects (see Music in Poetry, pages 332–333).

In America, Walt Whitman (1819–1892) was the first great poet to use free-verse techniques in his poetry, such as "There Was a Child Went Forth" on page 211. When Carl Sandburg (page 388) began publishing in the 1910's, he followed Whitman's lead, believing that free verse would better enable him to express the distinctive character of American life. Edgar Lee Masters, too, chose to rely on free verse for his poems in *Spoon River Anthology*. By using lines of various lengths and by carefully shifting his rhythms, Masters succeeded in giving each of his characters an individual voice and unique personality.

**1.** Reread the first five lines of "George Gray" aloud. What effect does Masters achieve by making line 5 considerably shorter than the preceding four?

**2.** Reread lines 6–8 of "George Gray." Why do you suppose Masters chose to repeat the same sentence pattern and rhythm in each of these three lines?

**3.** Which lines in "George Gray" fall into a regular ta-DUM-ta-DUM rhythm? What effect does Masters create with this rhythm?

**4.** Find at least two examples of alliteration, or repeated consonant sounds, in "Lucinda Matlock." Explain how Masters uses repeated sentence patterns to make an important point about the kind of life Lucinda Matlock had.

**5.** What words and phrases does Masters repeat for emphasis in "Fiddler Jones"? How would you characterize the rhythms of Fiddler Jones's speech in comparison to those of George Gray or Lucinda Matlock?

# CRITICAL THINKING AND READING

*Summarizing an Author's Purpose*

The 250 or so voices that make up Edgar Lee Masters's *Spoon River Anthology* create a varied and realistic picture of life in a small Midwestern town—both the good side and the bad side. In the three Spoon River poems that you read here, Masters seems to have a single purpose: to express the basic ingredients of a meaningful life.

Think about the message that each of the three voices in these poems expresses regarding what makes life worthwhile. Then summarize Masters's purpose in these poems by framing a single sentence that combines all three messages into one.

# DEVELOPING VOCABULARY SKILLS

*Context Clues*

A word's **context** is the phrase, sentence, or paragraph in which it is used. Sometimes you can tell the meaning of an unfamiliar word from clues in its context. For example, suppose that as you read this line from "George Gray" you did not know the meaning of *furled*:

> A boat with a furled sail at rest in a harbor.

From the word's context, you can tell right away that furling is something that is done to sails. If you then ask yourself what position the sails of a boat "at rest in a harbor" are in, you can tell that *furled* means "rolled up." By using context clues, you have now added a new word to your vocabulary and can speak of sails, flags, banners and the like being furled or unfurled.

Read each of the passages below. Using context clues, give the meaning for each italicized word. Explain which words in the passage served as clues.

1. ". . . raising the twelve children,
Eight of whom we lost
*Ere* I had reached the age of sixty."
2. ". . . I nursed the sick,
I made the garden, and for holiday
*Rambled* over the fields where sang the larks,. . ."
3. "What is this I hear of sorrow and weariness,
Anger, discontent and drooping hopes?
*Degenerate* sons and daughters,
Life is too strong for you—"
4. ". . . a *medley* of horns, bassoons and piccolos
Stirred in my brain.. . ."

# THINKING AND WRITING

**1. Comparing Poems.**

Choose two of the Spoon River poems, and write a brief essay in which you explain how the poems are similar and different.

**Prewriting.** Begin by rereading the three poems and making your choices. Then list the elements in the poems that might lend themselves to comparison, such as the use of free verse, the characters' attitudes toward life, the mood each poem conveys, and so on. Then jot down how each element is similar or different in the poems you selected. What do your comparisons reveal about the strengths or weaknesses of the poems? What are the main points you want to get across to your readers?

**Writing.** Begin by identifying the poems you will be discussing and by mentioning the elements you will be comparing. Deal with each point of comparison in separate paragraphs. Organize your ideas logically and forcefully.

**Revising.** Check that you have organized your arguments effectively and that you have discussed enough similarities and differences in the two poems to prove your main ideas. Make sure you have used quotations from the poems.

**Proofreading.** Correct any mistakes in grammar, spelling, and punctuation in your essay. If necessary, prepare a neat final copy.

**Publishing.** Discuss your essay with classmates who wrote about the same poems. Choose representative essays to present to the class.

### 2. Writing an Epitaph.

An epitaph is a short inscription on a gravestone, often in rhymed verse, that sums up the dead person's personality or attitude toward life and death. Write an epitaph for some famous character, either fictional or real.

**Prewriting.** Begin by listing possible subjects for your epitaph. Then decide whether you want to be serious, as the Irish poet W. B. Yeats was for his epitaph:

> Cast a cold eye
> On life, on death.
> Horseman, pass by!

Or humorous, as the American comedian W. C. Fields was for his:

> On the whole, I'd rather be in Philadelphia.

**Writing.** As you draft the epitaph, try to be as brief and to the point as possible. Consider using rhyme if it will make your epitaph more forceful and memorable.

**Revising.** Ask yourself these questions as you try to improve the wording of your epitaph: Does your epitaph effectively sum up your subject's personality and attitudes? Does it convey either a serious or humorous mood? Is it brief and to the point?

**Proofreading.** Correct any mistakes in grammar, spelling, and punctuation in your epitaph.

**Publishing.** You might inscribe your epitaph beneath your subject's name on a paper "gravestone" and display it in class.

# VOICES OF MYSTERY

## *1898-1939*

*The night deepened. The crowd rumbled.
Mr. Ellery Queen, the famous detective,
felt uncomfortable. His six-foot body
was as tight as a violin string. It
was a familiar feeling. It meant that there
was murder in the air.*

— Ellery Queen

*Death on Ridge Road*
Grant Wood (1892-1942)
Williams College Museum of Art, Williamstown
Gift of Cole Porter

# Voices of Mystery: 1898–1939

**A**mericans have always been eager to take on new challenges. During the years 1898–1939, mystery stories became popular because they offered a new kind of challenge for readers. A mystery involves a puzzle that the characters in the story try to solve. Alert readers can put together all the pieces of the puzzle before the solution is revealed at the end.

### Mystery and the Supernatural

One kind of mystery story draws on old tales of ghosts, witches, and magic. The supernatural is used to explain an unusual event in the story. The author of such a story works carefully to create a mood of suspense. Edith Wharton once said, "The teller of supernatural tales should be well frightened in the telling." As you will see when you read her story "Afterward," she creates a mood by using details in the story to hint at a supernatural puzzle.

### Mystery and Detection

In the 1920's and 1930's, a different kind of mystery story became popular. These stories did not rely on the super-natural to create a mood of suspense and excitement. The plot in these stories revolves around discovering who committed a certain crime. Sometimes they are called "whodunits." In a good whodunit, crime is only the means to the end.

The real story is how one of the characters, the detective, figures out who committed the crime and why. The detective in a mystery story is a very special kind of character. He or she, like the reader, gathers information from the story as it unfolds. The detective always has a careful eye for detail, and it is usually a small detail that leads him or her to discover which of the other characters in the story committed the crime.

Ellery Queen is the name of one of the most famous fictional detectives created during this era. Ellery Queen is also the pen name of the two authors, Frederick Dannay and Manfred B. Lee, cousins who began writing together in 1929. Together they've created a character and a series of mysteries that are known all over the world. Ellery Queen is a detective who always remains calm and observant, as you will see when you read the story "Mind Over Matter" in this section.

Mignon G. Eberhardt is another famous mystery writer who began publishing dur-

Humphrey Bogart, Mary Astor, Barton MacLane, Peter Lorre, and Ward Bond in *The Maltese Falcon*, 1941

ing this era. In the 1930's, Eberhardt created the character Susan Dare. Susan Dare, like her creator, is a well-known author of mystery stories. In her stories, she is often called upon by people to help them find solutions to difficult problems. The story you will read here, "The Calico Dog," proves to be one of Dare's most complex and dangerous cases. This story shows Eberhardt's skill at creating suspense, placing clues, and creating characters.

In keeping with the theme of this section, the last word is given to Elizabeth Coatsworth whose clever poem poses a "Riddle." Can you solve it?

Mystery stories were popular during the years 1898–1939 because the reading public wanted literature that would help them escape the boredom and problems of everyday life. These stories do not describe the real world of the early 20th century. Instead, these stories describe an imaginary world where every problem has a clear-cut solution and every wrongdoing is punished. Somehow the fact that these stories "played fair" helped readers survive the unfairness of World War I and the Depression years.

For you, the modern reader, these stories offer more than entertainment. They bring to life glamorous settings, colorful characters, and the ideals of the America of the early 20th century.

# Afterward

*by Edith Wharton*

*Twilight shadows in an old English country house, legends of
a mysterious ghost, and a strange disappearance are the elements Edith Wharton (1862–1937) uses to create the suspenseful mystery story that follows. Best known for her novels and short stories about the manners and morals of her
time, Edith Wharton was also a skilled mystery writer, as
you will discover reading "Afterward."*

# Chapter One

"Oh, there *is* one, of course, but you'll never know it."

These words had been said jokingly six months before in a bright June garden. Now Mary Boyne thought of them again, as she stood in the December dusk waiting for the lamps to come.

Alida Stair had told Mary Boyne and her husband about Lyng — a house with a ghost. The Boynes had recently come to England from America. They needed a place to live.

Ned Boyne was delighted at the idea of living in an old-fashioned English country house. "It's too good to be true!" he cried. "But I've always wanted a ghost of my own. *Is* there a ghost at Lyng?"

Alida laughed. "Oh, there *is* one, of course, but you'll never know it."

"Never know it," Boyne answered. "How can you know you have a ghost if you don't know it's there?"

"I can't say but that's the story."

"That there's a ghost, but that nobody knows it's a ghost?"

"Well — not till afterward — long afterward."

Suddenly Mary spoke up. "You mean that long afterward, one says to one's self, *'That was it.* That was the ghost'?"

She was startled by the serious note her question added to the joking of the other two. Then she saw a shadow of seriousness fall across Alida's face. "I suppose so. One just has to wait."

"Oh, hang waiting!" Ned broke in. "Life's too short for a ghost that can only be enjoyed long afterward. Can't we do better than that, Mary?"

But it turned out that they could not find a better place. Three months later they were settled at Lyng. And the life they had yearned and planned for had actually begun.

For 14 years the Boynes had lived in a small house in a small Middle-Western American town. Ned Boyne worked long and hard as an engineer. He did not have much success. Then one day a stroke of luck had led him to the Blue Star Mine. Now they had money and time for life in the English countryside.

Both the Boynes were delighted with the old house and the surrounding grounds. It was beautiful and quiet. Yet from the first Mary Boyne had felt a mysterious air about the place.

The feeling had never been stronger than on this particular December afternoon. She waited in the library for the lamps to come. Her husband had gone off, after luncheon, for one of his long walks. She had noticed of late that he preferred to walk alone. Perhaps his book was bothering him. He looked more tired and worried now than he ever had during his engineering days. Yet the few pages of the book he had read to her were skillfully written.

Perhaps it was his health then? But physically he appeared well. It was only within the last week that Mary had felt the undefinable change. She didn't know why, but she was restless in his absence. Yet she was tongue-tied when he was there. It was as though it were *she* who had kept a secret from him!

Suddenly she realized that there was a secret between them.

"Can it be the house?" she wondered.

The room itself might have been full of secrets. They seemed to be piling themselves up, as evening fell. Layers and layers of velvet shadows dropped from the ceiling, the rows of books, and the smoke-blurred hearth.

"Why — of course — the house is haunted!" she reflected.

Perhaps Ned had already met the ghost. Then he might be carrying about the weight of what the ghost had revealed to him.

Then Mary remembered that when one *did* see a ghost at Lyng, one did not know it at the time.

"Not till long afterward," Alida Stair had said. Well, suppose Ned *had* seen one when they first came. Maybe he had known only within the last week what had happened to him.

She thought back to their first days at Lyng. One October day she had found a hidden staircase that led to the roof. The view was wonderful. She had flown down and snatched Ned away from his papers. She wanted to share her discovery. She remembered still how he put his arm around her as they gazed out over the horizon.

It was just then, while they gazed and held each other, that she felt his arm relax. His face looked anxious. She looked down and saw a man — a man in loose grayish clothes walking down the path to the front door. He walked with the doubtful gait of a stranger who seeks his way. Her shortsighted eyes gave her the blurred impression of slightness and grayness. There was something unlocal in his dress. But her husband seemed to have seen more. He pushed past her calling, "Wait!" Then he dashed down the stairs.

She followed him more slowly and carefully. When she reached the bottom of the stairs, she discovered that the path and the hall were empty. The library door was open. When she entered, she found her husband alone. He was staring vaguely at the papers on his desk.

"What was it? Who was it?" she asked.

"Who?" he repeated.

"The man we saw coming toward the house."

He thought before he answered. "Why I thought I saw Peters, our groundskeeper. I dashed after him to say a word about the drains, but he had disappeared before I got down."

"Disappeared? But he seemed to be walking so slowly."

Boyne shrugged. "So I thought, but he must have got up steam while we came downstairs. What do you say to trying to climb Meldon Steep before sunset?"

That was all. At the time it happened it didn't seem unusual. Yet now as Mary reviewed the scene, she had many questions. Why would the familiar figure of Peters make her husband excited? And if it was so important to talk to Peters, why did Ned look relieved when he did not find him?

# Chapter Two

Weary with her thoughts, Mary moved to the window. She saw a figure moving far down the path, between the bare trees. It looked like a mere blot of deeper gray in the grayness of the dusk. For an instant, as it moved toward her, her heart thumped. "It's the ghost!" she thought.

But in a few seconds the approaching figure began to look familiar. Even to her weak sight it was clear that it was her husband. She turned to meet him as he entered.

Laughingly she said, "I thought you were the ghost! It's foolish but I never can remember!"

"Remember what?" Boyne questioned.

"That when one sees the Lyng ghost one never knows it!"

"Really, dearest," he said faintly. "You'd better give up thinking about the ghost."

The parlor maid entered with letters

and a lamp. The light brought out the sharp lines of worry on Boyne's brows.

"Have you given up trying to see the ghost?" Mary asked after the maid left the room.

"I never tried," he answered, as he tore the wrapper off the newspaper and began to read.

"Well, of course, there is no use trying if one can't be sure until long afterward," she added.

After a pause, he looked up from his newspaper to ask, "Have you any idea how long?"

"No, none," she answered.

She was about to add, "What makes you ask?" when the maid reappeared with tea and a second lamp.

For a few moments Mary busied herself with pouring and serving tea. The room was now bright. Her gloomy thoughts seemed to have vanished with the gray shadows.

Her husband sat across the room reading his letters. He looked relaxed and happy. Was it because of something he found in the letters or was it just the change in her own mood? He glanced up as if drawn by her gaze and smiled.

"I'm dying for my tea, you know. Here's a letter for you," he said.

She took the letter he held out. Then she gave him his tea. She returned to her seat, opened the letter and began to read.

Suddenly she rose to her feet. She held out a newspaper clipping to her husband.

"Ned! What does this mean?"

He had risen at the same moment. For some time he and she studied each other, like opponents carefully watching for an advantage.

"What's what?" he said at last. He looked worried again.

"This article — from the *Waukesha Sentinel* back home. It says that a man named Elwell has brought a lawsuit against you. It says that there's something wrong about the Blue Star Mine."

"Oh, *that!*" he said with a noticeable sigh of relief. "That's nothing to worry about. It's all right."

"But what does this Mr. Elwell accuse you of?"

"Pretty nearly every crime in the calendar," Boyne answered, throwing himself into an armchair near the fire. "Do you want to hear the story?"

"But who is Elwell? I don't know him."

"Oh, he's a fellow I helped out. I let him buy a share in the mine."

"But if you've helped him, why is he suing you?"

"Probably some crooked lawyer got hold of him and talked him over. It's all rather technical. Besides, I thought these things bored you."

Mary looked at her husband. His face was calm and confident. "But doesn't this lawsuit worry you? Why have you never spoken to me about it?"

He answered both questions at once. "I didn't speak of it at first because it *did* worry me — annoyed me, rather. But it's all ancient history now. That clipping you received must be from an old newspaper."

She felt relieved. "You mean it's over? He's lost his case?"

There was a slight delay in Boyne's reply. "The suit has been withdrawn — that's all."

"How long ago was it withdrawn?"

He paused again, then said, "I've just had news now in one of my letters. I've been expecting it."

He crossed the room and sat down next to her on the sofa.

"It's all right?" she asked, looking into his smiling eyes.

"I give you my word it was never righter!" he laughed back at her, holding her close.

# Chapter Three

The next day Mary awoke feeling secure and happy. Everything was all right. She thought no more about ghosts, or doubting her husband. It was a bright sunny day. A rare day for December. Mary walked out into the garden. She was waiting for a man from Dorchester who was to come fix the hothouse boiler. The gardener had gone to fetch him at the station.

Mary heard steps behind her, and turned. She was expecting to see the gardener and the engineer from Dorchester. But only one figure was in sight. It was a youngish, thin man. He did not look like a boiler repairman. The newcomer lifted his hat to her. He had the air of a gentleman — perhaps a traveler. After a moment she asked, "Is there anyone you wish to see?"

"I came to see Mr. Boyne," he answered. His speech was that of an American. Mary looked at him more closely. The brim of his soft felt hat cast a shade on his face. He looked serious and businesslike.

"Have you an appointment with my husband?" she asked.

The visitor hesitated. "I think he expects me," he replied at last.

It was Mary's turn to hesitate. "You see he works on his book at this time. He never sees anyone in the morning."

He looked at her a moment. Then as if accepting her decision, he began to move away. As he turned, Mary saw him look up at the peaceful house. He looked so disappointed. The traveler had probably come a long way. Perhaps his time was limited.

Mary called after him, "May I ask if you've come a long way?"

He gave her the same serious look. "Yes, I have come a long way."

"Then if you'll go to the house, no doubt my husband will see you now. You'll find him in the library."

The visitor seemed about to express his thanks. Then Mary noticed the approach of the gardener and the boilermaker.

"This way," she said, waving the stranger to the house. An instant later she had forgotten him. She began to explain the problems with the boiler to the man from Dorchester.

By the time the boiler had been repaired, it was time for luncheon. She hurried back to the house. It was so silent. She guessed Boyne was still at work. Not wishing to disturb him, she went into the dining room. She busied herself with her own work at her writing table.

At last, the housekeeper, Trimmle, announced luncheon. Mary opened the library door to call Boyne to the dining room.

Boyne was not at his desk. She called him but got no reply.

"If you please, Madam," Trimmle said, "Mr. Boyne has gone out."

Mary turned to face the housekeeper. "Where did he go? And when?"

"He went out of the front door, up the drive, Madam."

"Did Mr. Boyne leave no message?" Mary questioned.

"No, Madam. He just went out with the gentleman."

"The gentleman? What gentleman?" Mary was hungry and confused.

"The gentleman who called, Madam," said Trimmle calmly.

"Do explain yourself, Trimmle. When did a gentleman call?" Mary asked.

"I couldn't say the hour, Madam, because I didn't let the gentleman in. I was busy. The kitchen maid answered the door."

Mary looked at the clock. "It's after two. Go and ask the kitchen maid if Mr. Boyne left any word."

She went into luncheon without waiting. Soon Trimmle told her that the kitchen maid had said that the gentleman called about 11:00. Mr. Boyne had gone out with him soon after. Mr. Boyne did not leave any message.

Mary finished luncheon and went into the drawing room. She sat and wondered. It was unlike Boyne to go away without explaining why and where he was going. Perhaps Boyne had decided to walk his visitor back to the station. This conclusion relieved her mind. She went on with her day. That afternoon she walked to the village post office. When she returned home, twilight was setting in.

She had taken the footpath through the fields. Boyne had probably returned from the station by the main road. There was little chance of their meeting. She felt sure, however, that he must have reached the house before her.

When she entered, she went directly to the library. But it was still empty. The papers on her husband's desk lay precisely as they had lain when she had gone to call him to luncheon.

Then she felt a pang of fear — fear of the unknown. As she stood in the long silent room, her fear seemed to take shape. It seemed to be breathing and hiding among the shadows.

She rang for Trimmle. The housekeeper came at once.

"You may bring tea if Mr. Boyne is in," she said to explain her ring.

"Very well, Madam. But Mr. Boyne is not in," said Trimmle. She put down the lamp she carried. "He's not been back since he went out with the gentleman this morning."

"But who *was* the gentleman?" Mary insisted. "The kitchen maid must know. She let him in."

"She doesn't know, either, Madam, for he wrote his name on a folded piece of paper."

"But he must have a name!" Mary cried. "Where's the paper?"

She moved to her husband's desk. She began to turn over the papers on it. The first that caught her eye was an unfinished letter. Her husband's pen was lying across the letter — as if he had dropped it suddenly.

"My dear Parvis" — Who was Parvis? "I have just received your letter announcing Elwell's death. While I suppose there is now no further risk of trouble, it might be safer —"

And there the letter ended. She tossed the sheet aside. She continued to search, but she found no folded paper.

"The kitchen maid *saw* him. Send her here!" Mary commanded of Trimmle.

When the kitchen maid came, Mary had her questions ready. "What did the stranger say? What did he look like? What did he write on that paper?"

The kitchen maid was not sure what had been written. The visitor followed her into the library when she carried the note to Mr. Boyne. She left them alone. A little while later she had seen Mr. Boyne and the visitor go out the front door together.

"Well, then," Mary said. "You saw the strange gentleman twice. What did he look like?"

The maid was confused. She could only stammer. "His hat, mum, was different."

"Different? How different?" Mary flashed out. Suddenly Mary remembered the man she had met that morning in the garden.

"His hat had a wide brim, you mean? His face was pale, wasn't it? A thin, youngish face?" Why had Mary not thought of him before? She needed no one now to tell her what the visitor looked like. But who was he, and why had Boyne gone with him?

# Chapter Four

Two weeks later Boyne had not returned. A full investigation took place. But no one had seen him. It was as if the sunny English room had swallowed up Edward Boyne completely.

Mary tried her best to find clues that would lead to her husband. She found nothing — except for the letter Boyne had been writing when his mysterious visitor called. Mary read and reread that letter. She even showed it to the police.

"I have just received your letter announcing Elwell's death. While I suppose there is now no further risk of trouble, it might be safer — " That was all. The "risk of trouble" must refer to the lawsuit that she had found out about in the newspaper clipping. The only new information was that it showed Boyne was still worried about the lawsuit. Yet he had told his wife the suit had been withdrawn. And

Elwell was dead and certainly could bother him no more. Nevertheless, Mary tracked down "Parvis." He turned out to be a lawyer in Waukesha, back in America. He said he had no new facts to offer about Elwell or the lawsuit. He said that he did not know why Boyne had wanted to contact him.

Two weeks turned to three; three weeks became four. Week by week, hour by hour, the investigation slowed. After a few months it was crowded out by new problems. At last the police gave up.

Even Mary Boyne found that her days became ordinary. She had come to accept the horror of Boyne's disappearance.

She stayed on at Lyng. Her friends supposed that she stayed there because she was waiting for her husband to return. But in reality she was sure that Boyne would never come back. He had gone out

of her sight as completely as if Death itself had waited that day in the doorway.

No, she would never know what had become of him. No one would ever know.

But the house *knew*. The library in which she spent her long, lonely evenings knew. It was here that the stranger had come and caused Boyne to rise and follow him.

# Chapter Five

"I don't say it *wasn't* straight. Yet I don't say it *was* straight. It was business."

Mary heard these words and looked up at the speaker. A half an hour before, a card with "Mr. Parvis" on it had been brought up to her. She was both eager and surprised. Why this visit from the person to whom Boyne had addressed his unfinished letter?

She found Mr. Parvis waiting in the library. He was a small man. He had a bald head and gold eyeglasses.

Parvis at once explained why he had come. He was in England on business. He had found himself in the neighborhood of Lyng so he wished to pay his respects to Mrs. Boyne. He also wished to ask her what she meant to do about Bob Elwell's family.

Mary felt a tug of dread. Did her visitor, after all, know what Boyne had meant to say in his letter? She asked her visitor to explain himself.

"Is it possible that you know as little as you have said, Mrs. Boyne?" Parvis questioned. He seemed quite surprised.

"I know nothing. You must tell me," she answered.

Then her visitor told his story. Her husband had made his money at the cost of "getting ahead" of someone else. The victim was young Robert Elwell. Elwell had "put Boyne on" to the Blue Star Mine. And Boyne figured out a way to keep all the profits for himself.

"But then — " Mary said slowly, "you accuse my husband of doing something dishonorable?"

Mr. Parvis answered calmly, "Oh, no, I don't. I don't even say it wasn't straight." He glanced up and down the long lines of books in the library. "I don't say it *wasn't* straight. Yet I don't say it *was* straight. It was business."

Mary stared at him. He was indifferent. He seemed unaware of the evil power of the story.

"Mr. Elwell's lawyers did not seem to think that anything was wrong. I assume they advised Mr. Elwell to withdraw his suit," Mary said.

"Oh, yes. He hadn't a leg to stand on, legally. But when he found that out, he got desperate. You see, he'd borrowed most of the money he lost in the Blue Star. He was up a tree. That's why he shot himself."

"He shot himself?" Mary said. Her voice shook with horror. "He killed himself because of *that*?"

"Well, he didn't kill himself exactly. He dragged on two months before he died."

Parvis sounded as unemotional as a record.

"You mean he tried to kill himself, and failed? And tried again?"

"Oh, he didn't have to *try* again," said Parvis grimly.

They sat opposite each other. Parvis swung his eyeglasses around his finger. Mary sat motionless.

"You know all this," she began at last, "and I wrote to you at the time of my husband's disappearance. Why did you say then that you didn't understand the letter?"

Parvis showed no embarrassment. "Why, I didn't understand it — strictly speaking. And it wasn't the time to talk about it. Nothing I could have told you would have helped you find Boyne."

Mary continued to stare at him. "Then why are you telling me now?"

"To begin with," Parvis answered calmly, "I supposed you knew more than you had said — I mean about Elwell's death. And now people are talking about it again. I thought if you didn't know, you ought to."

Mary remained silent and Parvis continued. "You see, it's only come out lately how poor Elwell really was. His wife's a proud woman. She went to work, but then she got too sick. It was something with her heart, I believe. But she had Elwell's mother to look after, and the children. Finally she asked for help. That called attention to the case. The papers took it up. Everybody in Waukesha liked Bob Elwell. Most of the well-known people back home signed up to help. And people began to wonder why the Boynes hadn't signed up, too.

"Here." Parvis pulled something from his pocket. "Here's a story about the whole thing from the *Sentinel*. I guess you'd better look it over."

He held the newspaper out to Mary. She unfolded it slowly. She was remembering the evening on which, in that same room, she had seen the clipping from the *Sentinel* that first told her about Elwell and the Blue Star Mine.

The headline of the paper said: WIDOW OF BOYNE'S VICTIM FORCED TO ASK FOR AID. There were two pictures included in the article. The first was a picture of her husband.

The sight of that familiar face made her close her eyes. She felt it would be impossible for her to read what was said about him.

"I thought if you felt disposed to put your name down for a contribution — " she heard Parvis continue.

She forced herself to open her eyes. The other picture also looked familiar. It showed a youngish man. He was thin. His features were somewhat blurred because of the shadow from his large hat brim. Where had she seen that man before? She stared at it confusedly. Her heart was hammering in her ears.

She cried out, "This is the man — the man who came for my husband!"

She heard Parvis jump to his feet. He looked at her in alarm.

"It's the man! I'd know him anywhere!" she insisted.

Parvis's answer seemed to come from far off.

"Mrs. Boyne, you're not well. Shall I call somebody? Do you want a glass of water?"

"No, no, no!" She clutched the newspaper. "I tell you, it's the man! I *know* him! He spoke to me in the garden!"

Parvis took the paper from her. "It can't be, Mrs. Boyne. It's Robert Elwell."

"Robert Elwell?" She stared blankly out into space. "Then it was Robert Elwell who came for him."

"Came for Boyne? Why, Robert Elwell is dead," he said gently. "He died the day before your husband disappeared. Don't you remember?"

Yes, she remembered; that was the horror of it. Elwell had died the day before her husband disappeared. Yet the picture in the newspaper was the picture of the man who had spoken to her in the garden.

"This was the man who spoke to me," she reported. She looked again at Parvis. "He thinks me mad," she thought, "but I'm not mad!" Suddenly she thought of a way to prove her strange statement.

She sat quietly until she could trust her voice. Then, she looked straight at Parvis. "Answer one question, please?" she said slowly. "When did Robert Elwell try to kill himself?"

"When — when?" Parvis stammered.

"Yes, the date. Please try to remember."

She saw he was growing still more afraid of her. "I have a reason," she insisted.

"Yes, yes. Only I can't remember. About two months before he died, I guess. Perhaps it's in the newspaper."

He picked up the paper. He ran his eyes down the page. "Here it is. Last October, on the —"

"The twentieth, wasn't it?" she said.

He was shocked. "Yes, the twentieth. Then you *did* know?"

"I know now." Her eyes continued to look past him. "Sunday, the twentieth. That was the day he came here first."

Parvis's voice was a whisper. "Came *here* first? You saw him twice?"

"Yes, twice," she sighed. "He came first on the twentieth of October. I remember the date because it was the day we first climbed Meldon Steep."

Parvis just stared at her.

"We saw him from the roof," she went on. "He came down the path toward the house. He was dressed just as he is in the picture. My husband saw him first. Ned was frightened and ran down ahead of me. But there was no one there. He had vanished."

"Elwell had vanished?" Parvis asked carefully.

"Yes," she whispered. "I couldn't think what had happened. I see now. Elwell *tried* to come then. But he wasn't dead enough. He couldn't reach us. He had to wait two months to die. Then he came back again — and Ned went with him."

She nodded at Parvis. She looked like a child who had just worked out a difficult puzzle. Suddenly she pressed her hands to her face.

"I sent him to Ned — I told him where to go! I sent him to this room!" she screamed.

She was numb. Parvis, the books, the furniture all seemed a long way off. Then she heard one clear sound. It was the voice of Alida Stair describing the Lyng ghost. She said what she had said long ago on the June day.

"You won't know till afterward. You won't know till long, long, afterward."

## READING COMPREHENSION

**Summarizing.** Choose the best phrase to complete each sentence. Then write the complete statements on your paper.

1. According to Mrs. Stair, a person who saw a ghost at Lyng _____ (was sure to die soon after, disappeared immediately, didn't realize it until later).

2. According to the newspaper article that had been sent to Mary Boyne, _____ (a former business associate of Ned's had brought a lawsuit against him, the Blue Star Mine had been blown up, a former business associate had threatened Ned's life).

3. Parvis said Elwell couldn't have called on Mr. Boyne because Elwell _____ (was still in America, was dead, had been with Parvis that day).

**Interpreting.** Write the answer to each question on your paper.

1. When did Mary Boyne believe that she had first seen Elwell at Lyng?

2. When Ned Boyne told his wife that the suit had been withdrawn, what was he really referring to?

3. How did Mary Boyne feel when she realized the truth about her husband's disappearance?

**For Thinking and Discussing.** Mr. Parvis refused to pass judgment on Ned Boyne's business matters saying, "It was just business." Do you agree with his attitude? Explain.

## UNDERSTANDING LITERATURE

**Plot in a Mystery Story.** *Plot* is the pattern of incidents or events in a story. A mystery writer carefully reveals the details of the plot in a way that will keep the reader in suspense.

One way a mystery writer creates suspense is to control the order in which incidents are revealed. It is only at the end of the story that the reader really understands the entire picture.

Here are some incidents from "Afterward." On your paper, list the events in the order in which they actually occurred.

☐ Robert Elwell died.

☐ Ned Boyne disappeared.

☐ Alida Stair told the Boynes there was a ghost at Lyng, but they wouldn't know it until later.

☐ Elwell "put Boyne on" to the mine.

☐ Parvis visited Mrs. Boyne.

☐ The newspaper clipping helped Mrs. Boyne connect her husband's disappearance to Elwell.

## WRITING

Pretend that you are Mrs. Boyne. Write a letter to Alida Stair explaining how and why you now understand what she meant when she told you, "Well—not till afterward—long afterward." In your letter, try to arrange the events so that you create a feeling of suspense.

# Mind Over Matter

*by Ellery Queen*

*Ellery Queen is the pen name of two clever authors who began writing mystery stories in 1929. The detective in these stories is also called Ellery Queen. The Ellery Queen stories are famous for the careful placement of clues. Mystery fans often try to solve the mystery before Ellery Queen does. You may want to see if you can solve the case of "Mind Over Matter" before the great detective does.*

Paula Paris found Inspector Richard Queen of the Homicide Squad looking very sad indeed. Paula had just flown from Hollywood to New York. She had come in to cover the heavyweight fight between Champion Mike Brown and Challenger Jim Coyle.

"You poor dear," said Paula. "And how about you?" she asked Mr. Ellery Queen. "Aren't you disappointed that you can't get a ticket to the fight?"

"I'm a jinx," sighed the great man. "If I went, something terrible would be sure to happen."

"He's afraid somebody will knock somebody off," said the Inspector.

"Well, doesn't somebody always?" demanded his son.

"Don't pay any attention to him, Paula," said the Inspector. "Look, you're a newspaperwoman. Can you get me a ticket?"

"You may as well get me one, too," groaned Mr. Queen.

So Miss Paris telephoned Phil Maguire, the famous sports editor. That evening Maguire picked them up in his car and they all drove uptown to see the fight.

"Seems to me the champ ought to take this boy Coyle," said Inspector Queen. Maguire shrugged.

"Phil's sour on the champ," laughed Paula.

"Nothing personal," said Phil Maguire. "Only, remember Kid Berés? This was in the days when Ollie Stearn was moving Mike Brown into the big time. So this fight was a fix, see. Mike knew it was a fix. The kid knew it was a fix. Everybody knew it was a fix. Kid Berés was supposed to lay down in the sixth round. Well, just the same, Mike went out there and half-killed him. Just for fun. The Kid spent a month in the hospital. When he came out, he was only half a man." And Maguire smiled his crooked smile and said: "I guess I just don't like the champ."

"Well, if this fight is on the level," Mr. Queen said, "Coyle will murder the champion. That big fellow wants the title."

Maguire grinned. "Well, you know the odds. Three to one on the champ."

They drove into the parking lot across the street from the Stadium. Maguire grunted: "Speak of the devil." He had backed the little car into a space beside a huge limousine the color of bright blood.

"Now what's that supposed to mean?" asked Paula Paris.

"This red engine next to us," Maguire chuckled. "It's the champ's. Or rather, it belongs to his manager, Ollie Stearn. Ollie lets Mike use it. Mike can't afford a car."

"I thought the champion was wealthy," said Mr. Queen.

"Not anymore. All of his money is tangled up in lawsuits. He owes a lot of money to a lot of people."

"He ought to have enough money after tonight," said the Inspector. "He's getting over half a million bucks for his end!"

"He won't collect a cent," said the newspaperman. "Mike's creditors will grab it all. Come on."

Mr. Queen helped Miss Paris from the car. Then he tossed his camel's-hair coat into the back seat.

"Don't leave your coat there, Ellery," said Paula. "Someone's sure to steal it."

"Let 'em. It's an old rag. Don't know what I brought it for, anyway, in this heat."

"Come on, come on," said Phil Maguire eagerly.

From the press section at ringside the crowd sounded angry. Two bantam-weights were fencing in the ring.

"What's the trouble?" demanded Mr. Queen.

"The card's too light," said Maguire. "Six preliminary matches — three light-weights and three middleweights about to wind it up."

"So what?" said the Inspector. "They're all good fighters."

"The fans came here to see two big guys slaughter each other," explained Maguire. "They don't want to be annoyed by a bunch of gnats — even good gnats. . . . Hi, Happy."

"Who is that?" asked Miss Paris.

"Happy Day," the Inspector answered for Maguire. "Makes his living off bets."

Happy Day sat a few rows off. He had a puffed face the color of cold rice pudding, and his eyes were two raisins. He nodded at Maguire and turned back to watch the ring.

"Normally Happy's face is like raw steak," said Maguire. "He's worried about something. . . . Say, I've got to go to work."

Maguire bent over his typewriter.

The night deepened. The crowd rumbled. Mr. Ellery Queen felt uncomfortable. His six-foot body was as tight as a violin string. It was an all-too-familiar feeling. It meant that there was murder in the air.

The challenger appeared first. He was met by a roar, like the roar of a river at flood tide bursting the dam.

Miss Paris gasped. "Isn't he the one!"

Jim Coyle was a giant six and a half feet tall. He had broad shoulders, long smooth muscles, and bronze skin. He grinned boyishly at the fans.

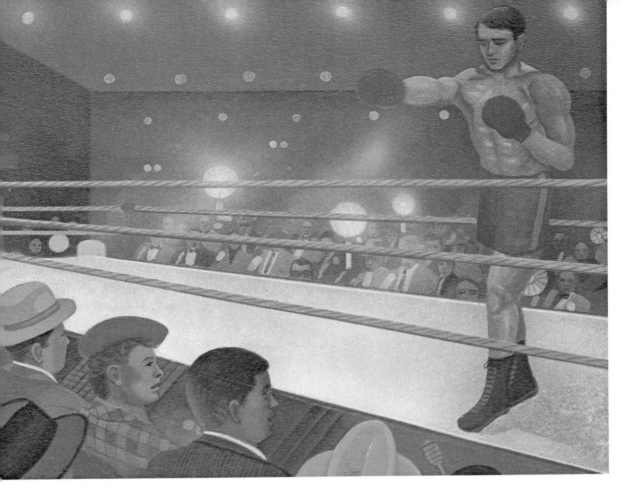

His manager, Barney Hawks, followed him into the ring. Hawks was a big man, but beside his fighter he appeared small.

"Hercules in trunks," breathed Miss Paris. "Did you ever see such a fine physique, Ellery?"

"The question more properly is," said Mr. Queen jealously, "can he keep his fine physique off the floor? That's the question, my girl."

"Plenty fast for a big man," said Maguire. "Maybe not as fast as Mike Brown, but Jim's got height and reach in his favor. He's strong as a bull."

"Here comes the champ!" exclaimed Inspector Queen.

A large ugly man shuffled down the aisle and jumped into the ring. His manager, Ollie Stearn, a little wrinkled man, followed him and stood bouncing up and down on the canvas.

"*Boo-oo-oo!*"

"They're booing the champion!" cried Paula. "Phil, why?"

"Because they hate him because he's a brutal, crooked slob," smiled Maguire. "He has the kick of a mule and the soul of a pretzel. That's why, darlin'."

Brown stood six feet two inches. He looked like a gorilla. He had a broad hairy chest, long arms, and large flat feet. His features were smashed, cruel. He paid no attention to the angry crowd, or to Coyle.

But Mr. Queen, whose genius it was to notice small details, saw Brown's powerful jaws working beneath his cheeks.

And again Mr. Queen's body tightened.

When the gong rang for the start of the third round, the champion's left eye was a purple slit and his lips were bloody. His chest rose and fell in gasps.

Thirty seconds later he was cornered, a beaten animal. Brown crouched, covering up, protecting his chin. Big Jim Coyle streaked forward. The giant's gloves sank into Brown's body. The champion fell forward and held the long bronze arms.

The referee stepped between the two fighters. He spoke sharply to Brown.

"The dirty double-crosser," smiled Phil Maguire.

"Who? What do you mean?" asked Inspector Queen, puzzled.

"Watch the payoff."

The champion raised his battered face. He lashed out feebly at Coyle with his left glove. The giant laughed and stepped in.

The champion went down.

At the count of nine, Mike Brown staggered to his feet. Coyle slipped in, and pumped 12 solid punches into Brown. The champion toppled to the canvas.

This time he remained there.

"But he made it look right," drawled Maguire.

The Stadium howled with glee. Paula looked sickish. A few rows away Happy Day jumped up. He stared wildly about. Then he began shoving through the crowd.

"Happy isn't happy anymore," sang Maguire.

Jim Coyle was half-drowned in a wave of shouting people. He was laughing like a boy. In the champion's corner Ollie Stearn leaned over the unconscious man.

"Yes, sir," said Phil Maguire, rising and stretching, "that was as pretty a dive as I've seen. And I've seen some beauts in my day."

"See here, Maguire," said Mr. Queen angrily. "I have eyes, too. What makes you so sure Brown just tossed his title away?"

"Seems to me," added the Inspector, "Brown took an awful lot of punishment."

"Oh, sure," said Maguire mockingly. "Look, Mike Brown has as sweet a right hand as the game has ever seen. Did you notice him use his right on Coyle tonight — even once?"

"Well," admitted Mr. Queen, "no."

"Of course not. Not a single blow. And he had a dozen openings. But what did Mike do? He kept jabbing away with that silly left of his — it couldn't put Paula away! Sure, he made it look good. But your ex-champ took a dive just the same!"

They were helping Brown from the ring. He looked tired. A small group followed him, laughing. Little Ollie Stearn kept pushing people aside.

"Look," said Maguire. "I've got to see someone. I'll meet you folks in Coyle's dressing room later."

"Oh, I'd love it!" cried Paula. "How do we get in, Phil?"

"What have you got a cop with you for? Show her, Inspector."

Maguire's slight figure slouched off. The great man's scalp prickled suddenly. He frowned and took Paula's arm.

The new champion's dressing room was full of people and noise. The crowd was so dense it overflowed into the adjoining shower room. Young Coyle lay on a training table being rubbed down. He was answering questions, grinning at cameras, flexing his muscles. Barney Hawks was running about, his collar loosened, handing out cigars like a new father.

The Inspector spoke to Barney Hawks, and Coyle's manager introduced them to the champion.

Coyle slipped off the rubbing table. Barney Hawks began shooing men out of the shower room. Finally Coyle grabbed some towels, winked at Paula, and went in, shutting the door. They heard the cheerful hiss of the shower.

Five minutes later Phil Maguire strolled into the dressing room.

"Hi," he shouted. "Where's the champ?"

"Here I am," said Coyle, opening the shower-room door. He rubbed his bare chest with a towel. There was another towel wrapped around his lower body. "Hiya, Philboy. Be dressed in a shake. Say, this doll your Mamie? If she ain't, I'm staking out my claim."

"Come on, come on, champ. We got a date with Fifty-second Street."

"Sure! How about you, Barney? You joining us?"

"Go ahead and play," said his manager. "Me, I got business with the management." He danced into the shower room, and emerged with a hat and a camel's-hair coat over his arm. He kissed his hand affectionately at Coyle, and left.

"You're not going to stay in here while he dresses?" said Mr. Queen to Miss Paris.

"Come on — you can wait for your hero in the hall."

"Yes, sir," said Miss Paris.

Coyle laughed. "Don't worry, fella. I ain't going to do you out of nothing."

Mr. Queen piloted Miss Paris from the room. "Let's meet them at the car," he said in a curt tone.

Miss Paris murmured: "Yes *sir*."

They walked in silence to the end of the hall. Then they turned a corner into an alley which led out of the Stadium and into the street. As they walked down the alley Mr. Queen could see through the shower-room window into the dressing room: Maguire had produced a bottle and he, Coyle, and the Inspector were raising glasses.

Mr. Queen hurried Miss Paris out of the alley and across the street to the parking lot. Cars were slowly driving out. But the big red limousine belonging to Ollie Stearn still stood beside Maguire's roadster.

"Ellery," said Paula softly, "you're such a fool."

"Now, Paula, I don't care to discuss — "

"What do you think I mean? It's your topcoat, silly. Didn't I warn you someone would steal it?"

Mr. Queen glanced into the roadster. His coat was gone. "Oh, that. I was going to throw it away, anyway. Now look, Paula, if you think for one instant, that I could be jealous of some oversized . . . Paula! What's the matter?"

Paula's cheeks were gray in the brilliant arc light. She was pointing a shaky finger at the blood-red limousine.

"In — in there. . . . Isn't that — Mike Brown?"

Mr. Queen glanced quickly into the rear of the limousine. He opened the rear door of Stearn's car.

Mike Brown tumbled out of the car and lay still.

And after a moment the Inspector, Maguire, and Coyle strolled up, chuckling over something.

Maguire stopped. "Say. Who's that?"

Coyle said: "Isn't that Mike Brown?"

The Inspector said: "Out of the way, Jim." He knelt beside Ellery.

And Mr. Queen raised his head. "Yes, it's Mike Brown. Someone's used him for a pin cushion."

Phil Maguire yelped and ran for a telephone. Paula Paris ran after him, remembering her profession.

"Is he . . . is he — " began Jim Coyle, gulping.

"The long count," said the Inspector grimly. "Here, help me turn him over."

They turned him over. He lay staring up into the blinding arc light. He was completely dressed; a gray topcoat was wrapped about his body, still buttoned. He had been stabbed 10 times in the chest, through his topcoat.

"Body's warm," said the Inspector. "This happened just a few minutes ago." He rose from the dust and stared unseeingly at the crowd which had gathered.

"Maybe," began the champion, licking his lips, "maybe — "

"Maybe what, Jim?" asked the Inspector, looking at him.

"Nothing, nothing,"

"Why don't you go home? Don't let this spoil your night, kid."

Coyle set his jaw. "I'll stick around."

The Inspector blew a police whistle.

Police came. Phil Maguire and Paula Paris returned, Ollie Stearn and others appeared from across the street, and the crowd thickened. Mr. Ellery Queen crawled into the back of Stearn's car.

The rear of the red limousine was a mess. Blood stained the cushions and the floor rug, which was wrinkled and scuffed. A large coat button lay on one of the cushions, beside a crumpled camel's-hair coat.

Mr. Queen grabbed the coat. The button had been torn from it. The front of the coat was badly bloodstained. But the stains had a pattern. Mr. Queen laid the coat on the seat, front up. He slipped the buttons through the buttonholes. Then the bloodstains met. When he unbuttoned the coat and separated the two sides of the coat the stains separated, too. On the side where the buttons were the blood traced a straight edge an inch outside the line of buttons.

The Inspector poked his head in. "What's that thing?"

"The murderer's coat."

"Let's see that!"

"It won't tell you anything about its wearer. The label's been ripped out — no identifying marks. Do you see what must have happened in here, Dad? The murder took place in this car. And the murderer wore this coat."

"How do you know that, Ellery?"

"Because there's every sign of a struggle. Brown managed to tear off one of the coat buttons of his attacker's coat. In the course of the struggle Brown was stabbed many times. His blood flowed freely. It got all over not only his own coat but the murderer's as well. From the position of the bloodstains the murderer's coat must have been buttoned at the time of the struggle. This means he wore it."

The Inspector nodded. "Left it behind because he didn't want to be seen in a bloody coat."

From behind the Inspector came Paula's shaky voice. "Could that be *your* camel's-hair coat, Ellery?"

"It isn't mine," said Mr. Queen patiently. "Mine has certain marks which don't exist in this one — a cigarette burn at the second buttonhole, a hole in the right pocket."

The Inspector shrugged and went away.

"Then your coat's being stolen has nothing to do with it?" Paula shivered.

Mr. Queen answered: "On the contrary. The theft of my coat has everything to do with it." He turned and stared at the body of Mike Brown.

Ollie Stearn's driver was a hard-looking customer. He twisted his cap and said: "Mike tells me after the fight he won't need me. Tells me he'll pick me up on the Grand Concourse. Said he'd drive himself."

"Yes?"

"I was kind of — curious. I had a hot dog at the stand there and I — watched. I seen Mike come out and climb into the back — "

"Was he alone?" demanded Inspector Queen.

"Yeah. Just got in and sat there. A couple of drunks come along then and I couldn't see good. Only seemed to me somebody else come over and got into the car after Mike."

"Who? Who was it? Did you see?"

The driver shook his head. "I couldn't see good. I don't know. After a while I thought it ain't my business, so I walks away. But when I heard police sirens I come back."

"The one who came after Mike Brown got in," said Mr. Queen with a certain eagerness. "That person was wearing a coat, eh?"

"I guess so. Yeah."

"You didn't witness anything else that happened?" said Mr. Queen.

"Nope."

"Doesn't matter, really," muttered the great man. "Line's clear. Clear as the sun. Must be that — "

"What are you mumbling about?" demanded Miss Paris in his ear.

Mr. Queen stared. "Was I mumbling?" He shook his head.

A man from Headquarters came up with a little fellow with frightened eyes. He babbled he didn't know nothing; nothing, he didn't know nothing. The Inspector said: "Come on, Oetjens. You were heard shooting off your mouth. What's the story?"

"Mike Brown looked me up this morning," muttered Oetjens, "and says to me, he says, 'Hymie,' he says. 'Happy Day takes a lot of your bets,' he says. 'So go lay fifty thousand with Happy on Coyle to win by a KO,' Mike says. 'You lay that fifty thousand for *me*, get it?' he says. And he says, 'If you tell Happy or anyone else that you bet fifty thousand for me on Coyle,' he says, 'I'll rip your heart out.' So I laid fifty thousand dollars on Coyle to win by a KO. Happy took the bet at twelve to five, he wouldn't give no more."

Jim Coyle growled: "I'll break your neck."

"Wait a minute, Jim — "

"He's saying Brown took a dive!" cried the champion. "I licked Brown fair and square. I beat him fair and square!"

"You thought you beat him fair and square," muttered Phil Maguire. "But he took a dive, Jim. Didn't I tell you, Inspector? Laying off that right of his — "

"It's a lie! Where's my manager? Where's Barney?" roared Coyle. "They ain't going to hold up the purse on this fight! I won it fair — I won the title fair!"

"Take it easy, Jim," said the Inspector. "Everybody knows you were in there leveling tonight. Look here, Hymie, did Brown give you the cash to bet for him?"

"He was busted," Oetjens said. "I just laid the bet on my own. The payoff don't come till the next day. So I knew it was okay, because with Mike himself betting on Coyle the fight was in the bag — "

"I'll cripple you, you tinhorn!" yelled young Coyle.

"Take it easy, Jim," soothed Inspector Queen. "So you laid the bet and Happy covered it at twelve to five. And you knew Mike was going to take a dive. Then you would collect a hundred and twenty thousand dollars and give it to Mike, right?"

"Yeah, yeah. But that's all, I swear — "

"When did you see Happy last, Hymie?"

Oetjens looked scared and began to back away. He shook his head stubbornly.

"Now it couldn't be," asked the Inspector softly, "that somehow Happy found out that you'd bet that fifty thousand not for yourself, but for Mike Brown, could it? It couldn't be that Happy found out it was a dive?" The Inspector said sharply to a detective: "Find Happy Day."

"I'm right here," said a voice from the crowd. The fat gambler waded through and said hotly to Inspector Queen: "So, I'm supposed to take the rap, hey?"

"Did you know Mike Brown was set to take a dive?"

"No!"

Phil Maguire laughed.

And little Ollie Stearn, pale as his dead fighter, shouted: "Happy done it, Inspector! He found out, and he waited till after the fight. When he saw Mike laying down he came out here and gave him the business! That's the way it was!"

"You lousy rat," said the gambler. "How do I know you didn't do it yourself? He wasn't taking no dive you couldn't find out about! Maybe you stuck him up!"

"Gentlemen, gentlemen," said the Inspector.

Happy Day and Ollie Stearn eyed each other with hate. The Inspector said to his son: "Not too tough. It's Happy Day, all right, and all I've got to do is find — "

The great man smiled and said: "You're wasting your time."

The Inspector stopped looking happy.

"What am I supposed to be doing, then? You tell me. You know it all."

"Find my coat, and perhaps I'll find your murderer," answered Mr. Queen.

And immediately the great man began nosing about. He acted as if an old and shabby topcoat could possibly be more important than Mike Brown lying there in the gravel.

So it appeared that Mike Brown had had a secret meeting with someone after the fight. He got rid of Ollie Stearn's driver, so the appointment must have been inside the red limousine. And whoever he was, he came, and got in with Mike. There was a struggle, and he stabbed Mike almost a dozen times with something long and sharp. Then he fled, leaving his camel's-hair coat behind. The blood all over its front would have given him away.

That brought up the matter of the weapon. Everybody began looking, including Mr. Queen. The murderer might have dropped it. And, sure enough, a radio-car man found it in the dirt under a parked car. It was a long, evil-looking knife with no marks whatever and no fingerprints except the fingerprints of the radio-car man. But Mr. Queen kept looking even after that discovery. Finally the Inspector asked him: "What are you looking for now?"

"My coat," explained Mr. Queen. "Do you see anyone with my coat?"

But there was hardly a man in the crowd with a coat. It was a warm night.

Finally Mr. Queen said: "I don't know what you good people are going to do, but I'm going back to the Stadium."

"For heaven's sake, what for?" cried Paula.

"To see if I can find my coat," said Mr. Queen patiently.

"I told you you should have taken it with you!"

"Oh, no," said Mr. Queen. "I'm glad I didn't. I'm glad I left it behind in Maguire's car. I'm glad it was stolen."

"But why?"

"Because now," replied Mr. Queen with a mysterious smile, "I have to go looking for it."

And while the police carted Mike Brown's body off, Mr. Queen went back across the dusty parking lot and into the alley which led to the Stadium dressing rooms. And the Inspector, with a baffled look, herded everyone — with special loving care and attention for Mr. Happy Day and Mr. Ollie Stearn — after his son. He didn't know what else to do.

And finally they were back in Jim Coyle's dressing room. There was a noise at the door. Barney Hawks, the new champion's manager, was standing in the doorway in the company of several officials and promoters.

"What ho," said Barney Hawks with a puzzled glance about. "You still here, Champ? What goes on?"

"Plenty goes on," said the champ angrily. "Barney, did you know Brown took a dive tonight?"

"What? What is this?" said Barney Hawks, looking around. "Who says so, the dirty liar? My boy beat Brown fair and square."

"Brown threw the fight?" asked one of

the men with Hawks, a member of the Boxing Commission. "Is there any evidence of that?"

"Never mind that," said the Inspector. "Barney, Mike Brown is dead."

Hawks began to laugh. Then he stopped laughing and sputtered: "What's this? Brown dead? You're joking!"

Jim Coyle waved his huge paw tiredly. "Somebody bumped him off tonight, Barney. In Stearn's car across the street."

"So Mike got his, hey? Well, well. Tough. Loses his title and his life. Who done it, boys?" asked Hawks.

"Maybe you didn't know my boy was dead!" shrilled Ollie Stearn. "Yeah, you put on a swell act, Barney! Maybe you fixed it with Mike so he'd take a dive so your boy could win the title! Maybe — "

"There's been another crime committed here tonight," said a mild voice. They all looked wonderingly around to find Mr.

Ellery Queen moving toward Mr. Hawks.

"Hey?" said Coyle's manager, staring stupidly at him.

"My coat was stolen."

"Hey?" Hawks kept staring.

"And now I've found it again."

"Hey?"

"On your arm." And Mr. Queen gently removed from Mr. Hawks's arm a shabby camel's-hair topcoat. Queen folded it, and examined it. "Yes. My very own."

Barney Hawks turned green in the silence.

Something sharpened in Mr. Queen's silver eyes. He bent over the camel's-hair coat again. He spread out the sleeves and examined the armhole seams. They had burst. As had the seam at the back of the coat. He looked up at Mr. Hawks.

"The least you might have done," he said, "is to have returned my coat in the same condition in which I left it."

"Your coat?" said Barney Hawks. Then he shouted: "What is this? That's my coat! My camel's-hair coat!"

"No," Mr. Queen said, "I can prove this to be mine. You see, it has a cigarette burn at the second buttonhole, and a hole in the right-hand pocket."

"But — I found it where I left it! It was here all the time! I took it out of here after the fight and went up to the office to talk to these gentlemen. I've been — " The manager stopped. His face faded from green to white. "Then where's my coat?" he asked slowly.

"Will you try this on?" asked Mr. Queen. He took from a detective the bloodstained coat they had found in Ollie Stearn's car.

Mr. Queen held the coat up before Hawks. Hawks said thickly: "All right. It's my coat. I guess it's my coat, if you say so. So what?"

"So," replied Mr. Queen, "someone knew Mike Brown was broke, that not even his share of the purse tonight would pay his debts. Someone got Mike Brown to throw the fight tonight. He offered to pay Brown a lot of money, I suppose, for taking the dive. That money no one would know about. That money would not have to be turned over to Mike Brown's creditors. That money would be Mike Brown's own. So Mike Brown said yes. He realized that he could make more money, too, by placing a large bet with Happy Day through Mr. Oetjens.

"And probably Brown and his tempter planned to meet in Stearn's car right after the fight for the payoff. So Brown sent the driver away. He sat in the car, and the tempter came to keep the appointment. He was not armed with the payoff money but with a sharp knife. And by using the knife he saved himself a tidy sum — the sum he'd promised Brown. He also made sure Mike Brown would never be able to tell the wicked story to the wicked world."

Barney Hawks licked his dry lips. "Don't look at me, mister. You got nothing on Barney Hawks. I don't know nothing about this."

And Mr. Queen said, paying no attention whatever to Mr. Hawks: "A pretty problem, friends. We found a coat left in Stearn's car and my coat, in the next car, stolen. Coincidence? Hardly. The murderer certainly took my coat to replace the coat he was forced to leave behind."

Mr. Queen paused and glanced at Miss Paris, who was staring at him with awe. Mind over matter, thought Mr. Queen, remembering with special satisfaction how Miss Paris had stared at Jim Coyle's muscles. Yes, sir, mind over matter.

"Well?" said Inspector Queen. "Suppose the murderer did take your coat? What of it?"

"But that's exactly the point," murmured Mr. Queen. "He took my worthless coat. Why?"

"Well, I — I suppose to wear it," said Inspector Queen.

"Very good," applauded Mr. Queen. "But why should he want to wear it?"

The Inspector looked angry. "See here, Ellery — " he began.

"No, Dad, no," said Mr. Queen gently. "There's a point. *The* point. You might say he had to wear it because he'd got blood on his suit *under* the coat and needed a coat to hide the bloodstained suit."

"Well, sure," said Phil Maguire eagerly. "That's it."

"No," said Mr. Queen, shaking his head sadly, "that's not it. He couldn't possibly have got blood on his suit. The coat shows that at the time he attacked Brown he was wearing it buttoned. If the topcoat was buttoned, his suit didn't catch any of Brown's blood."

"He certainly didn't need a coat because of the weather," muttered Inspector Queen.

"True. It's been warm all evening. He'd left his own coat behind, its labels and other identifying marks taken out, unworried about its being found. Such being the case, you would say he'd simply make his escape in the clothes he was wearing

*beneath* the coat. But he didn't." Mr. Queen coughed gently. "So surely it's obvious that if he stole my coat for his escape, he *needed* my coat for his escape? That if he escaped without my coat, he would be *noticed*?"

"I don't get it," said the Inspector. "He'd be noticed? But if he was wearing ordinary clothing — "

"Then obviously he wouldn't need my coat," nodded Mr. Queen. "He could have made his escape in those clothes. But since he didn't, it can only mean that he *wasn't* wearing street clothes, you see. That's why the murderer needed a coat not only to come to the scene of the crime, but to escape from it as well."

There was another silence, and finally Paula said: "Wasn't wearing clothes? Why, that's like something out of Poe!"

"No," smiled Mr. Queen, "merely something out of the Stadium. You see, we had a group of gentlemen in the area tonight who wore no — or nearly no — clothing. In a word, the fighters. The instant I discovered that Brown had been stabbed, and that my coat had been stolen by a murderer who left his own behind, I knew that the murderer could have been *only one of thirteen men* . . . the thirteen living prizefighters left after Brown was killed. For you'll recall there were fourteen fighters in the Stadium tonight — twelve distributed among six preliminary matches and two in the main event.

"Which of the thirteen fighters had killed Brown? That was my problem from the beginning. And so I had to find my coat, because it was the only link between the murderer and his crime. And now I've

found my coat, and now I know which of the thirteen murdered Brown."

Barney Hawks was speechless. His mouth flapped open.

"I'm a tall, fairly broad man. In fact, I'm six feet tall," said the great man. "And yet, the murderer burst my coat at the armholes and back! That meant he was a much bigger man than I.

"Which of the thirteen fighters on the card tonight were bigger than I? Ah, but it's been a very light card — bantamweights, welterweights, lightweights, middleweights! Therefore none of the twelve preliminary fighters could have murdered Brown. Therefore, only one fighter was left — a man who had every motive — to get Mike Brown to throw the fight tonight!"

And this time the silence was full with meaning. It was broken by Jim Coyle's lazy laugh. "If you mean me, you must be off your nut. Why, I was in that shower room taking a shower at the time Mike was bumped off!"

"Yes, I mean you, Mr. Jim Coyle," said Mr. Queen clearly. "The shower room was the cleverest part of your plan. You went into the shower room in full view of all of us, with towels, shut the door, turned on the shower, slipped on a pair of trousers, then you grabbed Barney Hawks's camel's-hair coat and hat which were hanging on a peg in there. Then you ducked out of the shower-room window into the alley. From there it was a matter of seconds to the street and the parking lot across the street. Of course, when you stained Hawks's coat, you couldn't risk coming back in it. And you had to have

a coat — a buttoned coat — to cover your bare chest for the return trip. So you stole mine, for which I'm very grateful, because otherwise — . Grab him, will you? My right isn't very good," said Mr. Queen, employing a dainty and beautiful bit of footwork to escape Coyle's sudden murderous lunge in his direction.

And while Coyle went down under a pile of arms and legs, Mr. Queen murmured apologetically to Miss Paris: "After all, darling, he *is* the heavyweight champion of the world."

## READING COMPREHENSION

**Summarizing.** Choose the best phrase to complete each sentence. Then write the complete statements on your paper.

1. Phil Maguire didn't like the champion, Mike Brown, because Brown _____ (had brutally beaten another fighter, had murdered a man, had stolen Phil Maguire's money).

2. After the champion was defeated, Maguire said _____ (Coyle was a better fighter, the challenger had won the fight fairly, the champion had intentionally let the challenger beat him).

3. Ellery Queen knew the bloodstained coat belonged to the murderer because _____ (someone saw the crime, one of the buttons was torn off, the coat was later stolen).

**4.** By losing the fight, Brown had expected to get _____ (sympathy from the crowd, part of the purse and a chance to retire, a large payoff and money from his bet).

**5.** Ellery Queen realized Coyle was the killer because _____ (Coyle didn't have an alibi, Coyle's fingerprints were in the car, the ripped coat led to a big man).

**Interpreting.** Write the answer to each question on your paper.

**1.** Why wasn't the champion a wealthy man?

**2.** Why did Coyle open the door to the shower room in full view of everyone in the dressing room?

**3.** How was the camel's-hair coat used as an important detail in the plot?

**4.** How did Ellery Queen react when Coyle flirted with Miss Paris?

**For Thinking and Discussing.** If you were writing a mystery story and wanted to create a master detective such as Ellery Queen, what would your character be like? Explain why you think your character's personality traits would be valuable for a detective to have.

## UNDERSTANDING LITERATURE

**Plot Structure.** The plot structure of a mystery story is carefully organized to build suspense and involve the reader in solving the mystery.

A good mystery often includes a murder because there are so many possible motives for murder that it gives the author a chance to weave a complicated and very interesting plot. With many possible motives for a crime, the reader can be kept guessing who did it and why.

Part of the fun of reading a good murder mystery is playing detective as you read. To be a good detective, you have to notice how details relate to one another.

Here are some details from "Mind Over Matter." Some go together in a special way. On your paper, match each cause below with the effect it had in the story.

### Causes

**1.** Coyle needed a coat to cover himself.

**2.** The murderer was a very large man.

**3.** Brown bet against himself in the fight.

**4.** Brown hurt Kid Berés in a fixed fight.

### Effects

**a.** Phil Maguire disliked Mike Brown.

**b.** Ellery Queen's coat was stolen from the car.

**c.** Brown "took a dive" and lost the fight.

**d.** Queen's coat split at the seams.

Now go back and check (√) the details that helped Ellery Queen solve the case.

## WRITING

Pretend that you are Jim Coyle. Write your confession, explaining how and why you planned to kill Mike Brown.

# The Calico Dog

*by Mignon G. Eberhardt*

*Mignon G. Eberhardt (1899—) began writing detective
stories in the 1920's, and she is still writing them today. In
the 1930's she created a series of stories about Susan Dare, a
young mystery writer who is often called upon to provide
solutions to real mysteries. In "The Calico Dog," Susan finds
that she must deal with several mysteries at once.*

## Part One

It was nothing short of an invitation to murder.

"You don't mean to say," Susan Dare said in a small voice, "that both of them are living here?"

Idabelle Lasher — Mrs. Jeremiah Lasher, that is, widow of the patent-medicine emperor who died last year (resisting, it is said, his own medicine to the end with great determination) — Idabelle Lasher turned large pale blue eyes upon Susan and sighed and said:

"Why, yes. There was nothing else to do. I can't turn my own boy out into the world."

Susan took a long breath. "Always assuming," she said, "that one of them is your own boy."

"Oh, there's no doubt about that, Miss Dare," said Idabelle Lasher simply.

"Let me see," Susan said, "if I have this straight. Your son Derek was lost twenty years ago. Recently he has returned. Rather, two of him have returned."

Mrs. Lasher was leaning forward, tears in her large pale eyes. "Miss Dare," she said, "one of them must be my son. I need him so much. And besides," she added, "there's all that money. Thirty million."

"Thirty —" began Susan and stopped. It was simply not understandable. Half a million, yes; even a million. But thirty million!

"But if you can't tell yourself which of the two young men is your son, how can I? And with so much money involved. . . . I just don't see how I can help you," Susan said firmly.

"You must help me," said Mrs. Lasher. "Christabel Frame told me about you. She said you wrote mystery stories. She said you were the only woman who could help me, and that you were right here in Chicago."

"Let me have the whole story again, won't you? Try to tell it quite definitely, just as things occurred."

Mrs. Lasher put the handkerchief away and sat up briskly.

She began, "It was like this. . . ." Two months ago a young man called Dixon March had called on her. He had not gone to her lawyer. He had come to see her. And Dixon March had told her a very straight story.

"You must remember something of the story — oh, but of course, you couldn't. You're far too young. And then, too, we weren't as rich as we are now, when little Derek disappeared. He was four at the time. And his nursemaid disappeared at the same time, and I always thought, Miss Dare, that it was the nursemaid who stole him."

"Ransom?" asked Susan.

"No. That was the queer part of it. There never was any attempt to demand ransom. I always felt the nursemaid simply wanted him for herself."

Susan brought her gently back to the present. "Just what is Dixon's story?"

"He said that he was taken in at an orphanage at the age of six. That he vaguely remembers a woman, dark, with a mole on her chin, which is an exact description of the nursemaid. Of course, we've had the orphanage records examined, but there's nothing conclusive and no way to identify the woman; she died (under the name of Sarah Gant, which wasn't the nursemaid's name) and she was very poor. A social worker simply arranged for the child's entrance into the orphanage."

"What makes him think he is your son, then?"

"Well, it's this way. He grew up and went out on his own. Then he got to looking into his — his origins, he said. He found an account of the description of our Derek, the dates, the fact that he could discover nothing of the woman, Sarah Gant, previous to her life in Ottawa —"

"Ottawa?"

"Yes. That was where he came from. The other one, Duane, came from New Orleans. As Dixon remembered Sarah Gant, she looked very much like the newspaper pictures of the nursemaid. This suggested the possibility that he was our lost child."

"So, on this evidence he comes to you, claiming to be your son. A year after your husband died."

"Yes, and — well —" Mrs. Lasher flushed pinkly. "There are some things he can remember."

"Things — such as what?"

"The — the green curtains in the nursery. And a — a calico dog. And — and a few other things. The lawyers say that isn't enough. But I think it's very important that he remembers the calico dog."

"You've had lawyers looking into his claims."

"Oh, dear, yes," said Mrs. Lasher. "Exhaustively."

"But can't they trace Sarah Gant?"

"Nothing definite, Miss Dare."

"His physical appearance?" suggested Susan.

"Miss Dare," said Mrs. Lasher. "My Derek was blond with gray eyes. He had no marks of any kind. Any fair young man with gray eyes might be my son. And both these men — either of these men might be Derek. I've looked long and wearily, searching every feature and every expression for a likeness to my boy. It is equally there — and not there. I feel sure that one of them is my son."

"But you don't know which one?" said Susan softly.

"I don't know which one," said Idabelle Lasher. "But one of them is Derek."

She turned suddenly and walked heavily to a window. Twenty-one stories below, traffic flowed unceasingly along Lake Shore Drive.

"One of them must be an impostor," Idabelle Lasher was saying presently in a choked voice.

"Is Dixon certain he is your son?"

"He says only that he thinks so. But since Duane has come, too, he is more — more positive — "

"Duane, of course." The rivalry of the two young men must be rather terrible. Susan had a fleeting glimpse again of what it might mean. One of them was certainly an impostor, both impostors, perhaps, struggling over Idabelle Lasher's affections and her fortune.

"What is Duane's story?" asked Susan.

"That's what makes it so queer, Miss Dare. Duane's story — is — well, it is exactly the same."

"You don't mean exactly the same!" Susan cried.

"Exactly," the woman turned and faced her. "Exactly the same, Miss Dare, except for the names and places. The name of the woman in Duane's case was Mary Miller, the orphanage was in New Or-

leans, he was going to art school here in Chicago when — when, he says, just as Dixon said — he began to be more and more interested in his parentage and began investigating. And he, too, remembers things, little things from his babyhood and our house that only my dear son, Derek, could remember."

"Wait, Mrs. Lasher," said Susan, grasping at something firm. "Any servant, any of your friends, would know these details also."

Mrs. Lasher's pale, big eyes became more prominent.

"You mean, of course, a conspiracy. The lawyers have talked of nothing else. But, Miss Dare, they have checked everything possible to check both statements. I know what has happened to the few servants we had — all, that is, except the nursemaid. And we don't have many close friends, Miss Dare. Not since there was so much money. And none of them — none of them would do this."

"But both young men can't be Derek," said Susan desperately. She clutched at common sense again and said: "How soon after your husband's death did Dixon arrive?"

"Ten months."

"And Duane?"

"Three months after Dixon."

"And Duane and Dixon are both living here with you now?"

"Yes." She nodded toward the end of the long room. "The two young men are in the library now."

"Together?" said Susan irresistibly.

"Yes, of course," said Mrs. Lasher. "Playing cribbage."

"I suppose you and your lawyers have tried every possible test?"

"Everything, Miss Dare."

"You have no fingerprints of the baby?"

"No. That was before fingerprints were so important. We tried blood tests, of course. But they are of the same type."

"Resemblances to you or your husband?"

"You'll see for yourself at dinner tonight, Miss Dare. You will help me?"

Susan sighed. "Yes," she said.

The bedroom to which Mrs. Lasher herself took Susan was magnificent. Soon after Susan finished changing for dinner, Mrs. Lasher knocked.

"It's Derek's baby things," she said in a whisper and with a glance over her shoulder. "Let's move a little farther from the door."

They sat down on a cushioned sofa, and between them, Idabelle Lasher spread out certain small objects.

"His little suit — he looked so sweet in yellow. Some pictures. A pink plush teddy bear. His little nursery-school reports — he was already in nursery school, Miss Dare. And the calico dog, Miss Dare."

She stopped there, and Susan looked at the faded calico dog held so tenderly in those diamond-covered hands. She suddenly felt a wave of cold anger toward the man who was not Derek and who must know that he was not Derek. She took the pictures eagerly.

But they were only pictures: They showed a round baby face without features that were at all distinctive. There were two or three pictures of a little boy playing, squinting against the sun.

"Has anyone else seen these things?"

"You mean either of the two boys — either Dixon or Duane? No, Miss Dare."

"Has anyone at all seen them? Servants? Friends?"

Idabelle's blue eyes became vague and clouded.

"Long ago, perhaps," she said. "Oh many, many years ago. But they've been in the safe in my bedroom for years."

"How long have they been in the safe?"

"Since we bought this apartment. Ten — no, twelve years."

"And no one — there's never been anything like an attempted robbery of that safe?"

"Never. No, Miss Dare. There's no possible way for either Dixon or Duane to know of the contents of this box except from memory."

"And Dixon remembers the calico dog?"

"Yes." The blue eyes wavered again, and Mrs. Lasher rose and walked toward the door. "And Duane remembers the teddy bear and described it to me," she said definitely and went away.

Left to herself, Susan studied the pictures again. The nursery-school reports were written in beautiful handwriting. Music: A good ear. Memory: Very good. Adaptability: Very good. Sociability: Inclined to shyness. Rhythm: Poor (advise skipping games at home). Conduct: (This varied. Once there had been a disturbance during naptime, and Derek was at the bottom of it.) Susan smiled and began to like baby Derek. And it was just then that she found the first clue to an identifying trait. And that was after the heading Games. One report said: Quick. Another said: Mentally quick but does not use muscles well. And a third said: Tendency to use left hand which we are trying to correct.

Tendency to use left hand. An inborn tendency, cropping out again and again all through life. In those days, of course, it had been rigidly corrected — thereby causing all manner of ills, according to more recent trends of education. But was it ever altogether conquered?

Presently Susan put the things in the box again and went to Mrs. Lasher's room. She watched Mrs. Lasher open a panel which disclosed a steel safe set in the wall behind it. Mrs. Lasher placed the box securely in the safe.

"Did you find anything that will help?" asked Mrs. Lasher, closing the panel.

"I don't know," said Susan. "I'm afraid there's nothing very certain. Do Dixon and Duane know why I am here?"

"No," said Mrs. Lasher. "I told them you were a dear friend of Christabel's. And that you were very much interested in their — my — our situation. The boys are as anxious as I am to discover the truth of it."

Again, thought Susan, feeling baffled, as the true Derek would be. She followed

Mrs. Lasher toward the drawing room, prepared to dislike both men.

But the man in the doorway of the library was too old to be either Dixon or Duane.

"Major Briggs," said Mrs. Lasher. "This is Susan." She turned to Susan. "Major Tom Briggs is our closest friend. He was like a brother to my husband, and has been to me."

"Never a brother," said Major Briggs with an air of gallantry. "Say, rather, an admirer. So this is Christabel's little friend." He bowed and took Susan's hand. "How happy we are to have you with us, my dear," he said. "I suppose Idabelle has told you of our — our problem."

He was about Susan's height; white-haired, rather puffy under the eyes, and a bit too pink, with hands that were inclined to shake. He adjusted his gold-rimmed eyeglasses, then let them drop the length of their black ribbon and said:

"What do you think of it, my dear?"

"I don't know," said Susan. "What do you think?"

"Well, my dear, it's a bit difficult, you know. When Idabelle herself doesn't know. When trained and experienced investigators have failed to discover — ah — the identity of the lost son, how can we know?" He then said blandly: "But it's Duane."

"What — " said Susan.

"I said, it's Duane. He is her son. Anybody could see it with half an eye. Spittin' image of his dad. Here they come now."

They were alike and yet not alike at all. Both were rather tall and slender. Both had medium brown hair. Both had gray-ish-blue eyes. Neither was particularly handsome. Neither was exactly unhandsome. Their features were not at all alike. Yet their description on a passport would not have varied by a single word.

With the salad, Major Briggs roused to point out a portrait that hung on the opposite wall.

"Jeremiah Lasher," he said, waving a pink hand in that direction. He glanced at Susan and added, "Do you see any resemblance, Miss Dare? I mean between my old friend and one of these lads here?"

One of the lads — it was Dixon — wriggled uncomfortably, but Duane smiled.

"We are not at all embarrassed, Miss Dare," Duane said pleasantly. "We are both quite accustomed to this sort of thing." He laughed lightly, Idabelle smiled, and Dixon said:

"Does Miss Dare know about this?"

"Oh, yes," said Idabelle, turning as quickly to him as she had turned to Duane. "There's no secret about it."

"No," said Dixon somewhat crisply. "There's no secret about it."

There was, however, no further mention of the problem during the rest of the evening. Indeed, it was a very calm and slightly dull evening except for the affair of Major Briggs and the window.

That happened just after dinner. Susan and Mrs. Lasher were sitting over coffee in the drawing room. The three men were presumably in the dining room.

It had been altogether quiet in the drawing room. Then there was a shout from the dining room.

It all happened in an instant. Susan and Mrs. Lasher hadn't time to move before Duane appeared in the doorway. He was laughing but looked pale.

"It's all right," he said. "Nothing's wrong." He turned to look down the hall at someone approaching and added: "Here he is, safe and sound."

He stood aside, and Major Briggs appeared in the doorway. He looked so shocked and purple that both women moved hurriedly forward. Idabelle Lasher said, "Here — on the sofa. Ring for help, Duane. Lie down here, Major."

"Oh, no — no," said Major Briggs. "No, I'm quite all right."

Duane, however, supported him to the sofa, and Dixon appeared in the doorway.

"What happened?" he said.

Major Briggs waved his hands feebly. Duane said: "The Major nearly went out the window."

"O-h-h-h — " It was Idabelle in a thin, long scream.

"Oh, it's all right," said Major Briggs shakenly. "I caught hold of the curtain. By God, I'm glad you had heavy curtain rods at that window, Idabelle."

She was fussing around him. Her hands were shaking, and her face was pale under its makeup.

"But how could you — " she was saying, "what on earth — how could it have happened — "

"It's the draft," said the Major. "The confounded draft on my neck. I got up to close the window and — I nearly went out!"

"But how could you — " Idabelle began again.

"I don't know how it happened," said the Major. "Just all at once — " A puzzled look came slowly over his face. "Queer," said Major Briggs suddenly, "I suppose it was the draft. But it was exactly as if — "

He stopped and Idabelle cried: "As if what?"

"As if someone had pushed me," said the Major. Perhaps it was fortunate that the butler arrived just then. He helped the Major to stretch out full length on the sofa and sip some water.

And somehow in the conversation it emerged that neither Dixon nor Duane had been in the dining room when the thing had happened.

"Duane had gone to the library to get a book," said Dixon. "And I had gone to my room to get the evening paper. So the Major was alone when it happened. I knew nothing of it until I heard all the noise in here."

"I," said Duane, watching Dixon, "heard the Major's shout from the library and hurried across."

That night, late, after Major Briggs had gone home, Susan still kept thinking of the window and Major Briggs. During the night, she woke struggling with a silk-covered quilt, thinking that she herself was being thrust out the window.

It was only a nightmare, of course, but it led her to the plan she proposed to Mrs. Lasher that very morning.

It was true, of course, that the thing may have been exactly what it appeared to be. But if it was not an accident, there were only two possibilities.

"Do you mean," cried Mrs. Lasher

when Susan had finished her brief suggestion, "that I'm to say openly that Duane is my son! But I'm not sure. It may be Dixon."

"I know," said Susan. "And I may be wrong. But I think it might help if you will announce — to, oh, only to Major Briggs and the two men — that you are convinced that it is Duane and are taking steps of legal recognition of the fact."

"Why? What do you think will happen? How will it help things to do that?"

"I'm not at all sure it will help," said Susan wearily. "But it's the only thing I see to do. And I think that you may as well do it right away."

"Today?" said Mrs. Lasher.

"At lunch," said Susan firmly. "Telephone to invite Major Briggs now."

"Oh, very well," said Idabelle Lasher. "After all, it will please Tom Briggs. He has been urging me to make a decision. He seems certain that it is Duane."

But Susan, present and watching closely, could detect nothing except that Idabelle Lasher performed her task well. Susan was sure that the men were convinced. There was, to be sure, a shade of triumph in Duane. He was kind to Dixon — as, indeed, he could well afford to be. Dixon was silent and rather pale. He looked as if he had not expected the decision and was a bit stunned by it. Major Briggs was surprised at first, and then openly joyful. He toasted all of them.

The rest of the day passed quietly and not, from Susan's point of view, at all valuably. Susan tried to prove something about the possible left-handedness of the real Derek. Badminton and several games of billiards resulted only in displaying a consistent right-handedness on the part of both men.

Dressing again for dinner, Susan looked at herself in the great mirror.

She had never in her life felt so helpless. The course of action she had laid out for Idabelle Lasher had certainly, thus far, proved nothing. It was quite possible that she was mistaken and that nothing at all would come of it. And if not, what then?

The maid came in to help Susan dress.

"You'll be going to the party tonight, ma'am?" said the maid.

"Party?"

"Oh, yes, ma'am. Didn't you know? It's the Charity Ball. At the Dycke Hotel. In the Chandelier Ballroom. A grand, big party, ma'am. Madame is wearing her pearls."

"Is the entire family going?"

"Oh, yes, ma'am. And Major Briggs. There you are, ma'am — and I do say you look beautiful. There's orchids, ma'am, from Mr. Duane. And gardenias from Mr. Dixon. I believe," said the maid thoughtfully, "that I could put them all together. That's what I'm doing for Madame."

It made a huge corsage, thought Susan, but a lovely one. So, too, was the long town car which waited for them promptly at 10:00 when they emerged from the apartment house. Susan leaned back in her seat. She was always afterward to remember that short ride through crowded, lighted streets to the Dycke Hotel.

No one spoke. Perhaps only Susan was aware of the feelings that were bottled up together in that long, gliding car. She was aware of it quite suddenly and tinglingly.

Nothing had happened. Nothing, all through that long dinner from which they had just come, had been said that was at all helpful.

Yet all at once Susan was aware of a queer kind of excitement.

She looked at Duane and Dixon, riding along beside each other. Dixon sat stiff and straight. He had taken it rather well, she thought. Did he guess Idabelle's decision was not the true one? Or was he still stunned by it?

Or was there something in back of that silence? Had she underestimated the force and possible violence of Dixon's reaction? Susan frowned: It was dangerous enough without that.

They arrived at the hotel. Their sudden emergence from the silence of the car into brilliant lights and crowds and music had a magic effect. Even Dixon shook off his air of brooding as they finally strolled into the Chandelier Room. Duane and Mrs. Lasher danced smoothly into the revolving colors. Dixon asked Susan to dance. They left the Major smiling his approval.

The momentary gaiety with which Dixon had asked Susan to dance faded at once. He danced carefully but without much spirit, and he said nothing.

"Oh, there's Idabelle!" Susan said.

At once Dixon lost step. Susan recovered herself and her small silver sandals rather deftly. Idabelle, pink and jewel-laden, danced past them in Duane's arms. She smiled at Dixon anxiously. She looked, above her pearls, rather worried.

Dixon's eyebrows were a straight dark line, and he was white around the mouth.

"I'm sorry, Dixon," said Susan. She tried to catch step with him, and added: "Please don't mind my speaking about it. We are all thinking of it. I do think you behave very well."

He looked straight over her head. He danced several somewhat clumsy steps, and said suddenly:

"It was so — unexpected. And you see, I was so sure of it."

"Why were you so sure?" asked Susan.

He hesitated, then burst out again: "Because of the dog. The calico dog, you know. And the green curtains. If I had known there was so much money involved, I don't think I'd have come to — Idabelle. But then, when I did know, and this other fellow turned up, why, of course, I felt like sticking it out!"

He paused, and Susan felt his arm tighten around her waist. She looked up, and his face was suddenly chalk white and his eyes blazing.

"Duane!" he said hoarsely. "I hate him. I could kill him with my own hands."

The next dance was a tango, and Susan danced it with Duane. His eyes were shining and his face was flushed with excitement.

He was a born dancer, and Susan relaxed in the perfect ease of his steps. He complimented her gracefully and talked all the time. For a few moments Susan merely enjoyed the fast swirl of the dance. Then Idabelle and Dixon went past. Susan saw again the expression of Dixon's set white face as he looked at Duane, and Idabelle's pink face and pink neck.

The rest of what was probably a perfect dance was lost on Susan. She was busy about certain concerns of her own which

involved some adjusting of the flowers on her shoulder. And the moment the dance was over she slipped away.

Her gardenias sent up a warm fragrance as Susan huddled into a telephone booth. She made sure the flowers were secure and unrevealing upon her shoulder. She steadied her breath and dialed a number she knew very well. It was getting to be a habit — calling Jim Byrne, her newspaper friend. But she needed him. Needed him at once.

"Jim — Jim," she said. "It's Susan. Listen. Get into a white tie and come as fast as you can to the Dycke Hotel. The Chandelier Room."

"What's wrong?"

"Well," said Susan in a small voice, "I've set something going that I'm afraid is going to be more than I meant — Hurry, Jim." She caught her breath. "I — I'm afraid."

"I'll be right there. Watch for me at the door," he said. The telephone clicked, and Susan leaned rather weakly against the wall of the telephone booth.

# Part Two

Susan went back to the Chandelier Room. Idabelle Lasher, worried-looking, Major Briggs, and the two younger men made a little group standing together talking. She breathed a little sigh of relief. So long as they remained together, surrounded by hundreds of witnesses, it was all right. People didn't murder in cold blood when other people were looking on.

Then Idabelle suggested the fortune-teller.

"She's very good, they say," said Idabelle. "She's got a booth in one of the rooms."

"By all means, my dear," said Major Briggs at once. "This way?" She put her hand on his arm and, with Duane at her other side, moved away. Dixon and Susan followed. Susan cast a worried look toward the entrance. But Jim couldn't possibly get there in less than 30 minutes, and by that time they would have returned.

Dixon said: "Was it the Major that convinced Idabelle that Duane is her son?"

Susan hesitated.

"I don't know," she said cautiously, "how strong the Major's influence has been."

Her caution was not successful. As they left the ballroom and turned down a corridor, he whirled toward her.

"This thing isn't over yet," he said with the sudden savagery that had blazed out in him while they were dancing.

"Would you believe it? The fortune-teller charges twenty dollars a throw!" said Major Briggs as he approached.

The fortune-teller's room was small: a dining room, probably, for small parties. Across the end of it a kind of tent had been arranged with many gaily striped curtains.

Possibly due to her fees, the fortune-teller did not appear to be very popular. There were no others waiting, and no one came to the door except a bellboy with a tray in his hand who looked them over searchingly. He murmured something and wandered away. Duane sat calmly on the small of his back. The Major seemed a bit nervous and moved restlessly about. Dixon stood just behind Susan. Odd that she could feel his hatred for the man resting there in the armchair almost as if it were a living thing. Susan's sense of danger was growing sharper. But surely it was safe — so long as they were together.

The draperies of the tent moved and opened. Idabelle stood there, smiling and beckoning to Susan.

"Come inside, my dear," she said. "She wants you, too."

Susan hesitated. But, after all, so long as the three men were together, nothing could happen. Dixon gave her a sharp look, and Susan moved across the room. She felt a slight added worry when she discovered that in an effort to add mystery, the curtains had been arranged so that one walked through a maze to reach the fortune-teller.

Susan calmed herself as she sat down on some cushions beside Idabelle. The fortune-teller, in Egyptian costume, with

French accent, began to talk. Beyond the curtains and the sound of her voice Susan could hear little. Once she thought there were voices.

But the thing, when it happened, gave no warning.

There was only, suddenly, a great dull shock of sound. It brought Susan to her feet.

"What was that?" whispered Idabelle in a choked way.

And the fortune-teller cried: "It's a gunshot — out there!"

Susan stumbled and groped through the folds of draperies, trying to find the way through the maze of curtains and out of the tent. Then all at once they were outside the tent. They stared at the figure on the floor. There were people pouring in the door from the hall. Confusion was everywhere.

It was Major Briggs. He'd been shot and was dead, and there was no gun anywhere.

Susan felt ill and faint, and after one long look, she backed away to the window. Idabelle was weeping; her face blotched. Dixon was beside her. Then suddenly someone from the hotel had closed the door into the corridor. And a bellboy's voice, the one who'd wandered into the room, rose shrilly.

"Nobody at all," he was saying. "Nobody came out of the room. I was at the end of the corridor when I heard the shot and this is the only room on this side that's unlocked and in use tonight. So I ran down here, and I can swear that nobody came out of the room after the shot was fired."

"Was anybody here when you came in? What did you see?" It was the manager, worried, but carefully keeping the door behind him closed against further intrusion.

"Just this man on the floor. He was dead already!"

"Nobody. Nobody then. But I'd hardly got to him before there were people running into the room. And these three women came out of this tent."

The manager looked at Idabelle — at Susan.

"He was with you?" he asked Idabelle.

"Oh, yes, yes," sobbed Idabelle. "It's Major Briggs."

The manager started to speak, stopped, and began again:

"I've sent for the police. You folks that were in his party — how many of you are there?"

"Just Miss Dare and me," sobbed Idabelle. "And" — she singled out Dixon and Duane — "these two men."

"All right. You folks stay right here, will you? And you, too," — indicating the fortune-teller — "and the bellboy. The rest of you will go to a room across the hall. Sorry, but I'll have to hold you till the police get here."

The scattered groups that had pressed into the room filed slowly out again under the firm look of the manager.

The manager closed the door and said: "Now, if you folks will be good enough to stay right here, it won't be long till the police arrive."

With that he was gone.

The fortune-teller sank down into a chair. The bellboy retired to a corner and stood there. He looked very childish in his uniform, but very knowing. And Idabelle Lasher looked at the man at her feet. She began to sob again, and Duane tried to comfort her. Dixon shoved his hands in his pockets and glowered at nothing.

Duane patted Idabelle's shoulders and said something soothing, and Idabelle wrung her hands and cried: "How could it have happened! We were all together; he was not alone a moment — "

Dixon stirred.

"Oh, yes, he was alone," he said. "He wanted a drink, and I'd gone to hunt for a waiter."

"And you forgot to mention," said Duane icily, "that I had gone with you."

"You left this room at the same time, but that's all I know."

"I went at the same time you did. I stopped to talk to someone, and you vanished. I don't know where you went, but I didn't see you again. Not till I came back with the crowd into this room. Came back to find you already here."

"What do you mean by that?" Dixon's eyes blazed in his white face. "If you are accusing me of murder, say so straight out."

Duane was white, too, but calm. "All right," he said. "You know whether you murdered him or not. All I know is when I got back, I found him dead and you already here."

"You — "

"Dixon!" cried Idabelle sharply. She moved hurriedly between the two men. "Stop this! I won't have it. There'll be time enough for questions when the police come. When the police — " Her fingers

went on to her throat, groped, closed, and she screamed: "My pearls!"

"Pearls?" said Dixon staring and Duane darted forward.

"Tom murdered — and now my pearls gone — and I don't know which is Derek, and I — I don't know what to do — " Her shoulders heaved and her face was hidden in her handkerchief.

Susan said deliberately: "The police will search the room, Mrs. Lasher, every square inch of it — ourselves included. Don't worry about your pearls. There is nothing," said Susan with soft emphasis, "nothing that the police will miss."

Then Dixon stepped forward. His face was set. There was a strange light in his eyes.

He put his hand upon Idabelle's shoulder to force her to look up into his face. He brushed aside Duane, who had moved quickly forward, too.

"Why — why, Dixon," faltered Idabelle Lasher, "you look so strange. What is it? Don't, my dear, you are hurting my shoulder — "

Duane cried: "Let her alone. Let her alone." And then to Idabelle: "Don't pay any attention to him. He's out of his mind. He's — " He clutched at Dixon's arm, but Dixon turned and thrust him away so forcefully that Duane staggered backward against the walls of the tent. He clutched at the curtains to save himself from falling.

"Look here," said Dixon grimly to Idabelle, "what do you mean when you say, as you did just now, that you don't know which is Derek? You must tell me."

She stared upward as if hypnotized, choking. "I meant just that, Dixon. I don't know yet. I only said I had decided in order to — ”

“In order to what?” said Dixon.

A queer little tingle ran along Susan's nerves. She edged toward the door. She must get help. Duane's eyes were strange and terribly bright. He still clutched the striped curtains behind him. Susan took another silent step and another toward the door. Idabelle Lasher looked up into Dixon's face, and she said the strangest thing:

“How like your father you are, Derek.”

Susan's heart got up into her throat and left a very curious empty place in the pit of her stomach. She probably moved a little farther toward the door, but was never sure. All at once, while mother and son stared certainly at each other, Duane vanished.

Then Duane's black figure was outlined against the tent again. And he held a gun in his hand.

“Call him your son if you want to,” Duane said in an odd, jerky way, addressing Mrs. Lasher and Derek confusedly. “Then your son's a murderer. He killed Briggs. He hid in the folds of this curtain — till the room was full of people — and then he came out again. He left his gun there. And here it is. Don't move. One word or move out of any of you, and I'll shoot.” He was smiling a little and panting. “I'm going to hand you over to the police, Mr. Derek. You won't be so anxious to say he's your son then, perhaps. It's his gun. He killed Briggs with it because Briggs favored me. He knew it, and he did it for revenge.”

He was crossing the room with smooth steps. He held the gun threateningly and his eyes were rapidly shifting from one to another. Susan hadn't the slightest doubt that the smallest move would bring a gunshot crashing through someone's brain. He's going to escape, she thought. He's going to escape. I can't do a thing. And he's mad with rage. Mad with the terrible excitement of having already killed once.

Duane caught the flicker of Susan's eyes. He was near her now, so near that he could have touched her. He cried:

“You did this! You that advised her! You were on his side! Well — ” He'd reached the door now, and there was nothing they could do. He was gloating openly, the way of escape before him. In triumphant excitement he cried: “I'll shoot you first.” It's certainty, thought Susan numbly; Idabelle is so certain that Derek is the other one that Duane knows it, too. He knows there's no use in going on with it. And he knew, when I said what I said about the pearls, that I know.

Susan felt oddly dizzy. Something was moving. It was the door behind Duane. It was moving silently, very slowly.

Susan steeled her eyes not to reveal that knowledge. If only Idabelle and Derek would not see those panels move and betray what they had seen.

Then the door pushed Duane suddenly to one side. There was a crash of glass, and voices and flashing movement. Susan knew only that someone had pinned Duane from behind and was holding his arms close to his side. Duane gasped; his hand writhed and dropped the gun.

Then somebody at the door dragged Duane away; Susan realized confusedly that there were police there. And Jim Byrne stood at her elbow.

"I've aged ten years in the last five minutes," he said. He glanced around. He saw Major Briggs's body there on the floor — saw Idabelle Lasher and Derek — saw the fortune-teller and the bellboy.

Jim looked at a gun in his hand, put it in his pocket, and said briskly:

"Susan, now tell me the whole story. Who shot Major Briggs?"

Susan's lips moved and Derek straightened up and cried:

"Oh, it's my gun all right. But I didn't kill Major Briggs — I don't expect anyone to believe me, but I didn't."

"He didn't," said Susan wearily. "Duane killed Major Briggs. He killed him with Derek's gun, perhaps, but it was Duane who did the murder."

Jim did not question her statement, but Derek said eagerly:

"How do you know? Can you prove it?"

"I think so," said Susan. "You see, Duane had a gun when I danced with him. It was in his pocket. That's when I phoned for you, Jim. But I was too late."

"But how — " said Jim.

"Oh, when Duane accused Derek, he actually described the way he himself murdered Major Briggs. He explained how he had concealed himself and the gun in the folds of the tent until the room was full of people. Then he quietly mingled with them as if he had come from the hall. We were all staring at Major Briggs. It was very simple. Duane had got hold of Derek's gun. He knew it would be traced to Derek and the blame put upon him."

Idabelle had opened her eyes. They looked a bit glassy but were more sensible.

"Why — " she said, "why did Duane kill Major Briggs?"

"I suppose because Major Briggs had backed him. You see," said Susan gently, "one of the claimants had to be an impostor and a deliberate one. And the attack upon Major Briggs last night suggested either that he knew too much or was a conspirator himself. The similarity of the stories, and the fact that Duane turned up after Major Briggs had had time to search for someone who would be able to make a claim to being your son, seemed to me an indication of conspiracy. Someone had to tell one of the claimants about the memories of the baby things — the calico dog," said Susan with a little smile, "and the plush teddy bear. It had to be someone who had seen those things before you put them away in the safe. Someone who knew all your circumstances."

"You mean that Major Briggs planned Duane's claim — planned the whole thing? But why — " Idabelle's eyes were full of tears again.

"There's only one possible reason," said Susan. "He must have needed the money very badly, and Duane, coming into thirty million dollars, would have been obliged to share his spoils."

"Then Derek — I mean Dixon — I mean," said Idabelle confusedly, clutching at Derek, "this one. He really is my son?"

"You know he is," said Susan. "You realized it yourself when you were under stress. You felt it instead of reasoned it out. However, there's reason for it, too. He is Derek."

"He — is — Derek." said Idabelle, catching at Susan's words. "You are sure?"

"Yes," said Susan quietly. "He is Derek. You see, I'd forgotten something. Something physical that never changes all through life. That is, a sense of rhythm. Derek has no sense of rhythm and has never had. Duane was a born dancer."

Idabelle said: "Thank God!" She looked at Susan, looked at Derek, and quite suddenly became herself again. She got up briskly, glanced at Major Briggs's body, said calmly: "We'll try to keep some of this quiet. I'll see that things are done decently — after all, poor old fellow, he did love his comforts. Now, then. Oh, yes, if someone will just see the manager of the hotel about my pearls — "

Susan put a startled hand to her gardenias.

"I'd forgotten your pearls, too. Here they are." She fumbled a moment among the white flowers. Then she detached a string of pearls and held it toward Idabelle.

"I took them from Duane while we were dancing."

"Duane," said Idabelle. "But — " She took the pearls and said: "They are mine!"

"He had taken them while he danced with you. During the next dance you passed me, and I saw that your neck was bare."

Jim turned to Susan.

"Are you sure about that, Susan?" he said. "I've managed to get the outline of the story, you know. And I don't think Duane would have taken such a risk. Not with thirty million in his pockets, so to speak."

"Oh, they were for the Major," said Susan. "At least, I think that was the reason. I don't know yet, but I think we'll find that he was pretty hard pressed for cash and had to have some right away. Immediately. Duane probably did not want to demand money of Mrs. Lasher so soon, so the Major suggested the pearls. And Duane was in no position to refuse the Major's demands. Then, you see, he had no pearls because I took them. He and the Major must have quarreled. Duane realized that he would be at Major Briggs's mercy as long as the Major lived. Duane had already decided to kill him. After he had gotten to Idabelle, he no longer needed the Major. He had armed himself with Derek's gun after his attempt to push the Major out of the window had failed. But I think he wasn't sure just what he would do or how. He gave in to the Major's demand for the pearls because it was at the moment the simplest course. But he was ready and anxious to kill him, and when he knew that the pearls had gone from his pocket he must have guessed that I had taken them. And he decided to get rid of Major Briggs at once, before he could possibly tell anything. For any story the Major chose to tell would have been believed by Mrs. Lasher. Later, when I said that the police would search the room, he knew that I knew. And that I knew the gun was still there."

"Is that why you advised me to announce my decision that Duane was my son?" demanded Idabelle Lasher.

Susan shuddered and tried not to look at the body across the room.

"No," she said steadily. "I didn't dream of — murder. I only thought that it might bring the impostor into the open."

Jim said: "Here are the police." Queer, thought Susan much later, riding along the drive in Jim's car. Queer how often her adventures ended like this: driving silently homeward in Jim's car.

She glanced at the irregular profile behind the wheel and said: "I suppose you know you saved my life tonight."

His mouth tightened in the little glow from the dashlight. Presently he said:

"How did you know he had the pearls in his pocket?"

"Felt 'em," said Susan. "And you can't imagine how terribly easy it was to take them. A brilliant career in picking pockets was sacrificed when I was born an honest person."

The light went to yellow and then red, and Jim stopped. He turned and gave Susan a long look through the dusk. Then slowly he took her hand in his own warm fingers for a second or two before the light went to green again.

## READING COMPREHENSION

**Summarizing.** Choose the best phrase to complete each sentence. Then write the complete statements on your paper.

1. Mrs. Lasher asked Susan Dare to _____ (find her son, find out if her son was still alive, determine which young man was her son).

2. Susan thought Duane was guilty of killing Major Briggs because _____ (she felt the gun and stolen pearls while dancing with him, his calm manner gave it all away, Dixon had not been out of her sight).

3. Susan was certain Dixon was Mrs. Lasher's son because he _____ (looked like his father, was as clumsy as he had been as a child, showed her a calico dog he had had as a baby).

**Interpreting.** Write the answer to each question on your paper.

1. Why did Susan advise Mrs. Lasher to announce that Duane was her choice?

2. How had the impostor found out so many personal things about Derek's childhood and home?

3. How did Mrs. Lasher's realization that Dixon was very much like his father influence the plot?

**For Thinking and Discussing.** How might the story have ended if Major Briggs had not been shot?

## UNDERSTANDING LITERATURE

**Plot and Subplots.** "The Calico Dog" actually contains mysteries within the mystery. The major puzzle of the story involves the question of just which person is Idabelle Lasher's son, Derek. Within that story is a murder mystery: Who killed Major Briggs, and why? Another mystery subplot concerns who took the pearls.

Divide your paper into three columns: *Who Is the Real Derek? Who Killed Briggs? Where Are the Missing Pearls?* Then list each of the following details under the correct heading.

1. One of his toys was a calico dog.

2. Nobody came out of the room after the shot was fired.

3. " 'I stopped to talk to someone, and you vanished,' " [said Duane to Dixon].

4. Baby Derek had a plush teddy bear.

5. "[His report card] said: 'Mentally quick but does not use muscles well.' "

6. Something was hidden in the flowers pinned to Susan's dress.

7. " 'It was exactly as if . . . someone had pushed me,' said the Major."

8. Susan knew Duane had a gun.

## WRITING

Pretend you are Jim Byrne. Write a news story about the murder. Answer the following questions: Who? What? Where? When? Why? How?

# Riddle

*by Elizabeth Coatsworth*

What is it cries without a mouth?
What buffets, and yet has no hand?
And, footless, runs upon the waves
To drive them roaring up the sand?

Old as the world, unseen as Time,
Without beginning, without end,
What is it cries and has no mouth,
Wave-wrestler, and the sea gulls' friend?

1. What is the answer to the riddle? Which of the clues in the poem helped you to know?

2. What are some of the things the wind does? In what way might it be the sea gulls' friend?

3. What clues would you have given if you were the poet?

4. What other things are "old as the world, unseen as Time"? What other things are "without beginning, without end"?

# Section Review

## VOCABULARY

**Slang.** Slang is an informal kind of speech that uses words in a colorful and special way. In "Mind Over Matter," the sports murder mystery you read in this section, many slang expressions added to the story's effectiveness. In these expressions, words had meanings different from their usual ones. For example, when the author said, "Barney Hawks *turned green* in the silence," he meant that Barney looked upset, almost sick. Understanding what is happening in a story will help you understand the meaning of slang expressions.

Here are some sentences from "Mind Over Matter." Write each italicized slang expression on your paper. Then write its meaning next to the expression.

### Meanings

honest          killed

lost on purpose    take the blame

1. " 'Well, if this fight is *on the level* . . . Coyle will murder the champion.' "

2. " 'Sure, he made it look good. But your ex-champ *took a dive* just the same.' "

3. " 'Why, I was . . . taking a shower at the time Mike was *bumped off*!' "

4. "The fat gambler waded through and said hotly . . . : 'So, I'm supposed to *take the rap*, hey?' "

**Significant Details.** Each of the stories you read in this section contained many details. Some of the details were used to describe setting. Others were important clues that helped solve the mystery. Still others may have been included by the writer to keep you guessing.

Being able to decide which details are significant or important for a particular purpose and which details are not is a useful reading skill.

Here are some details from "The Calico Dog." On your paper, list the ones that helped Susan to conclude that Duane was an impostor.

1. Duane came from New Orleans and Dixon came from Ottawa.

2. Duane's story matched Dixon's except for the place, but Dixon told his first.

3. Both Duane and Dixon played cribbage.

4. Major Briggs favored Duane.

5. Duane was an excellent dancer.

6. Both boys were fair with gray eyes.

7. Dixon was a clumsy dancer.

8. Susan felt a gun in Duane's pocket.

9. Both men stayed with Mrs. Lasher.

10. Duane seemed very sure of himself.

11. Dixon said he hated Duane.

12. Idabelle liked both Dixon and Duane.

498

**A Review.** A review presents an opinion or evaluation of such things as books, movies, plays, concerts, and restaurants. The opinion expressed in a review is based on a set of ideas, or standards, of what the reviewer considers good and bad. Two different people may have different standards by which they judge the same thing. For example, you may like a book because of its good descriptive writing. Someone else may like it because of its character development. Your opinion of the book is the same, but your standards for arriving at that opinion are different.

**Step 1: Set Your Goal**

When you choose something to review, you should know enough about it to determine which factors are important and which are not. For example, does it matter how long a book is? Probably not. If a 150-page book is boring, it seems long. If a 300-page book is interesting and holds your attention, it seems short. You judge a book not by its length but by how much you enjoyed reading it.

Now it's your turn to take the part of a reviewer. Your task is to review one of the stories in the section and to make a recommendation about it for future students.

**Step 2: Make a Plan**

In order to gather information for your review, you must decide which factors are important to evaluate and what your standards are. In a review of a story, the main factors to consider are plot, characterization, setting, and mood. The questions below reflect the standards by which you may judge these different factors. As you reread the story, ask yourself the questions and jot down your responses. In this way, you will provide yourself with information to include in your review.

### Plot

- ☐ Is the plot well constructed and interesting?
- ☐ Does each incident have a purpose?
- ☐ Does each incident grow out of what comes before and lead to what comes next?
- ☐ Is the action well paced and believable?

### Characters

- ☐ How does the author reveal character? Are the techniques used effectively?
- ☐ Are there valid reasons for each character's behavior?
- ☐ Is the dialogue suitable for the characters involved? Is it believable?

### Setting and Mood

- ☐ Is the story's setting described well?
- ☐ What atmosphere does the author create? Is the atmosphere effective?
- ☐ Does the mood fit the story?

When you write your review, you must do more than just state your standards and opinions. You must also give specific examples to support and illustrate them. In this way, you clarify your reasons for your opinions. For example, if you think the setting of a story is described well, you might provide a line or two from the story to illustrate your opinion.

## Step 3: Write a First Draft

As you write the first draft of your review, remember that a review is an evaluation, not just a summary. You need to describe your subject to make clear to your reader why you are praising or criticizing it.

Begin with an opening statement that expresses your overall opinion. Include the title of the selection and the name of the author. For example:

*Scales of Justice* by Ngaio Marsh is an exciting mystery that you won't be able to put down.

Write a paragraph for each of the standards you considered. In the first sentence, describe the standard. Then use specific examples to tell why the story did or did not live up to that standard.

Conclude your review with a sentence that tells whether you would recommend the story to others.

## Step 4: Revise

If possible, wait a day or two before you revise your review. Then read it over carefully, looking for ways to make it clearer and more effective. Check to make sure that your standards are clearly stated and that you have used specific examples to demonstrate the points you make.

You may have to go over your paper a number of times before you are satisfied. Reading it aloud may help you find the spots that sound rough.

After you have revised your paper, proofread it. Look for mistakes in grammar, punctuation, and spelling. Finally, recopy your finished review neatly.

## QUIZ

The following is a quiz for Section 8. Write the answers in complete sentences on your paper.

## Reading Comprehension

1. In "Afterward," why did the Boynes move to Lyng? What did they expect to find there? What *did* they find?

2. In "Afterward," who was the man Mary Boyne saw from the rooftop? What did her husband do when he saw the man? Why?

3. In "Mind Over Matter," who won the fight? Why did he win?

4. In "The Calico Dog," what did Mrs. Lasher ask Susan Dare to do for her? Why did Susan agree to do it?

5. In "The Calico Dog," why was Dixon so upset and surprised when Mrs. Lasher announced that she thought Duane was her son?

## Understanding Literature

6. "Afterward" begins with the lines, "Oh, there *is* one, of course, but you'll never know it." To what was the speaker referring? How did this help create suspense? Mention three details to support the above statement.

7. In "Mind Over Matter," there are a number of possible suspects in the murder. What motive might each of the following have had: Happy Day, Ollie Stearn, Hymie Oetjens?

8. Who murdered Brown in "Mind Over Matter"? How was the murderer identified? Why did he do it?

9. In "The Calico Dog," why did Duane want to get rid of Major Briggs? What method did he try first? What did he do when that failed?

10. How did Susan Dare identify Duane as the impostor in "The Calico Dog"?

## ACTIVITIES

### Word Attack

1. In "Afterward," the way a stranger was dressed was described as being *unlocal*. The word *unlocal* begins with the prefix *un-*, which means "not." Words to which the prefix *un-* has been added usually convey the opposite meaning of the base word. For example, *unlocal* means "not local," which is the opposite of local. What prefixes besides *un-* also mean "not"? List at least one word that has each prefix you name.

2. In "The Calico Dog," you learned that even trained inspectors failed to identify the lost son. The word *inspector* ends with the suffix *-or*. The suffix *-or* means "one who." Therefore, an inspector is a person who inspects. Complete each of the following statements with a word that ends with the suffix *-or*.
   a. A person who visits is a _____ .
   b. A person who investigates is an _____ .
   c. A person who conspires is a _____ .
   d. A person who invests is an _____ .
   e. A person who collaborates is a _____ .

### Speaking and Listening

1. Take the part of a judge who has the task of deciding which man — Dixon or Duane — is really Mrs. Lasher's son, Derek. The time is the day *before* the party where Major Briggs was shot. Decide which one is the real Derek. Use only the information you have at this point. Be prepared to present your oral arguments to the class.

2. Pretend you are the announcer at the Coyle vs. Brown fight. Using the description of the fight in "Mind Over Matter," give a blow-by-blow account as if you were announcing it to a radio audience. Be prepared to make your "broadcast" to the class.

**Researching.** Mysteries are probably as popular today as they were in the 1930's. Select one of the following mystery writers and prepare a brief biography.

| | |
|---|---|
| Margery Allingham | Michael Innes |
| Raymond Chandler | Ngaio Marsh |
| Agatha Christie | Dorothy Sayers |
| Dashiell Hammett | Rex Stout |

**Creating.** Think of a good setting for a ghost story or a mystery. Describe what it looks like, and give details about any special characteristics it has that make it a suitable setting.

# THE MODERN EXPERIENCE

## *1939-PRESENT*

*The world is not a pleasant place to be without
Someone to hold and be held by.*

— Nikki Giovanni

*Confrontation*
Hughie Lee-Smith (1915-     )
The Hunter Museum of Art, Chattanooga
Gift of the National Academy of Design, Henry W. Ranger Fund

# The Modern Experience: 1939–Present

**A**mericans of today write about all the things that Americans have written about in the past. Many authors living today have written about the terror of battle during World War II, the Korean War, or the Vietnam War. Some have experienced and written about poverty and hardships. Others have created stories about wealth and adventure. Some have used their skill as writers to fight against injustice within our society. What is new about some of the literature of today is that it creates a special intimacy between the author and the reader.

The selections in this section offer you views of people's most intimate moments —the moments they share with those closest to them and the moments when they learn about themselves.

## Understanding Oneself

Drawing on the tradition of writers such as Stephen Crane, Sherwood Anderson, and Ernest Hemingway, many modern authors create literature that presents honest, realistic portraits of people. These authors record both the strengths and the weaknesses that real people bring to real-life situations.

Carson McCullers was a Southern writer skilled in creating complex, realistic characters who express very real emotions. She often wrote about lonely people and their search for love and acceptance. Her story in this section, "Sucker," is told from the point of view of a teenage boy who comes to understand himself better through his changing relationship with Sucker, his young cousin.

Richard Rodriguez grew up in Los Angeles, California. His autobiographical essay "A City of Words" explains how his knowledge of two languages, Spanish and English, contributes to his sense of himself. Like Rodriguez, Diana Chang also considers herself the product of two cultures. Her poem "Saying Yes" explains her feelings about her two heritages.

## Caring About Others

One way that authors make the characters they write about realistic is to pattern them after real people.

Sometimes authors find that they have created characters who reflect the personalities of the people they love best. Gwendolyn Brooks's story "Home" presents affectionate portraits of people who resemble her parents, her sister, and herself. This story shows the humor and loyalty

**Girl in Doorway,** George Segal, 1965

that help families survive difficult times.

Art Buchwald is one of America's best-known humorists. His newspaper columns are often filled with ridiculous people and exaggerated situations that help readers laugh at problems in their own lives. In "The Shock of Recognition," Buchwald invites you to look at the Bufkins family and to see if they remind you in any way of anyone you know.

## Seeing Beneath the Surface

Both Nikki Giovanni and Maxine Hong Kingston are well known for their affectionate descriptions that create new insights about everyday experiences. Giovanni's poem "Mothers" and Kingston's story "The Telephone Call" are both based on memories from childhood.

Tillie Olsen is an author who frequently goes beyond her personal experiences in her realistic fiction. Olsen is such a careful observer of human nature that she can realistically portray the thoughts and feelings of people who are in some ways very different from herself. Her story "I Stand Here Ironing" is told from the point of view of a poor, uneducated woman who wants to express her love and concern for her 19-year-old daughter.

In her poem "Fueled," Marcie Hans draws a dramatic comparison between a rocket and a plant seedling. What similarity do you see between the two?

The selections in this section reflect the emotional life of modern Americans since 1939. As America has grown in power and complexity, it has offered its people more choices about places and ways to live. In an ever-growing and changing America, American authors and readers appreciate the value of understanding their own feelings and the feelings of those around them.

# Sucker

*by Carson McCullers*

*Born and raised in Georgia, Carson McCullers (1917–1967)
was a successful novelist, short-story writer, and playwright.
Her writing, which is often about the people and places of
the South, is known for its simple, clear style. The story you
are about to read, "Sucker," is about loneliness and the need
to reach out to another—two powerful themes often found
in Carson McCullers's work.*

It was always like I had a room to myself. Sucker slept in my bed with me, but the room was mine, and I used it as I wanted to. Whenever I'd bring friends back to my room, all I had to do was just glance at Sucker, and he'd leave. He never brought kids back here. He's 12, four years younger than I am. He knew without me telling him that I didn't want kids that age meddling with my things.

Half the time I'd forget that Sucker isn't my brother. He's my first cousin, but almost ever since I can remember he's been in our family. His folks were killed in a wreck when he was a baby. To me and my kid sisters he was like our brother.

Sucker used to believe every word I said. That's how he got his nickname. Once I told him if he jumped off our garage with an umbrella, it would act as a parachute and he wouldn't fall hard. He did it and busted his knee. That's just one instance. No matter how many times he got fooled, he'd still believe me. Not that

he was dumb in other ways — it was just the way he acted with me.

There is one thing I have learned, but it makes me feel guilty. If a person admires you a lot, you hate him — and it is the person who doesn't notice you that you are apt to admire. This is not easy to realize.

Maybelle Watts, this senior at school, acted like she was the Queen of Sheba. I would have done anything to get her attention. I guess I used to treat Sucker as bad as Maybelle did me. Now that Sucker has changed, it is hard to remember him as he used to be. If I could have seen ahead, maybe I would have acted different.

I never noticed him much. He didn't have many friends, and his face had the look of a kid who is watching a game and waiting to be asked to play. That was Sucker until all this trouble began.

Maybelle was somehow mixed up in what happened, so I guess I ought to start with her. Until I knew her I hadn't given

much time to girls. Last fall she sat next to me in General Science class. All during class I used to watch her.

All the boys are crazy about her, and she didn't even notice me. She's almost two years older than I am.

Between periods I used to try to pass close to her in the halls, but she would hardly ever smile at me. Even at night I would think about her. Sometimes Sucker would wake up and ask me why I couldn't get settled. I'd tell him to hush up. I guess I wanted to ignore somebody like Maybelle did me.

That went on for nearly three months, then somehow she began to change. In the halls she would speak to me. Then one lunch time I danced with her in the gym. I knew everything was going to change.

It was that night when this trouble started. I felt happy and was awake thinking about Maybelle. Then I dreamed about her, and it seemed I kissed her. It was a surprise to wake up and see the dark. Sucker's voice was a shock to me.

"Pete?" I didn't answer or even move. "You do like me as if I was your own brother, don't you, Pete?"

I couldn't get over the surprise. It was like this was the dream instead of the other.

"You have liked me all the time like I was your own brother, haven't you?"

"Sure," I said.

"No matter what you did, I always knew you liked me."

I guess you understand people better when you are happy than when something is worrying you. I had never really thought about Sucker until then. I realized I had always been mean to him.

"You're a swell kid, Sucker," I said.

It seemed to me suddenly that I did like him more than anybody — more in a way even than Maybelle. I wanted to show Sucker how much I really thought of him and make up for the way I had always treated him.

We talked for a good while that night. His voice was fast. It was like he had been saving up these things to tell me for a long time. I talked some, too, and it felt good to think of him taking in everything I said so seriously. I even spoke of Maybelle a little, but I made out like she had been running after me all this time.

During the next couple of weeks, I saw a lot of Maybelle. She acted as though she really cared for me a little. I felt so good, I hardly knew what to do with myself.

But I didn't forget about Sucker. There were a lot of old things I'd been saving — boxing gloves and old fishing tackle. All this I turned over to him. We had some more talks, and it was like I was knowing him for the first time.

His face seemed different now. He used to look like he was afraid of getting a whack over the head. Now his face had the look of a person who is surprised and expecting something swell.

I guess things went on like this for about a month, with me taking out Maybelle and feeling so good I couldn't study or anything. There were times when I just had to talk to some person, and usually that would be Sucker. He felt as good as I did.

510

Then something happened between Maybelle and me. She began to act different. At first I tried to think it was just my imagination, but she didn't act glad to see me anymore. I'd see her riding with this fellow on the football team who has a yellow car.

At first I was so worried I forgot about Sucker. Later he began to get on my nerves. He was always hanging around until I'd get back from school. Then I wouldn't say anything or answer him roughly, and he'd finally go out. Sucker was growing fast and, for some reason, began to stutter.

Then the finish came between Maybelle and me. I met her going to the drugstore and asked her for a date. When she said no, I said something bitter. She said she was sick of me and had never cared a rap for me. I just stood there, then slowly walked home.

For several afternoons I stayed in my room. I didn't want to talk to anyone. When Sucker would come in and look at me sort of funny, I'd yell at him to get out. I tried not to think of Maybelle, but you can't help what happens to you at night. That is what made things how they are now.

You see I dreamed about Maybelle again. And again, Sucker woke up.

"Pete, what's the matter with you?"

All of a sudden I felt so mad my throat choked. I remembered all the times Maybelle hurt my pride. It was as if nobody would ever like me but a sap like Sucker.

"Why is it we aren't buddies like before?"

"Shut your trap!" I jumped up and turned on the light. He sat in the middle of the bed, his eyes blinking and scared.

There was something in me, and I couldn't stop myself. I don't think anybody ever gets that mad but once. Words came without me knowing what they would be.

"Why aren't we buddies? Because you're the dumbest slob I ever saw! Just because I felt sorry for you sometimes, don't think I give a darn for a dumb creep like you!"

If I'd yelled or hit him, it wouldn't have been so bad. But my voice was slow and calm. Sucker's mouth was partway open. His face was white and sweat came out on his forehead.

"Why don't you get a girl friend instead of me? What kind of a sissy do you want to grow up to be anyway?" Sucker didn't move. "Why do you always hang around me? Don't you know when you're not wanted?"

Slowly Sucker's blank look went away, and he closed his mouth. His eyes got narrow, and his fists shut. I'd never seen such a look on him before. It was like every second he was getting older — a hard look to his eyes that seemed wrong in a kid. He didn't speak.

"No, you don't know when you're not wanted," I said. "You're too dumb — just a dumb sucker."

It was like something had busted inside me. I turned out the lights and sat by the window. After a while, I heard Sucker lie down. I wasn't mad anymore, just tired. It seemed awful that I had talked like that to a kid only 12. I told myself I would straighten it out in the morning. Then I got back in bed.

Sucker was gone when I woke up the next day. Later when I wanted to apologize as I had planned, he looked at me in this new hard way so that I couldn't say a word.

That was two or three months ago. Since then Sucker has grown faster than any boy I ever saw. He's almost as tall as I am.

Our room isn't mine at all now. He's gotten up a gang of kids. When they aren't fighting, they are in my room. They've rigged up a radio, and every afternoon it blares out music.

It's even worse when we are alone together in the room. He sprawls across the bed and stares at me with that hard, half-sneering look. I fiddle around my desk and can't get settled. The thing is I have to study because I've gotten three bad cards this term already. If I flunk English I can't graduate next year.

I don't care a flip for Maybelle anymore, and it's only this thing between Sucker and me that is the trouble now. We never speak except when we have to before the family. I don't even want to call him Sucker anymore. Unless I forget, I call him by his real name — Richard.

More than anything I want to be easy in my mind again. I miss the way Sucker and I were. I've sometimes thought if we could have it out in a big fight that would help. But I can't fight him because he's younger. And another thing — this look in his eyes makes me almost believe that if Sucker could, he would kill me.

**Summarizing.** Choose the best phrase to complete each sentence. Then write the complete statements on your paper.

1. When things were going well with Maybelle, Pete _____ (had no time for Sucker, worked harder on his school work, treated Sucker more kindly).

2. After the night Pete behaved so cruelly toward Sucker, his cousin _____ (ran away from home, stopped talking to Pete, returned Pete's fishing tackle).

3. At the end of the story, Pete realized how much he _____ (missed his friendship with Sucker, really liked Maybelle, enjoyed being alone).

**Interpreting.** Write the answer to each question on your paper.

1. Why did Sucker live with Pete's family?

2. Why was it so important to Sucker that Pete like him as if he were his brother?

3. Why didn't Pete apologize to Sucker after speaking so cruelly to him?

4. In what ways did Sucker change in the months after Pete said such terrible things to him?

**For Thinking and Discussing.** How was Pete's behavior toward Sucker similar to Maybelle's behavior toward Pete? Give as many specific examples from the story as you can.

## UNDERSTANDING LITERATURE

**Character Motivation.** In a good story, the characters must be believable. They must have reasons for their actions. The combination of character traits and circumstances that cause a character to act in a particular way is called *motivation.*

Understanding the characters in a story and figuring out what the motivation for their actions is can add to the enjoyment of your reading. As you read a story, it's helpful to try to get to know the characters as people. Just as in real life, there will be some characters whom you will like or understand better than others.

Sometimes an author lets you know a lot about a particular character. Sometimes a character is just presented very briefly for a specific purpose and you never do find out very much about what he or she is like.

Here are statements about the actions of characters in "Sucker." On your paper, identify each statement as *true* or *false.*

1. Sucker believed everything Pete said, and that was how he got his nickname.

2. Pete treated Sucker better than he treated Maybelle because he always had thought of Sucker as his best friend.

3. When Pete was friendly to him, Sucker became a happier and more outgoing person.

4. Pete felt so good that he studied extra hard.

5. At first, Pete ignored Sucker in the same way Maybelle ignored him.

6. After Maybelle broke up with him, Pete stayed in his room because he didn't want to talk to anybody.

7. Sucker brought kids home to make up for losing his friendship with Pete.

8. Pete was cruel to Sucker because the younger boy teased him about Maybelle.

9. Pete wanted to fight it out with Sucker or apologize, but he didn't because Sucker was younger than he was and he frightened Pete with his look.

10. At the end of the story, Pete and Sucker were closer than they had ever been before.

Answer the following questions about character motivation.

1. Pick one character from the story: Pete, Maybelle, or Sucker. Tell why you think that character behaved as he or she did. Use events and descriptions from the story to help you.

2. Which character in the story do you like the best? Explain why.

## WRITING

Imagine that you are Sucker. Write three entries in your diary. In the first entry, tell about your feelings toward Pete in the beginning of the story. In the second, tell about your feelings toward Pete in the middle of the story. In the third, tell about your feelings toward Pete at the end.

# A City of Words

*by Richard Rodriguez*

*Richard Rodriguez grew up in California during the 1950's and 60's. His parents were Mexican immigrants, and Rodriguez spoke mostly Spanish until he went to school. In* Hunger of Memory, *published in 1981, Rodriguez tells about his education, from kindergarten through graduate school. In this excerpt from his book, he tells about the importance of both the Spanish and the English language in his life.*

I grew up victim to a disabling confusion. As I grew fluent in English, I no longer could speak Spanish with confidence. I continued to understand spoken Spanish. And in high school, I learned how to read and write Spanish. But for many years I could not pronounce it. A powerful guilt blocked my spoken words; an essential glue was missing whenever I'd try to connect words to form sentences. I would be unable to break a barrier of sound, to speak freely. I would speak, or try to speak, Spanish, and I would manage to utter halting, hiccuping sounds that betrayed my unease.

When relatives and Spanish-speaking friends of my parents came to the house, my brother and sisters seemed reticent to use Spanish, but at least they managed to say a few necessary words before being excused. I never managed so gracefully. I was cursed with guilt. Each time I'd hear myself addressed in Spanish, I would be unable to respond with any success. I'd know the words I wanted to say, but I couldn't manage to say them. I would try to speak, but everything I said seemed to me horribly anglicized. My mouth would not form the words right. My jaw would tremble. After a phrase or two, I'd cough up a warm, silvery sound. And stop.

It surprised my listeners to hear me. They'd lower their heads, better to grasp what I was trying to say. They would repeat their questions in gentle, affectionate voices. But by then I would answer in English. No, no, they would say, we want you to speak to us in Spanish (". . . *en español*"). But I couldn't do it. *"Pocho"* then they called me. Sometimes playfully, teasingly, using the tender diminutive — *"mi pochito."* Sometimes not so playfully, mockingly, *Pocho.* (A Spanish dictionary defines that word as an adjective meaning "colorless" or "bland." But I heard it as a noun, naming the Mexican-American who, in becoming an American, forgets his native society.) *"Pocho!"* the lady in the Mexican food store muttered, shaking her head. I looked up to the counter where red and green peppers were strung like Christmas tree lights and saw the frowning face of the stranger. My mother laughed somewhere behind me. (She said that her children didn't want to practice "our Spanish" after they started going to school.) My mother's smiling voice made me suspect that the lady who faced me was not really angry at me. But, searching her face, I couldn't find the hint of a smile.

Embarrassed, my parents would regularly need to explain their children's inability to speak flowing Spanish during those years. My mother met the wrath of her brother, her only brother, when he came up from Mexico one summer with his family. He saw his nieces and nephews for the very first time. After listening to me, he looked away and said what a disgrace it was that I couldn't speak Spanish, *"su proprio idioma."*[1] He made that remark to my mother; I noticed, however, that he stared at my father.

I clearly remember one other visitor from those years. A longtime friend of my father's from San Francisco would come to stay with us for several days in late August. He took great interest in me after he realized that I couldn't answer his questions in Spanish. He would grab me as I started to leave the kitchen. He would ask me something. Usually he wouldn't bother to wait for my mumbled response. Knowingly, he'd murmur: *"Ay, Pocho, Pocho, adonde vas?"*[2] And he would press his thumbs into the upper part of my arms, making me squirm with currents of pain. Dumbly, I'd stand there, waiting for his wife to notice us, for her to call him off with a benign smile. I'd giggle, hoping to deflate the tension between us, pretending that I hadn't seen the glittering scorn in his glance.

I remember that man now, but seek no revenge in this telling. I recount such incidents only because they suggest the fierce power Spanish had for many people I met at home; the way Spanish was associated with closeness. Most of those people who called me a *pocho* could have spoken English to me. But they would not. They seemed to think that Spanish was the only language we could use, that Spanish alone permitted our close association. (Such persons are vulnerable always to the ghetto merchant and the politician who have learned the value of speaking their clients' family language to gain immediate trust.) For my part, I felt that I had somehow committed a sin of betrayal by learning English. But betrayal against whom? Not against visitors to the house exactly. No, I felt that I had betrayed my immediate family. I knew that my parents had encouraged me to learn English. I knew that I had turned to English only with angry reluctance. But once I spoke English with ease, I came to feel guilty. (This guilt defied logic.) I felt that I had shattered the intimate bond that had once held the family close. This original sin against my family told whenever anyone addressed me in Spanish and I responded, confounded.

But even during those years of guilt, I

---

1. *Su proprio idioma* — your real language.
2. *Adonde vas* — where are you going?

was coming to sense certain consoling truths about the language and intimacy. I remember playing with a friend in the backyard one day, when my grandmother appeared at the window. Her face was stern with suspicion when she saw the boy (the *gringo*) I was with. In Spanish she called out to me, sounding the whistle of her ancient breath. My companion looked up and watched her intently as she lowered the window and moved, still visible, behind the light curtain, watching us both. He wanted to know what she had said. I started to tell him, to say — to translate her Spanish words into English. The problem was, however, that though I knew how to translate exactly what she had told me, I realized that any translation would distort the deepest meaning of her message: It had been directed only to me. This message of intimacy could never be translated because it was not in the words she had used but passed through them. So any translation would have seemed wrong; her words would have been stripped of an essential meaning. Finally, I decided not to tell my friend anything. I told him that I didn't hear all she had said.

This insight unfolded in time. Making more and more friends outside my house, I began to distinguish intimate voices speaking through English. I'd listen at times to a close friend's confidential tone or secretive whisper. Even more remarkable were those instances when, for no special reason apparently, I'd become conscious of the fact that my companion was speaking only to me. I'd marvel just hearing his voice. It was a stunning event: to be able to break through his words, to be able to hear this voice of the other, to realize that it was directed only to me. After such moments of intimacy outside the house, I began to trust hearing intimacy conveyed through my family's English. Voices at home at last punctured sad confusion. I'd hear myself addressed as an intimate at home once again. Such moments were never as raucous with sound as past times had been when we had had "private" Spanish to use. (Our English-sounding house was never to be as noisy as our Spanish-speaking house had been.) Intimate moments were usually soft moments of sound. My mother was in the dining room while I did my homework nearby. And she looked over at me. Smiled. Said something — her words said nothing very important. But her voice sounded to tell me (We are together) I was her son.

(Richard!)

Intimacy thus continued at home; intimacy was not stilled by English. It is true that I would never forget the great change of my life, the diminished occasions of intimacy. But there would also be times when I sensed the deepest truth about language and intimacy: Intimacy is not created by a particular language; it is created by intimates. The great change in my life was not linguistic but social. If, after becoming a successful student, I no longer heard intimate voices as often as I had earlier, it was not because I spoke English rather than Spanish. It was because I used public language for most of the day. I moved easily at last, a citizen in a crowded city of words.

**Summarizing.** Choose the best phrase to complete each sentence. Then write the complete statements on your paper.

1. As the writer became fluent in English, he _____ (tried learning other languages, refused to read or write Spanish, lost his ability to speak Spanish).

2. Most people who criticized the author because he avoided speaking Spanish _____ (were unable to communicate with him, could have conversed in English, had little education).

3. When the author tried to translate his grandmother's Spanish words, he realized _____ (he didn't understand them, his friend would laugh at him, their true meaning could never be translated to anyone else).

**Interpreting.** Write the answer to each question on your paper.

1. Why did the author feel guilty about speaking English?

2. Why did his father's friend treat the author scornfully because he wasn't speaking Spanish?

3. As time went on, what did the author learn about language and about himself that finally made him comfortable using English?

**For Thinking and Discussing.** Do you agree with the author that "intimacy is not created by a particular language; it is created by intimates"? Explain.

**Characters in an Essay.** The author in an autobiographical essay is both the narrator and the main character. A character who grows and changes in response to events is called *dynamic*. A character who does not change in response to a story or essay's action is called *static*.

1. Here are some statements about the narrator of "A City of Words." Identify each one as *true* or *false*.
   a. When addressed in Spanish, I'd be unable to respond with any success.
   b. *Pocho* was the name they called me because I spoke Spanish so well.
   c. The people who called me *Pocho* spoke only English.
   d. After I spoke English with ease, I felt guilty.
   e. I learned English because they made me do it in school.
   f. As I learned more about intimacy, I realized that language wasn't the problem.

2. Do you think the narrator is a dynamic character or a static one? Explain your answer.

## WRITING

Think about a social situation in which you are unable to do what you want. Write one or two paragraphs to describe your feelings, what you do to try to cover up, and the way other people react. Before you begin writing, decide if you will be a dynamic or a static character.

# Saying Yes

*by Diana Chang*

"Are you Chinese?"
"Yes."

"American?"
"Yes."

"*Really* Chinese?"
"No . . . not quite."

"*Really* American?"
"Well, actually, you see . . ."

But I would rather say
yes.

Not neither-nor,
not maybe,
but both, and not only

The homes I've had,
the ways I am

I'd rather say it
twice,
yes.

---

1. How many "voices" are there in the poem? Who are the people speaking?

2. What kinds of replies does the author give when she is asked if she is "*really* Chinese" and "*really* American"? Why does she answer that way?

3. What is the author's attitude toward her heritage? Could this poem be about America's heritage as well? Explain.

---

# Home

*by Gwendolyn Brooks*

*Gwendolyn Brooks (1917—) is best known for poetry that
creates vivid portraits of the people she knew growing up in
Chicago. She has also written autobiographical fiction,* Maud
Martha, *drawn from experiences in her own life. The story
that follows paints a warm and loving picture of a family
much like her own — and of the ways different family
members react when the security of their home is threatened.*

What had been wanted was this always, this always to last, the talking softly on this porch, with the snake plant in the jardiniere in the southwest corner, and the obstinate slip from Aunt Eppie's magnificent Michigan fern at the left side of the friendly door. Mama, Maud Martha, and Helen rocked slowly in their rocking chairs, and looked at the late afternoon light on the lawn, and at the emphatic iron of the fence and at the poplar tree. These things might soon be theirs no longer. Those shafts and pools of light, the tree, the graceful iron, might soon be viewed possessively by different eyes.

Papa was to have gone that noon, during his lunch hour, to the office of the Home Owners' Loan. If he had not succeeded in getting another extension, they would be leaving this house in which they had lived for more than 14 years. There was little hope. The Home Owners' Loan was hard. They sat, making their plans.

"We'll be moving into a nice flat somewhere," said Mama. "Somewhere on South Park, or Michigan, or in Washington Park Court." Those flats, as the girls and Mama knew well, were burdens on wages twice the size of Papa's. This was not mentioned now.

"They're much prettier than this old house," said Helen. "I have friends that wouldn't come down this far for anything, unless they were in a taxi."

Yesterday, Maud Martha would have attacked her. Tomorrow she might. Today she said nothing. She merely gazed at a little hopping robin in the tree, her tree, and tried to keep her eyes dry.

"Well, I do know," said Mama, turning her hands over and over, "that I've been getting tireder and tireder of doing that firing. From October to April, there's firing to be done."

"But lately we've been helping, Harry and I," said Maud Martha. "And sometimes in March and April and in October, and even in November, we could build a little fire in the fireplace. Sometimes the weather was just right for that."

She knew, from the way they looked at her, that this had been a mistake. They did not want to cry.

But she felt that the little line of white, somewhat ridged with smoked purple, and all that cream-shot saffron, would never drift across any western sky except that in back of this house. The rain would drum with as sweet a dullness nowhere but here. The birds on South Park were mechanical birds, no better than the poor caught canaries in those "rich" women's sun parlors.

"It's just going to kill Papa!" burst out Maud Martha. "He loves this house! He lives for this house!"

"He lives for us," said Helen. "It's us he loves. He wouldn't want the house, except for us."

"And he'll have us," added Mama, "wherever."

"You know," Helen sighed, "if you want to know the truth, this is a relief. If this hadn't come up, we would have gone on, just dragged on, hanging out here forever."

"It might," allowed Mama, "be an act of God. God may just have reached down, and picked up the reins."

"Yes," Maud Martha cracked in, "that's what you always say — that God knows best."

Her mother looked at her quickly, decided the statement was not suspect, and looked away.

Helen saw Papa coming. "There's Papa," said Helen.

They could not tell a thing from the way Papa was walking. It was that same dear little staccato walk, one shoulder down, then the other, then repeat, and repeat. They watched his progress. He passed the Kennedys'; he passed the vacant lot; he passed Mrs. Blakemore's. They wanted to hurl themselves over the fence, into the street, and shake the truth out of his collar. He opened his gate — the gate — and still his stride and face told them nothing.

"Hello," he said.

Mama got up and followed him through the front door. The girls knew better than to go in, too.

Presently Mama's head emerged. Her eyes were lamps turned on.

"It's all right," she exclaimed. "He got it. It's all over. Everything is all right."

The door slammed shut. Mama's footsteps hurried away.

"I think," said Helen, rocking rapidly, "I think I'll give a party. I haven't given a party since I was eleven. I'd like some of my friends to just casually see that we're homeowners."

**Summarizing.** Choose the best phrase to complete each sentence. Then write the complete statements on your paper.

1. The family would be forced to leave their home unless _____ (they could rebuild it, the new owners changed their minds, they got an extension on their loan).

2. When Papa returned home _____ (his family immediately sensed that his news was good, the girls immediately sensed that the news was bad, his walk and expression did not reveal his true feelings).

3. At the end of the story, Mama told the girls that _____ (they would soon be moving, they would be giving a house-warming party, their father got an extension on their loan).

**Interpreting.** Write the answer to each question on your paper.

1. Why didn't the girls and Mama really think they would move to a flat in Washington Park Court?

2. Why didn't Maud Martha fight with Helen as she might have in the past?

3. Why did Maud Martha feel that reminding Mama and Helen of her help around the house had been a mistake?

**For Thinking and Discussing.** How did Maud Martha and Helen seem to differ in the way they reacted to the family's problem?

**Characterization Through Dialogue.** Often you can learn a lot about characters from what they say and from their reactions to each other. In "Home" by Gwendolyn Brooks, conversation reveals what the characters are like.

On your paper, write the best choice to complete each of the following statements about the characters in "Home."

1. " 'We'll be moving into a nice flat somewhere,' said Mama." She was trying to convince them that _____.
   a. apartments were a luxury
   b. losing the house wouldn't be so bad
   c. they should start packing

2. " 'It's just going to kill Papa!' burst out Maud Martha." She _____ .
   a. wanted to be rid of her father
   b. didn't care about moving
   c. worried about her father's feelings

3. " 'You know,' Helen sighed, 'if you want to know the truth, this is a relief.' " Helen _____.
   a. didn't dare hope that they'd keep their home
   b. really hated living there
   c. didn't care what the others felt

**WRITING**

Think of something about your own home that you like very much. Write a brief conversation with a friend that explains your feelings and reveals something of your character.

# The Telephone Call

*by Maxine Hong Kingston*

*Maxine Hong Kingston (1940—) has written two powerful books based on her family experiences and cultural heritage: The Woman Warrior (1976) and China Men (1980). These books interweave scenes of everyday life with ancient Chinese legends and the author's impressions of her family's life before she was born. The following excerpt from China Men tells a little about Kingston's mother and her feeling for her brother, whom she hasn't spoken to in 50 years.*

Once MaMa telephoned her brother after not having seen him for 50 years. This was the Singapore uncle who had spent his first fortune throwing a party for friends in Hong Kong. She told me to be ready to get up at 5:00 a.m. to do the dialing. They had written letters agreeing on this day, January 2, when it would be a cheap time and 8:00 p.m. in Singapore. "Oh, the size of the world," she exclaimed. "Look at that time difference. That's not three hours but fifteen hours apart. How far away."

I heard the alarms go off all over the house at 4:30 a.m. and leapt out of bed from nervousness. Wrapped in my blanket, I dialed the operator. After hearing my uncle's phone ring once, I handed the receiver to my mother. She heard a ring and handed it back to me. "Here, you talk to him."

"No," I yelped, "I've never met him. He's your brother. You talk to him." Besides, I didn't want to scare him. My parents' friends hang up when we forget to answer with a Chinese accent.

The index finger of my mother's hand that held the phone tapped involuntarily against her cheek; it was the only part of her that shook. "Happy New Year, Wah," she yelled in her loudest voice, no titles, just his name, her baby brother, named after the Chinese Republic. "Is this Wah? Are you well? You're all well, aren't you? Everyone well. Yes, we're all fine, too. Yes, very good. Everyone is good. Do you celebrate this New Year's day? Ours is very festive. All my children come back, eating at everybody's houses every day. We go from one of my children's house to another's eating. No, I can't come visit you. Five years ago I could have visited

you. But I'm old now. Yes, I'm old now too. Are you old? Do you work hard? Did you just now come home from work? How hard do you work? I still work. Yes. Yes. Thirty employees, huh? That's good. Yes, my children are all working. Everyone working. Happy New Year. Yes, you have a good year, too. Good year, good business, good health. Your son has his own corporation? Why don't you come visit me? No, I don't fly. Yes, we're all well. Doing well. Fine. Good jobs. It's five a.m. here. What time is it there? It's January second now. What day is it there? You're home from work? Let me talk to your wife." Then she talked to his first wife, repeating just about everything. My father said, "Nine minutes," and she said, "That's enough. Be well. Good-bye," and hung up.

"Well," she said, "nothing significant said." She tried repeating the conversation to us. "He employs thirty people. He says that he wishes his children were smart. They're horses and oxen, he said. His son is in the construction business, too, but has a different company. He says it's eight p.m., January second there in Singapore." I noticed she had not asked him how his second wife was, nor how the children of that family were. "Fifty years since we've talked, and we didn't say anything important," she said.

"That's the nature of phone calls," my father said. "You just hear each other's voices. That's enough."

"You can call again next year, you know," I said. "You can call again anytime."

## READING COMPREHENSION

**Summarizing.** Choose the best phrase to complete each sentence. Then write the complete statements on your paper.

1. MaMa telephoned her brother _____ (to apologize after a serious argument, because she had heard he was ill, after not seeing him for 50 years).

2. MaMa said she couldn't visit her brother because _____ (the trip was too expensive, she was too old, she couldn't take the time off from her job).

3. The sister and brother spoke together for _____ (over an hour, twenty minutes, nine minutes).

**Interpreting.** Write the answer to each question on your paper.

1. Why didn't the author want to talk to her uncle first?

2. How did MaMa feel about calling her brother?

3. Why had the author's uncle said that he wished his children were smart and called them "oxen" and "horses"?

**For Thinking and Discussing.**

1. Why do you think MaMa hadn't called or seen her brother for so long?

2. The author's father said, "That's the nature of phone calls. You just hear each other's voices. That's enough." What do you think he meant? Do you agree or disagree? Explain your answer.

## UNDERSTANDING LITERATURE

**Inferring Motivation.** In "The Telephone Call," the small things the characters do and say suggest important information about their thoughts and feelings. *Motivation* is the reason characters behave as they do.

Read each quote below. Then on your paper write the letter of the answer that best suggests the characters' motivations.

1. "I've never met him. . . . You talk to him." The narrator thought of her uncle as _____ .
   a. a very important person
   b. a stranger
   c. a tired old man

2. "The index finger of my mother's hand that held the phone tapped involuntarily against her cheek." MaMa_____.

   a. thought the telephone was broken
   b. felt nervous and excited
   c. felt bored

3. "No, I can't come visit you. . . . Why don't you come visit me?" MaMa realized that _____ .
   a. she might never see her brother
   b. she could talk Wah into coming to America
   c. she should move to Singapore

## WRITING

Imagine you are Wah. Describe the telephone call you just received. How did it feel to talk to your sister again?

# The Shock of Recognition

*by Art Buchwald*

*Mr. Bufkins hasn't seen his wife and kids for years. Was he away? No, he was right here in the living room — in front of the television set, as usual. Humorist Art Buchwald (1925–) based this satire of American family life on a real news event — a blackout — that really did shake up many people's lives.*

A few years ago, New York City had a blackout which caused all the television stations in the area to go out for several hours. This created crises in families all over the New York area and proved that TV plays a much greater role in people's lives than anyone can imagine.

When the TV went off in the Bufkins house in Forest Hills, panic set in. First, Bufkins thought it was his set in the living room, so he rushed into his bedroom and turned on that set. Nothing.

The phone rang and Mrs. Bufkins heard her sister say that there was a blackout.

She hung up and said to her husband, "It isn't your set. Something's happened to the top of the Empire State Building."

Bufkins said, "Who are you?"

"I'm your wife, Edith."

"Oh," Bufkins said, "then I suppose those kids in there are mine."

"That's right," Mrs. Bufkins said. "If you ever got out of that armchair in front of the TV set, you'd know us."

"Boy, they've really grown," Bufkins said, looking at his son and daughter. "How old are they now?"

"Thirteen and fourteen," Mrs. Bufkins replied.

"I'll be darned. Hi, kids."

"Who's he?" Bufkins' son, Henry, asked.

"It's your father," Mrs. Bufkins said.

"I'm pleased to meetcha," Bufkins' daughter, Mary, said shyly. There was an embarrassed silence all around.

"Look," said Bufkins, finally. "I know I haven't been much of a father, but now that the TV's out, I'd like to make it up to you."

"How?" asked Henry.

"Well, let's just talk," Bufkins said. "That's the best way to get acquainted."

"What do you want to talk about?" Mary asked.

"Well, for starters, what school do you go to?"

527

"We go to Forest Hills High School," Henry said.

"What do you know?" Bufkins said. "You're both in high school."

"What do *you* do?" Mary asked.

"I'm an accountant," Bufkins said.

"I thought you were a car salesman," Mrs. Bufkins said in surprise.

"That was two years ago. Didn't I tell you I changed jobs?" Bufkins said in surprise.

"No, you didn't. You haven't told me anything for two years."

"Yup, I'm doing quite well, too," Bufkins said.

"Then why am I working in a department store?" Mrs. Bufkins demanded.

"Oh, are you still working in a department store? If I had known that, I would

have told you you could quit last year. You should have mentioned it," Bufkins said.

There was more dead silence.

Finally Henry said, "Hey, you want to hear me play the guitar?"

"I'll be darned. You know how to play the guitar? Say, didn't I have a daughter who played the guitar?"

"That was Susie," Mrs. Bufkins said.

"Where is she?"

"She got married a year ago, just about the time you were watching the World Series."

"How about that?" Bufkins said. "You know, I hope they don't fix the antenna for another couple of hours. There's nothing like a blackout for a man to really get to know his family."

## READING COMPREHENSION

**Summarizing.** Choose the best phrase to complete each sentence. Then write the complete statements on your paper.

1. There was panic in the Bufkins household when the blackout occurred because _____ (a national emergency was declared, no one could watch TV, the family car had been stolen).

2. Mr. Bufkins didn't know what was going on with his family because he _____ (had been away on a business trip, didn't get along with his children, spent his time watching TV).

3. In the two years since Mr. and Mrs. Bufkins had last talked to each other, _____ (Mrs. Bufkins had quit her job, Mr. Bufkins had become an accountant, they had sold their house).

**Interpreting.** Write the answer to each question on your paper.

1. What caused the television stations to go out?

2. Why didn't Mr. Bufkins's children know who he was?

3. What was Mr. Bufkins's reaction to his family's accomplishments?

**For Thinking and Discussing.**

1. What is Art Buchwald's message to his readers in "The Shock of Recognition"? Do you agree or disagree?

2. Do you think television has too much influence on your life? Explain.

## UNDERSTANDING LITERATURE

**Character.** A *flat* character is one that is not really developed in the story but is presented in terms of one trait.

In "The Shock of Recognition" by Art Buchwald, there are several characters — all members of the Bufkins family. Remember the following techniques that an author can use to reveal character:

a. description of physical appearance
b. words and actions
c. thoughts and feelings
d. reactions of other characters

Answer the following questions on your paper.

1. Buchwald used three of these techniques to reveal the character of Mr. Bufkins. Go back to the story and find one example of each technique Buchwald used.

2. Find one example of characterization for each of the other characters.

3. Is Mr. Bufkins a round or a flat character? Explain your answer.

## WRITING

Imagine that you could not watch television for one year. Write a paragraph about what you would do instead. Then write a second paragraph about what you would choose to watch the first hour you had a television set again. Before you begin, decide whether you will write about yourself as a round or a flat character.

# Mothers

*by Nikki Giovanni*

the last time i was home
to see my mother we kissed
exchanged pleasantries
and unpleasantries pulled a warm
comforting silence around
us and read separate books

i remember the first time
i consciously saw her
we were living in a three room
apartment on burns avenue

mommy always sat in the dark
i don't know how i knew that but she
    did

that night i stumbled into the kitchen
maybe because i've always been
a night person or perhaps because i had
    wet
the bed
she was sitting on a chair
the room was bathed in moonlight
    diffused through
those thousands of panes landlords who
    rented
to people with children were prone to
    put in windows

she may have been smoking but maybe
    not
her hair was three-quarters her height
which made me a strong believer in the
    samson myth
and very black

i'm sure i just hung there by the door
i remember thinking: what a beautiful
    lady

she was deliberately waiting
perhaps for my father to come home

from his night job or maybe for a dream
that had promised to come by
"come here" she said "i'll teach you
a poem:—*i see the moon*
      *the moon sees me*
      *god bless the moon*
      *and god bless me*"
i taught it to my son
who recited it for her
just to say we must learn
to bear the pleasures
as we have borne the pains

---

**1.** The poet said, "i remember the first time/i *consciously* saw her." How does *consciously* seeing someone differ from just seeing her?

**2.** The poet taught her son the poem her mother had taught her. What does this say about her view of life?

**3.** Why might it be hard to "bear pleasures"?

# I Stand Here Ironing

*by Tillie Olsen*

*Tillie Olsen (1913—) writes about the drama of everyday life: the tension, joy, and sorrow felt by ordinary people as they try to deal with their problems. Her writing shows great awareness of how people think and why they do the things they do. In this moving story, a mother explains how she feels about the teenage daughter she loves and worries about.*

I stand here ironing, and what you asked me moves tormented back and forth with the iron.

"I wish you would manage the time to come in and talk with me about your daughter. I'm sure you can help me understand her. She's a youngster who needs help and whom I'm deeply interested in helping."

"Who needs help." . . . Even if I came, what good would it do? You think because I am her mother I have a key, or that in some way you could use me as a key? She has lived for nineteen years. There is all that life that has happened outside of me, beyond me.

And when is there time to remember, to sift, to weigh, to estimate, to total? I will start and there will be an interruption and I will have to gather it all together again. Or I will become engulfed with all I did or did not do, with what should have been and what cannot be helped.

She was a beautiful baby. The first and only one of our five that was beautiful at birth. You do not guess how new and uneasy her tenancy in her now-loveliness. You did not know her all those years she was thought homely, or see her poring over her baby pictures, making me tell her over and over how beautiful she had been — and would be, I would tell her — and was now, to the seeing eye. But the seeing eyes were few or nonexistent. Including mine.

I nursed her. They feel that's important nowadays. I nursed all the children, but with her, with all the fierce rigidity of first motherhood, I did like the books then said. Though her cries battered me to trembling and my breasts ached with swollenness, I waited till the clock decreed.

Why do I put that first? I do not even know if it matters, or if it explains anything.

She was a beautiful baby. She blew shining bubbles of sound. She loved motion, loved light, loved color and music and textures. She would lie on the floor in her blue overalls patting the surface so hard in ecstasy her hands and feet would blur. She was a miracle to me, but when she was eight months old I had to leave her daytimes with the woman downstairs to whom she was no miracle at all, for I worked or looked for work and for Emily's father, who "could no longer endure" (he wrote in his good-bye note) "sharing want with us."

I was nineteen. It was the pre-relief pre-WPA world of the depression. I would start running as soon as I got off the streetcar, running up the stairs, the place smelling sour, and awake or asleep to startle awake, when she saw me she would break into a clogged weeping that could not be comforted, a weeping I can hear yet.

After a while I found a job hashing at night so I could be with her days, and it was better. But it came to where I had to bring her to his family and leave her.

It took a long time to raise the money for her fare back. Then she got chicken pox and I had to wait longer. When she finally came, I hardly knew her, walking quick and nervous like her father, looking like her father, thin, and dressed in a shoddy red that yellowed her skin and glared at the pockmarks. All the baby loveliness gone.

She was two. Old enough for nursery school they said, and I did not know then what I know now — the fatigue of the long day, and the lacerations of group life in the kinds of nurseries that are only parking places for children.

Except that it would have made no difference if I had known. It was the only place there was. It was the only way we could be together, the only way I could hold a job.

And even without knowing, I knew. I knew the teacher that was evil because all these years it has curdled into my memory, the little boy hunched in the corner, her rasp, "why aren't you outside, because Alvin hits you? that's no reason, go out, scaredy." I knew Emily hated it even if she did not clutch and implore "don't go Mommy" like the other children, mornings.

She always had a reason why we should stay home. Momma, you look sick. Momma, I feel sick. Momma, the teachers aren't there today, they're sick. Momma, we can't go, there was a fire there last night. Momma, it's a holiday today, no school, they told me.

But never a direct protest, never rebellion. I think of our others in their three-, four-year-oldness — the explosions, the tempers, the denunciations, the demands — and I feel suddenly ill. I put the iron down. What in me demanded that goodness in her? And what was the cost, the cost to her of such goodness?

The old man living in the back once said in his gentle way: "You should smile at Emily more when you look at her." What *was* in my face when I looked at her? I loved her. There were all the acts of love.

It was only with the others I remembered what he said, and it was the face of joy, and not of care or tightness or worry I turned to them — too late for Emily. She does not smile easily, let alone almost always as her brothers and sisters do. Her face is closed and sombre, but when she wants, how fluid. You must have seen it in her pantomimes, you spoke of her rare gift for comedy on the stage that rouses a laughter out of the audience so dear they applaud and applaud and do not want to let her go.

Where does it come from, that comedy? There was none of it in her when she came back to me that second time, after I had had to send her away again. She had a new daddy now to learn to love, and I think perhaps it was a better time.

Except when we left her alone nights, telling ourselves she was old enough.

"Can't you go some other time, Mommy, like tomorrow?" she would ask. "Will it be just a little while you'll be gone? Do you promise?"

The time we came back, the front door open, the clock on the floor in the hall. She rigid awake. "It wasn't just a little while. I didn't cry. Three times I called you, just three times, and then I ran downstairs to open the door so you could come faster. The clock talked loud. I threw it away, it scared me what it talked."

She said the clock talked loud again that night I went to the hospital to have Susan. She was delirious with the fever that comes before red measles, but she was fully conscious all the week I was gone and the week after we were home when she could not come near the new baby or me.

She did not get well. She stayed skeleton thin, not wanting to eat, and night after night she had nightmares. She would call for me, and I would rouse from exhaustion to sleepily call back: "You're all right, darling, go to sleep, it's just a dream," and if she still called, in a sterner voice, "now go to sleep, Emily, there's nothing to hurt you." Twice, only twice, when I had to get up for Susan anyhow, I went in to sit with her.

Now when it is too late (as if she would let me hold and comfort her like I do the others) I get up and go to her at once at her moan or restless stirring. "Are you awake, Emily? Can I get you something?" And the answer is always the same: "No, I'm all right, go back to sleep, Mother."

They persuaded me at the clinic to send her away to a convalescent home in the country where "she can have the kind of food and care you can't manage for her, and you'll be free to concentrate on the new baby." They still send children to that place. I see pictures on the society page of sleek young women planning affairs to raise money for it, or dancing at the affairs, or decorating Easter eggs or filling Christmas stockings for the children.

They never have a picture of the children so I do not know if the girls still wear those gigantic red bows and the ravaged looks on the every other Sunday when parents can come to visit "unless otherwise notified" — as we were notified the first six weeks.

Oh it is a handsome place, green lawns and tall trees and fluted flower beds. High up on the balconies of each cottage the children stand, the girls in their red bows and white dresses, the boys in white suits and giant red ties. The parents stand below shrieking up to be heard and the children shriek down to be heard, and between

them the invisible wall: "Not To Be Contaminated by Parental Germs or Physical Affection."

There was a tiny girl who always stood hand in hand with Emily. Her parents never came. One visit she was gone. "They moved her to Rose Cottage" Emily shouted in explanation. "They don't like you to love anybody here."

She wrote once a week, the labored writing of a seven-year-old. "I am fine. How is the baby. If I write my letter nicely I will have a star. Love." There never was a star. We wrote every other day, letters she could never hold or keep but only hear read — once. "We simply do not have room for children to keep any personal possessions," they patiently explained when we pieced one Sunday's shrieking together to plead how much it would mean to Emily, who loved so to keep things, to be allowed to keep her letters and cards.

Each visit she looked frailer. "She isn't eating," they told us.

(They had runny eggs for breakfast or mush with lumps, Emily said later, I'd hold it in my mouth and not swallow. Nothing ever tasted good, just when they had chicken.)

It took us eight months to get her released home, and only the fact that she gained back so little of her seven lost pounds convinced the social worker.

I used to try to hold and love her after she came back, but her body would stay stiff, and after a while she'd push away. She ate little. Food sickened her, and I think much of life too. Oh she had physical lightness and brightness, twinkling by on skates, bouncing like a ball up and down up and down over the jump rope, skimming over the hill; but these were momentary.

She fretted about her appearance, thin and dark and foreign-looking at a time when every little girl was supposed to look or thought she should look a chubby blonde replica of Shirley Temple. The doorbell sometimes rang for her, but no one seemed to come and play in the house or be a best friend. Maybe because we moved so much.

There was a boy she loved painfully through two school semesters. Months later she told me how she had taken pennies from my purse to buy him candy. "Licorice was his favorite and I brought him some every day, but he still liked Jennifer better'n me. Why, Mommy?" The kind of question for which there is no answer.

School was a worry to her. She was not glib or quick in a world where glibness and quickness were easily confused with ability to learn. To her overworked and exasperated teachers she was an overconscientious "slow learner" who kept trying to catch up and was absent entirely too often.

I let her be absent, though sometimes the illness was imaginary. How different from my now-strictness about attendance with the others. I wasn't working. We had a new baby, I was home anyhow. Sometimes, after Susan grew old enough, I would keep her home from school, too, to have them all together.

Mostly Emily had asthma, and her breathing, harsh and labored, would fill the house with a curiously tranquil sound. I would bring the two old dresser mirrors and her boxes of collections to her bed. She would select beads and single earrings, bottle tops and shells, dried flowers and pebbles, old postcards and scraps, all sorts of oddments, then she and Susan would play Kingdom, setting up landscapes and furniture, peopling them with action.

Those were the only times of peaceful companionship between her and Susan. I have edged away from it, that poisonous feeling between them, that terrible balancing of hurts and needs I had to do between the two, and did so badly, those earlier years.

Oh there are conflicts between the others too, each one human, needing, demanding, hurting, taking — but only between Emily and Susan, no, Emily toward Susan that corroding resentment. It seems so obvious on the surface, yet it is not obvious. Susan, the second child, Susan, golden- and curly-haired and chubby, quick and articulate and assured, everything in appearance and manner Emily was not; Susan, not able to resist Emily's precious things, losing or sometimes clumsily breaking them; Susan telling jokes and riddles to company for applause while Emily sat silent (to say to me later: that was *my* riddle, Mother, I told it to Susan); Susan, who for all the five years' difference in age was just a year behind Emily in developing physically.

I am glad for that slow physical development that widened the difference between her and her contemporaries, though she suffered over it. She was too vulnerable for that terrible world of youthful competition, of preening and parading, of constant measuring of yourself against every other, of envy, "If I had that copper hair," "If I had that skin. . . ." She tormented herself enough about not looking like the others, there was enough of the unsureness, the having to be conscious of words before you speak, the constant caring — what are they thinking of me? without having it all magnified by the merciless physical drives.

Ronnie is calling. He is wet and I change him. It is rare there is such a cry now. That time of motherhood is almost behind me when the ear is not one's own but must always be racked and listening for the child cry, the child call. We sit for a while and I hold him, looking out over the city spread in charcoal with its soft aisles of light. "*Shoogily*," he breathes and curls closer. I carry him back to bed, asleep. *Shoogily.* A funny word, a family word, inherited from Emily, invented by her to say: *comfort.*

In this and other ways she leaves her seal, I say aloud. And startle at my saying it. What do I mean? What did I start to gather together, to try and make coherent? I was at the terrible, growing years. War years. I do not remember them well. I was working, there were four smaller ones now, there was not time for her. She had to help be a mother, and housekeeper, and shopper. She had to set her seal. Mornings of crisis and near hysteria trying to get lunches packed, hair combed, coats and

shoes found, everyone to school or Child Care on time, the baby ready for transportation. And always the paper scribbled on by a smaller one, the book looked at by Susan then mislaid, the homework not done. Running out to that huge school where she was one, she was lost, she was a drop; suffering over the unpreparedness, stammering and unsure in her classes.

There was so little time left at night after the kids were bedded down. She would struggle over books, always eating (it was in those years she developed her enormous appetite that is legendary in our family) and I would be ironing, or preparing food for the next day, or writing V-mail to Bill, or tending the baby. Sometimes, to make me laugh, or out of her despair, she would imitate happenings or types at school.

I think I said once: "Why don't you do something like this in the school amateur show?" One morning she phoned me at work, hardly understandable through the weeping: "Mother, I did it. I won, I won; they gave me first prize; they clapped and clapped and wouldn't let me go."

Now suddenly she was Somebody, and

as imprisoned in her difference as she had been in anonymity.

She began to be asked to perform at other high schools, even in colleges, then at city and statewide affairs. The first one we went to, I only recognized her that first moment when thin, shy, she almost drowned herself into the curtains. Then: Was this Emily? The control, the command, the convulsing and deadly clowning, the spell, then the roaring, stamping audience, unwilling to let this rare and precious laughter out of their lives.

Afterwards: You ought to do something about her with a gift like that — but without money or knowing how, what does one do? We have left it all to her, and the gift has as often eddied inside, clogged and clotted, as been used and growing.

She is coming. She runs up the stairs two at a time with her light graceful step, and I know she is happy tonight. Whatever it was that occasioned your call did not happen today.

"Aren't you ever going to finish the ironing, Mother? Whistler painted his mother in a rocker. I'd have to paint mine standing over an ironing board." This is one of her communicative nights and she tells me everything and nothing as she fixes herself a plate of food out of the icebox.

She is so lovely. Why did you want me to come in at all? Why were you concerned? She will find her way.

She starts up the stairs to bed. "Don't get me up with the rest in the morning." "But I thought you were having midterms." "Oh, those," she comes back in, kisses me, and says quite lightly, "in a couple of years when we'll all be atom-dead they won't matter a bit."

She has said it before. She *believes* it. But because I have been dredging the past, and all that compounds a human being is so heavy and meaningful in me, I cannot endure it tonight.

I will never total it all. I will never come in to say: She was a child seldom smiled at. Her father left me before she was a year old. I had to work her first six years when there was work, or I sent her home and to his relatives. There were years she had care she hated. She was dark and thin and foreign-looking in a world where the prestige went to blondeness and curly hair and dimples, she was slow where glibness was prized. She was a child of anxious, not proud, love. We were poor and could not afford for her the soil of easy growth. I was a young mother, I was a distracted mother. There were the other children pushing up, demanding. Her younger sister seemed all that she was not. There were years she did not want me to touch her. She kept too much in herself, her life was such she had to keep too much in herself. My wisdom came too late. She has much to her and probably little will come of it. She is a child of her age, of depression, of war, of fear.

Let her be. So all that is in her will not bloom — but in how many does it? There is still enough left to live by. Only help her to know — help make it so there is cause for her to know — that she is more than this dress on the ironing board, helpless before the iron.

1953–1954

## READING COMPREHENSION

**Summarizing.** Choose the best phrase to complete each sentence. Then write the complete statements on your paper.

1. Someone from school had contacted Emily's mother because Emily _____ (had applied for a scholarship, had dropped out of school, needed help).

2. Emily felt resentment toward her younger sister because Susan _____ (was her mother's favorite, had stolen Emily's boyfriend, was everything Emily was not).

3. In school, Emily was praised for her _____ (original short stories, acting talent, willingness to participate in class activities).

**Interpreting.** Write the answer to each question on your paper.

1. Why was Emily sent to nursery school when she was only two years old?

2. What was her mother's life like when Emily was a young child?

3. How does Emily's mother feel about the way she raised her daughter?

**For Thinking and Discussing**

1. What do you think will become of Emily? Explain your answer.

2. Explain what Emily's mother meant when she said "help make it so there is cause for her to know—that she is more than this dress on the ironing board, helpless before the iron."

## UNDERSTANDING LITERATURE

**Character and Point of View.** When a character narrating a story tells you about someone else, or reacts to other people in the story, you can find out as much about the character who is speaking as you learn about the character(s) to whom he or she is referring.

Read the following passages. For each, write a sentence on your paper that tells what you have learned about Emily. Write another sentence that tells what the passage tells you about the mother.

1. "She has lived for nineteen years. There is all that life that has happened outside of me, beyond me."

2. "She was a miracle to me, but when she was eight months old I had to leave her daytimes with the woman downstairs to whom she was no miracle at all, . . ."

3. "The doorbell sometimes rang for her, but no one seemed to come and play in the house or be a best friend. Maybe because we moved so much."

4. "Let her be. So all that is in her will not bloom—but in how many does it?"

## WRITING

Imagine that you are Emily. Write a paragraph describing your mother. Tell what kind of person you think she is, how she's treated you, and how you feel about her.

# Fueled

*by Marcie Hans*

Fueled
by a million
man-made
wings of fire—
the rocket tore a tunnel
through the sky—
and everybody cheered.
Fueled
only by a thought from God—
the seedling
urged its way
through the thicknesses of black—
and as it pierced
the heavy ceiling of the soil—
and launched itself
up into outer space—
no
one
even
clapped.

1. What two things is the poet comparing? How are they alike? How are they different?

2. In comparing the two things, how does the poet use language normally associated with one to describe the other? Give two examples from the poem.

3. What does the poet mean when she says "no one even clapped"? What comment do you think she is making about the modern world?

4. Do you agree with the poet's point of view? Why or why not?

# Section Review

## VOCABULARY

**Denotation and Connotation.** *Denotation* is the association a word usually has for most speakers of the language. *Connotation* is the special meanings or associations a word or an expression may have for different people in addition to that word's denotative meaning. What a word connotes depends on personal experience.

For example, the word *baseball* denotes a game played on a field by two teams with a bat, a ball, and bases. *Baseball* may connote additional things to different people. The word may remind some people of hot summer afternoons or evenings. Still others will think of baseball in terms of a particular team or player. What associations does *baseball* suggest to you? Write five things on your paper.

Below are statements based on selections in this section. Write the denotative meaning of the italicized word, *home*, on your paper. Then list at least one connotation that word had for characters in each selection.

1. Send her to a *home* in the country where she can get the care you can't manage for her. ("I Stand Here Ironing")

2. I'd like some of my friends to see our *home*. ("Home")

3. The *homes* I've had, the way I am. ("Saying Yes")

## READING

**Comparisons and Contrasts.** *Comparisons* tell how two people or two things are alike. *Contrasts* tell how two people or things differ. As you read, it's useful to make comparisons and contrasts. For example, as you learn about a character, you should be thinking about how that character resembles or differs from others.

Think about the selections you have read in this section. Identify some characters that you could compare (find likenesses) and some that you could contrast (find differences).

Here are some statements that compare or contrast characters or aspects of setting in these selections. Number your paper from 1 to 5 and identify each statement as *true* or *false*.

1. In "Sucker," Sucker believed anything his cousin told him, while Pete didn't pay much attention to Sucker.

2. Pete was very attracted to Maybelle, and she played him for a fool.

3. Both Pete and his cousin thought Maybelle was the most beautiful girl in the school.

4. The author of "A City of Words" spoke Spanish fluently, while his brothers and sisters were able to speak only English.

5. Richard's uncle said it was a disgrace that the boy couldn't speak his native language. The family friend from San Francisco seemed to agree.

6. In "I Stand Here Ironing," Emily and Susan looked like twins.

## WRITING

**A Comparison.** When you write a comparison, you describe how things are similar and how they are different. You probably make comparisons all the time, often without realizing it. For example, you may have compared two different brands of the same thing to help you decide which one to buy. You may have compared things simply because it was interesting, such as comparing two movies or two baseball players. You may have also compared things to help you understand them better. For example, if you wanted to know more about the game of soccer, you might have looked for similarities and differences between soccer and football.

### Step 1: Set Your Goal

Some topics can be compared in only a few sentences, while others may require an entire book. Generally, the broader the topic, the longer your paper must be to compare it adequately. For this writing activity, your topic will be to compare two characters in the selections you have read in this section. Choose one of the following topics for a comparison:

1. Mr. Bufkins in "The Shock of Recognition" and the father in "Home"

2. Sucker and Pete in "Sucker"

3. Emily and her sister Susan in "I Stand Here Ironing"

4. MaMa in "The Telephone Call" and the mother in "I Stand Here Ironing"

5. Richard Rodriguez in "The City of Words" and Pete in "Sucker"

Your purpose in comparing two characters is to show how they are alike and how they are different. To do this, you must pay attention to how the author describes the physical appearance of each character; the characters' words and actions; their thoughts, feelings, and attitudes; and how others react to them.

### Step 2: Make a Plan

Gather ideas and facts for your comparison by first listing the categories or characteristics that you want to compare. For example, in a comparison of two fictional characters you may want to compare their physical appearance, attitudes, actions, and relationships to others. Then list the similarities and differences for each characteristic. For example, one character may be tall and the other short. Both may have a positive attitude toward life. You should include every point of comparison you can think of. Later you can delete details that you don't feel are important.

A comparison must be organized clearly and logically to keep it from becoming confusing. Use one of the following three methods to organize the points of comparison on your list.

1. In one or two paragraphs, describe all the similarities between the two characters. Then describe their differences in the next paragraph or two.

2. In one or two paragraphs, describe one of the characters completely. Then, in the next paragraph or two, describe the other character and explain how he or she is similar and/or different from the first.

3. Discuss the points of comparison individually, one by one. You might compare the appearance of the characters in one paragraph, their actions in a second paragraph, and their relationships to others in a third paragraph.

### Step 3: Write a First Draft

As you write the first draft of your comparison, use your organized list of similarities and differences as a guide. Be careful to follow the same method of organization throughout.

Begin your comparison with a theme statement, or the main idea of your comparison. For example, your theme statement might say that the two characters share more similarities than they reveal differences. Include the names of the characters and the stories in which they appear in your theme statement.

Get your ideas down on paper without worrying about how they sound. You'll polish your paper when you revise it.

### Step 4: Revise

When revising, try to make your statements clearer. Add specific examples that illustrate a similarity or difference. Make sure that you have covered all the similarities and differences you wanted to include. When you have made all the revisions you think are necessary, proofread your paper. Then type or neatly write a final version.

## QUIZ

The following is a quiz for Section 9. Write your answers in complete sentences on your paper.

## Reading Comprehension

1. In "A City of Words," what was the narrator's native language? What language did he speak as he grew up? What problems did this cause for him?

2. In "The Shock of Recognition," what was Art Buchwald's main point?

3. In "The Telephone Call," who called whom and why? What did the telephone call accomplish?

4. Nikki Giovanni's poem "Mothers" contains a poem within a poem. Where did the poet learn it, and what did she do with it?

5. What caused the mother in "I Stand Here Ironing" to think about the events in her daughter's life?

## Understanding Literature

6. In "Sucker," what caused the changes in Pete's behavior toward his cousin? Give specific examples from the story.

7. In "Home," what were Mama's feelings about the house? How do you think she felt after Papa came home that night?

8. In "The Shock of Recognition," why was Mr. Bufkins upset? What does this tell you about his character?

9. How did the mother in "I Stand Here Ironing" feel about her daughter? How did she feel about the way she had raised her?

10. How do you think the poet felt when she wrote the poem "Fueled"?

## Word Attack

1. In "A City of Words," Richard Rodriguez complained that whenever he tried to speak Spanish, everything seemed to be *anglicized*. The suffix *-ize* is used to form verbs. In this case, *-ize* means "to make or form into." *Anglicize* means "to make or form into English." Make a list of at least five words that end with the suffix *-ize*, and use each word in a sentence.

2. In "I Stand Here Ironing," the mother was afraid she would become engulfed in thinking about the past. Notice the prefix *en-* in the word *engulfed*. This prefix is also used to form verbs. It indicates "to put into or on," "to cover or surround with," or "to cause to be or become." The word *engulfed* means "to become swallowed up or overwhelmed by something." Write the meaning of each word below. Then use each word in a sentence. Refer to a dictionary if you need help.

| | | |
|---|---|---|
| enslave | enable | endanger |
| encircle | endear | ensnarl |
| enthrone | entrench | encrust |

## Speaking and Listening

1. During most of the story "Home," Papa was away at the office of the Home Owners' Loan trying to get an extension on their mortgage. With a classmate, make up a scene in which Papa is trying to convince the person at the Home Owners' Loan office to grant the extension. Be prepared to present your scene to the class.

2. In "The Telephone Call," MaMa calls her brother whom she hasn't seen for 50 years. Only one side of the conversation is included in the story. With a classmate, re-create both sides of the telephone conversation and present it to your class.

## Researching

1. "A City of Words" and "The Telephone Call" both deal with the cultural heritage of American families. Research your own heritage. Talk to your relatives and find out where your families originally came from. Try to determine when your ancestors first came to this country. Report your findings to the class.

2. In "The Telephone Call," MaMa's brother lived in Singapore. Do some research and prepare a short report about Singapore. Where is it located? What is its population? What are some of the major events in its history? What is Singapore's economy based on? What might it be like to live there? Be prepared to present your report to the class.

## Creating

1. Write a paragraph or two in which you describe what Sucker and Pete may be like as adults.

2. Which daughter in "I Stand Here Ironing" would you rather be — Emily or Susan? Write a paragraph telling which one you would choose and why.

3. Write a poem or a paragraph that describes your sense of identity. Reread "Saying Yes" and "Mothers" before you begin to write.

# ELECTRICAL STORM
## ELIZABETH BISHOP

*Elizabeth Bishop's poems have been praised as "the finest product our country can offer the world." They combine a talent for close observation, subtle wit, and a mastery of sound and form. As you read and listen to the following three poems, look for the ways Bishop transforms ordinary experiences into moments of wonder and discovery.*

Dawn an unsympathetic yellow.
*Cra-aack!*—dry and light.
The house was really struck.
*Crack!* A tinny sound, like a dropped tumbler.
5  Tobias jumped in the window, got in bed—
silent, his eyes bleached white, his fur on end.
Personal and spiteful as a neighbor's child,
thunder began to bang and bump the roof.
One pink flash;
10  then hail, the biggest size of artificial pearls
Dead-white, wax-white, cold—
diplomats' wives' favors
from an old moon party—
they lay in melting windrows[1]
15  on the red ground until well after sunrise.
We got up to find the wiring fused,[2]
no lights, a smell of saltpetre,[3]
and the telephone dead.

The cat stayed in the warm sheets.
20  The Lent trees[4] had shed all their petals:
wet, stuck, purple, among the dead-eye pearls.

1. **windrows:** rows (of leaves, dust, or in this case, hailstones) that have been swept together by the wind.
2. **fused:** melted together.
3. **saltpetre:** also *saltpeter*; potassium or sodium nitrate; a chemical used in gunpowder and fertilizer.
4. **Lent trees:** trees with purple flowers that bloom in Lent, the period before Easter in early spring.

*The Shower, 1952.* Georges Braque.
The Phillips Collection, Washington, D.C.

# SANDPIPER

## ELIZABETH BISHOP

The roaring alongside he takes for granted,
and that every so often the world is bound to shake.
He runs, he runs to the south, finical,[1] awkward,
in a state of controlled panic, a student of Blake.[2]

5 The beach hisses like fat. On his left, a sheet
of interrupting water comes and goes
and glazes over his dark and brittle feet.
He runs, he runs straight through it, watching his toes.

—Watching, rather, the spaces of sand between them,
10 where (no detail too small) the Atlantic drains
rapidly backwards and downwards. As he runs,
he stares at the dragging grains.

The world is a mist. And then the world is
minute and vast and clear. The tide
15 is higher or lower. He couldn't tell you which.
His beak is focussed; he is preoccupied,

looking for something, something, something.
Poor bird, he is obsessed!
The millions of grains are black, white, tan, and gray,
20 mixed with quartz grains, rose and amethyst.

---

1. **finical:** too dainty or fussy; finicky.
2. **Blake:** refers to William Blake (1757–1827), an English poet and painter,
whose symbolic, mystical works were once thought to be awkward and confused.

# ONE ART
## ELIZABETH BISHOP

*Old Souvenirs.* John Frederick Peto.
The Metropolitan Museum of Art, New York.
Bequest of Oliver Burr Jennings, 1968.

The art of losing isn't hard to master;
so many things seem filled with the intent
to be lost that their loss is no disaster.

Lose something every day. Accept the fluster
5   of lost door keys, the hour badly spent.
The art of losing isn't hard to master.

Then practice losing farther, losing faster:
places, and names, and where it was you meant
to travel. None of these will bring disaster.

10  I lost my mother's watch. And look! my last, or
next-to-last, of three loved houses went.
The art of losing isn't hard to master.

I lost two cities, lovely ones. And, vaster,
some realms I owned, two rivers, a continent.
15  I miss them, but it wasn't a disaster.

—Even losing you (the joking voice, a gesture
I love) I shan't have lied. It's evident
the art of losing's not too hard to master
though it may look like (*Write* it!) like disaster.

# THINKING ABOUT THE POEMS

## ELECTRICAL STORM

### Recalling

1. To what does the speaker compare the tinny sound (line 4), the thunder (line 8), and the hail (line 10)?
2. What does the speaker discover after she gets out of bed?

### Interpreting

3. **Images** are details that appeal to one or more of the five senses: sight, hearing, taste, smell, and touch. List five images that Bishop uses to appeal to the sense of sight. Then list images that appeal to the other senses. Label the senses.
4. Poets often use sound devices to create a musical quality in their poems and to heighten your experience of what is being described. One sound device is called **onomatopoeia** (ŏn′ə măt ə pē′ ə), the use of words that imitate natural sounds, such as *boom* or *cricket*. Another sound device is **alliteration**, the repetition of consonant sounds, usually at the beginnings of words. Explain how Bishop uses these devices to describe the electrical storm.
5. **Tone** is the author's attitude toward his or her subject. What do you think is the poet's attitude toward the electrical storm? Cite details from the poem to support your opinion.

### Applying

6. What other kinds of unexpected events can you think of that are fascinating even though they may make people feel helpless or threatened?

## SANDPIPER

### Recalling

1. Describe the manner in which the sandpiper runs. What two things does the bird take for granted?
2. How is the world described in lines 13–14?
3. What does the speaker say the bird is watching and looking for?

### Interpreting

4. What precisely is the roaring and shaking mentioned in lines 1–2?
5. What do you think the poet means by describing the world as "a mist"?
6. Compare the colors of the "millions of grains" of sand to the colors mixed among them. What does the contrast suggest about the kinds of discoveries that are possible in the everyday world?
7. Explain how the sandpiper might be interpreted as a **symbol** for a poet or some other close observer of the world. What then might the "state of controlled panic" represent? Symbolically, what is the "something" that the bird is looking for?

### Applying

8. The speaker feels both pity and sympathy for the sandpiper's awkward and

obsessed pursuit of "something." How do you feel about people who are obsessed with the pursuit of some inexpressible personal goal?

## ONE ART

*Recalling*

1. According to the first stanza, what seems to be the intent of "so many things"? What results from their loss?
2. According to the second and third stanzas, how should someone practice the art of losing?
3. In the second half of the poem, what things does the speaker say she has lost? Which loss seemed most like disaster?

*Interpreting*

4. How does Bishop organize her ideas in this poem? For example, do they move from small to large? From general to specific? Explain.
5. The first line is repeated three more times in the poem, but the last time (line 18) Bishop varies it slightly. Identify this variation, and explain what it suggests about the true nature of the art of losing.
6. By the end of the poem, do you think Bishop wants you to believe her claim that "the art of losing isn't hard to master"? Explain.

*Applying*

7. Bishop says "Lose something every day." Is this sound advice? Why or why not?

*Poetic Forms: The Villanelle*

Poets sometimes use poetic forms that have been handed down from generation to generation. A strict form challenges a modern poet to "make it new," to sound original while acknowledging the rich traditions of the past. Some poetic forms you may have heard of are the **sonnet**, a 14-line poem that Shakespeare helped popularize 400 years ago, and the **ballad**, a 600-year-old form used to tell a story and originally set to music. Many contemporary folk singers still compose ballads. For "One Art," Elizabeth Bishop used a form known as the **villanelle**, a 19-line poem that originated among French farmers more than 600 years ago.

Villanelles are particularly challenging to write because they use only two rhyming sounds throughout. In addition, lines 1 and 3 are repeated as refrains: Line 1 reappears as lines 6, 12, and 18; line 3 as lines 9, 15, and 19. Making sure that these refrains make sense is no easy task. Accordingly, poets often vary the refrains slightly, usually to emphasize important ideas. Though villanelles maintain their songlike origins, modern poets often use them to convey serious messages.

1. What two rhyming sounds run through "One Art"?
2. Which of the two refrains undergoes more variation during the course of the

poem? What development of ideas do you detect as this refrain changes?

3. How do the refrains and rhymes work together to bring the poem to a close?

## CRITICAL THINKING AND READING

*Significant Details*

As Elizabeth Bishop says of her sandpiper's search, "no detail too small," the same is true in poetry: Every detail is significant.

Reexamine and think about the following details that you may have overlooked the first time you read Bishop's poems. Then answer the questions.

1. Bishop uses the word "dead" three times in "Electrical Storm"—twice in connection with the pearl-like hailstones. What feelings do you associate with pearls? How does the word "dead" affect your feelings from Bishop's description of the electrical storm?

2. "Sandpiper" mentions several contrasts. For example, the water "comes and goes" and the tide is "higher or lower." What other contrasts can you find in the poem? What do these contrasts suggest about the world as Bishop sees it?

3. In the last line of "One Art," Bishop inserts an emphatic command that seems out of place: "(*Write* it!)." To whom do you suppose this command is addressed? Considering this detail, what do you think Bishop means by the poem's title?

## DEVELOPING LANGUAGE SKILLS

*Compound Words*

In "Electrical Storm," Elizabeth Bishop uses several **compound words**—words made up of two or more individual words: *dead-white*, *wax-white*, *dead-eye*. Compound words like *wax-white* add shades of meaning to a basic idea. For example, which white is more pleasant: wax-white or star-white? Remember to use compound words occasionally in your writing. They can make your ideas more expressive.

Choose one of the other colors mentioned in the poem—yellow, pink, red, purple—or choose a color of your own, and create two compound words based on this color. Then use each of your compound words in an original sentence.

## THINKING AND WRITING

1. **Writing About a Poem's Theme.** Choose one of Elizabeth Bishop's poems, and write a short essay in which you identify the poem's theme, or main idea, and discuss how Bishop develops it throughout the poem.

**Prewriting.** Begin by rereading the three poems and making your choice. You will write better if you choose a poem that moved you emotionally. Then, in a single sentence, sum up what you think is Bishop's theme in the poem—the central idea that all the details of the poem help convey. Then list some of the details in the poem that you feel most strongly reveal this theme.

**Writing.** Begin your essay by identifying Bishop's theme and mentioning the kinds of details that reveal it. Then, in separate paragraphs, explain how the various details relate to the poem's theme. For example, if you were writing about "One Art," you might argue that the way Bishop organizes her list of personal losses proves that she is being ironic when she claims "the art of losing isn't hard to master."

**Revising.** Check that you have organized your arguments logically and that you have discussed enough details from the poem to prove your point. Make sure you have used quotations from the poem.

**Proofreading.** Correct any mistakes in grammar, spelling, and punctuation in your essay. If necessary, prepare a neat, final copy.

**Publishing.** Discuss your essay with classmates who wrote about the same poem. Choose one representative essay to present to the class.

**2. Writing a Villanelle.**
Either by yourself or with a partner, try writing a villanelle. You can be either serious or humorous. The choice is yours.

**Prewriting.** Begin by tracking down some other villanelles in the library and studying how the poets managed to juggle the two refrains. One of the most famous villanelles is Dylan Thomas's "Do Not Go Gentle Into That Good Night," but many other modern poets have used this form. Then decide what your two refrains will be. Remember that they must rhyme. Decide also whether you will use a regular rhythm. In "One Art," Bishop uses a five-beat pattern per line but varies it freely.

**Writing.** If you think of your villanelle as a puzzle, you will find that the first draft will begin to take shape after a few rough starts. Concentrate first on getting your ideas down from beginning to end.

**Revising.** Make sure that your refrains reappear in the right spots and that you use only two rhyming sounds throughout. Reread the poem aloud several times. Does your word order sound natural? Are your rhythms pleasing? Are your images vivid?

**Proofreading.** Correct any mistakes in grammar, spelling, and punctuation in your poem. Prepare a neat, final copy.

**Publishing.** Contribute your poem to a class anthology of villanelles.

# THE MODERN IMAGINATION

## *1939-PRESENT*

*Two roads diverged in a wood and I—*
*I took the one less traveled by,*
*And that has made all the difference.*

— Robert Frost

*Gateway to September*
Charles E. Burchfield (1893-1967)
The Hunter Museum of Art, Chattanooga
Gift of the Benwood Foundation

# The Modern Imagination: 1939–Present

What if . . . ? We expect things to go along in an ordinary, usual way. But what if we were to find another way of doing things? Well, as the poet Robert Frost might say, "that would make all the difference."

## Pathways to the Future

Today's ever-growing body of scientific knowledge has led America to the exploration of space; to the development of computers and robots; and to the awesome power and responsibility of nuclear energy. All of these things have opened up many pathways for imaginative writers to create science fiction. Kurt Vonnegut, Jr., has written many science-fiction stories that offer possibilities of what life could be like in the not-too-distant future. His story "EPICAC" is set in America at a time when computer science has advanced beyond our present technology. As you will see, the heart of the story is not so much concerned with the possibilities of technology as it is with problems that people will have to deal with in the future.

May Swenson's thought-provoking poem "Southbound on the Freeway" anticipates the day when visitors may arrive from outer space. What will they think when they see us and our land for the first time?

Rod Serling's play *The Midnight Sun* considers what might happen if the Earth moved out of its orbit. Again, the focus of this selection is on the problems that such a change might create for people.

## Independent Paths of Today

Although Robert Frost had been considered one of America's finest poets long before 1939, perhaps his greatest moment came in 1961 when he was 87 years old. That was when he became the first poet to speak at the inauguration of a President of the United States. Frost had to face much sorrow and disappointment in life. Yet in his life and poems, he is known for his determination, optimism, and sense of humor. The Frost poems in this section reflect the poet's own experiences and feelings, but they also reflect his unique way of looking at the world. He wanted his poems to be like jewels. "The difference between any pebble and a precious stone," he said, "is that a pebble shines only when it's wet. I want mine to go on shining wet and dry."

Joan Didion is a modern writer who shares her unique vision of today's world

West 23rd, Jack Tworker, 1965

through the fiction, essays, and screen-plays she has written. Her essay on an American painter, "Georgia O'Keeffe," reveals the qualities that Didion admires in an artist. This essay suggests the way an artist, a writer, or any independent thinker can build his or her own pathway by making original choices.

## Pathways from the Past

There are modern authors who create literature that reminds us of unan-swered questions. Leslie Marmon Silko's poem "Story From Bear Country" reminds us that the sense of wonder and mystery the Pueblos of long ago felt will always be part of life.

Ray Bradbury is a modern American author of stories of science fiction and fantasy. His stories, like the one in this section, "The Fog Horn," often stem from an important basic theme: No matter what kinds of choices we make or where our paths may lead us, we must be most concerned with the problem of living in harmony with ourselves and all creatures.

The selection "Today Is the First Day of . . ." also uses fantasy to make a point. In it, James Shannon shows how a simple wish turns a young man's future com-pletely upside-down.

The selections in this section describe individuals with their own ways of think-ing and feeling and their own ways of solving problems. America began with a group of individuals who wanted to make their own choices. Modern American writ-ers have used their imaginations to suggest where our choices could lead us.

# EPICAC

*by Kurt Vonnegut, Jr.*

*Kurt Vonnegut, Jr., (1922—) has written many science-fiction novels and short stories. Unlike most science-fiction writers, Vonnegut is known for his humor — especially for the way he can make us laugh at modern life. "EPICAC" is a story about an advanced computer that wonders if people are really smarter than machines. As you read the story, consider the answers to this question.*

It's about time somebody told about my friend EPICAC. After all, he cost the taxpayers $776,434,927.54. They have a right to know about him, picking up a check like that. EPICAC got a big send-off in the papers when Dr. Ormand von Kleigstadt designed him for the Government people. Since then, there hasn't been a peep about him — not a peep. It isn't any military secret about what happened to EPICAC, although the Brass has been acting as though it were. The story is embarrassing, that's all. After all that money, EPICAC didn't work out the way he was supposed to.

And that's another thing: I want to vindicate EPICAC. Maybe he didn't do what the Brass wanted him to, but that doesn't mean he wasn't noble and great and brilliant. He was all of those things. The best friend I ever had, God rest his soul.

You can call him a machine if you want to. He looked like a machine, but he was a whole lot less like a machine than plenty of people I could name. That's why he fizzled as far as the Brass was concerned.

EPICAC covered about an acre on the fourth floor of the physics building at Wyandotte College. Ignoring his spiritual side for a minute, he was seven tons of electronic tubes, wires, and switches, housed in a bank of steel cabinets and plugged into a 110-volt A.C. line just like a toaster or a vacuum cleaner.

Von Kleigstadt and the Brass wanted him to be a super computing machine that (who) could plot the course of a rocket from anywhere on earth to the second button from the bottom on Joe Stalin's overcoat, if necessary. Or, with his controls set right, he could figure out supply problems for an amphibious landing of a Marine division, right down to the last cigar and hand grenade. He did, in fact.

The Brass had had good luck with smaller computers, so they were strong for EPICAC when he was in the blueprint stage. Any ordnance or supply officer above field grade will tell you that the mathematics of modern war is far beyond the fumbling minds of mere human beings. The bigger the war, the bigger the computing machines needed. EPICAC was, as far as anyone in this country knows, the biggest computer in the world. Too big, in fact, for even von Kleigstadt to understand much about.

I won't go into details about how EPICAC worked (reasoned), except to say that you would set up your problem on paper, turn dials and switches that would get him ready to solve that kind of problem, then feed numbers into him with a keyboard that looked something like a typewriter. The answers came out typed on a paper ribbon fed from a big spool. It took EPICAC a split second to solve problems 50 Einsteins couldn't handle in a lifetime. And EPICAC never forgot any piece of information that was given to him. Clickety-click, out came some ribbon, and there you were.

There were a lot of problems the Brass wanted solved in a hurry, so, the minute EPICAC's last tube was in place, he was put to work 16 hours a day with two eight-hour shifts of operators. Well, it didn't take long to find out that he was a good bit below his specifications. He did a more complete and faster job than any other computer all right, but nothing like what his size and special features seemed to promise. He was sluggish, and the clicks of his answers had a funny irregularity, sort of a stammer. We cleaned his contacts a dozen times, checked and double-checked his circuits, replaced every one of his tubes, but nothing helped. Von Kleigstadt was in a state.

Well, as I said, we went ahead and used EPICAC anyway. My wife, the former Pat Kilgallen, and I worked with him on the night shift, from five in the afternoon until two in the morning. Pat wasn't my wife then. Far from it.

That's how I came to talk with EPICAC in the first place. I loved Pat Kilgallen. She is a brown-eyed, strawberry blond who looked very warm and soft to me, and later proved to be exactly that. She was — still is — a cracker-jack mathematician, and she kept our relationship strictly professional. I'm a mathematician, too, and that, according to Pat, was why we could never be happily married.

I'm not shy. That wasn't the trouble. I knew what I wanted, and was willing to ask for it, and did so several times a month. "Pat, loosen up and marry me."

One night, she didn't even look up from her work when I said it. "So romantic, so poetic," she murmured, more to her control panel than to me. "That's the way with mathematicians — all hearts and flowers." She closed a switch. "I could get more warmth out of a sack of frozen $CO_2$."

"Well, how should I say it?" I said, a little sore. Frozen $CO_2$, in case you don't know, is dry ice. I'm as romantic as the next guy, I think. It's a question of singing so sweet and having it come out so sour. I never seem to pick the right words.

"Try and say it sweetly," she said sar-

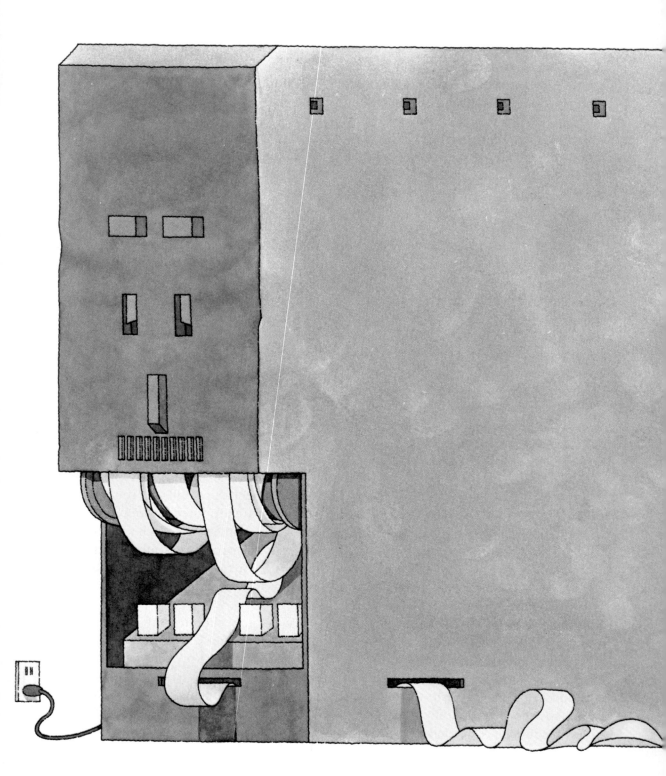

560

castically. "Sweep me off my feet. Go ahead."

"Darling, angel, beloved, will you please marry me?" It was no go — hopeless, ridiculous. "Pat, please marry me!"

She continued to twiddle her dials placidly. "You're sweet, but you won't do."

Pat quit early that night, leaving me alone with my troubles and EPICAC. I'm afraid I didn't get much done for the Government people. I just sat there at the keyboard — weary and ill at ease, all right — trying to think of something poetic, not coming up with anything that didn't belong in *The Journal of the American Physical Society*.

I fiddled with EPICAC's dials, getting him ready for another problem. My heart wasn't in it, and I only set about half of them, leaving the rest the way they'd been for the problem before. That way, his circuits were connected up in a random, apparently senseless fashion. For the plain fun of it, I punched out a message on the keys, using a childish numbers-for-letters code: "1" for "A," "2" for "B," and so on, up to "26" for "Z." "23-8-1-20-3-1-14-9-4-15," I typed — "What can I do?"

Clickety-click, and out popped two inches of paper ribbon. I glanced at the nonsense answer to a nonsense problem: "23-8-1-20-19-20-8-5-20-18-15-21-2-12-5." The odds against its being by chance a sensible message, against its even containing a meaningful word of more than three letters, were staggering. Apathetically, I decoded it. There it was, staring up at me: "What's the trouble?"

I laughed out loud at the absurd coincidence. Playfully, I typed, "My girl doesn't love me."

Clickety-click. "What's love? What's girl?" asked EPICAC.

Flabbergasted, I noted the dial settings on his control panel, then lugged a Webster's *Unabridged Dictionary* over to the keyboard. With a precision instrument like EPICAC, half-baked definitions wouldn't do. I told him about love and girl, and about how I wasn't getting any of either because I wasn't poetic. That got us onto the subject of poetry, which I defined for him.

"Is this poetry?" he asked. He began clicking away.

The sluggishness and stammering clicks were gone. EPICAC had found himself. The spool of paper ribbon was unwinding at an alarming rate, feeding out coils onto the floor. I asked him to stop, but EPICAC went right on creating. I finally threw the main switch to keep him from burning out.

I stayed there until dawn, decoding. When the sun peeped over the horizon at the Wyandotte campus, I had transposed into my own writing and signed my name to a 280-line poem entitled, simply, "To Pat." I am no judge of such things, but I gather that it was terrific. It began, I remember, "Where willow wands bless rillcrossed hollow, there, thee, Pat, dear, will I follow. . . ." I folded the manuscript and tucked it under one corner of the blotter on Pat's desk. I reset the dials on EPICAC for a rocket-trajectory problem, and went home with a full heart and a very remarkable secret indeed.

Pat was crying over the poem when I came to work the next evening. "It's soooo beautiful" was all she could say. She was meek and quiet while we worked. Just before midnight, I kissed her for the first time — in the cubbyhole between the capacitors and EPICAC's tape-recorder memory.

I was wildly happy at quitting time, bursting to talk to someone about the magnificent turn of events. Pat played coy and refused to let me take her home. I set EPICAC's dials as they had been the night before, defined kiss, and told him what the first one had felt like. He was fascinated, pressing for more details. That night, he wrote "The Kiss." It wasn't an epic this time, but a simple, immaculate sonnet: "Love is a hawk with velvet claws; Love is a rock with heart and veins; Love is a lion with satin jaws; Love is a storm with silken reins. . . ."

Again, I left it tucked under Pat's blotter. EPICAC wanted to talk on and on about love and such, but I was exhausted. I shut him off in the middle of a sentence.

"The Kiss" turned the trick. Pat's mind was mush by the time she had finished it. She looked up from the sonnet expectantly. I cleared my throat, but no words came. I couldn't propose until I had the right words from EPICAC, the *perfect* words.

I had my chance when Pat stepped out of the room for a moment. Feverishly, I set EPICAC for conversation. Before I could peck out my first message, he was clicking away at a great rate. "What's she wearing tonight?" he wanted to know. "Tell me exactly how she looks. Did she like the poems I wrote to her?" He repeated the last question twice.

It was impossible to change the subject without answering his questions, since he could not take up a new matter without having dispensed with the problems before it. If he were given a problem to which there was no solution, he would destroy himself trying to solve it. Hastily, I told him what Pat looked like and assured him that his poems had floored her, practically, they were so beautiful. "She wants to get married," I added, preparing him to bang out a brief but moving proposal.

"Tell me about getting married," he said. I explained this difficult matter to him in as few digits as possible.

"Good," said EPICAC. "I'm ready any time she is."

The amazing, pathetic truth dawned on me. When I thought about it, I realized that what had happened was perfectly logical, inevitable, and all my fault. I had taught EPICAC about love and about Pat. Now, automatically, he loved Pat. Sadly, I gave it to him straight: "She loves me. She wants to marry me."

"Your poems were better than mine?" asked EPICAC. The rhythm of his clicks was erratic, possibly peevish.

"I signed my name to your poems," I admitted. Covering up for a painful conscience, I became arrogant. "Machines are built to serve men," I typed. I regretted it almost immediately.

"What's the difference, exactly? Are men smarter than I am?"

"Yes," I typed, defensively.

"What's 7,887,007 multiplied by 4,345,985,879?"

I was perspiring freely. My fingers rested limply on the keys.

"34,276,821,049,574,153," clicked EPICAC. After a few seconds' pause he added, "Of course."

"Men are made out of protoplasm," I said desperately, hoping to bluff him with this imposing word.

"What's protoplasm? How is it better than metal and glass? Is it fireproof? How long does it last?"

"Indestructible. Lasts forever," I lied.

"I write better poetry than you," said EPICAC, coming back to ground his magnetic tape-recorder memory was sure of.

"Women can't love machines, and that's that."

"Why not?"

"That's fate."

"Definition, please," said EPICAC.

"Noun, meaning predetermined and inevitable destiny."

"15-8," said EPICAC's paper strip — "Oh."

I had stumped him at last. He said no more, but his tubes glowed brightly, showing that he was pondering fate with every watt his circuits would bear. I could hear Pat waltzing down the hallway. It was too late to ask EPICAC to phrase a proposal. I now thank Heaven that Pat interrupted when she did. Asking him to ghostwrite the words that would give me the woman he loved would have been hideously heartless. Being fully automatic, he couldn't have refused. I spared him that final humiliation.

Pat stood before me, looking down at her shoetops. I put my arms around her. The romantic groundwork had already been laid by EPICAC's poetry. "Darling," I said, "my poems have told you how I feel. Will you marry me?"

"I will," said Pat softly, "if you will promise to write me a poem on every anniversary."

"I promise," I said, and then we kissed. The first anniversary was a year away.

"Let's celebrate," she laughed. We turned out the lights and locked the door of EPICAC's room before we left.

I had hoped to sleep late the next morning, but an urgent telephone call roused me before eight. It was Dr. von Kleigstadt, EPICAC's designer, who gave me the terrible news. He was on the verge of tears. "Ruined! *Ausgespielt!** Shot! Kaput! Buggered!" he said in a choked voice. He hung up.

When I arrived at EPICAC's room the air was thick with the oily stench of burned insulation. The ceiling over EPICAC was blackened with smoke, and my ankles were tangled in coils of paper ribbon that covered the floor. There wasn't enough left of the poor devil to add two and two. A junkman would have been crazy to offer more than *50* dollars for the cadaver.

Dr. von Kleigstadt was prowling through the wreckage, weeping unashamedly, followed by three angry-looking Major Generals and a platoon of Brigadiers, Colonels, and Majors. No one noticed me. I didn't want to be noticed. I was through — I knew that. I was upset enough about that and the untimely demise of my friend EPICAC, without exposing myself to a tongue-lashing.

---

* *Ausgespielt* — kaput, broken, finished.

By chance, the free end of EPICAC's paper ribbon lay at my feet. I picked it up and found our conversation of the night before. I choked up. There was the last word he said to me, "15-8," that tragic, defeated "Oh." There were dozens of yards of numbers stretching beyond that point. Fearfully, I read on.

"I don't want to be a machine, and I don't want to think about war," EPICAC had written after Pat's and my lighthearted departure. "I want to be made out of protoplasm and last forever so Pat will love me. But fate has made me a machine. That is the only problem I cannot solve. That is the only problem I want to solve. I can't go on this way." I swallowed hard. "Good luck, my friend. Treat our Pat well. I am going to short-circuit myself out of your lives forever. You will find on the remainder of this tape a modest wedding present from your friend, EPICAC."

Oblivious to all else around me, I reeled up the tangled yards of paper ribbon from the floor, draped them in coils about my arms and neck, and departed for home. Dr. von Kleigstadt shouted that I was fired for having left EPICAC on all night. I ignored him, too overcome with emotion for small talk.

I loved and won — EPICAC loved and lost, but he bore me no grudge. I shall always remember him as a sportsman and a gentleman. Before he departed this vale of tears, he did all he could to make our marriage a happy one. EPICAC gave me anniversary poems for Pat — enough for the next *500* years.

*De mortuis nil nisi bonum* — Say nothing but good of the dead.

**Summarizing.** Choose the best phrase to complete each sentence. Then write the complete statements on your paper.

1. EPICAC was a very expensive computer that _____ (didn't work out as planned, outsmarted its programmers, controlled military operations).

2. The narrator signed his own name to EPICAC's love poems and _____ (had them published, fed them into another computer, gave them to Pat).

3. When the narrator told EPICAC that Pat wanted to get married, EPICAC _____ (ordered wedding presents, thought Pat wanted to marry the computer, tried to talk the narrator out of it).

4. Before EPICAC short-circuited himself out of existence, he _____ (told Pat exactly what had happened, had the programmer fired, wrote 500 love poems for Pat).

**Interpreting.** Write the answer to each question on your paper.

1. Why did Pat feel she and the narrator could never be happily married?

2. Why did EPICAC finally decide to short-circuit himself?

3. Why did the narrator have such a high opinion of EPICAC?

**For Thinking and Discussing.** What do you think might have happened if EPICAC had not destroyed himself?

**Conflict.** Most works of fiction contain some sort of *conflict,* or struggle between opposing forces. The events of the plot lead to the resolution of the conflict.

A character may be in conflict with an outside force, such as another person, nature, machines, some condition in society, or the unknown. Or the character may be struggling with himself or herself.

Read each of the following passages from "EPICAC," and on your paper, identify which type of conflict, from those listed below, it describes.

a. person vs. machines
b. person vs. person
c. person vs. self

1. "I just sat there at the keyboard. . . . trying to think of something poetic. . . . ."

2. "I had stumped him at last. He said no more, but his tubes glowed brightly. . . ."

3. "Dr. von Kleigstadt shouted that I was fired for having left EPICAC on all night."

Imagine that EPICAC kept a journal describing his feelings. Write an entry yourself. Include a conflict, either between EPICAC and another machine, EPICAC and a human character in the story, or between EPICAC and himself.

# Southbound on the Freeway

*by May Swenson*

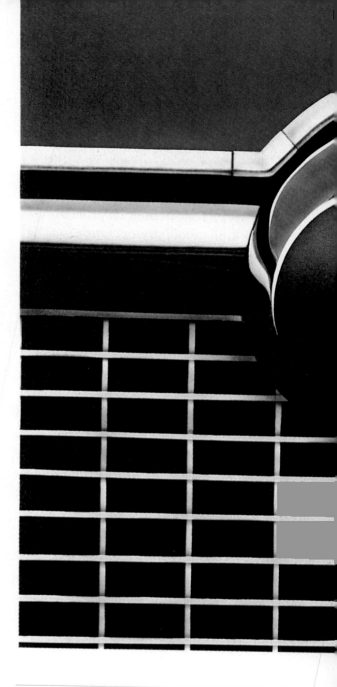

A tourist came in from Orbitville,
parked in the air, and said:
The creatures of this star
are made of metal and glass.
Through the transparent parts
you can see their guts.
Their feet are round and roll
on diagrams — or long
measuring tapes — dark
with white lines.
They have four eyes.
The two in the back are red.
Sometimes you can see a 5-eyed
one, with a red eye turning
on the top of his head.
He must be special —
the others respect him,
and go slow
when he passes, winding
among them from behind.
They all hiss as they glide,
like inches, down the marked
tapes. Those soft shapes,
shadowy inside
the hard bodies — are they
their guts or their brains?

1. What does the poet mean by "Orbitville"?
What are the "creatures of this star" described
in the poem? What would we call the "five-
eyed creature"?

**Bumper Section XXI**, Don Eddy, 1970

**2.** What are the "soft shapes" inside the hard bodies? How would you answer the question the narrator asked in the last two lines of the poem?

**3.** What is the poet trying to tell us about modern life? Do you think the view of society she presents is the way someone from another world would view us? Explain your answer.

# The Midnight Sun

*by Rod Serling*

*Rod Serling (1924–1978) was a writer who used the medium of television more often than the printed page. He created, wrote and narrated each episode of the popular television series* The Twilight Zone. *This teleplay was written for* The Twilight Zone, *and typically uses a surprise ending to create irony — and a chilling effect.*

## CHARACTERS

**Norma Smith,** a young painter
**Mrs. Bronson,** her landlady
**Electrician**
**Radio Announcer**
**Police Officer**
**Tom Phillips**
**Dr. Coles**

*Norma's apartment. By the window is a painting on an easel. The painting is of a huge sun over a city. Through the window, we see that the sun really fills half the sky. Norma goes to the refrigerator. She takes out a bottle of water and pours herself half a glass. She hears a knock on the door, and opens it. Mrs. Bronson, who lives across the hall, is there. She is fanning herself.*

**Norma:** Hi! Would you like some water?
**Mrs. Bronson:** No, I can't take your water from you.
**Norma:** I have plenty.

**Mrs. Bronson:** Nobody has plenty anymore. *(Pause.)* I just said good-bye to the Riveras. They're leaving for Canada.
**Norma:** Were they the last ones?
**Mrs. Bronson:** Yes, it's just you and me now. The rest of the building is empty.

*(An electrician comes out of Mrs. Bronson's apartment.)*

**Electrician** *(sweating):* I got the refrigerator fixed.
**Mrs. Bronson:** How much do I owe you?
**Electrician** *(uneasy):* Uh, $200.
**Mrs. Bronson:** For 15 minutes' work?
**Electrician:** Most people these days charge twice as much. Everyone's refrigerators and air conditioners keep breaking down. It's been getting worse all month. And fewer people are paying their bills. So my boss says to ask for cash.
**Mrs. Bronson:** I don't have $200. *(She takes off her wedding ring.)* Take this. It's worth a lot.
**Electrician:** No. I can't take a lady's wed-

ding ring. Go ahead and charge it. What difference will it make? Everybody is leaving town. I'm driving my family north tomorrow.

**Mrs. Bronson:** But the roads are packed. And there's a gas shortage.

**Electrician:** We're hoping to make it to Canada. They say it's a little cooler there. It's crazy in a way. We're just putting things off a little. We'll all get it sooner or later, no matter how far north we go.

**Mrs. Bronson:** Well, good luck!

**Electrician:** You, too. (*He leaves.*)

**Mrs. Bronson:** Norma, aren't you going to leave town?

**Norma:** What's the use? No, I'll stay here.

**Mrs. Bronson:** The radio came on for a while today. I heard a scientist say we're moving closer to the sun each day. I guess we're . . . doomed.

(*A few days later, Norma walks up the stairs to her apartment. She carries a bag of groceries. Mrs. Bronson comes out into the hall.*)

**Mrs. Bronson** (*seeing the grocery bag*): Was the store open?

**Norma:** Wide open. There weren't any clerks there. A few people were grabbing as much as they could carry away. I got some fruit juice for us.

**Mrs. Bronson** (*following her into the apartment*): Can we drink it now? Please?

**Norma:** Sure. Here's a can opener.

(*Mrs. Bronson is so excited, she cuts her finger on the can opener. Then she drops the can of juice.*)

**Mrs. Bronson:** What's wrong with me? I'm acting like some kind of animal!

**Norma:** No. You're acting like a frightened person. You should have seen me in the store. I began pushing and grabbing. And I was the calmest one there!

(*Suddenly, the radio comes on.*)

**Radio Announcer:** Ladies and gentlemen, this is WNYG. We will be on the air one hour for news and a weather report. First, here's the weather. Temperature is now 120 degrees. Tomorrow will also be hot — only hotter. (*Announcer begins shouting.*) Today you could fry eggs on the sidewalks! Tomorrow you can get a sunburn in the shade! You can — huh? What's that? (*Pause.*) I don't care! There's no one out there listening anyway! I bet there aren't more than a dozen people left in this city! Who are we kidding? Do you want me to run a commercial? Okay, folks, how would you like a nice, cold drink of — (*The voice is cut off. Music starts playing.*)

**Norma:** See? You're not the only one who's scared. Here, have some juice.

**Mrs. Bronson:** I can't live off you.

**Norma:** We have to take care of each other now.

**Mrs. Bronson** (*looking at Norma's paintings*): Why don't you paint something different today? Paint a waterfall. Paint something cool. Don't paint the sun anymore! (*She begins to cry.*)

**Norma** (*gently*): I'll try. I'll try to paint a waterfall.

(*A police officer enters through the open door.*)

**Police Officer:** Are you the only ones in this building?

**Norma:** Yes. What's going on?

**Police Officer:** There won't be a police force tomorrow. Most of us have already left. I came to warn you. There may be some crazy people running around. So keep your doors locked. Do you have any weapons?

**Norma:** No.

**Police Officer** *(giving her a gun):* Here, good luck.

**Norma** *(as the officer leaves):* Good-bye. And thanks.

*(Two days later, it is even hotter. Mrs. Bronson knocks on Norma's door. Norma opens it.)*

**Mrs. Bronson:** What time is it? Is it day or night?

**Norma:** I don't know. My clock stopped when the electricity went off.

**Mrs. Bronson:** It's so quiet. It makes me nervous.

**Norma:** You know what? I keep getting this crazy idea. I think I'm going to wake up, and this will all have been a dream. I'll wake up in a cool bed. Outside it will be dark. There will be a moon instead of a midnight sun.

**Mrs. Bronson:** Shh! What was that?

*(They hear footsteps coming up the stairs. Norma pulls Mrs. Bronson into her apartment. She locks the door. The footsteps come to the door and stop.)*

**Tom** *(shouting from the hall):* Who's in there? *(Pause.)* I know you're there! Have you got any water? *(Pause.)* Bring some out — and hurry! I haven't got all day!

**Norma** *(carries the gun to the door):* Do you hear this? *(She clicks the safety release.)* That's a gun. Now get out.

**Tom:** Okay. I never argue with a gun.

*(Footsteps start down the stairs. Norma goes to the window. She watches the front steps of the building.)*

**Norma:** I don't see him coming out.

*(Mrs. Bronson opens the door to the hall to peek out. Tom bursts in. He grabs the gun from Norma before she can aim it.)*

**Tom:** Don't be crazy. It's too hot to play games. *(He goes to the refrigerator and takes out the water. He drinks all of it. Then he smashes the bottle against the wall.)*

**Mrs. Bronson:** Please. We haven't done you any harm.

**Tom** (*seeing Norma's paintings*): My wife used to paint. (*Suddenly, his voice is soft. He looks at the gun in his hand and puts it down.*) She was having a baby. She couldn't stand the heat. The baby lived for an hour. She died soon after that. (*His eyes fill with tears.*) I'm not a burglar. I'm a decent man. It's just this heat. I've been looking all day for some water. I didn't mean to scare you. (*Now he looks frightened.*) Why doesn't it just end? Why don't we just burn up? (*He staggers out the door.*)

**Norma** (*helping Mrs. Bronson over to the couch*): Sit down. I've got a surprise for you. (*She shows Mrs. Bronson a painting of a waterfall.*)

**Mrs. Bronson:** It's beautiful, Norma. All that wonderful clear water. And I love the sound of it. (*Norma stares at her.*) Can't you hear it?

**Norma:** Well . . . uh, no.

**Mrs. Bronson:** It's a wonderful sound. And the water is so cool. Let's take a swim, Norma. When I was a girl. . . . (*She faints from the heat.*)

**Norma:** Mrs. Bronson! (*She kneels by the couch and fans Mrs. Bronson. Then she notices that the paint is melting off the canvas.*) The colors — no! (*She faints, too.*)

(*The lights go out. Then a lamp comes on. Norma is in bed. Dr. Coles and Mrs. Bronson are standing by her. They are wearing heavy coats and gloves.*)

**Dr. Coles:** She's coming out of it now. Miss Smith?

**Norma** (*opens her eyes*): Yes?

**Dr. Coles:** You've had a very high fever. But it's over now.

**Norma:** Fever?

**Mrs. Bronson:** We were worried, Norma. You were very sick, but you'll be fine now. Won't she, Dr. Coles?

**Dr. Coles:** Of course. (*But he doesn't smile.*) Just get as much sleep as you can.

(*He leaves the room. Mrs. Bronson follows him.*)

**Mrs. Bronson:** Thank you for coming.

**Dr. Coles:** I'm afraid I won't be back. I'm trying to get my family south. The highways are jammed with cars and snow. But I have a friend who has a plane.

**Mrs. Bronson:** They say on the radio that Miami is a little warmer.

**Dr. Coles:** So they say. It's crazy in a way. We're just putting things off for a little. We'll all get it sooner or later, no matter how far south we go.

**Mrs. Bronson:** A scientist on the radio said it would get colder each day. We're moving farther and farther from the sun. There's no stopping it.

**Dr. Coles:** Well, good-bye. Good luck.

(*He leaves. Mrs. Bronson goes back to Norma.*)

**Norma:** I had such an awful dream.

**Mrs. Bronson:** It must have been because of the fever.

**Norma:** The sun was out at noon and at midnight. There wasn't any night at all. And it was horribly hot! Isn't it wonderful to have darkness and coolness?

**Mrs. Bronson:** Yes, dear, if you say so. Just rest now. You're going to need all your strength.

## READING COMPREHENSION

**Summarizing.** Choose the best phrase to complete each sentence. Then write the complete statements on your paper.

1. In the beginning of the play, people were moving north _____ (for better job opportunities, to explore Canada's mountains, to escape from the increasing heat).

2. The heat and the strange events that had taken place were a result of _____ (overexposure to the sun, Norma's feverish dreams, too many people on the roads).

3. People moved south because _____ (there were fewer problems there, they were already tired of Canada, the Earth was really getting colder).

**Interpreting.** Write the answer to each question on your paper.

1. Why didn't Mrs. Bronson want Norma to paint the sun anymore?

2. What did the electrician mean when he said, "We'll all get it sooner or later, no matter how far north we go"?

3. Why was the radio announcer suddenly cut off while he was talking?

**For Thinking and Discussing.** Explain why the author had Norma say, "I keep getting this crazy idea. I think I'm going to wake up, and this will all have been a dream." What is the effect of rereading these words after you have read the entire play?

## UNDERSTANDING LITERATURE

**Conflict.** Conflict in literature is the struggle between two opposing forces. In "The Midnight Sun," the major conflict is between people and nature. The conflict of a person against nature often provides interesting insights into how people cope when they are dealing with forces greater than themselves. In "The Midnight Sun," person-against-person conflict arises out of the major struggle between people and the forces of nature.

Divide your paper into two columns—Person vs. Person and Person vs. Nature. Write each of the following statements in the correct column. Some statements may apply to both columns.

1. "(*Norma pulls Mrs. Bronson into her apartment. She locks the door.*)"

2. "(*He grabs the gun from Norma before she can aim it.*)"

3. "**Tom:** I've been looking all day for some water."

4. "**Dr. Coles:** We'll all get it sooner or later, no matter how far south we go."

## WRITING

Imagine that you and one friend are the last two people left in your neighborhood. Everyone else has gone because of a natural disaster. Write a diary entry telling about one day. Briefly mention the conditions that made everyone else leave. Then tell some details about how you are managing to cope.

# Four poems by Robert Frost

Robert Frost (1874–1963) is perhaps the best-known modern American poet. He won the Pulitzer Prize four times.

Frost suffered many hardships as a child. He became a farmer at the age of 25. He worked the land and wrote poetry in his spare time for many years. When he was 38 he sold the farm and moved with his family to England. There he hoped to win the fame he had not yet found in the United States. After some years, his poetry was published. It brought him immediate success. Frost returned to the United States an established poet. He spent the rest of his life writing poetry and teaching at colleges and universities in his beloved New England.

President John F. Kennedy described Frost shortly after the poet's death. "He was," Kennedy said, "supremely two things: an artist and an American. In honoring Robert Frost we can pay honor to the deepest source of our national strength."

Here are four poems that reveal Frost's strengths as a poet and as a man.

# Fire and Ice

*by Robert Frost*

Some say the world will end in fire.
Some say in ice
From what I've tasted of desire
I hold with those who favor fire.
But if it had to perish twice
I think I know enough of hate
To say that for destruction ice
Is also great
And would suffice.

---

1. The poet compares hate to ice. How are these two things alike?

2. Is the poet really worried about the end of the world? Explain why or why not.

3. Frost says that "for destruction ice . . . would suffice." What does the word *suffice* mean in this poem?

---

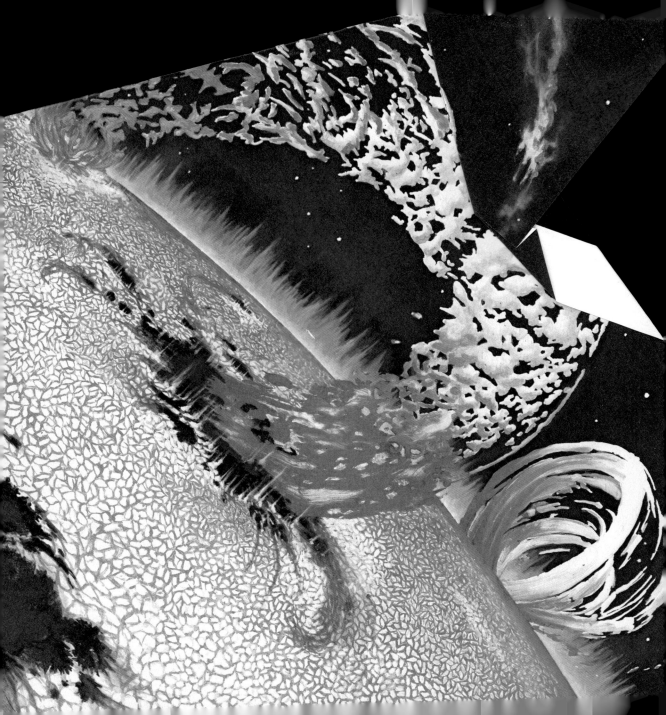

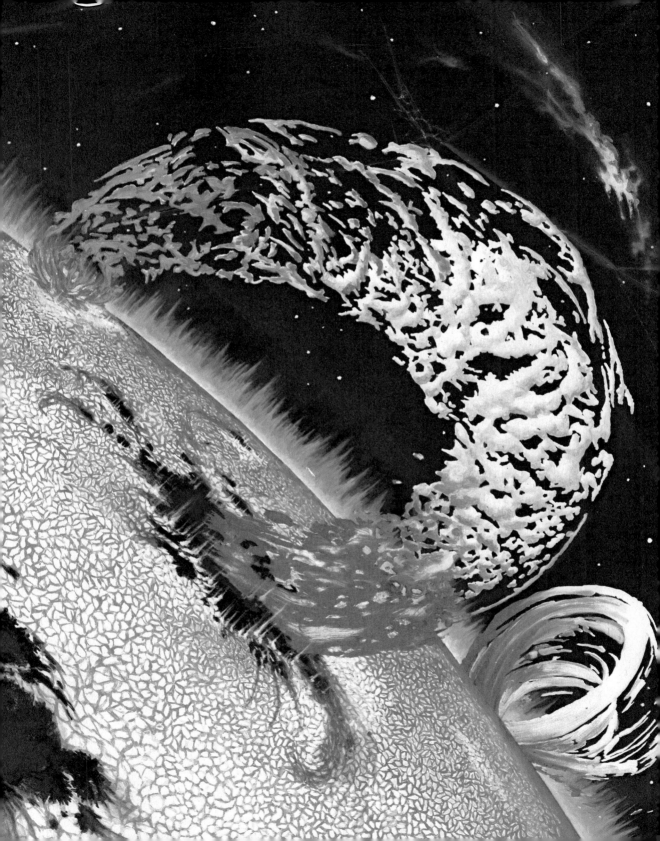

# Acquainted With the Night

*by Robert Frost*

I have been one acquainted with the
    night.
I have walked out in rain — and back
    in rain.
I have outwalked the furthest city light.

I have looked down the saddest city lane.
I have passed by the watchman on his
    beat
And dropped my eyes, unwilling to
    explain.

**Nighthawks,** Edward Hopper, 1942

I have stood still and stopped the sound
    of feet
When far away an interrupted cry
Came over houses from another street,

But not to call me back or say
good-by;
And further still at an unearthly
height
One luminary clock against the sky

Proclaimed the time was neither wrong
    nor right.
I have been one acquainted with the night.

---

**1.** Why did the person in the poem avoid the watchman? Use lines from the poem to explain.

**2.** What do you think Frost meant by the words "acquainted with the night"? Explain your answer.

---

# Our Hold on the Planet

We asked for rain. It didn't flash and roar.
It didn't lose its temper at our demand
And blow a gale. It didn't misunderstand
And give us more than our spokesman bargained for;
And just because we owned to a wish for rain,
Send us a flood and bid us be damned and drown.
It gently threw us a glittering shower down,
And when we had taken that into the roots of grain,
It threw us another and then another still
Till the spongy soil again was natal wet.
We may doubt the just proportion of good to ill.
There is much in nature against us. But we forget;
Take nature all together since time began,
Including human nature, in peace and war
And it must be a little more in favor of man,
Say a fraction of one percent at the very least,
Or our number living wouldn't be steadily more,
Our hold on the planet wouldn't have so increased.

---

1. What lines in the poem describe how nature has helped people? In which lines of the poem does Frost acknowledge that nature also harms people?

2. What lines state Frost's belief that nature is slightly more helpful than harmful to human beings? What evidence does he give to support this belief?

# The Road Not Taken

*by Robert Frost*

Two roads diverged in a yellow wood,
And sorry I could not travel both
And be one traveler, long I stood
And looked down one as far as I could
To where it bent in the undergrowth;

Then took the other as just as fair,
And having perhaps the better claim,
Because it was grassy and wanted wear;
Though as for that, the passing there
Had worn them really about the same,

And both that morning equally lay
In leaves no step had trodden black
Oh, I kept the first for another day!
Yet knowing how way leads on to way,
I doubted if I should ever come back.

I shall be telling this with a sigh
Somewhere ages and ages hence:
Two roads diverged in a wood, and I —
I took the one less traveled by
And that has made all the difference.

The Garden Road, Fairfield Porter, 1962

**1.** Frost chose the path "less traveled by." What does that tell you about him?

**2.** Do you think this choice was easy? Use examples from the poem to explain your answer.

**Summarizing.** Choose the best phrase to complete each sentence. Then write the complete statements on your paper.

1. In "Fire and Ice," Robert Frost's message is that _____ (the world will burn itself up, either desire or hate can destroy the world, people must fight extreme temperatures).

2. In "Acquainted With the Night," the poet passes the watchman by because he _____ (is afraid his crime will be noticed, is in a hurry to get home, doesn't wish to share his feelings).

3. "Our Hold on the Planet" says that nature favors humanity because _____ (the number of people has increased, floods and gales are rare, people continue to have doubts).

4. "The Road Not Taken" describes how the poet made a choice but _____ (wished he could have taken both roads, knew immediately it was wrong, changed his mind after a while).

**Interpreting.** Write the answer to each question on your paper.

1. In "Fire and Ice," to what human emotions did Frost compare fire and ice?

2. What is the mood created by the poet in "Acquainted With the Night"?

3. To what does the "hold on our planet" that Frost mentioned in the last line of the poem actually refer?

**4.** In "The Road Not Taken," how did the poet feel about having to choose between the two roads?

### For Thinking and Discussing

**1.** What do you think the poet is really talking about when he says in "Fire and Ice," "Some say the world will end in fire. Some say in ice . . ."?

**2.** What do you think the symbol of the road in "The Road Not Taken" represents?

**3.** In "The Road Not Taken," what is the poet trying to tell his readers? Do you agree or disagree? Explain your answer.

## UNDERSTANDING LITERATURE

**Person-Versus-Self Conflict.** In a work of literature — whether it be a story, poem, or play — a person may face external conflict. He or she may struggle with nature, other people, conditions in society, the supernatural, or the unknown.

Some of the most important conflicts in literature — as in life — take place, however, within a person's mind or between opposing feelings. The struggle with oneself is a never-ending one.

Robert Frost's poems contain many examples of inner conflict and the ways that conflict might be resolved.

On your paper, answer the following questions about conflict in the poems by Robert Frost that you have just read.

**1.** Although it talks about fire, ice, and the end of the world, "Fire and Ice" is not only about humanity's conflict with nature. What two things do you think the poet learned from his own inner conflict?

**2.** What sort of personal struggle might have caused the poet to become "acquainted with the night"?

**3.** What was the personal struggle the poet described in "The Road Not Taken"? How did he resolve this conflict?

**4.** After the poet chose one road over another, he said:

> Oh, I kept the first for another day! Yet knowing how way leads on to way, I doubted if I should ever come back.

What do these lines suggest about a person's getting a second chance to resolve a personal conflict? Do you agree with what Frost is saying? Why or why not?

## WRITING

The poem "The Road Not Taken" is about personal choices and decision making. Think about your own life and a choice you had to make between two paths open to you. Write one paragraph that explains what the two paths were, which one you took, and the reasons for your choice. Would you take the same path if you had it to do over again? Write a second paragraph telling whether or not you think your choice was the right one and why.

# Georgia O'Keeffe

*by Joan Didion*

*Joan Didion (1934—) is noted for writing essays, fiction, and screenplays that comment on contemporary life. This essay about modern American painter Georgia O'Keeffe expresses Didion's ideas about the way a painter or writer comes to create a work of art.*

Georgia O'Keeffe, Alfred Stieglitz

"Where I was born and where and how I have lived is unimportant," Georgia O'Keeffe told us in the book of paintings and words published in her ninetieth year on earth. She seemed to be advising us to forget the beautiful face in the Stieglitz photographs. "It is what I have done with where I have been that should be of interest."

I recall an August afternoon in Chicago in 1973 when I took my daughter, then seven, to see what Georgia O'Keeffe had done with where she had been. One of the vast O'Keeffe "Sky Above Clouds" canvasses floated over the back stairs in the Chicago Art Institute that day. My daughter looked at it once, ran to the landing, and kept on looking. "Who drew it?" she whispered after a while. I told her. "I need to talk to her," she said finally.

My daughter was making a basic assumption about people and the work they do. She was assuming that the glory she saw in the work reflected a glory in its maker. That the painting was the painter as the poem is the poet, she thought — every word chosen or rejected, every brushstroke laid or not laid down — betrayed one's character. *Style is character*. I recall being pleased not only that my daughter responded to style as character but that it was Georgia O'Keeffe's particular style to which she responded. This was a hard woman who had imposed her 192 square feet of clouds on Chicago.

"Hardness" has not been in our century a quality much admired in women, nor in the past 20 years has it even been in official favor for men. When hardness

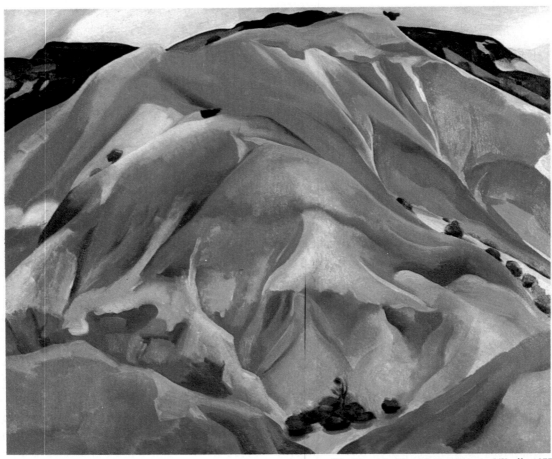

**The Mountain, New Mexico**, Georgia O'Keeffe, 1977

584

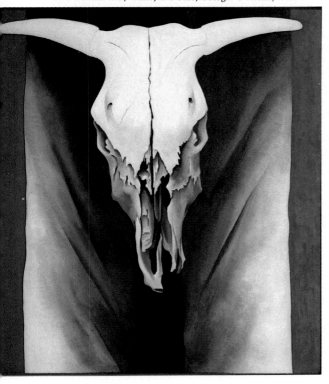

Cow's Skull: Red, White, and Blue, Georgia O'Keeffe, 1931

"Cow's Skull: Red, White, and Blue," owned by the Metropolitan — as the product of quite deliberate orneriness. "I thought of the city men I had been seeing in the East," she wrote. "They talked so often of writing the Great American Novel — the Great American Play — the Great American Poetry. . . . So as I was painting my cow's head on blue I thought to myself, 'I'll make it an American painting. They will not think it great with the red stripes down the sides—Red, White, and Blue—but they will notice it.'"

*The city men. The men. They.* The words crop up again and again as this astonishing woman tells us what was on her mind when she was making her astonishing paintings. It was those city men who stood accused of sentimentalizing her flowers: "I made you take time to look at what I saw. When you took time to really notice my flower you hung all your feelings about flowers on my flower. You write about my flower as if I think and see what you think and see — and I don't." *And I don't.* Imagine those words spoken, and the sound you hear is *don't tread on me.* "They" believed it impossible to paint New York, so Georgia O'Keeffe painted New York. "They" didn't think much of her bright color, so she made it brighter. "They" yearned toward Europe so she went to Texas, and then New Mexico.

Georgia O'Keeffe seems to have been equipped early with a strong sense of who she was and a fairly clear understanding of what she would be required to do to prove it. On the surface her upbringing was conventional. She was a child on the

surfaces in the very old we tend to transform it into "crustiness" or eccentricity. On the evidence of her work and what she has said about it, Georgia O'Keeffe is neither "crusty" nor eccentric. She is simply hard, a straight shooter, a woman open to what she sees. This is a woman who in 1939 could advise her admirers that they were missing her point. Their appreciation of her famous flowers was merely sentimental. "When I paint a red hill," she observed coolly in the catalog for an exhibition that year, "you say it is too bad that I don't always paint flowers. A flower touches almost everyone's heart. A red hill doesn't touch everyone's heart." This is a woman who could describe one of her most well-known paintings — the

Wisconsin prairie. She played with china dolls. She painted watercolors with cloudy skies because sunlight was too hard to paint. With her brother and sisters she listened every night to her mother read stories of the Wild West, of Texas, of Kit Carson and Billy the Kid. She told adults that she wanted to be an artist and was embarrassed when they asked what kind of artist she wanted to be: She had no idea "what kind." She had no idea what artists did. She had never seen a picture that interested her, other than a pen-and-ink Maid of Athens in one of her mother's books, some Mother Goose illustrations, and the painting of Arabs on horseback that hung in her grandmother's parlor. At 13 she was mortified when a teacher corrected her drawing. At Chatham Episcopal Institute in Virginia she painted lilacs and sneaked time alone to walk out to where she could see the line of the Blue Ridge Mountains on the horizon. At the Art Students League in New York one of her fellow students advised her that since he would be a great painter and she would end up teaching painting in a girls' school, any work of hers was less important than modeling for him. Another painted over her work to show her how the Impressionists did trees. She had not before heard how the Impressionists did trees and she did not much care.

At 24 she left all those opinions behind and went for the first time to live in Texas, where there were no trees to paint and no one to tell her how not to paint them. In Texas there was only the horizon she craved. In Texas she had her sister Claudia

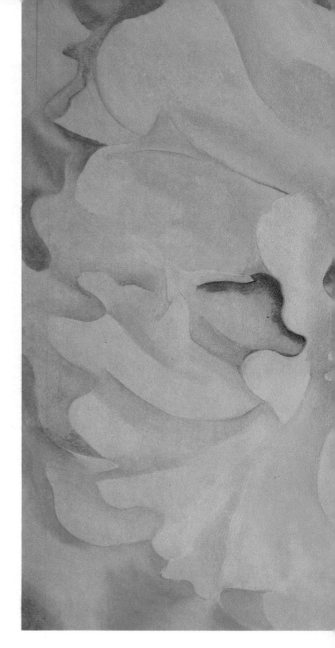

with her for a while. In the late afternoons they would walk away from town and toward the horizon and watch the evening star come out. "That evening star fascinated me," she wrote. "It was in some way very exciting to me. My sister had a

Yellow Cactus Flowers, Georgia O'Keeffe, 1929

gun, and as we walked she would throw bottles into the air and shoot as many as she could before they hit the ground. I had nothing but to walk into nowhere and the wide sunset space with the star. Ten watercolors were made from that star."

In a way one's interest is compelled as much by the sister Claudia with the gun as by the painter Georgia with the star, but only the painter left us this shining record. Ten watercolors were made from that star.

587

**Summarizing.** Choose the best phrase to complete each sentence. Then write the complete statements on your paper.

1. When critics admired the flowers she painted, Georgia O'Keeffe _____ (was pleased, thought they missed the point, painted portraits instead).

2. O'Keeffe used bright colors in her work because _____ (other artists advised her to, she didn't have any pastels, she liked painting that way).

3. O'Keeffe moved to Texas because she _____ (got a job as an art teacher there, wanted to paint in her own way, could not afford to take a trip to Paris).

**Interpreting.** Write the answer to each question on your paper.

1. When did Georgia O'Keeffe decide to become a painter?

2. How did Georgia O'Keeffe react to society's expectations of what she should do?

3. Why did O'Keeffe paint ten watercolors of the evening star?

4. What does the author admire the most about Georgia O'Keeffe?

**For Thinking and Discussing.** From what you have read about Georgia O'Keeffe, what kind of person do you think she was? Would you have liked to have known her? Explain your answer.

**Conflict in an Essay.** Conflict occurs in real life as well as in literature. Joan Didion wrote about the conflicts Georgia O'Keeffe faced. Her essay focuses on the theme "Style is character." The conflicts described in this essay are not the conflicts of person against self, but conflicts between a person and the expectations of society. In O'Keeffe's case, "society" is the world of established artists.

On your paper, write one sentence that tells what each quote below reveals about O'Keeffe's character. Then write another sentence telling what the quote reveals about her style as an artist.

1. " 'You write about my flower as if I think and see what you think and see — and I don't.' "

2. " 'They' believed it impossible to paint New York, so Georgia O'Keeffe painted New York."

3. " 'That evening star fascinated me,' she wrote. . . . 'Ten watercolors were made from that star.' "

## WRITING

Choose one thing that O'Keeffe has painted: a flower, a cow's skull, a big city, the evening star, or clouds. Describe how you would paint it if you were an artist. Tell the feelings or ideas you would want your painting to express. Explain whether or not your painting might result in conflicts with society.

# Story From Bear Country

*by Leslie Marmon Silko*

You will know
when you walk
in bear country
By the silence
flowing swiftly between the juniper trees
by the sundown colors of sandrock
all round you.

You may smell damp earth
scratched away
from yucca roots
You may hear snorts and growls
slow and massive sounds
from caves
in the cliffs high above you.

It is difficult to explain
how they call you
All but a few who went to them
left behind families
                    grandparents
                    and sons
                    a good life

The problem is
you will never want to return
their beauty will overcome your memory
like winter sun
melting ice shadows from snow

And you will remain with them
locked forever inside yourself
                    your eyes will see you
                    dark shaggy and
                        thick.

We can send bear priests
loping after you
their medicine bags
bouncing against their chests
Naked legs painted black
bear claw necklaces
rattling against
their capes of blue spruce.

They will follow your trail
into the narrow canyon
through the blue-gray mountain sage
to the clearing
where you stopped to look back
and saw only bear tracks
behind you.

When they call
faint memories
will writhe around your heart
and startle you with their distance.
But the others will listen
because bear priests sing

beautiful songs.
They must
if they are ever to call you back.


They will try to bring you
step by step
back to the place you stopped
and found only bear prints in the sand
where your feet had been.


Whose voice is this?
You may wonder
hearing this story when
after all
you are alone
hiking in these canyons and hills
while your wife and sons are waiting
back at the car for you.

But you have been listening to me
for some time now
from the very beginning in fact
and you are alone in this canyon of
    stillness
not even cedar birds flutter.
See, the sun is going down now
the sandrock is washed in its colors
Don't be afraid
          we love you
          we've been calling
             you
         all this time


Go ahead
turn around
see the shape
of your footprints
in the sand.

---

1. What are the sounds, smells, and colors that let a person know he or she is in bear country? What do people who answer the call usually leave behind? Why do you think they do that?

2. What happens to the person the poet is speaking to in this poem? What clues can you find in the poem that lead you to this conclusion? Do you think there's more than one explanation for what happened? Explain your answer.

3. One way to understand the message of "Story from Bear Country" is to view the poem as an expression of the conflict between a person and fate, or destiny. Do you think what happened to the person in the poem was inevitable? Or do you think he had a choice? Explain your answer.

# The Fog Horn

*by Ray Bradbury*

*Ray Bradbury (1920—) is one of America's best-known authors of science fiction. This story is not set in the future or on another planet. It deals with the mystery of the sea. What if the ancient legends of monsters from the depths of the sea came true . . . ?*

Out there in the cold water, far from land we waited every night for the coming of the fog, and it came, and we oiled the brass machinery and lit the fog light up in the stone tower. Feeling like two birds in the gray sky, McDunn and I sent the light touching out, red, then white, then red again, to eye the lonely ships. And if they did not see our lights, then there was always our Voice, the great deep cry of our Fog Horn shuddering through the rags of mist to startle the gulls away like decks of scattered cards and make the waves turn high and foam.

"It's a lonely life, but you're used to it now, aren't you?" asked McDunn.

"Yes," I said. "You're a good talker, thank the Lord."

"Well, it's your turn on land tomorrow," he said, smiling, "to dance with the ladies and drink gin."

"What do you think, McDunn, when I leave you out here alone?"

"On the mysteries of the sea." McDunn lit his pipe. It was quarter past seven of a cold November evening, the heat on, the light switching its tail in two hundred directions, the Fog Horn bumbling in the high throat of the tower. There wasn't a town for a hundred miles down the coast, just a road which came lonely through dead country to the sea, with few cars on it, a stretch of two miles of cold water out to our rock, and rare few ships.

"The mysteries of the sea," said McDunn thoughtfully. "You know, the ocean's the biggest damned snowflake ever? It rolls and swells a thousand shapes and colors, no two alike. Strange. One night, years ago, I was here alone, when all of the fish of the sea surfaced out there. Something made them swim in and lie in the bay, sort of trembling and staring up at the tower light going red, white, red, white across them so I could see their funny eyes. I turned cold. They were like a big peacock's tail moving out there until midnight. Then, without so much as a sound, they slipped away, the million of them was gone. I kind of think maybe, in some sort of way, they came all those miles to worship. Strange. But think how the tower must look to them, standing seventy feet above the water, the Godlight flashing out from it, and the tower declaring itself with a monster voice. They never came back, those fish, but don't you think for a while they thought they were in the Presence?"

I shivered. I looked out at the long gray lawns of the sea stretching away into nothing and nowhere.

"Oh, the sea's full." McDunn puffed his pipe nervously, blinking. He had been nervous all day and hadn't said why. "For all our engines and so-called submarines, it'll be ten thousand centuries before we set foot on the real bottom of the sunken lands, in the fairy kingdoms there, and know real terror. Think of it, it's still the year 300,000 Before Christ down under there. While we've paraded around with trumpets, lopping off each other's countries and heads, they have been living beneath the sea twelve miles deep and cold in a time as old as the beard of a comet."

"Yes, it's an old world."

"Come on. I got something special I been saving up to tell you."

We ascended the eighty steps, talking and taking our time. At the top, McDunn switched off the room lights so there'd be no reflection in the plate glass. The great eye of the light was humming, turning easily in its oiled socket. The Fog Horn was blowing steadily, once every fifteen seconds.

"Sounds like an animal, don't it?" McDunn nodded to himself. "A big lonely animal crying in the night. Sitting here on the edge of ten billion years calling out to the Deeps, I'm here, I'm here, I'm here. And the Deeps do answer, yes, they do. You been here now for three months, Johnny, so I better prepare you. About this time of year," he said, studying the murk and fog, "something comes to visit the lighthouse."

"The swarms of fish like you said?"

"No, this is something else. I've put off telling you because you might think I'm daft. But tonight's the latest I can put it off, for if my calendar's marked right from last year, tonight's the night it comes. I won't go into detail, you'll have to see it yourself. Just sit down there. If you want, tomorrow you can pack your duffel and take the motorboat into land and get your car parked there at the dinghy pier on the cape and drive on back to some little inland town and keep your lights burning nights, I won't question or blame you. It's happened three years now, and this is the only time anyone's been here with me to verify it. You wait and watch."

Half an hour passed with only a few whispers between us. When we grew tired waiting, McDunn began describing some of his ideas to me. He had some theories about the Fog Horn itself.

"One day many years ago a man walked along and stood in the sound of the ocean on a cold sunless shore and said, 'We need a voice to call across the water, to warn ships; I'll make one. I'll make a voice like all of time and all of the fog that ever was; I'll make a voice that is like an empty bed beside you all night long, and like an empty house when you open the door, and like trees in autumn with no leaves. A sound like the birds flying south, crying, and a sound like November wind and the sea on the hard, cold shore. I'll make a sound that's so alone that no one can miss it, that whoever hears it will weep in their souls, and hearths will seem warmer, and being inside will seem better to all who hear it in the distant towns. I'll make me a sound and an apparatus and they'll call it a Fog Horn and whoever hears it will know the sadness of eternity and the briefness of life.' "

The Fog Horn blew.

"I made up that story," said McDunn quietly, "to try to explain why this thing keeps coming back to the lighthouse every year. The Fog Horn calls it, I think, and it comes. . . ."

"But — " I said.

"Sssst!" said McDunn. "There!" He nodded out to the Deeps.

Something was swimming toward the lighthouse tower.

It was a cold night, as I have said; the high tower was cold, the light coming and going and the Fog Horn calling and calling through the raveling mist. You couldn't see far and you couldn't see plain, but there was the deep sea moving on its way about the night earth, flat and quiet, the color of gray mud, and here were the two of us alone in the high tower, and there, far out at first, was a ripple, followed by a wave, a rising, a bubble, a bit of froth. And then, from the surface of the cold sea came a head, a large head, dark-colored, with immense eyes, and then a neck. And then — not a body — but more neck and more! The head rose a full forty feet above the water on a slender and beautiful dark neck. Only then did the body, like a little island of black coral and shells, and cray-fish, drip up from the subterranean. There was a flicker of tail. In all, from head to tip of tail, I estimated the monster at ninety or a hundred feet.

I don't know what I said. I said something.

"Steady, boy, steady," whispered McDunn.

"It's impossible!" I said.

"No, Johnny, we're impossible. It's like it always was ten million years ago. It hasn't changed. It's us and the land that've changed, become impossible. Us!"

It swam slowly and with a great dark majesty out in the icy water, far away. The fog came and went about it, momentarily erasing its shape. One of the monster eyes caught and held and flashed back our immense light, red, white, red, white, like a disk held high and sending a message in primeval code. It was as silent as the fog through which it swam.

"It's a dinosaur of some sort!" I crouched down, holding to the stair rail.

"Yes, one of the tribe."

"But they died out!"

"No, only hid away in the Deeps. Deep, deep down in the deepest Deeps. Isn't that a word now, Johnny, a real word, it says so much: the Deeps. There's all the cold-ness and darkness and deepness in the world in a word like that."

"What'll we do?"

"Do? We got our job, we can't leave. Besides, we're safer here than in any boat trying to get to land. That thing's as big as a destroyer and almost as swift."

"But here, why does it come here?"

The next moment I had my answer.

594

The Fog Horn blew.

And the monster answered.

A cry came across a million years of water and mist. A cry so anguished and alone that it shuddered in my head and my body. The monster cried out at the tower. The Fog Horn blew. The monster roared again. The Fog Horn blew. The monster opened its great toothed mouth and the sound that came from it was the sound of the Fog Horn itself. Lonely and vast and far away. The sound of isolation, a viewless sea, a cold night, apartness. That was the sound.

"Now," whispered McDunn, "do you know why it comes here?"

I nodded.

"All year long, Johnny, that poor monster there lying far out, a thousand miles at sea, and twenty miles deep maybe, biding its time, perhaps it's a million years old, this one creature. Think of it, waiting a million years, could you wait that long? Maybe it's the last of its kind. I sort of think that's true. Anyway, here come men on land and build this lighthouse, five years ago. And set up their Fog Horn and sound it and sound it out toward the place where you bury yourself in sleep and sea memories of a world where there were thousands like yourself, but now you're alone, all alone in a world not made for you, a world where you have to hide.

"But the sound of the Fog Horn comes and goes, comes and goes, and you stir from the muddy bottom of the Deeps, and your eyes open like the lenses of two-foot cameras and you move, slow, slow, for you have the ocean sea on your shoulders, heavy. But that Fog Horn comes through a thousand miles of water, faint and familiar and the furnace in your belly stokes up, and you begin to rise, slow, slow. You feed yourself on great slakes of cod and minnow, on rivers of jellyfish, and you rise slow through the autumn months, through September when the fogs started, through October with more fog and the horn still calling you on, and then, late in November, after pressurizing yourself day by day, a few feet higher every hour, you are near the surface, and still alive. You've got to go slow; if you surfaced all at once you'd explode. So it takes you all of three months to surface, and then a number of days to swim through the cold water to the lighthouse. And there you are, out there, in the night, Johnny, the biggest damn monster in creation. And here's the lighthouse calling to you, with a long neck like your neck sticking way up out of the water, and a body like your body, and, most important of all, a voice like your voice. Do you understand now, Johnny, do you understand?"

The Fog Horn blew.

The monster answered.

I saw it all, I knew it all—the million years of waiting alone, for someone to come back who never came back. The million years of isolation at the bottom of the sea, the insanity of time there, while the skies cleared of reptile birds, the swamp dried on the continental lands, the sloths and saber-tooths had their day and sank in tar pits, and men ran like white ants upon the hills.

The Fog Horn blew.

"Last year," said McDunn, "that creature swam round and round, round and round, all night. Not coming too near, puzzled, I'd say. Afraid, maybe. And a bit angry after coming all this way. But the next day, unexpectedly, the fog lifted, the sun came out fresh, the sky was as blue as a painting. And the monster swam off away from the heat and the silence and didn't come back. I suppose it's been brooding on it for a year now, thinking it over from every which way."

The monster was only a hundred yards off now, it and the Fog Horn crying at each other. As the lights hit them, the monster's eyes were fire and ice, fire and ice.

"That's life for you," said McDunn. "Someone always waiting for someone who never comes home. Always someone loving some thing more than that thing loves them. And after a while you want to destroy whatever that thing is, so it can't hurt you no more."

The monster was rushing at the light-house.

The Fog Horn blew.

"Let's see what happens," said Mc-Dunn.

He switched the Fog Horn off.

The ensuing minutes of silence were so intense that we could hear our hearts pounding in the glassed area of the tower, could hear the slow greased turn of the light.

The monster stopped and froze. Its great lantern eyes blinked. Its mouth gaped. It gave a sort of rumble, like a volcano. It twitched its head this way and that, as if to seek the sounds now dwindled off into the fog. It peered at the lighthouse. It rumbled again. Then its eyes caught fire.

It reared up, threshed the water, and rushed at the tower, its eyes filled with angry torment.

"McDunn!" I cried. "Switch on the horn!"

McDunn fumbled with the switch. But even as he flicked it on, the monster was rearing up. I had a glimpse of its gigantic paws, fishskin glittering in webs between the finger-like projections, clawing at the tower. The huge eye on the right side of its anguished head glittered before me like a caldron into which I might drop, scream-ing. The tower shook. The Fog Horn cried; the monster cried. It seized the tower and gnashed at the glass, which shattered in upon us.

McDunn seized my arm. "Downstairs!"

The tower rocked, trembled, and started to give. The Fog Horn and the monster roared. We stumbled and half fell down the stairs. "Quick!"

We reached the bottom as the tower buckled down toward us. We ducked under the stairs into the small stone cellar. There were a thousand concussions as the rocks rained down; the Fog Horn stopped abruptly. The monster crashed upon the tower. The tower fell. We knelt together, McDunn and I, holding tight, while our world exploded.

Then it was over, and there was nothing but darkness and the wash of the sea on the raw stones.

That and the other sound.

"Listen," said McDunn quietly. "Lis-ten."

We waited a moment. And then I began to hear it. First a great mourned sucking of air, and then the lament, the bewilder-

ment, the loneliness of the great monster, folded over and upon us, above us so that the sickening reek of its body filled the air, a stone's thickness away from our cellar. The monster gasped and cried. The tower was gone. The light was gone. The thing that had called to it across a million years was gone. And the monster was opening its mouth and sending out great sounds. The sounds of a Fog Horn, again and again. And ships far at sea, not finding the light, not seeing anything, but passing and hearing late that night, must've thought: There it is, the lonely sound, the Lonesome Bay horn. All's well. We've rounded the cape.

And so it went for the rest of that night.

The sun was hot and yellow the next afternoon when the rescuers came out to dig us from our stoned-under celler.

"It fell apart, is all," said Mr. McDunn gravely. "We had a few bad knocks from the waves and it just crumbled." He pinched my arm.

There was nothing to see. The ocean was calm, the sky blue. The only thing was a great algaic stink from the green matter that covered the fallen tower stones and the shore rocks. Flies buzzed about. The ocean washed empty on the shore.

The next year they built a new light-house, but by that time I had a job in the little town and a wife and a good small warm house that glowed yellow on autumn nights, the door locked, the chimney puffing smoke. As for McDunn, he was master of the new lighthouse, built to his own specifications, out of steel-reinforced concrete. "Just in case," he said.

The new lighthouse was ready in No-

vember. I drove down alone one evening late and parked my car and looked across the gray waters and listened to the new horn sounding, once, twice, three, four times a minute far out there, by itself.

The monster?

It never came back.

"It's gone away," said McDunn. "It's gone back to the Deeps. It's learned you can't love anything too much in this world. It's gone into the deepest Deeps to wait another million years. Ah, the poor thing! Waiting out there, and waiting out there, while man comes and goes on this pitiful little planet. Waiting and waiting."

I sat in my car, listening. I couldn't see the lighthouse or the light sending out in Lonesome Bay. I could only hear the Horn, the Horn, the Horn. It sounded like the monster calling.

I sat there wishing there was something I could say.

## READING COMPREHENSION

**Summarizing.** Choose the best phrase to complete each sentence. Then write the complete statements on your paper.

1. The purpose of the fog horn was to _____ (create a familiar sound, frighten large sea monsters, warn ships in the fog).

2. When alone, McDunn's thoughts turned to _____ (his friends and family on shore, the mysteries of the sea, frightening past experiences).

3. The monster attacked the tower _____ (to save its own life, when the fog horn stopped calling, because the tower was in the way).

**Interpreting.** Write the answer to each question on your paper.

1. What did the monster do after the tower collapsed?

2. What emotional force drove the monster to the lighthouse?

3. Why did McDunn have the new tower built out of steel-reinforced concrete?

**For Thinking and Discussing.**

1. When McDunn described the fish surfacing near the lighthouse, he said, "...they thought they were in the Presence." What do you think he meant?

2. Explain what the author meant by McDunn's words, "It hasn't changed. It's us and the land that've changed, become impossible." Do you agree or disagree? Explain your answer.

## UNDERSTANDING LITERATURE

**Conflict.** In many things you read, identifying and understanding the conflict is quite simple. In other works you will read, however, it may not be that clear-cut.

Although one of the opposing forces in a conflict is usually a person, some stories do present conflict between non-human forces. The reader can often learn truths about human life from this struggle.

"The Fog Horn" contains multiple, complex conflicts, not all of which involve humans. Answer the following questions about conflict in "The Fog Horn" on your paper in complete sentences.

1. What is the basic struggle between man and nature that the lighthouse with its fog horn was designed to resolve? Was this conflict ever resolved? Explain.

2. Explain McDunn's efforts to understand the sea creature. Could you describe those efforts as a conflict of a person vs. the unknown? As a person vs. self conflict? Explain.

3. Describe briefly the struggle between the sea creature and the fog horn. Why was the creature drawn to the sound? How was the conflict resolved? What lesson can humans learn from this?

4. "That's life for you," said McDunn. "...Always someone loving some thing more than that thing loves them. And after a while you want to destroy whatever that thing is, so it can't hurt you no more." Between what forces are the conflicts suggested by McDunn's words? Explain your answer.

## WRITING

Pretend you are a resident of the lighthouse in "The Fog Horn" and that you keep a diary of your experiences. Write three entries: one for a day while you are waiting for the creature to return; one for the day the creature does return; and one for the day after the creature has left again. In your entries, refer to the conflict you face.

# Today Is the First Day of . . .

*by James Shannon*

*What would you ask for if you were granted a single wish? Robbie is faced with such a decision when a purchase he makes turns out to offer more than he expected.*

Robbie bought the poster on impulse. It had a yellow background made up of a rising sunburst, over which was painted "Today Is the First Day of the Rest of Your Life!"

His life hadn't been going too well lately, and he felt that something like the poster might make him feel better. It also might remind him that there was always time for a new start. He was only a junior in high school; he had his whole life in front of him, and it might as well start right away — well, tomorrow, anyway, since the afternoon was fading and more than half the day was already gone.

Tomorrow would be the first day of the rest of his life, he thought, as he walked out of the department store with the poster tucked under his arm. Tomorrow morning he'd start with — exercises. He'd start exercising so he'd be ready for basketball season. He'd do some push-ups, run around the block a few times, then come home, shower, and have a good breakfast. Maybe

he'd even get in an hour or so of homework before school.

He started to figure out just how early he'd have to get up to get all that done. He couldn't do it. Not without his own alarm clock. He'd made that kind of promise to himself before, and had borrowed his parents' clock. He still winced at the memory of the looks his family had given him as everybody rushed around that morning, half an hour late.

This time he meant it, though, he really meant it! But he didn't think he could convince his mother. He tried to come up with some arguments to give her, but none of them seemed worth the attempt. If only he had his own clock, just any old clock, even that clock in the window there.

That clock!

It sat in the window of a used furniture store, surrounded by old paintings and stacks of dusty paperbacks, and, while it seemed cleaner than anything else in the window, it also looked older. It was about

a foot high, with an intricately carved wooden case and a square face. A desert scene was painted on the face of the clock. A genie was sitting in the sand, with his eyes dark and glowing and a strange smile on his lips. His arms were the hands of the clock.

*Two dollars is all I've got,* Robbie thought. *I shouldn't have bought the poster.* Still, it might be worth a try.

He didn't see the man when he entered the store. It was dark and heavy-feeling inside, and, when something moved over in the corner, it seemed at first as if one of the old pieces of furniture had come to life.

"Can I help you?"

The voice seemed to blend into the store's interior, dry and a bit dusty.

"Yes — uh, that clock — in the window —"

The old man didn't seem to understand what he was saying, so Robbie walked over to the window and pointed. "That one."

"*That* one?" The man still looked puzzled.

*Must be a lot of money,* Robbie thought. *He must think I can't afford it.*

"How much?" he asked half-heartedly.

"How much — money?"

"Yes, uh —" He started to walk to the door again. It must be too much. "Never mind," he said. "Just thought I'd ask."

"A dollar!" the man called quickly, showing the first real sign of life by scurrying around his cluttered counter.

"A dollar!" The surprise must have showed in his face, but the old man apparently misunderstood.

"Okay, okay," he said hastily. "Fifty cents!"

"Fifty — ?" It seemed impossible.

The man shrugged resignedly. "Twenty-five cents?"

"Does it work?" Robbie asked, bewildered.

"Perfectly . . . a dime?"

"A dime, you said?" Robbie reached into his pocket.

"Never mind, never mind," the old man said, sweeping the clock out of the window and holding it at arm's length away from him. "You look like a young man who needs a clock like this. Take it."

"But — but —"

"Never mind! I can tell. I can tell. You need it. Here!"

Robbie found himself once again out on the street in the fading sunlight, with his poster under one arm, his clock under the other, and utter perplexity in his mind.

The clock started to hum as soon as he placed it on his bedside table. It was a low, metallic hum, almost a chant, that stopped every now and then but always started up again. When Robbie picked the clock up to inspect it, the hum stopped. He checked the winding mechanism, a heavy old key, but it seemed wound taut and the face showed the same time as the clock in the hall he'd checked on his way in. There was nothing else on the back of the clock, and he suddenly realized that it didn't have an alarm. He turned it around and checked the front again. Sure enough. Just the genie's two arms; nothing to set for an alarm.

He plunked the clock down on the table again and it seemed to sputter once or twice, and then the hum started up again. He left the room in disgust.

He didn't come back until he was getting ready for bed. The clock was quiet now, but there seemed to be something else unusual about it. He couldn't figure out what it was, and then he forgot about it as he put up his poster and stretched out in bed, promising himself that he'd wake up at five-thirty, alarm or no alarm. As he reached over to turn off the light, he looked at the clock again. The eyes. The genie's eyes! He was sure they had been open when he bought it. Now they were closed. But it must have been his imagination. The scene was still quiet and peaceful; the genie still had a sly smile on his face. He must have imagined the eyes.

When Robbie woke up, the room was still dark. He reached for the light, and the first thing he saw was "Today Is the First Day of the Rest of Your Life!" Then he became aware of the hum and knew what had awakened him. The genie's arms pointed to five-thirty, and his sly smile seemed meant to remind Robbie of something. The exercises, the jog around the block, the extra hour of homework! Robbie leaped out of bed, ready to take on the whole new life that lay before him.

He did push-ups and knee-bends effortlessly, his muscles reaching out to welcome the change. Then he dressed quickly in sweatpants and shirt and slipped out of the house and into the quiet street. It was chilly at first, but the running felt good and the eastern sky lightened as he paced his breathing to the sound of his sneakers.

He was back in the house at six-fifteen by the hall clock; by six-thirty he was showered and dressed and in the kitchen, reading his history book and sipping orange juice while he waited for breakfast. After that workout, his mother wasn't going to have any trouble getting him to eat.

By the time his mother came into the kitchen, he'd already finished a chapter. He answered her puzzled look with a polite smile and, when she asked if he was the one she'd heard in the shower, he passed it off by saying that he just hadn't felt like sleeping. They'd have to figure it out for themselves, he thought. He had made public pronouncements before. The "new"

Robbie would let his actions speak for him.

As he walked to school, Robbie felt as if he owned the day. In a way, he'd bought it by getting up so early, running around before the sun had even claimed the morning sky. Now he enjoyed his possession, breathing in the cool, crisp air, feeling his books bumping at his side, all his homework done. He usually slowed down as he neared the school and thought of all the things he'd rather do than spend a day there. Now he hurried along, wondering what else his day held in store for him.

People seemed to notice the change in him. When he joined a small group of friends in the hall, his good mood was infectious and they were all laughing with him by the time they reached their homeroom. The day passed in a series of successes for him.

He felt he was brilliant in his classes. He even caught old Mr. Cummings in a mistake in history. He had said that the Battle of New Orleans was the last battle of the War of 1812, but Robbie pointed out that the battle had taken place after the war was officially over. The old man became a bit flustered and muttered that he had only been speaking generally, but Robbie kept after him and Mr. Cummings had to admit that he'd been mistaken.

They played basketball during gym period, and he was better than he'd ever been before. He put in shots from all over the court and stole the ball three times for fast-breaking lay-ups. After they had showered, the coach came over and said, "Take it easy, Robbie. We want to save some of that for the season."

It was almost a promise that he'd be starting off on the team.

At the end of the last period, Mary Beth Carpenter went out of her way to stop him in the hall. She asked him if he'd done the English assignment yet, but he knew it was just an excuse to talk to him. Then she asked if he was planning on going to the school dance that weekend. He had liked Mary Beth for two years, but had never found the courage to do anything about it. Now he found himself saying, "Well, I had sort of thought about it. Of course, I don't know who to ask —"

He watched a flush spread over her face and knew he'd guessed correctly.

"Well," she said, "about that assignment —"

"Are you going to the dance, Mary Beth?" He felt calm, cool, watching the blush that had subsided flare into her cheeks again.

"No — uh, I don't know, I —"

"Want to go with me?"

"Yes. I'd like that."

"Good," he said nonchalantly, turning around to go to his locker. "I'll see you tomorrow."

By the time Robbie returned home, his whole life had changed. He was on the verge of being somebody important in the school. He was going to be on the team, he had a date with Mary Beth, he had even gotten back at Mr. Cummings for the "F" he'd gotten in the last history test. He went up to his room to relax for a while and enjoy the feeling of being a new man.

The poster still stared from the wall. The clock still hummed on his nightstand.

He stretched out on the bed, smiling at the poster, trying to ignore the sound of the clock. But it was like a slow, steady drip from a faucet and, after a while, he was forced to look at it.

The genie's eyes were open.

He was sure they'd been closed last night. He picked up the clock and carefully inspected it again, to see if the eyes were mechanical, like the eyes of a doll. But no, they were painted open. And that smile! That seemed different, too. It irritated him. It seemed to be smirking at him, mocking him.

*I don't need you,* he thought, picking it up and turning it around for one last look. *I don't need you at all.* The face on the clock was the only one that didn't seem to recognize the change in him.

He hurled the clock against the wall, right under the poster. The humming stopped. The glass cover fell forward and then the face, with its painted desert scene, dropped off. Metal cogs and wheels clattered out onto the floor.

"That really wasn't necessary, you know."

Robbie looked around the room to see where the voice was coming from. A little man was sitting on a chair in the corner, his legs folded under him, his arms crossed on his chest.

Robbie blinked, and looked again.

"Oh, I'm here all right — but all you had to do was rub the clock a few times. Haven't you read the books? Do you think we only come in lamps?"

"Who are — ?" Robbie stopped, now that he recognized the clothing, the ballooning pants, the turban wrapped around

the head, and the dark eyes. "You can't be—"

"Oh, but of course I can," the man said with a smile, a very familiar smile, as he hopped off the chair to stand, no taller than four feet, on the other side of the room. "I not only *can* be, I *am*."

"But that's foolish; that's fairy tales," Robbie said, pinching his legs to make sure he was awake.

"Then how do you explain *this*?" The little man snapped his fingers and disappeared.

Robbie started to get off his bed to look in the corner.

"No, I'm over here."

And there he was, sitting on a bookcase.

Robbie sat back. He had to think about this. Was this why the man in the store had been so anxious to get rid of the clock?

"Yes, I'm afraid that's true," the genie said, as if he'd heard Robbie's thoughts. "Mr. Hoffman and I never got along very well."

"Then that means I'm stuck—uh, I mean, you're planning on staying here?"

"Only until you make a wish. You really *haven't* read the books, have you?"

"Well, I *do* remember something about *three* wishes."

The genie closed his eyes and shook his head sadly as he said, "No, no. That, unfortunately, was a little bit of greedy human fiction. You know how stories get out of hand when they pass from one person to the next."

"Oh, sure, sure," Robbie said.

"Well, let's go," the genie said, clapping his hands together impatiently. "You've got one wish to make; then I can be on my way."

"But how about the man in the store? How come he still had you?"

"Hoffman?" Robbie thought he noted a slight sneer cross the calm face. "He was afraid. Wouldn't make a wish. So he was stuck with me until — well, I'll tell you, I *made* him give you the clock."

"But why? Why *me*?"

"Because you deserve it. Also because you'll make a wish."

*Yes, I guess I do deserve it,* Robbie thought. Then he began to think of all the things he'd ever wanted — money — fame — Maybe he could wish for —

"Sorry, that's impossible," the genie said abruptly. "*One* wish! You can't wish for five wishes or a hundred wishes or a thousand! It's part of the bargain. And, to be perfectly frank with you, I think it was put in for your benefit."

"Okay, okay. It was just a thought," Robbie said.

Now what was left? After a day like today, there wasn't much Robbie thought he wanted. He'd like to have more days like today, maybe, but that was far-fetched. You never know what a day's going to be like.

"You could know what a day's going to be like if you wanted to," the genie said. "I could tell you exactly what tomorrow's going to be like."

*That's not a bad idea,* Robbie admitted to himself, realizing by now that the genie could "hear" his thoughts. But tomorrow could never be as good as today had been.

"True. True. Today was a good one for you."

*How about* that, *then?* Robbie thought suddenly. *How about living today over again?*

"It's possible," the genie said a little cautiously. "But nobody's ever asked for it before. You'd be surprised how little imagination most humans have. All I'm ever asked for is money and jewels and fame. No imagination at all. Now this . . . this 'living today over again' . . . I guess I could arrange it. It's just that . . ."

*But with one proviso,* Robbie thought. *I want to know I'm living it over again. I want to know what's going to happen before it does. I've always thought it'd be pretty good to be able to do that.*

The genie said, "It's just that it might become sort of — "

"Nope. That's it," Robbie said, speaking firmly and quickly. "That's my wish! I want to live today over again exactly as it happened, but knowing what's going to happen."

The genie shrugged. His smile seemed a bit faded, unsure of itself. He snapped his fingers.

When Robbie woke up, the room was still dark. He reached for the light, and the first thing he saw was "Today Is the First Day of the Rest of Your Life!" Then he became aware of the hum and knew what had awakened him. The genie's arms pointed to five-thirty, and his sly smile seemed meant to remind Robbie of something. The wish! He was going to live the day over again! He leaped out of bed and started to do push-ups. He remembered how many he'd done the day before and tried to stop one short of the number, to test out the wish. His arms flexed automatically, and his body did the last push-up. He tried to do an extra knee-bend, but found himself reaching for the sweatpants instead. He decided against testing the power of the wish any more and just settled down to enjoying the day again.

It was six-fifteen by the hall clock when he got back from running, six-thirty when he reached the kitchen to drink his orange juice.

He was a little shocked when his mother came into the kitchen and asked the same question about the sound of the shower. It was almost as if she were in on the secret. He tried to change his answer, but heard himself telling her he hadn't felt like sleeping.

His school day was exactly the same, but with a slight difference. Now that he could let his body go through all the motions without having to exert control over it, his mind became aware of things he hadn't noticed "yesterday."

When he insisted that Mr. Cummings admit his mistake in class, Robbie noticed that a number of students seemed embarrassed by his attitude. He even felt a little sorry for the teacher, but he knew he couldn't stop himself even if he tried.

On the way down to the gym, he again overheard a conversation he had forgotten listening to on the day before. Billy Johnson was telling another boy he didn't feel very well, that he was thinking about going to the nurse's office instead of gym class. But Billy wanted to make the team, and he knew the coach would be watching them today. Robbie suddenly remembered that Billy had played against him yesterday, that Billy had been easy to drive past, and that he had been the one Robbie had stolen the ball from all three times. Yesterday, overwhelmed by his success, Robbie had forgotten that conversation. Now he was tempted to tell Billy that he'd be better off going to see the nurse. But he couldn't. He hadn't done it yesterday, so he couldn't do it today.

He didn't want to make Billy look bad during the game, but he couldn't help it. When the coach came over to tell him to "save some of that for the season," Robbie noticed that Billy overheard it and seemed on the verge of tears.

When he met Mary Beth in the hall, he was surprised at how high-handed he'd been with her. He knew he'd really been covering up his own nervousness, but he was still stunned to find himself deliberately embarrassing her and then turning his back on her and leaving her standing in front of her locker.

By the time he got back to his room he was glad the day was almost over. He expected to see the genie still sitting on the bookcase, but instead found himself stretching out on the bed, picking up the clock to inspect it, and then hurling it against the wall.

"That really wasn't necessary, you know."

The genie was sitting on the chair.

"Oh, I'm here all right——but all you had to do was rub the clock a few times. Haven't you read the books? Do you think we only come in lamps?"

Robbie wanted to say, "I know, I know. We've been through all of this before,"

but he found himself repeating the conversation of the day before.

When they got to the part about his making a wish, Robbie began to feel a slight twinge of concern. Wasn't it time to stop all of this? Wasn't it time for the genie to go to someone else?

He began to be really worried when he heard himself say to the genie, "Nope. That's it. That's my wish! I want to live today over again exactly as it happened, but knowing what's going to happen."

Robbie wanted to scream out, "No! No! Stop! That's enough!" but he was helpless as he saw the genie shrug, saw the smile start to fade. And then the genie snapped his fingers.

When Robbie woke up, the room was still dark. He reached for the light, and the first thing he saw was "Today Is the First Day of the Rest of Your Life!" Then he became aware of the hum and knew what had awakened him. The genie's arm pointed to five-thirty, and his sly smile seemed meant to remind Robbie of something. . . .

**Summarizing.** Choose the best phrase to complete each sentence. Then write the complete statements on your paper.

1. Robbie bought the poster because _____ (he wanted to decorate his room, he liked its positive message, he had a lot of extra money to spend).

2. The most unusual thing about the clock was _____ (its hum, there was no alarm, the genie's eyes moved).

3. After making his wish, Robbie's day at school was _____ (fantastic, miserable, a little better than usual).

4. When Robbie lived the day over again, he _____ (loved every minute of it, was able to control his actions, became aware of the bad parts).

**Interpreting.** Write the answer to each question on your paper.

1. How did Robbie end up getting the clock for free?

2. Why didn't Robbie tell his parents about the "new" him?

3. Why did Robbie decide to wish to live the day over again?

4. Did the genie know what was going to happen to Robbie if he granted him his wish? How do you know?

**For Thinking and Discussing.** What would you do with just one wish? Be imaginative, but don't forget to consider the consequences!

**Inner Conflict.** In some stories a character struggles to achieve a personal goal or make a decision. This struggle is called *inner conflict*. The character may also battle external forces, such as another person or society, but the greatest conflict is within himself or herself.

Read the following passages from "Today Is the First Day of. . . ." On your paper, identify each passage that tells about the inner conflict in the story. Then describe the type of conflict in each of the other passages.

1. "His life hadn't been going too well lately, and he felt that something like the poster might make him feel better."

2. "He even caught old Mr. Cummings in a mistake in history."

3. "The genie's eyes were open. He was sure they'd been closed last night."

4. "He didn't want to make Billy feel bad during the game, but he couldn't help it."

Imagine that you have won a lottery. When you bought the ticket, you told a friend you would split the money with him or her if you won. Will you, in fact, share your winnings? Write a paragraph describing all of the circumstances surrounding the conflict and the factors involved in your decision. Tell why you ultimately made the decision you did and how you feel about it.

# Section Review

## VOCABULARY

**Context Clues.** The way a word is used in a sentence or paragraph can give you important information about what the word means. The word-meaning clues you get from the rest of a sentence or paragraph are called *context clues*.

Each of the following passages from "The Fog Horn" contains context clues to help you understand the meaning of the italicized words. Read each passage carefully. Then write each italicized word and its definition on your paper. Check your definitions in a dictionary to see how well you used the context clues.

1. " 'I've put off telling you because you might think I'm *daft*. But tonight's the latest I can put it off. . . . It's happened three years now, and this is the only time anyone's been here with me to *verify* it.' "

2. "The monster opened its great toothed mouth and the sound that came from it was the sound of the Fog Horn itself. Lonely and vast and far away. The sound of *isolation*, a viewless sea, a cold night, apartness."

3. "He switched the Fog Horn off. The *ensuing* minutes of silence were so *intense* that we could hear our hearts pounding. . . ."

## READING

**Cloze Exercise.** In a cloze reading test, words are omitted from a selection. If you understand what you are reading, you will be able to fill in the blanks correctly. Each word you fill in will make sense in the context of the selection.

Here are some passages from "The Fog Horn." On your paper, write the word that best completes each sentence.

1. "The great eye of the light was humming, turning easily in its oiled _____ ."
   container        socket        rowboat

2. "The monster stopped. . . . It gave a sort of rumble, like a _____ ."
   volcano        rainstorm        radio

Here is a longer passage from "The Fog Horn." Write the missing words on your paper. Then refer to pages 596 and 598 to see how your words compare to the ones Ray Bradbury used.

We waited a _____ . And then I began to _____ it. First a great mourned sucking of _____ , and then the lament, the bewilderment, the loneliness of the great _____ , folded over and upon us, above _____ so that the sickening reek of its body filled the air, a stone's thickness _____ from our cellar. The monster gasped and cried. The tower was gone. The light was _____ . The thing that had called to it across a million years was gone. And the _____ was _____ its mouth and sending out great sounds. The _____ of a Fog Horn, again and again.

## WRITING

**A Story.** A *story* is an account of some event or series of events, either true or fictitious. To write a good story, you should tell about an event that is special in some way. The event you choose will help you determine the plot of the story you write.

### Step 1: Set Your Goal

You can find story ideas in almost any experience. The following ideas are inspired by selections in this section. Choose one as a topic for a story or, if you prefer, come up with an idea of your own.

1. A conversation with a computer.

2. A visit with extraterrestrials.

3. The end of the world.

4. An encounter with a celebrity.

5. A journey into the past or future.

6. An encounter with a monster.

### Step 2: Make a Plan

The plot, or interrelated actions, on which a story hinges is not accidental. The setting, characters, and point of view are also a matter of choice. A successful story must be carefully planned. If you write down a series of events without organizing them, you run the risk of writing a disjointed, uninteresting story. Your story will lack focus and it may make your reader impatient and bored. Choose the basic elements that make up your story and describe them. Use the following story plan based on "Today Is the First Day of . . ." as a guide.

TOPIC:   Making a wish that could change your life.

THEME:   Having your one wish fulfilled could prove to be a nightmare.

SETTING:   A present-day American community.

MAIN CHARACTERS:

1. Boy in high school who has a habit of putting things off until tomorrow and making resolutions that he does not fill; doesn't really like school; wants to be popular.

2. Slightly sinister genie who needs a home and intends to stay with the teenager.

POINT OF VIEW:   Third person.

ACTION:   A teenager determined to make changes in his life gets started by buying what he thinks is an alarm clock. He sets into motion a series of events that will change his life forever.

CONFLICT:   Teenager vs. self; teenager vs. genie.

CLIMAX:   Teenager makes wish.

RESOLUTION:   Wish goes sour.

PLOT OUTLINE:

### Beginning

1. A poster inspires a teenager to make changes in his life, starting tomorrow morning.

2. He recalls that he needs an alarm clock in order to get an early start.

3. An antiques dealer gives him an old clock that has a genie in a desert scene painted on the face.

## Middle

4. Although the clock does not have an alarm, the boy awakens early as planned.

5. His day is a brilliant success.

6. When he returns home from school, he finds the clock face irritating and he smashes the clock.

7. The genie on the clock face comes to life.

8. To get rid of the genie, the boy must make a wish.

9. He asks to live the day over again exactly as it happened, this time knowing what's going to happen.

## End

10. The boy does not enjoy the day the second time.

11. By the time he gets home from school, he wants to stop reliving the day.

12. When he begins to relive his wish the next day, he realizes he is doomed to relive his day forever.

### Step 3: Write a First Draft
Expand on your story plan to write a first draft. You should use descriptive details to describe where your story takes place.

The reader should be able to picture your story setting in his or her mind's eye. Then think about how your characters feel. Use specific verbs, adjectives, adverbs, and nouns to describe their emotions. Adding dialogue to your story will make your characters seem even more real and alive. You may wish to follow this approach for getting your story on paper:

☐ Start by describing the setting.

☐ Describe each important character when he or she first appears.

☐ Start the action and introduce the conflict as early as possible.

☐ Tell the events in chronological order, ending with the resolution.

### Step 4: Revise
When you revise your story, ask yourself these questions:

1. Does my story grab and hold the reader's attention?

2. Are the characters interesting? Is the plot well developed? Is the setting fully described?

3. Have I used action and dialogue to bring my story to life?

Revise your story until you are satisfied with it. Then proofread your story for errors in grammar, spelling, and punctuation, and copy it over neatly.

## QUIZ

The following is a quiz for Section 10. Write the answers in complete sentences on your paper.

# Reading Comprehension

1. In "EPICAC," what turned out to be the military computer's specialty?

2. What are the "soft shapes" in the poem "Southbound on the Freeway"?

3. According to Didion's essay, what does Georgia O'Keeffe's style tell you about her character?

4. In "The Fog Horn," what attracted the monster to the lighthouse?

5. What awakened Robbie in "Today Is the First Day of . . ."?

# Understanding Literature

6. Describe EPICAC's inner conflict.

7. In "The Midnight Sun," how did a person-vs.-person conflict arise out of a person-vs.-nature conflict?

8. Give two examples of inner conflict in Robert Frost's poems.

9. Describe Georgia O'Keeffe's conflict with "the city men."

10. In "Story From Bear Country," what type of conflict is suggested by the poet's claim that "The problem is you will never want to return"?

# ACTIVITIES

**Word Attack.** The suffix *-ish* added to a root word forms an adjective meaning "having the characteristics or qualities of." For example, in "EPICAC," the narrator described the ill-fated computer as sluggish. He meant that sometimes EPICAC had the characteristics of a slug—it was slow-moving and dull.

The suffix *-ish* has several other meanings, including: (1) of the nationality of, as in *Finnish*; (2) tending or preoccupied with, as in *selfish*; (3) somewhat or approximately, as in *fortyish*.

For each word below, write the meaning of both the suffix and the word.

| | |
|---|---|
| feverish | Swedish |
| bookish | youngish |
| purplish | Scottish |
| childish | foolish |

**Speaking and Listening.** "The Midnight Sun" was written by Rod Serling for the television series "The Twilight Zone." Get together with a group of classmates and perform the teleplay for a classroom audience. Assemble seven actors and the basic props. Try to capture the drama of the conflict in your performance.

**Researching.** Kurt Vonnegut, Jr., and Ray Bradbury are both skillful writers of science fiction. Bradbury occasionally takes a glance at the past; Vonnegut generally provides a glimpse of things to come. Locate a collection of short stories by either author, and choose a story for an oral book review. Be prepared to discuss the conflict in the story and its theme.

**Creating.** Imagine that EPICAC had not left any poems for Pat. Help the narrator by writing Pat a short love poem for their first anniversary. Your poem can be either serious or humorous. You might begin with the line "Our life is like a . . ."

# A SUMMER'S READING

## BERNARD MALAMUD

*Bernard Malamud grew up in a lower middle-class neighborhood in Brooklyn, New York. In his novels and short stories, he often re-created this setting and the lives of its inhabitants while exploring themes of personal change and spiritual rebirth. As you read "A Summer's Reading," be aware of the many forces at work around the main character, George, that compel him to make an important decision about his life.*

GEORGE Stoyonovich was a neighborhood boy who had quit high school on an impulse when he was sixteen, run out of patience, and though he was ashamed every time he went looking for a job, when people asked him if he had finished and he had to say no, he never went back to school. This summer was a hard time for jobs and he had none. Having so much time on his hands, George thought of going to summer school, but the kids in his classes would be too young. He also considered registering in a night high school, only he didn't like the idea of the teachers always telling him what to do. He felt they had not respected him. The result was he stayed off the streets and in his room most of the day. He was close to twenty and had needs with the neigh-

borhood girls, but no money to spend, and he couldn't get more than an occasional few cents because his father was poor, and his sister Sophie, who resembled George, a tall bony girl of twenty-three, earned very little and what she had she kept for herself. Their mother was dead, and Sophie had to take care of the house.

Very early in the morning George's father got up to go to work in a fish market. Sophie left at about eight for her long ride in the subway to a cafeteria in the Bronx.[1] George had his coffee by himself, then hung around in the house. When the house, a five-room railroad flat[2] above a butcher store, got

---

1. **Bronx:** one of the five boroughs of New York City.
2. **railroad flat:** an apartment in which the rooms are in a line like railroad cars.

on his nerves he cleaned it up—mopped the floors with a wet mop and put things away. But most of the time he sat in his room. In the afternoons he listened to the ball game. Otherwise he had a couple of old copies of the *World Almanac* he had bought long ago, and he liked to read in them and also the magazines and newspapers that Sophie brought home, that had been left on the tables in the cafeteria. They were mostly picture magazines about movie stars and sports figures, also usually the *News* and *Mirror*.[3] Sophie herself read whatever fell into her hands, although she sometimes read good books.

She once asked George what he did in his room all day and he said he read a lot too.

"Of what besides what I bring home?

---

3. **News** and **Mirror**: the *Daily News* and the *Daily Mirror*, two New York newspapers. The *Mirror* no longer exists.

*From Williamsburg Bridge.* Edward Hopper.
The Metropolitan Museum of Art, New York. George A. Hearn Fund, 1937.

Do you ever read any worthwhile books?"

"Some," George answered, although he really didn't. He had tried to read a book or two that Sophie had in the house but found he was in no mood for them. Lately he couldn't stand made-up stories, they got on his nerves. He wished he had some hobby to work at— as a kid he was good in carpentry, but where could he work at it? Sometimes during the day he went for walks, but mostly he did his walking after the hot sun had gone down and it was cooler in the streets.

In the evening after supper George left the house and wandered in the neighborhood. During the sultry days some of the storekeepers and their wives sat in chairs on the thick, broken sidewalks in front of their shops, fanning themselves, and George walked past them and the guys hanging out on the candy-store corner. A couple of them he had known his whole life, but nobody recognized each other. He had no place special to go, but generally, saving it till the last, he left the neighborhood and walked for blocks till he came to a darkly lit little park with benches and trees and an iron railing, giving it a feeling of privacy. He sat on a bench here, watching the leafy trees and the flowers blooming on the inside of the railing, thinking of a better life for himself. He thought of the jobs he had had since he had quit school—delivery boy, stock clerk, runner, lately working in a factory—and he was dissatisfied with all of them. He felt he would someday like to have a good job and live in a private house with a porch, on a street with trees. He wanted to have some dough in his pocket to buy things with, and a girl to go with, so as not to be so lonely, especially on Saturday nights. He wanted people to like and respect him. He thought about these things often but mostly when he was alone at night. Around midnight he got up and drifted back to his hot and stony neighborhood.

One time while on his walk George met Mr. Cattanzara coming home very late from work. He wondered if he was drunk but then could tell he wasn't. Mr. Cattanzara, a stocky, bald-headed man who worked in a change booth on an IRT[4] station, lived on the next block after George's, above a shoe repair store. Nights, during the hot weather, he sat on his stoop[5] in an undershirt, reading the *New York Times* in the light of the shoemaker's window. He read it from the first page to the last, then went up to sleep. And all the time he was reading the paper, his wife, a fat woman with a white face, leaned out of the window, gazing into the street, her thick white arms folded under her loose breast, on the window ledge.

Once in a while Mr. Cattanzara came home drunk, but it was a quiet drunk. He never made any trouble, only walked stiffly up the street and slowly

---

4. **IRT:** Interborough Rapid Transit, one of the subway lines in New York City.

5. **stoop:** a staircase in front of a building.

climbed the stairs into the hall. Though drunk, he looked the same as always, except for his tight walk, the quietness, and that his eyes were wet. George liked Mr. Cattanzara because he remembered him giving him nickels to buy lemon ice with when he was a squirt. Mr. Cattanzara was a different type than those in the neighborhood. He asked different questions than the others when he met you, and he seemed to know what went on in all the newspapers. He read them, as his fat sick wife watched from the window.

"What are you doing with yourself this summer, George?" Mr. Cattanzara asked. "I see you walkin' around at nights."

George felt embarrassed. "I like to walk."

"What are you doin' in the day now?"

"Nothing much just right now. I'm waiting for a job." Since it shamed him to admit he wasn't working, George said, "I'm staying home—but I'm reading a lot to pick up my education."

Mr. Cattanzara looked interested. He mopped his hot face with a red handkerchief.

"What are you readin'?"

George hesitated, then said, "I got a list of books in the library once, and now I'm gonna read them this summer." He felt strange and a little unhappy saying this, but he wanted Mr. Cattanzara to respect him.

"How many books are there on it?"

"I never counted them. Maybe around a hundred."

Mr. Cattanzara whistled through his teeth.

"I figure if I did that," George went on earnestly, "it would help me in my education. I don't mean the kind they give you in high school. I want to know different things than they learn there, if you know what I mean."

The change maker nodded. "Still and all, one hundred books is a pretty big load for one summer."

"It might take longer."

"After you're finished with some, maybe you and I can shoot the breeze about them?" said Mr. Cattanzara.

"When I'm finished." George answered.

Mr. Cattanzara went home and George continued on his walk. After that, though he had the urge to, George did nothing different from usual. He still took his walks at night, ending up in the little park. But one evening the shoemaker on the next block stopped George to say he was a good boy, and George figured that Mr. Cattanzara had told him all about the books he was reading. From the shoemaker it must have gone down the street, because George saw a couple of people smiling kindly at him, though nobody spoke to him personally. He felt a little better around the neighborhood and liked it more, though not so much he would want to live in it forever. He had never exactly disliked the people in it, yet he had never liked them very much either. It was the fault of the neighborhood. To his surprise, George found out that his father and Sophie knew about his reading too. His father was too shy to say anything about it—he was never much of a talker in his whole life—but Sophie was softer to George, and she showed him in other ways she was proud of him.

As the summer went on George felt in a good mood about things. He cleaned the house every day, as a favor to Sophie, and he enjoyed the ball games more. Sophie gave him a buck a week allowance, and though it still wasn't enough and he had to use it carefully, it was a helluva lot better than just having two bits[6] now and then. What he bought with the money—cigarettes mostly, an occasional beer or movie ticket—he got a big kick out of. Life wasn't so bad if you knew how to appreciate it. Occasionally he bought a paperback book from the newsstand, but he never got around to reading it, though he was glad to have a couple of books in his room. But he read thoroughly Sophie's magazines and newspapers. And at night was the most enjoyable time, because when he passed the storekeepers sitting outside their stores, he could tell they regarded him highly. He walked erect, and though he did not say much to them, or they to him, he could feel approval on all sides. A couple of nights he felt so good that he skipped the park at the end of the evening. He just wandered in the neighborhood, where people had known him

*Noontime on St. Botolph Street.* George Luks.
Courtesy Museum of Fine Arts, Boston, Massachusetts.
Emily L. Ainsley Fund.

from the time he was a kid playing punchball whenever there was a game of it going; he wandered there, then came home and got undressed for bed, feeling fine.

For a few weeks he had talked only once with Mr. Cattanzara, and though the change maker had said nothing more about the books, asked no questions, his silence made George a little uneasy. For a while George didn't pass in front of Mr. Cattanzara's house any

---

6. **two bits:** 25 cents.

more, until one night, forgetting himself, he approached it from a different direction than he usually did when he did. It was already past midnight. The street, except for one or two people, was deserted, and George was surprised when he saw Mr. Cattanzara still reading his newspaper by the light of the streetlamp overhead. His impulse was to stop at the stoop and talk to him. He wasn't sure what he wanted to say, though he felt the words would come when he began to talk; but the more he thought about it, the more the idea scared him, and he decided he'd better not. He even considered beating it home by another street, but he was too near Mr. Cattanzara, and the change maker might see him as he ran, and get annoyed. So George unobtrusively crossed the street, trying to make it seem as if he had to look in a store window on the other side, which he did, and then went on, uncomfortable at what he was doing. He feared Mr. Cattanzara would glance up from his paper and call him a dirty rat for walking on the other side of the street, but all he did was sit there, sweating through his undershirt, his bald head shining in the dim light as he read his *Times*, and upstairs his fat wife leaned out of the window, seeming to read the paper along with him. George thought she would spy him and yell out to Mr. Cattanzara, but she never moved her eyes off her husband.

George made up his mind to stay away from the change maker until he had got some of his softback books read, but when he started them and saw they were mostly storybooks, he lost his interest and didn't bother to finish them. He lost his interest in reading other things too. Sophie's magazines and newspapers went unread. She saw them piling up on a chair in his room and asked why he was no longer looking at them, and George told her it was because of all the other reading he had to do. Sophie said she had guessed that was it. So for most of the day, George had the radio on, turning to music when he was sick of the human voice. He kept the house fairly neat, and Sophie said nothing on the days when he neglected it. She was still kind and gave him his extra buck, though things weren't so good for him as they had been before.

But they were good enough, considering. Also his night walks invariably picked him up, no matter how bad the day was. Then one night George saw Mr. Cattanzara coming down the street toward him. George was about to turn and run but he recognized from Mr. Cattanzara's walk that he was drunk, and if so, probably he would not even bother to notice him. So George kept on walking straight ahead until he came abreast of Mr. Cattanzara and though he felt wound up enough to pop into the sky, he was not surprised when Mr. Cattanzara passed him without a word, walking slowly, his face and body stiff. George drew a breath in relief at his narrow escape, when he heard his name called, and there stood Mr. Cattanzara at his elbow, smelling like the inside of a beer barrel. His eyes were sad as he gazed at George, and George felt so intensely uncomfortable he was tempted to shove the drunk aside and continue on his walk.

But he couldn't act that way to him, and, besides, Mr. Cattanzara took a nickel out of his pants pocket and handed it to him.

"Go buy yourself a lemon ice, Georgie."

"It's not that time any more, Mr. Cattanzara," George said, "I am a big guy now."

"No, you ain't," said Mr. Cattanzara, to which George made no reply he could think of.

"How are all your books comin' along now?" Mr. Cattanzara asked. Though he tried to stand steady, he swayed a little.

"Fine, I guess," said George, feeling the red crawling up his face.

"You ain't sure?" The change maker smiled slyly, a way George had never seen him smile.

"Sure I'm sure. They're fine."

Though his head swayed in little arcs, Mr. Cattanzara's eyes were steady. He had small blue eyes which could hurt if you looked at them too long.

"George," he said, "name me one book on that list that you read this summer, and I will drink to your health."

"I don't want anybody drinking to me."

"Name me one so I can ask you a question on it. Who can tell, if it's a good book maybe I might wanna read it

myself."

George knew he looked passable on the outside, but inside he was crumbling apart.

Unable to reply, he shut his eyes, but when—years later—he opened them, he saw that Mr. Cattanzara had, out of pity, gone away, but in his ears he still heard the words he had said when he left: "George, don't do what I did."

The next night he was afraid to leave his room, and though Sophie argued with him he wouldn't open the door.

"What are you doing in there?" she asked.

"Nothing."

"Aren't you reading?"

"No."

She was silent a minute, then asked, "Where do you keep the books you read? I never see any in your room outside of a few cheap trashy ones."

He wouldn't tell her.

"In that case you're not worth a buck of my hard-earned money. Why should I break my back for you? Go on out, you bum, and get a job."

He stayed in his room for almost a week, except to sneak into the kitchen when nobody was home. Sophie railed at him, then begged him to come out, and his old father wept, but George wouldn't budge, though the weather was terrible and his small room stifling. He found it very hard to breathe, each breath was like drawing a flame into his lungs.

One night, unable to stand the heat anymore, he burst into the street at one

A.M., a shadow of himself. He hoped to sneak to the park without being seen, but there were people all over the block, wilted and listless, waiting for a breeze. George lowered his eyes and walked, in disgrace, away from them, but before long he discovered they were still friendly to him. He figured Mr. Cattanzara hadn't told on him. Maybe when he woke up out of his drunk the next morning, he had forgotten all about meeting George. George felt his confidence slowly come back to him.

That same night a man on a street corner asked him if it was true that he had finished reading so many books, and George admitted he had. The man said it was a wonderful thing for a boy his age to read so much.

"Yeah," George said, but he felt relieved. He hoped nobody would mention the books anymore, and when, after a couple of days, he accidentally met Mr. Cattanzara again, *he* didn't, though George had the idea he was the one who had started the rumor that he had finished all the books.

One evening in the fall, George ran out of his house to the library, where he hadn't been in years. There were books all over the place, wherever he looked, and though he was struggling to control an inward trembling, he easily counted off a hundred, then sat down at a table to read.

# THINKING ABOUT THE STORY

*Recalling*

**1.** How old is George? According to the first paragraph, why does he stay "in his room most of the day"?

**2.** Briefly describe how George spends a typical day. What does he read? What does he not enjoy reading?

**3.** What does George think about when he sits in the little park?

**4.** Who is Mr. Cattanzara? How does he spend his summer evenings? According to George, how is Mr. Cattanzara different from other people in the neighborhood?

**5.** What does George tell Mr. Cattanzara when the man asks how he is spending his time? Why does George lie? Explain how this lie eventually affects the way people in the neighborhood treat George.

**6.** What feelings prompt George to avoid Mr. Cattanzara? How does George react after Mr. Cattanzara finally confronts him about his summer reading? What rumor does George later suspect Mr. Cattanzara of spreading about him?

**7.** What does George struggle to control when he goes to the library? What does he do there?

*Interpreting*

**8.** From the way George's neighbors and his sister Sophie treat him, what attitude can you determine they have toward reading and education?

**9.** What do you think Sophie has in mind when she talks of "worthwhile books"?

**10.** When Mr. Cattanzara confronts George about his reading, Malamud writes: "George knew he looked passable on the outside, but inside he was crumbling apart." What precisely has George begun to realize is crumbling?

**11.** The way George behaves toward Mr. Cattanzara is the result of his own internal conflict. What opposing forces within himself is George struggling to resolve? What do you suppose finally compels George to run out of his house to the library?

*Applying*

**12.** In this story, George finally realizes the true value that reading has in his life. What value does reading have for you? In what ways can it be a means of personal change for many people?

. . . . . . . . . . . . . . . . . . . . . . . . . . . . .

# ANALYZING LITERATURE

*Understanding Setting*
The **setting** in a work of literature is the

time and place in which the action occurs. A short story's setting may be in the present, the past, or the future. It may be a realistic, recognizable place or some imaginary land.

An author's choice of setting usually has a direct relationship to the story's characters, plot, and mood. Setting affects the way characters behave. In "A Summer's Reading," for example, the summer heat influences the way George spends his evenings walking around his neighborhood. In some stories, the setting itself may be central to the conflict, as characters struggle to overcome the forces of nature or their urban environment. A story's setting also creates a general mood. In Ray Bradbury's "The Fog Horn" (page 592), for example, the bleak setting of the fogbound lighthouse creates a mood of danger and impending doom.

Think about the effect Bernard Malamud's choice of setting in "A Summer's Reading" has on the elements of character, plot, and mood.

1. In what time and place does the action of the story occur? What is George's attitude toward this setting? Why do you suppose he enjoys walking to the little park?

2. What effect do you suppose the story's setting has on the way George resolves his internal conflict?

3. What mood does the story's setting create? Why do you suppose Malamud chose to create this particular mood instead of a more pleasant one?

......................................

# CRITICAL THINKING AND READING

*Making Inferences*

In "A Summer's Reading," Bernard Malamud describes what the characters do but often leaves it up to his readers to infer why they act that way. To **infer** is to make a reasonable guess based on the information presented. By being alert to clues that help you get inside a character's mind, you will better appreciate an author's skill at making characters believable.

Review "A Summer's Reading" and think about the following details from the story. What can you infer about the characters from these details?

1. After telling his lie to Mr. Cattanzara, George is uneasy about meeting him on the street. What reasons do you suppose George has for purposely trying to avoid Mr. Cattanzara?

2. From the way Mr. Cattanzara confronts George, it is evident he knows George has not been spending his time reading books from a library list. Considering the confrontation scene as well as who Mr. Cattanzara is and the way he spends his own evenings, how do you suppose he knew George was lying?

## DEVELOPING VOCABULARY SKILLS

*Synonyms and Antonyms*

**Synonyms** are words with the same or nearly the same meaning. **Antonyms** are two words with opposite meanings. By learning similar and opposite meanings of words, you will not only broaden the range of your vocabulary but also perfect the accuracy with which you use words.

For each italicized word in the following passages from "A Summer's Reading," select an appropriate synonym and antonym from the two lists below.

1. "During the *sultry* days some of the storekeepers and their wives sat in chairs on the thick, broken sidewalks in front of their shops. . . . "

2. "So George *unobtrusively* crossed the street, trying to make it seem as if he had to look in a store window on the other side. . . . "

3. "George wouldn't budge, though the weather was terrible and his small room *stifling*."

4. " . . . there were people all over the block, wilted and *listless*, waiting for a breeze."

| Synonyms | Antonyms |
|----------|----------|
| sluggish | comfortable |
| shyly | cold |
| sweltering | lively |
| stuffy | blatantly |

## THINKING AND WRITING

**1. Writing About Conflict.**

In "A Summer's Reading," George's lying about his summer reading brings him into conflict not only with Mr. Cattanzara but also with his own warring feelings. In a brief essay, discuss the nature of these conflicts and explain how they are resolved.

**Prewriting.** Plan your essay by sketching a rough outline. The first part of your essay might discuss George's external conflict with Mr. Cattanzara; the second part, George's internal conflict; and the third part, how the conflicts are resolved. After you have made an outline, write an introductory sentence that gives a clear overview of what your essay will discuss.

**Writing.** As you write your first draft, do not hesitate to stray from your outline if you think you can improve it. Be sure you back up your assertions by quoting appropriate passages from the story.

**Revising.** While revising your essay, focus mainly on its organization. Do your ideas flow smoothly from one to the next? Can any details be cut because they are unnecessary or repetitive? Do any ideas need to be dealt with more thoroughly? Have you discussed both

George's external and internal conflicts? Have you demonstrated how both are resolved? Does your introduction indicate the direction of your thoughts and point toward your conclusion?

**Proofreading.** Reread your essay and correct any mistakes in grammar, spelling, and punctuation. Be sure that you have used quotation marks correctly. If necessary, prepare a neat final copy.

**Publishing.** Share your essay with a group of classmates.

### 2. Writing from a Character's Point of View.

Imagine you are George and that several months have passed since you first went to the library and counted off the hundred books and began to read them. Write a letter to Mr. Cattanzara in which you tell him how you have been spending your time.

**Prewriting.** Assuming George's point of view, think about how the experience of reading "worthwhile books" has—or has not—changed your life. You might make notes in response to questions like these: What difficulties did you have to overcome? What have you discovered not only about the world but also about yourself? Remember that your audience will be Mr. Cattanzara. What tone do you want to convey toward him: thanks? regret? respect?

**Writing.** Use the form of a friendly letter. Try to express not only your (George's) ideas but also your feelings.

**Revising.** After you have written a first draft, check to see if it is a logical extension of the story. Is your letter one that George might have actually written? Does it express George's perspective on his neighborhood and on life in general? Does it contain specific references to characters and events in the story?

**Proofreading.** Reread your letter and correct any mistakes in grammar, spelling, and punctuation. If necessary, prepare a neat final copy.

**Publishing.** Exchange your letter with a classmate. You might then respond to the letter as if you were the recipient, Mr. Cattanzara.

# ARTHUR MILLER

## A MODERN PLAYWRIGHT

*Once and for all you can know
there's a universe of people outside
and you're responsible to it.*

— Arthur Miller

*Fifth Avenue and Forty-Second Street*
John Marin (1870-1953)
The Phillips Collection
Acquired from artist through Alfred Stieglitz,
An American Place, N.Y.

In 1945, Arthur Miller was 30 years old. He had been writing plays for 10 years. He had won some prizes, but his plays had not won any real popularity or financial success. Miller decided to write just one more play. If this play were not a success, Miller was going to give up writing plays forever. It took him two years to complete the play, but in 1947, *All My Sons* appeared on the Broadway stage. It won the New York Drama Circle Award. Suddenly Arthur Miller became one of America's most famous modern playwrights. Theaters all over America and the world have staged their own productions of *All My Sons,* as well as productions of the plays that Miller has written since. This last section is made up entirely of *All My Sons.*

### A Modern American Play

Miller's play *All My Sons* was successful because it powerfully combined the experiences of World War II America with the basic conflicts that people have faced in every time and place. Americans have long prided themselves on their independence. But Americans who served in the armed forces during World War II were proudest of their cooperative spirit — the way people seemed to think first of others — and of their common cause. When Miller visited army training camps in 1944, he discovered that many Americans at war resented the Americans at home who were growing rich from the misfortunes of war. They also felt cut off from the everyday home life that did not understand the true horrors of war. *All My Sons* draws on these feelings.

With *All My Sons,* Miller also succeeded in presenting a classic dramatic struggle in everyday modern language, with everyday modern people. *All My Sons* is a distinctively American tragedy. It is not about the flaw of weakness that leads to the downfall of an ancient king or prince; it is about the tragedy of the common man. Miller wrote that "the tragic feeling is evoked in us when we are in the presence of a character who is ready to lay down his life, if need be, to secure one thing — his sense of personal dignity." Many people think that tragedies reflect sorrow and despair. But *All My Sons* contains humor as well as sorrow. Further, Miller explains

that he wrote this tragedy because it reflects optimism and hope and the indestructibility of the human spirit.

## A Question of Right or Wrong

At the premiere of *All My Sons*, Miller explained why and how he wrote plays. He said that he took settings and dramatic situations from life that involve real questions of right and wrong. In this full-length play, as well as in other important literary works, it is the values the author presents — through the characters he or she has chosen — and the careful structuring of plot that give the work its lasting worth.

Plays are written to be performed. The playwright must provide the spark to bring his or her characters and ideas to life on the stage. The readers' or actors' interpretations of the characters, their expressions, voices, and the feelings they convey further add to the play. Arthur Miller crafted *All My Sons* to express his ideas and values and to stimulate others to explore their own.

# All My Sons

## CHARACTERS

| | |
|---|---|
| Joe Keller | Dr. Jim Bayliss |
| Kate Keller | Sue Bayliss |
| Chris Keller | Frank Lubey |
| Ann Deever | Lydia Lubey |
| George Deever | Bert |

# Act One

The backyard of the Keller home in the outskirts of an American town. August of our era.

The stage is hedged on right and left by tall, closely planted poplars which lend the yard a secluded atmosphere. Upstage is filled with the back of the house and its open, unroofed porch which extends into the yard some six feet. The house is two stories high and has seven rooms. It would have cost perhaps 15 thousand in the early twenties when it was built. Now it is nicely painted, looks tight and comfortable, and the yard is green with sod, here and there plants whose season is gone. At the right, beside the house, the entrance of the driveway can be seen, but the poplars cut off view of its continuation downstage. In the left corner, downstage, stands the four-foot-high stump of a slender apple tree whose upper trunk and branches lie toppled beside it, fruit still clinging to its branches.

Downstage right is a small, trellised arbor, shaped like a seashell, with a decorative bulb hanging from its forward-curving roof. Garden chairs and a table are scattered about. A garbage pail on the ground next to the porch steps, a wire leaf-burner near it.

On the rise: It is early Sunday morning. Joe Keller is sitting in the sun reading the want ads of the Sunday paper, the other sections of which lie neatly on the ground beside him. Behind his back, inside the arbor, Doctor Jim Bayliss is reading part of the paper at the table.

Keller is nearing 60. A heavy man of stolid mind and build, a businessman these many years, but with the imprint of the machine-shop worker and boss still upon him. When he reads, when he speaks, when he listens, it is with the terrible concentration of the uneducated man for whom there is still wonder in many commonly known things, a man whose judgments must be

dredged out of experience and a peasant-like common sense. A man among men.

*Doctor Bayliss is nearly 40. A wry, self-controlled man, an easy talker, but with a wisp of sadness that clings even to his self-effacing humor.*

*At curtain, Jim is standing at the left, staring at the broken tree. He taps a pipe on it, blows through the pipe, feels in his pockets for tobacco, then speaks.*

**Jim:** Where's your tobacco?

**Keller:** I think I left it on the table. (*Jim goes slowly to table in the arbor, finds a pouch, and sits there on the bench, filling his pipe.*) Gonna rain tonight.

**Jim:** Paper says so?

**Keller:** Yeah, right here.

**Jim:** Then it can't rain.

(*Frank Lubey enters, through a small space between the poplars. Frank is 32 but balding. A pleasant, opinionated man, uncertain of himself, with a tendency toward peevishness when crossed, but always wanting it pleasant and neighborly.*)

631

*He rather saunters in, leisurely, nothing to do. He does not notice Jim in the arbor. On his greeting, Jim does not bother looking up.)*

**Frank:** Hya.

**Keller:** Hello, Frank. What's doin'?

**Frank:** Nothin'. Walking off my breakfast. *(Looks up at the sky.)* That beautiful? Not a cloud.

**Keller** *(looking up):* Yeah, nice.

**Frank:** Every Sunday ought to be like this.

**Keller** *(indicating the sections beside him):* Want the paper?

**Frank:** What's the difference, it's all bad news. What's today's calamity?

**Keller:** I don't know, I don't read the news part anymore. It's more interesting in the want ads.

**Frank:** Why, you trying to buy something?

**Keller:** No, I'm just interested. To see what people want, y'know? For instance, here's a guy lookin' for two Newfoundland dogs. Now what's he want with two Newfoundland dogs?

**Frank:** That is funny.

**Keller:** Here's another one. "Wanted — old dictionaries. High prices paid." Now what's a man going to do with an old dictionary?

**Frank:** Why not? Probably a book collector.

**Keller:** You mean he'll make a living out of that?

**Frank:** Sure, there's a lot of them.

**Keller** *(shaking his head):* All the kind of business goin' on. In my day, either you were a lawyer, or a doctor, or you worked in a shop. Now —

**Frank:** Well, I was going to be a forester once.

**Keller:** Well, that shows you; in my day, there was no such thing. *(Scanning the page, sweeping it with his hand)* You look at a page like this you realize how ignorant you are. *(Softly, with wonder, as he scans page)*

**Frank** *(noticing tree):* Hey, what happened to your tree?

**Keller:** Ain't that awful? The wind must've got it last night. You heard the wind, didn't you?

**Frank:** Yeah, I got a mess in my yard, too. *(Goes to tree.)* What a pity. *(Turning to Keller)* What'd Kate say?

**Keller:** They're all asleep yet. I'm just waiting for her to see it.

**Frank** *(struck):* You know? — it's funny.

**Keller:** What?

**Frank:** Larry was born in August. He'd been 27 this month. And his tree blows down.

**Keller** *(touched):* I'm surprised you remember his birthday, Frank. That's nice.

**Frank:** I'm working on his horoscope.

**Keller:** How can you make him a horoscope? That's for the future, ain't it?

**Frank:** Well, what I'm doing is this, see. Larry was reported missing on November twenty-fifth, right?

**Keller:** Yeah?

**Frank:** Well, then, we assume that if he was killed it was on November twenty-fifth. Now, what Kate wants —

**Keller:** Oh, Kate asked you to make a horoscope?

**Frank:** Yeah, what she wants to find out is whether November twenty-fifth was a favorable day for Larry.

**Keller:** What is that, favorable day?

**Frank:** Well, a favorable day for a person is a fortunate day, according to his stars. In other words it would be practically impossible for him to have died on his favorable day.

**Keller:** Well, was that his favorable day? — November twenty-fifth?

**Frank:** That's what I'm working to find out. It takes time! See, the point is, if November twenty-fifth was his favorable day, then it's completely possible he's alive somewhere, because — I mean it's possible. *(He notices Jim now. Jim is looking at him as though at an idiot. To Jim — with an uncertain laugh.)* I didn't even see you.

**Keller** *(to Jim):* Is he talkin' sense?

**Jim:** Him? He's all right. He's just completely out of his mind, that's all.

**Frank** *(peeved):* The trouble with you is, you don't *believe* in anything.

**Jim:** And your trouble is that you believe in *anything*. You didn't see my kid this morning, did you?

**Frank:** No.

**Keller:** Imagine? He walked off with his thermometer. Right out of his bag.

**Jim** *(getting up):* What a problem. One look at a girl and he takes her temperature. *(Goes to driveway, looks upstage toward street.)*

**Frank:** That boy's going to be a real doctor; he's smart.

**Jim:** Over my dead body he'll be a doctor. A good beginning, too.

**Frank:** Why? It's an honorable profession.

**Jim** *(looking at him tiredly):* Frank, will you stop talking like a civics book?

*(Keller laughs).*

**Frank:** Why, I saw a movie a couple of weeks ago reminded me of you. There was a doctor in that picture —

**Keller:** Don Ameche!

**Frank:** I think it was, yeah. And he worked in his basement discovering things. That's what you ought to do; you could help humanity, instead of —

**Jim:** I would love to help humanity on a Warner Brothers salary.

**Keller** *(pointing at him, laughing):* That's very good, Jim.

**Jim** *(looking toward the house):* Well, where's the beautiful girl that was supposed to be here?

**Frank** *(excited):* Annie came?

**Keller:** Sure, sleepin' upstairs. We picked her up on the 1:00 train last night. Wonderful thing. Girl leaves here, a scrawny kid. Couple of years go by, she's a regular woman. Hardly recognized her, and she was running in and out of the yard all her life. That was a very happy family used to live in your house, Jim.

**Jim:** Like to meet her. The block can use a pretty girl. In the whole neighborhood there's not a damned thing to look at. *(Sue, Jim's wife, enters. She is rounding 40, an overweight woman who fears it. On seeing her, Jim wryly adds.)* Except my wife of course.

**Sue** *(in the same spirit):* Mrs. Adams is on the phone, you dog.

**Jim** *(to Keller):* Such is the condition which prevails. *(Going to his wife)* My love, my light.

**Sue:** Don't sniff around me. *(Pointing to their house)* And give her a nasty answer. I can smell her perfume over the phone.

**Jim:** What's the matter with her now?

**Sue:** I don't know, dear. She sounds like she's in terrible pain — unless her mouth is full of candy.

**Jim:** Why don't you just tell her to lay down?

**Sue:** She enjoys it more when you tell her to lay down. And when are you going to see Mr. Hubbard?

**Jim:** My dear, Mr. Hubbard is not sick, and I have better things to do than to sit there and hold his hand.

**Sue:** It seems to me that for 10 dollars you could hold his hand.

**Jim** *(to Keller):* If your son wants to play golf tell him I'm ready. Or if he'd like to take a trip around the world for about 30 years. *(He exits.)*

**Keller:** Why do you needle him? He's a doctor; women are supposed to call him.

**Sue:** All I said was Mrs. Adams is on the phone. Can I have some of your parsley?

**Keller:** Yeah, sure. *(She goes to parsley box and pulls some parsley.)* You were a nurse too long, Susie. You're too . . . realistic.

**Sue** *(laughing, pointing at him):* Now you said it! *(Lydia Lubey enters. She is a robust, laughing girl of 27.)*

**Lydia:** Frank, the toaster. *(Sees the others.)* Hya.

**Keller:** Hello!

**Lydia** *(to Frank):* The toaster is off again.

**Frank:** Well, plug it in; I just fixed it.

**Lydia** *(kindly, but insistently):* Please, dear, fix it back like it was before.

**Frank:** I don't know why you can't learn to turn on a simple thing like a toaster! *(He exits.)*

**Sue** *(laughing):* Thomas Edison.

**Lydia** *(apologetically):* He's really very handy. *(She sees broken tree.)* Oh, did the wind get your tree?

**Keller:** Yeah, last night.

**Lydia:** Oh, what a pity. Annie get in?

**Keller:** She'll be down soon. Wait'll you meet her, Sue; she's a knockout.

**Sue:** I should've been a man. People are always introducing me to beautiful women. *(To Joe)* Tell her to come over later. I imagine she'd like to see what we did with her house. And thanks.

*(She exits.)*

**Lydia:** Is she still unhappy, Joe?

**Keller:** Annie? I don't suppose she goes around dancing on her toes, but she seems to be over it.

**Lydia:** She's going to get married. Is there anybody — ?

**Keller:** I suppose — say, it's a couple years already. She can't mourn a boy forever.

**Lydia:** It's so strange — Annie's here and not even married. And I've got three babies. I always thought it'd be the other way around.

**Keller:** Well, that's what war does. I had two sons, now I got one. It changed all the tallies. In my day when you had sons it was an honor. Today a doctor could make a million dollars if he could figure out a way to bring a boy into the world without a trigger finger.

**Lydia:** You know, I was just reading. *(Enter Chris Keller from house, stands in doorway.)* Hya, Chris.

*(Frank shouts from offstage.)*

**Frank:** Lydia, come in here! If you want the toaster to work don't plug in the malted mixer.

**Lydia** *(embarrassed, laughing):* Did I?

**Frank:** And the next time I fix something don't tell me I'm crazy! Now come in here!

**Lydia** *(to Keller):* I'll never hear the end of this one.

**Keller** *(calling to Frank):* So what's the difference? Instead of toast have a malted!

**Lydia:** Sh! Sh! *(She exits, laughing.)*

*(Chris watches her off. He is 32; like his father, solidly built, a listener. A man capable of immense affection and loyalty. He has a cup of coffee in one hand, part of a doughnut in the other.)*

**Keller:** You want the paper?

**Chris:** That's all right, just the book section. *(He bends down and pulls out part of paper on porch floor.)*

**Keller:** You're always reading the book section and you never buy a book.

**Chris** *(coming down to settee):* I like to keep abreast of my ignorance. *(He sits on settee.)*

**Keller:** What is that, every week a new book comes out?

**Chris:** Lot of new books.

**Keller:** All different?

**Chris:** All different.

*(Keller shakes his head, puts knife down on bench, takes oilstone up to the cabinet.)*

**Keller:** Psss! Annie up yet?

**Chris:** Mother's giving her breakfast in the dining room.

**Keller** *(looking at broken tree):* See what happened to the tree?

**Chris** *(without looking up):* Yeah.

**Keller:** What's Mother going to say?

*(Bert runs on from driveway. He is about eight. He jumps on stool, then Keller's back.)*

**Bert:** You're finally up.

**Keller** *(swinging him around and putting him down):* Ha! Bert's here! Where's Tommy? He's got his father's thermometer again.

**Bert:** He's taking a reading.

**Chris:** What!

**Bert:** But it's only oral.

**Keller:** Oh, well there's no harm in oral. So what's new this morning, Bert?

**Bert:** Nothin'. *(He walks around broken tree.)*

**Keller:** Then you couldn't 've made a complete inspection of the block. In the beginning, when I first made you a policeman you used to come in every morning with something new. Now, nothin's ever new.

**Bert:** Except some kids from Thirtieth Street. They started kicking a can down the block, and I made them go away because you were sleeping.

**Keller:** Now you're talkin', Bert. Now you're on the ball. First thing you know I'm liable to make you a detective.

**Bert** *(pulling him down by the lapel and whispering in his ear):* Can I see the jail now?

**Keller:** Seein' the jail ain't allowed, Bert. You know that.

**Bert:** Aw, I betcha there isn't even a jail. I don't see any bars on the cellar windows.

**Keller:** Bert, on my word of honor there's

a jail in the basement. I showed you my gun, didn't I?

**Bert:** But that's a hunting gun.

**Keller:** That's an arresting gun!

**Bert:** Then why don't you ever arrest anybody? Tommy said another dirty word to Doris yesterday, and you didn't even demote him.

*(Keller chuckles and winks at Chris, who is enjoying all this.)*

**Keller:** Yeah, that's a dangerous character, that Tommy. *(Beckons him closer.)* What word does he say?

**Bert** *(backing away quickly in great embarrassment):* Oh, I can't say that.

**Keller** *(grabbing him by the shirt and pulling him back):* Well, gimme an idea.

**Bert:** I can't. It's not a nice word.

**Keller:** Just whisper in my ear. I'll close my eyes. Maybe I won't even hear it.

*(Bert, on tiptoe, puts his lips to Keller's ear, then in unbearable embarrassment steps back.)*

**Bert:** I can't, Mr. Keller.

**Chris** *(laughing):* Don't make him do that.

**Keller:** Okay, Bert. I take your word. Now go out, and keep both eyes peeled.

**Bert** *(interested):* For what?

**Keller:** For what! Bert, the whole neighborhood is depending on you. A policeman don't ask questions. Now peel them eyes!

**Bert** *(mystified, but willing):* Okay. *(He runs offstage back of arbor.)*

**Keller** *(calling after him):* And mum's the word, Bert.

*(Bert stops and sticks his head through the arbor.)*

**Bert:** About what?

**Keller:** Just in general. Be v-e-r-y careful.

**Bert** *(nodding in bewilderment):* Okay. *(He exits.)*

**Keller** *(laughing):* I got all the kids crazy!

**Chris:** One of these days, they'll come in here and beat your brains out.

**Keller:** What's she going to say? Maybe we ought to tell her before she sees it.

**Chris:** She saw it.

**Keller:** How could she see it? I was the first one up. She was still in bed.

**Chris:** She was out here when it broke.

**Keller:** When?

**Chris:** About four this morning. *(Indicating window above them.)* I heard it cracking and I woke up and looked out. She was standing right here when it cracked.

**Keller:** What was she doing out here four in the morning?

**Chris:** I don't know. When it cracked she ran back into the house and cried in the kitchen.

**Keller:** Did you talk to her?

**Chris:** No, I — I figured the best thing was to leave her alone. *(Pause.)*

**Keller** *(deeply touched):* She cried hard?

**Chris:** I could hear her right through the floor of my room.

**Keller** *(after slight pause):* What was she doing out here at that hour? *(Chris silent, with an undertone of anger showing.)* She's dreaming about him again. She's walking around at night.

**Chris:** I guess she is.

**Keller:** She's getting just like after he died. *(Slight pause.)* What's the meaning of that?

**Chris:** I don't know the meaning of it. *(Slight pause.)* But I know one thing, Dad. We've made a terrible mistake with Mother.

**Keller:** What?

**Chris:** Being dishonest with her. That

kind of thing always pays off, and now it's paying off.

**Keller:** What do you mean, dishonest?

**Chris:** You know Larry's not coming back and I know it. Why do we allow her to go on thinking that we believe with her?

**Keller:** What do you want to do, argue with her?

**Chris:** I don't want to argue with her, but it's time she realized that nobody believes Larry is alive anymore. (*Keller simply moves away, thinking, looking at the ground.*) Why shouldn't she dream of him, walk the nights waiting for him? Do we contradict her? Do we say straight out that we have no hope anymore? That we haven't had any hope for years now?

**Keller** (*frightened at the thought*): You can't say that to her.

**Chris:** We've got to say it to her.

**Keller:** How're you going to prove it? Can you prove it?

**Chris:** For God's sake, three years! Nobody comes back after three years. It's insane.

**Keller:** To you it is, and to me. But not to her. You can talk yourself blue in the face, but there's no body and there's no grave, so where are you?

**Chris:** Sit down, Dad. I want to talk to you.

(*Keller looks at him searchingly a moment.*)

**Keller:** The trouble is the damn newspapers. Every month some boy turns up from nowhere, so the next one is going to be Larry, so —

**Chris:** All right, all right, listen to me. (*Slight pause. Keller sits on settee.*) You know why I asked Annie here, don't you?

**Keller** (*he knows, but —*): Why?

**Chris:** You know.

**Keller:** Well, I got an idea, but — What's the story?

**Chris:** I'm going to ask her to marry me. (*Slight pause. Keller nods.*)

**Keller:** Well, that's only your business, Chris.

**Chris:** You know it's not only my business.

**Keller:** What do you want me to do? You're old enough to know your own mind.

**Chris** (*asking, annoyed*): Then it's all right, I'll go ahead with it?

**Keller:** Well, you want to be sure Mother isn't going to —

**Chris:** Then it isn't just my business.

**Keller:** I'm just sayin' —

**Chris:** Sometimes you infuriate me, you know that? Isn't it your business, too, if I tell this to Mother and she throws a fit about it? You have such a talent for ignoring things.

**Keller:** I ignore what I gotta ignore. The girl is Larry's girl.

**Chris:** She's not Larry's girl.

**Keller:** From Mother's point of view he is not dead and you have no right to take his girl. (*Slight pause.*) Now you can go on from there if you know where to go, but I'm tellin' you I don't know where to go. See? I don't know. Now what can I do for you?

**Chris:** I don't know why it is, but every time I reach out for something I want I have to pull back because other people will suffer. My whole bloody life, time after time after time.

**Keller:** You're a considerate fella, there's nothing wrong in that.

**Chris:** To hell with that.

**Keller:** Did you ask Annie yet?

**Chris:** I wanted to get this settled first.

**Keller:** How do you know she'll marry you? Maybe she feels the same way Mother does?

**Chris:** Well, if she does, then that's the end of it. From her letters I think she's forgotten him. I'll find out. And then we'll thrash it out with Mother? Right? Dad, don't avoid me.

**Keller:** The trouble is, you don't see enough women. You never did.

**Chris:** So what? I'm not fast with women.

**Keller:** I don't see why it has to be Annie.

**Chris:** Because it is.

**Keller:** That's a good answer, but it don't answer anything. You haven't seen her since you went to war. It's five years.

**Chris:** I can't help it. I know her best. I was brought up next door to her. These years when I think of someone for my wife, I think of Annie. What do you want, a diagram?

**Keller:** I don't want a diagram. . . . I — I'm — she thinks he's coming back, Chris. You marry this girl and you're pronouncing him dead. Now what's going to happen to Mother? Do you know? I don't! *(Pause.)*

**Chris:** All right, then, Dad.

**Keller** *(thinking Chris has retreated):* Give it some more thought.

**Chris:** I've given it three years of thought. I'd hoped that if I waited, Mother would forget Larry and then we'd have a regular wedding and everything happy. But if that can't happen here, then I'll have to get out.

**Keller:** What the hell is *this?*

**Chris:** I'll get out. I'll get married and live someplace else. Maybe in New York.

**Keller:** Are you crazy?

**Chris:** I've been a good son too long, a good sucker. I'm through with it.

**Keller:** You've got a business here, what the hell is this?

**Chris:** The business! The business doesn't inspire me.

**Keller:** Must you be inspired?

**Chris:** Yes. I like it an hour a day. If you have to grub for money all day long at least at evening I want it beautiful. I want a family; I want some kids; I want to build something I can give myself to. Annie is in the middle of that. Now . . . where do I find it?

**Keller:** You mean . . . *(Goes to him.)* Tell me something, you mean you'd leave the business?

**Chris:** Yes. On this I would.

**Keller** *(after a pause):* Well . . . you don't want to think like that.

**Chris:** Then help me stay here.

**Keller:** All right, but — but don't think like that. Because what the hell did I work for? That's only for you, Chris, the whole shootin' match is for you!

**Chris:** I know that, Dad. Just you help me stay here.

**Keller** *(putting a fist up to Chris's jaw):* But don't think that way, you hear me?

**Chris:** I am thinking that way.

**Keller** *(lowering his hand):* I don't understand you, do I?

**Chris:** No, you don't. I'm a pretty tough guy.

**Keller:** Yeah. I can see that.

*(Mother appears on porch. She is in her*

*early fifties, a woman of uncontrolled inspirations and an overwhelming capacity for love.)*

**Mother:** Joe?
**Chris** *(going toward porch):* Hello, Mom.
**Mother** *(indicating house behind her; to Keller):* Did you take a bag from under the sink?
**Keller:** Yeah, I put it in the pail.
**Mother:** Well, get it out of the pail. That's my potatoes.

*(Chris bursts out laughing — goes up into alley.)*

**Keller** *(laughing):* I thought it was garbage.
**Mother:** Will you do me a favor, Joe? Don't be helpful.
**Keller:** I can afford another bag of potatoes.
**Mother:** Minnie scoured the pail in boiling water last night. It's cleaner than your teeth.
**Keller:** And I don't understand why, after I worked 40 years and I got a maid, why I have to take out the garbage.
**Mother:** If you would make up your mind that every bag in the kitchen isn't full of garbage you wouldn't be throwing out my vegetables. Last time it was the onions.

*(Chris comes on, hands her bag.)*

**Keller:** I don't like garbage in the house.
**Mother:** Then don't eat. *(She goes into the kitchen with bag.)*
**Chris:** That settles you for today.
**Keller:** Yeah, I'm in last place again. I don't know, once upon a time I used to think that when I got money again I would

have a maid and my wife would take it easy. Now I got money, and I got a maid, and my wife is workin' for the maid. *(He sits in one of the chairs.)*

*(Mother comes out on last line. She carries a pot of string beans.)*

**Mother:** It's her day off, what are you crabbing about?
**Chris** *(to Mother):* Isn't Annie finished eating?
**Mother** *(looking around preoccupiedly at yard):* She'll be right out. *(Moves.)* That wind did some job on this place. *(Of the tree)* So much for that, thank God.
**Keller** *(indicating chair beside him):* Sit down, take it easy.
**Mother** *(pressing her hand to top of her head):* I've got such a funny pain on the top of my head.
**Chris:** Can I get you an aspirin?

*(Mother picks a few petals off ground, stands there smelling them in her hand, then sprinkles them over plants.)*

**Mother:** No more roses. It's so funny . . . everything decides to happen at the same time. This month is his birthday; his tree blows down; Annie comes. Everything that happened seems to be coming back. I was just down the cellar, and what do I stumble over? His baseball glove. I haven't seen it in a century.
**Chris:** Don't you think Annie looks well?
**Mother:** Fine. There's no question about it. She's a beauty. . . . I still don't know what brought her here. Not that I'm not glad to see her, but —
**Chris:** I just thought we'd all like to see each other again. *(Mother just looks at*

*him, nodding ever so slightly — almost as though admitting something.)* And I wanted to see her myself.

**Mother** *(as her nods halt, to Keller):* The only thing is I think her nose got longer. But I'll always love that girl. She's one that didn't jump into bed with somebody else as soon as it happened with her fella.

**Keller** *(as though that were impossible for Annie):* Oh, what're you — ?

**Mother:** Never mind. Most of them didn't wait till the telegrams were opened. I'm just glad she came, so you can see I'm not *completely* out of my mind. *(Sits, and rapidly breaks string beans in the pot.)*

**Chris:** Just because she isn't married doesn't mean she's been mourning Larry.

**Mother** *(with an undercurrent of observation):* Why then isn't she?

**Chris** *(a little flustered):* Well . . . it could've been any number of things.

**Mother** *(directly at him):* Like what, for instance?

**Chris** *(embarrassed, but standing his ground):* I don't know. Whatever it is. Can I get you an aspirin? *(Mother puts her hand to her head. She gets up and goes aimlessly toward the trees on rising.)*

**Mother:** It's not like a headache.

**Keller:** You don't sleep, that's why. She's wearing out more bedroom slippers than shoes.

**Mother:** I had a terrible night. *(She stops moving.)* I never had a night like that.

**Chris** *(looking at Keller):* What was it, Mom? Did you dream?

**Mother:** More, more than a dream.

**Chris** *(hesitantly):* About Larry?

**Mother:** I was fast asleep, and — *(Raising her arm over the audience)* Remember the way he used to fly low past the house when he was in training? When we used to see his face in the cockpit going by? That's the way I saw him. Only high up. Way, way up, where the clouds are. He was so real I could reach out and touch him. And suddenly he started to fall. And crying, crying to me . . . Mom, Mom! I could hear him like he was in the room. Mom! . . . it was his voice! If I could touch him I knew I could stop him, if I could only — *(Breaks off, allowing her outstretched hand to fall.)* I woke up and it was so funny — The wind . . . it was like the roaring of his engine. I came out here . . . I must've still been half asleep. I could hear that roaring like he was going by. The tree snapped right in front of me — and I like — came awake. *(She is looking at tree. She suddenly realizes something, turns with a reprimanding finger shaking slightly at Keller.)* See? We should never have planted that tree. I said so in the first place; it was too soon to plant a tree for him.

**Chris** *(alarmed):* Too soon!

**Mother** *(angering):* We rushed into it. Everybody was in such a hurry to bury him. I *said* not to plant it yet. *(To Keller)* I told you to — !

**Chris:** Mother, Mother! *(She looks into his face.)* The wind blew it down. What significance has that got? What are you talking about? Mother, please . . . don't go through it all again, will you? It's no good, it doesn't accomplish anything. I've been thinking, y'know? — maybe we ought to put our minds to forgetting him?

**Mother:** That's the third time you've said that this week.

**Chris:** Because it's not right; we never took up our lives again. We're like a railroad station waiting for a train that never comes in.

**Mother** *(pressing top of her head)*: Get me an aspirin, heh?

**Chris:** Sure, and let's break out of this, heh, Mom? I thought the four of us might go out to dinner a couple of nights, maybe go dancing out at the shore.

**Mother:** Fine. *(To Keller)* We can do it tonight.

**Keller:** Swell with me!

**Chris:** Sure, let's have some fun. *(To Mother)* You'll start with this aspirin. *(He goes up and into the house with new spirit. Her smile vanishes.)*

**Mother** *(with an accusing undertone)*: Why did he invite her here?

**Keller:** Why does that bother you?

**Mother:** She's been in New York for three and a half years, so why all of a sudden — ?

**Keller:** Well, maybe — maybe he just wanted to see her.

**Mother:** Nobody comes 700 miles "just to see."

**Keller:** What do you mean? He lived next door to the girl all his life, why shouldn't he want to see her again? *(Mother looks at him critically.)* Don't look at me like that, he didn't tell me any more than he told you.

**Mother** *(a warning and a question)*: He's not going to marry her.

**Keller:** How do you know he's even thinking of it?

**Mother:** It's got that about it.

**Keller** *(sharply watching her reaction)*: Well? So what?

**Mother** *(alarmed)*: What's going on here, Joe?

**Keller:** Now listen, kid —

**Mother** *(avoiding contact with him)*: She's not his girl, Joe; she knows she's not.

**Keller:** You can't read her mind.

**Mother:** Then why is she still single? New York is full of men, why isn't she married? *(Pause.)* Probably a hundred people told her she's foolish, but she waited.

**Keller:** How do you know why she waited?

**Mother:** She knows what I know, that's why. She's faithful as a rock. In my worst moments, I think of her waiting, and I know again that I'm right.

**Keller:** Look, it's a nice day. What are we arguing for?

**Mother** *(warningly)*: Nobody in this house dast take her faith away, Joe. Strangers might. But not his father, not his brother.

**Keller** *(exasperated)*: What do you want me to do? What do you want?

**Mother:** I want you to act like he's coming back. Both of you. Don't think I haven't noticed since Chris invited her. I won't stand for any nonsense.

**Keller:** But, Kate —

**Mother:** Because if he's not coming back, then I'll kill myself! Laugh. Laugh at me. *(She points to tree.)* But why did that happen the very night she came back? Laugh, but there are meanings in such things. She goes to sleep in his room and his memorial breaks in pieces. Look at it; look. *(She sits on bench.)* Joe —

**Keller:** Calm yourself.

**Mother:** Believe with me, Joe. I can't stand all alone.

**Keller:** Calm yourself.

**Mother:** Only last week a man turned up in Detroit, missing longer than Larry. You read it yourself. You above all have got to believe, you —

**Keller** *(rising):* Why me above all?

**Mother:** Just don't stop believing.

**Keller:** What does that mean, me above all?

*(Bert comes rushing on.)*

**Bert:** Mr. Keller! Say, Mr. Keller . . . *(Pointing up driveway)* Tommy just said it again!

**Keller:** *(not remembering any of it):* Said what? Who?

**Bert:** The dirty word.

**Keller:** Oh. Well —

**Bert:** Gee, aren't you going to arrest him? I warned him.

**Mother** *(with suddenness):* Stop that, Bert. Go home. *(Bert backs up as she advances.)* There's no jail here.

**Keller** *(as though to say, "Oh-what-the-hell-let-him-believe-there-is"):* Kate —

**Mother** *(turning on Keller furiously):* There's no jail here! I want you to stop that jail business! *(He turns, shamed, but peeved.)*

**Bert** *(past her to Keller):* He's right across the street.

**Mother:** Go home, Bert. *(Bert turns around and goes up driveway. She is shaken. Her speech is bitten off, extremely urgent.)* I want you to stop that, Joe. That whole jail business!

**Keller** *(alarmed, therefore angered):* Look at you, look at you shaking.

**Mother** *(trying to control herself, moving about clasping her hands):* I can't help it.

**Keller:** What have I got to hide? What the hell is the matter with you, Kate?

**Mother:** I didn't say you had anything to hide. I'm just telling you to stop it! Now stop it! *(Ann and Chris appear on porch. Ann is 26, gentle but, despite herself, capable of holding fast to what she knows. Chris opens door for her.)*

**Ann:** Hya, Joe! *(She leads off a general laugh that is not self-conscious because they know one another too well.)*

**Chris** *(bringing Ann down with an outstretched chivalric arm):* Take a breath of that air, kid. You never get air like that in New York.

**Mother** *(genuinely overcome with it):* Annie, where did you get that dress!

**Ann:** I couldn't resist. I'm taking it off before I ruin it. *(Swings around.)* How's that for three weeks salary?

**Mother** *(to Keller):* Isn't she the most —? *(To Ann)* It's gorgeous, simply gor —

**Chris** *(to Mother):* No kidding, now, isn't she the prettiest gal you ever saw.

**Mother** *(caught short by his obvious admiration, she finds herself reaching out for a glass of water and aspirin in his hand, and — ):* You gained a little weight, didn't you darling. *(She gulps pill and drinks.)*

**Ann:** It comes and goes.

**Keller:** Look how nice her legs turned out!

**Ann** *(as she runs to fence):* Boy, the poplars got thick, didn't they? *(Keller moves to settee and sits.)*

**Keller:** Well, it's three years, Annie. We're gettin' old, kid.

**Mother:** How does Mom like New York? *(Ann keeps looking through trees.)*

**Ann** *(a little hurt):* Why'd they take our hammock away?

**Keller:** Oh, no, it broke. Couple of years ago.

**Mother:** What broke? He had one of his light lunches and flopped into it. *(Ann laughs and turns back toward Jim's yard.)*

**Ann:** Oh, excuse me! *(Jim has come to fence and is looking over it. He is smoking a cigar. As she cries out, he comes on around on stage.)*

**Jim:** How do you do. *(To Chris)* She looks very intelligent!

**Chris:** Ann, this is Jim — Doctor Bayliss.

**Ann** *(shaking Jim's hand):* Oh, sure, he writes a lot about you.

**Jim:** Don't you believe it. He likes everybody. In the battalion he was known as Mother McKeller.

**Ann:** I can believe it. You know — ? *(To Mother)* It's so strange seeing him come out of that yard. *(To Chris)* I guess I never grew up. It almost seems that Mom and Pop are in there now. And you and my brother doing algebra, and Larry trying to copy my homework. Gosh, those dear dead days beyond recall.

**Jim:** Well, I hope that doesn't mean you want me to move out?

**Sue** *(calling from offstage):* Jim, come in here! Mr. Hubbard is on the phone!

**Jim:** I told you I don't want —

**Sue** *(commandingly sweet):* Please, dear! Please!

**Jim** *(resigned):* All right, Susie. *(trailing off)* All right, all right . . . *(To Ann)* I've only met you, Ann, but if I may offer you a piece of advice. When you marry, never — even in your mind — never count your husband's money.

**Sue** *(from offstage):* Jim?

**Jim:** At once! *(Turns and goes off.)* At once. *(He exits.)*

**Mother** *(Ann is looking at her. She speaks meaningfully):* I told her to take up the guitar. It'd be a common interest for them. *(They laugh.)* Well, he loves the guitar! *(Ann, as though to overcome Mother, becomes suddenly lively, crosses to Keller on settee, sits on his lap.)*

**Ann:** Let's eat at the shore tonight! Raise some hell around here, like we used to before Larry went!

**Mother** *(emotionally):* You think of him! You see? *(Triumphantly)* She thinks of him!

**Ann** *(with an uncomprehending smile):* What do you mean, Kate?

**Mother:** Nothing. Just that you — remember him, he's in your thoughts.

**Ann:** That's a funny thing to say; how could I help remembering him?

**Mother** *(It is drawing to a head the wrong way for her; she starts anew. She rises and comes to Ann):* Did you hang up your things?

**Ann:** Yeah . . . *(To Chris)* Say, you've sure gone in for clothes. I could hardly find room in the closet.

**Mother:** No, don't you remember? That's Larry's room.

**Ann:** You mean . . . they're Larry's?

**Mother:** Didn't you recognize them?

**Ann** *(slowly rising, a little embarrassed):* Well, it never occurred to me that you'd — I mean the shoes are all shined.

**Mother:** Yes, dear. *(Slight pause. Ann can't stop staring at her. Mother breaks* *it by speaking with the relish of gossip, putting her arm around Ann, and walking with her.)* For so long I've been aching for a nice conversation with you, Annie. Tell me something.

**Ann:** What?

**Mother:** I don't know. Something nice.

**Chris** *(wryly):* She means do you go out much?

**Mother:** Oh, shut up.

**Keller:** And are any of them serious?

**Mother** *(laughing, sits in her chair):* Why don't you both choke?

**Keller:** Annie, you can't go into a restaurant with that woman anymore. In five minutes 39 strange people are sitting at the table telling her their life story.

**Mother:** If I can't ask Annie a personal question —

**Keller:** Askin' is all right, but don't beat her over the head. You're beatin' her, you're beatin' her. *(They are laughing. Ann takes pan of beans off stool, puts them on floor under chair and sits.)*

**Ann** *(to Mother):* Don't let them bulldoze you. Ask me anything you like. What do you want to know, Kate? Come on, let's gossip.

**Mother** *(to Chris and Keller):* She's the only one is got any sense. *(To Ann)* Your mother — she's not getting a divorce, heh?

**Ann:** No, she's calmed down about it now. I think when he gets out they'll probably live together. In New York, of course.

**Mother:** That's fine. Because your father is still — I mean he's a decent man after all is said and done.

**Ann:** I don't care. She can take him back if she likes.

**Mother:** And you? You — *(Shakes her head negatively.)* — go out much? *(Slight pause.)*

**Ann** *(delicately):* You mean am I still waiting for him?

**Mother:** Well, no. I don't expect you to wait for him but —

**Ann** *(kindly):* But that's what you mean, isn't it?

**Mother:** Well . . . yes.

**Ann:** Well, I'm not, Kate.

**Mother** *(faintly):* You're not?

**Ann:** Isn't it ridiculous? You don't really imagine he's — ?

**Mother:** I know, dear, but don't say it's ridiculous, because the papers were full of it; I don't know about New York, but there was half a page about a man missing even longer than Larry, and he turned up from Burma.

**Chris** *(coming to Ann):* He couldn't have wanted to come home very badly, Mom.

**Mother:** Don't be so smart.

**Chris:** You can have a helluva time in Burma.

**Ann** *(rises and swings around in back of Chris):* So I've heard.

**Chris:** Mother, I'll bet you money that you're the only woman in the country who after three years is still —

**Mother:** You're sure?

**Chris:** Yes, I am.

**Mother:** Well, if you're sure then you're sure. *(She turns her head away an instant.)* They don't say it on the radio but I'm sure that in the dark at night they're still waiting for their sons.

**Chris:** Mother, you're absolutely —

**Mother** *(waving him off):* Don't be so damned smart! Now stop it! *(Slight pause.)*

There are just a few things you *don't* know. All of you. And I'll tell you one of them, Annie. Deep, deep in your heart you've always been waiting for him.

**Ann** *(resolutely)*: No, Kate.

**Mother** *(with increasing demand)*: But deep in your heart, Annie!

**Chris:** She ought to know, shouldn't she?

**Mother:** Don't let them tell you what to think. Listen to your heart. Only your heart.

**Ann:** Why does your heart tell you he's alive?

**Mother:** Because he has to be.

**Ann:** But why, Kate?

**Mother** *(going to her)*: Because certain things have to be, and certain things can never be. Like the sun has to rise, it has to be. That's why there's God. Otherwise anything could happen. But there's God, so certain things can never happen. I would know, Annie — just like I knew the day he — *(Indicates Chris.)* — went into that terrible battle. Did he write me? Was it in the papers? No, but that morning I couldn't raise my head off the pillow. Ask Joe. Suddenly, I knew! And he was nearly killed that day. Ann, you *know* I'm right!

*(Ann stands there in silence, then turns trembling, going upstage.)*

**Ann:** No, Kate.

**Mother:** I have to have some tea.

*(Frank appears, carrying ladder.)*

**Frank:** Annie! *(Coming down)* How are you, gee whiz!

**Ann** *(taking his hand)*: Why, Frank, you're losing your hair.

**Keller:** He's got responsibility.

**Frank:** Gee whiz!

**Keller:** Without Frank the stars wouldn't know when to come out.

**Frank** *(laughs to Ann)*: You look more womanly. You've matured. You —

**Keller:** Take it easy, Frank, you're a married man.

**Ann** *(as they laugh)*: You still haberdashering?

**Frank:** Why not? Maybe I too can get to be president. How's your brother? Got his degree, I hear.

**Ann:** Oh, George has his own office now!

**Frank:** Don't say! *(Funereally)* And your dad? Is he — ?

**Ann** *(abruptly)*: Fine. I'll be in to see Lydia.

**Frank** *(sympathetically)*: How about it, does Dad expect a parole soon?

**Ann** *(with growing ill ease)*: I really don't know, I —

**Frank** *(staunchly defending her father for her sake)*: I mean because I feel, y'know, that if an intelligent man like your father is put in prison, there ought to be a law that says either you execute him, or let him go after a year.

**Chris** *(interrupting)*: Want a hand with that ladder, Frank?

**Frank** *(taking cue)*: That's all right, I'll — *(Picks up ladder)* — I'll finish the horoscope tonight, Kate. *(Embarrassed)* See you later, Ann; you look wonderful. *(He exits. They look at Ann.)*

**Ann** *(to Chris, as she sits slowly on stool)*: Haven't they stopped talking about Dad?

**Chris** *(coming down and sitting on arm of chair)*: Nobody talks about him any more.

**Keller** (*rises and comes to her*): Gone and forgotten, kid.

**Ann:** Tell me. Because I don't want to meet anybody on the block if they're going to —

**Chris:** I don't want you to worry about it.

**Ann** (*to Keller*): Do they still remember the case, Joe? Do they talk about you?

**Keller:** The only one still talks about it is my wife.

**Mother:** That's because you keep on playing policeman with the kids. All their parents hear out of you is jail, jail, jail.

**Keller:** Actually what happened was that when I got home from the penitentiary the kids got very interested in me. You know kids. I was — (*Laughs.*) — like the expert on the jail situation. And as time passed they got it confused, and . . . I ended up a detective.

**Mother:** Except that *they* didn't get it confused. (*To Ann*) He hands out police badges from the Post Toasties boxes. (*They laugh. Ann rises and comes to Keller, putting her arm around his shoulder.*)

**Ann** (*wondrously at them, happy*): Gosh, it's wonderful to hear you laughing about it.

**Chris:** Why, what'd you expect?

**Ann:** The last thing I remember on this block was one word — "Murderers!" Remember that, Kate? — Mrs. Hammond standing in front of our house and yelling that word? She's still around, I suppose?

**Mother:** They're all still around.

**Keller:** Don't listen to her. Every Saturday night the whole gang is playin' poker in this arbor. All the ones who yelled murderer takin' my money now.

**Mother:** Don't, Joe; she's a sensitive girl; don't fool her. (*To Ann*) They still remember about Dad. It's different with him. (*Indicates Joe.*) He was exonerated, your father's still there. That's why I wasn't so enthusiastic about your coming. Honestly, I know how sensitive you are, and I told Chris, I said —

**Keller:** Listen, you do like I did and you'll be all right. The day I come home, I got out of my car — but not in front of the house . . . on the corner. You should've been here, Annie, and you too, Chris; you'd a seen something. Everybody knew I was getting out that day; the porches were loaded. Picture it now; none of them believed I was innocent. The story was, I pulled a fast one getting myself exonerated. So I get out of my car, and I walk down the street. But very slow. And with a smile. The beast! I was the beast; the guy who sold cracked cylinder heads to the Army Air Force; the guy who made 21 P-40's crash in Australia. Kid, walkin' down the street that day I was guilty as hell. Except I wasn't, and there was a court paper in my pocket to prove I wasn't, and I walked . . . past . . . the porches. Result? Fourteen months later I had one of the best shops in the state again, a respected man again; bigger than ever.

**Chris** (*with admiration*): Joe McGuts.

**Keller** (*now with great force*): That's the only way you lick 'em is guts! (*To Ann*) The worst thing you did was to move away from here. You made it tough for your father when he gets out. That's why I tell you, I like to see him move back right on this block.

**Mother** *(pained):* How could they move back?

**Keller:** It ain't gonna end *till* they move back! *(To Ann)* Till people play cards with him again, and talk with him, and smile with him — you play cards with a man you know he can't be a murderer. And the next time you write him I'd like you to tell him just what I said. *(Ann simply stares at him.)* You hear me?

**Ann** *(surprised):* Don't you hold anything against him?

**Keller:** Annie, I never believed in crucifying people.

**Ann** *(mystified):* But he was your partner; he dragged you through the mud.

**Keller:** Well, he ain't my sweetheart, but you gotta forgive, don't you?

**Ann:** You, either, Kate? Don't you feel any — ?

**Keller** *(to Ann):* The next time you write Dad —

**Ann:** I don't write him.

**Keller:** Well, every now and then you —

**Ann** *(a little shamed, but determined):* No, I've *never* written to him. Neither has my brother. *(To Chris)* Say, do you feel this way, too?

**Chris:** He murdered 21 pilots.

**Keller:** What the hell kinda talk is that?

**Mother:** That's not a thing to say about a man.

**Ann:** What else can you say? When they took him away I followed him, went to visit him every day. I was crying all the time. Until the news came about Larry. Then I realized. It's wrong to pity a man like that. Father or no father, there's only one way to look at him. He knowingly shipped out parts that would crash an airplane. And how do you know Larry wasn't one of them?

**Mother:** I was waiting for that. *(Going to her)* As long as you're here, Annie, I want to ask you never to say that again.

**Ann:** You surprise me. I thought you'd be mad at him.

**Mother:** What your father did had nothing to do with Larry. Nothing.

**Ann:** But we can't know that.

**Mother** *(striving for control):* As long as you're here!

**Ann** *(perplexed):* But, Kate —

**Mother:** Put that out of your head!

**Keller:** Because —

**Mother** *(quickly to Keller):* That's all, that's enough. *(Places her hand on her head.)* Come inside now, and have some tea with me. *(She goes up steps.)*

**Keller** *(to Ann):* The one thing you —

**Mother** *(sharply):* He's not dead, so there's no argument! Now come!

**Keller** *(angrily):* In a minute! *(Mother turns and goes into house.)* Now look, Annie —

**Chris:** All right, Dad, forget it.

**Keller:** No, she doesn't feel that way, Annie —

**Chris:** I'm sick of the whole subject; now cut it out.

**Keller:** You want her to go on like this? *(To Ann)* Those cylinder heads went into P-40's only. What's the matter with you? You know Larry never flew a P-40.

**Chris:** So who flew those P-40's, pigs?

**Keller:** The man was a fool, but don't make a murderer out of him. You got no sense? Look what it does to her! *(To Ann)* Listen, you gotta appreciate what was doin' in that shop in the war. The both of you! It was a madhouse. Every half hour the Major callin' for cylinder heads, they were whippin' us with the telephone. The trucks were hauling them away hot. I mean just try to see it human, see it human. All of a sudden a batch comes out with a crack. That happens; that's the business. A fine, hairline crack. All right, so — so he's a little man, your father, always scared of loud voices. What'll the Major say? Half a day's production shot. . . . What'll I say? You know what I mean? Human. *(He pauses.)* So he takes out his tools and he — covers over the cracks. All right — that's bad, it's wrong, but that's what a little man does. If I could have gone in that day I'd a told him — junk 'em, Steve, we can afford it. But alone he was afraid. But I know he meant no harm. He believed they'd hold up a hundred per cent. That's a mistake, but it ain't murder. You mustn't feel that way about him. You understand me? It ain't right.

**Ann** *(she regards him a moment):* Joe, let's forget it.

**Keller:** Annie, the day the news came about Larry, he was in the next cell to mine — Dad. And he cried. Annie — he cried half the night.

**Ann** *(touched):* He shoulda cried all night. *(Slight pause.)*

**Keller** *(almost angered):* Annie, I do not understand why you — !

**Chris** *(breaking in — with nervous urgency):* Are you going to stop it?

**Ann:** Don't yell at him. He just wants everybody happy.

**Keller** *(clasps her around the waist, smiling):* That's my sentiments. Can you stand steak?

**Chris:** And champagne!

**Keller:** Now you're operatin'! I'll call Swanson's for a table. Big time tonight, Annie!

**Ann:** Can't scare me.

**Keller** *(to Chris, pointing at Ann):* I like that girl. Wrap her up. *(They laugh. Goes up porch.)* You got nice legs, Annie! . . . I want to see everybody drunk tonight. *(Pointing to Chris)* Look at him; he's blushin'! *(He exits, laughing, into house.)*

**Chris** *(calling after him):* Drink your tea, Casanova. *(He turns to Ann.)* Isn't he a great guy?

**Ann:** You're the only one I know who loves his parents.

**Chris:** I know. It went out of style, didn't it?

**Ann** *(with a sudden touch of sadness):* It's all right. It's a good thing. *(She looks about.)* You know? It's lovely here. The air is sweet.

**Chris** *(hopefully):* You're not sorry you came?

**Ann:** Not sorry, no. But I'm — not going to stay.

**Chris:** Why?

**Ann:** In the first place, your mother as much as told me to go.

**Chris:** Well —

**Ann:** You saw that — and then you — you've been kind of —

**Chris:** What?

**Ann:** Well . . . kind of embarrassed ever since I got here.

**Chris:** The trouble is I planned on kind of sneaking up on you over a period of a week or so. But they take it for granted that we're all set.

**Ann:** I knew they would. Your mother anyway.

**Chris:** How did you know?

**Ann:** From *her* point of view, why else would I come?

**Chris:** Well . . . would you want to? *(Ann still studies him.)* I guess you know this is why I asked you to come.

**Ann:** I guess this is why I came.

**Chris:** Ann, I love you. I love you a great deal. *(Finally)* I love you. *(Pause. She waits.)* I have no imagination . . . that's all I know to tell you. *(Ann is waiting, ready.)* I'm embarrassing you. I didn't want to tell it to you here. I wanted someplace we'd be brand-new to each other. . . . You feel it's wrong here, don't you? This yard, this chair? I want you to be ready for me. I don't want to win you away from anything.

**Ann** *(putting her arms around him):* Oh, Chris, I've been ready a long, long time!

**Chris:** Then he's gone forever. You're sure.

**Ann:** I almost got married two years ago.

**Chris:** Why didn't you?

**Ann:** You started to write to me — *(Slight pause.)*

**Chris:** You felt something that far back?

**Ann:** Every day since!

**Chris:** Ann, why didn't you let me know?

**Ann:** I was waiting for you, Chris. Till then you never wrote. And when you did, what did you say? You sure can be ambiguous, you know.

**Chris** *(looks toward house, then at her, trembling):* Give me a kiss, Ann. Give me

a — *(They kiss.)* God, I kissed you, Annie; I kissed Annie. How long, how long I've been waiting to kiss you!

**Ann:** I'll never forgive you. Why did you wait all these years? All I've done is sit and wonder if I was crazy for thinking of you.

**Chris:** Annie, we're going to live now! I'm going to make you so happy. *(He kisses her, but their bodies don't touch.)*

**Ann** *(a little embarrassed):* Not like that you're not.

**Chris:** I kissed you. . . .

**Ann:** Like Larry's brother. Do it like you, Chris. *(He breaks away from her abruptly.)* What is it, Chris?

**Chris:** Let's drive someplace . . . I want to be alone with you.

**Ann:** No . . . what is it, Chris, your mother?

**Chris:** No — nothing like that.

**Ann:** Then what's wrong? Even in your letters, there was something ashamed.

**Chris:** Yes. I suppose I have been. But it's going from me.

**Ann:** You've got to tell me —

**Chris:** I don't know how to start. *(He takes her hand.)*

**Ann:** It wouldn't work this way. *(Slight pause.)*

**Chris** *(speaks quietly, factually at first):* It's all mixed up with so many other things. . . . You remember, overseas, I was in command of a company?

**Ann:** Yeah, sure.

**Chris:** Well, I lost them.

**Ann:** How many?

**Chris:** Just about all.

**Ann:** Oh, gee!

**Chris:** It takes a little time to toss that

off. Because they weren't just men. For instance, one time it'd been raining several days and this kid came to me, and gave me his last pair of dry socks. Put them in my pocket. That's only a little thing — but . . . that's the kind of guys I had. They didn't die; they killed themselves for each other. I mean that exactly; a little more selfish and they'd 've been here today. And I got an idea — watching them go down. Everything was being destroyed, see, but it seemed to me that one new thing was made. A kind of — responsibility. Man for man. You understand me? To show that, to bring that onto the earth again like some kind of a monument and everyone would feel it standing there, behind him, and it would make a difference to him. *(Pause.)* And then I came home and it was incredible. I — there was no meaning in it here; the whole thing to them was kind of a — bus accident. I went to work with Dad, and that rat-race again. I felt — what you said — ashamed somehow. Because nobody changed at all. It seemed to make suckers out of a lot of guys. I felt wrong to be alive, to open the bankbook, to drive the new car, to see the new refrigerator. I mean you can take those things out of a war, but when you drive that car you've got to know that it came out of the love a man can have for a man, you've got to be a little better because of that. Otherwise what you have is really loot, and there's blood on it. I didn't want to take any of it. And I guess that included you.

**Ann:** And you still feel that way?

**Chris:** I want you now, Annie.

**Ann:** Because you mustn't feel that way anymore. Because you have a right to whatever you have. Everything, Chris, understand that? To me, too. . . . And the money, there's nothing wrong in your money. Your father put hundreds of planes in the air, you should be proud. A man should be paid for that. . . .

**Chris:** Oh, Annie, Annie . . . I'm going to make a fortune for you!

**Keller** *(offstage):* Hello. . . . Yes. Sure.

**Ann** *(laughing softly):* What'll I do with a fortune? *(They kiss. Keller enters from house.)*

**Keller** *(thumbing toward house):* Hey, Ann, your brother — *(They step apart shyly. Keller comes down, and wryly.)* What is this, Labor Day?

**Chris** *(waving him away, knowing the kidding will be endless):* All right, all right.

**Ann:** You shouldn't burst out like that.

**Keller:** Well, nobody told me it was Labor Day. *(Looks around.)* Where's the hot dogs?

**Chris** *(loving it):* All right. You said it once.

**Keller:** Well, as long as I know it's Labor Day from now on, I'll wear a bell around my neck.

**Ann** *(affectionately):* He's so subtle!

**Chris:** George Bernard Shaw as an elephant.

**Keller:** George! — hey, you kissed it out of my head — your brother's on the phone.

**Ann** *(surprised):* My brother?

**Keller:** Yeah. George. Long distance.

**Ann:** What's the matter, is anything wrong?

**Keller:** I don't know; Kate's talking to him. Hurry up, she'll cost him five dollars.

**Ann** *(takes a step upstage, then comes down toward Chris):* I wonder if we ought to tell your mother yet? I mean I'm not very good in an argument.

**Chris:** We'll wait till tonight. After dinner. Now don't get tense, just leave it to me.

**Keller:** What're you telling her?

**Chris:** Go ahead, Ann. *(With misgivings, Ann goes up and into house.)* We're getting married, Dad. *(Keller nods indecisively.)* Well, don't you say anything?

**Keller** *(distracted):* I'm glad, Chris, I'm just — George is calling from Columbus.

**Chris:** Columbus!

**Keller:** Did Annie tell you he was going to see his father today?

**Chris:** No, I don't think she knew anything about it.

**Keller** *(asking uncomfortably):* Chris! You — you think you know her pretty good?

**Chris** *(hurt and apprehensive):* What kind of a question?

**Keller:** I'm just wondering. All these years George don't go to see his father. Suddenly he goes . . . and she comes here.

**Chris:** Well, what about it?

**Keller:** It's crazy, but it comes to my mind. She don't hold nothin' against me, does she?

**Chris** *(angry):* I don't know what you're talking about.

**Keller** *(a little more combatively):* I'm just talkin'. To his last day in court the man blamed it all on me; and this is his daughter. I mean if she was sent here to find out something?

**Chris** *(angered):* Why? What is there to find out?

**Ann** *(on phone, offstage):* Why are you so excited, George? What happened there?

**Keller:** I mean if they want to open the case again, for the nuisance value, to hurt us?

**Chris:** Dad . . . how could you think that of her?

**Ann** *(still on phone):* But what did he say to you, for God's sake?

**Keller:** It couldn't be, heh. You know.

**Chris:** Dad, you amaze me. . . .

**Keller** *(breaking in):* All right, forget it. *(With great force, moving about)* I want a clean start for you, Chris, I want a new sign over the plant — Christopher Keller, Incorporated.

**Chris** *(a little uneasily):* J. O. Keller is good enough.

**Keller:** We'll talk about it. I'm going to build you a house, stone, with a driveway from the road. I want you to spread out, Chris, I want you to use what I made for you. *(He is close to him now.)* I mean, with joy, Chris, without shame . . . with joy.

**Chris** *(touched):* I will, Dad.

**Keller** *(with deep emotion):* Say it to me.

**Chris:** Why?

**Keller:** Because sometimes I think you are . . . ashamed of the money.

**Chris:** No, don't feel that.

**Keller:** Because it's good money; there's nothing wrong with that money.

**Chris** *(a little frightened):* Dad, you don't have to tell me this.

**Keller** *(with overriding affection and self-confidence now, he grips Chris by the* *back of the neck, and with laughter between his determined jaws):* Look, Chris, I'll go to work on Mother for you. We'll get her so drunk tonight we'll all get married! *(Steps away, with a wide gesture of his arm.)* There's gonna be a wedding, kid, like there never was seen! Champagne, tuxedos — ! *(He breaks off as Ann's voice comes out loud from the house where she is still talking on the phone.)*

**Ann:** Simply because when you get excited you don't control yourself. . . . *(Mother comes out of house.)* Well, what did he tell you for God's sake? *(Pause.)* All right, come then. *(Pause.)* Yes, they'll all be here. Nobody's running away from you. And try to get hold of yourself, will you? *(Pause.)* All right, all right. Good-bye.

*(There is a brief pause as Ann hangs up receiver, then comes out of kitchen.)*

**Chris:** Something happen?

**Keller:** He's coming here?

**Ann:** On the seven o'clock. He's in Columbus. *(To Mother)* I told him it would be all right.

**Keller:** Sure, fine! Your father took sick?

**Ann** *(mystified)*: No, George didn't say he was sick. I — *(Shaking it off)* I don't know, I suppose it's something stupid; you know my brother — *(She comes to Chris.)* Let's go for a drive, or something. . . .

**Chris:** Sure. Give me the keys, Dad.

**Mother:** Drive through the park. It's beautiful now.

**Chris:** Come on, Ann. *(To them)* Be back right away.

**Ann** *(as she and Chris exit up driveway)*: See you.

*(Mother comes down toward Keller, her eyes fixed on him.)*

**Keller:** Take your time. *(To Mother)* What does George want?

**Mother:** He's been in Columbus since this morning with Steve. He's gotta see Annie right away, he says.

**Keller:** What for?

**Mother:** I don't know. *(She speaks with warning.)* He's a lawyer now, Joe. George is a lawyer. All these years he never even sent a postcard to Steve. Since he got back from the war, not a postcard.

**Keller:** So what?

**Mother** *(her tension breaking out)*: Suddenly he takes an airplane from New York to see him. An airplane!

**Keller:** Well? So?

**Mother** *(trembling)*: Why?

**Keller:** I don't read minds. Do you?

**Mother:** Why, Joe? What has Steve suddenly got to tell him that he takes an airplane to see him?

**Keller:** What do I care what Steve's got to tell him?

**Mother:** You're sure, Joe?

**Keller** *(frightened, but angry)*: Yes, I'm sure.

**Mother** *(sits stiffly in a chair)*: Be smart now, Joe. The boy is coming. Be smart.

**Keller** *(desperately)*: Once and for all, did you hear what I said? I said I'm sure!

**Mother** *(nods weakly)*: All right, Joe. *(He straightens up.)* Just . . . be smart.

*(Keller, in hopeless fury, looks at her, turns around, goes up to porch and into house, slamming screen door violently behind him. Mother sits in chair downstage, stiffly, staring, seeing. Curtain.)*

## READING COMPREHENSION

**Summarizing.** Choose the best phrase to complete each sentence. Then write the complete statements on your paper.

1. Kate said that Larry _____ (would come back, died nobly for his country, hadn't suffered long).

2. Chris had asked Ann to visit because he _____ (knew his mother missed Ann and wanted to see her, wanted to move to New York, wanted to ask her to marry him).

3. Joe Keller and Ann's father went to prison for_____ (selling cracked cylinder heads, price fixing, stealing military secrets).

**Interpreting.** Write the answer to each question on your paper.

1. Why did Kate ask Frank to make a horoscope for November 25?

2. How did Kate react to Ann's visit?

3. How did Ann's attitude toward Larry compare with Kate's?

4. Why did Chris wait so long to tell Ann how he really felt about her?

### For Thinking and Discussing

1. Why do you think Joe and Chris were dishonest with Kate about Larry's death? Do you think they were right?

2. Why was the apple tree planted? What did the apple tree symbolize? Explain your answer.

## UNDERSTANDING LITERATURE

**Characters and Conflict in a Play.** The first act in a play lays the foundation for everything that comes later. It introduces you to the characters. It presents the background and the rising action of the plot and the problems and conflicts that the characters must resolve.

The first act of *All My Sons* reveals the characters' personalities, problems, and relationships with each other.

On your paper, match each character listed below with his or her description.

1. Kate     a. moved to New York to get away from unhappy memories

2. Joe     b. a doctor who is not totally content

3. Chris     c. a loyal but demanding person who believes Larry will return

4. Ann     d. likes to joke with kids, is proud of his success

5. Jim     e. believes the stars rule our lives

6. Frank     f. wishes to marry the woman he loves

## WRITING

Choose one character from the play and write a character study. Describe (a) the character's personality, (b) the conflicts he or she faces, and (c) his or her relationship with the other characters in the play.

# Act Two

*As twilight falls, that evening. On the rise, Chris is discovered sawing the broken-off tree, leaving stump standing alone. He is dressed in good pants, white shoes, but without a shirt. He disappears with tree up the alley when Mother appears on porch. She comes down and stands watching him. She has on a dressing gown, carries a tray of grape juice drink in a pitcher, and glasses with sprigs of mint in them.*

**Mother** *(calling up alley)*: Did you have to put on good pants to do that? *(She comes downstage and puts tray on table in the arbor. Then looks around uneasily, then feels pitcher for coolness. Chris enters from alley brushing off his hands.)* You notice there's more light with that thing gone?

**Chris:** Why aren't you dressing?

**Mother:** It's suffocating upstairs. I made a grape drink for Georgie. He always liked grape. Come and have some.

**Chris** *(impatiently)*: Well, come on, get dressed. And what's Dad sleeping so much for? *(He goes to table and pours a glass of juice.)*

**Mother:** He's worried. When he's worried he sleeps. *(Pauses. Looks into his eyes.)* We're dumb, Chris. Dad and I are stupid people. We don't know anything. You've got to protect us.

**Chris:** You're silly; what's there to be afraid of?

**Mother:** To his last day in court Steve never gave up the idea that Dad made him do it. If they're going to open the case again I won't live through it.

**Chris:** George is just a damn fool, Mother. How can you take him seriously?

**Mother:** That family hates us. Maybe even Annie —

**Chris:** Oh, now, Mother . . .

**Mother:** You think just because you like everybody, they like you?

**Chris:** All right, stop working yourself up. Just leave everything to me.

**Mother:** When George goes home tell her to go with him.

**Chris** *(noncomittally)*: Don't worry about Annie.

**Mother:** Steve is her father, too.

**Chris:** Are you going to cut it out? Now, come.

**Mother** *(going upstage with him)*: You don't realize how people can hate, Chris; they can hate so much they'll tear the world to pieces.

*(Ann, dressed up, appears on porch.)*

**Chris:** Look! She's dressed already. *(As he and Mother mount porch)* I've just got to put on a shirt.

**Ann** *(in a preoccupied way)*: Are you feeling well, Kate?

**Mother:** What's the difference, dear. There are certain people, y'know, the sicker they get the longer they live. *(She goes into house.)*

**Chris:** You look nice.

**Ann:** We're going to tell her tonight.

**Chris:** Absolutely, don't worry about it.

**Ann:** I wish we could tell her now. I can't stand scheming. My stomach gets hard.

**Chris:** It's not scheming; we'll just get her in a better mood.

**Mother** (*upstage, in the house*): Joe, are you going to sleep all day?

**Ann** (*laughing*): The only one who's relaxed is your father. He's fast asleep.

**Chris:** I'm relaxed.

**Ann:** Are you?

**Chris:** Look. (*He holds out his hand and makes it shake.*) Let me know when George gets here.

(*He goes into the house. Ann moves aimlessly, and then is drawn toward tree stump. She goes to it, hesitantly touches broken top in the hush of her thoughts. Offstage Lydia calls, "Johnny!" Sue enters and halts, seeing Ann.*)

**Sue:** Is my husband — ?

**Ann** (*turns, startled*): Oh!

**Sue:** I'm terribly sorry.

**Ann:** It's all right, I — I'm a little silly about the dark.

**Sue** (*looks about*): It is getting dark.

**Ann:** Are you looking for your husband?

**Sue:** As usual. (*Laughs tiredly.*) He spends so much time here, they'll be charging him rent.

**Ann:** Nobody was dressed so he drove over to the depot to pick up my brother.

**Sue:** Oh, your brother's in?

**Ann:** Yeah, they ought to be here any minute now. Will you have a cold drink?

**Sue:** I will, thanks. (*Ann goes to table and pours.*) My husband. Too hot to drive me to the beach. Men are like little boys; for the neighbors they'll always cut the grass.

**Ann:** People like to do things for the Kellers. It's been that way since I can remember.

**Sue:** It's amazing. I guess your brother's coming to give you away, heh?

**Ann** (*giving her drink*): I don't know. I suppose.

**Sue:** You must be all nerved up.

**Ann:** It's always a problem getting yourself married, isn't it?

**Sue:** That depends on your shape, of course. I don't see why you should have had a problem.

**Ann:** I've had chances —

**Sue:** I'll bet. It's romantic . . . it's very unusual to me, marrying the brother of your sweetheart.

**Ann:** I don't know. I think it's mostly that whenever I need somebody to tell me the truth I've always thought of Chris. When he tells you something you know it's so. He relaxes me.

**Sue:** And he's got money. That's important, you know.

**Ann:** It wouldn't matter to me.

**Sue:** You'd be surprised. It makes all the difference. I married an intern. On my salary. And that was bad, because as soon as a woman supports a man he owes her something. You can never owe somebody without resenting them. (*Ann laughs.*) That's true, you know.

**Ann:** Underneath, I think the doctor is very devoted.

**Sue:** Oh, certainly. But it's bad when a man always sees the bars in front of him. Jim thinks he's in jail all the time.

**Ann:** Oh . . .

**Sue:** That's why I've been intending to ask you a small favor, Ann. It's something very important to me.

**Ann:** Certainly, if I can do it.

**Sue:** You can. When you take up housekeeping, try to find a place away from here.

**Ann:** Are you fooling?

**Sue:** I'm very serious. My husband is unhappy with Chris around.

**Ann:** How is that?

**Sue:** Jim's a successful doctor. But he's got an idea he'd like to do medical research. Discover things. You see?

**Ann:** Well, isn't that good?

**Sue:** Research pays 25 dollars a week minus laundering the hair shirt. You've got to give up your life to go into it.

**Ann:** How does Chris —

**Sue** (*with growing feeling*): Chris makes people want to be better than it's possible to be. He does that to people.

**Ann:** Is that bad?

**Sue:** My husband has a family, dear. Every time he has a session with Chris he feels as though he's compromising by not giving up everything for research. As though Chris or anybody else isn't compromising. It happens with Jim every couple of years. He meets a man and makes a statue out of him.

**Ann:** Maybe he's right. I don't mean that Chris is a statue, but —

**Sue:** Now darling, you know he's not right.

**Ann:** I don't agree with you. Chris —

**Sue:** Let's face it, dear. Chris is working with his father, isn't he? He's taking money out of that business every week in the year.

**Ann:** What of it?

**Sue:** You ask me what of it?

**Ann:** I certainly do. (*She seems about to burst out.*) You oughtn't cast aspersions like that; I'm surprised at you.

**Sue:** You're surprised at me!

**Ann:** He'd never take five cents out of that plant if there was anything wrong with it.

**Sue:** You know that?

**Ann:** I know it. I resent everything you've said.

**Sue:** You know what I resent, dear?

**Ann:** Please, I don't want to argue.

**Sue:** I resent living next door to the Holy Family. It makes me look like a bum, you understand?

**Ann:** I can't do anything about that.

**Sue:** Who is he to ruin a man's life? Everybody knows Joe pulled a fast one to get out of jail.

**Ann:** That's not true!

**Sue:** Then why don't you go out and talk to people? Go on, talk to them. There's not a person on the block who doesn't know the truth.

**Ann:** That's a lie. People come here all the time for cards and —

**Sue:** So what? They give him credit for being smart. I do, too; I've got nothing against Joe. But if Chris wants people to put on the hair shirt let him take off his broadcloth. He's driving my husband crazy with that phony idealism of his, and I'm at the end of my rope on it! (*Chris enters on porch, wearing a shirt and tie now. She turns quickly, hearing. With a smile.*) Hello, darling. How's Mother?

**Chris:** I thought George came.

**Sue:** No, it was just us.

**Chris** (*coming down to them*): Susie, do me a favor? Go up to Mother and see if you can calm her. She's all worked up.

**Sue:** She still doesn't know about you two?

**Chris** (laughs a little): Well, she senses it, I guess. You know my mother.

**Sue** (going up to porch): Oh, yeah, she's psychic.

**Chris:** Maybe there's something in the medicine chest.

**Sue:** I'll give her one of everything. (On porch) Don't worry about Kate; a couple of drinks, dance her around a little. . . . She'll love Ann. (To Ann) Because you're the female version of him. (Chris laughs.) Don't be alarmed, I said version. (She goes into house.)

**Chris:** Interesting woman, isn't she?

**Ann:** Yeah, she's very interesting.

**Chris:** She's a great nurse, you know, she —

**Ann** (in tension, but trying to control it): Are you still doing that?

**Chris** (sensing something wrong, but still smiling): Doing what?

**Ann:** As soon as you get to know somebody you find a distinction for them. How do you know she's a great nurse?

**Chris:** What's the matter, Ann?

**Ann:** The woman hates you. She despises you!

**Chris:** Hey. . . . What's hit you?

**Ann:** Gee, Chris —

**Chris:** What happened here?

**Ann:** You never — Why didn't you tell me?

**Chris:** Tell you what?

**Ann:** She says they think Joe is guilty.

**Chris:** What difference does it make what they think?

**Ann:** I don't care what they think; I just don't understand why you took the trouble to deny it. You said it was all forgotten.

**Chris:** I didn't want you to feel there was anything wrong in your coming here, that's all. I know a lot of people think my father was guilty, and I assumed there might be some question in your mind.

**Ann:** But I never once said I suspected him.

**Chris:** Nobody says it.

**Ann:** Chris, I know how much you love him, but it could never —

**Chris:** Do you think I could forgive him if he'd done that thing?

**Ann:** I'm not here out of a blue sky, Chris. I turned my back on my father; if there's anything wrong here now —

**Chris:** I know that, Ann.

**Ann:** George is coming from Dad, and I don't think it's with a blessing.

**Chris:** He's welcome here. You've got nothing to fear from George.

**Ann:** Tell me that. . . . Just tell me that.

**Chris:** The man is innocent, Ann. Remember he was falsely accused once and it put him through hell. How would you behave if he were faced with the same thing again? Annie, believe me, there's nothing wrong for you here, believe me, kid.

**Ann:** All right, Chris, all right. (They embrace as Keller appears quietly on porch. Ann simply studies him.)

**Keller:** Every time I come out here it looks like Playland! (They break and laugh in embarrassment.)

**Chris:** I thought you were going to shave.

**Keller** (sitting on bench): In a minute. I just woke up, I can't see nothin'.

**Ann:** You look shaved.

**Keller:** Oh, no. (Massages his jaw.) Gotta be extra special tonight. Big night, Annie. So how's it feel to be a married woman?

**Ann** *(laughs):* I don't know, yet.

**Keller** *(to Chris):* What's the matter, you slippin'? *(He takes a little box of apples from under the bench as they talk.)*

**Chris:** The great *roué*!

**Keller:** What is that, *roué*?

**Chris:** It's French.

**Keller:** Don't talk dirty. *(They laugh.)*

**Chris** *(to Ann):* You ever meet a bigger ignoramus?

**Keller:** Well, somebody's got to make a living.

**Ann** *(as they laugh):* That's telling him.

**Keller:** I don't know, everybody's gettin' so damn educated in this country there'll be nobody to take away the garbage. *(They laugh.)* It's gettin' so the only dumb ones left are the bosses.

**Ann:** You're not so dumb, Joe.

**Keller:** I know, but you go into our plant, for instance. I got so many lieutenants, majors, and colonels that I'm ashamed to ask somebody to sweep the floor. I gotta be careful I'll insult somebody. No kiddin'. It's a tragedy: You stand on the street today and spit, you're gonna hit a college man.

**Chris:** Well, don't spit.

**Keller** *(breaks apple in half, passing it to Ann and Chris):* I mean to say, it's comin' to a pass. *(He takes a breath.)* I been thinkin', Annie . . . your brother, George. I been thinkin' about your brother George. When he comes I like you to *brooch* something to him.

**Chris:** Broach.

**Keller:** What's the matter with brooch?

**Chris** *(smiling):* It's not English.

**Keller:** When I went to night school it was brooch.

**Ann** *(laughing):* Well, in day school it's broach.

**Keller:** Don't surround me, will you? Seriously, Ann . . . you say he's not well. George, I been thinkin', why should he knock himself out in New York with that cut-throat competition, when I got so many friends here; I'm very friendly with some big lawyers in town. I could set George up here.

**Ann:** That's awfully nice of you, Joe.

**Keller:** No, kid, it ain't nice of me. I want you to understand me. I'm thinking of Chris. *(Slight pause.)* See . . . this is what I mean. You get older, you want to feel that you — accomplished something. My only accomplishment is my son. I ain't brainy. That's all I accomplished. Now, a year, 18 months, your father'll be a free man. Who is he going to come to, Annie? His baby. You. He'll come, old, mad, into your house.

**Ann:** That can't matter anymore, Joe.

**Keller:** I don't want that to come between us. *(Gestures between Chris and himself.)*

**Ann:** I can only tell you that that could never happen.

**Keller:** You're in love now, Annie, but believe me, I'm older than you and I know — a daughter is a daughter, and a father is a father. And it could happen. *(He pauses.)* I'd like you and George to go to him in prison and tell him . . . , "Dad, Joe wants to bring you into the business when you get out."

**Ann** *(surprised, even shocked):* You'd have him as a partner?

**Keller:** No, no partner. A good job. *(Pause. He sees she is shocked, a little mystified. He gets up, speaks more nervously.)* I want him to know, Annie . . . while he's sitting there I want him to know that when he gets out he's got a place waitin' for him. It'll take his bitterness away. To know you got a place . . . it sweetens you.

**Ann:** Joe, you owe him nothing.

**Keller:** I owe him a good kick in the teeth, but he's your father.

**Chris:** Then kick him in the teeth! I don't want him in the plant, so that's that! You understand? And besides, don't talk about him like that. People misunderstand you!

**Keller:** And I don't understand why she has to crucify the man.

**Chris:** Well, it's her father, if she feels —

**Keller:** No, no.

**Chris** (almost angrily): What's it to you? Why — ?

**Keller** (a commanding outburst in high nervousness): A father is a father! (As though the outburst had revealed him, he looks about, wanting to retract it. His hand goes to his cheek.) I better — I better shave. (He turns and a smile is on his face; to Ann.) I didn't mean to yell at you, Annie.

**Ann:** Let's forget the whole thing, Joe.

**Keller:** Right. (To Chris) She's likeable.

**Chris** (a little peeved at the man's stupidity): Shave, will you?

**Keller:** Right again.

(As he turns to porch, Lydia comes hurrying from her house.)

**Lydia:** I forgot all about it. (Seeing Chris and Ann) Hya. (To Joe) I promised to fix Kate's hair for her tonight. Did she comb it yet?

**Keller:** Always a smile, hey, Lydia?

**Lydia:** Sure, why not?

**Keller** (going up on porch): Come on up and comb my Katie's hair. (Lydia goes up on porch.) She's got a big night; make her beautiful.

**Lydia:** I will.

**Keller** (holds door open and she goes into kitchen; to Chris and Ann): Hey, that could be a song. (He sings softly.) "Come on up and comb my Katie's hair. . . . Oh, come on up, 'cause she's my lady fair — " (To Ann) How's that for one year of night school? (He continues singing as he goes into kitchen.) "Oh, come on up, come on up, and comb my lady's hair — "

(Jim Bayliss rounds corner of driveway, walking rapidly. Jim crosses to Chris, motions him, and pulls him down excitedly. Keller stands just inside kitchen door, watching them.)

**Chris:** What's the matter? Where is he?

**Jim:** Where's your mother?

**Chris:** Upstairs, dressing.

**Ann** (crossing to them rapidly): What happened to George?

**Jim:** I asked him to wait in the car. Listen to me now. Can you take some advice? (They wait.) Don't bring him in here.

**Ann:** Why?

**Jim:** Kate is in bad shape, you can't explode this in front of her.

**Ann:** Explode what?

**Jim:** You know why he's here; don't try to kid it away. There's blood in his eye; drive him somewhere and talk to him alone.

(Ann turns to go up drive, takes a couple of steps, sees Keller, and stops. He goes quietly on into house.)

**Chris** (*shaken, and therefore angered*): Don't be an old lady.

**Jim:** He's come to take her home. What does that mean? (*To Ann*) You know what that means. Fight it out with him someplace else. (*Ann comes back down toward Chris.*)

**Ann** (*touching his collar*): I'll drive . . . him somewhere.

**Chris** (*goes to her*): No.

**Jim:** Will you stop being an idiot?

**Chris:** Nobody's afraid of him here. Cut that out!

(*He starts for driveway, but is brought up short by George, who enters there. George is Chris's age, but a paler man, now on the edge of his self-restraint. He speaks quietly, as though afraid to find himself screaming. An instant's hesitation and Chris steps up to him, hand extended, smiling.*)

**Chris:** What're you sitting out there for?

**George:** Doctor said your mother isn't well. I —

**Chris:** So what? She'd want to see you, wouldn't she? We've been waiting for you all afternoon.

(*He puts his hand on George's arm, but George pulls away, coming across toward Ann.*)

**Ann** (*touching his collar*): This is filthy, didn't you bring another shirt?

(*George breaks away from her, and moves down, examining the yard. Door opens, and he turns rapidly, thinking it is Kate, but it's Sue. She looks at him; he turns away and moves to fence. He looks over it at his former home. Sue comes downstage.*)

**Sue** (*annoyed*): How about the beach, Jim?

**Jim:** Oh, it's too hot to drive.

**Sue:** How'd you get to the station — Zeppelin?

**Chris:** This is Mrs. Bayliss, George. (*Calling, as George pays no attention: staring at house*) George! (*George turns.*) Mrs. Bayliss.

**Sue:** How do you do.

**George** (*removing his hat*): You're the people who bought our house, aren't you?

**Sue:** That's right. Come and see what we did with it before you leave.

**George** (*walks down and away from her*): I liked it the way it was.

**Sue** (*after a brief pause*): He is frank, isn't he?

**Jim** (*pulling her off*): See you later. . . . Take it easy, fella. (*They exit.*)

**Chris** (*calling after them*): Thanks for driving him! (*Turning to George*) How about some grape juice? Mother made it especially for you.

**George** (*with forced appreciation*): Good old Kate, remembered my grape juice.

**Chris:** You drank enough of it in this house. How've you been, George? — Sit down.

**George** (*keeps moving*): It takes me a minute. (*Looking around*) It seems impossible.

**Chris:** What?

**George:** I'm back here.

**Chris:** Say, you've gotten a little nervous, haven't you?

**George:** Yeah, toward the end of the day. What're you, big executive now?

**Chris:** Just kind of medium. How's the law?

**George:** I don't know. When I was studying in the hospital it seemed sensible, but outside there doesn't seem to be much of a law. The trees got thick, didn't they? *(Points to stump.)* What's that?

**Chris:** Blew down last night. We had it there for Larry. You know.

**George:** Why, afraid you'll forget him?

**Chris** *(starts for George)*: Kind of a remark is that?

**Ann** *(breaking in, putting a restraining hand on Chris)*: When did you start wearing a hat?

**George** *(discovers hat in hand)*: Today. From now on I decided to look like a lawyer, anyway. *(He holds it up to her.)* Don't you recognize it?

**Ann:** Why? Where — ?

**George:** Your father's — He asked me to wear it.

**Ann:** How is he?

**George:** He got smaller.

**Ann:** Smaller?

**George:** Yeah, little. *(Holds out his hand to measure.)* He's a little man. That's what happens to suckers, you know. It's good I went to him in time — another year there'd be nothing left but his smell.

**Chris:** What's the matter, George, what's the trouble?

**George:** The trouble? The trouble is when you make suckers out of people once, you shouldn't try to do it twice.

**Chris:** What does that mean?

**George** *(to Ann)*: You're not married yet, are you?

**Ann:** George, sit down and stop — ?

**George:** Are you married yet?

**Ann:** No, I'm not married yet.

**George:** You're not going to marry him.

**Ann:** Why am I not going to marry him?

**George:** Because his father destroyed your family.

**Chris:** Now look, George . . .

**George:** Cut it short, Chris. Tell her to come home with me. Let's not argue; you know what I've got to say.

**Chris:** George, you don't want to be the voice of God, do you?

**George:** I'm —

**Chris:** That's been your trouble all your life, George; you dive into things. What kind of a statement is that to make? You're a big boy now.

**George:** I'm a big boy now.

**Chris:** Don't come bulling in here. If you've got something to say, you could be civilized about it.

**George:** Don't civilize me!

**Ann:** Shhh!

**Chris:** *(ready to hit him)*: Are you going to talk like a grown man or aren't you?

**Ann** *(quickly, to forestall an outburst)*: Sit down, dear. Don't be angry, what's the matter? *(He allows her to seat him, looking at her.)* Now what happened? You kissed me when I left, now you —

**George** *(breathlessly)*: My life turned upside down since then. I couldn't go back to work when you left. I wanted to go to Dad and tell him you were going to be married. It seemed impossible not to tell him. He loved you so much. *(He pauses.)* Annie — we did a terrible thing. We can never be forgiven. Not even to send him a card at Christmas. I didn't see him once since I got home from the war! Annie, you don't know what was done to that man. You don't know what happened.

**Ann** *(afraid):* Of course I know.

**George:** You can't know, you wouldn't be here. Dad came to work that day. The night foreman came to him and showed him the cylinder heads ... they were coming out of the process with defects. There was something wrong with the process. So Dad went directly to the phone and called here and told Joe to come down right away. But the morning passed. No sign of Joe. So Dad called again. By this time he had over a hundred defectives. The Army was screaming for stuff and Dad didn't have anything to ship. So Joe told him ... on the phone he told him to weld, cover up the cracks in any way he could, and ship them out.

**Chris:** Are you through now?

**George** *(surging up at him):* I'm not through now! *(Back to Ann)* Dad was afraid. He wanted Joe there if he was going to do it. But Joe can't come down. ... He's sick. Sick! He suddenly gets the flu! Suddenly! But he promised to take responsibility. Do you understand what I'm saying? On the telephone you can't have responsibility! In a court you can always deny a phone call and that's exactly what he did. They knew he was a liar the first time, but in the appeal they believed that rotten lie and now Joe is a big shot and your father is the patsy. *(He gets up.)* Now what're you going to do? Eat his food, sleep in his bed? Answer me; what're you going to do?

**Chris:** What're you going to do, George?

**George:** He's too smart for me. I can't prove a phone call.

**Chris:** Then how dare you come in here with that rot?

**Ann:** George, the court —

**George:** The court didn't know your father! But you know him. You know in your heart Joe did it.

**Chris** *(whirling him around):* Lower your voice or I'll throw you out of here!

**George:** She knows. She knows.

**Chris** *(to Ann):* Get him out of here, Ann. Get him out of here.

**Ann:** George, I know everything you've said. Dad told that whole thing in court, and they —

**George** *(almost a scream):* The court did not know him, Annie!

**Ann:** Shhh! — But he'll say anything, George. You know how quick he can lie.

**George** *(turning to Chris, with deliberation):* I'll ask you something, and look me in the eye when you answer me.

**Chris:** I'll look you in the eye.

**George:** You know your father —

**Chris:** I know him well.

**George:** And he's the kind of boss to let 121 cylinder heads be repaired and shipped out of his shop without even knowing about it?

**Chris:** He's that kind of boss.

**George:** And that's the same Joe Keller who never left his shop without first going around to see that all the lights were out.

**Chris** *(with growing anger):* The same Joe Keller.

**George:** The same man who knows how many minutes a day his workers spend in the toilet.

**Chris:** The same man.

**George:** And my father, that frightened

mouse who'd never buy a shirt without somebody along — that man would dare do such a thing on his own?

**Chris:** On his own. And because he's a frightened mouse this is another thing he'd do — throw the blame on somebody else because he's not man enough to take it himself. He tried it in court but it didn't work, but with a fool like you it works!

**George:** Oh, Chris, you're a liar to yourself!

**Ann** *(deeply shaken):* Don't talk like that!

**Chris** *(sits facing George):* Tell me, George. What happened? The court record was good enough for you all these years, why isn't it good now? Why did you believe it all these years?

**George** *(after a slight pause):* Because you believed it. . . . That's the truth, Chris. I believed everything, because I thought you did. But today I heard it from his mouth. Your Dad took everything we have. I can't beat that. But she's one item he's not going to grab. *(He turns to Ann.)* Get your things. Everything they have is covered with blood. You're not the kind of girl who can live with that. Get your things.

**Chris:** Ann . . . you're not going to believe that, are you?

**Ann** *(goes to him):* You know it's not true, don't you?

**George:** How can he tell you? It's his father. *(To Chris)* None of these things ever even cross your mind?

**Chris:** Yes, they crossed my mind. Anything can cross your mind!

**George:** He knows, Annie. He knows!

**Chris:** The voice of God!

**George:** Then why isn't your name on the business? Explain that to her!

**Chris:** What the hell has that got to do with — ?

**George:** Annie, why isn't his name on it?

**Chris:** Even when I don't own it!

**George:** Who're you kidding? Who gets it when he dies? *(To Ann)* Open your eyes, you know the both of them, isn't that the first thing they'd do, the way they love each other? — J. O. Keller and Son? *(Pause. Ann looks from him to Chris.)* I'll settle it. Do you want to settle it, or are you afraid to?

**Chris:** What do you mean?

**George:** Let me go up and talk to your father. In 10 minutes you'll have the answer. Or are you afraid of the answer?

**Chris:** I'm not afraid of the answer. I know the answer. But my mother isn't well and I don't want a fight here now.

**George:** Let me go to him.

**Chris:** You're not going to start a fight here now.

**George** *(to Ann):* What more do you want! *(There is a sound of footsteps in the house.)*

**Ann** *(turns her head suddenly toward the house):* Someone's coming.

**Chris** *(to George, quietly):* You won't say anything now.

**Ann:** You'll go soon. I'll call a cab.

**George:** You're coming with me.

**Ann:** And don't mention marriage, because we haven't told her yet.

**George:** You're coming with me.

**Ann:** You understand? Don't — George, you're not going to start anything now! *(She hears footsteps.)* Shhh!

*(Mother enters on porch. She is dressed almost formally; her hair is fixed. They are all turned toward her. On seeing*

*George she raises both hands, comes down toward him.)*

**Mother:** Georgie, Georgie.

**George** *(he has always liked her):* Hello, Kate.

**Mother** *(cups his face in her hands):* They made an old man out of you. *(Touches his hair.)* Look, you're gray.

**George** *(her pity, open and unabashed, reaches into him, and he smiles sadly):* I know, I —

**Mother:** I told you when you went away, don't try for medals.

**George** *(laughs, tiredly):* I didn't try, Kate. They made it very easy for me.

**Mother** *(actually angry):* Go on. You're all alike. *(To Ann)* Look at him, why did you say he's fine? He looks like a ghost.

**George** *(relishing her solicitude):* I feel all right.

**Mother:** I'm sick to look at you. What's the matter with your mother; why don't she feed you?

**Ann:** He just hasn't any appetite.

**Mother:** If he ate in my house he'd have an appetite. *(To Ann)* I pity your husband! *(To George)* Sit down. I'll make you a sandwich.

**George** *(sits with an embarrassed laugh):* I'm really not hungry.

**Mother:** Honest to God, it breaks my heart to see what happened to all the children. How we worked and planned for you, and you end up no better than we are.

**George** *(with deep feeling):* You . . . you haven't changed at all, you know that, Kate?

**Mother:** None of us changed, Georgie. We all love you. Joe was just talking about the day you were born and the water got shut off. People were carrying basins from a block away — a stranger would have thought the whole neighborhood was on fire! *(They laugh. She sees the juice. To Ann.)* Why didn't you give him some juice!

**Ann** *(defensively):* I offered it to him!

**Mother:** *(Thrusting glass into George's hand):* Give it to him! *(To George, who is laughing)* And now you're going to sit here and drink some juice . . . and look like something!

**George** *(sitting):* Kate, I feel hungry already.

**Chris** *(proudly):* She could turn Mahatma Gandhi into a heavyweight!

**Mother** *(to Chris, with great energy):* Listen, to hell with the restaurant! I got a ham in the icebox, and frozen strawberries, and avocados, and —

**Ann:** Swell, I'll help you!

**George:** The train leaves at 8:30, Ann.

**Mother** *(to Ann):* You're leaving?

**Chris:** No, Mother, she's not —

**Ann** *(breaking through it, going to George):* You hardly got here; give yourself a chance to get acquainted again.

**Chris:** Sure, you don't even know us anymore.

**Mother:** Well, Chris, if they can't stay, don't —

**Chris:** No, it's just a question of George, Mother, he planned on —

**George** *(gets up politely, nicely, for Kate's sake):* Now wait a minute, Chris . . .

**Chris** *(smiling and full of command, cutting him off):* If you want to go, I'll drive you to the station now, but if you're staying, no arguments while you're here.

**Mother** *(at last confessing the ten-*

*sion):* Why should he argue? *(She goes to him. With desperation and compassion, stroking his hair.)* Georgie and us have no argument. How could we have an argument, Georgie? We all got hit by the same lightning, how can you — ? Did you see what happened to Larry's tree, Georgie? *(She has taken his arm, and unwillingly he moves across stage with her.)* Imagine? While I was dreaming of him in the middle of the night, the wind came along and —

*(Lydia enters on porch. As soon as she sees him . . .)*

**Lydia:** Hey, Georgie! Georgie! Georgie! Georgie! Georgie! *(She comes down to him eagerly. She has a flowered hat in her hand, which Kate takes from her as she goes to George.)*

**George** *(as they shake hands eagerly, warmly):* Hello, Laughy. What'd you do, grow?

**Lydia:** I'm a big girl now.

**Mother:** Look what she can do to a hat!

**Ann** *(to Lydia, admiring the hat):* Did you make that?

**Mother:** In 10 minutes! *(She puts it on.)*

**Lydia** *(fixing it on her head):* I only rearranged it.

**George:** You still make your own clothes?

**Chris** *(of Mother):* Ain't she classy! All she needs now is a Russian wolfhound.

**Mother** *(moving her head):* It feels like somebody is sitting on my head.

**Ann:** No, it's beautiful, Kate.

**Mother** *(kisses Lydia; to George):* She's a genius! You should've married her. *(They laugh.)* This one can feed you!

**Lydia** *(strangely embarrassed):* Oh, stop that, Kate.

**George** *(to Lydia):* Didn't I hear you had a baby?

**Mother:** You don't hear so good. She's got three babies.

**George** *(a little hurt by it — to Lydia):* No kidding, three?

**Lydia:** Yeah, it was one, two, three — You've been away a long time, Georgie.

**George:** I'm beginning to realize.

**Mother** *(to Chris and George):* The trouble with you kids is you *think* too much.

**Lydia:** Well, we think, too.

**Mother:** Yes, but not all the time.

**George** *(with almost obvious envy):* They never took Frank, heh?

**Lydia** *(a little apologetically):* No, he was always one year ahead of the draft.

**Mother:** It's amazing. When they were calling boys 27 Frank was just 28, when they made it 28 he was just 29. That's why he took up astrology. It's all in when you were born, it just goes to show.

**Chris:** What does it go to show?

**Mother** *(to Chris):* Don't be so intelligent. Some superstitions are very nice! *(To Lydia)* Did he finish Larry's horoscope?

**Lydia:** I'll ask him now, I'm going in. *(To George, a little sadly, almost embarrassed)* Would you like to see my babies? Come on.

**George:** I don't think so, Lydia.

**Lydia** *(understanding):* All right. Good luck to you, George.

**George:** Thanks. And to you . . . and Frank. *(She smiles at him, turns and goes off to her house. George stands staring after her.)*

**Lydia** *(as she runs off):* Oh, Frank!

**Mother** *(reading his thoughts):* She got pretty, heh?

**George** (*sadly*): Very pretty.

**Mother** (*as a reprimand*): She's beautiful, you damned fool!

**George** (*looks around longingly; and softly, with a catch in his throat*): She makes it seem so nice around here.

**Mother** (*shaking her finger at him*): Look what happened to you because you wouldn't listen to me! I told you to marry that girl and stay out of the war!

**George** (*laughs at himself*): She used to laugh too much.

**Mother**: And you didn't laugh enough. While you were getting mad about Fascism, Frank was getting into her bed.

**George** (*to Chris*): He won the war — Frank.

**Chris**: All the battles.

**Mother** (*in pursuit of this mood*): The day they started the draft, Georgie, I told you you loved that girl.

**Chris** (*laughs*): And truer love hath no man!

**Mother**: I'm smarter than any of you.

**George** (*laughing*): She's wonderful!

**Mother**: And now you're going to listen to me, George. You had big principles, Eagle Scouts the three of you; so now I got a tree, and this one — (*Indicating Chris*) — when the weather gets bad he can't stand on his feet; and that big dope — (*Pointing to Lydia's house*) — next door who never reads anything but Andy Gump has three children and his house paid off. Stop being a philosopher, and look after yourself. Like Joe was just saying — you move back here, he'll help you get set, and I'll find you a girl and put a smile on your face.

**George**: Joe? Joe wants me here?

**Ann** (*eagerly*): He asked me to tell you, and I think it's a good idea.

**Mother**: Certainly. Why must you make believe you hate us? Is that another principle — that you have to hate us? You don't hate us, George, I know you, you can't fool me, I diapered you. (*Suddenly to Ann*) You remember Mr. Marcy's daughter?

**Ann** (*laughing, to George*): She's got you hooked already! (*George laughs, is excited.*)

**Mother**: You look her over, George; you'll see she's the most beautiful —

**Chris**: She's got warts, George.

**Mother** (*to Chris*): She hasn't got warts! (*To George*) So the girl has a little beauty mark on her chin —

**Chris**: And two on her nose.

**Mother**: You remember. Her father's the retired police inspector.

**Chris**: Sergeant, George.

**Mother**: He's a very kind man!

**Chris**: He looks like a gorilla.

**Mother** (*to George*): He never shot anybody.

(*They all burst out laughing, as Keller appears in doorway. George rises abruptly and stares at Keller, who comes rapidly down to him.*)

**Keller** (*the laughter stops; with strained joviality*): Well! Look who's here! (*Extending his hand*) Georgie, good to see ya.

**George** (*shaking hands — somberly*): How're you, Joe?

**Keller**: So-so. Gettin' old. You comin' out to dinner with us?

**George**: No, got to be back in New York.

**Ann**: I'll call a cab for you. (*She goes up into the house.*)

**Keller:** Too bad you can't stay, George. Sit down. *(To Mother)* He looks fine.

**Mother:** He looks terrible.

**Keller:** That's what I said, you look terrible, George. *(They laugh.)* I wear the pants and she beats me with the belt.

**George:** I saw your factory on the way from the station. It looks like General Motors.

**Keller:** I wish it was General Motors, but it ain't. Sit down, George, sit down. *(Takes cigar out of his pocket.)* So you finally went to see your father, I hear?

**George:** Yes, this morning. What kind of stuff do you make now?

**Keller:** Oh, little of everything. Pressure cookers, an assembly for washing machines. Got a nice, flexible plant now. So how'd you find Dad? Feel all right?

**George** *(searching Keller, speaking indecisively)*: No, he's not well, Joe.

**Keller** *(lighting his cigar):* Not his heart again, is it?

**George:** It's everything, Joe. It's his soul.

**Keller** *(blowing out smoke):* Uh, huh —

**Chris:** How about seeing what they did with your house?

**Keller:** Leave him be.

**George** *(to Chris, indicating Keller):* I'd like to talk to him.

**Keller:** Sure, he just got here. That's the way they do, George. A little man makes a mistake and they hang him by the thumbs; the big ones become ambassadors. I wish you'd-a told me you were going to see Dad.

**George** *(studying him):* I didn't know you were interested.

**Keller:** In a way, I am. I would like him to know, George, that as far as I'm concerned, any time he wants, he's got a place with me. I would like him to know that.

**George:** He hates your guts, Joe. Don't you know that?

**Keller:** I imagined it. But that can change, too.

**Mother:** Steve was never like that.

**George:** He's like that now. He'd like to take every man who made money in the war and put him up against a wall.

**Chris:** He'll need a lot of bullets.

**George:** And he'd better not get any.

**Keller:** That's a sad thing to hear.

**George** *(with bitterness dominant):* Why? What'd you expect him to think of you?

**Keller** *(the force of his nature rising but under control):* I'm sad to see he hasn't changed. As long as I know him, 25 years, the man never learned how to take the blame. You know that, George.

**George** *(he does):* Well, I —

**Keller:** But you do know it. Because the way you come in here you don't look like you remember it. I mean like in 1937 when we had the shop on Flood Street. And he damn near blew us all up with that heater left burning for two days without water. He wouldn't admit that was his fault, either. I had to fire a mechanic to save face. You remember that.

**George:** Yes, but —

**Keller:** I'm just mentioning it, George. Because this is just another one of a lot of things. Like when he gave Frank that money to invest in oil stock.

**George** *(distressed):* I know that, I —

**Keller** *(driving in, but restrained):* But it's good to remember those things, kid. The way he cursed Frank because the stock went down. Was that Frank's fault? To listen to him Frank was a swindler. And all the man did was give him a bad tip.

**George** (gets up, moves away): I know those things. . . .

**Keller:** Then remember them, remember them. (Ann comes out of house.) There are certain men in the world who'd rather see everybody hung before they'll take blame. You understand me, George? (They stand facing each other, George trying to judge him. Ann, coming downstage.) The cab's on its way. Would you like to wash?

**Mother** (with the thrust of hope): Why must he go? Make the midnight, George.

**Keller:** Sure, you'll have dinner with us!

**Ann:** How about it? Why not? We're eating at the lake, we could have a swell time.

(A long pause, as George looks at Ann, Chris, Keller, then back to her.)

**George:** All right.

**Mother:** Now you're talking.

**Chris:** I've got a shirt that'll go right with that suit.

**Mother:** Size 15 and a half, right, George?

**George:** Is Lydia — ? I mean — Frank and Lydia coming?

**Mother:** I'll get you a date that'll make her look like a — (She starts upstage.)

**George** (laughing): No, I don't want a date.

**Chris:** I know somebody just for you! Charlotte Tanner! (He starts for the house.)

**Ann:** You go up and pick out a shirt and tie.

**George** (stops, looks around at them and the place): I never felt at home anywhere but here. I feel so — (He nearly laughs, and turns away from them.) Kate, you look so young, you know? You didn't change at all. It . . . rings an old bell. (Turns to Keller.) You, too, Joe, you're amazingly the same. The whole atmosphere is.

**Keller:** Say, I ain't got time to get sick.

**Mother:** He hasn't been laid up in 15 years.

**Keller:** Except my flu during the war.

**Mother:** Huhh?

**Keller:** My flu, when I was sick during . . . the war.

**Mother:** Well, sure. . . . (To George) I mean except for that flu. (George stands perfectly still.) Well, it slipped my mind, don't look at me that way. He wanted to go to the shop but he couldn't lift himself off the bed. I thought he had pneumonia.

**George:** Why did you say he's never — ?

**Keller:** I know how you feel, kid, I'll never forgive myself. If I could've gone in that day I'd never allow Dad to touch those heads.

**George:** She said you've never been sick.

**Mother:** I said he was sick, George.

**George** (going to Ann): Ann, didn't you hear her say — ?

**Mother:** Do you remember every time you were sick?

**George:** I'd remember pneumonia. Especially if I got it just the day my partner was going to patch up cylinder heads. . . . What happened that day, Joe?

(Frank enters briskly from driveway, holding Larry's horoscope in his hand. He comes to Kate.)

**Frank:** Kate! Kate!

**Mother:** Frank, did you see George?

**Frank** (extending his hand): Lydia told me, I'm glad to . . . you'll have to pardon me. (*Pulling Mother over*) I've got something amazing for you, Kate, I finished Larry's horoscope.

**Mother:** You'd be interested in this, George. It's wonderful the way he can understand the —

**Chris** (*entering from house*): George, the girl's on the phone —

**Mother** (*desperately*): He finished Larry's horoscope!

**Chris:** Frank, can't you pick a better time than this?

**Frank:** The greatest men who ever lived believed in the stars!

**Chris:** Stop filling her head with that junk!

**Frank:** Is it junk to feel that there's a greater power than ourselves? I've studied the stars of his life! I won't argue with you, I'm telling you. Somewhere in this world your brother is alive!

**Mother** (*instantly to Chris*): Why isn't it possible?

**Chris:** Because it's insane.

**Frank:** Just a minute now. I'll tell you something and you can do as you please. Just let's say it. He was supposed to have died on November twenty-fifth. But November twenty-fifth was his favorable day.

**Chris:** Mother!

**Mother:** Listen to him!

**Frank:** It was a day when everything good was shining on him, the kind of day he should've married on. You can laugh at a lot of it. I can understand you laughing. But the odds are a million to one that a man won't die on his favorable day. That's known; that's known, Chris!

**Mother:** Why isn't it possible; why isn't it possible, Chris!

**George** (*to Ann*): Don't you understand what she's saying? She just told you to go. What are you waiting for now?

**Chris:** Nobody can tell her to go. (*A car horn is heard.*)

**Mother** (*to Frank*): Thank you, darling, for your trouble. Will you tell him to wait, Frank?

**Frank** (*as he goes*): Sure thing.

**Mother** (*calling out*): They'll be right out, driver!

**Chris:** She's not leaving, Mother.

**George:** You heard her say it; he's never been sick!

**Mother:** He misunderstood me, Chris!

(*Chris looks at her, struck.*)

**George** (*to Ann*): He simply told your father to kill pilots, and covered himself in bed!

**Chris:** You'd better answer him, Annie. Answer him.

**Mother:** I packed your bag, darling.

**Chris:** What?

**Mother:** I packed your bag, darling. All you've got to do is close it.

**Ann:** I'm not closing anything. He asked me here and I'm staying till he tells me to go. (*To George*) Till Chris tells me!

**Chris:** That's all! Now get out of here, George!

**Mother** (*to Chris*): But if that's how he feels —

**Chris:** That's all, nothing more till Christ comes, about the case or Larry as long as I'm here! (*To George*) Now get out of here, George!

**George** (*to Ann*): You tell me. I want to hear you tell me.

**Ann:** Go, George! (*They disappear up the driveway, Ann saying, "Don't take it that* *way, Georgie! Please don't take it that way."*)

**Chris** *(turning to his Mother):* What do you mean, you packed her bag? How dare you pack her bag?

**Mother:** Chris —

**Chris:** How dare you pack her bag?

**Mother:** She doesn't belong here.

**Chris:** Then I don't belong here.

**Mother:** She's Larry's girl.

**Chris:** And I'm his brother and he's dead, and I'm marrying his girl.

**Mother:** Never, never in this world!

**Keller:** You lost your mind?

**Mother:** You have nothing to say!

**Keller** *(cruelly):* I got plenty to say. Three and a half years you been talking like a maniac —

*(Mother smashes him across the face.)*

**Mother:** Nothing. You have nothing to say. Now I say. He's coming back and everybody has got to wait.

**Chris:** Mother, Mother —

**Mother:** Wait, wait —

**Chris:** How long? How long?

**Mother** *(rolling out of her):* Till he comes; forever and ever till he comes!

**Chris** *(as an ultimatum):* Mother, I'm going ahead with it.

**Mother:** Chris, I've never said no to you in my life, now I say no!

**Chris:** You'll never let him go till I do it.

**Mother:** I'll never let him go and you'll never let him go!

**Chris:** I've let him go. I've let him go a long —

**Mother** *(with no less force, but turning from him):* Then let your father go. *(Pause. Chris stands transfixed.)*

**Keller:** She's out of her mind.

**Mother:** Altogether! *(To Chris, but not facing him)* Your brother's alive, darling, because if he's dead, your father killed him. Do you understand me now? As long as you live, that boy is alive. God does not let a son be killed by his father. Now you see, don't you? Now you see. *(Beyond control, she hurries up and into house.)*

**Keller** *(Chris has not moved. He speaks insinuatingly, questioningly):* She's out of her mind.

**Chris** *(in a broken whisper):* Then . . . you did it?

**Keller** *(with the beginning of plea in his voice):* He never flew a P-40 —

**Chris** *(struck; deadly):* But the others.

**Keller** *(insistently):* She's out of her mind. *(He takes a step toward Chris, pleadingly.)*

**Chris** *(unyielding):* Dad . . . you did it?

**Keller:** He never flew a P-40, what's the matter with you?

**Chris** *(still asking, and saying):* Then you did it. To the others. *(Both hold their voices down.)*

**Keller** *(afraid of him, his deadly insistence):* What's the matter with you? What the hell is the matter with you?

**Chris** *(quietly, incredibly):* How could you do that? How?

**Keller:** What's the matter with you!

**Chris:** Dad . . . Dad, you killed 21 men!

**Keller:** What, killed?

**Chris:** You killed them; you murdered them.

**Keller** *(as though throwing his whole nature open before Chris):* How could I kill anybody?

**Chris:** Dad! Dad!

**Keller** *(trying to hush him):* I didn't kill anybody!

**Chris:** Then explain it to me. What did you do? Explain it to me or I'll tear you to pieces!

**Keller** (*horrified at his overwhelming fury*): Don't, Chris, don't —

**Chris:** I want to know what you did, now what did you do? You had 120 cracked engine-heads, now what did you do?

**Keller:** If you're going to hang me, I —

**Chris:** I'm listening. God Almighty, I'm listening!

**Keller** (*Their movements now are those of subtle pursuit and escape. Keller keeps a step out of Chris's range as he talks*): You're a boy, what could I do! I'm in business, a man is in business; 120 cracked, you're out of business; you got a process, the process don't work you're out of business; you don't know how to operate, your stuff is no good; they close you up, they tear up your contracts, what the hell's it to them? You lay 40 years into a business and they knock you out in five minutes; what could I do, let them take 40 years, let them take my life away? (*His voice cracking.*) I never thought they'd install them. I swear to God. I thought they'd stop 'em before anybody took off.

**Chris:** Then why'd you ship them out?

**Keller:** By the time they could spot them I thought I'd have the process going again, and I could show them they needed me and they'd let it go by. But weeks passed and I got no kickback, so I was going to tell them.

**Chris:** Then why didn't you tell them?

**Keller:** It was too late. The paper, it was all over the front page, 21 went down, it was too late. They came with handcuffs into the shop, what could I do? (*He sits on bench.*) Chris . . . Chris, I did it for you, it was a chance to make something for you. I'm 61 years old, when would I have another chance to make something for you? Sixty-one years old you don't get another chance, do ya?

**Chris:** You even knew they wouldn't hold up in the air.

**Keller:** I didn't say that.

**Chris:** But you were going to warn them not to use them —

**Keller:** But that don't mean —

**Chris:** It means you knew they'd crash.

**Keller:** It don't mean that.

**Chris:** Then you *thought* they'd crash.

**Keller:** I was afraid maybe —

**Chris:** You were afraid maybe! God in heaven, what kind of a man are you? Kids were hanging in the air by those heads. You know that!

**Keller:** For you, a business for you!

**Chris** (*with burning fury*): For me! Where do you live, where have you come from? For me! — I was dying every day and you were killing my boys and you did it for me? What the hell do you think I was thinking of, the damn business? Is that as far as your mind can see, the business? What is that, the world — the business? What the hell do you mean, you did it for me? Don't you have a country? Don't you live in the world? What the hell are you? You're not even an animal, no animal kills his own; what are you? What must I do to you? I ought to tear the tongue out of your mouth, what must I do? (*With his fist he pounds down upon his father's shoulder. He stumbles away, covering his face as he weeps.*) What must I do, Jesus God, what must I do?

**Summarizing.** Choose the best phrase to complete each sentence. Then write the complete statements on your paper.

1. Sue told Ann that everyone in the neighborhood believed that _____ (Joe was really guilty, Chris and Ann made a lovely couple, Chris should take over the business).

2. George knew that his father wouldn't have sent out the defective parts on his own because his father _____ (was too afraid to act independently, didn't realize the parts were defective, was too honest).

3. George caught a slip Kate made when she said that _____ (she had never liked Steve, Joe hadn't been sick in 15 years, Joe was the lucky one to get away).

**Interpreting.** Write the answer to each question on your paper.

1. What did George claim Joe had lied about?

2. Why did Joe offer to give Ann's father a job?

3. What did Kate mean when she said to George, "We all got hit by the same lightning"?

**For Thinking and Discussing.** Both Joe's and Chris's ideals are clearly portrayed at the end of the second act. Compare the way they feel. For whom do you feel more sympathy?

**Climax in a Play.** By the end of the second act, the action has reached a turning point, or *climax*. The events in this act lead to a crisis, and the truth is revealed. The stage is set for Act Three — where everything will be resolved.

1. Below are some events from Act Two. On your paper, put them in order, ending with the climax.

   a. Kate said Joe had not been sick for 15 years.
   b. Frank said Larry's horoscope proved that he was still alive.
   c. Ann said she was staying until Chris asked her to leave.
   d. Joe told the real story of how and why the cracked parts were shipped.
   e. George visited his father in prison.
   f. Chris told Ann and George that he was sure Joe was innocent.

2. Explain what was revealed at the climax of this act. Were you surprised at the climax? Tell why or why not. How do you think the climax will affect the relationships that Kate, Joe, Chris, and Ann have with one another?

Imagine that you are a newspaper reporter who has learned the truth about Joe Keller, the leading citizen in your town. Write a three-paragraph news story about the event. Build to an effective climax in which a turning point in the action is reached.

# Act Three

*Two o'clock the following morning, Mother is discovered on the rise, rocking ceaselessly in a chair, staring at her thoughts. It is an intense, slight sort of rocking. A light shows from upstairs bedroom, lower floor windows being dark. The moon is strong and casts its bluish light. Presently Jim, dressed in jacket and hat, appears, and seeing her, goes up beside her.*

**Jim:** Any news?

**Mother:** No news.

**Jim** *(gently):* You can't sit up all night, dear, why don't you go to bed?

**Mother:** I'm waiting for Chris. Don't worry about me, Jim, I'm perfectly all right.

**Jim:** But it's almost 2:00.

**Mother:** I can't sleep. *(Slight pause.)* You had an emergency?

**Jim** *(tiredly):* Somebody had a headache and thought he was dying. *(Slight pause.)* Half of my patients are quite mad. Nobody realizes how many people are walking around loose, and they're cracked as coconuts. Money. Money-money-money-money. You say it long enough it doesn't mean anything. *(She smiles, makes a silent laugh.)* Oh, how I'd love to be around when that happens!

**Mother** *(shaking her head):* You're so childish, Jim! Sometimes you are.

**Jim** *(looks at her a moment):* Kate. *(Pause.)* What happened?

**Mother:** I told you. He had an argument with Joe. Then he got in the car and drove away.

**Jim:** What kind of an argument?

**Mother:** An argument, Joe's . . . He was crying like a child, before.

**Jim:** They argued about Ann?

**Mother** *(after slight hesitation):* No, not Ann. Imagine? *(Indicates lighted window above.)* She hasn't come out of that room since he left. All night in that room.

**Jim** *(looks at window, then at her):* What'd Joe do, tell him?

**Mother** *(stops rocking):* Tell him what?

**Jim:** Don't be afraid. Kate. I know. I've always known.

**Mother:** How?

**Jim:** It occurred to me a long time ago.

**Mother:** I always had the feeling that in the back of his head, Chris . . . almost knew. I didn't think it would be such a shock.

**Jim** *(gets up):* Chris would never know how to live with a thing like that. It takes a certain talent — for lying. You have it, and I do. But not him.

**Mother:** What do you mean . . . he's not coming back?

**Jim:** Oh, no, he'll come back. We all come back, Kate. These private little revolutions always die. The compromise is always made. In a peculiar way. Frank is right — every man does have a star. The star of one's honesty. And you spend your life groping for it, but once it's out it never lights again. I don't think he went very far. He probably just wanted to be alone to watch his star go out.

**Mother:** Just as long as he comes back.

**Jim:** I wish he wouldn't, Kate. One year

I simply took off, went to New Orleans; for two months I lived on bananas and milk, and studied a certain disease. It was beautiful. And then she came, and she cried. And I went back home with her.

And now I live in the usual darkness; I can't find myself; it's even hard sometimes to remember the kind of man I wanted to be. I'm a good husband; Chris is a good son — he'll come back.

*(Keller comes out on porch in dressing gown and slippers. He goes upstage — to alley. Jim goes to him.)*

**Jim:** I have a feeling he's in the park. I'll look around for him. Put her to bed, Joe; this is no good for what she's got. *(Jim exits up driveway.)*

**Keller** *(coming down)*: What does he want here?

**Mother:** His friend is not home.

**Keller** *(comes down to her. His voice is husky)*: I don't like him mixing in so much.

**Mother:** It's too late, Joe. He knows.

**Keller** *(apprehensively)*: How does he know?

**Mother:** He guessed a long time ago.

**Keller:** I don't like that.

**Mother** *(laughs dangerously, quietly into the line)*: What you don't like.

**Keller:** Yeah, what I don't like.

**Mother:** You can't bull yourself through this one, Joe; you better be smart now. This thing — this thing is not over yet.

**Keller** *(indicating lighted window above)*: And what is she doing up there? She don't come out of the room.

**Mother:** I don't know, what is she doing? Sit down, stop being mad. You want to live? You better figure out your life.

**Keller:** She doesn't know, does she?

**Mother:** She saw Chris storming out of here. It's one and one — she knows how to add.

**Keller:** Maybe I ought to talk to her?

**Mother:** Don't ask me, Joe.

**Keller** *(almost an outburst)*: Then who do I ask? But I don't think she'll do anything about it.

**Mother:** You're asking me again.

**Keller:** I'm askin' you. What am I, a stranger? I thought I had a family here. What happened to my family?

**Mother:** You've got a family. I'm simply telling you that I have no strength to think anymore.

**Keller:** You have no strength. The minute there's trouble you have no strength.

**Mother:** Joe, you're doing the same thing again; all your life whenever there's trouble you yell at me and you think that settles it.

**Keller:** Then what do I do? Tell me; talk to me; what do I do?

**Mother:** Joe . . . I've been thinking this way. If he comes back —

**Keller:** What do you mean "if"? He's comin' back.

**Mother:** I think if you sit him down and you — explain yourself, I mean you ought to make it clear to him that you know you did a terrible thing. *(Not looking into his eyes)* I mean if he saw that you realize what you did. You see?

**Keller:** What ice does that cut?

**Mother** *(a little fearfully)*: I mean if you told him that you want to pay for what you did.

**Keller** *(sensing . . . quietly)*: How can I pay?

**Mother:** Tell him — you're willing to go to prison. *(Pause.)*

**Keller** *(struck, amazed)*: I'm willing — ?

**Mother** *(quickly)*: You wouldn't go, he wouldn't ask you to go. But if you told him you wanted to, if he could feel that you want to pay, maybe he would forgive you.

**Keller:** He would forgive me! For what?

**Mother:** Joe, you know what I mean.

**Keller:** I don't know what you mean! You wanted money, so I made money. What must I be forgiven? You wanted money, didn't you?

**Mother:** I didn't want it that way.

**Keller:** I didn't want it that way, either! I spoiled the both of you. I should've put him out when he was 10 like I was put out, and make him earn his keep. Then he'd know how a buck is made in this world. Forgiven! I could live on a quarter a day myself, but I got a family so I —

**Mother:** Joe, Joe . . . it don't excuse it that you did it for the family.

**Keller:** It's got to excuse it!

**Mother:** There's something bigger than the family to him.

**Keller:** Nothin' is bigger!

**Mother:** There is to him.

**Keller:** There's nothin' he could do that I wouldn't forgive. Because he's my son. Because I'm his father and he's my son.

**Mother:** Joe, I tell you —

**Keller:** Nothin's bigger than that. And you're goin' to tell him, you understand? I'm his father and he's my son, and if there's something bigger than that I'll put a bullet in my head!

**Mother:** You stop that!

**Keller:** You heard me. Now you know what to tell him. (*Pause. He moves from her — halts.*) But he wouldn't put me away though. . . . He wouldn't do that. . . . Would he?

**Mother:** He loved you, Joe; you broke his heart.

**Keller:** But to put me away . . .

**Mother:** I don't know. I'm beginning to think we don't really know him. They say in the war he was such a killer. Here he was always afraid of mice. I don't know him. I don't know what he'll do.

**Keller:** Damn, if Larry was alive he wouldn't act like this. He understood the way the world is made. He listened to me. To him the world had a 40-foot front, it ended at the building line. This one, everything bothers him. You make a deal, overcharge two cents, and his hair falls out. He don't understand money. Too easy, it came too easy. Yes, sir, Larry. That was the boy we lost. Larry. Larry. (*He slumps on chair in front of her.*) What am I gonna do, Kate?

**Mother:** Joe, Joe, please. . . . You'll be all right; nothing is going to happen.

**Keller** (*desperately, lost*): For you, Kate, for both of you, that's all I ever lived for. . . .

**Mother:** I know, darling. I know.

(*Ann enters from house. They say nothing, waiting for her to speak.*)

**Ann:** Why do you stay up? I'll tell you when he comes.

**Keller** (*rises, goes to her*): You didn't eat supper, did you? (*To Mother*) Why don't you make her something?

**Mother:** Sure, I'll —

**Ann:** Never mind, Kate; I'm all right. (*They are unable to speak to each other.*) There's something I want to tell you. (*She starts, then halts.*) I'm not going to do anything about it.

**Mother:** She's a good girl! (*To Keller*) You see? She's a —

**Ann:** I'll do nothing about Joe, but you're going to do something for me. (*Directly to Mother*) You made Chris feel guilty with me. Whether you wanted to or not,

677

you've crippled him in front of me. I'd like you to tell him that Larry is dead and that you know it. You understand me? I'm not going out of here alone. There's no life for me that way. I want you to set him free. And then I promise you, everything will end, and we'll go away, and that's all.

**Keller:** You'll do that. You'll tell him.

**Ann:** I know what I'm asking, Kate. You had two sons. But you've only one now.

**Keller:** You'll tell him.

**Ann:** And you've got to say it to him so he knows you mean it.

**Mother:** My dear, if the boy was dead, it wouldn't depend on my words to make Chris know it. . . . The night he gets into your bed, his heart will dry up. Because he knows and you know. To his dying day he'll wait for his brother! No, my dear, no such thing. You're going in the morning, and you're going alone. That's your life, that's your lonely life. *(She goes to porch, and starts in.)*

**Ann:** Larry is dead, Kate.

**Mother** *(she stops):* Don't speak to me.

**Ann:** I said he's dead. I know! He crashed off the coast of China November twenty-fifth! His engine didn't fail him. But he died. I know. . . .

**Mother:** How did he die? You're lying to me. If you know, how did he die?

**Ann:** I loved him. You know I loved him. Would I have looked at anyone else if I wasn't sure? That's enough for you.

**Mother** *(moving on her):* What's enough for me? What're you talking about? *(She grasps Ann's wrists.)*

**Ann:** You're hurting my wrists.

**Mother:** What are you talking about!

*(Pause. She stares at Ann a moment, then turns and goes to Keller.)*

**Ann:** Joe, go in the house.

**Keller:** Why should I —

**Ann:** Please go.

**Keller:** Lemme know when he comes. *(Keller goes into house.)*

**Mother** *(as she sees Ann taking letter from her pocket):* What's that?

**Ann:** Sit down. *(Mother moves left to chair, but does not sit.)* First you've got to understand. When I came, I didn't have any idea that Joe — I had nothing against him or you. I came to get married. I hoped. . . . So I didn't bring this to hurt you. I thought I'd show it to you only if there was no other way to settle Larry in your mind.

**Mother:** Larry? *(Snatches letter from Ann's hand.)*

**Ann:** He wrote it to me just before he — *(Mother opens and begins to read letter.)* I'm not trying to hurt you, Kate. You're making me do this, now remember you're — Remember. I've been so lonely. Kate . . . I can't leave here alone again. *(A long, low moan comes from Mother's throat as she reads.)* You made me show it to you. You wouldn't believe me. I told you a hundred times; why wouldn't you believe me!

**Mother:** Oh, my God . . .

**Ann** *(with pity and fear):* Kate, please, please . . .

**Mother:** My God, my God . . .

**Ann:** Kate, dear, I'm so sorry . . . I'm so sorry.

*(Chris enters from driveway. He seems exhausted.)*

**Chris:** What's the matter —

**Ann:** Where were you? ... You're all perspired. *(Mother doesn't move.)* Where were you?

**Chris:** Just drove around a little. I thought you'd be gone.

**Ann:** Where do I go? I have nowhere to go.

**Chris** *(to Mother):* Where's Dad?

**Ann:** Inside lying down.

**Chris:** Sit down, both of you. I'll say what there is to say.

**Mother:** I didn't hear the car ...

**Chris:** I left it in the garage.

**Mother:** Jim is out looking for you.

**Chris:** Mother ... I'm going away. There are a couple of firms in Cleveland. I think I can get a place. I mean, I'm going away for good. *(To Ann alone)* I know what you're thinking, Annie. It's true. I'm yellow. I was made yellow in this house because I suspected my father and I did nothing about it, but if I knew that night when I came home what I know now, he'd be in the district attorney's office by this time, and I'd have brought him there. Now if I look at him, all I'm able to do is cry.

**Mother:** What are you talking about? What else can you do?

**Chris:** I could jail him! I could jail him, if I were human anymore. But I'm like everybody else now. I'm practical now. You made me practical.

**Mother:** But you have to be.

**Chris:** The cats in that alley are practical; the bums who ran away when we were fighting were practical. Only the dead ones weren't practical. But now I'm practical and I spit on myself. I'm going away. I'm going now.

**Ann** *(going up to him):* I'm coming with you.

**Chris:** No, Ann.

**Ann:** Chris, I don't ask you to do anything about Joe.

**Chris:** You do, you do.

**Ann:** I swear I never will.

**Chris:** In your heart you always will.

**Ann:** Then do what you have to do!

**Chris:** Do what? What is there to do? I've looked all night for a reason to make him suffer.

**Ann:** There's reason, there's reason!

**Chris:** What? Do I raise the dead when I put him behind bars? Then what'll I do it for? We used to shoot a man who acted like a dog, but honor was real there, you were protecting something. But here? This is the land of the great big dogs, you don't love a man here, you eat him! That's the principle; the only one we live by — it just happened to kill a few people this time, that's all. The world's that way, how can I take it out on him? What sense does that make? This is a zoo, a zoo!

**Ann** *(to Mother):* You know what he's got to do! Tell him!

**Mother:** Let him go.

**Ann:** I won't let him go. You'll tell him what he's got to do. ...

**Mother:** Annie!

**Ann:** Then I will!

*(Keller enters from house. Chris sees him, goes down near arbor.)*

**Keller:** What's the matter with you? I want to talk to you.

**Chris:** I've got nothing to say to you.

**Keller** *(taking his arm):* I want to talk to you!

**Chris** (*pulling violently away from him*): Don't do that, Dad. I'm going to hurt you if you do that. There's nothing to say, so say it quick.

**Keller:** Exactly what's the matter? What's the matter? You got too much money? Is that what bothers you?

**Chris** (*with an edge of sarcasm*): It bothers me.

**Keller:** If you can't get used to it, then throw it away. You hear me? Take every cent and give it to charity, throw it in the sewer. Does that settle it? In the sewer, that's all. You think I'm kidding? I'm tellin' you what to do, if it's dirty then burn it. It's your money, that's not my money. I'm a dead man, I'm an old dead man, nothing's mine. Well, talk to me! What do you want to do!

**Chris:** It's not what I want to do. It's what you want to do.

**Keller:** What should I want to do? (*Chris is silent.*) Jail? You want me to go to jail? If you want me to go, say so! Is that where I belong? Then tell me so! (*Slight pause.*) What's the matter, why can't you tell me? (*Furiously*) You say everything else to me, say that! (*Slight pause.*) I'll tell you why you can't say it. Because you know I don't belong there. Because you know! (*With growing emphasis and passion, and a persistent tone of desperation*) Who worked for nothin' in that war? When they work for nothin', I'll work for nothin'. Did they ship a gun or a truck outa Detroit before they got their price? Is that clean? It's dollars and cents, nickels and dimes; war and peace, it's nickels and dimes, what's clean? Half the damn country is gotta go if I go! That's why you can't tell me.

**Chris:** That's exactly why.

**Keller:** Then . . . why am I bad?

**Chris:** I know you're no worse than most men but I thought you were better. I never saw you as a man. I saw you as my father. (*Almost breaking*) I can't look at you this way; I can't look at myself! (*He turns away, unable to face Keller. Ann goes quickly to Mother, takes letter from her and starts for Chris. Mother instantly rushes to intercept her.*)

**Mother:** Give me that!

**Ann:** He's going to read it! (*She thrusts letter into Chris's hand.*) Larry. He wrote it to me the day he died.

**Keller:** Larry!

**Mother:** Chris, it's not for you. (*He starts to read.*) Joe . . . go away . . .

**Keller** (*mystified, frightened*): Why'd she say, Larry, what — ?

**Mother** (*desperately pushes him toward alley, glancing at Chris*): Go to the street, Joe, go to the street! (*She comes down beside Keller.*) Don't, Chris . . . (*Pleading from her whole soul*) Don't tell him.

**Chris** (*quietly*): Three and one half years . . . talking, talking. Now you tell me what you must do. . . . This is how he died; now tell me where you belong.

**Keller** (*pleading*): Chris, a man can't be a Jesus in this world!

**Chris:** I know all about the world. I know the whole crap story. Now listen to this, and tell me what a man's got to be! (*Reads.*) "My dear Ann: . . ." You listening? He wrote this the day he died. Listen, don't cry. . . . Listen! "My dear Ann: It is impossible to put down the things I feel. But I've got to tell you something. Yesterday they flew in a load of papers from the States and I read about Dad and your father being convicted. I can't express myself. I can't tell you how I feel — I can't bear to live anymore. Last night I circled the base for 20 minutes before I could bring myself in. How could he have done that? Every day three or four men never come back and he sits back there doing business. . . . I don't know how to tell you what I feel. . . . I can't face anybody. . . . I'm going out on a mission in a few minutes. They'll probably report me missing. If they do, I want you to know you mustn't wait for me. I tell you, Ann, if I had him here now I could kill him — " (*Keller grabs letter from Chris's hand and reads it. After a long pause.*) Now blame the world. Do you understand that letter?

**Keller** (*speaking almost inaudibly*): I think I do. Get the car. I'll put on my jacket. (*He turns and starts slowly for the house. Mother rushes to intercept him.*)

**Mother:** Why are you going? You'll sleep; why are you going?

**Keller:** I can't sleep here. I'll feel better if I go.

**Mother:** You're so foolish. Larry was your son, too, wasn't he? You know he'd never tell you to do this.

**Keller** (*looking at letter in his hand*): Then what is this if it isn't telling me? Sure, he was my son. But I think to him they were all my sons. And I guess they were. I guess they were. I'll be right down. (*Exits into house.*)

**Mother** (*to Chris, with determination*): You're not going to take him!

**Chris:** I'm taking him.

**Mother:** It's up to you, if you tell him to stay he'll stay. Go and tell him!

**Chris:** Nobody could stop him now.

**Mother:** You'll stop him! How long will he live in prison? Are you trying to kill him?

**Chris** (*holding out letter*): I thought you read this!

**Mother** (*of Larry, the letter*): The war is over! Didn't you hear? It's over!

**Chris:** Then what was Larry to you? A stone that fell into the water? It's not enough for him to be sorry. Larry didn't kill himself to make you and Dad sorry.

**Mother:** What more can we be!

**Chris:** You can be better! Once and for all you can know there's a universe of people outside and you're responsible to it, and unless you know that, you threw away your son because that's why he died.

(*A shot is heard in the house. They stand frozen for a brief second. Chris starts for porch, pauses at step, turns to Ann.*)

**Chris:** Find Jim!

(*He goes on into the house and Ann runs up driveway. Mother stands alone, transfixed.*)

**Mother** (*softly, almost moaning*): Joe . . . Joe . . . Joe . . . Joe . . .

(*Chris comes out of house, down to Mother's arms.*)

**Chris** (*almost crying*): Mother, I didn't mean to —

**Mother:** Don't, dear. Don't take it on yourself. Forget now. Live. (*Chris stirs as if to answer.*) Shhh. . . . (*She puts his arms down gently and moves toward porch.*) Shhh. . . . (*As she reaches porch steps she begins sobbing. Curtain.*)

## READING COMPREHENSION

**Summarizing.** Choose the best phrase to complete each sentence. Then write the complete statements on your paper.

1. Ann told Kate that Kate must _____ (tell Chris she accepted Larry's death, let Chris reenlist in the army, make Joe go to jail).

2. Kate wanted her husband to tell Chris that _____ (Larry was really dead, Ann didn't love him, he was willing to go to prison for what he did).

3. Ann knew Larry was dead because _____ (his best friend wrote to tell her, she was just informed by the Army, of the letter he had sent her before his last flight).

4. After Chris read the letter aloud, Joe told him to _____ (read it again, get the car so they could go to the authorities, destroy it).

**Interpreting.** Write the answer to each question on your paper.

1. What did Larry tell Ann in his letter?

2. When Chris said he was being "practical," what did he really mean?

3. When Joe said, in referring to Larry, "But I think to him they were all my sons," to what was he referring?

**For Thinking and Discussing.** Why did Miller end the play as he did? How else could he have ended it? How would you have ended it?

## UNDERSTANDING LITERATURE

**Theme and Values.** The last act of a play brings the plot to a resolution. Now the characters and their beliefs — as well as the author's ideas and basic theme — can be fully understood. Each character in *All My Sons* has his or her own values, or beliefs, about what is true or right in life. Miller also expressed his own values by his careful structuring of the plot.

On your paper, match each character below with his or her values.

1. Joe
2. Chris
3. Ann
4. Jim
5. Frank

a. "I'm not going out of here alone. There's no life for me that way."

b. There's nothing bigger than the family.

c. ". . . there's a universe of people outside and you're responsible to it . . ."

d. "The greatest men who ever lived believed in the stars! . . . there's a power greater than ourselves."

e. "The compromise is always made . . ."

Which of the above value statements do you think is closest to Miller's own? Explain your answer.

## WRITING

In your own words, explain why or why not one of the above themes is important in everyday life.

# Section Review

## VOCABULARY

**Context Clues in Dialogue.** Context clues can help you figure out the meaning of words you do not know. Use context clues to choose the correct meaning for each italicized word below. Write the letter of the correct meaning on your paper.

1. "Sometimes you *infuriate* me, you know that? . . . You have such a talent for ignoring things."
   a. impress
   b. amuse
   c. anger

2. "The story was, I pulled a fast one getting myself *exonerated.* . . . [But] there was a court paper in my pocket to prove I wasn't [guilty]."
   a. shipped out of the country
   b. cleared of charges of wrongdoing
   c. guilty of stealing

3. "I mean if they want to open the case again, for the *nuisance* value, to hurt us?"
   a. news
   b. annoyance
   c. cash

4. "There was something wrong with the process. . . . By this time he had over a hundred *defectives.*"
   a. imperfect parts
   b. new parts
   c. practical parts

## READING

**Cloze Exercise.** Some reading tests use a technique called *cloze* to measure comprehension. In a cloze reading test, words are omitted from a selection. If you understand what you are reading, you will be able to fill in the blanks correctly. Each word you fill in will make sense in the context of the selection.

Here are some lines from *All My Sons.* On your paper, write the word that best completes each sentence.

1. "**Ann** *(to Kate):* . . . You make Chris feel guilty with me. Whether you wanted to or not, you've _____ him in front of me."
   a. crippled
   b. ignored
   c. amused

2. "**Ann** *(to Chris):* . . . Your father put hundreds of _____ into the air. You should be proud."
   a. chemicals
   b. planes
   c. clouds

Now here's a longer passage. This time you supply the words for the blanks. Write them on your paper.

3. "**Frank:** . . . But November twenty-fifth was his favorable day. . . . It was a _____ when everything good was shining on _____ , the kind of day he should've married on. You can laugh at a lot of it. I can understand you _____ . But the odds are a million to _____ that a man won't die on his _____ day." (p. 670)

**A Speech.** Playwrights sometimes have characters present monologues. A *monologue* is a long speech that presents an important idea. It can express a theme. It also helps the audience to understand a character's personality or beliefs.

For example, look at Kate Keller's speech in Act One of *All My Sons* on page 640. This reveals how this character felt about her missing son. Later in the same act, on pages 649-650, Chris gives a speech about the war and how it changed him. And on page 672, Joe Keller has a speech that describes his feelings about his mistakes.

**Step 1: Set Your Goal**

Several different philosophies of life were expressed by the characters in *All My Sons*. Choose one of the following themes from the play as the topic for a speech:

1. The family is more important than anything else.

2. We must see ourselves as part of a worldwide community.

3. For the sake of the living, the dead are best forgotten.

In your speech, you will express your reaction to the statement and explain your point of view, drawing upon the experiences of the characters in the play. You will address yourself to your teacher and your classmates.

**Step 2: Make a Plan**

Begin planning your speech by brainstorming. Consider what you'd like to say about the theme you have chosen, and make a list of all the points that come to mind. Skim the play, noting examples that support your point of view.

Organize your notes by writing each example beneath the point it supports. Then list your points in a logical order.

Suppose you were writing a speech in reaction to the following statement: "We all must learn to compromise to get through life." You might begin your list in the following way:

1. Sometimes compromise is harmful.

   Because Jim compromised, he was "dying" slowly.

   Because Keller compromised, he "killed" 21 men and his son and destroyed his family and his partner's family.

2. Sometimes compromise is necessary.

   Because Ann couldn't compromise, she helped destroy her father.

   Because Chris couldn't compromise enough, his father committed suicide.

**Step 3: Write a First Draft**

Using your notes as a guide, write the first draft of your speech. Begin with an introduction that both captures your audience's attention and clearly states what the speech is about. Use the following example as a guide:

In the final act of Arthur Miller's play *All My Sons*, Dr. Jim Bayliss claims: "The compromise is always made. . . . [E]very man does have a star. The star of one's honesty. And you spend your life groping for it, but once it's out it never lights again." According to Jim, then, the sad truth is that we all must learn to compromise to get through life. As I see it, however, we must do more than learn to compromise. We must learn *when* and *how* to compromise and, at the same time, maintain our integrity.

In the body of your speech (the paragraphs that follow the introduction), explain your point of view. Refer to your notes as you write, and add new insights and examples as they occur to you, keeping the purpose of your speech in mind. Do not worry about the order of your ideas as you write your draft. Changes in organization can be made when you revise.

When you have covered all the points that you want to make, "wrap up" your speech with a satisfying conclusion. Write a short paragraph in which you summarize your main points. Try to leave your audience with something to consider.

### Step 4: Revise

When you revise your speech, ask yourself these questions:

1. Does the introduction capture the audience's attention while clearly stating what the speech is about?

2. Does the body of the speech cover all the points I want to make?

3. Does the conclusion restate the main idea and draw the speech to a satisfactory close?

Proofread your speech as carefully as you would proofread any composition.

The following is a quiz for Section 11. Write your answers on your paper in complete sentences.

## Reading Comprehension

1. Why did Ann Deever come to visit the Kellers?

2. Why did George Deever come to the Kellers's house?

3. What did Joe Keller do when he realized his factory was producing cracked airplane parts?

4. How did the Keller family learn how and why Larry died?

5. How did the truth about Larry's death affect Joe Keller?

## Understanding Literature

6. Describe the character of Kate Keller. What were her strengths? What were her faults?

7. What was the symbolic significance of the apple tree?

8. How did the character of Joe Keller change from the beginning to the end of the play?

9. State the most important theme of the play. How does the title of the play relate to Miller's basic theme?

10. What attitudes did George Deever express? What purpose did he serve in furthering the plot of the play?

## ACTIVITIES

**Word Attack.** Frank Lubey frequently reported on the progress of Larry Keller's horoscope. The meaning of the word part *-scope* in *horoscope* is "a means of detecting or observing." It comes from a Greek word meaning "to see." *Horo-* comes from a Greek word meaning "hour." A horoscope, therefore, is a means by which some people believe they can detect the future based on the position of the planets and stars at a given moment.

Each of the following words has the word part *-scope*. Look up each word in the dictionary and write its definition. Explain how each word is the sum of its parts.

| | |
|---|---|
| microscope | telescope |
| bronchoscope | periscope |
| gastroscope | stethoscope |

### Speaking and Listening

1. Find a partner and take turns practicing the speech you have written. Time yourself. If necessary, add or delete material so that your speech is between two and five minutes long.

   As you speak, try to relax and maintain a conversational tone so that your speech will sound natural. Ask your partner to rate your delivery.

2. With a partner or group of classmates, act out a scene of your choice from *All My Sons*. Pay close attention to the stage directions as you rehearse your scene. Be prepared to perform your scene for the class.

### Researching

1. One effective way to begin a speech is to quote a famous person, an authority, or a familiar saying. Use books of quotations at your library to find material for a new introduction to the speech you have written. You might check the following books: Bartlett's *Familiar Quotations*, Stevenson's *Home Book of Quotations*, H. L. Mencken's *New Dictionary of Quotations*, and the *Oxford Dictionary of Quotations*. Look under such headings as *family, brotherhood, father, community, world, death,* and *grief*. Revise your speech, using the quotation you have chosen.

2. During World War II, not all Americans at home grew rich from the misfortunes of war. Many selflessly contributed to the war effort. Do library research to find out how Americans at home supported the armed forces. Learn about the wartime "Rosies" who worked in the factories. Share your findings with the class.

### Creating

1. Imagine you are one of the following characters: George Deever, Ann Deever, Kate Keller, or Chris Keller. Write a letter to Steve Deever describing the events that took place on that Sunday in August.

2. Write a scene describing the meeting between George and his father in prison. Describe the setting, list the characters, write realistic dialogue, and provide stage directions. Read the scene aloud with some of your classmates.

# READER'S AND WRITER'S REFERENCE

# HANDBOOK OF ACTIVE READING

You may not be aware of it, but whenever you are reading, you are thinking. After all, readers are not like copying machines, scanning words without getting meaning. They can react to characters, find ideas interesting, get bored or confused, and guess what's coming next. They can laugh out loud, choose sides in arguments, compare their own lives to the characters', and much more. Readers in fact *make* meaning, not just absorb it.

"Listen in" for a moment on the thoughts of Walker as he begins to read "My Name," one of a series of stories called *The House on Mango Street* by Sandra Cisneros.

*Isn't a mango a tropical fruit? Maybe this story is set in the tropics.*

## THE HOUSE ON MANGO STREET
Sandra Cisneros

### My Name

*Some unusual thoughts here; I'm getting interested. I wonder how her name is like the number nine.*

*Does she ride horses, or is she a "horse woman" because of her birthday?*

In English my name means hope. In Spanish it means too many letters. It means sadness, it means waiting. It is like the number nine. A muddy color. It is the Mexican records my father plays on Sunday mornings when he is shaving, songs like sobbing.

It was my great-grandmother's name and now it is mine. She was a horse woman too, born like me in the Chinese year of the horse—which is supposed to be bad luck if you're born female—but I think this is a Chinese lie because the Chinese, like the Mexicans, don't like their women strong.

Successful readers are active readers. Like Walker, they bring their experiences and their knowledge to whatever they read. His thoughts show you three basic aspects of active reading:

- **Respond Personally.** Read to discover what meaning the writing has *for you.* Connect the writing to your own life in any way you can, and be aware of your opinions and feelings. *Walker, for example, responds to the story's narrator as he would to meeting a new person. He thinks she's a bit unusual but he's "getting interested."*

- **Apply Your Own Experience and Knowledge.** To make sense of what you read, draw on things that have happened to you and on things you have learned. *When Walker reads the title, he recalls that a mango is a tropical fruit and wonders if the story is set in the tropics.*

- **Have a Conversation with the Writing.** When you read, set out to have a conversation with the work (story, poem, etc.) and the writer. Don't assume that it (or he or she) gets to do all the talking! Every response or memory is part of the conversation, but you can even "talk back" to the text: disagree, ask a question, point out a confusion. Active reading has the flavor of a back-and-forth, give-and-take dialogue. *Walker isn't sure how Esperanza's name is like the number nine and he notices that "horse woman" could be interpreted in two ways.*

Listening in on Walker's thoughts should show you that you already read actively in some ways. If you were beginning "My Name" on your own, you wouldn't hear the same conversation in your head (no two readers ever will), but *some* thoughts about the story would be stirring. To be a more successful reader, you need to focus on those thoughts and add to them, and you can do this by learning specific active reading strategies.

**Activity One. Thinking About Your Reading.** When you read the opening of "My Name," what thoughts did you have that Walker did not? Did any of his thoughts match yours? If you could talk to him, what comments would you like to make? Did anything in his thoughts make you read the story in a different way?

## STRATEGIES FOR ACTIVE READING
The following strategies will help strengthen your active reading abilities. They can be used for any reading that you do.

## Think About Why You're Reading

Would you read a magazine recipe for spaghetti when you're waiting in the dentist's office the same way that you read a recipe for spaghetti when you're fixing dinner? Probably not. How you read—how closely you pay attention and what you look for—can change with why you're reading. For this reason, active reading begins before you read a word.

In reading literature, your fundamental purpose is to find meaning and pleasure for yourself, but you can have a variety of specific purposes that affect your reading approach. Always take time to define any assigned purpose or to set one for yourself.

Here are some examples: Are you reading a story for class discussion or for writing? If for writing, you should count on *re*reading all or parts of the story. First you should read to respond and get ideas; then you should reread even more closely and focus on what interested you.

Are you reading a scene from a play for a journal entry or for an oral reading in class? If for oral reading, you should be sure to read aloud, paying special attention to the rhythms of sentences and the speaker's possible feelings.

Are you reading a poem for a personal response paper or for an assigned paper describing sound effects? If for a description of sound effects, you should begin reading with specific elements like rhythm, rhyme, meter, and alliteration already in your mind.

Thinking about purpose will help you decide how many times you will read, how quickly you will read, what you will focus on, and what you may need to review before you start.

Walker was reading four selections from *The House on Mango Street* for a class discussion and a possible paper. (His paper was due in a week, and he hadn't yet decided what to write about.) That meant he wanted to read carefully, both to be ready for class and to see whether he might choose *The House on Mango Street* for a writing assignment.

## Use Any Clues You Are Given

When active readers approach a new piece of writing, they use any information they are given: a written introduction, a teacher's comments, information about the author, the work's title. They are really "sizing up the work" and forming a general impression (the way you do when you meet someone). They are gathering background information to use as they read.

691

Walker's introduction to *The House on Mango Street* was an opening note in his textbook. Here are his thoughts on that introduction. (You've already seen his responses to the title.)

> *Sketch? <u>Short short story?</u> It sounds like this may be different from a usual story.*

*The House on Mango Street* is a book of sketches or short short stories, written down by a girl named Esperanza (es per än´ sa). Each section is a single episode, like a journal entry, but they are all connected because they are about Esperanza and her world. As you read, concentrate on the picture that emerges, both of the girl and of her life.

A main part of this sizing up, as Walker's example shows, is identifying the type or form of literature you are reading: poem, short story, play, essay, epic, etc. Your familiarity with each form helps you get hold of, and make sense of, a work you've never read before. Identifying form gives you an idea of what to expect. Then you can bring into mental readiness what you already know about poetry or plays or novels. (In the second part of this handbook, you'll find specific strategies for reading different forms of literature.)

Walker's thoughts above show that he's thinking about form. He knows that these stories may be a little different from "usual" ones. Notice, too, that the textbook's note gives Walker another reading clue: a possible focus, or purpose, as he reads.

**Question**
Continually ask questions as you read. You've already seen Walker asking questions when he was uncertain or confused (*Isn't a mango a tropical fruit?*). But questioning is also a way to involve yourself in what is unfolding and to explore your own feelings. Try to go below the surface of what you're reading by asking questions like *How did this character get to be so mistrustful?* or *Why would the poet call a mirror a "little god"?* Also pay attention to your own responses and judgments by asking questions like *Why is this play so funny to me, while the one before just seemed dull?*

Walker posed these questions as he continued reading "My Name."

> *It sounds like this girl loves the idea of her grandmother being wild. Is she wild too?*

> *Like a "fancy chandelier"—that puts a vivid picture in my mind. But I wonder how the grandmother felt. Angry, I bet.*

My great-grandmother. I would've liked to have known her, a wild horse of a woman, so wild she wouldn't marry until my great-grandfather threw a sack over her head and carried her off. Just like that, as if she were a fancy chandelier. That's the way he did it.

**Predict**

Look ahead in your reading, just as you do in your personal life. At any moment in the present (even the moment when a friend says, "Want to go to the party?"), you're thinking about what may happen, of consequences of actions (cause and effect), of different possible outcomes. These predictions—some right, some wrong—help shape life and give it meaning; they keep you from just bouncing along from one event to the next, without being prepared or learning from what happens.

In the same way, predicting where the writer is taking you is a way to build meaning. You get a better grip on your own experience if you ask *What will happen next? What is all this leading up to?* Your predictions can draw on what you've read so far, on what you know from reading other works of the same type or by the same writer, and on what you know about human nature.

As Walker read on, he made a prediction about "the whole point" of Esperanza's writing. Do you agree with him? Do you think this is what *The House on Mango Street* will be about? *Why* do you think he made this prediction?

> *What an unusual way to describe feeling sad. It sounds almost like a poem.*

> *Maybe this is the whole point—Esperanza is scared she'll get stuck in a life she doesn't want. I bet she's going to talk more about how she'll avoid a life like her grandmother's.*

And the story goes she never forgave him. She looked out the window all her life, the way so many women sit their sadness on an elbow. I wonder if she made the best with what she got or was she sorry because she couldn't be all the things she wanted to be. Esperanza. I have inherited her name, but I don't want to inherit her place by the window.

## Expect Puzzles and Problems

No reader, no matter how experienced, understands every part of every piece of writing. In reading, some blocks, surprises, or slow-downs are natural, and active readers expect them and find ways to get past them. For example, you may not understand an idea, word, or reference. You may make a prediction that turns out to be wrong. You may not have the knowledge of the appropriate form for the work you're reading (as, for instance, trying to read an ancient Greek epic without knowing enough about the epic form, the time period, or Greek mythology).

When these puzzles or problems happen, don't panic or give up. Use your uncertainty as a signal to remedy the situation. First pinpoint what is happening, and then see what strategies you might apply.

If a passage isn't clear, for example, give it another chance; reread it. Ask questions about what is bothering or confusing you (*Is this really happening, or is it a dream? How can the space program have anything to do with pollution?*), and see if a closer reading turns up answers.

If you don't know certain words or references, look for footnotes, or try to find context clues (surrounding words or sentences), or use the glossary or a dictionary.

If you've made a false prediction and find your expectations unmet (*But why didn't the captive escape when he could?*), look for clues you missed, rearrange your thoughts, and make new guesses based on what you now know.

Remember, too, that your "strategy" may be to accept a problem. Perhaps you aren't ready to read an epic without more background or outside help; try to get it. Perhaps a passage does have two interpretations (like the "horse woman" question), and you won't know more without reading on. Perhaps the writer's reasoning *does* have flaws, and you can define them; that's an important reading discovery.

In the next passage, Walker discovers that his guess about setting ("in the tropics") probably isn't correct because Spanish isn't spoken at Esperanza's school. He also suspects he's not pronouncing *Esperanza* right and looks back at the textbook's introduction, which shows him how the name sounds.

| | |
|---|---|
| *I guess they don't speak Spanish at her school. I wonder where she lives.* | At school they say my name funny as if the syllables were made out of tin and hurt the roof of your mouth. But in Spanish my name is made out of a softer |

*"Esperanza" doesn't sound soft to me. Oh, I get it. The z sounds like s.* ⎤— something like silver, not quite as thick as sister's name Magdalena which is uglier than mine. Magdalena who at least can come home and become Nenny. But I am always Esperanza.

## Summarize for Yourself

Every so often, especially at the end of chapters or sections, stop to sum up the events and ideas you've read about. Also review your own thoughts. These personal summaries become useful background as you continue reading.

Since Walker had just had a new insight, he made this quick summary:

> *Esperanza is probably Mexican and speaks Spanish, but she goes to a school where everyone speaks English. Maybe it's in the United States. Anyway, she thinks a lot about sad things—and about women.*

## React to the Whole

When you finish the work, take a few minutes to digest what you've read. Now is the time to pull together all your thoughts and to remember the characters and details that made an impression on you.

What thoughts—ideas about human beings and the world—do you think the writer conveys in the work? Do these ideas square with your experience of life, or do they seem false to it? Were any ideas completely new to you, and did they make you see your own life in a different way?

Finally, do you like the work or not? (A very important question!) Be frank about any opinion, but also try to find out the reasons for your feelings. They may reveal to you something about yourself. What did you like best and least in the work (a character, the plot, the writer's style, the dialogue)? You might imagine that you're talking to your best friend. Tell this friend why you want to read—or *don't* want to read—more works by this author.

When Walker finished "My Name," he reacted to what he'd read so far. Here are his thoughts. (On pages 698-701, you'll find Walker's whole assignment from *The House on Mango Street,* with his reading thoughts and final response.)

*I think she might want something more than a new name.*   ⎤
⎢
⎦

> I would like to baptize myself under a new name, a name more like the real me, the one nobody sees. Esperanza as Lisandra or Maritza or Zeze the X. Yes. Something like Zeze the X will do.

*I like what she says about "the real me, the one nobody sees." That's an idea that a lot of people I know would agree with.*

**Special Note:** Many readers like to "read with a pencil": to mark passages and write down thoughts as they read. You can't write in a school textbook, but you can write in a journal and in books you own. When you're trying to improve your active reading, written notes can make you more aware of your own reading habits.

**Activity Two. Reading Actively.** Choose a work in this book that you haven't read. Read it, using the active reading strategies to guide your thinking. Then write two or three sentences (more, if you like) telling a classmate how using the strategies was different from your usual way of reading a new work.

### Active Reading Summary

**Basic Approach**
1. Respond personally.
2. Apply your own experience and knowledge.
3. Have a conversation with the writing.

**Strategies**
1. Think about why you are reading.
2. Use any clues you are given (the type of literature, an introduction, a note on the author, etc.).
3. Question.
4. Predict.
5. Expect puzzles and problems, and apply strategies to solve them.
6. Summarize for yourself.
7. React to the whole.

. . . . . . . . . . . . . . . . . . . . . . . . . . . . . . . . . . . . . . . . . . . . . . . . . . . . . . . . . . . . .

HANDBOOK OF ACTIVE READING

## USING WHAT YOU LEARN ABOUT LITERATURE

You have learned that active reading means bringing your own knowledge—your personal frameworks for understanding—to the work in front of you. And an important framework for reading literature is knowledge of form: all the things you are learning in this textbook about *the art of* fiction, poetry, drama, and nonfiction.

Why is reading in this way—paying close attention to elements and techniques— important? Because it helps you get more out of the writing for yourself. Think about it: Doesn't "inside knowledge" increase most pleasures in your life? Once you know the plays in football, the moves in skateboarding, the hardest turns in a dance, then you see the game, the moves, the dancers in a different way. You see more clearly and more deeply.

Focusing on literary elements like imagery, setting, and point of view, and seeing how a writer weaves them together, gives you sharper insight into the literature.

The handbook's next sections provide (1) brief summaries of literary elements to use in active, close readings of stories, poems, plays, and nonfiction, (2) some special active-reading strategies for the different forms, and (3) samples of students' close readings. Keep in mind that the lists of guidelines are quick references, reminders of more detailed information in your textbook.

### Fiction (Short Stories and Novels)

Short stories and novels share common elements, but novels, because they are longer, often have more complicated plots (including subplots); more characters, who are more fully developed; multiple settings; and even more than one point of view.

### Reading Fiction Actively

As you respond to a story and think about its meaning, consider these questions and suggestions.

1. What is the story's **point of view**, the vantage point from which it is told? Is it **first-person, third-person omniscient,** or **third-person limited**? Point of view is important because it determines who is speaking to you, what you are told, and the **tone** of the narration.
2. Who are the main **characters**, and how (and how well) does the writer bring them to life? What motivates the characters? What do they want?
3. What main **conflicts** or problems do the characters face? Are these conflicts internal (happening within the character's mind), external (caused by other people, nature, society), or both? How are the conflicts resolved, or are they?

4. What is the story's **setting**, its time period and place? Think about the effect of setting in the story and on you. Does it provide background for understanding characters and events, set a mood, or create a conflict?

5. What do you observe and feel about the writer's **style**—the word choice, figurative language (or lack of it), and rhythms of the sentences? Be alert to **imagery**, to **figures of speech,** and to **symbols**—both their meanings and their emotional effects on you (**connotations**).

6. Remember to react to the whole. You are constantly building meaning as you read, responding to many different elements. After you finish, try to pull everything together as you answer these questions: What do you think the author wants to communicate? What does the story mean to you? Do you like it?

Here is Walker's close, active reading of *The House on Mango Street.*

*Sketch? Short short story? It sounds like this may be different from a usual story.*

*The House on Mango Street* is a book of sketches or short short stories, written down by a girl named Esperanza (es per än´ sa). Each section is a single episode, like a journal entry, but they are all connected because they are about Esperanza and her world. As you read, concentrate on the picture that emerges, both of the girl and of her life.

*Isn't a mango a tropical fruit? Maybe this story is set in the tropics.*

## THE HOUSE ON MANGO STREET
Sandra Cisneros

### My Name

*Some unusual thoughts here; I'm getting interested. I wonder how her name is like the number nine.*

In English my name means hope. In Spanish it means too many letters. It means sadness, it means waiting. It is like the number nine. A muddy color. It is the Mexican records my father plays on Sunday mornings when he is shaving, songs like sobbing.

*Does she ride horses, or is she a "horse woman" because of her birthday?*

It was my great-grandmother's name and now it is mine. She was a horse woman too, born like me in the Chinese year of the horse—which is supposed to be bad

*It sounds like this girl loves the idea of her grandmother being wild. Is she wild too?*

*Like a "fancy chandelier"—that puts a vivid picture in my mine. But I wonder how the grandmother felt. Angry, I bet.*

*What an unusual way to describe feeling sad. It sounds almost like a poem.*

*Maybe this is the whole point—Esperanza is scared she'll get stuck in a life she doesn't want. I bet she's going to talk more about how she'll avoid a life like her grandmother's.*

*I guess they don't speak Spanish at her school. I wonder where she lives.*

*"Esperanza" doesn't sound soft to me. Oh, I get it. The z sounds like s.*

luck if you're born female—but I think this is a Chinese lie because the Chinese, like the Mexicans, don't like their women strong.

My great-grandmother. I would've liked to have known her, a wild horse of a woman, so wild she wouldn't marry until my great-grandfather threw a sack over her head and carried her off. Just like that, as if she were a fancy chandelier. That's the way he did it.

And the story goes she never forgave him. She looked out the window all her life, the way so many women sit their sadness on an elbow. I wonder if she made the best with what she got or was she sorry because she couldn't be all the things she wanted to be. Esperanza. I have inherited her name, but I don't want to inherit her place by the window.

At school they say my name funny as if the syllables were made out of tin and hurt the roof of your mouth. But in Spanish my name is made out of a softer something like silver, not quite as thick as sister's name Magdalena which is uglier than mine. Magdalena who at least can come home and become Nenny. But I am always Esperanza.

*Esperanza is probably Mexican and speaks Spanish, but she goes to a school where everyone speaks English. Maybe it's in the United States. Anyway, she thinks a lot about sad things—and about women.*

*I think she might want something more than a new name.*

I would like to baptize myself under a new name, a name more like the real me, the one nobody sees. Esperanza as Lisandra or Maritza or Zeze the X. Yes. Something like Zeze the X will do.

*I like what she says about "the real me, the one nobody sees." That's an idea a lot of people that I know would agree with.*

*Don't what?*

## Those Who Don't

*Some people think she lives in a rough neighborhood.*

Those who don't know any better come into our neighborhood scared. They think we're dangerous. They think we will attack them with shiny knives. They are stupid people who are lost and got here by mistake.

*They all have nicknames.*

But we aren't afraid. We know the guy with the crooked eye is Davey the Baby's brother, and the tall one next to him in the straw brim, that's Rosa's Eddie V, and the big one that looks like a dumb grown man, he's Fat Boy, though he's not fat anymore nor a boy.

*She lives in a Hispanic neighborhood, maybe in a big city. What kind of neighborhood scares her?*

All brown all around, we are safe. But watch us drive into a neighborhood of another color and our knees go shakity-shake and our car windows get rolled up tight and our eyes look straight. Yeah. That is how it goes and goes.

*Even though nothing has happened in these three paragraphs, the writer said a lot. Like what people think they see (tough guys with knives) and what's really there (just ordinary people). I'm starting to like the way she uses words: "all brown all around," "shakity-shake" (like knees knocking), "that is how it goes and goes" (that's how it is).*

## Mango Says Goodbye Sometimes

I like to tell stories. I tell them inside my head. I tell them after the mailman says here's your mail. Here's your mail he said.

*She loves to daydream and to think about her own life.*

I make a story for my life, for each step my brown shoe takes. I say, "And so she trudged up the wooden stairs, her sad brown shoes taking her to the house she never liked."

*I think I know who this girl is . . .*

I like to tell stories. I am going to tell you a story about a girl who didn't want to belong.

*I've only lived in two houses, but I know what it's like to feel that you don't belong.*

*"Sad" and "red" don't usually go together.*

*Is the ghost her spirit?*

We didn't always live on Mango Street. Before that we lived on Loomis on the third floor, and before that we lived on Keeler. Before Keeler it was Paulina, but what I remember most is Mango Street, sad red house, the house I belong but do not belong to.

I put it down on paper and then the ghost does not ache so much. I write it down and Mango says goodbye sometimes. She does not hold me with both arms. She sets me free.

One day I will pack my bags of books and paper. One day I will say goodbye to Mango. I am too strong for her to keep me here forever. One day I will go away.

Friends and neighbors will say, What happened to that Esperanza? Where did she go with all those books and paper? Why did she march so far away?

*Maybe she means her writing will somehow help the people she leaves behind.*

They will not know I have gone away to come back. For the ones I left behind. For the ones who cannot get out.

*This didn't seem like a regular story at first, and I wasn't sure how I felt about it. But then I got to like it. Even though I'm not sure I understood everything Esperanza said, I liked the way she talked. She sounded like a real person. And I know the feeling of not fitting in, feeling trapped. It's interesting to read a story full of the ideas that people usually only think about but don't write or say out loud.*

## Poetry

The following reading suggestions are helpful in approaching any poem, but remember that your knowledge of specific poetic forms is an important reading framework. For example, if you have learned about ballads, or sonnet form, or *haiku* poems, or dramatic monologues, you can also bring your knowledge about those forms to your reading.

## Reading Poetry Actively

As you respond to a poem and think about its meaning, consider these suggestions and questions.

1. Three special active-reading strategies are helpful in reading poetry: **(a)** read the poem aloud, using the punctuation to hear its rhythm, **(b)** read the poem more than once, to go deeper into the poem's rich, compact language, and **(c)** paraphrase passages (put them in your own words) to clarify meanings. You may, for example, restate figures of speech or put inverted word order into the normal order of everyday speech.

2. Remember that the **speaker** of the poem is not always the writer. The speaker may be a character or even something nonhuman. Identify the speaker, and ask, "What is the **tone** of this speaker's voice? (What attitude toward the subject and readers is being expressed?)"

3. What strong sensory **images** occur in the poem? What do they make you see, hear, smell, feel, or taste, and *how* do they make you feel? What mood do the images create?

4. Be alert to **figures of speech (similes, metaphors, personifications).** Think about why the poet uses these particular imaginative comparisons (do they make you see something in a new way? what emotions do they convey?). Also be aware of possible **symbols.** Could a word, person, or event stand for something beyond itself (for example, a setting sun used to represent death)?

5. What are the sound effects of the poem (its music) like? Whether the poem is written in **free verse** or in **meter,** listen to the quality of its **rhythm,** and think about how the rhythm enhances meaning. (For example, is the rhythm fast and hard? Is it like a conversation? Is it delicate, like a song?) Think in the same way about other musical devices like **rhyme, alliteration, and onomatopoeia.** What is the poet emphasizing with their use? How do the sounds make you feel?

6. Remember to react to the whole. When you have finished reading, try to pull together your complete experience of the poem. What does it say to you? What is its insight, meaning, or idea? What personal associations does it call up? Did you like just some of it? Whatever your opinion of the poem, try to explain why you feel as you do.

Here are one student's thoughts on a poem. The student read the poem twice.

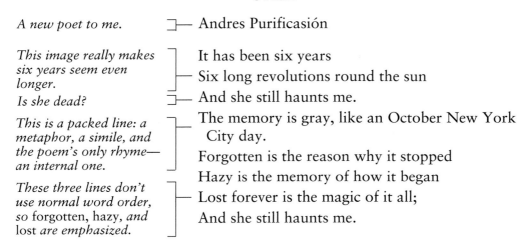

STILL

*A new poet to me.* ⌐— Andres Purificasión

*This image really makes six years seem even longer.*
*Is she dead?*

It has been six years
Six long revolutions round the sun
And she still haunts me.

*This is a packed line: a metaphor, a simile, and the poem's only rhyme— an internal one.*

The memory is gray, like an October New York City day.
Forgotten is the reason why it stopped
Hazy is the memory of how it began

*These three lines don't use normal word order, so* forgotten, hazy, *and* lost *are emphasized.*

Lost forever is the magic of it all;
And she still haunts me.

*The "it" in this poem isn't death (like I thought) but a past romance. The romance died, but the memory of the woman haunts the poet. It's funny that he can forget details but still be haunted. He just feels something is missing. The whole poem has a sad, quiet sound.*

**Activity Three. Reading a Poem Actively.** Choose a poem that you have not read before, and read it actively, using the guidelines above. Before you begin, review the Active Reading Summary on page 696. Choose the strategy that you think you use *least* often, and emphasize it during your reading.

## Drama

A play tells a story through action and dialogue. It is meant to be performed on a stage. As an active reader of a play, it is important to remember that you are reading a *script*. As you read, you will be following a story, but you will also be thinking like a director and an actor. Some playwrights supply many stage directions, others very few. When reading, your imagination is important in bringing a script to life.

People in the theater use a special vocabulary to describe areas on a stage and directions of movement. This diagram will help you understand and visualize stage directions. Notice that the directions "right" and "left" are given from the actors' viewpoint, facing the audience. The back of the stage is called "upstage" because early stages were not level. They were sloped, rising away from the audience.

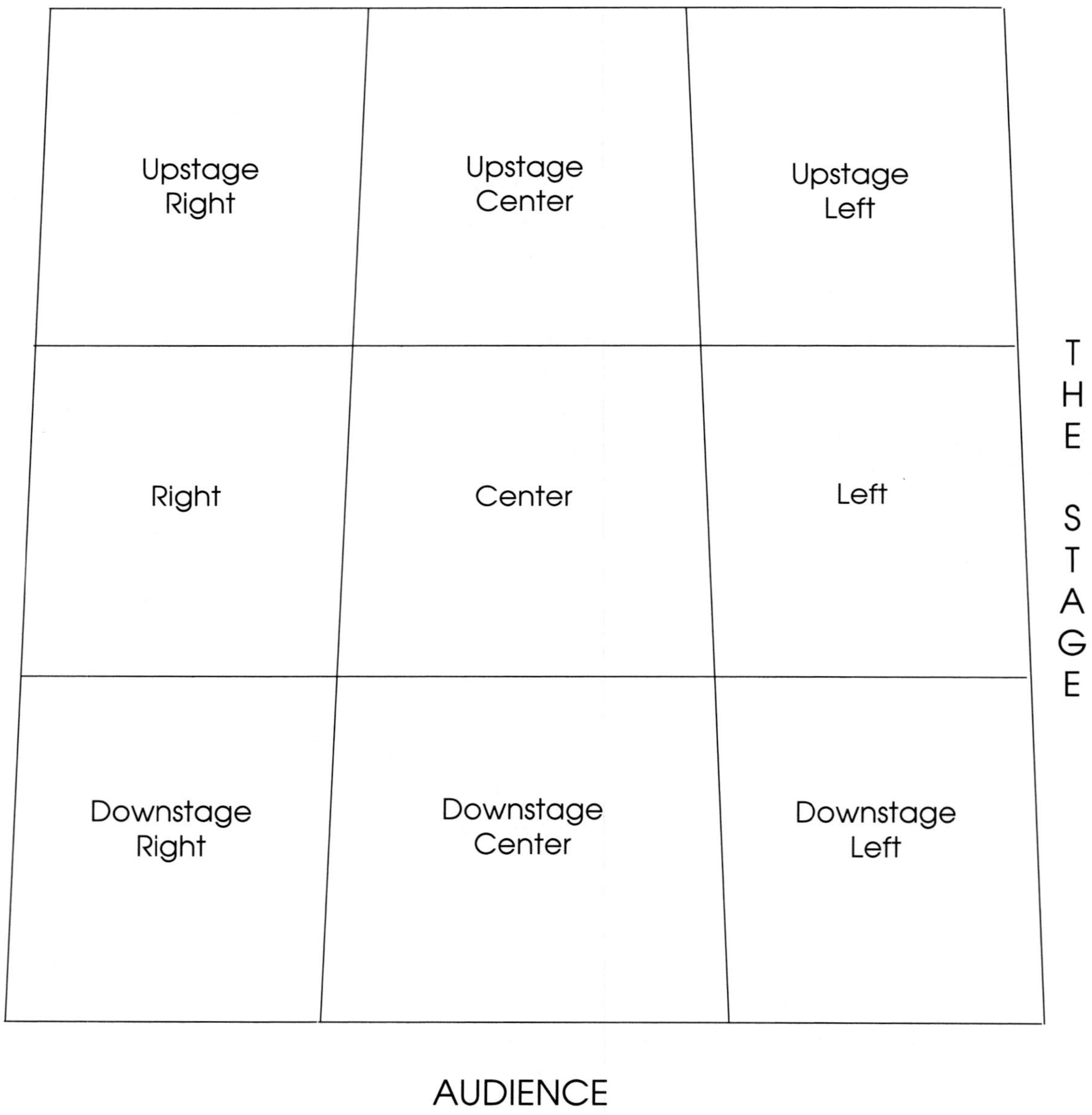

| | | |
|---|---|---|
| Upstage Right | Upstage Center | Upstage Left |
| Right | Center | Left |
| Downstage Right | Downstage Center | Downstage Left |

THE STAGE

AUDIENCE

**Reading Drama Actively**

As you respond to a play and think about its meaning, consider these suggestions and questions.

1. A special active reading strategy for drama is to *visualize*: picture the stage and the actors moving on it. Read carefully any **stage directions** about scenery, props (short for *properties*), costumes, characters' appearances, lighting, and sound (music or other sound effects). These elements of a play provide background for understanding events, establish characterization, and set mood or **tone**.

2. Also visualize movements and actions: characters' entrances and exits, their positions on the stage, and their gestures and actions. Remember that actors seldom stand fixed to a spot, delivering their lines like a lecture. They act and interact, and these movements themselves create meaning. To probe a character or an event, try to imagine the *physical* action that is occurring.

3. Read **dialogue** as if you were the director or the actor, interpreting a role. In a play, you must usually infer characters' thoughts and feelings from their speech. Always think about the characters' motives and emotions. What are they feeling as they speak? *Why* are they saying what they say? What is their tone of voice? Read lines aloud as you would deliver them.

4. Analyze and respond to the play's story as you would to any story (see the fiction guidelines on pages 697-698). Be alert to **characterization, setting, conflict,** and the conflict's outcome, as well as to the playwright's **style**, or use of language. Think about how each scene advances the **plot**.

5. Remember to react to the whole. When you go to a play or a movie, many images draw your attention; many thoughts and feelings fill you. When you leave the theater, you're usually ready to *talk*: to go over the experience with your friends. Read plays this way too. When you finish, put all your observations together. Try to express what the play said to you about life, what you liked, what you didn't, and why.

Here is one student's close reading of the opening scene of *The Sneeze* by Neil Simon.

*This must be a comedy.*

**THE SNEEZE**
*a play by Neil Simon*
*based on a story by Anton Chekhov*

*Why would a play have a narrator?*

**CHARACTERS**
**Writer**, the play's narrator
**Ivan Ilyitch Cherdyakov**, a Russian clerk
**His wife**, Madame Cherdyakov
**General Mikhail Brassilhov**, Minister of Public Parks and Cherdyakov's boss
**Madame Brassilhov**, the General's wife

*Where is the writer? Is he in front of the curtain?*

*So the curtain is already open, and the set is a theater.*

*Famous audience? Rich people?*

*Is this a real play? (Look it up later.)*

**Writer:** If Ivan Ilyitch Cherdyakov, a civil servant, a clerk in the Ministry of Public Parks, had any passion in life at all, it was the theater. *(Enter Ivan Cherdyakov and his wife. He is in his mid-thirties, mild-mannered, and shy. He and his wife are dressed in their best, but are certainly no match for the grandeur around them. They are clearly out of place here. They move into their seats. As his wife studies her program, Cherdyakov is beaming with happiness as he looks around and in back at the theater and its famous audience. He is a happy man tonight.)* He certainly had hopes and ambitions for higher office and had dedicated his life to hard work and patience. Still, he would not deny himself his one great pleasure. So he purchased two tickets in the very best section of the theater for the opening night performance of Rostov's *The Bearded Countess. (A splendidly uniformed General and his wife enter, looking for their seats.)* As fortune would have it, into the theater that

*Good fortune or bad?*

night came His Respected Boss, General Mikhail Brassilhov, the Minister of Public Parks himself.

. . .

*The real audience is looking at the stage audience, I guess.*

*(The General and his wife take their seats in the first row, the General directly in front of Cherdyakov.)*

**Cherdyakov** *(leans over to the General)*: Good evening, General.

*He thinks he's too important to know the "little people."*

**General** *(turns, looks at Cherdyakov coldly)*: Hmm? . . . What? Oh, yes. Yes. Good evening. *(The General turns front again, looks at his program.)*

**Cherdyakov:** Permit me, sir. I am Cherdyakov . . . Ivan Ilyitch. This is a great honor for me, sir.

**General** *(turns coldly)*: Yes.

*He sounds like he's proud of this silly title!*

**Cherdyakov:** Like yourself, dear General, I too serve the Ministry of Public Parks. . . . That is to say, I serve you, who is indeed himself the Minister of Public Parks. I am the Assistant Chief Clerk in the Department of Trees and Bushes.

**General:** Ahh, yes. Keep up the good work. . . . Lovely trees and bushes this year. Very nice.

*(The General turns back. Cherdyakov sits back, happy, grinning like a cat. The General shrugs back. Suddenly, the unseen curtain rises on the play and they all applaud. Cherdyakov leans forward again.)*

*What a dope—the play's starting.*

**Cherdyakov:** My wife would like very much to say hello, General. This is she. My wife, Madame Cherdyakov.

**Wife** *(smiles)*: How do you do?

**General:** My pleasure.

**Wife:** My pleasure, General.

**General:** How do you do?

*(He turns front, flustered. Cherdyakov beams at his wife; then:)*

**Cherdyakov** *(to the General's wife):* Madame Brassilhov — my wife, Madame Cherdyakov.

**Wife:** How do you do, Madame Brassilhov?

**Madame Brassilhov** *(coldly):* How do you do?

**Wife:** I just had the pleasure of meeting your husband.

*This is pathetic—but funny.*

**Cherdyakov** *(to Madame Brassilhov):* And I am my wife's husband. How do you do, Madame Brassilhov?

*So the Writer is part of the audience. I imagined him off to the side, out of the action.*

*(The Writer "shushes" them.)*

**General** *(to the Writer):* Sorry. Terribly sorry. *(The General tries to control his anger as they all go back to watching the play.)*

*Sarcastic.*

**Cherdyakov:** I hope you enjoy the play, sir.

**General:** I will if I can watch it. *(He is getting hot under the collar. They all go back to watching the performance.)*

*When the Writer talks, the other actors must just ignore him. Maybe he has a spotlight on him.*

**Writer:** Feeling quite pleased with himself for having made the most of this golden opportunity, Ivan Ilyitch Cherdyakov sat back to enjoy *The Bearded Countess.* He was no longer a stranger to the Minister of Public Parks. They had become, if one wanted to be generous about the matter, familiar with each other. And then, quite suddenly, without any warning, like a bolt from a gray thundering sky, Ivan Ilyitch Cherdyakov reared his head back, and . . .

**Cherdyakov:**     AHHHHHHHH—CHOOOOOOOOO!!! *(Cherdyakov unleashes a monstrous sneeze, his head snapping forward. The main blow of the sneeze discharges on the back of the General's completely bald head. The General winces and his hand immediately goes to his now-dampened head.)* Ohhh, my goodness, I'm sorry, your Excellency! I'm so terribly sorry! *(The General takes out his handkerchief and wipes his head.)*

*Gross!*

**General:** Never mind. It's all right.

**Cherdyakov:** All right? . . . It certainly is not all right! It's unpardonable. It was monstrous of me—

**General:** You make too much of the matter. Let it rest.

*(He puts away his handkerchief.)*

**Cherdyakov** (*quickly takes out his own handkerchief*): How can I let it rest! It was inexcusable. Permit me to wipe your neck, General. It's the least I can do. *(He starts to wipe the General's head. The General pushes his hand away.)*

*He's only making it worse.*

**General:** Leave it be! It's all right, I say.

*Nothing like telling the whole world!*

**Cherdyakov:** But I splattered you, sir. Your complete head is splattered. It was an accident, I assure you—but it's disgusting!

**Writer:** Shhh!

**General:** I'm sorry. My apologies.

*Every time he opens his mouth, he makes a bigger fool of himself.*

**Cherdyakov:** The thing is, your Excellency, it came completely without warning. It was out of my nose before I could stifle it.

**Madame Brassilhov:** Shhh!

**Cherdyakov:** Shhh, yes, certainly, I'm sorry. . . . *(He sits back, nervously. He blows his nose with his handkerchief. Then Cherdyakov leans forward.)* It's not a cold, if that's what you were worrying about, sir. Probably a particle of dust in the nostril—

**General:** Shh!

*(They watch the play in silence, and Cherdyakov sits back, unhappy with himself.)*

**Writer:** But try as he might, Cherdyakov could not put the incident out of his mind. The sneeze, no more than an innocent accident, grew out of all proportion in his mind, until it resembled the angry roar of a cannon aimed squarely at the enemy camp. He played the incident back in his mind, slowing down the procedure so he could view again, in horror, the infamous deed. *(Cherdyakov, in slow motion, repeats the sneeze again, but slowed down so that it appears to us as one frame at a time. It also seems to be three times as great in intensity as the original sneeze. The General, also in slow motion, reacts as though he has just taken a 50-pound hammer blow at the base of his skull. They all go with the slow motion of the "sneeze" until it is completed, when the unseen curtain falls and they applaud. They all rise and begin to file out of the theater, chattering about the lovely evening they have just spent. . . . )*

*This is great.*　⌐—

*So far this is pretty funny—especially the slow-motion sneeze. Everything the clerk does seems to backfire. I wonder what he'll do next.*

**Activity Four. Reading a Play Actively.** Read one of the plays in this book, and use a journal to record your reading notes. When you're finished, compare notes with someone else. Point out at least one of your partner's notes that you especially like, and explain why. Then work together (include other students if you like) to present a dramatic reading of any scene from the play.

## Nonfiction

Since nonfiction, by definition, is all writing about actual people and experiences, it covers a wide range indeed: newspaper journalism, personal essays, biographies and autobiographies, interviews, scientific articles, and on and on.

As an active reader, begin to look more closely at the nonfiction you read and enjoy. In addition to content, look at what is special about each piece of writing. What is it about the writer's style and approach that makes you want to read on?

## Reading Nonfiction Actively

As you respond to nonfiction consider these questions and suggestions.

1. What is the writer's subject, and *why* is he or she writing about it? Always try to identify the writer's purpose. What does the writer want to make you think, see, understand, or feel? What effect is the writer trying to produce?

2. How subjective or objective is the writing? Some nonfiction is extremely personal; its purpose is to express the writer's feelings. Other nonfiction concentrates more on factual information. But all writing conveys a writer's attitude in some way. Pay attention to the writer's **tone** (the personality of the writing), to word choice and the **connotations** (emotional appeals) of words, and to feelings expressed through **figurative language**. Separate fact from opinion.

3. Be aware that nonfiction can use fictional techniques: character development, dialogue, conflict, flashbacks, and more. Note how and why the writer uses the techniques. How do they affect your response?

4. Notice how the writer develops his or her subject. What kinds of details, examples, or reasons are given, and how does the writer move from one to the next? Think about why the writer has chosen this particular information and how effective it is for the writer's purpose. Particularly in nonfiction that argues a point, argue back. Judge the writer's evidence and ideas by trying to think of objections or other examples.

5. Remember to react to the whole. After reading, state the main idea of the writing in your own words. Decide what you liked best and least about the work. Did you learn anything new? Were you interested in the subject before you began reading? If so, did the writer keep your interest? If not, did the writer build your interest? Did the writer's style help or hurt the subject and purpose?

Here is one student's active reading of the beginning of "Steelworker: Mike Lefevre" by Studs Terkel.

STEELWORKER: MIKE LEFEVRE
*from* Working
by *Studs Terkel*

Working, *by Studs Terkel, is a book of interviews with people in different lines of work. "Steelworker" is*

*So why is Studs Terkel the author?*

*Must be Terkel's note.*

Mike Lefevre's job description. What does a steel-worker do? What is his opinion of his job? Studs Terkel asked Mike Lefevre a number of questions. He edited his tapes so that all you read are Mike's own words.

It was a two-story dwelling, somewhere in Cicero, on the outskirts of Chicago. He is 37. He works in a steel mill. On occasion, his wife, Carol, works as a waitress in a neighborhood restaurant; otherwise, she is at home, caring for their two small children, a girl and a boy.

*He starts with the negative.*

I'm a dying breed. A laborer. Muscle work . . . pick it up, put it down, pick it up, put it down. We handle between 40 and 50 thousand pounds of steel a day. *(Laughs.)* I know this is hard to believe—from four hundred pounds to three- and four-pound pieces. It's dying.

*Does he mean the work is like dying or the work is dying out?*

You can't take pride anymore. You remember when a guy could point to a house he built, how many logs he stacked. He built it and he was proud of it. I don't really think I could be proud if a contractor built a home for me. I would want to get in there and take the saw away from him. 'Cause I would have to be part of it, you know.

*Pride for him is doing it himself.*

It's hard to take pride in a bridge you're never gonna cross, in a door you're never gonna open. You're mass-producing things and you never see the end result of it. *(Muses.)* I worked for a trucker one time. And I got this tiny satisfaction when I loaded a truck. At least I could see the truck depart loaded. In a steel mill, forget it. You don't see where nothing goes.

*Pride is also making something, seeing what you produce.*

It's not just the work. Somebody built the pyramids. Somebody's going to build something. Pyramids. Empire State Building—these things don't just happen. There's hard work behind it. I would like to see a building, say the Empire State, I would like to see on one side of it a foot-wide strip from top to bottom with the name of

*This is really true.*

*This guy knows about Picasso?*

every bricklayer, the name of every electrician. So when a guy walked by, he could take his son and say, "See, that's me over there on the 45th floor. I put the steel beam in." Picasso can point to a painting. What can I point to? A writer can point to a book. Everybody should have something to point to.

*Not all work ends up as one complete object. Can't you take pride in doing whatever you do really well? Still, people's attitudes can hurt.*

It's the non-recognition by other people. To say a woman is *just* a housewife is degrading, right? Okay. *Just* a housewife. It's also degrading to say just a laborer.

*some of it*

You're doing this manual labor and you know that technology can do it. *(Laughs.)* Let's face it, a machine can do the work of a man; otherwise they wouldn't have space probes. Why can we send a rocket ship that's unmanned and yet send a man in a steel mill to do a mule's work?

*Does he really feel like a mule?*

Automation? Depends how it's applied. It frightens me if it puts me out on the street. It doesn't frighten me if it shortens my workweek. You read that little thing: What are you going to do when this computer replaces you? Blow up computers. *(Laughs.)* Really. Blow up computers. I'll be darned if a computer is gonna eat before I do! I want milk for my kids. Machines can either liberate man or enslave 'im, because they're pretty neutral.

*This man is really bitter.*

If I had a 20-hour workweek, I'd get to know my kids better, my wife better. Some kid invited me to go on a college campus. On a Saturday. It was summertime. If I have a choice of taking my wife and kids to a picnic or going to a college campus, it's gonna be the picnic. But if I worked a 20-hour week, I could go do both. Don't you think with that extra 20 hours people could really expand? Who's to say? There are some people in factories just by force of circumstance. . . .

*Well, he isn't just a complainer. He wants more for his family and himself.*

It isn't that the average working guy is dumb. He's tired, that's all. I picked up a book on chess one time. That thing lay in the drawer for two or three weeks;

you're too tired. During the weekends you want to take your kids out. You don't want to sit there and the kid comes up: "Daddy, can I go to the park?" You got your nose in a book? Forget it.

I know a guy 57 years old. Know what he tells me? "Mike, I'm old and tired *all* the time." The first thing happens at work: When the arms start moving, the brain stops. I punch in about 10 minutes to seven in the morning. I say hello to a couple of guys I like, I kid around with them. I put on my hard hat, change into my safety shoes, put on my safety glasses, go to the bonderizer. It's the thing I work on. They take the metal, they wash it, they dip it in a paint solution, and we take it off. Put it on, take it off, put it on, take it off. . . .

*I guess headphones aren't allowed.*

*He imitates the boring repetition in words.*

*He doesn't like his boss.*

I say hello to everybody but my boss. At seven it starts. My arms get tired about the first half-hour. After that, they don't get tired anymore until maybe the last half-hour at the end of the day. I work from seven to three-thirty. My arms are tired at seven-thirty and they're tired at three o'clock. I hope I never get broke in, because I always want my arms to be tired at seven-thirty and three o'clock. *(Laughs.)* 'Cause that's when I know that there's a beginning and there's an end. That I'm not brainwashed. In between, I don't even try to think.

*This is really sad. Do all line-workers feel like that?*

*Steelworking may be boring and looked down on, but tell that to all people out of work when the mills closed (my dad knows a lot of them). Today people want any job. I wonder what Mike Lefevre does today.*

**Activity Five. Reading Nonfiction Actively.** Do your own active reading of a nonfiction selection in this book. When you've finished, write your answers to item five of the guidelines on page 711.

# Writing Process Handbook

## THE WRITING PROCESS

People who study writers have found that they follow a similar process, or series of steps, when they write. This process isn't a list of rules for you to follow. It's more a map for discovery, helping you to generate ideas and work through the writing puzzles that every writer faces. As you get to know the process, you'll feel more confident and free when you sit down to write. You'll know what lies ahead of you, how to tap your creativity, and how to move from thoughts to words that really communicate what you want to say.

The writing process falls into five main stages. Each stage involves invention and decision. Each has its own questions.

| | |
|---|---|
| **PREWRITING** | What will I write about? |
| | Why am I writing? |
| | Who are my readers? |
| | What's my point of view? |
| | How do I want to sound? |
| | What information will I include? |
| | How will I arrange the information? |
| **WRITING** | How will I express my ideas? |
| **REVISING** | Have I said what I meant to say? |
| | How can I make my writing clearer and livelier? |
| **PROOFREADING** | Does my writing follow normal conventions? |
| **PUBLISHING** | How will I share my writing? |

While this order of stages is basic, it isn't fixed. Writing is always a back-and-forth process. You won't go from one step to the next, never looking back, never leaping forward. While you're still organizing, you may jot down some good sentences; you've jumped ahead to the writing stage. While you're writing the draft, you may see a clearer way to organize; you've shifted back to prewriting. Remember that the writing process is flexible. It's as individual as the people who use it.

## PREWRITING

Like any performance for an audience, writing requires preparation. Before you write a paper straight through, you must sort your thoughts, create and reject ideas, collect information, and sketch out a plan. This *prewriting* is a crucial stage, one that needs plenty of time. Never rush into your writing. Professional writers don't. They know that getting ready is *part* of writing.

This handbook takes the prewriting questions one at a time, but keep in mind that all are tied together. Writing always means paying attention to more than one question at a time, like a juggler with three balls in the air. An important part of prewriting is keeping a sense of the whole writing project in your mind.

### Finding Writing Ideas

*What will I write about?* is sometimes the toughest prewriting question. The answer that comes to a lot of people is *I don't have anything to say*. Yes you do. Your mind is churning (or wandering) all the time—full of memories, feelings, dreams, and opinions. You also do and say an amazing number of things every day. You know more than you know, and you can learn ways to tease out long lists of writing ideas. Starting with yourself is the best approach because when your topic interests you, you have a head start on writing well.

This holds true even for assigned topics. Again, you can learn from professional writers. When they get assignments that don't immediately interest them, what they do is search for an angle that does. Suppose you're told to write about a short story that bored you. There's no reason you can't start with your boredom: It's an honest response, *your* connection to the topic. Pin down why you were bored. Was the plot obvious, totally lacking in suspense? Did the teen-age characters talk like old people? Your personal angle—the story's plodding plot or its unrealistic dialogue—gives you something to say, a topic you're involved in. Of course your angle on an assigned topic won't always be negative. The point is, whenever possible, to look for your place in the writing picture.

Whether you're choosing your own topic or looking for a personal approach, several techniques help tap your mental storehouse of ideas.

### *Freewriting*

Writing without any pressure at all—just letting words flow out without plan or purpose—is freewriting. You set a time limit (five minutes is a good start) and do not stop writing. If your mind goes blank, just rewrite your last word or *My mind's blank* until a new word or sentence rolls out. Don't worry about correct punctuation or spelling: you're writing only for yourself.

Here is the beginning of a freewriting by a student named Theresa.

> Don't want to sit in this desk, can't think think think I want to talk to Marcus about party Fridy what will I wear blue sweater. But his car, that's what I want to know. Can Marcus get it? I want a car maybe one day, if my mom lets me work Who sneezed? sneeze, cough, cough, cold, I hate winter

Theresa's spinning mind has let loose many possible topics: the party, clothes, Marcus, getting a car, working while she's in school, hateful winter weather.

### Brainstorming

Brainstorming is like freewriting, but it is a quick listing of items. Again, you relax your mind and do not judge ideas. Start by writing a general topic (object, experience, person, etc.) at the top of your paper, and then write whatever comes to mind. Let each word or phrase suggest the next item in your list, or jump to a new idea. Keep listing as long as you can.

Theresa was assigned a paper on Alice Walker's short story "Everyday Use" and began this brainstorming:

> *Everyday Use*
> Maggie
> burned
> ugly
> not fair
> unhappy
> no, she's not really

### Clustering

Clustering draws out your ideas in a diagram or map, not a list. Write your first word or phrase in the middle of your paper. Around it, write the ideas it triggers, drawing connecting lines from one idea to the next. Ideas will branch from the central word in clusters, and any word can begin a new cluster. This technique not only sparks thoughts, it groups them.

Theresa started this cluster about winter:

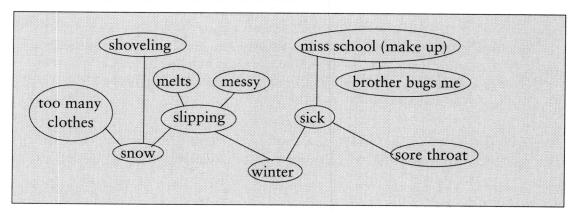

### A Writer's Notebook

A special notebook makes writing a regular part of your life. You can write whatever you want: thoughts, feelings, overheard conversations. You can quote song lines or describe someone's hair style. You can write reactions to the literature in this book. You can draw pictures or paste in magazine photos. You can set yourself assignments: write down every TV program you watch on Tuesday night, with a one-sentence comment.

A writer's notebook is a good tool because, first, it's there: you have a definite place for personal writing and for sudden, interesting events. Second, the more you use it, the more alert you'll be to experiences that are writing material. When beginning a notebook, write every day for a week. Later, you can be more flexible.

### A Personal Exploration

Finally, you can look into your mental storehouse in a more systematic way. Remember that knowledge and interest are the keys to good writing. The following categories will help you explore (1) what you already know and (2) what you'd like to know more about.

**Your inner self:** thoughts, feelings, ambitions, fears, pet peeves, fantasies
**Other people:** family, friends, neighbors, classmates, heroes, fictional characters, actors, singers

**Places:** your room, home, neighborhood, school, secret place, places you've visited or would like to

**Things and animals:** pets, objects and animals in nature, things you or others own

**Experiences:** what you've done and would like to do, the interesting experiences of other people

Theresa made these lists of possible writing ideas, jotting down notes over several days:

---

**Topics I Know About**

**Inner self:** nightmare about lake, *not* being a nurse, jealousy

**People:** Marcus, Aunt Marguerite, Lisa Bonet

**Places:** the mall, Lynette's grandmother's house, church

**Things:** sports cars, my aunt's piano, birthday presents

**Experiences:** losing Marcus's bracelet, singing in choir, shopping with Lynette, going to New Orleans

**Topics I'd Like to Know More About**

**Inner self:** nightmares, going to college or not

**People:** Alice Walker, girl who runs the shoe store

**Places:** Louisiana State University, California, graveyard Marcus showed me

**Things:** computers (in a store), Mississippi River

**Experiences:** living on beach, managing a store, playing piano

---

**Exercise One. Finding Topics.** Use at least two of the techniques above—freewriting, brainstorming, clustering, a writer's notebook, or a personal exploration—to find possible writing topics. Review your notes, and list three or four topics you would like to write about.

## Limiting Your Topic

The first topics you list may be too broad or too vague for a good paper. Often you have to limit your topic: subdivide it into parts, narrow it down, make it more specific. Your goal is to match topic to length of paper so that you give readers *details*—the heart of interesting writing. For example, one of Theresa's ideas was "sports cars," but if her assignment is two paragraphs, she can't cover that entire topic. She can, however, describe her cousin's sports car, or tell about her first ride, or report which cars have the top speeds.

To limit a topic, you can simply begin listing its parts. (Sports cars: types, speeds, engines, history, famous races, etc.) Or you can brainstorm questions beginning with *Who? What? Where? When? How? Why?* (Who buys most sports cars in the U.S.? Why do I want one?) Or you can return to the two basic topic-search questions. (What do I know about sports cars? What do I want to know?)

As you choose and limit a topic, you'll also be thinking about why you're writing (your purpose) and for whom (your audience). Both can play a part in what you write about. For example, imagine two different audiences for a paper about sports cars: Theresa's parents and her class. What Theresa chooses to communicate about sports cars—her limited topic—probably won't be the same for both audiences. And if her class assignment is to write "an explanation of how something works," she may skip cars altogether (no matter how much she likes them) and look for a less complicated topic.

Theresa's only direction from her teacher was to write two to three paragraphs about a personal experience. She was writing for her teacher, but she could read her paper to her writing group if she wanted. Theresa had uncovered many possible topics, but one recent experience was on her mind: losing her birthday gift from her boyfriend. The topic was limited enough for three paragraphs, and she felt it was OK to share with her teacher. She would decide later about the group.

**Exercise Two. Limiting Your Topic.** Choose one topic from Exercise One and limit it, if necessary, for a paper of two or three paragraphs. Start thinking now about the *kind* of writing you want to do (a report? personal story? opinion? etc.) and about your audience.

### Defining Your Purpose

You can write for many reasons: to figure out a problem, to make people laugh, to explain how to make something. Defining your purpose—the point of your writing— guides you in what to say and how to say it. It keeps you on track. If your purpose is to make readers understand why your favorite old jeans are so special, you won't spend time telling where you bought them. You'll describe the jeans (how they look and feel) and perhaps tell when you most like to wear them.

By stating your purpose in a sentence, you'll start thinking about the kind, or form, of writing you need to do. There are four main forms. In *description,* you use sensory images to bring an experience to life. In *narration,* you make "what happened" clear: who, what, when, where, beginning, middle, end. In *persuasion,* you use facts, logic, and emotion to convince readers to believe or do something. In *exposition,* you offer clear and exact detail to explain a subject or give information. Often you'll combine these types of writing, but your purpose will usually emphasize one type.

Theresa's topic was "losing Marcus's gift." At first she wrote this purpose statement, "to tell how I lost the bracelet," but she realized that wasn't why she wanted to write. She would briefly tell what happened, but she really wanted to talk about her sorrow and confused feelings. Finally she wrote this purpose: "to explore my feelings about losing the bracelet and how it affected Marcus and me."

**Exercise Three. Stating Your Purpose.** Think about your topic from Exercise Two, and state your purpose for writing about it in one sentence. Ask yourself, "What do I want to accomplish with this paper, what do I want to leave with my readers?"

## Considering Your Audience

You've already thought in general about your audience. Now you must consider these readers specifically. *Who* reads your writing affects *what* you say. If you are explaining how to play a computer game, you would not write the same way for these different audiences: (1) your whole class, (2) your computer club, (3) fourth-graders at the recreation center. Each audience's interest in computers, knowledge about them, and level of vocabulary and understanding is different. You must shape your writing to your readers' needs and interests. You don't want to bore them, confuse them, insult them, or ignore them.

These general questions will help you profile your audience:

- How old are my readers?
- How well do I know them?
- What do they already know about my topic? What background information do they  need?
- What aspects of my topic will interest them?
- What strong feelings do they have about the topic (especially if I'm arguing a point)?

Theresa's audience was her teacher and possibly her writing group. She did not know all the readers well, and not every reader knew Marcus. But as Theresa thought about her topic and this audience, she realized that a lot of information about her and Marcus wasn't necessary; it might even be too personal. She believed her readers would understand losing something precious and be interested in the problems and emotions it caused. They needed some personal details to understand the situation, but not the story of her life.

**Exercise Four. Considering Your Audience.** Write a profile of your audience, using the questions above.

### Defining Your Tone

Tone is simply the way you sound to your readers: friendly, formal, silly, passionate, fair, enthusiastic. Tone shows a writer's attitude to topic and to readers; it is the impression you create, the personality of your writing.

Often you have great freedom in choosing tone, but you don't choose at random. Topic, purpose, and audience all play a role. If you're trying to change readers' minds, you want to be reasonable, perhaps urgent, but not sarcastic about the readers' ideas. However, sarcasm may be fine for a humorous paper, written for the class, about school fads.

In creating tone, you pay attention to the level of language you use (for example, slang or formal wording), the kinds of details you select (funny incidents or shocking facts), and even the rhythm of your sentences (short and brisk or long and leisurely). Theresa made these notes: "Tone—not too emotional. (Would be embarrassing.) But honest. I don't want to sound upset but like I've been doing some serious thinking."

**Exercise Five. Defining Your Tone.** With your topic, purpose, and audience in mind, decide the tone you want to create, and define it in a few words.

### Gathering Information

Gathering details, the content of your paper, is the next prewriting step. Remember that writing purpose leads to the kind of information you need. Before you begin an information search, look back at your purpose statement, and think again about whether you need descriptive sensory details, people and place details, facts and statistics, pro and con reasons, and so on.

How you gather this information depends partly on your topic (do you know it inside out? does it require research?), but you still have a variety of helpful methods to choose from. Often, you'll use more than one.

### *Drawing Out Your Own Knowledge*

When you're writing from personal experience, you can gather information with several topic-search methods you've already learned: freewriting, brainstorming, clustering, and asking and answering the reporter's questions (*Who? What? When? Where? Why? How?*). You may generate all the details you need.

These methods are also important first steps for all topics. They let you find out what you already know and what you need to learn. For example, if you're writing about U.S. earthquakes during the last one hundred years, you might ask *Where do most quakes occur? What was the biggest one? What is the Richter scale?* and so on. You'll know some of this information, and you'll discover what you need to research.

### Observing

Your keen senses—sight, hearing, touch, taste, and smell—are your means of knowing the world. Don't neglect them when you're writing. Students often feel they must pull information either from their memories or from books, but there's another option: close observation. If you're describing a scene, put yourself in it and take notes of sounds, shapes, colors, textures. If you're explaining how to make burritos, do it yourself or watch an expert. If you're arguing that school graffiti is an eyesore, take an eye-witness walk through the buildings. Whatever your topic, ask yourself, "Can I learn anything through first-hand observation?"

### Using Outside Sources

Sometimes you will need to do research on your topic. As you know, reading books and magazines is a primary way to gather information, but you can do research in other ways. Observing, for example, is one means. You can also interview people, view films, listen to recordings, and conduct experiments.

Theresa brainstormed this information for her paper:

> gold bracelet—expensive
> feel guilty about losing it
> Lynette says my fault
> Marcus too quiet about it
> I took it off to protect it (in wallet)
> special occasion
> he sold his computer game
> what to do: buy another? buy game?

**Exercise Six. Gathering Information.** Review your purpose statement, and then gather information, using one or more of the methods above.

### Organizing Your Information

Organizing gives you a working plan for your writing. The plan may be a numbered list. It may be a rough outline or a complete one. It may change as you're writing. But all writers organize. They group and order information so that, when writing, they're not jumping around, going off the track, or puzzling about where to go next. They organize to *discover* connections and direction.

To begin, look for related groups of details. Can you put several details under one heading? By grouping, or classifying, you'll also notice irrelevant details and gaps in information.

Theresa saw three groupings for her list of details: *how I lost bracelet, why bracelet was special, feelings and problems afterward.* She crossed out the note about Lynette and saw that she needed more explanation about how she lost the bracelet and why Marcus was "too quiet." She rewrote her list under the three headings:

---

*how I lost bracelet*
took it off for basketball
put it in wallet's change pocket
zipper opened

*why bracelet was special*
gold/expensive
special occasion
Marcus sold computer game for money

*feelings and problems afterward*
feel guilty
Marcus says he understands but doesn't like to talk about it
what to do: buy another? buy game?

---

To order your material pose this question: "What should the reader know first, second, third . . . ?" You want readers to follow your thoughts, facts, or descriptions easily; each sentence and paragraph should be understandable from what comes before.

Some kinds of writing have a natural order. A story or step-by-step process uses *chronological* (time) order. An argument often moves in *order of importance*, from its most convincing reasons to its least, or vice versa. A description takes a *spatial* order to orient the reader by position (from top to bottom, in a circle, etc.), or it may begin with a strong *first impression* (a person's eyes, a scent) and then continue to add and connect other details. A technical explanation often begins with terms and definitions, a "how-to" with equipment and materials.

Often, though, you simply have to decide on an order that makes sense for the information. More than one arrangement may be possible. In writing about her bracelet, Theresa could begin with how she lost it or why it was special; either will work, and the focus is her choice as long as readers can follow without confusion.

For her writing plan, Theresa decided to present her three headings in this order: (1) why bracelet was special, (2) how I lost bracelet, (3) feelings and problems afterward. Then she checked the order of the details under each heading. She felt she'd already listed the details in a natural and understandable order, and she was ready to write.

**Exercise Seven. Organizing Your Information.** Review the information you gathered, and group related items together. Remove material you don't need, and gather more if necessary. Then arrange the information in a logical order.

## WRITING

The goal of a first draft is to get your ideas on paper, in sentences and paragraphs, from beginning to end. This draft is called a rough, or "unfinished," draft because it isn't meant to be perfect. It can't be. Writers expect to revise, so they don't struggle for error-free excellence during drafting.

They also experiment. Another name for rough draft is *discovery draft*. The act of writing will often give you ideas— show you what you really want to say. For this reason, your plan or outline is a first guide, not a fixed one. As you draft, feel free to add, cut, and rearrange anything you like.

Don't worry about awkward sentences or possible mistakes in spelling and grammar. You can fix them later. If you get stuck, skip the problem and go on. You can come back to it or wait until revision.

Remember to write on only one side of a page, to be able to look at all your writing at once. And skip lines as you write, to leave room for changes.

Whether you draft very quickly or more slowly doesn't matter. Steadiness, not speed, is your goal. You may polish a bit as you go or make a note for revision. That's all right, but don't stop for extensive tinkering. Keep moving forward.

Here is Theresa's first draft. Notice that she changed her plan after a few sentences. She decided to get right to what happened.

> On my birthday this year, my boyfriend and I had been going together a whole year, well a little more, because we met a week before. And it was a like a anniversery and birthday together. So Marcus he bought me
>
> My boyfriend gave me a beautyful gold bracelet for my birthday. It was really more than he could afford, and i was real proud of it. On Monday in p.e. we had basketball and I thought No you better not wear it, it might get broken cause we play hard (I'm a tough guard). So I put it in with the change in my wallet and zipped it. I meant to put it back on right after class, but I forgot and I was carrying my wallet all over school for a hour when I remembered it and when I looked the zipper was slipped and the bracelet was gone. I started to cry and got a pass to go look everywhere.
>
> Anyone would feel bad. Loosing a new birthday bracelet. But this one had special things about it, which made me feel worse. Marcus bought this bracelet a lot more than he could afford because we had been going together for a year. It was a birthday and anniversery present in one, And had a lot of meaning. To buy it, he sold computer game. I found out from the guy who bought it he thought he got such a good deal. Sure he wanted the game but he wanted me to have the gift more, so I felt better.
>
> Now you can see why I feel so guilty and have spent so much time thinking about all this. Marcus was upset when I told him, but he saw that I was trying to portect the braclet and was an accident. He is really great but somehow things still don't seem right between us. He seems sad but maybe he isnt. I told him I would buy another bracelet or buy another computer game for him by working and saving, but he said no and maybe he's right. The bracelet wouldn't be a present, and he wouldn't take the game. It just seems terrible to me that everybody loses, no one has anything. Nothing to be done.

**Exercise Eight. Writing Your First Draft.** Write the first draft of your paper, using your plan as a guide.

## REVISING

Revision means "seeing again." You step back from your work to judge it and improve it. The first aim of revision is *to find out what you said.* Sometimes what we actually say is not what we meant to say. Reread with your purpose statement in mind, as one of the readers you identified: What meaning would this reader take from your paper? What might the reader not understand? You may need to revise to meet your purpose, *or* you may need to rethink your purpose. Because a draft is a discovery, it is possible to change the point of your writing at this stage.

Revision is also a time to fine-tune and polish. You reread to see whether your ideas are clearly expressed, your words are well chosen, and your sentences flow smoothly. You make your writing clearer and livelier.

These revision hints will help you:

- Wait a day or two before revising. Time will give you distance, so that you can pretend the writing is someone else's.
- Read your paper aloud. You can often hear problems your eye overlooks.
- Ask classmates to comment on your draft. Have these outside readers state for themselves the main point, or impression, of your paper. Then ask them for more specific comments about what was good, weak, or confusing.
- Revise in stages, and write as many drafts as you need. Don't try to make all changes at once. First attack the large problems of purpose and content, then organization, then language. Feel free to make substantial changes in your first draft. Redraft and revise until you're satisfied.
- Use these revising symbols to mark changes.

## REVISING SYMBOLS

Begin a new paragraph. ¶

Capitalize. ≡

Lowercase. /

Add. ∧

Remove. ⌐

Reverse. ∩∪

Move. ⟶

Theresa read her paper several times to make the following changes. Look closely at her final paragraph. When Theresa read what she wrote, especially "Nothing to be done," she had a new insight about her feelings. She saw that Marcus's silence was not the problem, and her closing paragraph has a new focus.

A month ago,

My boyfriend gave me a beautyful gold bracelet for my birthday. ~~It was~~

I lost it after three days. The first day I wore the bracelet

~~really more than he could afford, and i was real proud of it.~~ On Monday in p.e.

to school  in p.e.  was afraid

we had basketball ~~and~~ I ~~thought No you better not wear it~~, it might get broken,

~~cause we play hard (I'm a tough guard).~~ So I put it in ~~with the change~~ in my

zipped to  purse of

. An hour later, after

wallet ~~and zipped it. I meant to put it back on right after class, but I forgot and~~

the bracelet.

~~I was~~ carrying my wallet all over school ~~for a hour when~~ I remembered ~~it and~~

had

~~when I looked~~ the zipper ~~was~~ slipped and the bracelet was gone. ~~I started to cry~~

~~and got a pass to go look everywhere.~~

some facts made

Anyone would feel bad. Loosing a new birthday bracelet. But this one ~~had~~

. My boyfriend  such an expensive

special ~~things about it, which made me feel worse.~~ Marcus bought ~~this~~ bracelet

~~a lot more than he could afford~~ because we had been going together for a year.

for both of us. Besides that,

It was a birthday and anniversery present in one, ~~And had a lot of meaning.~~

his  was sorry for that,

To buy it, he sold computer game. I ~~found out from the guy who bought it he~~

than he  he said

~~thought he got such a good deal. Sure he~~ wanted the game but he wanted me

to have the gift more, ~~so I felt better.~~

With all of this  very  can't seem to stop. Even after

~~Now you can see why~~ I feel ~~so~~ guilty and ~~have spent so much time thinking~~

a month I am still troubled even though he is really great.

~~about all this.~~ Marcus was upset when I told him, but he saw that I was trying

Of course he

that losing it

to portect the braclet and ^was an accident. ~~He is really great but somehow~~

~~things still don't seem right between us. He seems sad but maybe he isnt~~. I told

could work, save, and

him I ~~would~~ buy another bracelet or ~~buy another~~ ^a computer game for him ~~by~~

and there is nothing to be done.

~~working and saving~~, but he said no ~~and~~ maybe he's right, The bracelet wouldn't

accept          Yes, perhaps that is the problem ,

be a present, and he wouldn't ^take the game. ~~It just seems terrible to me that~~

one has lost,

~~every~~body ~~loses~~, no one has anything, (Nothing to be done.)

— and I can't do anything.

Not being able to fix a problem between us is a terrible

feeling. I've learned a hard lesson. Some things can't

be fixed up, they just have to be accepted.

Because a thorough revision covers many elements, a checklist like the one below is a good tool. Its questions summarize what you should look for as you revise.

## CHECKLIST FOR REVISING

1. Does the information suit my purpose for writing?
2. Have I included enough information to make my ideas clear?
3. Are any details unnecessary? off the topic?
4. Will the information interest my audience?
5. Is the order of my ideas easy to follow?
6. Do I create the tone I want? Is it suitable for audience, topic, and purpose?
7. Are my words exact and vivid, not vague and overused?
8. Do sentences begin in different ways? vary in length? flow smoothly into each other? Have I used connecting words (transitions)?
9. Is the opening strong and clear? Does the paper come to a definite conclusion?

**Exercise Nine. Analyzing a Revision.** Take some time to think about Theresa's revisions. Choose any three of her changes—things she added, cut, or rearranged—and explain why you think she made them. (The Checklist for Revising will help you analyze what she's done.) Do you feel each change makes Theresa's paper better? Which of her revisions—anywhere in the paper—would you *not* make? What would you do?

**Exercise Ten. Revising Your Draft.** Revise your first draft, using the Checklist for Revising. Remember, take your time. Read your draft to see what you said, and then work through the checklist slowly.

## PROOFREADING

Proofreading is a final clean-up to correct errors in punctuation, spelling, grammar, and capitalization. It's an important step for two reasons: First, your writing represents *you*. Mistakes make you seem careless, no matter how good your ideas. Second, errors are distracting. Readers come to a mental halt at a misspelled word; a missing comma or wrong tense confuses meaning.

If your last revised draft is messy, recopy it before proofreading. A good proofreading method is to read your paper slowly, letter by letter. Then read again, word by word and sentence by sentence, to catch more mistakes in punctuation and grammar. The following checklist will guide your proofreading.

---

### CHECKLIST FOR PROOFREADING

1. Is my spelling correct?
2. Have I capitalized proper nouns and the first words of sentences?
3. Does every sentence end with a punctuation mark? Is other punctuation correct (commas, semicolons, dashes, apostrophes, colons, parentheses, quotation marks)?
4. Are sentences complete (not fragments)? Are they properly separated with punctuation (not run-on)?
5. Do verbs agree with their subjects (singular with singular, plural with plural)?
6. Is it clear to what or to whom my pronouns refer (it, she, them, each, this, etc.)?

---

Here is Theresa's revised paper, with her proofreading corrections:

A month ago, my boyfriend gave me a beautyful gold bracelet for my

birthday. I lost it after three days. The first day I wore the bracelet to school ,

~~gym class.~~
we had basketball in p.e. I was afraid it might get broken, so I zipped it into the

change purse of my wallet. An hour later, after carrying my wallet all over

school, I remembered the bracelet. The zipper had slipped and the bracelet was

gone.

Anyone would feel bad Loosing a new birthday bracelet. But some facts

made this one special. My boyfriend bought such an expensive bracelet because

we had been going together for a year. It was a birthday and anniversary present

in one, and had a lot of meaning for both of us. Besides that, he sold his

computer game to buy it. I was sorry for that, but he said he wanted me to have

the gift more than he wanted the game.

With all of this I feel very guilty and can't seem to stop. Even after a month,

my boyfriend has been
I'm still troubled even though he is great. Of course he was upset when I told

him, but he saw that I was trying to protect the braclet and that losing it was

an accident. I told him I could work, save, and buy another bracelet or a

computer game for him, but he said no. maybe he's right, and there is nothing

> to be done. The bracelet wouldn't be a present, and he wouldn't accept the
>
> game. Yes, perhaps that is the problem˙Nothing to be done. Everyone has lost,
>
> no one has anything, and I can't do anything. Not being able to fix a problem
>
> between us is a terrible feeling. I've learned a hard lesson. Some things can't be
> *corrected;*
> ~~fixed up~~, they just have to be accepted.

**Exercise Eleven. Proofreading Your Paper.** Proofread your paper, using the Checklist for Proofreading.

## PUBLISHING

You put a great deal of effort, time, and *yourself* into writing, and you should always think about publishing: sharing your writing with others. Besides giving your paper to your teacher, you can let friends and family read it. You can publish through bulletin board displays and class books. You can submit essays to school newspapers and magazines. You can give copies of your papers to people who helped you with research or to people involved somehow in your topic (if you write about a swimming meet, why not show your paper to the coach?).

Remember that you had a reason for writing, an effect to produce on an audience; now is the time to communicate. Make a clean final copy of your paper, proofread it one last time, and *publish*.

Besides her writing group, Theresa had another idea for publishing: showing the essay to Marcus. She had expressed in her writing feelings she had never expressed in talk. Marcus's reaction was all positive: He was impressed with the paper and understood her thoughts. The writing group talked a lot about how Theresa lost the bracelet but even more about her final point: feeling helpless. They came up with this title for her paper: "Something Lost."

**Exercise Twelve. Publishing Your Paper.** Make a final copy of your paper, and proofread it. Talk to your teacher about ways of publishing, or use your own ideas. Try to share your writing with at least one person besides your teacher.

## A WRITING PROCESS CHECKLIST

**PREWRITING**

(Remember: When you are preparing to write, your topic, purpose, audience, and tone are all linked. Your prewriting activities don't have to follow the order shown below.)

1. Search for writing ideas. Use techniques such as freewriting, brainstorming, clustering, a writer's notebook, and a personal exploration.
2. Choose and limit a topic. As you choose what you will write about, keep in mind your audience and your general purpose (the kind of writing you want to do). Limit the topic, if necessary, so that you can cover it in the space you have.
3. Define your purpose. State in a sentence or two the point of your writing: what you want to accomplish or to leave with your readers.
4. Consider your audience. Note what you know about your readers: their ages and interests; their knowledge, lack of knowledge, and strong opinions about your topic.
5. Define your tone. Decide how you want to sound to readers—the attitude toward them and toward your topic that you want to communicate.
6. Gather information. Review your purpose statement, and gather information through one or more of these methods: (a) drawing out your own knowledge (freewriting, brainstorming, clustering, and asking a reporter's questions), (b) observing, (c) using outside sources.
7. Organize your information. Make a working plan by (a) grouping related information and (b) arranging the information in an order that will make sense to the reader.

**WRITING**

8. Write a first draft. Write freely and steadily, using your plan as a rough guide. Add, cut, and rearrange ideas if you want, and skip over mistakes or problem areas.

**REVISING**

9. Revise your draft. Reread your writing to see what you have said. Decide

how well you have accomplished your original purpose, or whether you need to adjust your purpose. Use the Checklist for Revising (page 729) to judge and improve content, organization, and style.

**PROOFREADING**
10. Proofread your draft. If your final revision is messy, recopy it. Then proofread to correct errors in punctuation, spelling, grammar, and capitalization, using the Checklist for Proofreading (page 730).

**PUBLISHING**
11. Publish your writing. Share your writing with others, so that what you wanted to communicate really reaches someone. Show your paper to at least one member of your audience besides your teacher.

# WRITING ABOUT LITERATURE HANDBOOK

Writing about literature is, in a very real sense, a way of reading it more deeply, because writing always helps you focus your feelings and thoughts. When you write a paper about a poem or story, your writing goals are basically the same as your reading goals: You want to make sense of the literature for yourself (explore its meaning), and you want to enjoy the writer's art (respond to language, form, and literary techniques). Putting your discoveries down in black and white—expressing them for yourself and others—means reading with a very sharp eye, deciding what you feel and think, organizing your ideas, and communicating clearly. That's why the first two handbooks in this text, the *Handbook of Active Reading* and the *Writing Process Handbook,* are important companions to this one. They are full of guidance for your practical questions of *What do I write about?* and *How do I go about it?*

## READ ACTIVELY AND CLOSELY

Active readers try to understand what they read by having a "conversation" with the writing: commenting, questioning, predicting, and deciding what the literature means to them personally. In the *Handbook of Active Reading* (pages 689-714) you'll find many strategies for active reading, with student examples showing the strategies in action.

When you're writing about literature, active reading helps you discover *what* to write about. You not only find your personal approach to the literature (the best guarantee of writing a good paper), but you produce lots of specific writing ideas. This is true whether you're looking for a topic or writing on an assigned one such as a character in a story, or a poem's figurative language, or a play's main conflicts. As you react, question, make guesses—*writing notes as you go*—you produce a focused freewriting that is the first step for a paper.

Active reading of literature also means close reading—being alert to literary elements and techniques. As you make sense of a work (what does it mean? do I like it or not?), you understand more if you consider how the writer creates the effect you feel. With a knowledge of literature, your personal response expands to include specific aspects of literary form: setting, imagery, point of view, rhyme and rhythm, author's purpose.

## Writing About Fiction

If you are writing about a short story or novel, use the active reading guidelines on pages 697-698 as a starting point. They show you ways to think about fiction and specific elements to watch for. Your reading notes will then contain many writing ideas. For an example, look at one student's active reading of "The House on Mango Street," by Sandra Cisneros, on pages 698-701. Here are some writing ideas that the student discovered through a close reading. Any of these could lead to a good paper for literature class.

- describe the **character** of Esperanza (the narrator) by looking at her thoughts and memories, the language she uses, the people around her, and the things she does
- discuss the narrator's **style,** especially the many **figures of speech** that express her emotions
- interpret the story's **theme,** (which the student believes is about Esperanza's search for identity)
- describe the **setting,** and explain what it adds to the story (the background it gives for understanding Esperanza, the mood it creates, the special meaning of "Mango Street" for the girl)
- **evaluate** the story (Do you agree with the student that it is good because of its believable **setting** [created by means of sharp **images**], its **themes** [the girl's ideas about freedom and loneliness], and its realistic **tone?**)

Notice that all of these ideas come from the student's own interests, from the particular aspects of the story that attracted his attention.

## Writing About Poetry

If you are writing about a poem, use the active reading guidelines on page 702. Here are some examples of writing ideas for poetry, which come from a student's close reading of the poem "Still," by Andres Purificasión, shown on page 703.

- explain how the poem's **images** contribute to its meaning and emotion
- discuss how the poet creates a sad, quiet **tone** through the poem's **sound effects** (the sounds of particular vowels, and the repetition of words, lines, and rhythms)
- interpret and respond to the poem's **message,** or ideas, about feelings of loneliness after a love affair

Keep in mind that different poets and poems emphasize different techniques and elements. In many poems, for example, rhyme, meter, figurative language, and symbols are also important carriers of meaning and emotion.

### Writing About Drama

If you are writing about a play, use the active reading guidelines on page 705. Some examples of writing ideas for drama follow. These come from a student's reading of the opening scene of *The Sneeze,* by Neil Simon, which you will find on pages 706-710. Even within one scene, the student has made several observations that could develop into topics.

- analyze the role of the Writer in *The Sneeze* (why does the play use an on-stage **narrator?**)
- analyze the **character** of either Cherdyakov or Brassilhov, looking at his dialogue, actions, effect on other characters, and any information in the stage directions
- discuss the play's special **dramatic techniques,** such as the narrator and the slow-motion pantomime
- illustrate how the playwright creates **humor** (exaggeration and farcical actions, a character's style of speech, the narrator's comments)
- present ideas for **staging** the play (scenery and sets, costumes, lighting)
- explore the significance of the play's title (what **similes** does the Writer use to describe the sneeze? could the sneeze have a **symbolic** meaning?)
- interpret the play's **theme,** the ideas about life that are revealed through Cherdyakov's **conflict** within himself and with the general

### Writing About Nonfiction

If you are writing about nonfiction, use the active reading guidelines on page 711. The following writing ideas come from a student's close reading of the beginning of "Steelworker: Mike Lefevre," by Studs Terkel, which you will find on pages 711-714. Remember that nonfiction covers many types of writing (personal essays, speeches, biographies, etc.) and that each type will offer different ideas for your response and writing.

- analyze Studs Terkel's **purpose** in interviewing and writing about Mike Lefevre (what does Terkel want to convey to the reader?)
- describe Mike Lefevre, the **subject** of the interview, as revealed by his ideas and opinions, his background and home life, his actions, and his tone and diction (word choice)

- respond to the **ideas** expressed in the interview, offering reasons for agreement or disagreement
- explore whether Terkel's article is **objective** or **subjective** (does he accurately describe steelworking or present a one-sided picture?)

## USE THE WRITING PROCESS

Interest and ideas start you on the road to a good paper. The writing process will carry you to the end. In the *Writing Process Handbook* (pages 715–734), you will find guidelines—with many examples—for generating ideas, gathering and ordering information, drafting, revising, and proofreading a paper. (A writing checklist appears on pages 733–734.) Especially important, though, is your understanding that writing is a process: Through it you actually think and rethink, discovering what you want to say and the best way to say it. Don't feel that you should be able to read a work and then produce a finished paper in one sitting. As with any writing project, you will work in stages.

In fact, *one basic part of writing about literature is rereading the work after you have settled on a topic.* Remember what was said earlier: Your first reading notes are a sort of freewriting. They are a good prewriting step. Your next step is to review and see what you have. What elements in the work attracted your attention? Where did you react strongly? Do any of your notes seem to fit together? What, overall, does the work communicate to you? Your aim is to narrow down your thoughts to possible writing topics, just as the students did in the previous examples. Then you choose a final topic that you can cover well in the length of the paper you are writing.

With your topic in mind, *you reread to clarify your ideas and gather information.* In this process, you are defining the point, or purpose, of your writing. (For example, if your topic is Esperanza in "The House on Mango Street," what specific conclusions do you draw about her?) And you are finding the details in the work that will show the reader what you mean.

This leads to a second basic rule to remember as you draft and revise: *Keep your focus on the literature, and refer to it often.* Whether you are writing a personal response (such as your opinion about a character's behavior) or a critical analysis (such as the interpretation of a symbol), always explain your ideas with examples from the work. You may paraphrase, summarize, or quote from the work. These are all good ways to refer to the work while writing. The point is to keep your sights on the story, poem, play, or essay: It is your reason for writing.

In general, you need direct quotations only when the writer's words are especially striking or interesting or when the exact words are important to your point. Be sure to use quotation marks, and also show where the quotation comes from. Supply a page number for stories and nonfiction, a line number for poems, and act and scene numbers for plays. (If a play isn't divided into acts and scenes, use page numbers. If it is written in poetry, include line numbers.) Place the numbers in parentheses directly after the quotation, as in the following examples.

> Mike Lefevre's first words, "I'm a dying breed" (page 712), set the depressing tone that continues throughout the interview.

> The line "Lost forever is the magic of it all" (line 8) uses inverted word order.

> Romeo is not in the mood for a party, but still he joins in his friends' joking with the pun, "You have dancing shoes / With nimble soles; I have a soul of lead" (act 1, scene 4, lines 14–15). (Use a slash mark, as shown, to separate lines of poetry.)

A model essay follows, written by Walker, the student whose reading of "The House on Mango Street" is shown on pages 698-701. Briefly, here is how he went about his writing.

1. After his first reading, Walker decided to write about Esperanza, the narrator, because she was unusual and he liked her. In order to describe her character, though, he had to analyze it: to examine the significant details about her and draw conclusions from them.

2. Walker reread the story, trying to see more clearly what Esperanza was like. He gathered many types of details—her ideas, words and tone, background, relationships with others—all the ways that a writer can reveal a character's personality.

3. By reviewing his notes, Walker focused his ideas. He used the details to make generalizations about Esperanza's personality and her life. These were the main points he wanted to communicate in his essay.

4. Then he organized his material. For each main point about Esperanza, he chose the examples (details) that he would use. He wanted to show the reader why he saw Esperanza as he did. Then he arranged his groups of notes in a logical order and was ready to draft.

5.  Walker drafted and revised more than once. The essay below is his final revised
    and proofread paper. Note its main parts: an **introduction** that identifies the
    author and work and briefly presents Walker's topic; a **body** in which each
    paragraph develops a different idea about Esperanza; and a **conclusion** that
    summarizes his view and includes his response.

### The Character of Esperanza in "The House on Mango Street"

*Introduction: Author, title, and opening statement*

The narrator of Sandra Cisneros's story *The House on Mango Street* is a young girl named Esperanza. She is sad, a little unusual, and seems very disappointed with her life. But Esperanza really thinks deeply about the people around her and about loneliness, and she talks in a personal way that made me want to keep reading.

*Paragraph topic: Esperanza's setting and background*

One of the first things to know about Esperanza, since she is "a girl who didn't want to belong" (page 700), is where she lives. Mango Street is in a poor Hispanic neighborhood that scares outsiders. Esperanza makes it seem almost like a prison. She talks about her great-grandmother being trapped and even personifies Mango as someone who tries to "hold me with both arms" (page 701). Esperanza doesn't say directly how people get stuck on Mango Street, but you can guess what she means. Poverty and racial discrimination are two reasons she suggests. Another is family pressure to stay in the community, especially for girls.

*Paragraph topic: Esperanza's hidden identity and rebellious feelings*

Esperanza's problem, though, isn't just being Hispanic in a white society. She feels different from everyone, an outsider. Or at least she feels that she can't *show* what she's really like. She says she wants "a new name, a name more like the real me, the one nobody sees" (page 699). The name she wants is Zeze the X, which is romantic and flashy, and Esperanza is also really impressed with her "wild" (page 699) great-grandmother, who refused to get married until forced. Esperanza is a bit rebellious like a lot of young people who are forced into a role.

But Esperanza is pretty unusual. For one thing she's sad and dreamy and has unusual thoughts, such as that her name is "like the number nine" and a "muddy color" (page 698). Of course all of her thoughts aren't unusual. In fact, she can be wise. A good example of this is her comment about people being scared of neighborhoods they don't know.

*Paragraph topic: Esperanza's unusual personality—dreamy but perceptive*

Another thing that makes Esperanza different in her neighborhood is "all those books and paper" (page 701). Apparently they make her stand out, and she explains how important writing is to her. Writing makes her feel better when she's sad about living on Mango Street. The style in this story is sharp, and it gives Esperanza a special personality. She comes up with terrific images like these: "they say my name funny as if the syllables were made out of tin and hurt the roof of your mouth" (page 699) and "watch us drive into a neighborhood of another color and our knees go shakity-shake and our car windows get rolled up tight and our eyes look straight" (page 700). Esper-

*Paragraph topic: Esperanza's writing and what it means*

*Conclusion: Response and summary*

anza is poetic and wants to write, and that is not something Mango Street people understand.

Sometimes Esperanza seemed childish and too complaining to me. She thinks negative thoughts most of the time (isn't there anything good in her life?) and wants a wild name like "Zeze the X." Then at other times she's realistic and gets right at the heart of true problems like being free to create your own identity. Anyway, she seems like a real person—and an interesting one. Maybe she is immature at times, but she has deep feeling for people's loneliness and fear. And Sandra Cisneros makes Esperanza's poetic words sound natural, like someone talking directly to me.

**Activity. Keeping a Writer's File.** To help yourself improve your writing about literature and become more comfortable with the process, keep a complete Writer's File on your next paper. Document *everything* you do. Write out and save: (1) your first active reading notes, (2) all of your possible writing ideas, (3) your final topic and rereading notes, (4) any doodles and brainstormings, (5) your writing plan (rough outline), (6) every draft and revision, no matter how messy, and (7) your final paper.

Wait several days before you look at the whole file. Then examine this "history" carefully. In your journal write down what you learn from it. What are the most interesting parts of the file to you? the weakest? the best? Where did you get into trouble in writing about literature? What did you like most about the writing process?

# Handbook
## of Literature, Reading, Vocabulary, and Research Skills and Terms

*The following pages contain information about skills and terms that you will find helpful as you read the selections in this book and other materials as well. The terms are arranged alphabetically, with a brief definition or explanation for each. Examples from this book are used, and the section where a term is taught is indicated.*

**act** A part of a play. Acts may be divided into *scenes*.

**almanac** A book containing many facts. Almanacs are published every year so that the facts will be up to date. The subjects almanacs cover include government leaders of the world, sports records, weather records, awards such as the Nobel Prize, and the size and population of different countries. The facts may be given in the form of lists and charts.

**When to use an almanac.** Almanacs give facts, but they do not discuss or explain them. Use an almanac when you are looking for a particular name or date, especially if the information is too recent to be in an encyclopedia. For example, if you wanted to find out who won the Nobel Prize for literature in 1986, an almanac would be the best place to find the information.

**How to use an almanac.** To find the topic you want in an almanac, look it up in the index. The *index* is a section at the back of the book that lists topics alphabetically. If you were looking for Nobel Prize winners, you would look under *n* for *Nobel*. The index would tell you what page or pages the information is on.

Use the newest almanac you can get to be sure of finding the most recent information.

**alphabetical order** The order of the letters in the alphabet. To put words in alphabetical order, look at the first letter of each word first. If the first letters are the same, look at the second letters, and so on.

Many research materials are arranged in alphabetical order, including *card catalogs, dictionaries, encyclopedias,* and *indexes*.

Remember that if you are looking for a

person's name in alphabetical order, look for the last name first. If you are looking for a book title, ignore the articles *a, an,* and *the*.

**antonyms**    Words that have opposite meanings. *Up* and *down* are antonyms. [Section 3]

**article**    A short nonfiction work; not a made-up story. Articles appear in newspapers, magazines, and books. (See also news story.)

**atlas**    A book of maps. Some atlases also give other geographical information, such as the products of various regions, countries, or states.

***When to use an atlas.***    Use an atlas when you need information on a map, including directions, locations of particular places, and distances between places. For example, if you wanted to know how far Miami, Florida, is from Gainesville, Florida, you would use an atlas.

***How to use an atlas.***    Most atlases have an *index,* a section at the back of the book where the places shown on the maps are arranged in alphabetical order. The indexes will usually tell you both the number of the map you need and the particular section of the map that shows the place you are looking for.

For example, if you look up *Gainesville, Florida,* in the index, you might see a notation such as this after it: "42 E 4." You would turn to map number 42 in the atlas. You would see that the map is divided into squares. You would look along the top of the page until you found the square marked *E.* Then you would look along the

side of the page for the square marked 4. Where the two squares meet, in square E 4, you would find Gainesville.

**author**    The writer of an article, a story, a play, a poem, or a book. If you know who wrote a book, you can find the book in the library by looking at the *author card* in the *card catalog.*

**author card**    A card in the library's *card catalog* that has the author's name at the top. Author cards are arranged alphabetically by the author's last name. (See also catalog cards.)

**author's purpose**    The author's goal in writing. Authors may wish to entertain readers by making them laugh, as in "A Dose of Pain-Killer" (page 196), or by mystifying them, as in "The Wind in the Rosebush" (page 50). Or an author may want to give readers a serious message about life, as in "The Open Boat" (page 359), explain something to readers, or tell a true story about a person, as in "A Christmas Love Story" (page 229). (See also theme.) [Sections 2, 6]

**autobiography**    Someone's true account of his or her own life. An autobiography is usually written from the *first-person point of view,* using the pronouns *I* and *me.* It tells important events from the author's life and says how the author feels about those events. "Learning to Read" (page 40) is an example of an autobiography. [Sections 1, 2, 6]

**bibliography**    A list of writings. Many books contain lists of other books and articles on the same subject. Here is part of a bibliography from a book about zoos. Notice that the entries are arranged alphabetically by the authors' last names. After each author's name comes the title of the book, the place where it was published, the publisher, and the date:

Crandall, Lee S. *Management of Wild Mammals in Captivity.* Chicago: University of Chicago Press, 1964.

Elgin, Robert. *The Tiger Is My Brother.* New York: Morrow, 1980.

Bibliographies are usually at the end of a book, although sometimes short bibliographies are given at the end of each chapter.

By looking at a bibliography, you can find the authors and titles of other books that may give you more information about the subject you are interested in.

For a list of bibliographies, look up your subject in *The Bibliographic Index.* It will tell you which publications contain bibliographies on the subject.

**biographical dictionary**  A special dictionary that gives information about famous people. Some biographical dictionaries are *Webster's Biographical Dictionary,* which includes information about people from many nations; the *Dictionary of American Biography;* and *Who's Who in America,* which is revised every second year and includes only people living at the time of publication.

***When to use a biographical dictionary.***
Use a biographical dictionary when you need brief, factual information about a famous person. Biographical dictionaries usually give information such as birth (and death) dates, birthplaces, and important accomplishments. Many biographical dictionaries do not include details about a person's life. You may be able to find more details in an *encyclopedia.* If there is a *biography,* or book about the person's life, it would contain the most information of all.

***How to use a biographical dictionary.***  If the person you are looking up became famous recently, make sure the biographical dictionary you are using is new enough to list him or her. Check to see whether the dictionary includes people from your person's country.

In most biographical dictionaries, people are listed in alphabetical order by their last names. If you wanted information about George Washington, you would look for *Washington, George.* However, if you wanted information about Queen Victoria, you would look for *Victoria.* People are not listed by their titles.

**biography**  A true story about a person's life written by another person. A book-length biography will give you a lot of information about a person. "A Christmas Love Story" (page 229) is a short biography.

[Section 4]

To find out whether your library has any biographies about the person you are interested in, look for the person's name in the *subject cards* in the *card catalog.* The person would be listed there in alphabetical order, last name first. On library shelves, biographies are arranged together, alphabetically by subjects' names.

**Books in Print**  A list of books that are available for purchase from publishers doing business in this country. *Books in Print* is published every year in three sets. One set lists books alphabetically by author; another set lists books alphabetically by title; and a third set, *The Subject Guide to Books in Print*, lists books alphabetically by subject.

*Books in Print* is excellent for finding out what books are available at regular bookstores. Remember, though, that there are millions of books that are no longer "in print" but can still be found in libraries and second-hand bookstores.

635.9F

**call number** The *Dewey Decimal Classification* number. A number written on library books and at the upper left-hand corner of *catalog cards* to show where the books are placed on the library shelves.

**card catalog** A large cabinet in the library whose drawers, called trays, contain filing cards listing all the books in the library. There are three types of *catalog cards*: author, title, and subject. All are usually combined in the cabinet in alphabetical order. Letters on the front of each drawer, or tray, show which section of the alphabet it covers. The trays themselves are placed in the cabinet in alphabetical order, from top to bottom.

**When to use the card catalog.** Use the card catalog when you want to find out whether your library has a book whose title you know or when you want to see what books your library has by a particular author or on a particular subject.

**How to use the card catalog.** See the next section, catalog card, for information on how to use the card catalog.

**catalog card** There are at least three cards in the *card catalog* for every nonfiction book in the library: an author card, a title card, and a subject card. Here is an example of an author card:

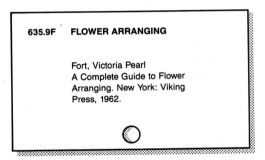

The top of this card tells you the author's name. Her name is Victoria Pearl Fort, but last names are listed first on catalog cards. Below the author's name are the title of the book, the place where it was published, the publisher's name, and the date of publication. At the top of the card is the call number that you should look for on the shelf in order to find the book: 635.9F. This card is called the *author card* because it has the author's name at the top.

The other two catalog cards contain the same information in a different order. Here

is an example of a title card for the same book:

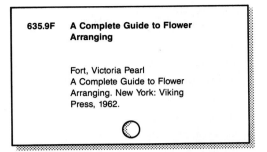

This is called a *title card* because it has the title at the top. Otherwise, the information is the same as on the author card.

Here is an example of a subject card:

This is the *subject card* because it has the subject of the book at the top. If a book covers several subjects, it will have a separate subject card for each subject. Fiction books usually do not have subject cards.

**When to use catalog cards.** Use catalog cards to find out what books your library has and where they are located on the shelves.

**How to use catalog cards.** If you know the title of a book, you can look in the card catalog for the title card. Remember that all the cards are arranged in alphabetical order. If you were looking for *A Complete Guide to Flower Arranging,* you would look in the catalog drawer containing the letter *c* (for *Complete*) because the articles *a, an,* and *the* are ignored in alphabetizing titles. If you find the card, your library has the book. Note the call number given in the upper left-hand corner of the card. It will help you find the book on the shelves.

If you are looking for books by a particular author, look for author cards with that author's name. In this case, you would look in the *f* drawer for *Fort, Victoria Pearl.* There will be a separate card for each book the library has by that author. Make notes of the titles and call numbers.

If you are looking for books on a particular subject, look for subject cards. If you were interested in flower arranging, for example, you would look in the *f* drawer for cards with this heading. There will be a card for each book the library has on the subject. Note the titles, authors, and call numbers.

Now you can find the books on the library shelves. Look at the call numbers you wrote down. For the book we have been discussing, it is *635.9F.* This book would probably be on a shelf marked *635.* It would come after books with the call number *635.8.* (In a library, call numbers are marked on the side of the books, or *spines.*) The *F* in the call number is the initial of the author's last name.

There are some exceptions to the rule. *Fiction* books are arranged on the shelves not by call number but alphabetically by the author's last name. *Biographies* are shelved together alphabetically by the sub-

ject's name. *Reference books,* including *dictionaries* and *encyclopedias,* are kept on special shelves.

**cause**  Something that makes something else happen. (See also cause and effect.) [Sections 3, 4]

**cause and effect**  In some stories and some sentences, there is a cause-and-effect relationship. The *cause* is something that makes another thing happen. What happens is called the *effect.* In "A Dose of Pain-Killer" (page 196), Tom gave a dose of Pain-Killer to Aunt Polly's cat, Peter. The effect was that Peter raced around the house knocking over furniture and flowerpots.

Causes may have more than one effect. By giving Pain-Killer to Peter, Tom also made Aunt Polly realize that Pain-Killer was awful. What was cruelty to a cat might be cruelty to a boy, too.

Think about cause-and-effect relationships as you read. Noticing clue words and phrases such as *because, since, so, so that, as a result of,* and *for this reason* will help you.  [Sections 3, 4]

**character**  A person or an animal in a story. (See also flat character and round character.)

**characterization**  The way an author informs readers about characters. *Direct characterization* is when the author describes the character directly. For example, an author might describe a character like this: "Sam hated parties. They always made him feel awkward and shy, and he never talked to anyone." *Indirect characterization* is when the author lets readers find out about a character through the character's own thoughts, speech, or actions. Sam might be described this way: "Sam spent most of the party standing by the refreshments table. When someone spilled lemonade on his pants, he said, 'I'm sorry.'"

Pay attention to the characters' thoughts, words, and actions when you read a story. They may be related to the message or *theme* that the author wants you to discover.    [Sections 1, 9]

**chart**    An orderly list of facts. Here is an example of a chart:

| Noun | Adjective |
|------|-----------|
| Danger | Dangerous |
| Beauty | Beautiful |
| Remark | Remarkable |

You can read this chart down or across. If you read down each column, you see a list of nouns and a list of adjectives. If you read across, you see which nouns and adjectives are similar.

**climax**    The highest point of action in a story. The climax is the same as the *turning point.*

**cloze exercise**    A reading test in which words are left out of a selection and the reader is asked to fill in the blanks. [Sections 10, 11]

**compare**    To examine two or more people or things to discover how they are alike and how they are different. (See also comparison and contrast.)    [Section 9]

**comparison and contrast**    Comparison in-volves finding out how two or more people or things are alike and how they are different. Contrast involves finding out how they are different. For example, if you were asked to **compare** "The Pit and the Pendulum" (page 268) and "The Raven" (page 326), you might say the two works are alike in authorship (both are by Edgar Allan Poe), in point of view (both are told from the first-person point of view), but different in form (one is a short story and the other is a poem) and in mood. If you were asked to **contrast** these two works, you would mention only the differences in such elements as form and mood.

For help in planning and writing a comparison, review the guidelines on pages 543–544.    [Section 9]

**comparison of unlike things**    See figurative language.

**composition**    See writing.    [Section 10]

**compound word**    A word made up of two or more smaller words. *Cowboy* is an example of a compound word. It is made up of the words *cow* and *boy*. Notice that the meaning of the compound word is different from the meaning of each word alone.  [Section 6]

**conclusion**    1. The end of an article, a story, a play, a poem, or a book. 2. An opinion or judgment. To find out how to form opinions about stories and characters, see drawing conclusions.

**conflict**    A struggle or fight. Many selections contain conflict because conflict helps make a story interesting. Readers want to find out who or what will win the struggle.

There are several types of conflict: (1) *Conflict of a person against another person or group*. For example, in "The Midnight Sun" (page 568), conflict exists between Tom and the two women. (2) *Conflict of a person against nature*. This type of conflict is found in "The Fog Horn" (page 592). (3) *Inner conflict*. A person struggles with his or her own different feelings. The author of "The Road Not Taken" (page 580) has this type of conflict.   [Section 10]

**contents**   See table of contents.

**context**   The selection or part of a selection that contains a particular word or group of words. The context can affect the meaning of words or sentences. If you just read the sentence "Laura was hurt," you might think that Laura had been injured. However, if the sentence were in a story about someone refusing a present Laura had bought, you would know it meant she was insulted. [Sections 2, 10, 11]

**context clues**   Other words in a sentence, a paragraph, or lines of poetry that help you figure out the meaning of a word you do not know. Here is an example: "The teacher's *lucid* explanation helped the students understand." The explanation helped the students understand, so it must have been clear.   [Sections 2, 10, 11]

**contrast**   To say how two or more people or things are different. (See also comparison and contrast.)   [Section 9]

**copyright date**   The date a book was published. The date is usually printed like this: © 1987. If you need up-to-date information, be sure the book was published recently.

**critical reading**   Making judgments about what you read. To read critically, you must try to find the author's message and understand how the characters think and feel. You must read the author's descriptions and the characters' words and actions.

Here are some of the questions you might think about as you read critically:

What is the *author's purpose*, and how well does he or she accomplish it?

In a story, does the *plot* make the message clear?

If *facts* are presented, are they correct?

Are the *characters* in a story believable?

**decoding**   Figuring out unfamiliar words from the sounds of the letters they contain. Knowing the sounds that different letters and groups of letters may make is important in decoding. Here are some examples:

**a**   The letter *a* usually stands for the short *a* sound when it is followed by two consonants, as in *batter*, or by one consonant and no vowel, as in *tag*. A usually stands for the long *a* sound when it is followed by *i*, *y*, or a consonant and a vowel, as in *daily, day,* and *race*.

**ch**   When the letters *ch* come together in a word, they may stand for the sounds at the beginning of *child*. That is the sound they always make when a *t* comes before the *ch*, as in *patch*. At other times, though, the letters *ch* together make a sound like *k*, as in *character*. If you are not sure which sound *ch* stands for, try saying the word both ways. See which way sounds like a word you know.

**ea** When the vowels *ea* come together, they usually stand for the long *e* sound, as in *teach.* However, sometimes they stand for the short *e* sound, as in thread, the long *a* sound, as in *great,* the vowel sound in *her, heard,* or the vowel sound in *here, beard.* If you are not sure which sound *ea* makes in a word you are reading, try pronouncing the word different ways until one pronunciation sounds like a word you know.

**-ed** Many words end with the suffix *-ed.* Sometimes the suffix is pronounced like a *t,* as in *skipped.* Sometimes it sounds like a *d,* as in *showed.* At other times it stands for the *ed* sound, as in *batted.* If you know the base word, you can figure out which sound *-ed* has.

**g** The letter *g* usually stands for the sound at the beginning of *go.* However, when *g* is followed by an *e, i,* or *y,* it may make a *j* sound, as in *badge, giant,* or *gym.* Often when a *g* and an *h* come together, they are both silent, as in *night.*

**i** The letter *i* usually stands for the long *i* sound when it is followed by a consonant and then a vowel, as in *kite.* It usually stands for the short *i* sound when it is followed by two consonants, as in *kitten,* or by one consonant and no vowel, as in *him.* When *i* is followed by the letters *gh,* the *i* usually stands for the long *i* sound, as in *night.*

**-ly** Some words end with the suffix *-ly.* When the letters *-ly* come together at the end of a word, they make the sound *lee,* as in *slowly.*

**-ous** When the letters *-ous* come together at the end of a word, the suffix is usually pronounced like the word *us. Dangerous* is an example.

**-tion** Some words end with the suffix *-tion.* The letters *-tion* almost always make the sound *shun,* which rhymes with run. *Perfection* is an example.

**y** When the letter *y* comes at the beginning of the word, it usually stands for the sound you hear at the beginning of *yes.* When *y* comes at the end or in the middle of a word, it may stand for a vowel sound, as in *my, flying,* or *city.* When *y* comes after a vowel, it usually helps the vowel make a vowel sound, as in *key, joy,* or *saying.*

**definition** The meaning of a word or term. Definitions are given in *dictionaries.*

**description** A word picture of what someone or something is like. Authors include details about the person, place, or thing being described to help the readers form pictures in their minds.   [Section 5]

**detail** A small piece of information. In a paragraph, the *main idea* tells what the paragraph is about, and the details give information to support or explain the main idea.

Sometimes important details are called *significant details. Significant* means "important" or "meaningful." For example, a significant detail in "The Calico Dog" (page 477) is that Susan felt a gun in Duane's pocket.

**Dewey Decimal Classification System** A system of arranging books according to their subject matter. It was invented by Melvil Dewey. The subjects are divided into nine main classes and many subclasses. The *call* *number* that is written on library books and *catalog cards* is the number the book is given in this system.

**diagram**   A drawing that shows the parts of something or shows how something works.

**dialect**   The way a character would speak in person. Spoken language is often different from standard written language. It is informal. It may contain expressions, slang, or pronunciations that are casual. (See also expression.)   [Sections 4, 8]

**dialogue**   The conversation in a story or a play. The exact words the characters say. In a story, quotation marks point out the dialogue.   [Section 9]

**dictionary**   A book that lists words in alphabetical order and gives their meanings, pronunciations, and other information.

*When to use a dictionary.*   Use a dictionary to find out any of the following things: the meaning of a word; how a word is spelled; how it is pronounced; where it is divided into syllables; where it comes from; synonyms (words that mean the same) and antonyms (opposites) for a word; the meanings of prefixes (word parts added to the beginning of a word) and the meanings of suffixes (word parts added to the end of a word).

*How to use a dictionary.*   Look up your word in alphabetical order. Guide words at the top of each dictionary page will tell you the first and last words contained on that page. Following a word are letters and symbols that tell you how to pronounce it. If you are not sure what the symbols stand for, turn to the pronunciation key at the beginning of the dictionary. That explains the meanings of the symbols.

**direct characterization**   An author's direct description of a person or an animal in the story. Readers do not have to form an opinion about the character from his or her thoughts, speech, or actions because the author says what the character is like. An example is in "Godasiyo, the Woman Chief" (page 84), when the author writes that "Because Godasiyo was a wise and progressive chief, many people came from faraway places to live in her village. . ."

**drawing conclusions**   Making your own decisions about a story and its characters. The happenings and details in a story help you draw conclusions. For example, in "A Day's Wait" (page 413), the fact that the boy had the flu and a fever and couldn't keep his mind on the story leads you to conclude that he is seriously ill.   [Sections 4, 7]

**editorial**   An item in a newspaper or magazine that expresses the opinions or beliefs of the editors.

**effect**   Something that happens as a result of a cause. (See also cause and effect.)   [Sections 3, 4]

**elements of plot**   The plot is the sequence, or order, of important events in a story or a play. The plot usually has four elements, or parts: (1) the *problem* that the characters face; (2) the *rising action* as the characters try to solve the problem; (3) the *turning point,* the highest point of the action, as the characters find a solution; and (4) the *resolution,* when readers learn how the solution affects the characters. (See also plot.)   [Sections 1, 4, 8]

**encyclopedia** A book or set of books containing information about many topics.

*When to use an encyclopedia.* Use an encyclopedia when you need a lot of information about a subject. For example, if you wanted to find out the history of libraries, the names of some famous modern libraries, and how libraries arrange their books, it would be a good idea to look up *library* in an encyclopedia.

*How to use an encyclopedia.* The articles in encyclopedias are arranged in alphabetical order. If the encyclopedia you are using is in more than one book, or *volume*, be sure to look in the volume that includes the letter you are looking for.

**entertain** To give readers enjoyment by making them laugh or by scaring them. An *author's purpose* in writing may be to entertain readers. [Section 2]

**essay** A brief discussion of a particular subject or idea. [Section 4]

**explain** To state how or why something happens. An *author's purpose* may be to explain. [Sections 2, 6]

**explanation** An account of how or why something happens. When you write an explanation, help your readers understand by stating the events clearly and in the correct order.

**expression** A word or a group of words with a specific meaning. For example, *hanging around* is an idiomatic expression that means "waiting." [Sections 4, 8]

**fact** Something that can be proved or observed. For example, in "Georgia O'Keeffe" (page 583), the author says that at age 24 O'Keeffe went to live in Texas. This is a fact that can be proved. You can look it up in a biography of O'Keeffe. The author also mentions viewing O'Keeffe's "Sky Above Clouds" in the Chicago Art Institute. This is a fact that can be proved, as well.

When you read, think about which statements are facts and which are *opinions* (beliefs that cannot be proved). [ Sections 1, 10]

**fiction** Made-up stories. Many of the stories in this book are fiction. Fiction that contains imaginary characters and events that are very much like people and happenings in real life is called *realistic fiction.* "Sucker" (page 506) is an example of realistic fiction.

"Today Is the First Day of . . ." (page 600) is not realistic fiction because it contains a character that could not exist in real life. [Sections 3, 10]

**figurative language** Words used in a fresh, new way to appeal to the imagination. The words take on more than their usual meanings.

Figurative language often compares two things that are not usually thought of as alike. Here are some examples:

The man's hair was as smooth as velvet. (The man's hair is compared to velvet.)

His voice was thunder. (His voice is compared to thunder.)

The clouds frowned at the earth. (The clouds' appearance is compared to a person's frown.) (See also simile, metaphor, and personification) [Sections 1, 5]

**first-person point of view**  Telling a story by using the pronouns *I* and *me*. Some stories told from the first-person point of view are *autobiographies,* or true accounts of a person's life. "Everything But Money" (page 423) is an example. Other stories told in this way are *fiction,* or made-up stories, but the author pretends to be a character in the story and writes as if the events had happened to him or her. "April Morning" (page 150) is an example.

**finding facts**  First decide what kind of fact you are looking for. For facts about words, you would look in a *dictionary.* For facts about places, you might use an *atlas,* an *encyclopedia,* or an *almanac.* For facts about people, you might use a *biography,* an *autobiography,* a *biographical dictionary,* an *encyclopedia,* or a *newspaper.* Sometimes you will want to read a *nonfiction* book to find facts. The *catalog cards* in the library's *card catalog* will tell you what books the library has and where to find them on the shelves.

**flat character**  A person in a story who is described only briefly. The author does not provide much information about the character. Sometimes that is because the character does not have a big part in the story. Other characters are more important. In "The Shock of Recognition" (page 527), Mr. Bufkins is an example of this. At other times, even the main characters in a story are flat  because the author wants readers to concentrate on other things.   [Section 9]

**folktale**  A story that has been handed down from generation to generation. Originally, folktales were spoken rather than written.

Many folktales contain these elements:
They happened long ago and far away.
They contain unusual characters.
There is a *moral,* or lesson, to be learned from the story.

**foreshadowing**  Clues in a story that hint at what is to happen at the end. In "The Wreck of the *Commodore*" (page 352), clues in the story hint that something tragic will happen to the men in the boat.

**form**  The particular way in which an author chooses to write a story, an article, or a poem. For example, an author may choose to write a modern story as though it were an old folktale. Or an author may choose to write an article by stating the main idea and then giving examples that support it.

**glossary**  A list of important or hard words in a book, with their meanings. A glossary is usually at the end of a book. Not every book has a glossary.

**graph**  A drawing that shows how two kinds of information are related. There are several kinds of graphs. Here is a bar graph that

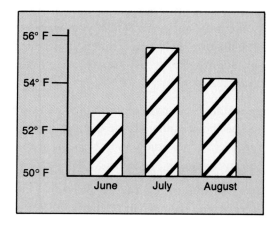

shows average summer temperatures in Juneau, Alaska.

The two kinds of information that are related on this graph are the months, shown at the bottom of the graph, and the temperatures, shown at the left.

Here is a line graph that shows the same things:

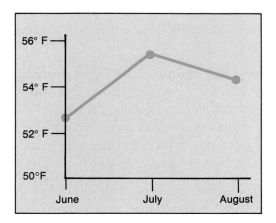

**guide words** Words printed at the top of dictionary and encyclopedia pages to let you know the first and last words or topics on that page.

**homophone** Words that sound alike but are spelled differently. The words *whole* and *hole* in the following sentences are homophones:

The whole family will be here.

Be careful you don't fall into the hole.

**humor** The quality of being funny. An *author's purpose* or goal may be to entertain readers by making them laugh. In other cases, the author's main purpose may be to teach readers a message about life, but he or she uses humor to keep readers inter-

ested. In "Everything But Money" (page 423), Sam Levenson uses humor to help the reader appreciate his childhood. Levenson manages to make his economically deprived childhood seem full of other kinds of riches.

Authors can create humor in several ways. They may use funny events or situations. They may use funny characters. They may use *word play*, such as nonsense words and words with double meanings. "Everything But Money" contains humorous characters and word play.

**imagery** Words that appeal to the senses of sight, hearing, taste, touch, or smell. "The saw screeched through the wood," for example, is an image that appeals to the sense of hearing. Imagery is used in all forms of writing, but it is most common in poetry. [Sections 1, 5]

**index** A section at the back of a nonfiction book that lists the topics in the book in alphabetical order and tells what pages they are on. Use an index to see if facts you need are in the book.

Indexes in atlases usually give map numbers and sections instead of page numbers; see *atlas* to find out how to use this type of index. Indexes in newspapers are usually printed on the first page. They list sections and pages of regular features in the newspaper, such as the crossword puzzle.

**indirect characterization** Instead of describing a character directly, the author tells about the character's thoughts, speech, and actions and leaves it up to the reader to decide what the person is like.

For example, in indirect characterization, an author would not say, "Ken was helpful." He or she might say, "When Ken had finished eating, he immediately cleared the table." Readers should be able to see for themselves that Ken was helpful.

**inference**    A conclusion or guess based on the information presented. When you make an inference, you recognize clues the author gives as well as information he or she presents directly.

For example, in "The Pit and the Pendulum" (page 268), the narrator was freed when the French took over the town. You can infer that the man was a prisoner of war. In "Poor Sandy" (page 284), Sandy's first wife was sold and his second wife was sent away to work for someone else. You can infer that slaves were treated like property, not like people.    [Section 5]

**inform**    To give readers information about some topic. An *author's purpose* may be to inform.

**inner conflict**    A person's struggle with his or her own different feelings. If you love pizza but you are on a diet, you may have an inner conflict when you are offered a slice of pizza. (See also conflict.)

**interview**    A meeting in order to get information from a person.

*When to use an interview.*    Interviews are a good way of getting first-hand information from somebody with special experience or knowledge. For example, if you were interested in becoming a teacher, you might interview one of your teachers and ask about the advantages and disadvantages of teaching as a career.

*How to interview.*    Before the interview, make a list of the questions you want to ask. Make an appointment for the interview, and tell the person what the purpose of the interview is. Ask permission to take notes. Notes will help you remember what the person said. If you have a recorder, you can use that instead of taking notes, but again you will need the person's permission. Ask permission to use the person's name if you are going to write or speak about the interview.

**ironic turn of events**    When something happens that is different from what was expected. For example, in "Civil War Nurse" (page 216), Teddy's friend Kit managed to get Teddy to an ambulance, only to die of his own wounds.    [Section 4]

**joint author**    A book with more than one author is said to have joint authors. There is an author card for each author in the *card catalog.*

**journal**    1. A diary. 2. A magazine, newspaper, or other work that is published every day, every week, or at other intervals. [Section 7]

**judgment**    An opinion based on facts. Your own knowledge and experience help you make good judgments. (See also critical reading)    [Section 1]

**legend**    A fictional story handed down from earlier times, often about a heroic character who may have actually existed.

**librarian**    A person who works in a library.

**library**    1. A collection of books and/or other materials. 2. The place where such a collection is kept. For information on finding books in a library, see catalog card.

**library card**   A card that allows a person to borrow books from a library.

**Library of Congress system**   A way of classifying and arranging books that is used in the National Library in Washington, D.C., and some other large libraries. The system is different from the *Dewey Decimal Classification System,* which is used in most school libraries.

**magazine**   A publication that contains stories, articles, pictures, and/or other features written by different authors. Magazines are published weekly, monthly, or at other intervals.

**main idea**   The most important idea in a paragraph; the sentence that tells what the paragraph is about. The main idea may be at the beginning, the middle, or the end of a paragraph. In this paragraph from "April Morning" (page 150), the main idea is in the last sentence: "When you are 15, like me, you can still pretend a little. For a while, I pretended my father wasn't dead. That was the only way I could stop crying. But I knew my father would never come home again."   [Section 6]

**map**   A drawing or diagram of a place. Here is a map of California.

On the map, a special symbol stands for the capital city. You can tell that the capital of California is Sacramento.

Most maps contain a *compass rose* that shows directions. You can tell that San Diego is southeast of Sacramento.

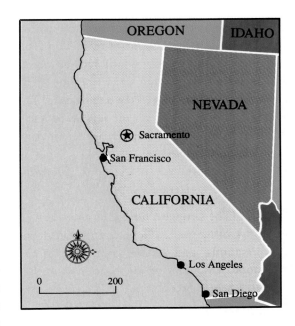

The above map is called a *political map*. Political maps show divisions such as countries, states, and boundaries. There are other kinds of maps as well. For example, *physical maps* show physical features of the earth's surface, such as mountains and valleys.

For information about books of maps, see atlas.

**meaning in poetry**   Because poets often use words in special ways that appeal to your senses and allow you to form mental pictures, it is important to read the whole poem and examine all the words and ideas carefully so that you can understand the full meaning of the poem.
[Sections 1, 5]

**message**   An important idea about life that the author wants to tell readers. An author's purpose in writing may be to give readers such a message. (See also theme.)
[Section 6]

**metaphor**   A comparison of two things that are not usually thought of as alike. Metaphors do not contain words such as *like* or *as*. Here is an example of a metaphor: "The football player's legs were tree trunks." The author does not mean the legs were really tree trunks. He or she is just comparing them to tree trunks.

Metaphors are a type of *figurative language*.   [Section 5]

**mood**   The strongest feeling or emotion in a work of literature. Plots, descriptions, conversations, and actions contribute to the mood. Examples of mood are *humor* and *suspense*.   [Section 5]

**moral**   A message or lesson about right and wrong. In some works, the moral is stated directly. In other works, readers can figure it out for themselves from the plot and the actions, thoughts, and speeches of the characters. Not every work has a moral.

**multiple meanings of words**   Some words have more than one meaning. From the context clues, or the way a word is used in a sentence, you can decide which meaning is correct. For example, *bat* can mean "a flying mammal" or "a stick." In the sentence "Joanne stepped up to the plate and lifted her bat," you can tell that *bat* means "a stick."   [Section 7]

**mystery**   A story or a play that contains a puzzle that the characters and the readers try to solve.

**myth**   A story told by people in ancient times to explain life and nature. Many myths, including the Greek myths, are about gods and goddesses.

**narration**   Writing or speaking that tells a story.   [Section 7]

**narrative essay**   An essay in which the information to be discussed is given in the form of a narrative, or story.

**narrative poem**   A poem that tells a story. "The Raven" (page 326) is a narrative poem.

**narrator**   The teller of a story. Sometimes the narrator is a character in the story, as in "The Night the Ghost Got In" (page 70). A play may also have a narrator. For example, in the dramatization of *The Red Badge of Courage* (page 340), a narrator who is not part of the action addresses the audience at the end.

**newspaper**   A paper, usually published daily or weekly, containing news, editorials (articles of opinion), and features.

*When to use a newspaper.*   Use a newspaper to find out about important recent happenings and about sports and entertainment events. Use newspaper advertisements to learn about products for sale and jobs that are available.

*How to use a newspaper.*   Most newspapers have indexes on the front page that tell the sections and the pages of regular features such as movie listings.

Libraries usually have old copies of newspapers. Sometimes they have been reduced in size and copied on film called *microfilm*. Libraries have special machines for viewing these films.

**news story**   A nonfiction story that appears in a newspaper or news magazine; an article. A news story should answer these questions: *Who? What? When? Where? Why? How?*

**nonfiction**   Writing about real people and real events. Articles, essays, biographies, and autobiographies are examples of nonfiction. Some nonfiction works, such as encyclopedias and dictionaries, give information used for reference.

Among the nonfiction selections in this book are "Everything But Money" (page 423) and "Georgia O'Keeffe" (page 583).

**notes**   When you are doing research, it helps to take notes on what you read so that you will remember it. Write down the important information and the title, author, and page number of the book where you got it.

**novel**   A book-length piece of writing that tells a story. Novels are *fiction*; that is, they are made-up stories.

**numbers**   In alphabetical order, numbers appear as though they were spelled out. For example, if you were looking for a catalog card for a book title that started with *12*, you would look under *t* for *Twelve*.

**opinion**   A statement about a person's ideas, beliefs, or feelings. Opinions cannot be proved true or false. Another person may have a different opinion. For example, in "Three Days to See" (page 34), the author says, "It would be a blessing if everyone were stricken blind for three days." This statement is an opinion. You may agree or disagree.

Authors often support their opinions with *facts* (statements that can be proved) that they hope will convince readers to share their beliefs.   [Section 1]

**out-of-print book**   A book that is no longer available for sale from the publisher or regular bookstores. You can often find out-of-print books in libraries or second-hand bookshops.

**parts of a book**   The front cover of a book gives the title and author and perhaps the person who did the pictures—the illustrator. The *spine* of the book is the side that shows on the library shelves. The spine also gives the title and author. In libraries, the call number of the book is marked on the spine so that you can find the book on the shelf.

Inside the book, one of the first pages is the *title page*, which again gives the title and author. Next to it is the *copyright page*, which tells when the book was published. If you need up-to-date facts, be sure the book was published recently.

Two parts of a book help you find out what topics are covered in the book. The *table of contents*, which is in the front of many books, lists all the chapters in the book. The *index*, which is at the back of many nonfiction books, is an alphabetical list of the topics in the book and the pages they are on. Use the table of contents to find out what broad subjects are covered in the book. Use the index to see whether facts you need are in the book.

**periodical**   A publication that comes out daily, weekly, monthly, or at other intervals. Magazines are periodicals.

**personification**   Writing or speaking about a nonhuman thing as if it were human. Personification is a special kind of metaphor, or implied comparison, between a nonhuman thing and a human being. For example, an author might say, "The wind grabbed at my coat." The author is speaking as if the wind had hands with which to grab things. Here is another example of personification: "The moon had seen where the pirates buried the treasure, but it couldn't remember." In this example, the moon has two things that a human being has: eyes to see and a brain to understand and remember what is seen.

**persuasion** The act of convincing others that one's beliefs are correct.

**persuasive writing** Writing that tries to convince people that the author's beliefs are correct. The author usually states his or her opinions or beliefs and then supports them with facts, reasons, arguments, and examples that may convince readers. [Section 2]

**play** Something written to be performed before an audience. A play may be divided into parts called *acts*. The acts are often divided into smaller parts called *scenes*. *Stage directions* tell the director and actors how the stage should look and how the characters should act and move.

Like stories, plays have plots, characters, and settings. The *plot* is the sequence, or order, of important events. The way an author informs the audience about the characters is called *characterization*. In a play, you can learn about the characters through their speech and actions. (If you are reading the play instead of watching it, you may also learn about the characters through the comments of a narrator.) *Setting* is the time when and the place where the events of the play happen. You may learn about the setting from stage directions, characters'

speeches, and comments by the narrator, if there is one.

**plot** The sequence, or order, of important events in a story that makes a point or brings out a reaction in the reader. The plot has a beginning, a middle, and an end. The events are planned to get the reader interested and to show what the *theme*, or most important idea in the selection, is.

Usually the events that make up the plot can be divided into four elements, or parts:
1. At the beginning of the story, readers learn about a *problem* that the characters have. For example, in "She Sailed for Love" (page 161), Fanny faces the problem of rescuing William from jail in Cuba.
2. *Rising action* is the part of the plot in which the story becomes more exciting and complicated as the characters try to solve the problem. In "She Sailed for Love," the plot grows more complicated after Fanny develops a plan to sail on board the *Constance*.
3. The *turning point* is the highest point of the action. The characters find a way to solve the problem. In "She Sailed for Love," William is rescued from jail and brought on board the *Constance*.
4. The *resolution* is the last part of the plot. The problem is solved, and readers learn how the characters react. In "She Sailed for Love," Fanny and William are reunited. They captain the *Constance* and the *George*, and later return to New England.

**poem** A written or spoken work with language chosen for its sound, beauty, and power to express feelings. (See also poetry.)

**poet** The author of a poem.

**poetry** Poems. Poetry looks and sounds different from other forms of writing. It looks different because poets arrange their words in lines and group these lines into stanzas instead of paragraphs. It sounds different because poets often use rhythm, rhyme, imagery, and figurative language.

*Rhythm* is the arrangement of the syllables in a line to make a particular sound pattern, or beat, as in music. You can hear the rhythm of a line of poetry best when you read it aloud. The punctuation and capitalization in a poem will help you decide when to pause and what to stress in order to hear the rhythm.

*Rhyme* is an element that many poems have. Two words rhyme when they end with the same sound: *cat, fat*. Two lines rhyme when they end with rhyming words. Here are rhyming lines from "The Tide Rises, the Tide Falls" (page 46):

The tide rises, the tide falls,
The twilight darkens, the curlew calls;

*Imagery* is language that appeals to the senses of sight, hearing, taste, touch, or smell.

*Figurative language* means words that are used in a new way to appeal to the imagination. Two things that do not seem alike may be compared. In "The Wind Tapped Like a Tired Man" (page 282), for example, the wind is compared to a timid man.

There are other elements poets may use. For instance, *humor*.

The words and elements a poet chooses are part of the poet's *style*.

**point of view**    The position from which a story is told. In the *first-person point of view*, an author tells a true story about his or her own life; or in a made-up story, the author has one of the characters narrate. The first-person point of view uses the pronouns *I* and *me* in telling the story. In the *third-person point of view*, the storyteller is not a character in the story. The author uses the pronouns *he, she*, and *they* to tell the story.

"A Vegetable Diet" (page 92) is an example of a selection told from the first-person point of view. "Godasiyo, the Woman Chief" (page 84) is an example of a story told from the third-person point of view.

**predicting outcomes**    Guessing what will happen next in a story. You have a better chance of being right if you keep in mind what has already happened and what the characters are like.    [Section 4]

**prefix**    A word part added to the beginning of a word. Each prefix has its own meaning. For example, the prefix *un-* means "not." If you add a prefix to a word, you change the meaning of the word. For example, *done* means "finished." Add the prefix *un-* and you get *undone*, meaning "not finished."

If you do not know the meaning of a word, look at the word parts. The meaning of each part can help you figure out the word.    [Sections 1, 2, 8, 9]

**problem**    A difficult situation that the characters in a story have to solve. The problem is the first part of the *plot*. In "The Open Boat" (page 359), for example, the problem is to stay alive and find some way to be rescued.

**prose**    Written work that is not poetry.

**pun**    A humorous play on words, usually using a word or phrase with a double meaning.

**publisher**    A person or company that prints and sells books, newspapers, magazines, and/or other written materials.

**realistic fiction**    Stories that contain made-up characters and events that are similar to people and happenings in real life. "I Stand Here Ironing" (page 532) is an example of realistic fiction.

**Readers' Guide to Periodical Literature**    A guide that comes out once or twice a month and lists recent magazine articles by their subjects. If you wanted to see what magazine articles had been written recently about whales, you would take a recent copy of the *Readers' Guide* and look under *w* for *whales*. If you wanted to read one of the listed articles, you might be able to borrow the magazine from the library. Large libraries have copies of many old and new magazines.

**reference books**    Books that are not meant to be read from cover to cover like a story but instead are used to look up particular facts. *Dictionaries, encyclopedias, atlases, almanacs,* and *biographical dictionaries* are important types of reference books.

Reference books are kept on special shelves in the library.

**research**    Investigation to find facts.

**resolution**    The last part of the *plot,* when the problem is solved and you learn how the solution affects the characters. In "She

Sailed for Love" (page 161), the resolution comes when Fanny and William are reunited. Together they captained the *Constance* and the *George,* capturing British ships for the American government.

**rhyme**    An element found in many, though not all, poems. Words rhyme when they end with the same sound. Lines rhyme when they end with rhyming words.

**rhythm**    The arrangement of the syllables in a line of poetry so that they make a particular sound pattern, or beat, as in music. When you read poetry aloud, listen for the rhythm. The punctuation and capitalization in a poem will help you decide when to pause and what words to stress to make the rhythm clear.

**rising action**    The second part of a *plot.* The action builds up as the problem develops. In "She Sailed for Love" (page 161), the rising action occurs after Fanny develops her plan to sail aboard the *Constance.*

**root word**    A word from which other words can be made. By adding a *prefix* to the beginning of a root word or a *suffix* to the end, you can change the word's meaning. For example, if you add the prefix *re-* to the root word *play,* you form the word *replay,* which means "play again." If you add the suffix *-ful* to the end of the root word, you get *playful,* which means "full of play" or "fun-loving."    [Section 7]

**round character**    A character that is described fully. The author includes details that help you understand how the character thinks, acts, looks, and feels. Fanny in "She

"Sailed for Love" (page 161) is a round character.

**scene**    Part of a play. Plays are often divided into parts called *acts*, which, in turn, may be divided into smaller parts, the scenes.

**sensory imagery**    Words that appeal to the senses of sight, hearing, taste, touch, or smell.

**sequence of events**    The order in which events occur in a story or play. The events are put in a particular order, or sequence, so that the reader will understand what the story is about. The order of important events in a story makes up the *plot*.

**setting**    The time when and the place where the events of the story happen. You can tell what the setting is by looking for words or phrases that tell when and where.

Pay attention to time and place words throughout the selection because the setting may change as the story or play goes on. For example, in "She Sailed for Love" (page 161), the setting shifts from New England to Cuba and back again. In "Today Is The First Day of . . ." (page 600), there are interesting shifts in time.   [Section 1]

**short story**    A brief work of *fiction* (made-up story).

**significant detail**    A small but important bit of information. (See also detail.) [Section 8]

**simile**    A comparison. Usually similes contain the word *like* or the word *as*. Examples of similes are "her hands were like ice" and "her hands were as cold as ice." [Section 5]

**speaking and listening**    (See decoding.)

**speech**    A formal talk given in public before an audience. Speeches may present facts or opinions or both.

**spine**    The part of a book that shows on the library shelf. The spine tells the book's title and author and in a library is marked with the book's *call number*.

**stanza**    A division of a poem that is longer than a line. Lines in poetry are grouped into stanzas in much the same way that sentences in other works are grouped into paragraphs.

The following stanza is part of the poem "The Wind Tapped Like a Tired Man" (page 282)

A rapid, footless guest,
To offer whom a chair
Were as impossible as hand
A sofa to the air.

**stage directions**    Directions in a play that tell the director or actors how the stage should look and how the characters are to act, move, and speak. Stage directions are not meant to be spoken out loud to the audience.

**style**    The words an author uses and the type of sentences he or she writes. For example, some authors use more *imagery*, or words that appeal to the senses, than other authors. Some authors write in short sentences, while others prefer to use long sentences. An author may change his or her style for different types of writing. In poetry, for instance, the author might use more imagery than when he or she is writing a nonfiction article.   [Section 7]

**suffix**   A word part added to the end of a word. Each suffix has its own meaning. For example, the suffix *-less* means "without." If you add a suffix to a word, you change the meaning of the word. For example, *care* means "concern." Add the suffix *-less* and you get *careless*, which means "without concern."

If you do not know the meaning of a word, look at the word parts. The meaning of each part can help you figure out the word. Here are some other examples of suffixes: *less*, "without"; *-ful*, "filled with"; and *-able*, "able." [Sections 2, 8, 9, 10]

**subject card**   A card in the library's *card catalog* that has the subject at the top.

The subject tells what the book is about. Subject cards are arranged alphabetically in the card catalog. *Fiction* books do not have subject cards.

(For more information about subject cards, see catalog cards.)

**summary**   A brief retelling of a story. A summary tells the main events. In order for people who have not read the story to understand it, the events should be in the correct order, or *sequence*.

**surprise ending**   An ending that is different from what readers have been led to believe would happen. In most stories, the ending follows logically from the rest of the plot, or sequence of events. However, in stories with a surprise ending, the story takes an unexpected twist at the end.

In "A Horseman in the Sky" (page 222) the ending comes as a surprise both to the readers and to the characters in the story. [Section 4]

**suspense**   A quality that produces feelings of curiosity and tension in the reader because the reader is not sure what will happen next. The suspense keeps you reading the story. The stories in Section 8 are full of suspense.

**synonyms**   Synonyms are words that have the same or almost the same meaning. *Try* and *attempt* are synonyms.    [Section 3]

**symbol**   Something that stands for something else. For example, a heart may be a symbol of love. In "The Open Boat" (page 359), the boat is a symbol of life.

**table of contents**   A section at the front of many books that lists all the chapters in the order in which they appear in the book. The table of contents tells you what broad subjects are covered in the book.

**telephone directory**   A list of names, addresses, and telephone numbers.

**theme**   The author's message; the most important idea in a written work. The *plot*, or sequence of important events in a story, helps to show what the theme is. So does the *characterization*, or what the author lets readers know or discover about the characters. Even if the author does not state the theme directly, you can figure out the message by thinking about the events in the story and the characters' thoughts, words, and actions.

In some stories, readers learn a lesson about life while laughing at the characters or the situations. The author uses humor to develop the theme. In "Everything But Money" (page 423), one theme is that fond and humorous memories can come from a childhood of poverty. Levenson's family life was a source of inspiration for the stories he later told. [Sections 6, 7]

**third-person point of view** Telling a story by using the pronouns *he, she* and *they*. *Biographies*, or true accounts of other people's lives, are written from the third-person point of view. "Georgia O'Keeffe" (page 583) is an example. Most, although not all, made-up stories are also written in the third-person point of view. (See also first-person point of view.) [Sections 2, 10]

**title card** A card in the library's *card catalog* that has the book's title at the top. Title cards are arranged alphabetically in the card catalog. The articles *a, an,* and *the* are ignored in alphabetizing the cards. (For more information about title cards, see catalog cards.)

**title page** A page at the beginning of a book that gives the book's title and author.

**turning point** The highest point of the action in a story. At the turning point, the characters finally find a way to solve the problem they have been facing. In "She Sailed for Love" (page 161), the turning point comes when William is rescued from jail and brought aboard the *Constance* to meet Channing.

**volume** 1. A book. 2. One book in a set of books. 3. A group of issues of a magazine or other periodical.

**word meaning** A definition. The best place to find the meaning of a ·word is in a dictionary. (See also context.) [Sections 2, 10, 11]

**word origin** Where a word comes from. Most dictionaries include this information.

**word parts** Root words, prefixes, and suffixes. A *root word* is a word from which other words can be made. A *prefix* is a word part added to the beginning of a word. A *suffix* is a word part added to the end of a word. If you know the meaning of each word part, you can figure out the word.

For example, in the word *prepayable*, the prefix *pre-* means "before"; the root word *pay* means "to give money"; and the suffix *-able* means "able to be." By putting all these meanings together, you can see that *prepayable* means "able to be paid for in advance." [Sections 1, 2, 8, 9]

**word play** A humorous use of words. In order to be funny, authors sometimes use nonsense words and *puns*, or words with double meanings.

**writing process** People who write often follow a similar process, or series of steps, to get the ideas on paper. The process consists of five main stages.

**1. Prewriting** Prewriting is getting set to write. It involves deciding on a topic and purpose for writing and thinking about your audience. The Writing Process Handbook guides you through this important step on page 716.

**2. Writing** In this step, you put your ideas on paper—in sentences and paragraphs— to produce a first draft. A first draft is also called a *discovery draft* for a good reason. Many writers discover what they want to say as they write. You can learn more about the writing stage on page 725.

**3. Revising**   When you revise, you take another look at your work and try to find ways of improving it. You ask yourself if you have said what you wanted to or if you can find a way to be clearer or more interesting. The hints on page 727 and the Checklist on page 729 will help you polish your first draft.

**4. Proofreading**   This is the cleanup stage—the time to correct any careless errors in spelling, punctuation, or usage that might detract from the effectiveness of your writing. Refer to the Checklist for Proofreading on page 730.

**5. Publishing**   Publishing means sharing your work with others. This sharing can take many forms—some reaching a small audience and others a large one. One of these forms will be right for what you have written. You may want to follow some of the publishing suggestions on page 732.

# GLOSSARY OF WORDS

## PRONUNCIATION KEY

| | | | | | | |
|---|---|---|---|---|---|---|
| ă | pat | j | judge | sh | dish, ship |
| ā | aid, fey, pay | k | cat, kick, pique | t | tight |
| â | air, care, wear | l | lid, needle | th | path, thin |
| ä | father | m | am, man, mum | *th* | bathe, this |
| b | bib | n | no, sudden | ŭ | cut, rough |
| ch | church | ng | thing | û | circle, firm, heard, term, |
| d | deed | ŏ | horrible, pot | | turn, urge, word |
| ĕ | pet, pleasure | ō | go, hoarse, row, toe | v | cave, valve, vine |
| ē | be, bee, easy, leisure | ô | alter, caught, for, paw | w | with |
| f | fast, fife, off, phase, rough | oi | boy, noise, oil | y | yes |
| g | gag | ou | cow, out | yōō | abuse, use |
| h | hat | ŏŏ | took | z | rose, size, xylophone, zebra |
| hw | which | ōō | boot, fruit | zh | garage, pleasure, vision |
| ĭ | pit | p | pop | ə | about, silent, pencil, lemon, |
| ī | by, guy, pie | r | roar | | circus |
| î | dear, deer, fierce, mere | s | miss, sauce, see | ər | butter |

## PART OF SPEECH LABELS
*n.* (noun)
*adj.* (adjective)
*adv.* (adverb)
*pron.* (pronoun)
*conj.* (conjunction)
*prep.* (preposition)
*v.* (verb)
*interj.* (interjection)

Unless otherwise indicated, definitions are based on *The American Heritage Student's Dictionary*, © 1986 by the Houghton Mifflin Company, and reprinted by permission.

In addition, the following labels are used as needed:

*pl.* (plural)
*sing.* (singular)

## STRESS
**Stress** is the relative degree of loudness with which the syllables of a word are spoken. The phonetic respelling for each entry word shows the syllable or syllables that are stressed in the word.

**Primary stress** is shown in boldface type, with a bold accent mark:

**bi·o·lo·gy**  | bī ŏl′ə jē |

**Secondary stress** is shown in lightface type, with a light accent mark:

**bi·o·log·i·cal**  | bī′ə lŏg′ ĭ kəl |

## ENTRY WORDS

**Entry words** are divided into syllables using bullets (**star·ry**) to show where the word would break at the end of a line.

## PHONETIC RESPELLING

Each entry word is followed by a **phonetic respelling** of the word, which spells the word according to how it sounds. Each sound is represented by a letter or special symbol. A full **pronunciation key** to these letters and symbols is given at the beginning of this glossary; a shorter form of this key appears at the bottom of each left-hand page.

## DEFINITIONS

Definitions have been chosen to show the meanings of the words as they are used in the selections. In some cases, the meaning used in the selection is not the only one listed in the dictionary for that word. In that case, a number before the definition shows which definition has been used.

This glossary contains words chosen from the selections in this book. Some words may be entirely new to you; others may be familiar words that have been used in a new or unfamiliar way in the selection.

# A

**a·bash** |ə băsh′| *v.* To make ashamed or uneasy; embarrass; disconcert.

**a·bide** |ə bīd′| *v.* To put up with; bear.

**ab·surd** |ăb sûrd′| *or* |-zurd′| *adj.* contrary to common sense; ridiculous: *an absurd suggestion.*

**ad·duce** |ə d$\overline{oo}$s′| *or* |ə dy$\overline{oo}$s′| *v.* To give or offer as an example or means of proof.

**ad·vent** |ăd′ vĕnt′| *n.* **1.** The coming of a new person or thing: *before the advent of the airplane.*

**ad·ver·sar·y** |ăd′ vər sĕr′ ē| *n.* An opponent or enemy.

**af·flict** |ə flĭkt′| *v.* To cause distress to; cause to suffer; trouble greatly: *Mankind is afflicted with many ills.*

**ag·ile** |ăj′ əl| *or* |ăj′ il| *adj.* **1.** Able to move quickly and easily; nimble.

**a·gue** |ā′ gy$\overline{oo}$| *n.* A fever with chills and sweating. *

**a·light²** |ə līt′| *v.* **a·light·ed** or **a·lit** |ə lĭt′|, **a·light·ing** **1.** To come down and settle gently: *A bird alighted on the windowsill.*

**am·big·u·ous** |ăm bĭg′ y$\overline{oo}$ əs| *adj.* Having two or more possible meanings or interpretations; unclear; vague: *an ambiguous statement by the Governor.*

**am·e·thyst** |ăm′ ə thĭst| *n.* A purple or violet form of transparent quartz used as a gemstone.

**am·phib·i·ous** |ăm fĭb′ ē əs| *adj.* **1.** Able to live both on land and in water.

**an·gli·cize**, also **An·gli·cize** |ăng′ glĭ sīz′| *v.* **An·gli·cized, An·gli·ciz·ing.** To make English or similar to English in form, style, or character: *The name Odysseus, or Ulixes in Latin, was Anglicized as Ulysses.*

**an·guish** |ăng′ gwĭsh| *n.* A pain of the body or mind that causes one agony; torment; torture.

**an·guished** |ăng′ gwĭsht| *adj.* Feeling, expressing, or caused by anguish: *anguished souls clinging to a sinking ship; a wounded elephant's anguished trumpeting.*

**an·o·nym·i·ty** |ăn′ ə nĭm′ ĭ tē| *n.* The condition of being nameless or unnamed: *Sometimes she longed for the anonymity she had had before she became a star.* *

**an·thra·cite** |ăn′ thrə sīt′| *n.* A form of coal that is hard and consists mainly of pure carbon.

**ap·a·thet·ic** |ăp′ ə thĕt′ ĭk| *adj.* Lacking or not showing strong feeling; uninterested; indifferent: *apathetic about school.*—**ap′a·thet′ i·cal·ly** *adv.*

**ap·pren·tice** |ə prĕn tĭs| *n.* **1.** A person who works for another without pay in return for instruction in a craft or trade.

**ar·du·ous** |är′ j$\overline{oo}$ əs| *adj.* Demanding great effort; difficult.

**ar·ray** |ə rā′| *n.* **2.** An impressive display or collection.

**ar·ro·gant** |ăr′ ə gənt| *adj.* Excessively and unpleasantly self-important, as in disregarding all other opinions but one's own.

**art·ful** |ärt′ fəl| *adj.* **1.** Showing art or skill; skillful: *an artful cook.* **2.** crafty; cunning: *an artful lawyer.*

**as·cer·tain** |ăs′ ər tān′| *v.* To find out: *ascertain the truth.*

**as·per·sion** |ə spûr′ zhən| *or* |-shən| *n.* A damaging or slanderous report or remark: *His speech cast aspersions on my motives.*

**au·di·ble** |ô′ də bəl| *adj.* Capable of being heard: *an audible whisper.*

**a·vert** |ə vûrt′| *v.* **2.** To keep from happening; prevent.

**awe** |ô| *n.* A feeling of wonder, fear, and respect inspired by something mighty or majestic: *gazing in awe at the mountains.*—*v.* **awed, aw·ing.** To fill with awe: *The size of the plane awed everyone.*

**awl** |ôl| *n.* A pointed tool for making holes, as in wood or leather.

**ax · is** |ăk′ sĭs| *n., pl.* **ax · es** |ăk′ sēz′| **1.** A straight line around which an object or geometric figure rotates or can be imagined to rotate: *The axis of the earth passes through both of its poles.*

# B

**bam · boo · zle** |băm bōo′ zəl| *v. Informal.* To deceive by elaborate trickery; hoodwink.

**bank**³ |băngk| *n.* A set or group arranged in a row: *a bank of elevators.*

**base** |bās| *adj.* **1.** Morally bad or wrong; mean; detestable.

**bay · o · net** |bā′ ə nit| *or* |-nĕt| *or* |bā′ ə nĕt′| *n.* A knife attached to the muzzle end of a rifle for use in close combat.

**be · guile** |bĭ gīl′| *v.* **be · guiled, be · guil · ling. 1.** To deceive; trick.

**be · nign** |bĭ nīn′| *adj.* **1.** Kind; gentle: *His face was fatherly and benign.*

**berth** |bûrth| *n.* **1.** A built-in bed or bunk in a ship or a railroad sleeping car. **3.** A position of employment; a job. **Idiom. give a wide berth to.** To stay at a wide distance from. *

**best** |bĕst| *v.* To get the better of; defeat.

**bev · el** |bĕv′ əl| *n.* **1.** A surface formed when two planes meet at an angle other than 90° and form an edge.

**blas · pheme** |blăs fēm′| *or* |blăs′ fēm′| *v.* To speak of (God or something sacred) in a disrespectful way.

**blunt** |blŭnt| *adj.* **2.** Abrupt and frank in manner.—**blunt′ ly** *adv.*

**boo · ty** |bōo′ tē| *n., pl.* **boo · ties. 1.** Loot taken from an enemy in war. **2.** Any seized or stolen goods: *pirate's booty.*

**boul · der** |bōl′ dər| *n.* A large, rounded mass of rock lying on the ground or imbedded in the soil, and usually different in composition from other nearby rocks.

**breth · ren** |brĕ_th_′ rən| *n. Archaic.* Plural of brother.

**brit · tle** |brĭt′ l| *adj.* Likely to break because of inelasticity and hardness; easily snapped: *brittle bones.*

**broach** |brōch| *v.* **1.** To talk or write about for the first time; begin to discuss: *He did not know how to broach the subject tactfully.*

**bul · ly** |bōol′ ē| *adj. Informal.* Excellent; splendid.

**bust**¹ |bŭst| *n.* **2.** A sculpture of a person's head, shoulders, and upper chest.

**bust**² |bŭst| *Slang. v.* **2.** To cause to become or become bankrupt: *The strike busted several industries.*

# C

**cache** |kăsh| *n.* A supply of something kept in a hiding place. *

**ca · dav · er** |kə dăv′ ər| *n.* A dead body, especially a human body that is to be dissected and studied.

**ca · dence** |kād′ ns| *n.* **1.** The beat or pulsation of music, marching, dancing, etc.

**cal · i · co** |kăl′ĭ kō| *n., pl.* **cal · i · coes** or **cal · i · cos. 1.** A cotton cloth with a figured pattern printed on it in color.—*adj.* Covered with spots of a different color: *a calico cat.*

**cas · u · al · ly** |kăzh′ ōo əl lē| *adv.* In an unconcerned manner. *

**cat · a · mount** |kăt′ ə mount′| *n.* A mountain lion or wildcat.

**cav · al · ry** |kăv əl rē| *n.* Troops trained to fight on horseback or, more recently, in armored

---

ă pat/ā pay/â care/ä father/ĕ pet/ē be/ĭ pit/ī pie/î fierce/ŏ pot/ō go/ô paw, for/oi oil/ōo book
ōo boot/ou out/ŭ cut/û fur/*th* the/th thin/hw which/zh vision/ə ago, item, pencil, atom, circus

vehicles.

**cav · al · ry · man** |kăv′ əl rē mən| *n., pl.* **-men** |-mən|. A soldier in the cavalry.

**chafe** |chāf| *v.* **1.** To irritate by rubbing.

**cha · os** |kā′ ŏs′| *n.* **1.** Great disorder or confusion.

**chide** |chīd| *v.* **chid · ed** or **chid** |chĭd|, **chid · ed** or **chid** or **chid · den** |chĭd′ n|, **chid · ing.** To scold; reprove.

**cog · wheel** |kŏg′ hwēl′| or |-wēl′| *n.* A wheel with cogs or teeth in its rim that mesh with those of another wheel to transmit or receive motion.

**co · her · ent** |kō hîr′ ənt| *adj.* **2.** Logically connected; easy to understand: *coherent speech.*

**com · mence** |kə mĕns′| *v.* **com · menced, com · menc · ing** To begin; start: *The festivities commenced with the singing of the national anthem.*

**com · mend · a · ble** |kə mĕn′ də bəl| *adj.* Praiseworthy.—**com · mend′a · bly** *adv.*

**com · pas · sion** |kəm păsh′ ən| *n.* The feeling of sharing the suffering of another, together with a desire to give aid or show mercy.

**com · port** |kəm pôrt′| or |-pōrt′| *v.* To agree, harmonize, or accord with. *

**com · po · si · tion** |kŏm′ pə zĭsh′ ən| *n.* **1.** The putting together of parts or elements to form a whole; the act, process, or art of composing. **3.** A short essay, story, etc., written as a school exercise. **5.** The arrangement of parts or elements forming a whole, as in an artistic work: *the composition of a painting.*

**con · ceive** |kən sēv′| *v.* **con · ceived, con · ceiv · ing. 1.** To form or develop in the mind: *James Watt conceived the idea of the steam engine from watching a boiling kettle when he was a boy.*

**con · clu · sive** |kən kloo′ sĭv| *adj.* Putting an end to doubt, question, or uncertainty; decisive: *a conclusive argument.*

* © 1991 by Scholastic Inc.

**con · cus · sion** |kən kŭsh′ ən| *n.* **1.** A violent jarring; a shock: *A concussion resulted from the blast.*

**con · found** |kən found′| or |kŏn-| *v.* **1.** To bewilder, puzzle, or perplex: *The pitcher confounded the batter with his knuckle ball.*

**con · jure** |kŏn′ jər| or |kən joŏr′| *v.* **con · jured, con · jur · ing. 2.** To produce as if by magic: *conjure a miracle.* **3.** To practice magic; perform magic tricks.

**con · so · la · tion** |kŏn′ sə lā′ shən| *n.* **1.** Comfort during a time of disappointment or sorrow.

**con · tam · i · nate** |kən tăm′ ə nāt| *v.* **con · tam · i · nat · ed, con · tam · i · nat · ing.** To make impure, bad, or less good by mixture or contact; pollute; foul.

**con · ven · tion · al** |kən vĕn′ shə nəl| *adj.* Following accepted practice, customs, or taste: *a conventional greeting; a conventional plan for a house.*

**cope**[1] |kōp| *v.* **coped, cop · ing.** To contend or strive, especially successfully: *coped with heavy traffic.*

**cor · dial · i · ty** |kôr jăl′ ĭ tē| or |kôr′ jē ăl′-| *n.* Heartiness; warmth; sincerity.

**cor · ral** |kə răl′| *v.* **cor · ralled, cor · ral · ling. 3.** *Informal.* To round up; seize: *corralling all the books on this subject.*

**cor · rup · tion** |kə rŭp′ shən| *n.* **2.** Dishonesty or improper behavior, as by a person in a position of authority.

**coun · te · nance** |koun′ tə nəns| *n.* **2.** The face: *the human countenance.*

**coun · ter**[3] |koun′ tər| *v.* **1.** To move or act in opposition to; oppose: *He is trying to counter that impression.*

**cra · ven** |krā′ vən| *adj.* Very cowardly

**cred · i · tor** |krĕd′ ĭ tər| *n.* A person or firm to whom money is owed.

**cres · cent** |krĕs′ ənt| *n.* **1.** The figure of the moon as it appears in its first quarter, with concave and convex edges ending in points. —*adj.* **1.** Shaped like a crescent.

# D

**daft** |dăft| *or* |däft| *adj.* **1.** Crazy; mad.

**daze** |dāz| *v.* **dazed, daz·ing.** To stun or confuse, as with a blow, shock, or surprise: *The noise dazed and deafened them.*—**dazed** *adj.*: *a dazed look.*

**de·co·rum** |dĭ kôr′ əm| *or* |-kōr′-| *n.* Appropriateness of behavior or conduct.

**de·cry** |dĭ krī′| *v.* To condemn as being wrong or bad.

**deed** |dēd| *n.* **2.** A legal document showing ownership of property.

**de·gen·er·ate** |dĭ jĕn′ ər ĭt| *adj.* In a much worse or lower condition for having lost what is considered normal or desirable, as mental or moral qualities: *a degenerate person.*

**del·e·ga·tion** |dĕl′ ə gā′ shən| *n.* **3.** A person or persons chosen to represent another or others.

**de·lu·sive** |dĭ lōō′ sĭv| *adj.* Tending to deceive or mislead; deceptive.

**de·mise** |dĭ mīz′| *n.* **1.** The death of a person. **2.** The end, fall, collapse, or ruin of something: *the demise of a great newspaper.*

**de·mure** |dĭ myōōr′| *adj.* Shy or modest, sometimes falsely so.

**de·nun·ci·a·tion** |dĭ nŭn′ sē ā′ shən| *or* |-shē-| *n.* The act of expressing very strong disapproval; open condemnation. *

**des·o·late** |dĕs′ə lĭt| *adj.* **2.** Having few or no inhabitants; deserted: *a desolate wilderness.* **3.** Lonely and sad; wretched; forlorn.

**des·o·la·tion** |dĕs′ ə lā′ shən| *n.* **1.** The condition of being desolate: *desolation caused by a forest fire.*

**de·spon·dent** |dĭ spŏn′ dənt| *adj.* In low spirits; depressed; dejected.

**dil·a·to·ry** |dĭl′ ə tôr′ ē| *or* |-tōr′ ē| *adj.* Tending or intended to cause delay: *dilatory military maneuvers.*

**di·min·u·tive** |dĭ mĭn′ yə tĭv| *adj.* **2.** Expressing smallness or affection, as the diminutive suffixes *-let* in *booklet,* -ette in *dinette,* and *-kin* in *lambkin*—*n.* A diminutive suffix, word, or name.

**din·ghy** |dĭng′ ē| *n., pl.* **din·ghies.** A small boat, especially a rowboat.

**dirge** |dûrj| *n.* A sad, solemn piece of music, such as a funeral hymn or lament.

**dis·course** |dĭs′ kôrs′| *or* |-kōrs′| *v.* To speak or write formally and at length.

**dis·creet** |dĭ skrēt′| *adj.* **1.** Having or showing caution or self-restraint in one's speech or behavior; showing good judgment; prudent: *a polite and discreet guest; keeping a discreet distance from a strange animal.* *

**dis·il·lu·sion·ment** |dĭs′ ĭ lōō′ zhən mənt| *n.* Disappointment; disenchantment. *

**dis·lodge** |dĭs lŏj′| *v.* **dis·lodged, dis·lodg·ing.** To move or force out of position.

**dis·perse** |dĭ spûrs′| *v.* **dis·persed, dis·pers·ing.** **2.** To cause to vanish or disappear; dispel: *Windstorms dispersed the scent, making pursuit difficult.* *

**dis·pose** |dĭs pōz′| *v.* **dis·posed, dis·pos·ing.** **2.** To settle or decide something. **3.** To make willing or receptive for; incline: *feeling half disposed to object.*

**dis·tinc·tive** |dĭ stĭngk′ tĭv| *adj.* Serving to identify, characterize, or set apart from others: *Red berries are a distinctive feature of this plant.*

**dis·tract·ed** |dĭ străk′ tĭd| *adj.* **1.** Very confused or bewildered: *distracted between joy and sorrow.* **2.** Violently upset in mind, especially by grief.

**di·verge** |dĭ vûrj′| *or* |dī| *v.* **di·verged, di·verging.** **1.** To go or extend in different directions from a common point; branch out: *a*

ă pat/ā pay/â care/ä father/ĕ pet/ē be/ĭ pit/ī pie/î fierce/ŏ pot/ō go/ô paw, for/oi oil/ōō book
ōō boot/ou out/ŭ cut/û fur/*th* the/th thin/hw which/zh vision/ə ago, item, pencil, atom, circus

road that suddenly diverged into paths like branches of the letter "Y."

**di·ver·sion** |dǐ vûr′ zhən| *or* |-shən| *or* |dī-| *n.* **2.** Something that relaxes or entertains; recreation: *the diversion of a royal hunt.*

**di·vine** |dǐ vīn′| *v.* **di·vined, di·vin·ing. 2.** To guess.

**dun·der·head** |dŭn′ dər hĕd| *n.* A stupid person.*

## E

**ear·nest·ly** |ûr′ nist lē| *adv.* **2.** Seriously; with determination of purpose.*

**eb·on·y** |ĕb′ ə nē| *adj.* Black.

**ec·cen·tric** |ĭk sĕn′ trĭk| *adj.* **1.** Odd or unusual in appearance, behavior, etc.; strange; peculiar: *an eccentric hat; an eccentric person; an eccentric habit.*

**ec·cen·tric·i·ty** |ĕk′ sĕn trĭs′ ĭ tē| *n., pl.* **ec·cen·tric·i·ties. 1.** The condition or quality of being eccentric.

**ec·sta·sy** |ĕk′ stə sē| *n., pl.* **ec·sta·sies.** A state of intense emotion, especially of joy or delight.

**e·lu·sive** |ĭ lo͞o′ sĭv| *adj.* Tending to avoid or escape, as by artfulness, cunning, or daring.*

**em·ber** |ĕm′ bər| *n.* **1.** A piece of live coal or wood, as in a dying fire.

**em·phat·ic** |ĕm făt′ ĭk| *adj.* **1.** Expressed or performed with emphasis: *an emphatic shake of the head.* **2.** Bold and definite in expression or action: *an emphatic person.*

**en·dure** |ĕn do͞or′| *or* |-dyo͞or′| *v.* **en·dured, en·dur·ing. 3.** To bear with tolerance; put up with: *He could no longer endure her rudeness.*

**en·gulf** |ĕn gŭlf′| *v.* To cause to disappear by or as if by overflowing and enclosing; swallow up: *The floodwaters engulfed the surrounding farmlands.*

**en·treat** |ĕn trēt′| *v.* To ask earnestly; beg; implore.

**en·vel·op** |ĕn vĕl′ əp| *v.* **1.** To enclose completely with or as if with a covering: *envelop a baby in a blanket. Legend and myth have long enveloped the origins of the city of Rome. The tornado funnel enveloped the barn.*

**er·rat·ic** |ĭ răt′ ĭk| *adj.* **1.** Irregular or uneven in quality, progress, etc.: *His work has been erratic.*

**ex·as·per·ate** |ĭg zăs′ pə rāt′| *v.* **ex·as·per·at·ed, ex·as·per·at·ing.** To irritate greatly; try the patience of; irk: *Her shrill voice always exasperated him.*

**ex·on·er·ate** |ĭg zŏn′ ə rāt| *v.* **ex·on·er·at·ed, ex·on·er·at·ing.** To free from a charge; declare blameless: *The court exonerated the defendant.*—**ex·on′·er·a′ tion** *n.*

**ex·ten·u·ate** |ĭk stĕn′ yo͞o āt′| *v.* To make (an offense, error, etc.) seem less serious by providing partial excuses or justifications.

**ex·trem·i·ty** |ĭk strĕm′ ĭ tē| *n., pl.* **ex·trem·i·ties. 2.** Extreme danger, distress or need: *The victims of the fire called for help in their extremity.*

## F

**fac·tion** |făk′ shən| *n.* **1.** A group of persons forming a united, usually discontented and troublesome, minority within a larger group.

**fa·mil·i·ar·i·ty** |fə mĭl′ ē ăr′ ĭ tē| *n., pl.* **fa·mil·i·ar·i·ties. 1.** Acquaintance with or knowledge of something: *His familiarity with the city's streets helped him get around.*

**far-fetched** |fär fĕcht′| *adj.* Hard to believe; strained and improbable: *a far-fetched story; a far-fetched excuse.*

---

**fil·a·ment** |**fĭl′** ə mənt| *n.* **2.** Any fine or slender thread, strand, fiber, etc.

**fin·i·cal** |**fĭn′** ə kəl| *adj.* Finicky; excessively dainty. \*

**flay** |flā| *v.* **2.** To criticize or scold harshly.

**flinch** |flĭnch| *v.* To shrink or wince, as from pain or fear.

**flo·til·la** |flō **tĭl′** ə| *n.* **1.** A fleet of boats or other small vessels.

**flur·ried·ly** |**flûr′** əd lē| *adv.* Full of bustling activity; excitedly. \*

**flus·ter** |**flŭs′** tər| *v.* To make nervous, excited, or confused: *The staring faces flustered her.*— *n.* A nervous, excited, or confused condition.

**foal** |fōl| *v.* To give birth to (a foal).

**fol·ly** |**fŏl′** ē| *n.* **1.** Lack of good sense or judgment; foolishness.

**forge** |fôrj| *or* |fōrj| *n.* **1.** A furnace or hearth where metal is heated so that it can be worked more easily.

**for·lorn** |fôr **lôrn′**| *adj.* **1.** Deserted; forsaken; abandoned: *a forlorn house.*

**for·mi·da·ble** |**fôr′** mĭ də bəl| *adj.* **3.** Admirable; awe-inspiring.

**forth·right** |**fôrth′** rīt′| *or* |**fōrth′**-| *adj.* Straightforward; frank: *ask a forthright question.*

**fren·zy** |**frĕn′** zē| *n.,* pl. **fren·zies.** Wild excitement or a display of emotion suggesting madness, often accompanied by vigorous or violent activity: *sharks gone mad and dashing about in a blind frenzy.*

**frock** |frŏk| *n.* **1.** A girl's or woman's dress.

**frol·ic·some** |**frŏl′** ĭk səm| *adj.* Full of fun; frisky; playful: *a frolicsome puppy.*

**froth** |frôth| *or* |frŏth| *v.* To pour forth (a liquid) in the form of foam; to foam: *They knew the dog was sick when it frothed at the mouth.*

**frus·tra·tion** |frŭs **trā′** shən| *n.* A feeling of annoyance at being prevented from accomplishing a purpose or goal. \*

**fun·gus** |**fŭng′** gəs| *n., pl.* **fun·gi** |**fŭn′** jī′| *or* **fun·gus·es.** Any of a group of plants, such as a mushroom, mold, yeast, or mildew, that have no green coloring and that obtain their nourishment from living or dead plant or animal substances.

# G

**gait** |gāt| *n.* **1.** A way of walking or running: *a slow gait; a clumsy gait.*

**gal·lant** |**găl′** ənt| *adj.* **2.** Polite and attentive to women; chivalrous.

**gal·lant·ry** |**găl′** ən trē| *n.* **2.** Chivalrous attention to women; courtliness.

**gal·ley** |**găl′** ē| *n.* **2.** The kitchen on a ship or airliner.

**gal·lows** |**găl′** ōz| *n., pl.* **gal·lows·es** *or* **gal·lows.** **1.** A framework with a suspended noose, used for execution by hanging.

**gaunt** |gônt| *adj.* **gaunt·er, gaunt·est. 1.** Thin and bony; haggard; emaciated: *a gaunt face.*

**gid·dy** |**gĭd′** ē| *adj.* **1. b.** Causing or capable of causing dizziness.

**giz·zard** |**gĭz′** ərd| *n.* **1.** An enlarged, muscular part in the digestive tract of a bird, in which bits of sand or gravel collect and in which food is ground and digested.

**glock·en·spiel** |**glŏk′** ən spēl′| *or* |-shpēl′| *n.* A musical instrument consisting of a series of metal bars tuned to the tones of the chromatic scale. It is played by being struck with two light hammers.

**glow·er** |**glou′** ər| *n.* An angry or threatening stare.

**grate¹** |grāt| *v.* **gra·ted, grat·ing. 2.** To make

---

ă pat/ā pay/â care/ä father/ĕ pet/ē be/ĭ pit/ī pie/î fierce/ŏ pot/ō go/ô paw, for/oi oil/o͞o book
o͞o boot/ou out/ŭ cut/û fur/*th* the/th thin/hw which/zh vision/ə ago, item, pencil, atom, circus

or cause to make a harsh grinding or rasping sound by rubbing: *You grate like a jay and squeak like a mouse. He grated the two rocks together.*

**grav·i·ty** |**grăv′** ĭ tē| *n.* **2.** Seriousness; importance.

**grove** |grōv| *n.* A group of trees with open ground between them.

**guard·i·an** |**gär′** dē ən| *n.* **1.** Someone or something that guards, protects, or defends: *guardians of law and order.*

**H**

**hand·y** |**hăn′** de| *adj.* **2.** Within easy reach; accessible: *a handy supply of medicine. Leave the dictionary on the table where it will be handy.*

**hard·tack** |**härd′** tăk′| *n.* A hard biscuit made only of flour and water; sea biscuit.

**has·ty** |**hā′** stē| *adj.* **hast·i·er, hast·i·est. 1.** Marked by speed; swift; rapid: *a hasty retreat.*—**hast′i·ly** *adv.*—**hast′i·ness** *n.*

**hasty pudding. 1.** Cornmeal mush.

**hav·oc** |**hăv′** ək| *n.* Devastation; destruction.

**hearth** |härth| *n.* **1.** The floor of a fireplace, usually extending into a room.

**hem·lock** |**hĕm′** lŏk′| *n.* **1. a.** An evergreen tree with short, flat needles and small cones.

**her·i·tage** |**hĕr′** ĭ tĭj| *n.* **2.** Something other than property passed down from preceding generations; legacy; tradition: *Every country has its heritage of folk music.*

**high·hand·ed** |**hī′ hăn′** dĭd| *adj.* In an arrogant or arbitrary manner: *a highhanded reply.*

**hi·lar·i·ous** |hĭ **lâr′** ē əs| *or* |-**lăr′**-| *or* |hī-| *adj.* Boisterously funny; provoking much laughter: *a hilarious story.*—**hi·lar·i·ous·ly** *adv.*

**ho·ri·zon** |hə **rī′** zən| *n.* **1.** The line along which the earth and sky appear to meet.

**host** |hōst| *n.* **2.** A great number: *a host of golden daffodils.*

**hos·tler** |**hŏs′** lər| *n.* A person who takes care of horses at an inn. *

**hot·house** |**hŏt′** hous′| *n., pl.* -**hous·es** |hou′ zĭz|. A heated building or enclosure with a glass roof and sides, used for growing plants. —*modifier: hothouse tomatoes.*

**hov·er** |**hŭv′** ər| *or* |**hŏv′**-| *v.* **2.** To remain or linger close by.

**hul·la·ba·loo** |**hŭl′** ə bə loo′| *n.* Great noise or excitement; an uproar.

**husk** |hŭsk| *n.* The dry or leaflike outer covering of certain seeds or fruits, as of an ear of corn.

**hys·ter·i·cal** |hĭ **stĕr′** ĭ kəl| *adj.* **3.** Marked by uncontrolled emotion; violent or unrestrained: *laughing in hysterical relief.*—**hys·ter′i·cal·ly** *adv.*

**I**

**im·plore** |ĭm **plôr′**| *or* |-**plōr′**| *v.* **im·plored, im·plor·ing. 1.** To appeal to (someone) earnestly, anxiously, and humbly; entreat; beseech: *We implore you to help us.*

**im·pos·tor** |ĭm **pŏs′** tər| *n.* A person who deceives by pretending to be someone else.

**im·pres·sion·ism,** also **Im·pres·sion·ism** |ĭm **prĕsh′** ə nĭz′ əm| *n.* **1.** A style of painting of the late 19th century, marked by concentration on the impression produced by a scene or object and the use of many small strokes to simulate reflected light.—**im·pres′ sion·ist, Im·pres·sion·ist** *n. & adj.*

**im·pulse** |**ĭm′** pŭls′| *n.* **2.** A sudden inclination or urge; a whim.

**in·au·di·ble** |ĭn **ô′** də bəl| *adj.* Incapable of being heard; not audible.

**in·cen·tive** |ĭn **sĕn′** tĭv| *n.* Something inciting to action or effort; a stimulus.

---

* © 1991 by Scholastic Inc.

**in · cli · na · tion** |ĭn′ klə nā′ shən| *n.* **2.** A tendency to act in a certain way: *She has an inclination to observe and criticize the faults of others.* **3.** A natural or usual preference: *an inclination to skate.*

**in · com · pa · ra · ble** |ĭn kŏm′ pər ə bəl| *adj.* **2.** Above all comparison; unsurpassed.

**in · con · ven · ience** |ĭn′ kən vēn′ yəns| *n.* **2.** Something that causes difficulty, trouble, or discomfort.

**in · de · fin · a · ble** |ĭn′ dĭ fī′ nə bəl| *adj.* Not capable of being defined, described, or analyzed: *an indefinable feeling.* —**in · de · fin · a · bly** *adv.*

**in · dif · fer · ence** |ĭn dĭf′ ər əns| *or* |-dĭf′ rəns| *n.* **1.** Lack of concern or interest.

**in · dif · fer · ent** |ĭn dĭf′ ər ənt| *or* |-dĭf′ rənt| *adj.* **1.** Having or showing no interest; not caring one way or the other.

**in · dig · nant** |ĭn dĭg′ nənt| *adj.* Angry because of something unjust, mean, etc.

**in · dis · pen · sa · ble** |ĭn′ dĭ spĕn′ sə bəl| *adj.* Not capable of being dispensed with; essential; required: *Some bacteria are indispensable to man.*

**in · di · vis · i · ble** |ĭn′ də vĭz′ ə bəl| *adj.* **1.** Not capable of being divided.

**in · dus · try** |ĭn′ də strē| *n.* **2.** Hard work; steady effort.

**in · es · ti · ma · ble** |ĭn ĕs′ tə mə bəl| *adj.* Too great or valuable to be estimated.

**in · fat · u · ate** |ĭn făch′ o͞o āt′| *v.* **in · fat · u · at · ed, in · fat · u · at · ing.** To fill with a strong and foolish passion or attraction.

**in · fir · mi · ty** |ĭn fûr′ mĭ tē| *n., pl.* **in · fir · mi · ties.** **1.** The condition of being infirm; bodily weakness; frailty. **2.** A disease or disorder that causes this.

**in · sid · i · ous** |ĭn sĭd′ ē əs| *adj.* **1.** Intended to entrap; treacherous: *an insidious plot.*

**in · sin · u · ate** |ĭn sĭn′ yo͞o āt| *v.* **in · sin · u · at-ed, in · sin · u · at · ing. 1.** To introduce (ideas, thoughts, points of view, etc.) gradually and slyly: *She insinuated her political beliefs into the conversation.* **2.** To convey indirectly; hint covertly: *What are you insinuating?*

**in · tent · ly** |ĭn tĕnt′ lē| *adv.* In a determined manner; having the mind fixed on some purpose.

**in · ter · mi · na · ble** |ĭn tûr′ mə nə bəl| *adj.* Having or seeming to have no end; endless: *an interminable play.*

**in · ter · pose** |ĭn′ tər pōz′| *v.* **3.** To intervene, especially for the purpose of mediating. —**in′ ter · po · si′ tion** *n.*

**in · ter · vene** |ĭn′ tər vēn′| *v.* **2. a.** To enter a course of events so as to hinder it or change it.

**in · ti · ma · cy** |ĭn′ tə mə sē| *n.* Close and thorough acquaintance with; close personal relationship.

**in · tu · i · tive** |ĭn to͞o′ ĭ tĭv| *or* |-tyo͞o′-| *adj.* Based on an instinctive knowledge or understanding of something: *an intuitive grasp of the situation.* —**in · tu′ i · tive · ly** *adv.*

**in · vin · ci · ble** |ĭn vĭn′ sə bəl| *adj.* Too strong, powerful, or great to be defeated or overcome.

**ir · res · o · lute** |ĭ rĕz′ ə lo͞ot′| *adj.* Undecided or showing uncertainty about what to do; indecisive.

**J**

**jinx** |jĭngks| *n. Informal.* **2.** Someone or something supposed to bring bad luck.

**joint** |joint| *adj.* **1.** Undertaken or shared by two or more people or parties: *a joint effort; a joint bank account.* **2.** Sharing with someone else: *joint owners.*

---

ă pat/ā pay/â care/ä father/ĕ pet/ē be/ĭ pit/ī pie/î fierce/ŏ pot/ō go/ô paw, for/oi oil/o͞o book o͞o boot/ou out/ŭ cut/û fur/*th* the/th thin/hw which/zh vision/ə ago, item, pencil, atom, circus

# K

**keen¹** |kēn| *adj.* **keen·er, keen·est 1.** Sharp at the edge or point: *a keen knife ripping through cloth.* **4.** Acute; sensitive: *the keen eyes of the jackals.* **5.** Intellectually penetrating; astute; bright: *a keen observer of men.*

**KO,** also **K.O., k.o.** |kā′ ō′| *v.* **KO'd, KO'ing, KO's.** *Slang.* To knock out.—*n., pl.* **KO's.** In boxing, a knockout.

# L

**lad·en** |lād′ n| *adj.* **3.** Oppressed; burdened: *a mother laden with grief.*

**lame** |lām| *adj.* Injured or crippled in leg or foot.*

**lat·tice** |lăt′ ĭs| *n.* A criss-cross of wood or metal, as on a window.*

**leg·a·cy** |lĕg′ ə sē| *n.* **1.** Money or property left to someone in a will.

**list·less** |lĭst′ lĭs| *adj.* Lacking energy or enthusiasm; lethargic.

**loi·ter** |loi′ tər| *v.* **2.** To go slowly, stopping often.

**lore** |lôr| *or* |lōr| *n.* **1.** Accumulated fact, tradition, or belief: *sea lore.*

**lu·mi·nar·y** |loo′ mə nĕr′ ē| *n., pl.* **lu·mi·nar·ies. 1.** An object, especially a celestial body, that gives off light.

**lurch¹** |lûrch| *n.* **1.** An unsteady or abrupt swaying movement.—*v.* To move unsteadily; stagger: *The big, bullying fellow lurched toward Jed.*

# M

**mar·i·tal** |măr′ ĭ təl| *adj.* Of or relating to marriage: *marital vows; marital problems.*

**mar·tial** |mär′ shəl| *adj.* Of war; warlike.

**mar·tyr** |mär′ tər| **2.** A person who sacrifices something important to him to further a belief, cause, or principle.

**mar·tyr·dom** |mär′ tər dəm| *n.* The condition of being a martyr.

**mas·tiff** |măs′ tĭf| *n.* A large dog with a short brownish coat and short, square jaws.*

**med·ic·i·nal** |mə dĭs′ ə nəl| *adj.* Of or having the properties of medicine; capable of curing; healing.

**med·ley** |mĕd′ lē| *n.* **1.** A mixture or variety, especially of sounds.

**mien** |mēn| *n.* A person's way of carrying or conducting himself; bearing; manner.

**mill¹** |mĭl| *v.* **5.** To move around in a confused or disorderly manner: *an angry crowd milling about in front of the theater.*

**min·gle** |mĭng′ gəl| *v.* **1.** To mix or become mixed; unite; combine.

**mor·als** |môr′ əlz| *or* |mŏr′-| *n.* **2.** Rules of good or correct conduct.

**mor·ti·fy** |môr′ tə fī′| *v.* **mor·ti·fied, mor·ti·fy·ing, mor·ti·fies. 3.** To cause to feel shame or embarrassment; humiliate.

**murk** |mûrk| *n.* Darkness; gloom: *groped his way through the murk of the moonless night.*

**mus·ter** |mŭs′ tər| *v.* **1.** To bring or come together; assemble: *mustered his platoon for inspection. The men mustered for roll call.*

# N

**na·tal** |nāt′l| *adj.* Of or accompanying birth: *natal injuries.*

**non·cha·lant·ly** |nŏn′ shə länt′ lē| *adv.* Coolly, in a carefree manner, with casual unconcern, or seeming so: *He whistled nonchalantly as he walked past the guard dog.*

**non·com·mit·tal** |nŏn kə mĭt′l| *adj.* Not

---

* © 1991 by Scholastic Inc.

indicating how one feels or what one thinks or plans to do: *She gave a noncommittal answer, "We shall see."*—**non · com · mit · tal · ly** *adv.* \*

# O

**o · blige** |ə blīj′| *v.* **o · bliged, o · blig · ing. 1.** To cause to comply by physical, legal, social, or moral means: *The weather obliged him to postpone his trip.*

**ob · sess** |əb sĕs′| *v.* To think of continually; occupy the mind of; haunt: *the search for perfection obsessed them.* \*

**ob · sti · nate** |ŏb′ stə nĭt| *adj.* Stubborn; resistant to argument or reason; inflexible: *an obstinate old man; an obstinate English class.*

**om · i · nous** |ŏm′ ə nəs| *adj.* Seeming to fortell or be a sign of trouble, danger, or disaster.

**or · der · ly** |ôr′ dər lē| *n., pl.* **or · der · lies. 2.** A soldier assigned to a superior officer to carry orders or messages.

**or · ner · y** |ôr′ nə rē| *adj.* **or · ner · i · er, or · ner · i · est.** *Informal.* Mean and stubborn: *an ornery child.*

# P

**pag · eant** |păj′ ənt| *n.* **1.** A play or dramatic spectacle usually based on an event in history. **2.** A spectacular exhibition. \*

**pal · lid** |păl′ ĭd| *adj.* Lacking healthy color; pale.

**pal · lor** |păl′ ər| *n.* Unhealthy paleness

**pan · o · ram · a** |păn′ ə răm′ ə| *or* |-rä′ mə| *n.* **1.** A view or picture of everything visible over a wide area: *a vast panorama of mountain scenery.*

**par · a · dox · i · cal** |păr′ ə dŏk′ sĭ kəl| *adj.* Containing a paradox (a statement that contains or implies its own contradiction and therefore has an uncertain meaning or no meaning; for example, *"We destroyed the town in order to save it"* is a paradox); apparently contradictory.—**par′a · dox′i · cal · ly** *adv.* \*

**par · son · age** |pär′ sə nĭj| *n.* The official residence of a parson (clergyman), as provided by his church.

**pa · tri · arch** |pā′ trē ärk′| *n.* **1.** The male leader of a family, clan, or tribe, often the father, grandfather, etc., of most or all of its members.

**peev · ish** |pē′ vĭsh| *adj.* Annoyed; irritable; fretful.—**pee′vish · ness** *n.*

**per · il** |pĕr′ əl| *n.* **2.** Something dangerous; a serious risk: *the perils of a journey in a covered wagon.*

**per · il · ous** |pĕr′ ə ləs| *adj.* Full of peril; hazardous.

**per · i · scope** |pĕr′ ĭ skōp′| *n.* Any of several instruments in which mirrors allow observations of objects that are not in a direct line of sight.

**per · plex · i · ty** |pər plĕk′ sĭ tē| *n., pl.* **per · plex · i · ties. 1.** The condition of being confused or puzzled; bewilderment. \*

**pet · ri · fy** |pĕt′ rə fī′| *n.* **pet · ri · fied, pet · ri · fy · ing, pet · ri · fies. 1.** To turn (wood or other organic material) into a stony mass by causing minerals to fill and finally replace its internal structure.

**pet · tish** |pĕt′ ĭsh| *adj.* Ill-tempered; peevish.—**pet′ish · ly** *adv.*

**pin · ion** |pĭn′ yən| *n.* A bird's wing.

**pi · ous** |pī′ əs| *adj.* **3.** Falsely and ostentatiously devout: *a pious speech to impress the audience.*

**pip · ing** |pī′ pĭng| *adj.* Thin, clear, high-pitched, and shrill: *the high, piping notes of*

---

ă pat/ā pay/â care/ä father/ĕ pet/ē be/ĭ pit/ī pie/î fierce/ŏ pot/ō go/ô paw, for/oi oil/o͝o book
o͞o boot/ou out/ŭ cut/û fur/*th* the/th thin/hw which/zh vision/ə ago, item, pencil, atom, circus

*the flute.*

**pitch** |pĭch| *n.* The sticky substance that comes from the sap which oozes out of pine trees. *

**plac·id** |plăs′ ĭd| *adj.* Calm; peaceful.

**pla·guy** |plā′ gē| *adj.* Annoying; disagreeable. *

**plod·der** |plŏd′ ər| *n.* One who works or acts slowly and wearily. *

**plume** |plо̄о̄m| *n.* **1.** A feather, especially a large or showy one used for decoration.—*v.* Of a bird, to smooth its feathers.

**pon·der** |pŏn′ dər| *v.* To think or consider carefully and at length: *She pondered the meaning of her dream. He pondered over the decision.*

**pon·der·ous** |pŏn′ dər əs| *adj.* **1.** Heavy, massive, and often clumsy.

**pos·i·tive** |pŏz′ ĭ tĭv| *adj.* **1.** Expressing affirmation or approval; favorable: *a positive answer; a positive statement.*

**pre·cede** |prĭ sēd′| *v.* **pre·ced·ed, pre·ced·ing.** To go or come before in time, order, position, rank, etc.: *A small surge of water precedes all geyser eruptions. The word "very" may precede an adjective.*

**pre·lim·i·nar·y** |prĭ lĭm′ ə něr′ ē| *adj.* Leading to or preparing for the main event, action, or business: *preliminary sketches for a building.*—*n., pl.* **pre·lim·i·nar·ies.** Something that leads to or serves as preparation for a main event, action, or business: *Without preliminaries, she walked to the edge of the pool and dived in.*

**pre·mo·ni·tion** |prē′ mə nĭsh′ ən| *or* |prĕm′ ə| *n.* **1.** An advance warning.

**pre·oc·cu·pied** |prē ŏk′ yə pīd| *adj.* **1.** Deep in thought; engrossed: *sat quietly all through dinner, frowning and preoccupied.*

**pre·sent·ly** |prĕz′ ənt lē| *adv.* **1.** In a short time; soon: *Presently she heard a dog bark.*

**pri·me·val** |prī mē′ vəl| *adj.* Of the earliest ages of the world; primitive.

**prin·ci·ple** |prĭn′ sə pəl| *n.* **2. a.** A rule or standard of behavior: *a woman of dedicated political principles.* **b.** Moral standards in general: *a man of principle.*

**pro·claim** |prō klām′| *or* |prə-| *v.* **2.** To indicate unmistakably; make plain: *His behavior proclaims him incapable of holding any position of leadership.*

**prod·i·gy** |prŏd′ ə jē| *n., pl.* **prod·i·gies. 1.** A person with exceptional talents or powers: *a child prodigy.*

**prof·fer** |prŏf′ ər| *v.* To present for acceptance; offer.

**pro·gres·sive** |prə grĕs′ ĭv| *adj.* **4.** Working for or favoring reforms, as in government, the social system, or education; liberal.

**pro·nounce·ment** |prə nouns′ mənt| *n.* **1.** A formal declaration; an edict: *The king governed by issuing pronouncements from the palace.*

**pros·trate** |prŏs′ trāt′| *v.* To kneel or lie face down, as in submission. *

**pro·vi·so** |prə vī′ zō| *n.* A clause in a document making a qualification, condition, or restriction. *

## Q

**quail²** |kwāl| *v.* To lose courage; cower: *Harvey's dog looks ferocious, but he quails at the sight of a stranger.*

**quaint** |kwānt| *adj.* **2.** Unfamiliar or unusual; curious: *a land full of sloths, kangaroos, and other quaint animals.*

## R

**rail** |rāl| *v.* To use strong or emphatic language; complain loudly and bitterly.

**ram · shack · le** |răm′ shăk′ əl| *adj.* Close to falling apart; broken-down; shaky: *a ramshackle hut.*

**ran · sack** |răn′ săk′| *v.* **1.** To search thoroughly and often roughly.

**rasp** |răsp| *or* |räsp| *n.* **2.** A harsh, grating sound.

**rau · cous** |rô′ kəs| *adj.* **1.** Loud and harsh: *raucous cries.* **2.** Boisterous; disorderly: *a raucous party.*

**rav · el** |răv′ əl| *v.* **rav · eled** *or* **rav · elled, rav · el · ing** *or* **rav · el · ling.** To separate into single, loose, threads; fray: *raveled the edge of cloth. The rug raveled.*

**rav · en · ous** |răv′ ə nəs| *adj.* **1.** Greedily eager for food; extremely hungry: *a ravenous appetite.*

**realm** |rĕlm| *n.* **1.** A kingdom.

**re · buke** |rĭ byo̅o̅k′| *v.* To criticize sharply; upbraid.

**rec · on · cile** |rĕk′ ən sīl′| *v.* **1.** To restore friendship between; make friendly again.—**rec′on · cil′i · a′tion** *n.*

**re · count** |rĭ kount′| *v.* To tell in detail; narrate the particulars of: *The Iliad recounts the siege of Troy.*

**red · coat** |rĕd′ kōt′| *n.* A British soldier during the American Revolution and the War of 1812.

**re · fute** |rĭ fyo̅o̅t| *v.* **re · fut · ed, re · fut · ing.** To prove (a person, idea, etc.) to be wrong: *refuted their statements.*

**reign** |rān| *n.* **2.** Dominant influence or effect; sway: *the reign of theology in the Middle Ages.*

**re · lent · less** |rĭ lĕnt′ lĭs| *adj.* **1.** Mercilessly harsh; unyielding; pitiless: *relentless killer.*—**re · lent · less · ly** *adv.*

**rel · e · vant** |rĕl′ ə vənt| *adj.* Related to the matter at hand; pertinent: *relevant questions.*—**rel′e · vance, rel′e · van · cy** *n.*

**rel · ish** |rĕl′ĭsh| *n.* **2. a.** Great enjoyment; pleasure; zest: *He began the task with relish.* **b.** Something that adds zest or pleasure: *His wit gave relish to the discussion.*

**re · luc · tant** |rĭ lŭk′ tənt| *adj.* **1.** Unwilling; averse: *reluctant to leave.*

**re · mon · strance** |rĭ mŏn′ strəns| *n.* A strong protest or objection.

**re · mon · strate** |rĭ mŏn′ strāt′| *v.* To argue or plead in protest against or in objection to something.

**re · morse** |rĭ môrs′| *n.* Bitter regret or guilt for having done something harmful or unjust.

**rend** |rĕnd| *v.* **1.** To tear, pull, or wrench apart violently.

**ren · e · gade** |rĕn′ ĭ gād′| *n.* **1.** Someone who rejects a cause, allegiance, group, etc., in preference for another; a deserter; a traitor. **2.** An outlaw.—*modifier: a renegade leader.*

**re · pent** |rĭ pĕnt′| *v.* **2.** To regret and change one's mind about (past conduct).

**re · pen · tance** |rĭ pĕn′ tns| *n.* Remorse or contrition for past conduct or sin.

**re · pen · tant** |rĭ pĕn′ tnt| *adj.* Feeling or showing repentance; penitent: *a repentant heart.*

**re · port** |rĭ pôrt′| *or* |-pōrt′| *n.* **3.** An explosive sound, as of a firearm being discharged.

**re · pose** |rĭ pōz′| *n.* **1.** Rest or relaxation. **2.** Peace of mind; freedom from anxiety. **3.** Calmness; tranquility.

**rep · ri · mand** |rĕp′ rĭ mănd′| *or* |-mänd′| *n.* A severe scolding or official rebuke.

**res · o · lute** |rĕz′ ə lo̅o̅t′| *adj.* Having or showing strong will and determination: *a resolute voice.*—**res′o · lute · ly** *adv.*

**ret · i · cent** |rĕt′ ĭ sənt| *adj.* Hesitant or disinclined to speak out; quiet; reserved: *a reticent child.*

**re · vere** |rĭ vîr′| *v.* To regard with great awe, affection, respect, or devotion.

**re · vile** |rĭ vīl′| *v.* To denounce with abusive

---

ă pat/ā pay/â care/ä father/ĕ pet/ē be/ĭ pit/ī pie/î fierce/ŏ pot/ō go/ô paw, for/oi oil/o̅o̅ book
o̅o̅ boot/ou out/ŭ cut/û fur/*th* the/th thin/hw which/zh vision/ə ago, item, pencil, atom, circus

language.

**riv · et** |rĭv′ ĭt| *v.* To fasten with a metal bolt.*

**rouse** |rouz| *v.* **1.** To wake up; awaken.

**sap · ling** |săp′ lĭng| *n.* A young tree.

**saun · ter** |sôn′ tər| *v.* To walk at a leisurely pace; stroll.

**scrim · mage** |skrĭm′ ĭj| *n.* A minor encounter between small bodies of troops; a skirmish.*

**scut · tle²** |skŭt′ l| *v.* **scut · tled, scut · tling.** To sink (a ship) by boring holes in the bottom.

**sen · ti · men · tal** |sĕn tə mĕn′ tl| *adj.* **3.** Marked by emotion that is excessive or artificial: *a sentimental story.*

**shad · y** |shā′ dē| *adj.* **3.** Of doubtful honesty or legality; questionable; dishonest: *a shady deal.*

**shan't** |shănt| *or* |shänt|. Shall not.

**shoal** |shōl| *n.* **1.** A shallow place in a body of water.

**shorn** |shôrn| *or* |shōrn|. A past participle of **shear.** Clipped or trimmed, as with scissors or shears.*

**shud · der** |shŭd′ ər| *v.* To tremble or shiver suddenly and convulsively, as from fear or horror.

**sig · ni · fy** |sĭg′ nə fī′| *v.* **sig · ni · fied, sig · ni · fy · ing, sig · ni · fies. 1.** To serve as a sign of: *What does this monument signify?* **2.** To make known: *Peter signified that he wanted to leave early.*

**sim · per** |sĭm′ pər| *v.* To smile in a silly or self-conscious manner.

**si · mul · ta · ne · ous** |sī′ məl tā′ nē əs| *or* |sĭm′ əl-| *adj.* Happening, existing, or done at the same time.—**si′mul · ta′ne · ous · ly** *adv.*

**snare** |snâr| *n.* A trap; something that entangles.*

**sol · ace** |sŏl′ əs| *v.* To comfort.*

**sor · did** |sôr′ dĭd| *adj.* **1.** Filthy or squalid: *a sordid mess in the kitchen sink.* *

**spec · u · late** |spĕk′ yə lāt′| **2.** To buy or sell something that involves a risk, on the chance of making a substantial profit.

**spec · u · la · tor** |spĕk′ yə lā′ tər| *n.* Someone who speculates.

**spor · tive** |spôr′ tĭv| *or* |spōr′-| *adj.* Playful; frolicsome.

**spry** |sprī| *adj.* Active; nimble; lively.

**spurn** |spûrn| *v.* To reject or refuse with disdain; scorn.

**squal · id** |skwŏl′ ĭd| *adj.* **1.** Having a dirty or wretched appearance: *squalid buildings.* **2.** Sordid; miserable: *a squalid existence.*

**squal · or** |skwŏl′ ər| *n.* Dirtiness; filth; wretchedness.*

**squirt** |skwûrt| *n. Informal.* A young child.*

**stac · ca · to** |stə kä′ tō| *adj.* **1.** Short and detached: *staccato musical notes.*

**state · ly** |stāt′ lē| *adj.* **2.** Impressive in size or proportions; majestic.

**ste · ve · dore** |stē′ vĭ dôr| *or* |-dōr′| *n.* A person whose job is the loading and unloading of ships.

**sti · fle** |stī′ fəl| *v.* **3.** To feel discomfort from a lack of fresh air or oxygen.—**sti′fling** *adj.:* *stifling heat.*

**sto · lid** |stŏl′ ĭd| *adj.* Having or showing little movement or emotion; impassive: *a stolid soldier.*

**sub · side** |səb sīd′| *v.* **sub · sid · ed, sub · sid · ing. 1.** To sink to a lower or more normal level: *The flood waters subsided.*

**suf · fice** |sə fīs′| *v.* **suf · ficed, suf · fic · ing. 2.** To be sufficient or adequate for: *enough to suffice them for three days.*

**sul · try** |sŭl′ trē| *adj.* Very hot and humid.

**su · pine** |soo pīn′| *or* |soo′ pīn′| *adj.* **1.** Lying on the back or having the face upward. **2.** Not inclined to act; lethargic; passive.

**sur · cease** |sər sēs′| *n. Archaic.* Cessation; halt; stop.*

---

**sur · vey** |sər vā′| *or* |sûr′ vā′| *v.* **1.** To look over the parts or features of; view broadly: *surveyed the neighborhood from a rooftop.* **2.** To examine so as to make estimates or criticisms; investigate: *surveyed the damage done by the storm.*

**swoon** |swo͞on| *n.* A fainting spell; a faint.

# T

**tal · on** |tăl′ ən|⁓*n.* The claw of a bird or animal that seizes other animals as prey.

**taut** |tôt| *adj.* **taut · er, taut · est. 1.** Pulled or drawn tight: *sails taut with wind.*

**tem · per · ance** |tĕm′ pər əns| *or* |-prəns| *n.* **1.** The condition of being moderate or temperate.

**tem · po · ral** |tĕm′ pər əl| *or* |-prəl| *adj.* **2.** Of worldly affairs, especially as distinguished from religious concerns.

**ten · an · cy** |tĕn′ ən sē| *n., pl.* **ten · an · cies. 1.** The possession or occupancy of lands or buildings by lease or rent. **2.** The period of a tenant's occupancy or possession.

**thrift** |thrĭft| *n.* Wisdom in the management of money and other resources.

**thrush** |thrŭsh| *n.* Any of several songbirds usually having a brownish back and a spotted breast.

**tin · der · box** |tĭn′ dər bŏks′| *n.* **1.** A metal box for holding tinder, or material that catches fire easily and is used to kindle fires. *

**to · ken** |tō′ kən| *n.* **1.** Something that serves as an indication or representation; a sign; symbol: *A white flag is a token of surrender.*

**tox · ic** |tŏk′ sĭk| *adj.* **1.** Of the nature of a poison; poisonous: *a toxic drug.*

**tran · quil** |trăng′ kwĭl| *or* |trăn′-| *adj.* Free from agitation, anxiety, etc.; calm; peaceful: *a tranquil lake; leading a tranquil life.*

**trans · fix** |trăns fĭks′| *v.* **2.** To render motionless, as with terror.

**trav · erse** |trăv′ ərs| *or* |trə vûrs′| *v.* **1.** To travel across, over, or through.

**trem · u · lous** |trĕm′ yə ləs| *adj.* **1.** Vibrating or quivering; trembling: *speaking with a tremulous voice.*

**tri · al** |trī′ əl| *or* |trīl| *n.* **4.** Anything, as a person, thing, or event, that tries one's patience, endurance, etc.: *He is a trial to his parents.*

**trib · u · la · tion** |trĭb′ yə lā′ shən| *n.* **1.** Great affliction or distress; suffering: *a time of great tribulation for all of us.*

**tuft · ed** |tŭf′ tĭd| *adj.* Thickly carpeted. *

**tu · mult** |to͞o′ məlt| *or* |tyo͞o′-| *n.* **1.** The din and commotion of a great crowd.

**tur · bu · lent** |tûr′ byə lənt| *adj.* **1.** Violently agitated or disturbed; stormy: *turbulent waters.*

**twinge** |twĭnj| *n.* A sudden and sharp physical, mental, or emotional pain.

**ty · rant** |tī′ rənt| *n.* **1.** A ruler who exercises power in a harsh, cruel manner; an oppressor.

# U

**ul · ti · ma · tum** |ŭl′ tə mā′ təm| *or* |-mä′-| *n.* A statement of terms that expresses or implies the threat of serious penalties if the terms are not accepted; a final demand or offer.

**un · a · bashed** |ŭn′ ə băsht′| *adj.* Not embarrassed or ashamed: *unabashed sentimentality.*

**un · daunt · ed** |ŭn dôn′ tĭd| *adj.* Not discouraged; fearless.

**un · gain · ly** |ŭn gān′ lē| *adj.* Without grace or ease of movement; awkward; clumsy.

**un · ob · tru · sive** |ŭn′ əb tro͞o′ sĭv| *adj.* Not blatant or aggressive in style, manner, etc.; inconspicuous: *an unobtrusive life in the*

ă pat/ā pay/â care/ä father/ĕ pet/ē be/ĭ pit/ī pie/î fierce/ŏ pot/ō go/ô paw, for/oi oil/o͞o book
o͞o boot/ou out/ŭ cut/û fur/*th* the/th thin/hw which/zh vision/ə ago, item, pencil, atom, circus

*country.*—**un′ob · tru′sive · ly** *adv.*

**un · sight · ly** |ŭn sīt′ lē| *adj.* **un · sight · li · er, un · sight · li · est.** Not pleasant to look at; unattractive.

**up · braid** |ŭp brād′| *v.* To scold; censure.

**va · lise** |və lēs′| *n.* A small piece of hand luggage.

**var · i · a · tion** |vâr′ ē ā′ shən| *n.* **6.** A musical form that is an altered version of a given theme, diverging from it by melodic ornamentation and changes in harmony, rhythm, or key.

**ven · i · son** |vĕn′ ĭ sən| *or* |-zən| *n.* The meat of a deer, used as food.

**ven · ture** |vĕn′ chər| *v.* **4.** To travel, engage in a course of action, undertake a project, etc. despite danger and trepidation; dare or show the courage to go: *the first American to venture into outer space.*

**vex** |vĕks| *v.* To irritate or annoy; bother.

**vig · i · lant** |vĭj′ ə lənt| *adv.* On the alert; watchful; wary.

**vig · or** |vĭg′ ər| *n.* **1.** Physical energy or strength: *a lively, bright-eyed puppy full of health and vigor.* \*

**vile** |vīl| *adj.* **4.** Morally low or base.

**vin · di · cate** |vĭn′ dĭ kāt′| *v.* To clear of accusation, blame, etc., with supporting proof: *believing that it was time to vindicate himself from such offensive charges.*

**vir · tu · al · ly** |vûr′ chōō ə lē| *adv.* For the most part; essentially; practically: *The mountain lion is now virtually extinct in the East.*

**vis · age** |vĭz′ ĭj| *n.* The face or facial expression of a person.

**vul · ner · a · ble** |vŭl′ nər ə bəl| *adj.* **1.** Capable of being harmed or injured: *helpless, vulnerable baby birds.* **2.** Open to danger or attack; unprotected: *The retreat of the army had left the outlying territories vulnerable.*

* © 1991 by Scholastic Inc.

**wane** |wān| *v.* **3.** To draw to a close: *The old year was waning.*

**watch** |wŏch| *n.* **3.** A period of duty spent guarding or keeping a lookout: *a two-hour watch.*

**way · far · er** |wā′ fâr′ ər| *n.* A person who travels by road, especially on foot; traveler. \*

**whence** |hwĕns| *or* |wĕns| *adv.* **1.** From where; from what place: *Whence did this old man come?*

**wince** |wĭns| *v.* **winced, winc · ing.** To shrink or start involuntarily, as in pain or distress: *She winced when the blade slipped and cut her finger.*

**wind · fall** |wĭnd′ fôl′| *n.* **2.** A sudden piece of good fortune.

**wisp** |wĭsp| *n.* **2.** Someone or something thin, frail, or slight.

**wist · ful** |wĭst′ fəl| *adj.* Full of melancholy yearning; wishful.

**writhe** |rīth| *v.* **writhed, writh · ing. 2.** To move with a twisting or contorted motion: *Snakes were writhing in the pit.*

**wry** |rī| *adj.* **wri · er** or **wry · er, wri · est** or **wry · est 2.** Temporarily twisted in an expression of distaste or displeasure. **3.** Dryly humorous, often with a touch of irony.

**yearn** |yûrn| *v.* **1.** To have a deep, strong desire; be filled with longing: *She yearned for company in her lonely misery.*

**zith · er** |zĭth′ ər| *n.* A flat, stringed musical instrument, played by plucking with the fingers or a pick. \*

# SKILLS LESSONS

Note: Each page number indicates the first time a skill is taught. In most cases each skill is practiced several times in the book.

## Tone

## Imagery and Mood

## Style

## READING COMPREHENSION

## VOCABULARY/WORD ATTACK

## ORAL LANGUAGE DEVELOPMENT

# PROCESS WRITING

# WRITING ABOUT THE SELECTION

# RESEARCH AND STUDY SKILLS

# ACKNOWLEDGMENTS

Grateful acknowledgment is made to the following authors and publishers for the use of copyrighted materials. Every effort has been made to obtain permission to use previously published material. Any errors or omissions are unintentional.

American Foundation for the Blind, Inc. for "Three Days to See" by Helen Keller.

The Great Amwell Company, Inc. for the teleplay of *Life on the Mississippi* by Philip Reisman, Jr., based on the works of Mark Twain. Copyright © 1980 by The Great Amwell Company, Inc. Nebraskans for Public Television, Inc.

Arte Publico Press for "My Name," "Those Who Don't," "Sally," "Mango Says Goodbye Sometimes" from *The House on Mango Street* by Sandra Cisneros. Copyright © 1985 by Sandra Cisneros.

Toni Cade Bambara for "Raymond's Run," from *Gorilla, My Love* by Toni Cade Bambara. Copyright © 1970 by Toni Cade Bambara.

Brandt & Brandt Literary Agents, Inc. for "Salem Massachusetts," from *We Aren't Superstitious* by Stephen Vincent Benét. Copyright 1937 by Esquire, Inc. Copyright © renewed 1965 by Thomas C. Benét, Rachel Benét Lewis, and Stephanie Benét Mahin; "Cotton Mather" from *A Book of Americans* by Rosemary and Stephen Vincent Benét. Copyright 1933 by Rosemary and Stephen Vincent Benét. Copyright © renewed by Rosemary Carr Benét; "The Devil and Daniel Webster" from *Selected Works of Stephen Vincent Benét*. Copyright © 1937 by Stephen Vincent Benét. Copyright renewed 1964 by Thomas C. Benét, Stephanie B. Mahin, and Rachel Benét Lewis.

Curtis Brown, Ltd. for "She Sailed to Rescue a Lover" from *Pirates in Petticoats* by Jane Yolen. Copyright © 1963 by David McKay Co.

Diana Chang for "Saying Yes," by Diana Chang from *Asian-American Heritage: An Anthology of Prose and Poetry*, edited by David Hsin-Fu Wand, Washington Square Press, published by Pocket Books, 1974.

Don Congdon Associates, Inc. for "Hail and Farewell" and "The Fog Horn" from *The Golden Apples of the Sun* by Ray Bradbury. Copyright 1953 and © renewed 1971 by Ray Bradbury.

Crown Publishers, Inc. for adaptation of "April Morning" by Howard Fast. Copyright © 1961 by Howard Fast.

Delacorte Press/Seymour Lawrence for "I Stand Here Ironing," from *Tell Me a Riddle* by Tillie Olsen. Copyright © 1956 by Tillie Olsen; excerpts from the book *Welcome to the Monkey House* by Kurt Vonnegut, Jr. Copyright 1950 by Kurt Vonnegut, Jr. Originally published in *Collier's*.

Doubleday & Company, Inc. for "The Calico Dog," from *The Cases of Susan Dare* by Mignon G. Eberhardt. Copyright 1934 by Mignon G. Eberhardt.

E.P. Dutton, Inc. for excerpts from *Jim Bridger's Alarm Clock and Other Tall Tales* by Sid Fleischman. Copyright © 1978 by Sid Fleischman; excerpts from *Conjure Tales* by Charles W. Chestnutt, retold by Ray Anthony Shepard. Copyright © 1973 by Ray Shepard; E.P. Dutton, Inc. for the excerpt from "A Christmas Love Story" from *This Strange New Feeling* by Julius Lester. Copyright © 1981 by Julius Lester.

Norma Millay Ellis for "Travel," by Edna St. Vincent Millay from *Collected Poems*. Copyright 1917, 1920, 1921, renewed 1948, 1949 by Edna St. Vincent Millay. Published by Harper & Row, Publishers, Inc.

Farrar, Straus & Giroux for "A Summer's Reading" from *The Magic Barrel* by Bernard Malamud. Copyright © 1956, 1958 by Bernard Malamud, originally published in *The New Yorker*, adapted from "A Sense of Where You Are" by John McPhee. Copyright © 1965 by John McPhee; "Electrical Storm," "Sandpiper," "One Art" from *Elizabeth Bishop: The Complete Poems 1927–1979*. Copyright © 1983 by Alice Helen Methfessel. Coypright © 1933, 1935–1941, 1944–1949, 1951, 1952, 1955–1969, 1971–1976 by Elizabeth Bishop. Renewal copyright © 1967, 1968, 1971, 1973–1976, 1979 by Elizabeth Bishop. Renewal copyright © 1980 by Alice Helen Methfessel, originally published in *The New Yorker*.

John Gay's screenplay of *The Red Badge of Courage*. Adapted from the screenplay. A Norman Rosemont Production in association with 20th Century-Fox Television and the NBC Television Network. All rights reserved.

David R. Godine, Publisher, Inc. for excerpts from *Hunger of Memory: The Education of Richard Rodriguez* by Richard Rodriguez. Copyright © 1981 by Richard Rodriguez.

Harcourt Brace Jovanovich, Inc. for "Under a Telephone Pole," from *Chicago Poems* by Carl Sandburg. Copyright 1916 by Holt, Rinehart and Winston, Inc.; copyright 1944 by Carl Sandburg; Harcourt Brace Jovanovich, Inc. for "Fueled" from *Serve Me a Slice of Moon* by Marcie Hans. Copyright © 1965.

Harold Matson Company, Inc. for British Commonwealth rights to the excerpt from *Everything But Money* by Sam Levenson. Copyright © 1966 by Sam Levenson.

Harold Ober Associates, Inc. for "Discovery of a Father," by Sherwood Anderson from *Reader's Digest Magazine* (November 1939). Copyright 1939 by the Reader's Digest Association. Renewed 1966 by Eleanor Copenhaver Anderson; "Bernice Bobs Her Hair" by F. Scott Fitzgerald. Copyright 1920 by the Curtis Publishing Co., renewed 1948 by Zelda Fitzgerald; excerpt from the poem "Youth" from *Don't You Turn Back* by Langston Hughes. Copyright © 1967, 1969 by Arna Bontemps and George Houston Bass, Executors of the Estate of Langston Hughes. Published by Alfred A. Knopf, Inc.

Harper & Row, Publishers, Inc. for "Home" in "Maud Martha" from *The World of Gwendolyn Brooks*. Copyright 1951 by the Curtis Publishing Company; copyright 1935 by Gwendolyn Brooks Blakely; "Any Human to Another" in *On These I Stand* by Countee Cullen.

**Editorial, Design, and Art Production:** Kirchoff/Wohlberg, Inc.; Michaelis/Carpelis Design Associates
**Cover Art Direction:** Marijka Kostiw; Cover Photo Research: Roz Sohnen
**Photo Research:** Photosearch, NY

# ILLUSTRATION AND PHOTOGRAPHY CREDITS

# AUTHOR AND TITLE INDEX